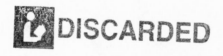

PROMISE OF GREATNESS

PROMISE
OF GREATNESS

———◆◆◆———

THE WAR OF 1914-1918

Edited by George A. Panichas

Foreword by Sir Herbert Read

CASSELL LONDON

CASSELL & COMPANY LTD.
35 Red Lion Square, London WC1
Melbourne, Sydney, Toronto
Johannesburg, Auckland

S.B.N. 304 93300 7

Copyright © 1968 by The John Day Company, Inc.
First published 1968

PRINTED IN THE UNITED STATES OF AMERICA
AND BOUND IN GREAT BRITAIN
F. 768

Foreword

THE CONTRIBUTORS to this volume, most relating their experiences of
a war that took place fifty years ago, speak as witnesses or students of
an event that has had no parallel in recorded history. Wars there
have been since the beginning of human history, and all have been
desperate, bloody, and futile. Sometimes they have been redeemed
by heroism, by self-sacrifice, and by what, with many qualifications,
we may call patriotism.[1] The peculiarity of the First World War
was that, as the name we now give it indicates, it was the first *world*
war; more than that it was, as Edwin Erich Dwinger indicates in the
title of his contribution, the first *civil* war within Europe: a war
that apart from preliminary skirmishes by professional troops was
fought by hastily trained civilians for reasons that were never clear
to them at the time, for causes that have only been obscured or
made ambiguous by subsequent historical research. Most of our
contributors bear witness to the fact, baffling to the warmongers at
home, that no specific hatred was felt on one side for the combatants on the other side of what we called no-man's-land. Among the
British soldiers the common name for the Germans opposite them
was Jerry, almost a term of affection. Brutalities in the heat of
battle did occur; men went berserk, an animal intoxication that
comes from the smell of blood and powder, the drumbeat of the
guns, and the instinct for self-defense. But such face-to-face
encounters took place at relatively long intervals. The normal
condition of the soldier on the western front was one of stoical
endurance: an endurance of prolonged physical hardships that was
perhaps a severer ordeal than any fear of death in combat.

The fear of death, as most of our contributors testify, was not for
the majority an obsession or even a persistent worry. Such fear is

---

[1] A word acceptable only in this sense: "Our peasants love their villages. The
Romans were ardent patriots, when Rome was a mere township. When it became
more powerful, their patriotism was not so keen. A city that was mistress of the world
was too vast for the hearts of its citizens. Men are not made to love immensity."
(Vauvenargues, *Reflections and Maxims,* trans. by F. G. Stevens [London, 1940].)

dissipated in companionship, and companionship, or camaraderie, came as a revelation to most participants: It was a human relationship and a reality that had not existed in times of peace. It overcame (or ignored) all distinctions of class, rank, or education. We did not call it love; we did not acknowledge its existence; it was sacramental and therefore secret.

If we did not feel fear, we knew instinctively that we were doomed. A few of us might survive—and did survive (as this book testifies). But we had no hope of survival, and that made our destiny tragic, as tragic as the destiny of the heroes of a Greek drama. We were participants in such a pre-Christian unredemptive tragedy: the gods in their malice and jesting being represented by the invisible generals who commanded us; the obscene chorus being the politicians and journalists of a country that was so remote that we British gave it a new name, Blighty. We played out that tragedy to the end, never knowing what the end might be. A future, from 1916 onward, did not exist for us. We learned how to live from day to day, from hour to hour, believing that the only future was death, a future to which we were indifferent.

Simone Weil, in her great essay on the *Iliad*, says: "That men should have death for their future is a denial of nature. As soon as the practice of war has revealed the fact that each moment holds the possibility of death, the mind becomes incapable of moving from one day to the next without passing through the specter of death. Then the consciousness is under tension such as it can only endure for short intervals." The daily sufferance of such violence in war, she concludes, "wipes out every conception of a goal, even all thoughts concerning the goals of war."[2] We thought, on the western front, that we had lost any conception of a goal because (as again almost all the contributors to this volume remark) our generals never confided in us, and we were altogether out of touch with those who directed the war from London or Paris. But perhaps Simone Weil is right: The real reason was a kind of insensibility induced by the ever-present specter of death. At the time we would have been too proud or too stupid to admit such a psychological explanation.

The sense of doom varied in intensity according to the quality of one's experience of war. A field surgeon, such as Sir Geoffrey Keynes, was too busy patching up the mutilated bodies that came down from the trenches in their thousands to have anything but a sense of mercy or of pity. Pity was Wilfred Owen's word; the subject of his poems, he wrote, is war, and the pity of war. "The poetry is in

---

[2] *Intimations of Christianity Among the Ancient Greeks,* trans. by Elisabeth Chase Geissbuhler (London, 1957), p. 41.

the pity." But he admitted there was no consolation in such poetry; pity was irrelevant to the truth about war—all the truthful poet could do was to warn.

And yet, it will be said, many people survived the war without experiencing the tragic emotions I have attributed to the common soldier. If I understand Charles Carrington's contribution rightly, he is of the opinion that it is only "literary men" who "agonize" about war. Certainly we may have been disillusioned by the war, all of us who saw it nakedly, but it is better to follow Horace's advice and not to blab about it. "Honest silence brings a sure reward." That might have been good counsel to give to a Roman hero or even to a Roman coward, but any comparisons from the past (even from Homer, the first and greatest realist of warfare) is invalid for the war that broke out in 1914. It was a war of an unparalleled kind: not only, as we have observed, a civil war on an unparalleled scale, but a genocidal war, waged by each side against women and children no less than against conscripted men. That fact alone made it tragic, in a sense in which even the Trojan War was not tragic. But tragedy, let us admit, is an artifact and always man-made; it is the supreme human effort to redeem life from absurdity.

This book is not a tragedy or written in a tragic spirit: It is a collection of reminiscences and reflections that are the raw material for tragedy. The First World War, in any literary sense, will not be made the subject of a tragedy by any of its survivors, and it is doubtful if such a tragedy will be written for many generations. There have been intimations of an epical treatment of these events (such as David Jones' *In Parenthesis*), but all major forms of art require (in the words of Georges Poulet) a "plenitude which is no longer secured by the operation of a personal memory but by the operation of a general memory which, in one state of consciousness, takes in the life of all humanity."[3] About three centuries are supposed to separate Homer from the war he made the subject of his *Iliad*. According to some of our contemporary prophets, poetry as an art will not survive long. These fragments, therefore, are doubly precious, in that they record the substance of a world tragedy and for a long time, perhaps forever, may have to serve (with similar fragments already published) as a substitute for a work of art that would give universal significance to a unique historical event.

April, 1968

HERBERT READ

---

[3] *Studies in Human Time,* trans. by Elliott Coleman (Baltimore, 1956), p. 30.

Acknowledgments

THIS VOLUME of essays could not have been assembled without the assistance of my colleagues and friends. Thus it gives me pleasure to thank them for the help and the time which they so generously gave to this project in the course of the last two years.

To my colleagues in the Department of English, University of Maryland, College Park, Professors Charles Manning, dean of the College of Arts and Sciences; Morris Freedman, head of the department; Kurt G. Weber; and Raymond Thorberg—I am grateful for their support, which they demonstrated variously and abundantly. I am especially proud to be associated with the University of Maryland—its staff, its administration, and its student body—and I wish to acknowledge for the public record its steadfast interest in and endorsement of my research and teaching.

To Miss Martha Seabrook, of the University of Maryland Library —I want to express appreciation not only for her advice and friendship, but also for her painstaking reading of my Introduction, which, because of her invariably perceptive editing, was saved from stylistic and factual errors. Throughout my tenure in the University of Maryland, I have derived much benefit from her consideration of my work, and she has also shared with me her wide and discerning knowledge of literature, particularly the modern British novel.

To Miss Mary E. Slayton, of the Library of Congress, I want once again to voice my gratitude for her diligence and industry in aiding me in the immense correspondence and secretarial work necessitated by such a big and "international" volume of essays; in typing and retyping many of the manuscripts; and, not least of all, in reading and correcting galley proofs. Her patience and constant and selfless readiness to assist me with these, as well as with other, innumerable chores, can be deservingly cited but can never be fully estimated.

To Mrs. Alda W. Brincefield, Miss Linda L. Koelker, Joseph Lalley, Miss Susan Myerberg, N. Frederick Nash, Andrew Panichas, Mrs. Miriam B. Wood, and Professors Carl Bode, Richard B. Hovey, Lewis A. Lawson, and Charles D. Murphy—I am indebted for their kindnesses. And to Alan Tucker, editor, the John Day Company, I want to give thanks for his belief in this project. From beginning to end he was sensitive to the historical and literary significance of the book, and I gladly salute him.

Finally, words fail me in assessing the collaboration of the distinguished contributors to this volume. It remains for their own essays to testify to their willingness to write for the book and to the enthusiasm with which they responded to its aims. Their own lives and accomplishmens are what have made possible the publication of *Promise of Greatness* as a gift to history.

Contents

SOCIAL-HISTORICAL PERSPECTIVES 377

LITERATURE OF WAR   477

THE GUILT   557

*A map of part of the western front precedes
the essay by Robert Graves.*

Introduction

No ONE who was born and has lived in the twentieth century has been spared from war, from either the reality or the constant thought and threat of war. This century has seen wars fought with ever-increasing ferocity. Perhaps no other war stirs the emotions more or exerts more lasting interest than does World War I—the Great War of 1914–18, the Great War for Civilization. Although a half century has passed since the Armistice of November 11, 1918, not only in the memories of the survivors, those who fought and those who did not fight, but also in the imaginations of those who were not living at the time, the Great War holds a place of importance which grows stronger as the events of the war come gradually to belong to a distance in the past which gives rise to legend and song and poetry, to the tale of war: the mingling of romance and history into which war has merged from the earliest of times.

War as we have experienced it in this century can hardly arouse exaltation. We have come to see the utter devastation and meaninglessness of war, those cruel realities that the bloodstained face of history has taken on. We have had to learn to confront war not as abstraction but as actuality, "the great unequal battle . . . between the forces of terror and the forces of dialogue," as Albert Camus expressed it. War has made us and our age harder and more cynical. Certainly men today refuse to connect the waging of war with the mystique of adventure: the fulfillment of some inborn promise, the matchless opportunity to display a chivalrous temper. It seems that we have learned war's lessons of illusion and disillusion. The rhetoric of war, which we find as deplorable as it is irresponsible, has no place in a world where nuclear annihilation poses the final menace—and the final madness.

Our attitude toward war that is expressed nowadays in such militant and clamorous ways underlines the fact that the twentieth

century is no longer young or naïve. Indeed, when we consider some
of the immediate responses to the declaration of war in August,
1914, we recognize innocence, the innocence of youth on the
threshold of a new age in an old world with which this century
began, when as C. E. Montague later wrote in *Disenchantment*, "All
the air was ringing with rousing assurances."[1] "The air is better to
breathe than it has been for years . . . ," declared (Sir) Walter
Raleigh, professor of English literature at Oxford University.[2] In
Vienna, Sigmund Freud exclaimed, "All my libido is given to
Austro-Hungary."[3] In France one writer expected that the war
would be "amusing," another that it would provide the opportunity
to "picnic on the grass."[4] And in Germany one thinker asserted
that because his nation had discovered the factor of a higher organization, the war would provide the occasion for reorganizing
Europe—and, concurrently, for realizing the German dream of the
Kolossal.[5] Time and history had not yet run out of promises for the
generation of 1914–18. The experience of the war harmonized with
the language of heroism, as the early years of the war amply demonstrated. These years held golden moments, "the eve of our crowning
hour," according to a soldier-poet. Many men who enlisted in that
war felt they were fighting not only for age-old concepts but also
for the sake of changing the world and shaping a new destiny.

From a vantage point fifty years later we come to realize that the
Great War in its early stages was fought not so much to destroy an
enemy as to defend and to extend the possibilities of civilization,
and precisely that civilization which Henry James envisioned as the
way "to find and to make the earth a friendlier, an easier, and
especially a more various sojourn."[6] It is on transcendent levels of
the abstract and the ideal and the romantic that we first view the
waging of this war. Comradeship, splendor, glory, honor, love,
sympathy were still to retain those values vital to a humane civilization. The war was seen in 1914 as a conflict "between sisters, between Martha and Mary, the efficient and intolerant against the
casual and sympathetic,"[7] between the real and the unreal, the effete

---

1 (New York, 1922) , p. 3.

2 Quoted in Virginia Woolf, "Walter Raleigh," in *Collected Essays*, (London, 1966) ,
Vol. I, p. 327.

3 Ernest Jones, *The Life and Work of Sigmund Freud*, ed. and abridged by Lionel
Trilling and Steven Marcus (New York, 1963 [1961]) , p. 327.

4 See Julien Benda, *The Betrayal of the Intellectuals*, trans. by Richard Aldington
with an Introduction by Sir Herbert Read (Boston, 1955 [1928], p. 140.

5 Romain Rolland, *Above The Battle*, trans. by C. K. Ogden (Chicago, 1916) , pp.
111 ff.

6 *Within the Rim* (London, 1918) , p. 90.

7 *The Letters of Charles Sorley*, W. R. Sorley, ed. (Cambridge, England, 1919) ,
p. 232.

and the vital, the conscious and the unconscious, the *homo contra-humanus* and the *homo humanus*. As such for many of its partici-pants, and for its nonparticipants, too, this war acted as "a great remedy" and "a great experience," a breakthrough at long last from the dreamworld of the nineteenth century. "You won't catch me complaining of any war—much less of a great war like this that we wage on both sides like mystics for a reason beyond reason," Robert Frost wrote in a letter dated September 17, 1914.[8]

Combatants were characterized again and again by an enthusiasm bordering on religious frenzy. For not a few the war at the front was transposed into a religious experience which provided in its own forms a heightening and a lucidity and a freedom, emerging from shared suffering and death, that no human action could approxi-mate. In battle one experienced a "compelling fascination . . . that lies . . . [in] War's power": "Once you have lain in her arms you can admit no other mistress. You may loathe, you may execrate, but you cannot deny her."[9] Likewise, the war served as a baptism into reality, as it were, a tragic, even ecstatic dimension of life that a soldier-priest, Pierre Teilhard de Chardin, who was cited as "an outstanding stretcher-bearer," envisioned as "an urgent invitation to prayer" while one lived "in a forward-looking tension." Only at the front, with "its noble struggles" and "its impassioned quests," in the ever-present shadow of danger, Teilhard de Chardin believed, could one attain a fully conscious state, a new form of soul, "to be healed and made perfect," and experience there, in "the thick of human endeavour, and with no stopping for breath," what he could not experience anywhere else: that sense of exaltation which comes with "fulfilling a function far higher than that of the individual."[10] Charles Hamilton Sorley, despite a "mute and burning rage and annoyance and sulkiness," felt something of the same when he confessed that in battle "one learns to be a servant. The soul is disciplined."[11]

This was far from assuming some merely sentimental attitude or some lingering heroic dream evoked by schoolboy memories of the "plains of windy Troy," which elated Rupert Brooke upon his de-parture for the Dardanelles in late February, 1915. "Will Hero's Tower crumble," he asked, "under the 15″ guns? Will the sea be polyphloisbic and wine-dark and unvintageable? Shall I loot

8 *Selected Letters of Robert Frost,* Lawrance Thompson, ed. (New York, 1964), p. 134.

9 Guy Chapman, *A Passionate Prodigality* (London, 1965 [1933]), p. 226.

10 Pierre Teilhard de Chardin, *The Making of a Mind,* trans. by René Hague (New York, 1961), p. 205, and *Hymn of the Universe,* trans. by Simon Bartholomew (New York, 1961), p. 54.

11 *The Letters of Charles Sorley,* pp. 220, 312.

mosaics from St. Sophia, and Turkish Delight, and carpets? Should
we be a Turning Point in History? Oh God!"[12] For many of the
fighting men the war was much more than the excitation of the
"confident and glorious hopes"—and questions—that stirred in
Brooke. And it was much more, surely, than what H. G. Wells described with commanding import when he asserted: "This, the
greatest of all wars, is not just another war—it is the last war!"[13] If
for some men the war meant the renovation of mankind by the
creation of a "great society," as well as "a new map of Europe,"
when, as a young French novelist wrote to Romain Rolland,
"History will tell of us, for we are opening a new era in the
world,"[14] for others it signified the ultimate confrontation of the
realities which lie far beyond and far deeper than just "a necessity
of honour," for which one statesman pleaded, or an opportunity
to "travel along the road of human destiny and progress, at the end
of which we shall see the patient figure of the Prince of Peace, pointing to the Star of Bethlehem that leads us on to God," as an
English journalist averred.[15]

Hence for some of the fighting men the war—"the whole sad man-
made complication," as Rainer Maria Rilke termed it—transcending
the romantic and idealistic, transcending, too, what some fighting
men designated as "a state of primal innocence," the war enabled
one to grasp a better concept of the nature of man and of life as a
whole. Above all, it disclosed that evil in the world is not rooted
merely in oppression but is an intrinsic part of the nature of things.
The realities of the condition of man and of life at the front; the
nightmare of slaughter and wooden crosses that the Great War became—these were facts that unmasked the demonic character of man
who had sinned and fallen. Life at the front was thus the furthest
extension of man's essential condition: his weakness and imperfecti-
bility strained to their most extreme limits. "In this war, then, we
are fighting for no great *liberation* of mankind," T. E. Hulme wrote
from the trenches, "for no great jump upward, but are merely accomplishing a work, which, if the nature of things was ultimately
'good,' would be useless, but which in this actual 'vale of tears' becomes from time to time necessary, merely in order that bad may
not get worse."[16]

The war suddenly awakened the 1914 generation from the com-

---

[12] Edward Marsh, *Rupert Brooke. A Memoir* (New York, 1926), p. 163.
[13] *The War That Will End War* (New York, 1914), p. 14.
[14] *Above the Battle, op. cit.,* p. 39.
[15] Julian Symons, *Horatio Bottomley* (London, 1955), p. 174.
[16] *Further Speculations,* Sam Hynes, ed. (Lincoln, Nebraska, 1962), p. 184.

parative ease and comfort and orderliness of an older and more stable way of life. Left behind was the leisurely world of European society before 1914—when education was centered in the classics, when cricket and the hunt often meant much more than international affairs, when private life was valued, when writing poetry and exploring the countryside were sources of quiet joy—a world still close to Thomas Hardy's "indispensable conditions of existence [which] are attachment to the soil of one particular spot by generation after generation."[17] Even as it caused incredulity, disarray, anguish, the declaration of war awakened dreams of glorious exploits echoing once more to the roll of drums. Stefan Zweig, reflecting on the reasons why Europe went to war, suggests that it was not because of ideologies or even provocative acts but rather because of a "surplus of force, a tragic consequence of the internal dynamism that had accumulated in those forty years of peace and now sought violent release."[18] Those who had come to manhood under the discipline of the old tradition had suddenly to face the demands of a new age. Indeed, the war was as much an awakening to these demands as it was a military event. And one of the clearest demands after that "monstrous August" was that the war must correspond with the essential character of a civilization which was becoming increasingly industrialized.

The military conduct of the war mirrored a great transition. Dreams of cavalry charges, of open warfare with dashing officers leading not conscripts but professional soldiers into the fray, into a struggle of strength and skill and courage, had to give way, and at a tremendous expense of lives and material, to the grim exigencies of a fighting front thick with barbed wire and gashed by trenches. This was a new war in a new age. It was a total, an absolute, war; it involved many nations and war fronts and was fought with revolutionary tactics and with new weapons of annihilation—airplanes, submarines, tanks, trench bombs, poison gas. In short, modern warfare was to prescribe the methods of wholesale violence. At the same time, disclosing the denial of personality, it was a struggle directed against men as objects. As such, this war was to be a portent of an age progressively sacrificing the personal to the needs of machine-made mass civilization. "As a man as of a knife: does it cut well? Nothing else mattered," D. H. Lawrence wrote in *Women in Love*, which "took its final shape in the midst of the war."[19] His

---

17 "Preface," *Far from the Madding Crowd* (New York, 1960 [1874]), p. vii.
18 *The World of Yesterday. An Autobiography* (New York, 1943), p. 197.
19 (New York, Modern Library Edition [1920]), p. 254; Foreword, p. ix.

words instance the objectivization that war in the modern industrial world has since procured on demand time and time again.

That the Great War was to be the source of many achievements in prose, in poetry, in drama, and in autobiography and memoirs is not surprising. Literature, after all, reflects both the values and the impulses of an age. For the generation of 1914 these impulses were eminently generous. The drabness of mechanical civilization had not yet conditioned men who, even in the cockpit of slaughter and in the darkness of battle, still apprehended the call of beauty, the passage of the seasons, the spirit of place. Just as war had a deeply religious dimension for some of its combatants, so too did it have a deeply poetic dimension when the creative and destructive instincts, imagination and power, strove for expression. Undoubtedly the immediate scenes of fighting, the desolate, defiled, charred, scarred landscape, now beyond description, strange and dead, inhuman, empty—empty of hope and abandoned by God—were not without their communicable, and incommunicable, impressiveness. Men who had lived in Arcadia were now trapped in Armageddon, but the past lingered precariously in their memory. In the tension between terror and memory was born art, which, as André Gide has told us, "if born of constraint, lives by struggle, dies of freedom."

The literature of the war, as written by participants and by survivors both during and after the conflict, invariably reflects a yearning for truth, a struggling search for some deep understanding of war that, never ignoring the passion of the experience, yet attains the detachment necessary to measure it. What we detect so often in the generation and in the literature of 1914–18 is an intensity of awakening to reality and to truth. Many of the combatants recognized as never before the problematic human situation and likewise discovered truth of self. Bodily and mentally, men rose through the experience of war to the experience of self-meaning. Many of the recollections of the war verbalize the process of discovering some truth of self, of life. Thus, for many soldiers, regardless of nation, the Great War as the home of their youth dramatized in extremity what the world included.

If the war meant anguish, it also meant "the infinite pain of self-realization," to use a phrase of William Butler Yeats, who, incidentally, dismissed the war as a "bloody frivolity." In one sense, perhaps, true heroism was to be experienced precisely in such an awakening. There was the growing awareness of the elemental value of dogged hanging on in an interminable conflict of great military "offensives" and "deadlocks." Reading the reminiscences of life at the front, we are struck by the fact that soldiers had to wait so long for things to happen; that determination itself was tested by a war in which time had come to a desperate standstill. "There really seems no reason why the Germans and ourselves," said French President Raymond Poincaré at the end of the first year, "should not stand facing one another for all eternity."[20] Indeed, it was a war in which there was as much a despair of time as there was of death. Time is associated with an agonizing sense of unreality often arising from an awareness of an isolated world reduced to utter devastation and putrefaction. The picture of this world, where life and death at last became one, represented for some of the soldiers a nightmarish eternity. At the front, time stopped for violence to pass, and the alternating periods of violence and of still-ness, of savage bombardments followed by sudden silence, blended to render time dimensionless, indistinct. Time, it seems, had also become the victim of the irreversibility of destruction and death. And endurance, if anything, had to take its place and the place of faith.

But the war also meant a more passionate awakening than just learning how to endure. This was an experiential awareness of men sharing dangers, undergoing the drudgery of trench warfare, having the same fears, disappointments, complaints, resentments, irrita-tions, disgusts, the same hopes and dreams and enthusiasms, fighting and surviving, or dying, in a world which they alone knew. Endur-ance, which must inevitably consist in physical and spiritual weari-ness that defies death and nothingness, was made more achievable by a confraternity of men in arms and by a sense of identity that could be grasped only in the most extraordinary of human situa-tions. This shared identity was not established just on the fact of youth in sight of chaos or on intense comradeship emerging in a world from which there was no easy escape. After all, no lines of discrimination based on class or favor could exist among men thrown together in a war that imposed on them an equivalent danger and equivalent conditions of fighting and of dying. When time had no meaning and when civilized living had been necessarily reduced in space to the rubble of no-man's-land, men sought their remaining human identity through communion with one another. Beyond this identity there could be nothing else that counted.

In one another, it can be said, the soldiers fighting at the front

---

[20] *The Memoirs of Raymond Poincaré,* trans. by Sir George Arthur (London, 1929), Vol. III, p. 295.

grew to greatness. In a world where everything seemed to be in a
state of collapse, ranging from the failures of leadership at home and
at the front to the failures of the announced promise of "victory"
battles, they looked for something surer than mere promises or the
vagaries of faith. And they found this assurance in fellowship with
their comrades. Exposed to maximum dangers, the men in the front
lines learned to speak a language based on a unity of experience.
They had found promise and truth in one another, even as they
learned to accept and inspire one another. Not seldom, in fact,
soldiers who had been returned to civilian areas for rest and re-
cuperation yearned to be sent back to the battlefield. (Recovering
from war wounds in England, Siegfried Sassoon felt the "awful
attraction" that the war held over his mind, and he was "disquieted
by a craving to be back on the Western Front as an independent
contemplator."[21]) Their feelings for one another were a mixture of
respect and pity, based on an experience of life born and tested and
renewed in the heat of conflict. As their accounts demonstrate, these
men did not hate utterly. For them the war, much deeper than the
fastness of hate, was the passion of its suffering, when in the course
of cruel history "I hear, through dead men's drums, the riddled
lads/Strewing their bowels from a hill of bones,/Cry Eloi to the
guns"[22]—the suffering, that is to say, mitigated by a common human
identity and fulfilled in a common judgment: When all are to
blame, all are accused.

The many brave acts of the men who fought in this war must not
be judged by the traditional criterion of prowess or the old concept
of the heroic man of action. This was an altogether new and mechanized war, ungraced by those inexpressibly strange felicities and
nobilities engendered by older wars, even at their most savage
heights. The Nietzschean view of men who wage war for the
"pleasures of victory and cruelty" so as to be "purified" by their
triumphs over the elements and other men and thus become "the
archetypes of moral beauty" could hardly be defended or exempli-
fied in a war that wrought indiscriminate annihilation. There was
nothing beautiful or glorious about this war. Bravery was no longer
some spectacular process; when it appeared, it was usually against a
dehumanized background of ugliness and disbelief. Essentially a
brave act had to be achieved not in some encounter with other men
but against the mechanical might of the weapons of destruction
produced by a new science and engineering. Bravery, like heroism,
was radically transformed in act and meaning in a conflict in which,

---

21 *Siegfried's Journey. 1916–1920* (London, 1945), pp. 69–70.
22 Dylan Thomas, "My World Is Pyramid," in *Collected Poems. 1934–1952* (London, 1966), p. 26.

as it transpired, there could be neither complete victory nor complete defeat.

By no means should these observations imply that the soldiers in this war were not as brave as the soldiers in past wars. On the contrary, the men at the front disclosed a bravery all the more astonishing when one considers their inexperience and the awesome surprise that they must have often felt in contending not with other human beings but with the depersonalized ways of modern warfare. The opportunity for individual acts of bravery gave way to the requirements of collective military efforts, now made necessary by a war based on tactics and maneuvers and executed by great armored forces. Under these circumstances bravery became more a matter of holding on tenaciously, even miraculously, against innumerable forms of mechanized power that could bring death swiftly, unexpectedly, at any time, in any place. For many soldiers bravery became a realized inner experience of surmounting fear of the senseless and the pitiless, while at the same time appreciating such things as chance and luck and fate. It became passive, rather than exhibitive. In other words, bravery was something that a soldier had first to search for and discover and exert in himself, and as such it was to be attained anonymously: in the common soldier—the "nobody" as he was sometimes known—struggling to survive a mass killing process which ultimately flouted any distinction between bravery or cowardice.

As the war went on, especially after the Battle of the Somme and the failure of the "Great Advance" in 1916, and as the casualties, the disappointments, and the horrors accumulated, the realization grew that this was a "murder war" now further and further removed from any struggle for civilization, certainly from that phantom civilization which Matthew Arnold once saw as the humanization of man in society. At the front, in the midst of endless barbed-wire entanglements, of advances counted by the inches, of murderous artillery bombardments that led to the disappearance of entire villages and to the creation of cemeteries of mud for men and animals alike, the presage of death became the most immediate fact of life. Military leadership, professionally—and professedly—concerned with what T. E. Lawrence has described as "the whole house of war in its structural aspect, which was strategy, in its arrangements, which were tactics, and the sentiment of its inhabitants, which was psychology,"[23] frequently failed to sustain the soldiers' enthusiasms and trust and, worse, to understand the hell of this war. Errors in judgment, inexcusably inadequate communication,

---

23 *Seven Pillars of Wisdom* (New York, 1966 [1926]) , pp. 162–63.

recklessness, bungling, stubbornness, caprice, irresponsibility, amateurishness, stupidity, especially on the part of the military mandarins, led to unnecessary death and maiming, as well as to the cynicism that the fighting men increasingly felt and that in some French Army units even erupted into mutiny. . . . In "the house of war" the meed of valor must yet inevitably vie with the spirit's ruin.

Of all the experiences of war, what remains unwavering in the survivors' recollections is the omnipresence of death. And it is the immensity and ugliness and horror of death that haunt their memories. The scenes in which the soldiers depict death are touched not so much by mystery or fear as by incomprehensibility. At the front, death was to come suddenly and with a wide range of devastation. Often it was the unnaturalness of the scenes of death that seemed so grotesque. Death came with mechanical force, with an objective relentlessness and an instantaneousness beyond belief. Though some of the survivors recall separate examples of death wounds and death experiences, it is more usual for them to depict scenes of collective death. We are thus reminded of a war in which entire armies disappeared; death was as massive in its results as it was incontrovertible in its power. Awesomeness and powerlessness, consequently, characterize the responses of the fighting men to the constant danger of death cheaply but efficiently accomplished by the engines of war.

Oftentimes the survivors recall scenes in which the living and the dead come together. A soldier seeking refuge and protection in some pithole finds his only other companion to be a dead soldier. Or, as he threads his way in the dark, he stumbles against a dying man. Or, as he is digging, he unearths a khaki-clad corpse covered by debris in the wake of an earlier artillery bombardment. And too, there are the memories of mass graves, of burying parties, of smelling corpses being eaten by packs of roaming dogs, of young and strong bodies deformed beyond recognition. And we are ever aware of the appalling number of casualties, in a war in which one day alone could bring death and wounds to many thousands of men and one year to well over a million. At the front death is the overwhelming fact. The magnitude of death creates speechless horror; the thought of death fills immensity. There is hardly a boundary line between the dead, the dying, and the living. It has been said that although death destroys a man, the idea of death saves him. But for the men at the front, death held no comfort of theory by which one could leap over death as destruction or as salvation. For them it was the major presence of life: The incessant vision of the wounded and the dying exceeded pity and prayer alike.

Yet self-pity and sentimentality, offshoots of great spiritual and physical crises, are singularly lacking in these responses. Even where the scenes of death become dread images of mass slaughter, they reflect immense pain felt and a stark recognition of some tremendous force let loose, bringing infinite ruin. Often, therefore, death is seen in the metaphorical guise of madness; it is what could not possibly be real because of its sheer inhumanness, but which in its enormity and momentum moves at last beyond the consciousness of the real and the moral. That life has been violated and blasphemed in man's least sacrosanct moments is what often informs some of the immediate responses to the scenes of death. The victory of a profane spirit becomes an overarching fact. That the word "monstrous" appears repeatedly in the survivors' recollections is not without its significance here: This power that brings death is mechanical and conscienceless; it inflicts death with a kind of measured, passionless intensity. The battle scenes of death reveal the marks of a power that crushes once it strikes, reaping men in swaths.

In the concluding pages of *The Magic Mountain*, Thomas Mann describes the Great War as "The historic thunder-peal, of which we speak with bated breath, [and which] made the foundations of the earth to shake. . . ."[24] Certainly by the time of the Armistice the war had become an experience of the abyss, not only for the fighting men on both sides, but also for entire civilian populations, especially in the immediate areas of the hostilities. This shaking of the foundations of European civilization was brutally evident in every phase of life. After 1918 the values of a settled civilization were gone. The years of the war remained as the chief remembrance of things past, and the future was uncertain. The war had destroyed a sense of security and stability, and 1918 was to become a date signaling the crises of civilization that have marked the rest of the twentieth century. Those who lost their lives lost all their bitterness. But those who survived felt sorrow without end. Recalling the upheavals of the war, Leonard Woolf remarks in *Downhill All the Way*: "In 1914 in the background of one's life and one's mind there was light and hope; by 1918 one had unconsciously accepted a perpetual public menace and darkness and had admitted into the privacy of one's mind or soul an iron fatalistic acquiescence in insecurity and barbarism."[25]

Here Mr. Woolf underlines what can be described as the "deaths in belief" that the generation of 1914–18 suffered. The war was

---

24 (Harmondsworth, England, 1960 [1924]) , p. 709.
25 (London, 1967) , p. 9.

especially disastrous for idealistic thought, for the innocence of an optimist faith, for the liberal doctrine, for the humanist creed, and for the old ideals of classicism and education. More than anything else, the war had unmasked the most diabolic tendencies and weaknesses of man and his society. Neither the values of a civilization founded on what the English philosopher G. E. Moore termed the "divine voice of a plain common-sense" nor G. Lowes Dickinson's melioristic vision of a world in which man can stretch "feelers into the Dark, laying hold there of stuff, and building mythologies and poems, the palaces of splendid hopes and desires," could possibly withstand the ravages of the war. Modern civilization, in the wake of war, was to become the hostage of a world in which a glorified "authentic present" and a "massive incertitude" (to use here a phrase of Ezra Pounds) agitated to replace the traditions and values that the war had destroyed. Civilization in the period following 1918, then, was a witness both to a dying order and to a world striving to be reborn. But the possibility of resurrection in a world defiled beyond recognition was not without its frightening limitations: "The post-war generation had to live," one writer lamented, "and the war-generation had nothing to give them to live by."[26]

There are always those, of course, who, like Conrad Aiken in *The Soldier*, suggest that "The history of war/is the history of mankind":[27] who suggest that war in the historical process is ultimately a dynamic, cleansing, and creative experience which helps to teach nations and humanity self-knowledge and to release new energy. But surely the Great War was to destroy such a myth! After the Armistice nothing could be more painfully obvious than the absurdity of the promises of war. For what remained—had to remain—was the physical and spiritual shattering that this war had brought to European civilization, not the least of which were the staggering statistics of nearly 9,000,000 men in uniform killed and more than 21,000,000 wounded. Figures by themselves undoubtedly cannot relate a tragedy. Nor indeed can mere descriptions of a holocaust convey its full meaning. The outer crisis of this war—the death of man by man, the destruction, the absurdity, the defilement—was inevitably transcribed into an inner crisis of mind and soul: the alienation, the meaninglessness, the cynicism, the hate, the despair, the confusion, the suspicion, the fear, the doubt that possess modern man even in the midst of his triumphs in science and technology. The legacy of the Great War, as its survivors' reminiscences reveal

---

[26] J. Middleton Murry, *Looking Before and After* (London, 1948), p. 155.
[27] (Norfolk, Connecticut, 1944), p. 16.

and as history attests, was the death of man in flesh and in spirit. Perhaps this is the one truth that can be discovered in the midst of struggle and destiny in those years of conflict.

When the war ended, a feeling of futility set in—a realization that, in the end, little had been gained, much had been lost. This sense of futility is communicated by the survivors over and over again: It haunts their memories and stamps their apprehension of the emptiness of life. A broken promise and a broken world were the most direct results of the war. The war dramatized disorder and divisions and catastrophes. Beyond these tangible manifestations of an annihilative spirit, it also led to a deadening process in the hearts of men. Civilized living, it can be asserted, is nourished by a sense of discrimination, which war blunts and gradually displaces. "Pathos, piety, courage—they exist, but are identical, and so is filth. Everything exists, nothing has value."[28] Thus E. M. Forster sums up the senselessness of existence, and no words could better capture what the Great War finally legislated. More than anything else, in the collapse of the discriminating, civilizing faculty, the war revealed that barbarism is a force which constantly threatens civilization, that civilization itself must occupy a tenuous position in a world in which supreme acts of might instance not only the relative worth of life but its worthlessness as well. For the survivors the war was to produce a clearer and more terrifying recognition of the finite conditions of man's existence.

Barbarism was not confined to the fronts. Nor was it merely resorted to and executed in the service of force and slaughter. Barbarism is as much a dehumanizing process as it is a brutal action or reaction; its eruptions and effects are to be measured in terms not of one area of antagonisms but of a total human situation. If barbarism, then, quickens in the midst of the cannonade and the battle cries of the killing instinct—if, that is, it is a special condition, even requirement, of what happens in warfare—it is also something that embraces what can be called the public life, or the everyday life distant from the war front. During the Great War civilian populations could hardly escape the impact of the war either physically or spiritually. The barbarism of the war was thus extended to include those men and women not immediately involved. Perhaps one of the most far-reaching, brutalizing effects of the war was the bringing to the surface of a crisis of trust between participant and nonparticipant, a breakdown of communication between them. One of the soldiers in Henri Barbusse's *Under Fire,* returning to

---

28 *A Passage to India* (London, 1953 [1924]) , p. 156.

the front after two months' sick leave, brings out this lack of communication when he cries: " 'I'm fed up—*that's* what I am! The people back there, I'm sick of them—they make me spew, and you can tell 'em so!' "[29] It was in the very nature and irrationality of the war, thus, to make more difficult the possibility of authentic dialogue between those who were fighting and those not fighting. (G. E. Moore, for example, admitted that he never felt anything about the war at all. To him it made no difference: "None. Why should it?" he snapped to Lytton Strachey.) [30]

The barbarism of the war at the front, hence, was not without its counterpart in the public life that managed to go on in the apparent safety behind the lines. And among the civilian populations the Great War brought out some of the least desirable qualities and responses. Writing from London in October, 1917, D. H. Lawrence bitterly complained that "People are not people any more: they are factors, really ghastly, like lemures, evil spirits of the dead."[31] For Lawrence the war signified "destruction and dying and corruption," "so much hate . . . and disintegration," when "massive creeping hell is let loose." Lawrence did not serve in the war, but his visionary insights into the condition of the men and women who lived during the war years have a special significance, insofar as they help convey the spirit of the barbarism that possessed whole populations. Its manifestations were numerous: "Talkers," "word makers of war," statesmen, and profiteers (war's "vested interests bawling patriotically and making money"[32]) united to oil the propaganda machines and to inflame public opinion with atrocity stories and spy scares. Religious leaders, preaching "the Gospel of the Spiked Helmet" and exhorting "Christ-loving soldiers," claimed that the choice had to be made between "the nailed hand" and "the mailed fist." Young women presented white feathers to men who for one reason or another were not serving in the armed forces. And some parents publicly displayed their sons' military medals—and their sons—with a sense of pride tantamount to the most glossy barbarism.

Nothing ever remains sacred in war, which embodies disorder and affliction *ne plus ultra*. It generates habits of violence. It muddles human consciousness. It accentuates, above all, the ceaseless struggle between barbarism and its proper opposite, civilization.

29 Trans. by Fitzwater Wray (New York, 1917) , p. 112.

30 Michael Holroyd, *Lytton Strachey. A Critical Biography* (New York, 1968) . Vol. II, p. 148.

31 *The Collected Letters of D. H. Lawrence*, Harry T. Moore, ed. (New York, 1962) , Vol. I, p. 528.

32 Desmond MacCarthy, *Memories* (New York, 1953) , p. 141.

The Great War proved that the barbaric element, far from having been refined out of existence, in a world of immense technological progress, remains a perpetual threat. Europe in the course of the war saw the deterioration of rational, civilizing values, particularly the value of life, not only in the destruction and death on the war fronts, but also in the widespread demoralization of life distant from the front. The Great War increasingly absorbed the energies of soldier and civilian alike. No one was to be immune from the barbarism that war provokes or blameless in the savageries committed against civilized life and thought. Tested and pressured by a war augmented by the inexorable powers of the newly evolved, and evolving, technique and apparatus of an industrial society, the very structure and consciousness of Europe crumbled. For European civilization, therefore, the Great War meant both death and world-weariness: death for the soldier, world-weariness for the civilian. It compelled the depersonalization of life, as well as its sacrifice to a mechanized materialism abrogating all human value. "The terrible, terrible war," to cite Lawrence once more, "made so fearful because in every country practically every man lost his head, and lost his own centrality, his own manly isolation in his own integrity, which alone keeps life real."[33]

The war, transforming men, transformed Europe. More than anything else, it shattered man's inner life by destroying faith in himself and in his own worth. By 1918 the soul had been humiliated. With the end of the war European man was to be acutely aware of the deceptiveness of his prewar belief, fashioned in more spacious, less thought-tormented days, that his refinement and essential civilization had at last, in this century and in this world, defeated barbarism. Immunity from the barbarism of the subhuman and the antihuman was to be one of modern man's serious deaths in belief. For the "European spirit" and the "European mind" the Great War showed civilization disintegrating—that "rhythm of disintegration," as Arnold Toynbee calls it[34]—which was equated with "breakdown," "collapse," "paralysis." The war consituted a multiple barbarism of might, the fundamental, most exhaustive consequence of modern man's capacities and progress, his technical resources, his industries—his audacity. Europe submitted to this might, to this technique, and the disaster was incalculable: It had to be appraised on a scale of conflict and consequence and change manifoldly greater than in any previous conflict, involving not localized objectives and limited fighting numbers and fronts, but

---

[33] *Kangaroo* (Harmondsworth, England, 1960 [1923]) , p. 236.
[34] *A Study of History,* abridged by D. C. Somervell (New York, 1946) , Chap. XXI.

a total society, in which the whole was at war with its parts. Superseding the "old geometry of history" and "the old mechanics of power," the war showed that "melodic history" was no longer possible.[35] The meaning of history, like the spirit and mind of Europe, could hardly remain the same after the events of 1914–18.

"We later civilizations . . . we too now know that we are mortal," Paul Valéry wrote in the *Athenaeum* in 1919, his famous words arising from the depths of the ruins and the anguish of the Great War.[36] The passage from war to peace, he believed, was darker and more dangerous than the passage from peace to war. "'Peace,'" he continued, "is perhaps that state of things in which the natural hostility between men is manifested in creation, rather than destruction as in war."[37] Valéry's remarks stress the mortality of European civilization and of the European psyche that the war had evinced. The problems of the "great peace" after the military crisis was over were to agonize the conscience of Europe throughout the years before the next war. The war itself was an omen of the peace that ensued: the exhaustion of a civilization in spirit and in mind, as much as in body.

Sir Herbert Read notes that the Great War has not yet been, nor in all probability will be, the subject of a tragedy or of a great epic work by any of its survivors: Rather, the war's tragic meaning will have to be discovered, and its total human drama rendered, in the various reminiscences and reflections that have been appearing since 1914. Yet if the Great War, with the passage of half a century, has not lent itself to tragic or epic expression, it has, in the divers literary forms of the fragments that have been written, disclosed what is just as imperishable and just as sacred a manifestation of the creative spirit: prophetic vision. This vision arises from a special knowledge, in itself a result of experiencing some historical happening in civilization at its midnight hour, and communicates with a sense of urgency a special revelation, that burden of vision which a Hebrew prophet depicted as his responsibility to "Write the vision and make it plain, upon tables, that he may run that readeth it."[38] No less than other celebrated writers in the great prophetic tradition which extends back to the ancient Hebrews, the survivors of the Great War often "see" and "speak" in their writings with a prophetic power that reveals hidden truths. And like great prophets

---

35 Paul Valéry, *History and Politics,* trans. by Denise Folliot and Jackson Mathews (New York, 1962), pp. 115, 116.

36 *Ibid.,* as reprinted, p. 23.

37 *Ibid.,* p. 29.

38 Habakkuk 2:2.

who see more than they ought to see, they speak directly from the inner fact of things with an immediacy of experience and concern endowing their vision with a truth no less significant or imperative than that with which the ancient prophet demanded of his people, "Hear this word."

Prophetic literature is a "literature of crisis." It emerges in the midst of breakdown. It is addressed to men who do not know, who do not understand. It decries the violation of the dignity of life. It protests against human debasement. It speaks not only of what is happening or has happened, but also of what can happen. The prophetic voice has no finality in the historical setting in which suffering is uncircumscribed. With the pain of experience and with a compassion and a pathos that endure, the prophet's words register a special awareness, beyond experience itself—even beyond man himself. Prophets, Paul Tillich suggests, "are like the refined instruments which register the shaking of the earth on far-removed sections of its surface."[39] These words crystallize some of the essential qualities and functions of the writings of those who fought in the Great War. For these writings summon us to take part in a time of crisis of a guilt-ridden epoch, to recognize a historical situation, and to fathom its disaster as it is re-created and reflected in words— in the vision—that echo the Hebrew prophet's own lament: "The harvest is past, the summer is ended, and we are not saved."[40] The prophetic spirit, Martin Buber maintains, "instils the vision in the people for all time to come. It lives within the people from then on as a longing to realize a truth."[41] Approached from this view, the literature of war becomes prophecy. Such literature, we can well agree with Sir Herbert, contains "the raw material for tragedy," "the substance of a world tragedy"; but it remains for prophecy to give to it universal significance.

Far from simplifying or sentimentalizing the problem of war, as Douglas Jerrold feared,[42] these writings are prophetic in their warnings. They are quintessentially part of the historical process and witness to "the rebelliousness of the hour" rather than to "the struggle for revelation." Once the war had ended, Rilke remarked, "the world passed out of the hands of God into the hands of men." In an age that has been increasingly concerned with the problematic relation between man and man, not between man and God, it is to

---

39 *The Shaking of the Foundations* (New York, 1948) , p. 7.
40 Jeremiah 8:20.
41 *Pointing the Way: Collected Essays,* trans. by Maurice S. Friedman (New York, 1956) , p. 190.
42 See his *The Lie About the War* (Criterion Miscellany, no. 9; London, 1930) .

this truth that the war writers turn our attention. The war writer as prophet unveils the spirit of an age in which man, cut off from God and the old value system, is also cut off from other men. The war itself epitomized this schism. The soldier-prophet registers its pain and terror. Indeed, the experience and the forces of terror in this century are announced, are prophesied, in the writings that came out of 1914–18. An event like Virginia Woolf's suicide in 1941 can be connected with the terror, the fanaticism, the violence, which the Great War unleashed. Her suicide note summarizes the terror that appeared with such "unparalleled" savagery in 1914 and was to continue into World War II. Besides, it shows how defenseless a private life, and civilization with it, is in the presence of fear and force, "the last arguments" which, Clive Bell says in *Civilization*,[43] the Great War confirmed. "I feel certain [Mrs. Woolf wrote] that I am going mad again. I feel we can't go through another of those horrible times. And I shan't recover this time. I hear voices and cannot concentrate on my work. I have fought against it, but I cannot fight any longer."[44]

Military despotism, the herd instinct, barbarism—the Great War signaled the entry of these forces of terror into modern life, as the wheels of the universe seemed to roll backward. When the Belgian city of Louvain, with its great library, its art treasures, its famous public buildings, was burned and devastated and its civilian population mercilessly slaughtered in the early days of the war, it was made clear that in a modern "murder war" nothing is preservable, least of all the amenities and sanctities of civilization. From the very beginning of the conflict, the pleas of a Hermann Hesse, in Berne, to artists and thinkers not to be engulfed by the war spirit—"*O Freunde, nicht diese Töne!*"[45]—or the counsel of a Romain Rolland, in Geneva, to remain "*au-dessus de la mêlée*," were destined by and large to be ignored or to be received as the foolish ideas of "pacifists" and "defeatists." Any expectation of discovering after 1914 "the moral equivalent of war" became redundant. As the war dragged on year in and year out, so did all hope and faith vanish. In the resultant conditions of life, the boredom and the dreariness at the front and away from the front, 1914–18 may be seen as years that lie, in Barbara Tuchman's words, "like a band of scorched earth dividing that time from ours."[46] There died in those lost years— *lost,* for they were years wrenched from the body of life—the hopes

---

43 Middlesex, England, 1947 [1928], p. 137.
44 Quoted in James Hafley, *The Glass Roof* (Berkeley, 1954), pp. 6–7.
45 *Above the Battle, op. cit.* p. 157.
46 *The Proud Tower* (New York, 1966), p. xiii.

for civilization that life in itself enjoins. This war served as a pro-
logue to an age—particularly to that modern spirit of discontent and
of an endless groping for meaning, for values that the conflict had
all along proved valueless.

As some of the survivors stress, perhaps the greatest casualty of the
war was the collapse of the established values of a social order, of
European civilization, extending back to the French Revolution.
Although it had survived the conflagrations of 1830, 1848, and 1870,
this civilization was unequal to the struggle posed by the Great War.
It was unequal to this struggle not because the struggle was no
longer considered necessary or right but because civilization was
unready for the radical nature of a time when history was being
emptied of its past. The Great War degraded the civilizing reti-
cences, whether in the methods and weapons of modern warfare
or in the cause and manner of death. What the survivors often decry
in their writings is the obscenity of the war and, in turn, the obscenity of the "modern mind." On the front lines, as well as at the home,
among statesmen, priests, generals, among soldiers, their parents,
their wives—allies and enemies alike—everyone had submitted to
the obscene process of the war, to that "modern mind" that, out-
distancing itself in its inventions and capacity for invention, had
depraved itself. A war that for many started somehow with a vague
dream of a better world gradually brought the realization that civilization was reverting to the obscenities of life at its most primitive
level. That this shock was overpowering and even impossible to
fathom becomes the burden of the message of the literature of the
Great War and the source of its prophecy.

Many writers depict the Great War as a tragedy in the history of
European civilization. Certainly when the period of this "war-
disease" is examined; when the war's barbarism, both "scientific"
and "systematic," is seen in all its pain and horror; when European
society was reduced to a collective state of destruction or one of
awaiting destruction; when the spirit of the time was no more than
a "hymn to hate," with the voices of reason and compassion giving
way to those of violence—"Have no fear, our force will slay theirs,"
the French philosopher Henri Bergson asserted,[47] and his words
summed up the sentiments on both sides, as even intellectuals and
academicians affirmed that force contains the only solutions—it is
not difficult to detect the tragic ramifications of this war: the calamity, the anguish, the despair, the oppressiveness, the pathos, the
fatefulness which are the constants of all tragedy, classical and

---

47 *The Meaning of the War* (London, 1915) , p. 47.

modern. Characterized by ugliness, cynicism, insensitivity, scorn, criminality, it was tragedy that was mean-spirited, without the beauty, without the wisdom, without the nobility and humanism that redeem tragedy and man. In the tragedy of this war, man's puniness was laid bare with devastating contempt: Man was nothing, degraded as he was to instrumentality by an obscene mechanical process. In a word, the tragedy of the Great War was a modern tragedy of obscenity, when neither man's understanding nor his virtues could resemble or equal those endemic to the ascendant rhythm of ancient tragedy. Such a tragedy could hardly conclude except on the humiliating note of insult and sneer, as the spectacle of the postwar period, right up to 1939, iterated with multiplying examples.

By no means should these remarks imply that the generation of 1914–18 was unequal to or incapable of tragedy. Their writings on the war show only too clearly a grasp of the tragic elements that no survivor of World War II has yet to disclose. From every standpoint the generation that fought in the Great War was a generation made for suffering and heroism in a "war against war." That they were an unsuspicious generation with a passion for idealism and justice and freedom; that they were responsive to "cause" and "principle" and "duty"; that they were as proud and self-confident as they were romantic and naïve; that they were a generation that believed in creative reason, in progress, in civilization, and hence in man's destiny are qualities that the men of 1914 reveal without conscious effort. But if this generation was worthy of heroic attitudes and gestures that still looked back to early times, they were not ready for the changes that affected tragic experience in the modern world. For millions of men the experience of the war was tragic in its physical and mental suffering; in its exposure of the inchoate evil and the chaos existent in the visible world; in its desperation and dilemma, as well as in its hopelessness. But although the phenomenal experience of the war was for many men tragic, the vision implicit in tragedy was not. The mechanical nature of modern warfare had neutralized not only men, but also values. Life had been terribly cheapened; suffering itself had been devalued. The ultimate meaning of the war had been translated into something soulless, into a state that gravitated not to a higher recognition of human value but to meaninglessness.

The war finally constituted an unelevated tragedy, lifted to no noble scale or design, and thus holding no visionary, no revivifying, meaning for man and his world. In place of magnanimity, which is intrinsic to the experience of tragedy with its "divine worth of tones and tears," the war ordained a squalid human destiny, one of bondage to distortions and perverseness. If, therefore, the historical situation was conducive to tragic experience, with the warning to man not to boast in his strength as applicable to European man in 1914–18 as it was to the ancient Greek heroes, the unnatural and immoral conditions of the war failed, necessarily, to produce vision. A war that violated and scorned the dignity of and a reverence for life precluded tragic vision—precluded, that is, the possibility of a deep, redeeming awareness of man's place in the modern world. A sense of nothingness, of futility, of cynicism, of alienation from the past (now there would be "no more parades!" "No more Hope, no more Glory, no more parades for you and me any more," wrote Ford Madox Ford[48]), which the conflict resulted in, signified not the attainment of vision, and thus of truth and value, but the impasse of despair and the death of hope in the midst of the obscene. The Great War became tragedy without vision, the experience of evil and suffering without value, without the culminating affirmation and decisiveness that bring with them even a fleeting comprehension of victory over the seal of man's betrayal and condemnation.

"The war," wrote Benedetto Croce, "which had been announced to the peoples with the promise of a general catharsis, in its course and its end was completely untrue to this promise."[49] Not a transfiguring nobility but a sense of disgust beyond despair marked the temper of Europe by November 11, 1918. The very sordidness of the war, the whole demeaning process of its rapacity, had cheated man of any positiveness of a tragic vision, of something valuable and lasting in life and in the universe, some conception of wisdom and regeneration. In short, war, once again, but on a more monstrous scale, had not enlarged the meaning of life, had not, in an integrally tragic sense, revealed either humility or enlightenment, or shown man, trapped by conflict, a different shape of his destiny. No longer was it even a matter of optimism or pessimism. At the end of the war, man's apathy, his smallness, and, indeed, his loathsomeness informed the prevailing view of events and consequences. More than life itself had died in the conflict. Max Ernst, the German painter who had fought at the front and had been wounded, said that the question that the war finally posed for him was: "How to overcome the disgust and fatal boredom that military life and the horrors of war create. Howl? Blaspheme? Vomit?"[50] His words epitomize the feelings of men who, recognizing the fact that with

48 *No More Parades*, in *Parade's End* (New York, 1961 [1925]) , p. 307.

49 *History of Europe in the Nineteenth Century,* trans. by Henry Furst (New York, 1933) , p. 350.

50 *Max Ernst,* William S. Lieberman, ed. (New York, 1961) , p. 11.

this war, senselessness had made its appearance in society, wanted to spit in the eye of the world, as well as the mood that swept over postwar Europe, when, as Aldous Huxley was to write, "To-morrow . . . will be as awful as to-day."[51]

That the Great War could go beyond a tragedy of phenomena to become a tragedy of vision and knowledge, that tragedy which Karl Jaspers defines as "the measure of man's greatness in breakdown and failure"[52] and which transcends man's "limit-situation," was a promise that never materialized. The promise of greatness with which the war was identified at the outset when, as a poet rhapsodized, the time was ripe "To win Eternity/ And claim God's kiss,"[53] was dead by 1918. As undoubtedly an experience of failure dramatizing the precariousness of human meaning and truth, the war had in the end hardly affirmed "the measure of man's greatness." History since 1914 has reinforced man's view of a world adying and of an existence more deeply despised, even as new cataclysms appear. More than at any other time in the history of civilization, what happened in 1914–18 imparted the force of the truth that "Every truth we may think complete will prove itself untruth at the moment of shipwreck."[54] The Great War, marking the triumph of such a "moment"—a moment that now spans more than fifty years as a chronicle of an age and a condition of a civilization—negated not alone the human possibility, as war must always negate it, but also man's expedition toward the goal which Jaspers sees as carrying the only promise of greatness which can overcome the fear and the expiration of hope itself: "This is the vision of a great and noble life: to endure ambiguity in the movement of truth and to make light shine through it; to stand fast in uncertainty; to prove capable of unlimited love and hope."[55]

,
GEORGE ANDREW PANICHAS

Winter-Spring, 1967–1968

---

51 *Antic Hay* (New York, 1965 [1923]) , p. 283.

52 *Tragedy Is Not Enough,* trans. by Harald A. T. Reiche, Harry T. Moore, and Karl W. Deutsch (Boston, 1952) , p. 45.

53 "The Dead Heroes," in *The Collected Poems of Isaac Rosenberg,* Gordon Bottomley and Denys Harding, ed. (New York, 1949) , p. 42.

54 *Tragedy Is Not Enough, op. cit.,* p. 104.

55 *Ibid.,* p. 105.

A Total View

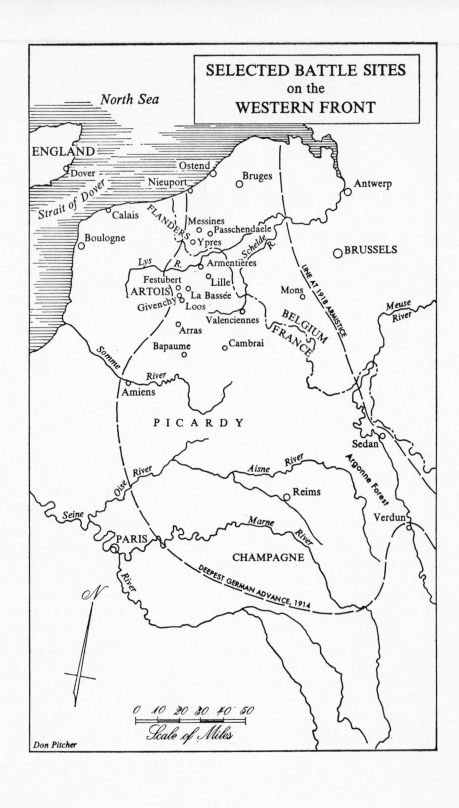

SELECTED BATTLE SITES
on the
WESTERN FRONT

North Sea

ENGLAND

Dover

Strait of Dover

Ostend

Nieuport

Bruges

Antwerp

Calais

FLANDERS

Messines

Passchendaele

Ypres

Schelde R.

BRUSSELS

Boulogne

Lys R.

Armentières

Festubert

Lille

ARTOIS

La Bassée

Mons

Givenchy

Loos

Valenciennes

BELGIUM

Meuse River

Arras

Cambrai

FRANCE

Bapaume

Somme River

Amiens

PICARDY

Sedan

Oise River

Aisne River

Argonne Forest

Reims

Seine River

Marne River

Verdun

PARIS

CHAMPAGNE

River

LINE AT 1918 ARMISTICE

DEEPEST GERMAN ADVANCE, 1914

N

0 10 20 30 40 50

Scale of Miles

Don Pitcher

Robert Graves

ROBERT GRAVES' *autobiography* Good-bye to All That (1927) *has been termed* "*a permanently valuable work of literary art, and indispensable for the historian either of the First World War or of modern English poetry.*" *What Mr. Graves speaks of in this book as his* "*conditioning in the Protestant morality of the English governing classes, though qualified by mixed blood, a rebellious nature, and an overriding poetic obsession, . . . not easily out-grown*" *can be seen in his contributions to literature. His books of mythology and collected essays are admired by scholars and used in college courses, and he has composed many distinguished translations from Latin, Greek, German, French, and Spanish texts. He is frequently invited to the United States to lecture and read from his work, especially from his famous poetry. In 1963 he was poet in residence at the Massachusetts Institute of Technology, where he enjoyed teasing the* "*scientific mind.*"

Born in London in 1895, Mr. Graves fought with the Royal Welch Fusi-liers in France during World War I and then earned a degree at Oxford. In 1926 he was professor of English literature at Cairo University in Egypt. He has lived in Majorca since 1929, except for a period which he describes in the Epilogue to Good-bye to All That: "*The one serious set-back to my quiet life [in Majorca] came with the Spanish Civil War in 1936, when all British subjects were advised to leave, by warship. I wandered around Europe and the United States for three years; and spent the Second World War in England, because three of my children had joined the Armed Forces—the fourth, Sam, being prevented by deafness from doing the same.*" *His oldest son, David, having joined the First Royal Welch in World War II, was shot and killed on the Arakan peninsula, Burma, in March, 1943, while rushing a Japanese strongpoint single-handed.*

Mr. Graves, his second wife, and the youngest of his eight children now live in Deyá, Majorca, a section where tourists are seldom seen. Long hours at his desk are interrupted by swimming in the Mediterranean and leisurely con-versations with his family and friends. Majorca Observed *eloquently expresses his love of that island. As for the rest of his work, however, Mr. Graves affirms,* "*I think it has nothing in it that is not fundamentally English. There is perhaps one olive tree in my poems; otherwise, they are from my native island—not my adopted one.*"

THE KAISER'S WAR:
A BRITISH POINT OF VIEW

WHEN THE NEWSPAPER PLACARDS on August 4, 1914, read: ENGLAND DECLARES WAR ON GERMANY—"Britain" being a word not yet in current use—there was no prouder nation in the world than ours. Though possessing the greatest Empire ever known and ruling it, on the whole, humanely, we nevertheless supplemented the national anthem with "Land of Hope and Glory":

> Wider still and wider
> Shall thy bounds be set!
> God who made thee mighty
> Make thee mightier yet!

As successors of the Romans, it suited our governing classes to continue their imperial tradition. The nobility and landed gentry sent their sons to public schools and the major universities for the discipline of Latin, Greek, and the birch rod. The unassuming and ultrarespectable "middle class" enjoyed a shorter but more practical education. Our profane laboring classes struggled against ignorance and dire poverty, spent a large part of their wages on drink, and nursed a stubborn pride in being English. Socialism seemed on the decline: Labour had lost ten seats in the general election of 1910 and now held a mere 41 out of 670. Women could not vote; neither, for that matter, could millions of men who lacked substantial property—such as the lower ranks in the Army and Navy.

Motorcars had not yet seriously challenged horse traffic; filthy street crossings were still swept by ragged, barefoot boys for button-booted ladies to negotiate with raised skirts. Electric light was a rare domestic luxury, the telephone rarer; laborsaving devices were limited to carpet sweeper, meat grinder, knife-cleaning machine; and the racks worked by a pulley for drying wet clothes over the kitchen range. Airplanes in their infancy; jerky, silent, moving pictures enlivened by piano music; no broadcasting. Untarred main roads; slums of appalling horror in every big city. A powerful Liberal Party. Eire not yet a republic. Free trade; no check on immigration; a minimal income tax. The civil service about a fiftieth of its present size, working short hours and still using quill pens and red tape. Divorces unusual and disgraceful. . . .

We were the envy of the world, especially of our "German cousins" who, because of their preeminence in music, philosophy, and social sciences, believed themselves chosen by God to succeed us. Their temperamental Kaiser, a grandson of Queen Victoria, had declared that Germany's future lay on the sea and undertaken never to rest until her fleet was as strong as her army—already the most powerful in the world. In 1900 he told German troops whom he sent to defend the Peking foreign legations against Boxer rebels that they must emulate the terrible Huns of old: hence the newspaper use of "Huns" for Germans. His frequent "saber rattling," from the time of the Boer War until the Agadir incident in 1912, his attempt to break the Anglo-French Entente Cordiale, and the covetous eye he threw at our colonies annoyed us almost beyond endurance. His excuse for Germany's invasion of Belgium—the murder of an Austrian archduke in the Balkans—seemed cynically irrelevant. We felt relieved when *Der Tag*, solemnly toasted by German naval officers, dawned at last.

Most historians present the war as a sort of chess game between rival supreme commands: the united British, French, Belgian, Russian, and Serbian commands on one hand, and the united German, Austrian, Turkish, and Bulgarian on the other. But what a game! Each group of players in persistent disunity, everyone new to the game, fresh pieces continually introduced, and fresh rules extemporized. . . .

None of us had the least presentiment of coming catastrophe. The Fleet had taken up its battle station at Scapa Flow; the British Expeditionary Force had landed in France. Our French and Russian allies were mobilizing twice as many divisions as the Germans; the Austrian Army seemed a liability rather than an asset to the Kaiser's forces; Italy had declared herself neutral and later joined us. "War will be over by Christmas." "Business as Usual!" Which was like saying: "The best cure for a cold is hot rum and a couple of days in bed."

Memories of the Boer War—only twelve years behind us—came flooding back. The heroic departure of the City Imperial Volunteers:

> Duke's son, cook's son, son of a hundred kings:
> Fifty-thousand horse and foot going to Table Bay—
> Each of them doing their country's work. . . .

The glorious bonfires of Mafeking night:

> We're the soldiers of the King, my lad;
> The King, my lad; the King, my lad:
> We shall fight for England's glorious name
> Like the soldiers of the King. . . .

All our generals were cavalrymen, for in this respect alone the English did not imitate the Romans, who had treated infantry as their most honorable arm, with cavalry as mere flank protection supplied by subject allies. Not until A.D. 378, when Gothic heavy cavalry broke the legions at Adrianople, did European horsemen count themselves superior beings. Then arose the code of chivalry, borrowed from Islam by our Norman ancestors. In medieval times, King Arthur and his Knights of the Round Table—commemorated in the Order of the Garter—meant more to our chivalrous governing classes than all the saints in the calendar except their patron, St. George. Every duke led out his mounted vassals; every lesser peer his knights; every knight his rabble of footmen armed with bows, bills, and long knives, whom he called "my dear children," or "infantry." And, blind to change, Generals French, Haig, Plumer, Cavan, and the rest still thought of war as a succession of heroic cavalry charges: their territorial gains consolidated by slow-marching infantry.

They made a point of opposing every mechanical innovation that might disturb this dream. They loved horses; they excelled in polo; they hated motorcars and lorries—nasty-smelling things at which horses shied. Apart from a few traction engines for pulling heavy siege guns, the B.E.F. was completely unmechanized until, at the last moment, a couple of Royal Engineer officers were sent to commandeer a few score brewery lorries. No provision had, of course, been made for a supply of magnetos, and the disgraceful story of how the War Office obtained them by secret trading with the Bosch Company of Stuttgart has never yet, I believe, been told! The German Army was equipped with 500 lorries, each towing a trailer: Mercedes-Benz, Dürkopp, and others. Their plan of attack had been prepared down to the last detail.

In late August the British Expeditionary Force—which the Kaiser described as "that contemptible small army" (hence the "Old Contemptibles") —were forced by French defeat on their flank to a headlong retreat from Mons. Small, yes: six divisions, compared with the Germans' eighty-seven. Yet when in October the Germans —now held at the Aisne—decided to smother the B.E.F. by a mass attack at Ypres and seize the Channel ports, they suffered fantastic casualties from musketry so rapid and accurate that they mistook it for machine-gun fire. There were no British reserves, however. On November 14, our 1st and 7th Divisions had been practically annihilated, and Prussian troops poured through a gap. They were met by the Royal Field Artillery firing over open sights, and then counterattacked by a scratch force: cooks, tailors, transportmen, headquarter clerks—being the thirty survivors from the 2d Queens and forty from the 1st Royal Welch Fusiliers, commanded by a second lieutenant named Orme (just arrived from Sandhurst) whose death left the battalion officerless. The Prussians hesitated and dug in. Heavy rain fell; the line held.

More then half our Army had become casualties at Ypres. The ranks were refilled with Special Reservists who could at least form fours and use their rifles. Comfortable West End clubmen argued that although the Germans had overrun all Belgium and a great part of northern France and beaten the Russians decisively at Tannenberg, they had now shot their bolt. Our French and Russian allies would soon grind them to powder.

What began as an ordinary old-fashioned campaign took on, by the spring of 1915, the nightmare quality of total war. The period of fluid fighting—enjoyed by Uhlans, Hussars, and Lancers—had ended in the previous September, and every month of stalemate now made it more difficult for the Germans to break our front, which ran from the North Sea to Switzerland. Formed accidentally by the useless attempts of both sides to outflank one another, it consisted of a front line protected by barbed-wire entanglements, machine-gun nests, and listening posts, and behind it support lines, rear lines, and tactical reserves. Soon all the higher commands caught the same obsessional madness: a conviction that the enemy line could be breached by intense bombardment, with cavalry held in readiness to gallop through, fan out, and pave the way for an infantry advance. But the German General Staff, still set on capturing the Channel ports, decided to fortify their artillery fire with a surprise weapon banned by the Hague Convention: poison gas.

They tried it on April 22 at the Ypres Salient. The 1st Canadian Division, its principal victims, did not panic—as their French-Algerian neighbors had done—and the line, though flattened, remained unbroken. This shocking event, and the later German use of flame throwers, made us so credulous of German atrocity stories served up by official war correspondents that any compromise peace became unthinkable.

Our declared policy was now "attrition," meaning the daily and nightly bombardment of trenches to weaken enemy morale. That needed an unlimited supply of shells (but David Lloyd George, our new Minister of Munitions, saw to it) and, since the Germans might imitate our strategy, an unlimited supply of cannon fodder: namely, conscripts. We had suffered 500,000 casualties by the summer of 1915, and at the Battle of the Somme—Sir Douglas Haig's first attempt at a breakthrough—another 500,000. Yet he claimed (untruly) that our losses were inconsiderable compared with the Germans', and the Military Service Act soon swelled his command to a generous 1,500,000. Haig grudged the divisions sent away to "sideshows"—facing the Austrians in Italy, the Turks in Egypt, the Bulgarians in Greece—believed that the war could be won only on the western front, and wrote in his diary that Almighty God Himself seemed to guide whatever decisions he made.

The British despised Continental armies on the grounds that one volunteer was a match for four conscripts. But in a war of attrition, the volunteer's prowess was not often put to the test by hand-to-hand fighting. Besides, conscripts soon acquired the appearance of volunteers by wearing the same uniforms and sharing the same discomforts.

Each army in turn attempted the knockout punch: that glorious swing from hip to jaw. Each failed. The most unspeakably horrible, pointless, and costly campaign ever fought by British troops was Haig's 1917 offensive. He told the Cabinet that he had "no intention of entering into a tremendous offensive involving heavy loss," and told his Army commanders that "opportunities for the employment of cavalry in masses are likely to occur." Although warned by Engineer experts that prolonged shelling of the Ypres area would inevitably destroy the drainage system and return the land to swamp, he subjected the enemy trenches to a fortnight's bombardment: 4,500,000 shells. Even this failed to silence the German machine guns ensconced in concrete pillboxes on higher ground. We made gains of a few hundred yards, but the Engineers' prediction was fulfilled. The Passchendaele battlefield became a quagmire in which not only hundreds of men, but even mules, were drowned, guns disappeared, and to dig a trench was merely to create a canal. . . . Another 400,000 casualties; yet Haig was not superseded.

He had ridiculed tanks—a British invention—as impracticable toys, and lost their surprise effect on the Somme, in September, 1916, by wasting the first small consignment on a purely local gain. It was not until November 20, 1917, that he permitted a mass attack by 380 tanks across hard ground near Cambrai, without preliminary bombardment. They made an advance of 5 miles, breaking through to open country; but our cavalry were not alerted, and Haig, with no reserves left after Passchendaele, had proudly refused Foch's offer of a French Army corps to exploit the breach, which the Germans did not close for several hours.

This was the month of the Bolshevik Revolution, when Russia's armies ceased fighting. The Germans would soon be able to transfer 2,000,000 men from their eastern front to the west. Meanwhile, they further alienated themselves from the rest of the world by a more serious defiance of international law. Their submarines were ordered to torpedo merchant vessels on the high seas, including neutrals, without examining their cargoes or allowing the crews time to escape in lifeboats. They even sank hospital ships and justified this on the ground that our blockade had been starving children and noncombatants. Thus the United States was eventually brought into the war; but by April, 1917, the Allies lost nearly 1,000,000 tons of shipping each month, despite the 3,000 destroyers and other light craft allotted to submarine chasing. Fortunately, by autumn, the convoy system and American naval help had reduced these losses to 200,000 a month.

England was transformed. Rationing, for the first time in history: unbuttered muffins, wedding cakes without sugar. Golf links commandeered as drill grounds. Country houses turned into hospitals. Servant girls deserting ducal kitchens for the munitions factory. Class distinctions disappearing, as when wounded officers promoted from the ranks fell in love with aristocratic V.A.D. (Voluntary Aid Detachment) nurses. Zeppelin raids, and boy scouts blowing the all clear on bugles. Women enrolled as Army cooks, typists, *chauffeuses*: saluting like men, instead of curtsying. The universities taken over by cadet battalions. Expansion of the Royal Flying Corps and the Royal Naval Air Services into the world's largest air force, though suffering immensely high training losses, and without parachutes. War babies; hated war profiteers; despised conscientious objectors. An alarming increase in venereal disease. A sudden boom in poetry. . . .

We were now shouldering the heaviest burden of the war, America's new armies being still untrained and short of weapons; the French Army having mutinously refused any more offensives; and the Italians not having recovered from their fearful defeat at Caporetto. Attrition, attrition, attrition! One thousand men killed daily, and a daily 7,000,000 pounds of war debt. Trench life was as obsessive as alcohol. Only in the trenches did we feel free—from generals, staff officers, military police, drill sergeants, lead-swingers, journalists, civilian bores, patriots, or religious fanatics. . . . But continuous shell fire and the lesser nuisances of machine guns, trench mortars, rifle grenades so stimulated our adrenal glands that, after three months, we became mentally off-center; after six, certifiably insane. We welcomed an occasional ten days' leave but, if lightly wounded, soon grew bored with hospital and depot and schemed to get back again, our wounds half-healed. The trenches made us feel larger than life: only there was death a joke rather than a threat.

The better divisions, which could take up to 90 percent casualties without breaking, were thrown into every important attack. A soldier who had the honor to serve with one of them could count on no more than three months' trench service before being wounded or killed; a junior officer, on a mere six weeks. This difference was largely caused by the officer's being condemned, as an honorary horseman, to wear riding breeches and a swordless leather sword belt and thus to provide a tempting target for German marksmen.

We held two irreconcilable beliefs: that the war would never end and that we would win it. Eventually it was won, not by us infantrymen so much as by the naval blockade—which starved the Germans into surrender while still occupying Belgium and a great part of France. Their troops on the western front were withdrawing to the Rhine, but in excellent order, as even Haig admitted. They accepted an Armistice on November 11th, 1918, and peace was proclaimed in the following July.

At the Peace Conference attended by President Wilson, God, who made us mighty, made us mightier yet: on paper. The seizure of German colonies added immense new tracts to our Empire; but we had lost 1,000,000 dead, and as many permanently disabled, besides incurring some 5,000,000,000 pounds' worth of war debts. The Americans, who had sent 2,000,000 men to our rescue and lost 800,000, now led the world and were in a position to take over our lost foreign markets and turn their backs on Europe. Why not? The original quarrel had not been theirs. In May, 1920, the Senate refused to ratify the peace treaty signed by the President and, in 1921, withdrew their representative from the Council of Ambassadors at Paris, thus opting out of the Supreme Council at the League of Nations. The policing and rehabilitation of Germany were left to the French and us.

A generation later the Germans, driven to despair by the wreck of their sacred ambitions, made a second bid for world mastery. Although in Hitler's war our armies were commanded by prudent and capable infantry generals, the subsequent peace reduced us

from a second-class power to a third-. We were forced at last to stop
thinking like Romans and jettison all but a few fragments of our
Empire. Thanks to the nuclear bomb, however, we have been
spared a third world war and, in our quiet way, are sane again:
prosperous, lively, inventive, and unresentful. Class distinctions
have all but vanished; so has real poverty; we are seldom deceived
by political handouts; religion is a matter of choice, not social
pressure; and though oppressed by hordes of faceless bureaucrats,
we have preserved our national liberty, our Crown, and our sense of
humor. Nor have we yet forgotten our debt to the United States for
having saved us, in Hitler's war, from an infinitely worse fate than
the Kaiser ever threatened.

Myself, I value the Kaiser's war as having given me not only an
unsurpassable standard of danger, discomfort, and horror by which
to judge more recent troubles, but a confidence in the golden-
heartedness and iron endurance of my fellow countrymen (proved
again during Hitler's war) , which even the laxity of this new plastic
age cannot disturb.

Roland Dorgelès

In the eyes of World War I veterans, Roland Dorgelès is the writer who has best described their common memories, their courage, their misery, and fifty years after the war, his books have become pages of history. He may be said to symbolize a generation.

Born at Amiens in the Somme on June 15, 1885, prior to 1914 he led a happy, though often difficult, life in Montmartre which was later to inspire absorbing writings. But his destiny was cast, and suddenly, at the mobilization.

Classified as unfit to serve because of pulmonary illness by the draft board in 1906, and thus exempted from all military duty, he nonetheless enlisted in the infantry in August, 1914. Assigned to the 74th Infantry (Rouen), he asked to leave for the front immediately; and with neither the instruction nor the training that would have followed, he reached the combat zone at the beginning of September and was assigned to the 39th Infantry.

In the Artois attacks of June, 1915, he received the Croix de guerre with this first citation: "Remarkable asset to morale. Under heavy bombardment and though all his machine gunners were disabled, alone assured the functioning of his piece. Himself wounded, refused to be evacuated and continued to fire."

At the end of 1915, he was called into the Air Force. After a serious crash, he was assigned to the auxiliary forces and classified as definitively unfit, then appointed to be an instructor.

When he was discharged, in April, 1919, he published Les Croix de bois, a work that brought him immediate fame. Two years later, having brought out a second war book, Le Cabaret de la Belle Femme, he was made a chevalier of the Legion of Honor.

Since then, Dorgelès has published twenty volumes—novels, travel books, memoirs—all of which have proved to be resounding successes: Partir, La Caravane san chameaux, Vive la liberté, Sous le casque blanc, Bouquet de Bohème, Portraits sans retouche, Tout est à vendre, A Bas l'argent, and others.

Early during the Occupation several of his books were banned. The author was officially notified that the Germans would authorize the reprinting of

these war books, provided certain cuts were made. He refused emphatically.
Soon after the liberation, moreover, Dorgelès wrote Carte d'identité, *describing how he was tracked by the Gestapo to the Haute-Garonne village where he had taken refuge and from which he had to flee after an inquiry.*

Dorgelès was elected to the Académie Goncourt in 1929, to fill the seat left vacant by Georges Courteline, and succeeded Colette in the presidency of that body. He was made a grand officer of the Legion of Honor in 1962.*

---

* The Legion of Honor, the order of merit instituted by Napoleon in 1802, consists of the ranks (in ascending order) of chevalier (or knight) , officer, commander, grand officer, and grand cross.—Tr.

AFTER FIFTY YEARS*

———◆———

FIFTY YEARS!

It has already been fifty years since the thunder of the shells fell silent, more than half a century since the war exploded upon a frightened world.

For us who lived those exalting hours, this past is very close. In the bat of an eyelid it rises again; the events are revived; faces that have disappeared are resurrected. This is a page of history we are unresigned to turning. Our musing leads us back to August, 1914. A terrible date in the young century.

For a week Paris had been living in a fever. We swung from anguish to hope in the wake of telegrams coming from the four corners of Europe:ultimatum to Serbia . . . the English intercede . . . Berlin refuses . . . appeal to The Hague . . . mobilization in Russia . . . state of war in Germany—then Saturday, August 1, in the afternoon, the suffocating time of storms, the terrible news broke like a lightning bolt.

"It's come! It's posted at the district mayor's office," a passerby shouted to me as he ran.

I reached the Rue Drouot in one leap and shouldered through the mob that already filled the courtyard to approach the fascinating white sheet pasted to the door. I read the message at a glance,

---

* Translated from the French by Sally Abeles.

then reread it slowly, word for word, to convince myself that it was true:

THE FIRST DAY OF
MOBILIZATION WILL BE
SUNDAY, AUGUST 2

Only three lines, written hastily by a hand that trembled. It was an announcement to a million and a half Frenchmen.

The people who had read it moved away, stunned, while others crowded in, but this silent numbness did not last. Suddenly a heroic wind lifted their heads. What? War, was it? Well, then, let's go! Without any signal, the "Marseillaise" poured from thousands of throats, sheaves of flags appeared at windows, and howling processions rolled out on the boulevards. Each column brandished a placard: ALSACE VOLUNTEERS, JEWISH VOLUNTEERS, POLISH VOLUNTEERS. They hailed one another above the bravos of the crowd, and this human torrent, swelling at every corner, moved on to circle around the Place de la Concorde, before the statue of Strasbourg banked with flowers, then flowed toward the Place de la République, where mobs from Belleville and the Faubourg St. Antoine yelled themselves hoarse on the refrain from the great days, *"Aux armes, citoyens!"* (To arms, citizens!) But this time it was better than a song.

To gather the news for my paper, I ran around the city in every direction. At the Cours la Reine I saw the fabled cuirassiers in their horsetail plumes march by, and at the Rue La Fayette footsoldiers in battle garb with women throwing flowers and kisses to them. In a marshaling yard I saw guns being loaded, their long, thin barrels twined around with branches and laurel leaves, while troops in red breeches piled gaily into delivery vans they were scrawling with challenges and caricatures. Young and old, civilians and military men burned with the same excitement. It was like a Brotherhood Day.

Dead tired but still exhilarated, I got back to *L'Homme libre* and burst into the office of Georges Clemenceau, our chief.[1]

"What is Paris saying?" he asked me.

"It's singing, sir!"

"Then everything will be all right. . . ."

His old patriot's heart was not wrong; no cloud marred that fabulous day. Yet anything could have happened. The workers,

---

[1] *L'Homme libre* (The Free Man) was but one of several periodicals Clemenceau founded and directed during his long political career.—Tr.

overwhelmed by Jean Jaurès' death,[2] might demand revenge. The day before, a few minutes after the attack, I had leaned over the eloquent leader's body, stretched out on two marble-top tables at the Croissant Bar; I had read the anger in the faces of the workers who had surged out of the neighboring printshops. A word, a gesture and there would have been a riot; but an associate of Jaurès', standing in the vehicle where they were laying the tall body, exhorted the men, many of whom were weeping, to contain their rage, and heads lowered, teeth clenched, they watched in silence as the first death of the war was carried away in the night.

Less than twenty-four hours later, seeing their old dreams of peace crumble, they would stream out into the boulevards to demonstrate. But this time they would break into the "Marseillaise," not the "Internationale"; they would cry, "To Berlin!," not "Down with war!"

What did they have to defend, these black-nailed patriots? Not even a shack, an acre to till, indeed hardly a patch of ground reserved at the Pantin Cemetery; yet they would depart, like their rivals of yesterday, a heroic song on their lips and a flower in their guns. No more poor or rich, proletarians or bourgeois, right-wingers or militant leftists; there were only Frenchmen.

Beginning the next day, thousands of men eager to fight would jostle one another outside recruiting offices, waiting to join up. Men who could have stayed home, with their wives and children or an imploring mama. But no. The word "duty" had a meaning for them, and the word "country" had regained its splendor.

I close my eyes, and they appear to me, those volunteers on the great day; then I see them again in the old kepi or blue helmet, shouting, "Here!" when somebody called for men for a raid, or hurling themselves into an attack with fixed bayonets, and I wonder, and I question their bloody shades.

Tell me, comrades in eternal silence, would you have besieged the enlistment offices with the same enthusiasm, would you have fought such a courageous fight had you known that fifty years later those men in gray knit caps or steel helmets you were ordered to kill would no longer be enemies and that we would have to open our arms to them? Wouldn't the heroic "Let's go!" you shouted as you cleared the parapets have stuck in your throats? Deep in the grave where you dwell, don't you regret your sacrifice? "Why did we fight? Why did we let ourselves get killed?" This is the murmur of a million and a half voices rising from the bowels of the earth, and we, the survivors, do not know what to answer.

---

2 French Socialist, politician, and labor figure.—Tr.

Were they dupes, then, the men who valiantly offered themselves to the massacre? Were they being gulled when they were taught from childhood that dying for their country was the noblest of fates? Must we trample down the frontiers for which they were killed? Does duty continuously change meaning, depending on how the whimsical wind blows? So many questions we don't dare ask those heads with empty sockets. I would like to cry out to them, "No, your sacrifice was not in vain! Your valiance saved not only your country but the entire universe, which Germany would have crushed under her iron heel; the final victory is only an offspring of yours, and the great men of our time remain in your debt." But what would be the use? You don't console the dead with speeches. . . .

Taught by the events, we know today that we must forget. France and Germany are penned up in Europe like animals in a cage; if they do not come to terms, they will eat into each other till the end of time. Even if the heart is mute, reason gives us the word: We must cross out the years of war and occupation. Yes, I want to forget.

But the others, whose young mouths are sealed forever, who gave their lives to take a scrap of French soil back from the enemy, would they also be forgiving?

I feel no hatred for the hardy fighters whom I saw with my own eyes fire a shot or throw a grenade at me—they were tending to their terrible trade, as I to mine—but are all our dead equally at peace? I ask this question of my cousin, whom I went to dig up with my hands near Château-Thierry. He had a black hole in the back of his neck: the mark of the bullet fired from behind, coward fashion, when he had just been taken prisoner. Would you hold out your hand, your skeleton of a hand, to your murderer?

And you, gentle René Blum, you, proud François de Tessan, my closest friends, dead in Nazi camps, would you have the funereal courage to murmur, "Enough, let's be friends"?

All of us, of course, have had men before us who were not brutes. To allay my bitterness, I will evoke that bloodless wounded man our stretcher-bearers put down in front of the colonel's quarters late one night. His raiding party had slipped noiselessly up to our barbed wire, a handkerchief tied around their arms so as not to kill each other in the dark, and when they reached our zigzag trench they leaped at it shouting. This one had slumped over our parapet, wounded in the belly, and now, motionless under the brown blanket, he had stopped groaning. As the stretcher-bearers waited for his last breath, he made an effort and opened his eyes once more and begged in a hollow voice, "I want to die looking toward my country." A liaison officer who understood German translated, and lifting the dying man by the shoulders, my comrades, holding back their tears, propped him up facing his lines. The last flares were fading in the gray sky. He looked at that pale frontier a long moment, and then, murmuring perhaps a good-bye, he fell back heavily. We did not have to close his eyes. . . .

Along with him, I recall another. Not dying, this one; not even wounded. Quite sound, in fact, and almost provocative. Captured between the lines when he was on patrol, he had been taken to the colonel to be interrogated. He had been brought up in a school in Neuilly and spoke our language perfectly, but he refused to answer. He was asked what regiments were in his sector: "I don't know." Whether reinforcements were coming in: "I don't know." Whether they were digging attack trenches, whether the Brimont artillery was changing its emplacements: "I don't know." The colonel finally got angry: "If you don't speak, I'll have you shot!" The threat did not shake the prisoner. Then, shifting his tactics, our chief broke off a chunk of the still warm bread the orderly had just brought from the neighboring village and held it out to him: "It's good, huh, the bread of France. It makes your mouth water. Here, eat!"

The hungry soldier stood at attention. "Thank you, Colonel, I like black bread better. . . ."

Can we despise such men? Can we impute the crimes of the swastikaed butchers to them? I ask myself this uneasily; I ask it of my comrades of *Les Croix de bois*, the wooden crosses,[3] who fought at my side. Of my gunner pal, a Norman kid, I remember, who when the mist suddenly dissipated on the Loire plain spotted some men on fatigue duty in the German lines. Thinking they were invisible, they had come out of the communication trench to go faster and were moving toward their own trench across open ground.

"Fire! Mow them down!" our lieutenant ordered.

The gunner hesitated a second, then said resolutely, "No, Lieutenant. They aren't armed. You don't fire at sitting ducks."

The officer insisted, threatened, spoke of refusing to obey orders. Nothing worked. Our stubborn gunner had his concept of war and would not fire on defenseless men. The Germans, seeing they had been discovered, took to their heels and leaped into a sap. Do you know, poor Prussian or Bavarian devils, that if you are still alive, you owe it to this obstinate *Franzose* who risked a court-martial for you?

I could give other examples like these. Christmas night when Frenchmen and Germans on patrol came together between the

---

[3] Roland Dorgelès, *Les Croix de bois*, Paris, A. Michel, 1919; *Wooden Crosses*, G. P. Putnam's Sons, New York, 1921.—Ed.

lines, rifles slung on shoulders, and shook one another's hands and exchanged greetings they did not understand. Headquarters denounced these attempts to fraternize and threatened severe reprisals. On the German side the repressive measures were undoubtedly worse. Yet these soldiers were not mutineers who refused to fight. They proved it six weeks later in a savage attack which left hundreds of corpses on the ground. Perhaps the very ones who had shaken one another's hands Christmas night. . . .

To gird my loins, I appeal to the dead. To Edmond Adam, a clerk in the bridges and roads department, an infantry enlistee, a simple engineer they had made into a lieutenant, killed in Champagne at the end of the war. Between hard drives he scribbled poems in his shelter, and if they are unknown, I have not forgotten them. This one especially, which he dedicated to a combatant across from him:

> I bear you little ill will, you know,
> It's four years you've done your bit
> Behind your lookout slit. . . .
> Well, us, too, it's four years we've worked
> To knit these great meshes of nets
> And cut them the eve of attacks,
> To get through and chase you
> From your trenches.
> You see, we are neighbors,
> Almost buddies, in our labors.
> We sweat for rival houses.
> Agh! Maybe they deserve each other,
> Nobody knows. . . .

"Buddies," he wrote the word. . . . This one, I'm sure, would be forgiving.

Doubtless I haven't his greatness of soul: I still hesitate. The hand I would like to extend stays in a fist in my pocket. Not from the memory of my own wrath but from the thought of those who cursed them in agony. "You do not have the right," they could say in reproach.

This idea tormented me when I found myself in Berlin shortly before the last war. I had been invited to the final meeting of a veterans' conference presided over by the Duke of Saxe-Coburg-Gotha, and after a speaker had sounded my praises, I was pushed to the rostrum. Not wanting, not able, to talk of reconciliation to them, I said:

"As you have just been told, I belong to a generation which left its fields, its factories, its desks, its schools in August of 1914 to run for the frontier shouting, 'To Berlin!' " Here I paused a moment. Then: "Excuse me for getting to the appointment twenty-two years late."

They could have taken this as braggadocio and booed me, but General von Armin, seated in the first row, gave the signal for applause, and everyone followed.

I looked down on those aging men from the dais and thought I recognized them. Weren't they the same men, with their scars and campaign ribbons, whom I found each spring in the Invalides chapel attending the mass for my regiment? Yes, "neighbors, almost buddies, in our labors," the poet wrote.

Like us, they ran in frenzy through the flag-decked avenues of Munich and Hamburg in August, 1914, waving banners, brandishing placards. Their "Marseillaise" was the "Deutschland über Alles," and instead of shouting, "À Berlin!" they yelled, "Nach Paris!" The two roads led to the same slaughterhouse. . . .

They, too, fifty years later, must be questioning themselves about their reasons for fighting, and weighing the wasteful horror of those massacres. They, too, must be wondering at this moment whether our two countries are condemned to hate each other eternally and repay their ruins with the ruin of the neighbor. So I make an effort; I try to tender this resisting hand. I force myself to believe that men of my age have understood the last wars, that tomorrow's nations, reconciled at last, will form only a single great bloc, united for peaceful pursuits. I repeat to myself: "Brothers all!" I write it to convince myself of it.

But I love my country too much to accept the notion that it can lose its identity and become merely a district in a flat-faced Europe. I want it always to be as it was in the geography book of my boyhood, a pretty rose color, scored with blue rivers, protected by dark mountains, and wearing a mourning band along the border showing the lost provinces we were to liberate. Nothing can obliterate this map etched in me. So too do I remain loyal to the history of glorious events we marveled at, and so am I proud that men of my age added to it a chapter worthy of the past.

And if all peoples must dissolve one day in a uniform mold where they will blend together, I cling to the hope that centuries and centuries from now teachers will still read to children, like a fairy tale, "Once upon a time, between the Rhine and the Atlantic, there was a valiant little country which was called *France.*"

The Fighting Fronts

Edmund Blunden

EDMUND BLUNDEN, the son of Charles Edmund Blunden, schoolmaster, and Georgina Margaret Blunden, née Tyler, was born in London on November 1, 1896. He was educated at Christ's Hospital School and Queen's College, Oxford. Serving in the Royal Sussex (infantry) Regiment in World War I from 1915 to 1919, he was awarded the Military Cross in 1916.

He was professor of English from 1924 to 1927 in the University of Tokyo, and returned to Japan to be cultural adviser with the British Liaison Mission, in Tokyo, from 1947 to 1950. The Order of the Rising Sun, Third Class, was conferred on him in Japan. From 1930 to 1943 he was a fellow of Merton College, Oxford, and from 1953 to 1964 he was professor of English in the University of Hong Kong. For his distinguished accomplishments he was made a C.B.E. (Commander of the British Empire).

His first publications were small collections of verse, Poems 1913–1914, The Harbingers (1916), and Pastorals (1916). The Waggoner (1920) and The Shepherd (1922) made his name known; for The Shepherd he was given the Hawthornden Prize. Of many other volumes the latest is A Hong Kong House (1962).

The best known of his prose books is Undertones of War (1928). He assisted his former wife, Sylvia Norman, in an experiment called We'll Shift Our Ground: Almost a Novel (1933). His many literary biographies include those of Charles Lamb, Shelley, Leigh Hunt, Keats' publisher (John Taylor), and Thomas Hardy. Miscellaneous essays were collected in The Mind's Eye and Votive Tablets. He published many works chiefly for Japanese readers in Japan.

In 1945 Mr. Blunden married Claire Margaret Poynting; they have four daughters, and live in Long Melford, Suffolk. He has written a short guide to its much admired ancient church.

INFANTRYMAN PASSES BY

———◆———

I

IN THE EARLY MONTHS of 1941 I was very little concerned with
world affairs, except that my mother used sometimes to caution us
under the rubric "when you go out into the world" which we told
her meant at the moment the small market town 2 or 3 miles off.
The scene of her repeated admonition was the schoolhouse in a very
small village in Sussex, in the south of England, within comfortable
reach—by bicycle—of the seacoast and above all the enchantments of
"London by the Sea," Brighton. Heroic expeditions to that city
with all its huge hotels and piers and fashion parades along the
seafront were sometimes managed, but my leadership could only be
infrequent and while I was on holiday from my school.

The school was in the same county of Sussex and also inland,
about as far away from the sea as our village, and that geographical
detail used to matter in one's feelings. It is strange now to think
what a distance lay between the schoolhouse and the English
Channel in a sense of security (Napoleon having gone away) and
equally between Christ's Hospital, Horsham, and those waters.
That noble foundation had been removed from its ancient premises
near St. Paul's Cathedral, in London, to the former estate of the
poet Shelley's family near sleepy Horsham in Sussex. It was (and is)
a magnificent, mighty school, but the scholars were by charter boys
whose parents were poor, though not all of the same social degrees.
In 1914 I had been at this school, which is known for such literary
representatives as S. T. Coleridge and Charles Lamb and for all
sorts of others in all walks of life, for six years and was on the
staircase to the university. Lucky boys could look to Oxford or
Cambridge in particular as they rose in classes in the school and
could count on school exhibitions so long as at the finish they
carried off university scholarships. Those would usually be concerned with classics or mathematics. They were worth about seventy
or eighty pounds a year—amazing opulence!—or "just enough."

All at school went happily, occasionally hungrily, in most pastoral alluring surroundings and in an air well blending ancient and
modern. There was a clear division between two tracks of education—classical and modern. A boy had to be placed, on his entering

the school, in one of these two sides. My father firmly replied, "Classical," to the headmaster's question on my first appearing, and probably that decision affected the unexpected experiences which were to follow. I missed, for instance, except for a few terms, the German classes, though French somehow was a stylish study abundantly available. That perhaps was due to an eager enthusiasm on the part of some masters for French literature and particularly French poetry. "Modern" boys seemed rather to be involved in a commercial language.

Our acceptance of anything in classrooms can be imagined, and equally of our daily life altogether, well occupied from the early waking bell to the evening prayers called duty, and I must here note the description of our school, "The religious, royal and ancient foundation of Christ's Hospital"—the temper of the place was distinctive. After nearly 400 years it could hardly be otherwise, even though we had been transplanted from town to country, wisely no doubt. The peace of the boys' lives would have been the same in the buildings of the old Greyfriars in London. These "echoing cloisters pale," which are celebrated in a poem by Coleridge, remained, and they still do, as the calm pathway of the learned youths at the head of the school.

I have spoken of the peace which quite simply ruled our lives in our very orderly school, with its centuries of family spirit and useful duty continuing, and our Tudor uniform, the blue coats and yellow stockings, seeming to express a particular unity and concord among us; but there was one matter which did not harmonize, or so I used to feel in 1914. It looked to me as an influence directing the world, in its limited way, out of the paths of peace. All the boys—this was a recent ordinance—at quite an early age were required to become members of an officers training corps. This "fine body of men" regularly paraded in accurate khaki uniform and often went afield for sham fights, charging over fields and up hillsides and letting off some noisy blank ammunition and generally trying to imagine what war itself would be like. From time to time these young warriors were paraded on the playing fields and inspected by a real general, who perhaps made a speech at the conclusion and might utter a view which I confess seemed to me a gloomy, even horrible view: We were not just playing soldiers; we should be "wanted." At school camp, in the holidays, with its diversions and realistic excitements, that note could be heard even without speeches. "You'll be a man, my son."

As the year 1914 wore on, the newspapers in the dayroom made us aware of troubles in Ireland which were regarded as capable of

bringing on a fighting war, but for most of the busy little readers
the political side of that crisis was too difficult. Presently, far away it
was and seemed, a brutal assassination in some strange capital came
into the news. To interpret its consequences was beyond us, but the
occurrence was not to be forgotten in a moment or two even while
our beautiful peace and our almost untiring industry and great
events like cricket cup ties and swimming sports went on. The
summer holidays came into the prospect, and sunshine seemed
likely to abound. Our military carbines would soon be stacked away
in the armory, and our blue clothes, which made us rather conspicuous, except I suppose in London, could be exchanged for less
antique and ornamental clothes at home.

We had our meals in the great dining hall, and at the midday
meal the housemasters would take their places at the top of the long
tables. One day my own senior housemaster came in, and as he sat
down, with a curious ambiguous look, he said in a quiet way,
"Well, boys, it looks as though within a month the whole of Europe
will be at war." This from him was something to be taken seriously,
and it was. But I do not remember that any of us had any spoken
comment to make. We were not prophets. In a way not all of us
were surprised. But perhaps things would take another turn, and
we had plenty on our hands—the immediate trouble was probably
how to borrow a bicycle for the next enchanting Sunday afternoon
ride through the rich byways of Sussex.

> Beat! beat! drums!—blow! bugles! blow!
> Through the windows—through doors—burst like a ruthless force,
> Into the solemn church, and scatter the congregation,
> Into the school where the scholar is studying:
> Leave not the bridegroom quiet—no happiness must he have now
>   with his bride,
> Nor the peaceful farmer any peace, ploughing his field or gathering
>   his grain,
> So fierce you whirr and pound you drums—so shrill you bugles blow.

When World War I was declared, Walt Whitman's poems of
1861 did not obviously correspond to all that happened within my
own observation in England in 1914, but they describe the effect of
all as the new age established itself on our old world. When the
diplomats gave up their riddle, and the word "ultimatum" had
become like the last trumpet or nearly, I was at home in our gentle
village, and for a time—it would have been "invasion country" if
any were—there was excitement. My father even declared his intention of confronting any invaders at his front door, not the back

door. The cleverest of all rumors was widely believed—the Russian Army, having dealt with Germany, would shortly be over the Channel and dealing with the United Kingdom. Meanwhile, some of our untalkative farm laborers and tradespeople quietly disappeared from the scene, having "jowned up" in one of the services or another. And some young men who had come home from business desks for summer holidays, masters of the great world, suddenly looked quite as brilliant in well-fitting uniforms.

Weeks were soon drifting by, and I could do much as I liked, discovering other villages, catching carp, reading and writing—and always listening to some wiseacre announcing that the war would be over by Christmas. The war somehow dodged our observation very annoyingly. Summer holidays passed, and great victories went to sleep again, and wearisome new songs drew attention to sewing socks for soldiers or the long way to Tipperary. I was now writing verses with great eagerness, but not often on the war; what was near at hand usually started me off, and a friendly bookseller in Shelley's old town was so kind as to print a little volume or two for me, which at least kept me from thinking too long about the prospect for those of my age. The poems by the older generation in periodicals which I came upon were mostly admonitions to us to join the forces at once and be killed with all cheerfulness. The penalties invented for not doing these things were severe:

> What will you lack, sonny, what will you lack
>   When the girls line up the street,
> Shouting their love to the lads come back
>   From the foe they rushed to beat?
> Will you send a strangled cheer to the sky
>   And grin till your cheeks are red?
> But what will you lack when your mates go by
>   With a girl who cuts you dead?

However, it was decided that the boys at our school who were working for places in the universities should complete their courses, which meant staying with one's books until the summer of 1915. The girls whom I knew did not punish me for that or present me with white feathers, as was a reported fashion of those days.

On a glorious day that August I got out my bicycle for a longish ride across our county to Chichester, where the renowned Royal Sussex Regiment had its headquarters. I was equipped with papers which were to support my application for His Majesty's commission, and however dusty I was on arrival, the guard received me in the dignified way of an ancient regiment. A less bellicose place could hardly be imagined, and there seemed hardly any soldiers in it, but one was deputed to lead me to the major in charge of the barracks that day. He, too, put me at my ease at once, and I began to think the war was remarkably friendly after all. He told me to go over to the sergeant major and get him to run a tape measure round my chest and then come back for a drink and lunch. What promotion! The sequel perhaps a fortnight after was my receiving a commission and the outfit allowance—fifty pounds in that period was liberal. It easily covered the price—incidentally—of a sword.

Wearing this embarrassing romantic weapon, before many days I was traveling with other new subalterns to a training outfit at Weymouth, and still it was a pleasant war. We rose early for physical training on the beach, which exercise was broken off one morning by news that the British Army on the western front had made a successful attack at a place called Loos. It might be true; anyway it ended boredom, and following days gave the skeptics their opportunity. Altogether we were enjoying Weymouth without the holiday multitude when our orders arrived for doing something somewhere else, and I was one of those consigned to a large camp on the Sussex coast. We were so many that there were not enough "other ranks" for us to play at officering, and the medical officer was exceedingly sympathetic in excusing us from duty, which let us disappear into joyous Brighton—or I would sometimes walk home, 20 miles, in those days.

Some of the second lieutenants in my hut had seen a bit of active service and had their curious experiences to tell, but not much about the small battles which I heard of as making life miserable on the western front. The idea of everybody seemed to be to recite more outrageous limericks and ballads than anybody else. Lectures and exercises there were indeed, but it was argued that nothing in training was in the least like the actual war, so why worry? I was permitted without interference to collect around my bed a library of books, some even of the eighteenth century, the spoils of Brighton bystreets. These, however, could not go with me on the next stage of this odd indolent training—toward the end of 1915 the young officers found themselves crossing a very angry midnight Irish Sea. The destination was not many miles from Cork, a park with a large ruined mansion and plenty of huts, a rifle range, and very nice surrounding scenery.

Other arrangements had not been completed, and for some days the most enterprising officers were searching the country for supplies; I remember one of the plumpest of them driving some fat pigs into camp; it was surprising how soon the amateur organization for food and drink was working. We were in this place, we gathered, partly because of the state of Ireland and partly so as to be trained in earnest by some powerful Guardsmen, one of whom was soon nicknamed the Human Machine Gun. It came out that we were to take at an early date an examination: To fail would be, perhaps, not to be shot at dawn; to succeed would mean to be sent promptly to that almost forgotten place, the western front. So (and there were other reasons) night schemes were better attended now than in the region of Brighton, England.

In this camp, it is curious but pleasant to recall, I had quite an allowance of talk about the English poets, ancient and modern. The bed next to mine was occupied by one of the descendants of Keats' friend Richards, a learned reader indeed. Then one evening I was surprised and just a shade frightened by a message from the adjutant, desiring me to go see him. The reason was that he had heard something of my scribbling verses at the expense of some prominent personalities in the camp, which he even applauded, and soon we fell into serious discourse on poetry. He could quote very choicely, and his taste then was for the sadder tones:

> O to recall—
> What to recall?

or "Through the dark postern of time long elapsed. . . ." I never saw Gordon Reah after this Irish episode, though once in the ramparts of Ypres in Belgium I had an affectionate note from him, and I did my utmost to get along the chaos and see him—but the attempt failed. It was an event, by the way, when I bought an edition of some of Tom Moore's Irish songs in Fermoy for one penny, "as new."

Early spring over southern Ireland and our songs as we ventured on the River Blackwater were disputing poetic rights in my mind when, having passed the threatened examination, I was with many friends on the way back to England, and once again the destination was that vast camp at Shoreham. This time I was given a daily job, marching a company of convalescent soldiers anywhere out of the way. They would not talk, though they were most amiable and humble, of their war. So I was still in the dark about it, more or less, when I found my name on the notice board in the mess among those of subalterns who would "proceed" to the British Expeditionary Force in two or three days. I should have been noisily glad, of course, but—some other time!

II

The scene has changed indeed, and the month is May (1916).
With two other young officers who have been on training with me, I
am finding my way about in a quiet sector of the western front (but
it has seen its bitter fighting) with one of our county battalions. A
few miles east of these trenches (most of them are more or less
passages between low embankments of sandbags) there is the big
city of Lille, but except for hearing the city-hall clock strike
midnight (or so we believe), it does not enter into our thoughts.
Our landscape is flat, mostly, agricultural, and after nearly two
years of war something of a wilderness. Here and there as we near
the firing line we find a permanent-looking machine-gun emplacement built largely of brick, and the company headquarters look
solid enough; but we also see a few ruins to suggest that artillery
can swiftly obliterate such shelters.

The cheerfulness and attention to detail of those already experienced infantrymen with whom I now was have sounded on through
my life as a simple music of an excellent old England. Even allusions to the Germans facing us over shattered fruit trees, deserted
farm roads, hedges of crowded barbed wire, were quiet in tone and
in thought. The ordinary references were to the Alleymans, Jerry,
or Fritz. Even the two machine guns which were the greatest
nuisance, at night, from the German strongpoints had nicknames.
As for firing, at that time and place the artillery took only a share
now and then; but there was a strange and unforgettable performance from the rifles of both sides as day broke. Every man who
had ammunition, on both sides, seemed to join in a great wave of
shooting across no-man's-land, which swelled up and traveled along
the line for ten minutes or a quarter of an hour and died down.
This meant that about a mile behind the trenches the oddest noises
of bullets swishing over or spinning from anything they hit surrounded us, walking from keep to dump, and the puzzle was, so far
as we could observe, how seldom they caused casualties.

Danger there was in less obvious forms or methods. The firing
lines twisted about so that often the enemy was able to look into a
stretch of the other trenches, and from the snipers' posts a deadly
shot might find its mark at any time. This uncertainty led to a
superstitious quality in otherwise steady enough coming and going.
The sun might glow long hours on a peaceful, even drowsy scene,
but something was always lurking besides those frogs with their
nightlong croaking and the more detested myriads of mosquitoes

also claiming their ancient rights to the swampy pools. So, when it began to be remarked that the battalion was due to be relieved, and actually some officers and men had been named as an advance party to go back and arrange the company's billets, there was a slightly anxious thankfulness among us all, not simply owing to a need of rest. Nor was monotony quite the cause.

At that date, long-range firing was not much tried, and billets in small towns or villages were pleasant places, with the luxury of *estaminets* almost able to vie with the locals in England as scenes of mild refreshment and many anecdotes. But the war was not to be kept away even from rest areas, and often within a few hours of arrival in a more or less comfortable barn its requirements changed the outlook. Finding guards, for example, and drill and training almost caused revolutions, but no: Much worse things could happen. There was "something in the air." Raids were perhaps being thought out, and indeed one of those operations on a grimly large scale was staged by the whole brigade with a great display of grenades, guns, trench mortars—and all to no purpose.

This attack was of the kind sometimes called Chinese attacks, or feints, and occurred on the day before the French and British armies began the Battle of the Somme, many miles south; its object was thought to have been the deceiving of the Germans into keeping some of their artillery away from that huge challenge, awaiting a new stroke in the north of the long line. Our battlefield adjoined the remains of the village Neuve-Chapelle, then famous as the objective of a greater assault a year and more earlier. But what was more conspicuous to our eyes, looking over the top of our breastwork front line for some days, was a gloomy wood, the Bois du Biez, with a few innocent-looking cottages along its hitherward edge, and in some way a legend emanated and circulated that this solid deep-green wood had been entered by British troops before in a "censured" attack and not a man had come out of it.

Still, the new assault. . . . A beautiful darkness ended, a sweet morning began, and there were some of us in a recognizable brewery ruin, waiting for the wonders. Right on the moment the flashes and thunders of our (then not too frightful) artillery began, and instantly from eastward quite an equivalent amazed us; where had been silence there seemed endless supplies of death, flame, and noise. We were saved at the moment in a small tunnel which the enemy himself had dug long ago. Then the slow day began; the poor chaps who were crossing no-man's-land and some of them carrying wooden bridges to defeat the deep drains dividing fields of rye or even tobacco, apart from "the wire," were stopped. Some hobbled and crawled home at last, as horrified by what they had seen happen to men (of whatever nation) as had almost happened to them. Their clothing and equipment told that part of the story. "And I live."

The June day grew quieter, and the sinister wood kept its secret. It seemed as though the Germans had forgotten the episode, but perhaps they had merely taken away the batteries that were to have been detained. Our front line had been, in spite of knocks, kept scrupulously neat, almost domesticated; now it was punched shapeless, scarcely passable, but in those days the farmlands which it traversed had their harmless look still, apart from some ancient deserted trenches with a reputation for horrors, mysteries.

All this may be termed in its context elementary education. So too other passages in that summer of siege warfare slightly revised. Hamlet commented some time earlier that:

> . . . 'tis the sport to have the engineer
> Hoist with his own petard

and I believe he was alluding to the kind of war fought by the tunnelers with the cooperation of us footsoldiers, probably never again to achieve its vast, infernal perfections. Our chief observation of that kind of fighting came when we were sent into the line one side or another of the canal from Béthune to La Bassée (unprovocative little towns with Marlborough's wars of two centuries before haunting them quite without ghostly representatives in 1916). Here the landscape was fierce in a glaring sunlight, and industrial buildings in ruin hovered through the haze. When we took over a section of the parching front line, I talked with a philosophical engineer officer who remarked on the number of German mines known or suspected to be in construction underneath these trenches. And we, it was presumed, would have to occupy the place for a fortnight! In the end we emerged from that region and the one on the far side of the canal with mere examples of what might happen; we had had one small mine blown by the Germans underneath us, but a little short of a length, and had taken part in a loud bombing dispute following our own sappers' exploding a "small mine" again, defensively, toward the enemy position. The first incident on a night streaming with rain and resounding and lanterning with scores of shellbursts was a bad one. "It might have been worse," but even Germans miscalculated. I remember that I had to make my way from our headquarters in a shaky brick cellar along glistening, soaked trenches I had never seen, and to find the real way after so many shells, until I was trying to say a word to a dying man, whose quiet manner by the dark canal bank was beyond any words then or now.

We grew, you may say cynically, accustomed to having things of this kind befall us, until we had seen many miles of the northward front line of the British Expeditionary Force and knew the unnatural history of numbers of death-dealing "aerial torpedoes"—the word may serve for a whole genus of larger and smaller monsters—better than that of the rats who shared our trenches and equipment and evaded revolver shots in miraculous fashion. We had spells of emancipation, and out of the trenches an officer had a right to an actual bedroom and a humpy but exquisitely clean bed in a cottage or perhaps a mansion. The summer of 1916 almost made it a throne. The real throne was perhaps the incomparable lovingkindness of all, officers and all, who lived and worked so much together, grumbling away at times, seeing past the war yet never judging their own fate. "The British Army will all go home in one boat." . . . "When this war ends, we shall see four blue lights go up." "No, mate, four black lights." . . . "Here they come again, throwing gun and all at us." . . . "They were shooting at our post with iron foundries." . . . "Wind favorable for whizbangs, Jim?" The last was a mild joke on the gas warnings, "wind favorable" and the rest, which had become an ordinary part of the soldier's reading hereabouts.

To the next phase of our campaigning I shall not devote so much detail; the bewildering Battle of the Somme has been so often copiously described. We marched south toward it in golden weather and through what might have been described as France at peace. The roads were all cobblestone roads, and after our months in the mud of trenches the feet of many high-spirited soldiers were low-spirited; we passed the Guards marching equally, and indeed in the splendid heat and along those stone roads even they also seemed to be weary. We reached our attack area after an interval of rehearsals in a woodland and plowland place west of Arras, said to be a facsimile of our assigned "over the top." If it was, it was no help in the frantic realities of the day when it came, then called Z day. The village which gave us a home during our exercises was perfect eighteenth century, a peasant picturesque dream, in Corot's country. But soon, onward into a solitude; there the inhabitants had been withdrawn, and our position in a dusky wood was not only gas-scented but ghost-ridden—the sense of some intolerable presences had nothing to do with us, presumably, but that wood was deadly in gunfire fact and in some other way. Mailly Wood.

From here or near it the first of our three main ordeals in the
Somme battles was begun. Begun, but the misery of being ordered
up to the line and sent back for postponement was repeated a time
or two. The first actual attack on a glowing autumn day—it opened
before daylight and hardly a man had any chance of knowing the
ups and downs of the hollow to be crossed on the way to the
enemy's line—was an obliteration. It was completely mysterious; the
troops just disappeared. Perhaps the Germans' deep dugouts, especially those under a railway embankment on our right, were too
many for the bombers especially. No message came from those
merry boys, no acknowledgment of new supplies of hand grenades.
Further, as we were on the little hills sloping toward the Ancre
River's north side, the German guns on the hills opposite, their
destruction of the unlucky British infantry attacking there having
been easy for them, had no trouble in switching to us, and the
network camouflage over our little slit trenches soon vanished, and
our headquarters were simple targets.

So we were "a complete failure," and there were miles of that;
but southward the armies made some progress over the most terrifying devastated area perhaps ever yet seen on our planet. I remember
coming in sight of it for the first time; gunnery had extinguished
every sign of life every step to the horizon and left a specimen
of a world without a God. But the battle went on. We were
used as a holding battalion, securing miles of front, as the autumn
also went on. Late in October our function changed, and we again
attacked. "We" now meant almost a new battalion, so many reinforcements had been called for, poor fellows, many of whom made
their short acquaintance with modern war in the moment of mad
battle itself. They largely fell in the next two days. The battle took
place in white frost and began in full daylight. Underfoot was mud
or corpses. We somehow gained Stuff Trench, and such was its
desolation that the battalion relieving us (they had to be led in
almost individually) hated it and us, too (a rare thing) .

November brought clammy fogs and deeper mud, besides war
itself, and a third attack was required of us. It was successful! The
Germans were betrayed by their enormous deep dugouts. But
nothing much came of that. The *Sommeschlacht* (Battle of the
Somme) was somehow wearing out. It had introduced the tanks to
the fighting man's world. We saw some examples, heard of their
wonders, and dragged ourselves along. Then one night our grand
colonel for once spoke out and said that we were to be taken out of
the Somme battle, immediately. And we were—those who then
made up "we"—and again were men marching, with even our band

playing us into unspoiled Doullens (the stretcher-bearers formed the band) . Where were we going?

North this time, to a city with a glory about it but also an air of mortality—Ypres in Belgium. Of course, in incurable ruins, but serviceable as the stronghold of the Ypres Salient, a pattern of trenches of all sorts defying any advance of the German powers that way to the Channel ports. It had been tolerably quiet during 1916 but was constantly under observation and frequently under heavy fire. It was managed by the British garrison in a businesslike way, thanks especially to the ancient ramparts which guarded the gray, lifeless city on the east side. They are still standing over the lovely moat, which even in war was beautiful with swans. They conceal many spacious excavations, usually safe protections, in our time—at any time since perhaps the Romans held outposts here.

But we had no leisure or inspiration to think of other legions in Flanders. A dismal and painful winter was seizing the Ypres Salient when we rather amazedly arrived. Going out of the place to the area of Hill 60 on reconnaissance, my dear Sergeant Wally Ashford, walking with me through a grove of skeleton trees, remarked, with his ambiguous grin, "Looks just like the Somme . . . well, rather worse." It bore the strange title Sanctuary Wood. It had been no sanctuary to generations of doomed young soldiers of several nationalities.

Intense winter ended the year 1916 in those parts and went on without mercy until sudden kind spring poured sunshine over the snow and ice. Fighting and digging had gone on, but now that mercy seemed to descend, it was apparent that the year 1917 was to produce war of a new ferocity and, as many ordinary soldiers thought, futility. The name Passchendaele is inscribed on that page of war history. It was intended at first that, from Ypres, the low ridge of Passchendaele and other uninteresting farmland round it should be captured in the spring. The ridge was said to overlook the English Channel, and if it did, it could not worry the British Navy. But it had a good view, and so did other low uplands, of everything in or around mutilated Ypres. A further intention of the battle was to advance as far as Ostend.

"That agony returns." On July 31 the worst and most hated of the British offensives was begun, against all reason, all around or nearly all around Ypres. Reason had had no luck for weeks before; the preparations, including new roads and railways everywhere into the forward area, had been fantastically shown off, as though the Germans would be scared by the exhibition. The farmlands over which we were to advance had been drained in former times with minute care, and now that honest, wise labor was all lost with the increasing bombardments—and the weather. It was well known that at the end of July Flanders weather almost inevitably became foul.

On July 31 then, as the darkness was dying, the Passchendaele battle began with an orgy of gunfire and of machine-gun barrages which I thought noisier than all the artillery, and on our share of the line we were surprised to get across entanglements and tattered trenches without extraordinary difficulty. We soon found the concrete blockhouses which the Germans had been building for their defense system, often within barns and farmhouses, great and small, but the principle of the opening of the defense was mainly to withdraw the majority of the troops. At any rate we moved forward and, when we had reached the positions to be seized were even bewildered by having done so—at a price. But we for a moment felt that success had beamed on us. The other side's guns were not doing much just then. Another enemy came into action. Almost silently the rain began. It went on, grew heavier, and the vision of victory dissolved in the grayness.

To try to chronicle the miseries and destructions of the days thus begun would be to invite sleepless nights or insane dreams, which have been exorcised, in any event, during the half century, and the battle with its variations of place and problem had my attention until summer had become winter, and however I was released from it (the authorities had not been altogether monsters, but had laid on a scheme of schools behind the line which were perhaps rest stations, as well as places of instruction), I was still back among the captured concrete pillboxes. The natural history of these was that their entrances, once we had possession, faced the German guns, and so always a direct hit from them was especially murderous. It was so on the celebrated Menin Road, in royal autumn sunshine, at the end of September, 1917. We could not avoid these concrete shelters, but the German gunners had them before them whenever they cared to bump them. Sunshine and irony united then. But late in the year a brilliant surprise far to the south, a tank battle toward Cambrai, diverted the war proper for a few days. "Think we shall win?" It was almost a possibility.

What ideas were now going around among the fighting men? Not many more than usual, but that America's armies were in the business was knowingly mentioned by some not loquacious sergeants. Our performances became a little less urgent, I thought, though hardly less deathly. At the end of that year of pain, 1917, it was strange for me to be in freezing starshine, staring east over the death-strewn miles, waiting for the rival guns to say something. They did, but as though bored. "How long, O Lord, how long?"

Before long we had moved far south to the Cambrai battlefield and been happy to find comparatively dry green ground and firm roads around our front line. The remains of the recent contest, which was a wonderful performance on both sides, offered no early end to the war. My expectation of being on the scene, God willing, through the new year, 1918, was simple; old friends were still there; the comforts were tolerable, and it was said we should soon have leave to visit Amiens even. But a system of transferring some who had a certain front-line length of experience had begun, and it included me. It happened so while we were digging miles of trenches and putting out entanglements of barbed wire apparently against a German offensive of considerable depth. It was assigned to me to prepare defense orders for our front. That done, and even approved by our commanding officer, I was—away!

The hope of returning to the line may seem to have been a symptom of madness, but such a hope stirred in me in a camp in England, and I nearly got back, when the German attack antici-pated had roared itself along far beyond our trace trenches. The half-starved German soldiery and civilians could not now quite win, and my next contribution to the declining battle was in November, 1918, when the war was slackening from several causes into its mortification. A godforsaken winter followed the Armistice, but at any rate the guns were silent; the starvation state of affairs went on but could not go on forever; the last booby trap of the German retreat had at length compelled amazement if it had failed to kill.

What out of all this miscellany abides after so long? The war cemeteries. But somebody was saying lately, when viewing one of them with 20,000 graves in it (near Passchendaele) , such a total was only chick feed in comparison with other displays of inhumanity. Then, perhaps what goes on is the memory of anonymous heroes, who personally had nothing to hope for and who had nothing "patriotic" to say and went on day after day with a countenance of invincibility, not notably referring to any known enemy, just facing whatever gods may be.

Gerald Brenan

"I was born in Malta in 1894 of an English father and a Scottish-Irish mother from Ulster and spent my early childhood in South Africa, India, and Ireland. Then in 1902 my parents settled in a remote village in Gloucestershire. From there I went to the usual private and public schools, but not to a university because I was intended for the family career of the Army. However, I had come under the spell of poetry and travel books, so in 1912, having just passed into Sandhurst, I ran away from home with the idea of traveling by land to China. I got as far as Bosnia, where I was forced to turn back, and then was put by my parents to cram for the Indian police. I was awaiting the result of my exam when the war broke out.

"After the war I settled with several thousand books in a mountain village in Spain, which I have described in South from Granada. Later I lived in London, where I got to know the literary group known as Bloomsbury. Then in 1930, having come into a little money, I married an American poetess from South Carolina and three years later bought the house near Málaga where we still live. I have written four books on Spanish subjects: The Spanish Labyrinth (1943); The Literature of the Spanish People (1951); The Face of Spain (1950); and South from Granada (1957). I have also written under my own name two novels, A Holiday by the Sea (1961) and The Lighthouse Always Says Yes (1960), and an autobiography up to 1919, entitled A Life of One's Own (1962). This last contains a fuller account of my war experiences than is given here."

A SURVIVOR'S STORY

IN AUGUST, 1914, I was staying at my parents' house in the Cotswolds. The weather was fine and warm, the wheat stood ready for cutting in the fields, and a deep peace hung over everything. Then the German Army invaded Belgium, and a shock of dismay and horror ran through the country as the first reports of the fighting came through. It seemed incredible that in our orderly, civilized world such things could happen.

Since I was going through a period of adolescent revolt against school and parents, I was not in a very patriotic frame of mind, but I wished to be in the war because I felt it would be a great experience. I was therefore delighted when my father returned from Gloucester with a commission for me in the local Territorials. As soon as my uniform was ready I joined my battalion, the 5th Gloucesters, at Chelmsford. Except that I had done a little drill at my public school, I knew nothing of soldiering, but in those days the division between officers and men was one of class. Almost at once I was put to a sharp test. On my third day after arriving I had to take my company onto battalion parade because the other officers were absent on courses. I had to shout the correct orders, drill and maneuver my company, and salute with my sword. Somehow I got through it, but nothing in the whole course of the war was to frighten me so much.

We now settled down to training. On three mornings a week we marched our companies about on the parade ground in massed formations as though we were preparing to fight in the Marlborough wars. On other mornings we practiced in open formations for the Boer War. But we were not taught how to fight in trenches. These, we were told, were merely a temporary phase. In the spring, when our new armies were ready, we would break out of the trench line and chase the Germans back to the Rhine, while the Russian steamroller advanced slowly but surely on the other side. Our chief fear was that the war might be over before we got out to it.

Our adjutant rightly took a poor view of my efficiency so that in December I found myself seconded to a cyclist company which our division, the 48th, was forming. These companies were intended to serve the same purpose as the mounted infantry had done in the Boer War. With their superior mobility they could be rushed to any point of danger or else used as advance guards. I now found myself messing with eight young officers, all of them except our company commander under twenty-one, who for various reasons had made themselves disliked in their battalions. We got on well, so that for the first time I began to feel confidence in myself and to enjoy training my platoon. Then one day in March, 1915 we embarked for France.

A week later we found ourselves in billets in a farmhouse just behind Armentières on the Belgian frontier. Spring had already come. The trees were bursting into leaf; the grass was scattered with flowers; the fruit blossoms coming out. The country around was green and lush, with more civilians to be seen than soldiers. In contrast with this was the continual roll of the guns. When on my first night I walked down the lane, I could see the sky lit up for miles on either side by flashes and the Very lights floating like water lilies above them. At that moment the war seemed beautiful.

The 4th Division was holding the line in front of us. They had been in these trenches all winter, and the 48th was to relieve them. As it happened, I had a great friend called Taylor in that division, and I got leave to go look for him. I found him only 3 miles away at Le Bizet. He was the brigade machine-gun officer with six machine guns in his charge, and he offered to take me down at once to the front line.

The approach lay through a long row of red brick workmen's houses, in which a hole had been knocked in every partition wall. From this one emerged into the front trenches, which were not trenches at all, because the ground was waterlogged, but a narrow parapeted lane built of sandbags. It had a few strands of barbed wire in front of it and ended suddenly in a field. One had to talk in whispers because the Germans were only 30 yards away, and if they heard voices they would send over a rifle grenade or a jam jarful of shrapnel. In fact, as we stood there, a trench mortar shell burst above us, and a piece of metal tore my breeches and drew a few drops of blood. It was my twenty-first birthday, and I was delighted to feel I had been initiated.

Taylor had a long tale to tell of the sufferings of the troops during the previous winter. The trenches had been deep in water, the shelters had not kept out the rain, and casualties had been heavy. But now that spring had come, he was feeling more cheerful. I myself was in the highest spirits. In small doses danger is a great stimulant, and as I watched the shells exploding close by or heard the bullets whistling overhead, that old feeling of the romance of war took hold of me. Besides, the whole scene was so fantastic. All around me there were shattered houses with new pieces being knocked out of them as I watched, and this appealed to a repressed destructive instinct. As in a Chaplin film, the continual breaches of the ordinary usages of civilized life released a flood of excitement—almost of gaiety. To make it stranger, civilians were still living in many of these houses. For example, just behind our front trench there was a cottage that might have come out of a painting by Brueghel which was occupied by an old woman who could not go out by day without being sniped. Her cows lay around her dead on their sides; but she would not leave, and the Army had no authority to move her. Then it seemed incredible that those tall buildings one saw only a few hundred yards away were as inaccessible as the summit of Everest because they lay behind the German lines. The absolute impossibility of reaching them fascinated me, all the more as one never saw a German.

A few days after this my company had a short spell in the trenches opposite Messines. As at Le Bizet, they did not form a continuous line, but a string of unconnected positions. There was hardly any wire, so that the only things that prevented us from going forward and occupying the village on the hill above us were a few rifles and machine guns. In other days troops had had shields and armor, and it did not seem to me beyond the wit of man to devise some mechanical means of advancing under shelter. As I stood there considering this, the sentry next to me was shot in the head and fell back dead. But I was too excited by the novelty of everything to be affected by this, my first sight of death. I was young and full of life—it could not happen to me.

I saw a good deal of my friend Taylor during the next two weeks. Either I went down to the trenches with him or he rode over on his horse to my farm, where we drank coffee with fresh cream and ate cakes and talked poetry. I read him my favorite pieces from Rimbaud and Laforgue or spouted from *Also sprach Zarathustra,* which he admired in English but could not read in German. Then one night, as I lay sleeping in the orchard, where I had spread my sleeping bag under a pear tree in blossom, I was awakened by the trampling of boots and the rumble of vehicles along the great cobbled road. It was, I guessed, the 4th Division marching north to fill the gap left by the German gas attack at Ypres. Taylor must be there riding on his horse among them.

Meanwhile, we were given little to do, and I had most of my afternoons to myself. Armentières, a large ugly manufacturing town, was only a couple of miles away. The German lines ran through its farther suburbs, and shells fell on it all the time; but in spite of that, it was full of civilians. Close to the station there was a restaurant patronized by officers which became very gay in the evenings. The lovely spring weather put everyone in good spirits, and as in previous wars, there was a pervasive feeling of sex in the air which quickened the senses. The girls seemed to feel it, too. When a party of men bathed—naked, of course—in the Lys, they would gather around and make their comments. Then at the delousing baths that had been set up in a brewery we would see the eyes of the laundry girls who worked next door peering at us through the gaps in the wooden partition and hear their excited giggles. In the yard of the restaurant the men queued up to have the waitresses, who charged nothing.

But this pleasant lazy life did not last for long. Soon we were put to digging a redoubt on a hill opposite Messines. Since it was not far from the German lines, we worked by night, and every time a flare went up, we had to freeze. The nightingales, excited by the whistle of the machine-gun bullets, sang loudly, and we had a few casualties. Then sometimes, instead of returning to our billets, we would bivouac in the grounds of a chateau nearby. The front of the building had been ripped off by a shell, which had also destroyed the staircase, and looking up, we could see the brass bedsteads still heaped with sheets and a mirrored wardrobe disgorging female garments. In the garden below, the peonies, irises, and tulips were in full flower, along with rhododendrons and lilacs. The men wandered about like children on a school feast, picking bunches of them and green gooseberries to cook.

Toward the middle of May I had word that Taylor had been killed in the fighting near Ypres, and I got leave to ride up with my batman and learn how it had happened. I had already visited Ypres a few days before the gas attack. Then it had been crowded with people and little damaged, but now it was completely deserted and out-of-bounds to troops. Whole streets were burning, and packs of dogs roamed around, feeding on the corpses that one could smell everywhere. In the great market square the shattered cathedral and Cloth Hall stood up out of a pile of rubble, while in the bars and cafés half-filled glasses still stood on the tables, for with the first rumor of gas the population had fled in panic. We found Taylor's battalion holding the line near St.-Julien and came back.

A few weeks later I rode up to Ypres again to look for the grave of a cousin of mine who had been killed at Hill 60. This time I found the city more shattered than ever, its towers jagged and broken and its walls gleaming in the damp air like marble. The notorious Hill 60 turned out to be an inconspicuous lump rising a few feet above the pockmarked plain and containing an immense mine crater on its summit. It had been continuously fought over, both above- and belowground, so that its surface had taken on that pitted, tormented look which was later to characterize the whole of the Ypres Salient. Shell craters, mounds, rotting sandbags, coils of wire, latrines, graves with rats and flies, and the faint, inescapable smell of putrefaction mingling with that of chloride of lime and, where a shell had burst, the fumes of picric acid.

During the last days of June we moved south to Picardy, where a new British army was taking over the sector that stretched from Arras to the Somme. We established ourselves in the ruins of Hébuterne, a village that stood just behind the front line, and were assigned the task of repairing the communication trenches. Later we were given a piece of the line to hold, and I got a certain pleasure from going out on night patrols. The front was very quiet, and the trenches were more comfortable than those at Armentières, as well as drier.

The Somme region consists of long rolling valleys sown with wheat, with every few miles a village surrounded by apple orchards. It is a monotonous country, and our lives became monotonous to match it, for in the autumn we were moved back to billets 6 miles behind the line and put onto repairing roads. The romance of the war had now departed, and boredom set in. To relieve it, I and my friend Partridge would ride into Amiens on Sunday afternoons, have a good dinner, and look for girls. *La chasse aux filles* became our only serious activity; but the villages around had filled up with troops, and success was difficult. Then in the spring we returned to Hébuterne, and I was put in charge of an observation post just outside it.

Soon after this the divisional cyclist companies were broken up to form the 8th Corps Cyclist Battalion. Some of my fellow officers, among them Partridge, went back to the infantry, but when I applied to do this, I was told that I must stay with my O.P. (observation post). Meanwhile, the preparations had begun for the great push that was to roll the Germans back 100 miles. Every day new batteries would arrive and begin registering, new light railways would spring up, new shell dumps and notice boards, while the whole countryside began to teem with khaki figures till it looked like an overstocked rabbit warren. Through my telescope I could see mounds of white chalk appearing in the German support trenches. Evidently they were building deep shellproof dugouts in preparation for our expected attack.

The 8th Corps, which was commanded by a spit-and-polish ma-

ιc called General Hunter-Weston, was to form the left hinge of
υur advance, and its first objective was the hamlet of Serre, which
stood on the skyline some 900 yards from our front trenches. My
O.P. was immediately opposite it and about a mile away. The battle
opened a little after sunrise on July 1, 1916, with a bombardment
that shook the air with its roar and sent up the earth on the German
trenches in gigantic fountains. It seemed as if no human being
could live through that. Then our men climbed by short ladders
onto the parapet and began to move forward, shoulder to shoulder,
one line behind the other, across the rough ground. They went
slowly because each of them carried a weight of 66 pounds. A
moment later the German barrage fell on our trenches, and their
machine guns began to rattle furiously. Clouds of blue and gray
smoke from the bursting shells, mingling with a light ground mist,
hid the general view, but through the gaps I could see the little
antlike figures, some of them keeping on, others falling, creeping,
writhing, lying still. Each of them carried on his back a tin triangle
to assist in his identification by our artillery, and the early morning
sun shone on these triangles and made them glitter. But as the
hours passed, I could not see that any of them had reached the
German support line, and later I knew why: The Boche machine
gunners had come out of their deep dugouts and were mowing
them down.

All this time the barrage that had fallen on our shallow assault
trenches had continued and was churning up the earth all around.
As I learned later, they were still packed with troops because they
had been manned in the wrong order, and two of the waves had
been caught by the barrage and had never got off. Slowly the sun
rose higher and higher in the sky, and the heat of that scorching day
grew and grew; but I could detect no movement on the slope in
front of me except that here and there a wounded man could be
seen creeping toward a shell hole. It became clear that our attack
had failed. Then, when darkness fell, terrible stories began to come
in. They told of appalling casualties, of whole battalions reduced to
thirty or forty men, and I have since read that no British Army
corps had ever before suffered such losses in a single day. The pick
of our young men, the first to volunteer for the war, were dead, and
on our corps front not a yard had been gained.

Ten days later I was brought face to face and in the most repellent way with the consequences of this battle. My platoon was detailed for a burying party. The bodies of our men who had been
mashed to pieces in the assault trenches had been brought up by
night on a trench railway and bundled out onto the ground. Legs

had broken off from trunks, heads came off at a touch, and nauseous liquids oozed out of the cavities. The stench was overpowering. Our job was to cut off the identity disks and bury these decomposing corpses in shallow trenches. After a few hours of this the fear of death had so entered into me that if I had been ordered to go over the top next morning I should not have been able to.

Meanwhile, as there was no more observing to be done, I had some time off. I decided to use it by looking up my friend Partridge, who was with his battalion in the new ground that had been won to the east of Albert. As, accompanied by my batman, I crossed the old front line, I seemed to be leaving a gale-swept, yet solid shore for a treacherous, chaotic region recently abandoned by the tide. The farther we went, the more desperate and confused the landscape became—shattered woods and villages, shattered trenches, abandoned equipment, and then unburied bodies. But it was also thickly populated: There was a heavy traffic of mule-drawn limbers and wagons choking the roads, and around us batteries were firing and soldiers camping by companies and battalions around their stacked rifles in open bivouacs. Then the numbers thinned out, and after a little we came to Mametz Wood, which had been the scene of heavy fighting. Its trees were torn and shattered, its leaves had turned brown, and there was a shell hole every 3 yards. This was a place where something unheard of in this war had taken place— hand-to-hand fighting in the open with bombs and bayonets. What seemed extraordinary was that all the dead bodies there lay just as they had fallen, as though they were being kept as exhibits for a war museum. Germans in their field gray uniforms, British in their khaki, lying side by side, their faces and their hands a pale waxy green, the color of a rare marble. Some of these figures still sat with their backs against a tree, and two of them stood locked together by their bayonets, which had pierced each other's bodies; they were sustained in that position by the tree trunk against which they had fallen. I felt that I was visiting a room in Madame Tussaud's Chamber of Horrors, for I could not imagine any of those corpses having ever been alive.

We kept on across the battlefield—dead bodies of men, dead mules and horses, rifles, hand grenades, German spiked helmets, gas masks, haversacks, scattered like the debris on a beach after a winter storm—till we came to Trones Wood, which, though greatly battered, had kept its green leaves. Here we were close to the front line, and since the machine-gun bullets began to whistle round us and I could hear no word of my friend's battalion, we turned back. After this we ran into a nasty patch of shelling and were glad to find ourselves in Albert again and to recover our cycles. Although I had failed to find Partridge, I had now learned where he was.

A few days later therefore—it was around July 21—I went back and, after crossing again the old front line, turned left toward Ovillers. Everything here was in a terrible state, the ground torn up by shells and littered with dead bodies from the attack on July 1. The wounded, who could not be brought in, had crawled into shell holes, wrapped their waterproof sheets round them, taken out their Bibles, and died like that. The stench from all these corpses was unbearable. I found Partridge commanding a company. The farther end of the trench he was occupying was held by the Germans. What was needed, he said, was to bomb up it so as to reach a machine gun that was holding up our advance, but his men were tired and not out to take risks. As usual, he said, the staff was execrable. It took hours to get a message back to brigade H.Q., and the orders they received from them were usually impossible to carry out because they came too late. I had lunch, washed down by a bottle of German champagne, with him in his deep German dugout and came away.

The letter I wrote home two days later is, in a way that amazes me today, a eulogy of battle. War was, of course, horrible, yet I could not help liking it because it was a great challenge. Only exceptional people were capable of rising to its worst moments, for the majority had no heart for it. These were Partridge's views, and since I admired his soldierly qualities, I was temporarily inclined to share them. Yet although I envied him for being in the thick of things, I wondered how I would come out of the supreme test of battle. I knew that I could take shellfire, for I was doing it all the time, but how should I stand going over the top and facing machine guns? That was a question which every infantryman in this war asked himself.

A few days after this my battalion got its marching orders. We were to move to Poperinge, behind the Ypres Salient. After a few weeks there, spent in reading Gibbon's *Decline and Fall*, I was again put onto observation work. My new O.P. was on the bank of the Ypres Canal, a little to the north of the city and not far from where the German lines came down to it and the Belgian sector began. This canal was a decidedly unprepossessing place. Enclosed by high banks and frequently shelled, it had taken on the baleful aspect of the front region and grew more sinister and tainted as it approached the point where it became the boundary between the lines. With the destruction of the locks most of the water had run out, leaving only a few feet of oily liquid resting on a bed of black and even oilier mud. Rotting branches and nameless objects of twisted metal rose out of its surface, and the rats had made their tunnels in the banks and swarmed in their thousands. I and my observers were given two dugouts which were dry and comfortable, as well as reasonably safe. Since our O.P. commanded only a small sector of the German trenches, I took to moving about with a small telescope and periscope and in this way got to know the whole northern half of the salient. It was a dismal region of mud and shell holes with only an occasional tree stump to relieve the monotony.

I was also expected to report on British and German raids. As soon, therefore, as I heard a German barrage come down, I would pull on my clothes and hurry to the front line. These occasions were apt to be unpleasant. The shattered trenches, the reek of powder, the black darkness fitfully lit up by a flare, the dead or dying that one stumbled over were unnerving, as was the possibility that the raiders might not yet have gone back. Then one saw by torchlight the shattered looks of the men who had survived and perhaps heard the moaning and sobbing of a poor fellow who had broken down. On one occasion I was caught in the German barrage. I do not think that anyone who has not lived through one of these can form a conception of what they were like. The earth appears to rock and tremble. The air is filled by a persistent rushing sound, broken by the crash of explosions. The mind cannot think, the arms and legs tremble automatically, and the tough man is the one who recovers quickest. I have read that concentrations of artillery fire such as these were never attained in the Second World War.

After spending the whole winter like an anchorite in my canal dugout, I was given another O.P. a couple of miles away. This was in a disused brickyard known as La Brique, standing on a low hill just beyond the Menin Gate. To get a better view, we hammered horseshoes into a thin elm tree and installed our telescope 30 feet above the ground. As the summer drew on, we learned that our big attack of the year was going to be on this sector. The Germans evidently knew it, too. Most of the traffic that supplied the salient had to pass through Ypres, and so morning, noon, and night the heavy shells fell on it, scattering clouds of white and rose-colored dust from the great shapeless mounds of the cathedral and Cloth Hall. I had watched this beautiful city crumble slowly away through the past two years, and now nothing but rubble was left.

The attack was to take place at dawn on July 31. I was to go over the top with the second wave and send reports back. But on the twenty-ninth I was wounded in the arm and side by a piece of shell. When I walked over to the dressing station to get myself bandaged, the major in charge sent me off, in spite of my strong protests, to a base hospital. It was not exactly that I was looking forward to the battle, for I had not forgotten the Somme, but no one likes to have his plans upset.

I found the atmosphere in England intensely unpleasant. The women were all agog for atrocity stories, while the hatred of the Germans that had been worked up by the Northcliffe press boded ill for the eventual peace. I soon got tired of peacetime soldiering and asked my C.O. in Belgium to apply for my return.

By February I was back in Poperinge. A long-distance shell burst at the railway station as I arrived, but though I ducked like a staff officer, I was not sorry to be back in the old haunts again. War was hateful, but if it had to be, the best place for a young unmarried man was in the front line. And there I went—to another O.P.

The five months' battle that was to have sent the Germans scurrying back to Antwerp had carried us less than 6 miles forward over an expanse of mud to what had once been the village of Passchendaele. This place with the beautiful name crowned a low ridge which provided cover from view until one was almost in the front line. My O.P. was a tiny ramshackle affair 50 yards behind it, but our living quarters were some way back in a large white pillbox built by the Germans. It was completely shellproof, but unfortunately it was sinking in the mud, so that one had to stoop low to enter it. A few weeks later it had sunk so far that we left it and went back to La Brique.

The country around was as strange to look at as anything I had ever seen. All about us stretched a broad, slightly undulating plain of brown sodden earth and shell craters filled to the brim with water. These craters touched and intersected so frequently that it sometimes seemed as if there were more water than mud. The valleys were completely flooded, and there was no sign of houses or trees and no grass or vegetation. The only objects that stood out from the morass were the white German pillboxes, massive and rounded as elephants, and now and then in the back regions a half-buried tank. It goes without saying that there were no support or communication trenches. The way up to the front line was by 4-mile-long footways made of duckboards and raised on piles above the mud. If one fell off, one would sink to one's waist or deeper, which made them unhealthy places on which to be caught by shellfire. The villages marked on the map had completely vanished: not a stone of them remained.

I had not been here long when we learned that the Germans had attacked and broken through our line opposite Amiens and then, which was more dangerous, between Armentières and Messines. To shorten our front, we gave up all we had gained in the last battle and withdrew to the outskirts of Ypres. The 8th Corps handed over its divisions to another corps, and I went back to Cassel.

How was it, every soldier asked himself, that while we had been attacking on the largest scale, at enormous cost, without obtaining any significant results, the Germans had in a few days smashed through our front in two places? Obviously our generals were bad, and the morale of the troops fell accordingly. Living in comfort far behind the lines and rarely seen where shells were falling, these haughty brass hats had always been unpopular. But I had no time to dwell on these matters, for I was sent out with a small patrol to keep in touch with the situation around Mount Kemmel.

After two and a half years of being penned up in the trenches it was strange to see fighting taking place in the open country—men lying behind hedges or advancing by sections across fields, signal-men semaphoring, field guns cantering along and then unlimbering and firing. French cavalry uniforms alternated with British ones, but the only shelling was from 18-pounders because the Germans had not yet brought up their heavy artillery. Instead one heard the sharp *rat-tat-tat* of machine guns and the crack of rifle fire. No one seemed to know where the front line was—indeed it was changing all the time.

My memory of these days is very hazy. I find that I have a tendency to forget unpleasant experiences unless I record them soon afterward. What I chiefly remember is the green leafy country with its old brick farmhouse, its tangled lanes, and its English flowers—and then the dead and wounded in their blue or khaki uniforms, sprinkled with blood. I got mixed up in a German attack and then in a French one, and two of the three men with me were killed. The reports I sent back must have been quite useless.

I had been a captain for some time, and when, as now happened, I returned to my battalion, I was given the command of a company. A week later we entrained for a place far to the south—Châlons-sur-Marne in the Champagne. Here we were attached to the French, and so we settled down to learn how to fire their machine guns. Then suddenly the news of a fresh German advance came through. They had attacked on the Chemin des Dames and within three days had reached the Marne. We rode off and a few hours later were digging in between Vandières and Châtillon with our left flank on that river. At dawn on the following day I sent out a patrol of five men to watch a farmhouse that stood halfway between the lines and that I suspected was occupied by the enemy. The lance corporal, after keeping it under observation for a time, surprised the seven Germans who were holding it while they were eating their lunch and brought them back. They belonged to a *corps d'élite*, the Prussian Guard, and the French were very pleased.

I wanted to take some offensive action with my company, and my C.O. gave me a free hand. The first attempt was a fiasco, for at the last moment I realized that we were attempting too much and, after an agony of indecision, canceled the attack. But two nights later I led out a patrol of three men from the French lines opposite a hamlet called Trotte, and after crawling painfully on our bellies across a stubble field, we struck a gap in the German lines and got right through.

This was for me the most exhilarating moment of the war. Here we were, after staring at that impassable frontier for three years, walking about in safety behind it. An almost mystical feeling of release and liberation came over me. Moving down the slope, I could see the broad valley lit up by the dim moonlight and hear the sound of heavy motor traffic at the bottom. What should we do with our discovery? Wild schemes rushed through my head, but then I saw that our best plan would be to capture the hamlet of Trotte from behind. It offered a much better defensive position than the wood held by the French because it overlooked the main German communications with the rear and could only be approached up a long open slope. We therefore made a careful reconnaissance of it, creeping up in the shadow of the barns to locate two machine-gun posts and then returning by the way we had come.

On the following night I went back with a sergeant and two men to reconnoiter the further end of the place. We located a third machine gun and what seemed to be a company headquarters; we were just about to leave when a sentry came down the sunk road which served as their front line toward us. We were crouching one behind the other in the shadow of a wall, and he did not see us until he was within a few yards. I covered him with my revolver, but instead of putting up his hands, he slowly and deliberately unslung his rifle from his shoulder and aimed at me. I watched him do this in a sort of trance, for, seeing his young face with its blue saucer eyes in the moonlight, I felt unable to pull the trigger. I could no doubt kill a German in hot blood or at a distance, but I was not a homicide. Then his shot rang out, I felt a blow in my side, and said, "I'm hit." But I was not hit, for the bullet had only torn my tunic. My men finished him off, and we ran out over the stubble field toward the French lines. About 50 yards on we came to the carcass of a cow and, just as a machine gun opened fire, threw ourselves down behind it. As we did so, a dozen rats leaped out of its belly and scurried away over our backs. There we lay for a long time, pressed into the earth, with the bullets, each time the gun traversed, passing just over us, almost shaving us. But at last they ceased, and very slowly we crept off to the wood, where we narrowly escaped being shot by the French sentry.

The prospects for capturing Trotte were no longer so good because the Germans had been alerted, yet I reckoned that they could not know that we had passed behind their lines. I decided, therefore, to go through with the attack that night. I would lead the first patrol—with only a couple of men in case they set an ambush. Two larger patrols would follow, and the rest of the company would stand by to await the signal to rush forward. As soon as it was dark then, our faces and hands blackened with charcoal, we left the wood for the haystack that marked the gap. We had got within 20 or 30 yards of it, crawling on our bellies over the prickly stubble, when I saw a German raise his head over the bank and heard the clink of metal. They were waiting for us, and there was nothing to be done but fade out. Since we were plainly visible as dark blotches on the pale background, this meant that we must wriggle backward, waiting to move till a passing shell would deaden our sound. It took us two hours to do the couple of hundred yards, and then I found that the officer in charge of the second patrol had returned to the village with all the men and reported that we had been either killed or captured.

So I had failed twice. Disgusted at this and ashamed at my failure over the German sentry, I took out a fighting patrol on the following night in a new sector where the lines were a mile apart, in the hope of getting a German alive or dead for identification. But it was blowing and raining hard, and though we thought we saw an enemy patrol on the skyline, we failed to intercept it. Then, on the next night, my battalion was asked by the French to raid two machine-gun posts that were annoying them. My company was detailed to take on one of them, and my C.O. told me to put a junior officer in charge. But after my last night's experience I did not trust the only one I had, so though I was very tired, I persuaded him to let me lead it. Just as we were starting, the Germans began to shell our village, and a whizbang hit a man just outside company headquarters. We carried him in on a stretcher and found that the whole of the lower part of his face had been carried away, leaving a red palpitating hole. But he was still alive, and his eyes were moving about in a serious, inquiring way as if he did not understand what had happened to him. He was very young, perhaps not more than nineteen, and as I trudged up the road with my men, I kept seeing those eyes, and they gave me a bad feeling.

We got to the French front line, which was along the edge of a wood, and saw the poilus sitting around in easy attitudes. But the sergeant in charge said that he had strict orders not to let any patrol go out. We must wait for the company commander. So we squatted down in the ditch, and then, from the gray open country beyond, a machine gun began to fire from close range. The bullets swished by overhead, bringing down small twigs and leaves, and I knew that they came from the post that we had orders to raid and which I had reconnoitered that afternoon. As I sat there in the moist, warm trench with the dark trees clustering thickly around, listening to that ear-shattering stutter, a very unpleasant feeling came over me. I had never had quite that sensation in the pit of my stomach before.

We sat there for some time, and then the French captain arrived. He said he could not possibly allow us to do our raid that night because he had a working party out. I asked him to sign a paper to that effect and with unspeakable relief led my men back.

I had now been out on patrols for six nights in succession and had been far too busy to lie down by day. I was therefore very tired and slept for twelve hours without waking. When I did wake, I learned that the other company's raid had been a failure and that an officer and several men had been killed trying to rush a machine gun. But we were being relieved next day, so that I should not have to go out on patrol again. Within a week we were in billets on the Somme. Here I went down with the Spanish flu that was sweeping through the Army and was invalided back to England. I was still there when the Armistice came.

Jacques Meyer

Born in 1895 at Valenciennes, to a modest family of Alsatian origin, Jacques Meyer got his secondary schooling first at the Lycée de Valenciennes and then in Paris at the Lycée Charlemagne and, to prepare for the École Normale Supérieure, the Lycée Louis-le-Grand. He applied to the École Normale and was accepted in 1914, eight days before the war.

All the members of Jacques Meyer's class, including himself, enlisted immediately, and after a short training program he was commissioned as an officer in the infantry and went to the front, where he spent a number of months in a first-line unit. Badly wounded in the Somme attack, he was mentioned in dispatches several times and was named a chevalier of the Legion of Honor.

After the war he finished his studies, earned a doctorate in law, and passed the examination in philosophy. Then he went into journalism. General manager of Paris' biggest evening paper, L'Intransigeant, in 1931, he became the president of a privately owned broadcasting station, Radio-Cité.

The Second World War found him a captain at general headquarters. After the fall of France, he was able to reach Gibraltar and join the Free French government in Algiers. He participated in the Provence landing as the chief of intelligence services of General Jean de Lattre de Tassigny's army, and reorganized the press and broadcasting facilities in the southern zone of liberated France. His military activities led to his being named a commander of the Legion of Honor.[1]

In September, 1944, he became general manager of Radio Française. He was appointed a government adviser in 1949, a post he retained until 1963.

His intellectual activity has found expression in a number of books. One treats French politics—Question de confiance (1948)—but most of his works concern the war of 1914–18 and have earned him a reputation as an expert in this field. In 1928 he wrote La Biffe (The Infantry) and in 1931 La Guerre, mon vieux. . . . His Vie et mort des Français, 1914–1918 was written jointly with two former classmates from the École Normale Supérieure and carried an introduction by Maurice Genevoix, the permanent secretary of the Académie Française. Meyer's Le 11 Novembre came out in 1964 and La Vie quotidienne des soldats pendant le Grande Guerre in 1966.

---

[1] He had been named an officer of the Legion of Honor in 1935, in his capacity as a writer.

VERDUN, 1916*

Verdun was a whole war, inserted into the Great War. . . . It was also
a kind of duel before the universe, a singular and almost symbolic
tourney.   —PAUL VALÉRY

I. THE THEATER OF OPERATIONS

THE GREAT German sweep on Verdun in February, 1916, first
checked through the strength of sheer despair and then arrested
after months of superhuman resistance and pushed back to its point
of departure at the end of the year, cannot be separated from the
great French-English attack on the Somme of July 1. The latter,
initially undertaken for another purpose—to break through on a
larger scale than in the unsuccessful offensives of 1915—had the
effect above all of relieving Verdun. The Germans, who had had
grounds for believing the war finished in 1914, made an enormous
effort in 1916, which they hoped would be decisive, to bring it to an
end. In their view, Britain's staying power depended entirely on the
French Army. It was thus the French Army's men and matériel they
had to exhaust, so as to deprive England of its "best sword,"[1] in
bullfighting parlance. Moreover, Russia's strength had already been
considerably reduced by its reverses, aggravated by the check at the
Dardanelles, the closing of the Black Sea by the Turks, and the
crushing of Serbia.

On their side, the French government and General Staff had to
take into account in their planning the delay of the English conscription and consequently the slow dispatch of British divisions.
Nonetheless, after General Sir Douglas Haig took command in
December, 1915, they replaced our troops in the north of France
little by little. And it was primarily the offensive which Major
General Erich von Falkenhayn expected from the Anglo-French
forces in the spring or summer that prompted him to launch a
preventive attack against Verdun on February 21.

Why was Verdun chosen by the German high command? It was
not simply to heighten the glory of his dynasty that the Kaiser
detailed the army led by his son, the Crown Prince, for the "victory

---

* Translated from the French by Sally Abeles.
[1] Major General von Falkenhayn's phrase.—Tr.

offensive." The main reasons were of a strategic and psychological order. The front, as it had been defined by the battles of the Marne and the fighting in the winter of 1914–15, followed a large salient between Argonne and Lorraine which embraced the fortified region at Verdun and continued southward along advance posts in the Woëvre plain. The position, almost closed in on three sides, was all the more vulnerable because it straddled a river, which could make communications from one bank to the other tricky.

A system of fourteen major railway lines served the German front; Verdun, on the contrary, could no longer use its two lines when it was attacked; the one from the south had been cut at St.-Mihiel since the end of 1914, and the other, from the west, would be severed by the bombardments of the left bank of the Meuse. Only the winder,[2] a narrow-gauge line from Bar-le-Duc to Verdun by way of Souilly, the Army's headquarters, remained to ensure the food supply (800 tons a day). Fortunately, the parallel road, which had been widened to seven meters by March, 1915, was immediately activated by Captain Doumenc's vehicle transport service, alerted on February 18. It became the Sacred Road, and its special width is today marked out for the attention of indifferent motorists. As of the twentieth, Captain Doumenc committed himself to transporting munitions and men, the foodstuff of battle, provided that he remained absolute master of the road. It was set up like a two-track railway line, divided into sections, each with its own organization. At noon on February 20, the 20th Army Corps debarked at the Bar-le-Duc station, the 1st Army Corps being already en route to Verdun. Beginning on February 29, eight days after the German attack was launched, 3,000 trucks—the count rose to 3,500 shortly—divided into 51 groups carried 50,000 tons of munitions and 90,000 men toward the front each week. If we add the light vans, ambulances, touring cars, tractors, and the like to the trucks, 11,500 vehicles were using the road in June—one every fourteen seconds, sometimes even one every five seconds. This endless chain, this "bucket conveyor," ran along the 75 miles of the artery that brought to Verdun the generous blood of the reinforcements and carried back the exhausted troops and the pitiable wounded. The 8,500 men and 300 officers of the 2d Army Transport Service could claim full credit for this success. Their chief, Captain-become-Major Doumenc, had decided that:

We will totally exclude horse or foot convoys, by shuttling them off onto parallel routes; finally, we will in no case interrupt traffic to make

---

2 The popular name given to trains serving a local line and stopping at every station.

systematic repairs of the roadway. . . . Nonmotor convoys will cross it, but without being allowed to turn onto it. . . . Any vehicle that cannot be towed off must be pushed into the ditch. No one has the right to stop, except for a serious breakdown; no truck may pass another.

If Von Falkenhayn decided to launch his attack—which he hoped to be conclusive—on Verdun, it was because he adjudged it so important from the standpoint of morale that the French command would be forced to engage every last man in its defense. "Verdun is the heart of France," the Crown Prince had said. In addition to these considerations, the Verdun region, with its numerous woods where artillery and infantry could hide from sight, even from the air, lent itself admirably to the camouflaging of preparations for attack. Thus was the German 5th Army able to keep its deployment utterly invisible. Not a single parallel takeoff trench had been dug. The assault troops lay covered in deep shelters. The average distance between the two lines, 800 to 1,000 meters, was such that the French command, though on the alert, could only believe that the preparations were incomplete, judging by precedent. Bombardment without range setting, directed against individual objectives corresponding to each artillery cluster, was made possible thanks to the German supremacy in aerial observation by planes and balloons (*Drachen*). This had the purpose of crushing everything that might oppose the advance of the assault troops. German reconnaissance was to make sure that nothing was left before three waves— each more dense than the preceding—moved forward to occupy the position, equipped with matériel to overthrow it and munitions to defend it. If the objective had not been totally destroyed, the guns were to go to work again.

On the French side, the obtuseness of the general headquarters (G.H.Q.) intelligence service, despite an abundance of warning signs, allowed an attack known about throughout the Crown Prince's army and signaled by numerous deserters to be turned into a surprise. At a time when all the defenders of Verdun sensed a gigantic attack on Verdun coming, the high command proceeded with the disarmament of the forts, because they had been shown up as worthless in the early days of the war, at Liège and Maubeuge. It was thought that their artillery would be put to better use in preparing new offensives. The surroundings of the town brought to mind an abandoned construction yard, rather than a stronghold on the alert. General Henri Pétain, who was to take command of the Army at Verdun, later described the disorganization of the sector in these words:

The fortified region had not been the object of any undertaking on the adversary's part since 1914; military activity there seemed less in 1914 than it had been in peacetime. The forts rose silent and as if abandoned. Between the forts and beyond, there was only ruin: trenches largely caved in; barbed wire cut to pieces, its inextricable tangles covering the Côtes de Meuse woods and the muddy Woëvre plains; roads and tracks turned into quagmires; equipment scattered about, wood rotting and metal rusting in the rain.

Yet there had been no lack of warnings. General Herr, who commanded the fortified region of Verdun, had issued them repeatedly. Much movement of German troops and great activity on the rail lines in the area had been reported by aerial observers. Letters taken from prisoners and the prisoners themselves referred to a review the Kaiser was going to hold at Verdun the end of February and to the peace that would follow. Reinforcements were requested, to work on strengthening the positions, as well as to hold the lines. Feverishly, at the front as in the rear, positions were blocked out again and again without any being settled on and without a fixed idea of what line of resistance to choose. The line of the forts should stand in good stead, though no attempt had been made to put their solid concrete masses to full use. We know that their artillery, though well aimed and protected, had had most of its guns withdrawn. The infantry garrisons, reduced in number, now included only Territorial troops. Behind an unsubstantial first line poorly defended by intermittent wire fencing, the support and redoubt lines comprised only widely separated and inadequately manned trenches. The second-position works were embryonic; they had not been begun until fourteen days before the attack. There were no communication trenches between the positions or linking them with the forts.

Yet Deputy Émile Driant, an infantry lieutenant colonel who would die in glory early in the day, had notified his fellow members of the Chamber of Deputies' Commission of the Army of these conditions on December 1. On December 12, General Joseph Simon Galliéni, the Minister of War, had written Field Marshal Joseph Joffre to tell him what he had learned about the lack of organization at Verdun. Joffre had replied, "Nothing justifies the fears expressed," and he made it clear that he would resign if "the complete confidence of the government" was not vested in him and if it tolerated practices which would diminish his moral authority. He admitted only that the barbed-wire fencing was inadequate. Joffre's chief of staff, General Édouard de Curières de Castelnau, was sent to inspect the area on January 25, and he found: "The organization of the first position *on the right bank* of the Meuse corresponds exactly with the directives given by the commanding general in his instructions." He nonetheless ordered the construction of shelters for the Reserves and the reinforcement of the flanks and the second position. On his return, he began to send reinforcements, but the work could not be carried out owing to lack of time. Leaves were, of course, canceled on February 9. But G.H.Q., misled by a series of diversionary actions that took place January 9–February 21 from Artois to the upper Alsace and through the Somme region and Champagne, and showered with calls for reinforcements from all these points, continued to think that German activity would boil up again primarily on the eastern front instead, "even if the Allies do not retain the initiative on operations until next summer."

Two days after the opening of the attack, Joffre again declared, with his unshakable optimism, "All precautions have been taken." Fortunately, Castelnau was able to get himself sent to Verdun immediately with full powers. Surveying the situation at firsthand, he decided to put the fortified region of Verdun under the command of the head of the 2d Army, General Pétain, who was then available, arranging a meeting at Souilly. Pétain had already received the order to send his General Staff toward Bar-le-Duc and made contact with Joffre at Chantilly. The conversation ended with this comment by Joffre: "So, my friend, now you're at ease." But it was already too late for this; the enemy had cut the standard-gauge rail lines to Verdun, and the drama was ended—the Crown Prince's troops, outnumbering the defenders five to two, bowled over the first lines of the French defense. Driant was killed in the midst of his infantrymen, and Fort Douaumont was taken (February 21–25).

The reorganized high command made the necessary decisions. But what could the soldier, even the subordinate officer, know of what was happening in that other world? From February 21 at least until the Somme attack—that is, for more than four months—the fighters at Verdun were almost constantly cut off, by German fire, from their own command, which began at the battalion level, and even more so from the artillery and the air units. The Battle of Verdun, for those who fought it in the flesh, was a battle of very small units, each directing its own fate, to the degree that the enemy fire did not totally destroy them. The actions of the head men, taken very late and often by default, were in any case remote, incapable of reaching the fighting men. The combatants were most often left to their own devices, and thus was the soldier of Verdun molded.

II. THE SOLDIER OF VERDUN

THE NARROWNESS of the terrain, the jumbling of the lines, the pounding of enemy, and, alas, friendly artillery which the sketchily dug trenches could not withstand made the war at Verdun something it rarely was elsewhere, even during the big attacks: a war fought by small isolated groups, living—and dying—in shell holes. If the positions were no more than precarious slopes of sandbags, and the communicating trenches furrows barely begun before they were stopped, they still gave an illusion of psychological protection, for they could save one from bullets and shrapnel. It was in the craters hollowed by the shells that "groups piled in the bottom . . . invisible to each other . . . form the first line. Crisscrossing of gray craters (the German *Feldgrau*) and blue craters (the French *bleu-horizon*), indistinguishable one from another. . . . Farther on, other groups, other regiment numbers."[3] There they waited; there they slept and defended themselves with tossed grenades. There they took shelter in the vague belief that two shells never fall in the same hole, a belief that often proved false.

Verdun was most often a war of abandoned men, a few men around a chief, a junior officer, a noncom, even a simple soldier whom circumstances had shown capable of leadership. Sometimes it was a single man reduced to leading himself. Handfuls of men or individuals forced to act, to take the initiative of defense—or withdrawal. Failures of nerve—there were some—generally occurred in bigger units, which were not always the most hardened but were the most shocked by the unexpectedness of the disaster. Decisive and courageous acts were mainly individual, leaving most of them unknown.

By day, impossible to make a move without emerging waist-high and being pitilessly popped off. On the left bank of the Meuse, around Hill 304, no food came in; no wounded could be taken out for two days. Nightfall hardly freed the soldiers: "Flares burst out of the darkness every minute to make sure that not a shovelful of earth was shifted by the victims designated for crushing shellfire."[4] Farther to the rear, reinforcements wandered about for hours because of the darkness before finding their positions:

The guide who was leading us was making his last turn of duty with this trip, and he quickened his pace, spurred by the anticipation of being

---

[3] Joseph Jolinon, *Le Valet de gloire* (Paris, F. Rieder) .

[4] Charles L. Delvert, *Histoire d'une compagnie* (Paris-Nancy, Berger-Levrault, 1918) .

relieved. He was our only safeguard; without him we would have been a herd of blind men. Our fate hung on his memory and his cool nerve. . . . It wasn't rare for units to wander all night among the shell holes, unable to find their place. It even happened that roving companies ran into Boche lines in the morning, where they were surrounded and slaughtered.[5]

What could have brought a measure of order into the infantry movements, active *command,* no longer existed, as we have seen. When bombardment reached the dimensions it had for months at Verdun, telephone communications were completely cut off; liaison personnel, wounded or dead, could no longer do their job. Regimental and battalion leaders, sometimes even company commanders no longer knew where their men were, nor did the men know where their lines were. Day, as well as night, in the fog of gas and the smoke of explosions, on torn-up ground where advances and partial retreats made it impossible to fix a continual line, who could tell whether the flames of firing and the whistling bullets were French or German? And the same was true on the other side.

The battered earth bore nothing but groaning wounded who couldn't be helped, distended bodies that your foot sank into, among broken guns, punctured helmets, scattered equipment. You advanced by leaping from shell hole to shell hole, their bottoms covered with muddy water and often dead men, half-buried by an explosion. Sometimes no one was in them, sometimes there were men, who welcomed you with muttered curses because you would get their precious shelter spotted. A spectral, semiconscious life, interrupted only by the eruption of danger: sudden attacks, periodic bombardments, the insidious accumulation of gas in gullies and hollows, machine guns discovered by surprise—everything overwhelmed the footsoldier. All this explains the eternal fame of Verdun—as hell, created as much by misery as by danger.

Yet the bucket conveyor, also called the pulley, of trucks from the Sacred Road continued to provide Verdun with men for devouring, whose divisions were relieved after some days. All they needed to do for this was to lose at least a third, if not half, of their strength; then their blood-sucked regiments again took their places on the too-roomy benches of the trucks that had brought them. All the *bonhommes*[6] knew this, and yet the system was less demoralizing than that of the Germans: most of their units assigned at the outset were kept at Verdun all during 1916. So those who had escaped

---

5 Pierre Chaîne, *Les Mémoires d'un rat* (Paris, Payot, 1930) .

6 The popular name generally given to soldiers at the front; the term "hairy" poilu was used mainly in the rear.

death and capture or had not been evacuated had to endure a like hell for months on end.

Doubtless it came about that both sides exaggerated the losses. The figure of 1,000,000 men was given. Actually, despite the heat of the fighting at Verdun and the Somme, the year 1916 took less of a toll than 1915, the year of nibbling actions and insane attempts at breakthroughs. At Verdun, the trenches were reduced to such inconsequence that the enemy did not know our exact positions, which were in the balance very thin and irregular. "He was therefore forced to shower a whole sector with shells instead of concentrating his fire on target areas."[7] The probable figure of losses at Verdun for both sides nonetheless reached some 700,000, with 300,000 killed or definitely missing, and the French share a little higher. All this ending with the two adversaries only a few kilometers from their original positions, after ten months of savage fighting. But the same axiom ruled on both sides: *Every position lost must be retaken.* Thus, the town of Fleury changed hands sixteen times between June 23 and July 17. Thousands of deaths for a few hundred yards of ground: On February 28, after two days of attack, 98 of Driant's men remained out of 1,200; and 64 men were standing out of eight companies of the 362d Infantry Regiment. Counterattacking Le Mort-Homme on May 24, 6th Company of the 60th Infantry was reduced from 143 men to 11. The losses among junior officers were proportionally higher, for their role was enlarged by the isolation of the battlefield. From July 13 to 28, the 115th Infantry lost 24 officers:

Lieutenant V——, who arrived for support a few days ago, has just been killed . . . two minutes after shaking my hand; a shell fragment hit his haversack full of grenades and reduced him to pulp. Cadet S——, 19, has been killed. Likewise Cadet M——, the same age, and Sergeant Major C——. They are stretched out here side by side, all three of them, my poor buddies, in front of my aid station.[8]

The superior officers who were close by their men, like Driant, did not escape death. Captain Imhaus, who had joined up again at the age of sixty, was killed in a 163d Infantry counterattack on March 30. Three of his sons were already dead at the front; the fourth was to be killed in August, 1918.

For the rest, the usual miseries of men at the front—the cold, the smell of corpses, too little and often no food when the men on field

---

7 Chaîne, *op. cit.*
8 Delvert, *op. cit.*

kitchen duty were killed before they returned—were heightened at Verdun. The mud following the rain, which fell until the summer, had tragic consequences. Wounded men drowned in shell holes filled to the brim with water. More often, the living sank into the mud near the planks that lined the pathways or the bottom of communication trenches in a very few places.

For the injured, there was no such thing as a "good wound." Even those who could try to get away from the battlefield on their own were not necessarily saved. Their trip down was as risky as their trip up to the line: How many of them were killed en route! If they had the luck to be stretcher-borne, the danger multiplied with the number of men grouped together, making a target for the machine guns or a "bundle" for a shell falling on the heap. Getting killed on a stretcher and surviving alongside a smashed stretcher and dead bearers came to the same thing. Worst of all, many wounded could not be picked up and died of gangrene or exhaustion, either where they fell or as they dragged themselves from hole to hole. This explains why the figures on Verdun include twice as many missing—that is, unidentified dead—as certain dead. Moreover, the daily inoculation of horror inevitably bred insensitivity.

In June, which was the peak of the battle, the men were not so much hungry as tired and, above all, thirsty, a thirst that the poisoned dust made a torture. Hunger would have been easier to satisfy, if only because the dead could be relieved of their reserve rations; but when a man had a few biscuits and a can of monkey meat[9] in hand, he might hesitate to eat them for fear of getting thirsty. The loss of sleep at night, spent in relief work, duty, anxious watches, was not made up by catnaps during the day, subject to the fracas of bombardments and to sudden alerts. Of course, the intensity of the bombardment could itself cause a semiconscious torpor which might let a man slip into sleep, his head between his knees or on a comrade's shoulder—or on a corpse that hadn't been discovered when the dead were being picked up. This torpor often became a kind of apathy or insensitivity in the face of death.

No distinction between the shells that blew you up. All the witnesses have said the same thing: One out of five times—some claimed one out of four or three—it was fragments from our 75 shells that shredded our *bonhommes,* the blast of our 155's that crushed the shelters. Nor were the Germans spared shells falling short. So the infantrymen in the two camps could have joined in

---

9 Popular name for canned processed beef.

muttering the same imprecations against the artillery. Ours especially, blinded by the haze and smoke and almost totally deprived of
observation posts, most often could not reply either to the red flares
summoning a barrage or to the green calling for a lengthening of
range. The German gas shells in particular hounded the artillery
gun crews, although starting with the first days of attack the
Germans did not neglect also to shoot tear gas and asphyxiating gas
into all the ditches and woods, where the branches held the fumes
in suspension.

Another agony, almost exclusively visited on the footsoldiers, for
it required close quarters: the flamethrower. Its use was not initiated at Verdun. But it was there that the Germans applied it whole
scale, and the more effectively in that its dreadful operation generally followed a heavy bombardment. It contributed to the German success in the February attack. After that, the footsoldiers
learned how to defend themselves; they tried to explode the fuel
tanks with a grenade, which transformed the carriers into living
torches, or if they could fell the sapper who held the flamethrower,
the jet of flame, no longer aimed, would then wash over its immediate surroundings.

The solidarity among the men—old and young, soldiers and the
officers near them—was never more important than at Verdun. This
moral force, said Pétain, consisted "less of ardor than of hardy
determination, and lay mainly in an inflexible will to defend their
families and their goods against the invader." And this was true, for
at Verdun, the simplest fellow felt obscurely that he had a *mission*
to protect what was for him, quite unpretentiously, "the sacred soil
of our country," a mission which, at the worst moments, the chiefs
did not hesitate to call sacrificial. But unlike what devolved after
the unsuccessful 1915 offensives, the men at Verdun were no longer
haunted by the feeling that they were dying for nothing. For the
first and only time, in fact, between the Germans' invasion arrested
at the Marne in September, 1914, and their do-or-die onslaught
stopped at the same river in May, 1918, the Germans were attempting a widescale attack, with the aim of "bleeding the French
Army," in Von Falkenhayn's phrase. And once again, as the first
time, the soldiers knew they had to dam the mounting tide, by
raising a wall of their own bodies against it, "so that they will not
pass." They will not pass became the motto of Verdun.

In the mutual exhaustion of a mercilessly prolonged struggle, this
time it was the Germans' turn to weigh the vanity of war. The
Germans, who in the early days had thought they would break our
resistance without a fight, crushing us with their *Trommelfeuer*,

their "drum-roll" fire, began to suffer the same miseries as deeply as our soldiers, with the added mortification of not having finished the war upon penetrating Verdun. They crumbled as we regained our feet. As the loss of Douaumont, through confusion and surprise, had long demoralized the French, its recapture in the autumn of 1916 sealed the reverse of the Germans and definitively destroyed their hopes. "That hill of Douaumont has become our destiny," said the German writer and military man Werner Beumelburg. They would not take Verdun; they would not yet finish a war which might never end. Thus was Verdun, which was a French victory only in the sense of an invincible resistance, a defeat of Germany before the final defeat, the only one after the Marne.[10]

But in exhausting itself, the German Army had almost succeeded in "bleeding the French Army," and the land was so crammed with corpses that Henry de Montherlant could write: "You walk on the ground of Verdun as though on the face of the Country." For the rest, the living themselves were only dead men reprieved, living an epic—the epic of suffering.

Verdun was martyrdom for its men, its footsoldiers especially, in an almost unmitigated hell, where the hours of so-called respite, in the Tavanne tunnel, for instance, were at best a purgatory. The men of the field kitchens very often could not satisfy the hunger and especially the thirst of their comrades, for, humble unsung heroes, they were struck down on the unsafe terrain among their scanty cooking pots. The calvary of the liaison men, Verdun's runners, and the litter-bearers was even worse, because it went on all night for the stretcher men and recurred at least once a day for the liaison personnel.

As for those who had to go to earth, immobile and passive and awaiting the worst under the infernal pounding, it seemed impossible to expect them to rise, exhausted, from the debris of their departure points or shell holes when the enemy attack finally rolled in, following the flamethrowers, and fire on an attacker who thought our positions were deserted, their occupants crushed. And yet almost every time, despite the lack of possible help, with their distress signals unseen, their guns plugged up, the machine guns jammed, the survivors pulled themselves up to try to check the flood. For aside from a rare and understandable panic, these men seemed still to prefer death or capture to the safety of flight.

The image that formed of this "war within the war" came to

---

[10] The final relief of Verdun was accomplished on September 12, 1918, by the American 1st Army.

create a sort of myth of Verdun. That special aura was the basis of a state of mind among the soldiers which can be divided into three successive stages. When a man went up there, he felt a dim fear. When he left, he no longer was afraid of being afraid. When he left for good, he carried a sense of pride away in his memory. An officer recounts that once he was reading his men the day's communiqué, and it told about a German reverse near the Thiaumont farm where his regiment had stayed. "Don't say nothing about our losses," growled a *bonhomme*. But he was the only one to grumble. The others had a little flame of pride in their eyes: "That's us, it is!" Human beings draw their pride from their worst sufferings.

Vivian de Sola Pinto

VIVIAN DE SOLA PINTO *was born in Hampstead, England, in 1895, and was educated at University College School, London, and Christ Church, Oxford. In World War I he served as an officer in the Royal Welch Fusiliers in Gallipoli, Egypt, France, and Belgium, and was wounded twice on the western front. In the summer of 1918 he was second-in-command to Captain Siegfried Sassoon, the late poet, in the 25th Royal Welch. In 1921 he graduated with first-class honors from Oxford University and in 1926 was awarded the degree of Doctor of Philosophy. He was professor of English at University College, Southampton, from 1926 till 1938 and at the University of Nottingham from 1938 till 1961. He was elected a fellow of the Royal Society of Literature in 1929. In World War II he served as a captain in the British Intelligence Corps and the Royal Engineers. He has lectured in Belgium, Holland, India, Italy, the United States, and Yugoslavia, and he spent the academic year 1965–66 as visiting professor at the University of California, Davis. He married Irène Adeline Pittet in 1922 and has two sons. His publications include* Sir Charles Sedley (1927), Peter Sterry, Puritan and Platonist (1934), The English Renaissance (1938), Crisis in English Poetry (1951), Restoration Carnival (1954), Enthusiast in Wit (1962), The Restoration Court Poets (1965), William Blake (1965), *as well as two volumes of verse,* The Invisible Sun (1934) *and* This Is My England (1941). *He has also edited* The Poetical and Dramatic Works of Sir Charles Sedley, The Poems of John Wilmot, Earl of Rochester, *and (with Warren Roberts)* The Complete Poems of D. H. Lawrence.

MY FIRST WAR: MEMOIRS OF A SPECTACLED SUBALTERN

IN THE SUMMER of 1914 I was a tall, lanky, spectacled youth of eighteen; I had just left school and was to go up to Oxford in October. At the end of July, I went with my father and sister to spend our usual summer holiday on the Scottish coast. When we left London, we had just heard of the assassination of the Austrian archduke at Sarajevo. By the end of the month the news was becoming not merely exciting but alarming. At first it seemed as if the conflict might be confined to the Balkans, but the refusal of the German government to cooperate with Sir Edward Grey's strenuous efforts to damp down the flames and the successive mobilizations of the Austrian, Russian, German, and French armies soon made it clear that a major European war was inevitable.

In the last days of July, however, and even in the first two of August, it was by no means certain that Britain would be drawn into the conflict. On Monday the third we read Grey's speech in the Commons in which he declared that the British Fleet would oppose any attempt of the German Navy to sail down the Channel and attack the French ports and indignantly rejected the German attempt to buy British neutrality by promising to restore French territorial integrity after the war. Then came in quick succession the German violations of France, Luxembourg, and, finally, Belgium, the country whose neutrality Britain was pledged to defend, the ultimatum and declaration of war on August 4.

A comparison at once suggests itself between the way in which the news of these world-shaking events was received by our little party at Dunbar in 1914 and the impact of the declaration of World War II twenty-five years later. Then, too, I was holiday making. I was with my wife and two young sons at a farmhouse in north Wales when we heard on a primitive radio set Mr. Chamberlain's announcement that we were at war with Hitler's Germany. In 1939 our reaction, like that, I believe, of most English people, was one of grim acceptance of a terrible necessity. Our mood in August, 1914, was very different. It was a mixture of relief, enthusiasm, and, I must admit, something like exultation.

Of course, we had no idea of the horrors of modern warfare. What we felt was relief from an intolerable tension, a sense of liberation from the deadly stuffiness of a commercialized civilization and of participation in a heroic adventure. Here, it seemed, was a chance for a wonderful renovation of human life, almost an apocalypse. At last we were being asked to fight and suffer not for imperial aggrandizement or material gain but for justice and liberty. Not only would we save the French and the Belgians, but we would rebuild our own society on a basis of social justice. This confused, nebulous, but fundamentally generous and humane enthusiasm was certainly the mood of millions of young Britons in the first weeks of the war. Rupert Brooke gave it a rather strained and melodramatic expression in his sonnet beginning "Now, God be thanked, Who has matched us with His Hour." Thomas Hardy, a much greater poet, alone found the right words for it in his "Song of the Soldiers":

> What of the faith and fire within us
> Men who march away
> Ere the barn-cocks say
> Night is growing grey,
> Leaving all that here can win us;
> What of the faith and fire within us
> Men who march away?

I find it hard to understand how people whom I respect, like Bertrand Russell, can still argue that we could and should have stood aside from the European conflict in 1914. If the pacifist minority in the Liberal government had had its way and we had failed to fulfill our legal obligation to Belgium and our moral obligation to France, the nation would certainly have been split from top to bottom. The Germans would, doubtless, have overrun western Europe as they did in 1940; but in the meantime, I have no doubt that thousands of British volunteers without adequate arms or organization would have streamed across the Channel to help the resistance, and the tragedy of the International Brigade in Spain in 1936–37 would have been anticipated on a much larger scale in France and Flanders. In the meantime, the German militarists controlling the resources of the whole Continent would have dictated their own terms to a divided and isolated Britain without a friend in the world, and the next victim would certainly have been the wealthy and, at that time, almost defenseless American democracy.

The feelings that I have tried to describe were certainly shared by many older English people, but in their minds they were often mixed, doubtless half-consciously, with less idealistic motives. Here was a unique opportunity to militarize the whole nation, to put a stop to all democratic progress and to use the naïve idealism of the young to buttress the domination of the privileged classes and enlarge and strengthen the British Empire. At the beginning of the war perhaps only a few crusted old colonels and the like would have explicitly accepted this view of the situation, but very soon such ideas began to gain ground especially among the "hard-faced men" who, as usual in times of national crisis, soon occupied key positions. More and more the war became *their* war, and not that of the young enthusiasts of August, 1914, and the results were tragic for Britain and the world. The betrayal of "the faith and fire within us" of August, 1914, is surely one of the great disasters of history and was to lead inevitably to the miserable reversion to the old game of power politics in the postwar period and the terrible results that followed.

We cut short our holiday at Dunbar and returned to London immediately after the declaration of war. I remember the next few weeks in our suburban home as a strange, feverish time. As there was no radio or television in those days, our only source of information about the war was the newspapers. I spent much of my time buying and reading the numerous editions of the morning and evening papers which appeared at all sorts of odd times. The smooth routine of middle-class suburban life seemed quite unreal. I felt that this world was now dead, a sort of ghastly simulacrum from which I must escape as soon as possible. Soon we heard of the landing of the B.E.F. in France, the retreat from Mons, the"miracle of the Marne," and the "race to the sea." Kitchener became War Minister, and his heavily moustached face appeared on all the hoardings, making his famous appeal for 1,000,000 recruits (conscription was still politically impossible under a Liberal government) . I waited in a long queue at a local recruiting office; when my turn came to be medically examined, I was told to remove my glasses for the eyesight test, and it was found that I could only with difficulty decipher the top letter on the card at the prescribed distance. So, like other myopic enthusiasts, at the time I was promptly rejected. I tried again at other recruiting offices with the same result, and I learned that only men who could read the first four lines without glasses were accepted. The British Army had no use for spectacled soldiers in 1914.

I went up to Oxford in October and joined the senior division of the O.T.C. to prepare myself for the time when the rigid rule debarring myopics from the fighting forces should be relaxed, as I was sure it would be if the war continued for any length of time.

Life at Oxford was pleasant but, like everything else in England at that time, seemed unreal. By the autumn the great line stretching from the North Sea to Switzerland had been established, Antwerp had been lost; but the old British Regular Army had withstood the German onslaught at Ypres, and the Channel ports had been saved. We heard now for the first time of the strange new phenomenon of trench warfare, and Bruce Bairnsfather's drawings helped us visualize its humors and miseries. I loved Oxford, but my demon kept telling me that I must get away from it and take my place among the men who were fighting and suffering. Paradoxically, at that moment it seemed that the only real life was to be found where there was the greatest chance of meeting a violent death.

When I came home for the Christmas vacation, London seemed to wear its usual appearance except for the recruiting posters and the number of men in uniform in the streets. It was the period of "business as usual," and so far there had been no air raids and no rationing. In fact, for a great part of the population it was a lovely war. Wages were high, unemployment had disappeared, profiteers were making huge profits, and money was flowing freely. Conscription was still far off, and numerous recruiting meetings were addressed by all sorts of people ranging from Cabinet ministers to music hall stars. Hysterical young women persecuted men of military age seen in the street in "civvies," and to protect myself from their attentions, I used to wear my O.T.C. uniform.

At the end of my second term I felt that it was impossible to live any longer in the Oxford dreamworld. In March I made several more assaults on recruiting offices with the same result as before. Then I heard that I might have a chance of being accepted by a unit called the Inns of Court O.T.C., which was a sort of offshoot of the famous Artists' Rifles. At this time officer cadet schools had not yet been organized, and the Inns of Court Battalion was being used to help with the supply of junior officers for the rapidly expanding Army. When I was medically examined at their headquarters, I was confronted by a kindly doctor who tactfully left me alone for a few minutes with the eyesight testing card before he asked me to remove my glasses. In these few minutes I memorized the first four lines of letters on the card and was able to recite them glibly when the doctor returned and my glasses were removed. So I became a private or rather rifleman in the Inns of Court Battalion and remained with them for a few weeks. My memory of those weeks is of strenuous drilling mostly at the double and being shouted at by a foulmouthed Cockney corporal who initiated us into the mysteries of the drill of the rifle regiments, which differed from the ordinary infantry drill which I had learned in my school and university O.T.C.'s. We also had bayonet practice which consisted of charging with rifle and fixed bayonet at a sack stuffed with straw suspended from a wooden frame and shouting imprecations at this imaginary enemy. Later, I believe, red paint was used to simulate blood on these sacks, but this charming refinement had not been introduced in the spring of 1915.

My fellow riflemen-cadets were constantly leaving to take up commissions, and soon my turn came. I was summoned to the orderly room and asked by the C.O. if I would accept a commission in a Territorial battalion of the Royal Welch Fusiliers. I suspected that this invitation may have been due to a Major M——, an officer in that battalion who had some acquaintance with my father. I knew nothing of the Royal Welch except that their officers wore a bunch of black ribbons on the backs of their tunics; but Major M—— was a kind, fatherly sort of person, and I thought I might as well enter this new and somewhat alarming world under his wing.

It is October, 1915. The scene is the rocky coast of the Gallipoli Peninsula in Turkey. The shy young undergraduate has been transformed into a second lieutenant in the Royal Welch Fusiliers dressed in dirty khaki drill uniform. He has recently arrived with a draft of junior officers to replace those killed or wounded at the August landings. His battalion is at present in a so-called rest camp consisting (I quote a diary kept at the time) "of numerous holes dug in the side of a hill called Ghazi Baba overlooking the sea. The holes are for the most part about 6 × 3 feet covered with a single ground sheet. Senior officers have somewhat larger ones with walls of sandbags or stones covered with several ground sheets stitched together. The place has the appearance of a huge antheap swarming with greyshirted, khaki-trousered tommies, mostly wearing woollen 'cap-comforters' on their heads (as yet there are no steel helmets). Looking southward, there is a magnificent view across Suvla Bay and Anzac Cove with the promontory called Lala Baba jutting out between them and behind it the sheet of water called the Salt Lake. On the right across the Aegean we can see the islands of Imbros and Samothrace and on the left, across a sandy plain dotted with a few stunted trees and ruined farmhouses, are the heights held by the Turks with the village of Anafarta Sagir (this name is naturally the subject of many lewd jests). The sea is full of allied warships, including a queer-looking Russian cruiser with four funnels called by our men 'the packet of woodbines,' which constantly shell the Turkish positions. Just out of range of the Turkish guns are a number of hospital ships painted green and white with large red crosses which are illuminated at night."

I am talking to a friendly Irish subaltern called Close, one of the survivors of the August landings, who tells me how the incompetent corps commander, General Stopford, kept our division, the 53d

Welch, and the Scottish 51st on the beach for nearly forty-eight hours after landing, during which time the Turks and Germans brought up heavy reinforcements. Even then our men reached Anafarta Sagir and could have pressed on across the peninsula to the straits if they had received adequate support and supplies.

Our food, mainly tinned stuff, is always full of sand and grit and infested with swarms of flies. Practically the whole Army is suffering from diarrhea and dysentery. The latrines are poles stretched across open trenches. On these poles rows of scarecrows, many of them dying of dysentery, sit continuously. It is a sight to which Goya at his most macabre might have done justice.

On the night of October 19 the Turkish field guns (which included many of the deadly French 75's) get the range of our camp and shell it with shrapnel, killing four men in the dugouts, including one of the subalterns who has come with me from England. The wounds are mostly in the head and could have been avoided if we had had steel helmets. The next night our battalion goes up to the front line, which is less than 100 yards from the Turkish trenches. Now for the first time I become acquainted with the routine of trench warfare: daylight hours of enforced idleness in trenches or dugouts, alternating with nights of activity with working parties and patrols and subalterns taking their turns as officers of the watch between the two important rituals of standing to arms at an hour before sunset and an hour before sunrise. The Turks are well supplied with ammunition and keep up a pretty incessant rifle and machine-gun fire during the hours of darkness. By daylight their very competent snipers were active, and we were warned not to expose any part of our anatomies above the parapet of the front-line trenches by day.

A jolly red-haired boy in my platoon called "Ginger" Jenkins disregarded this injunction on our first morning in the front line. I was in the next bay when I heard the crack of a rifleshot and found poor Ginger lying in a pool of blood on the fire step. As the body was being carried away by the stretcher bearers the platoon sergeant said, "Strong as a little 'orse 'e was. 'E never got no dysentery." I thought of Rupert Brooke: "If I should die, think only this of me. . . ." and Sergeant Cooper's epitaph seemed to me far more to the point than Brooke's highfalutin fancy. On November 18 I was sent with a working party in the early morning to a place some way behind the front line near the Salt Lake. We found there on the brown grass and buried a number of corpses of men of the Worcesters which had been there since the landings in August. The stench was horrible; I describe them in my diary as "gruesome black masses of decomposition with pitiful, loose arms and legs, their white sunhelmets lying beside them adding to the nightmare quality of the scene." This sight haunted my memory, and henceforward I was proof against all the clichés about "sacrifice," "glory," and "never sheathing the sword." All such expressions were for me now permanently tainted by the thought of those vigorous young bodies turned into objects of horror.

Toward the end of November the weather broke. On the twenty-seventh rain fell in torrents, and it turned very cold. It was the beginning of the worst winter known in the Aegean for many years, a grimly appropriate conclusion to the ill-starred Gallipoli campaign. We were flooded out of our trenches, which were knee-deep in water. The Turks probably suffered as much as we did, and their rifle and machine-gun fire ceased. We had no dry clothes or hot rations, our tobacco and matches were soaked so that we could not smoke, and we spent the night shivering in the fields behind the trenches. The next day some hot food was brought to us and that night we were relieved by a Scottish battalion of the 51st Division.

We marched in single file in pitch-darkness down endless waterlogged communication trenches. When we emerged into open country, the word was passed down that we were to halt and bivouac for the night. "Bivouac" was a grim joke as, with wonderful foresight, our waterproof sheets and blankets had been collected before we left the trenches. An icy wind was now blowing, and the rain had turned to sleet. Soon it was freezing and snowing, and our clothes were caked with mud and frozen stiff. In the early morning I helped another subaltern, my friend Vernon Anson, and his batman, John Evans, enlarge a shell hole over which we stretched an old blanket and secured the edges with stones. The three of us huddled together in this improvised dugout. Anson had a tin of condensed milk, and I had a flask with a little brandy, and we shared these scanty supplies for the rest of the day while a blizzard swept over us. This was November 30, the day long remembered by survivors of the Gallipoli army as "frozen foot day," when more than 200 British soldiers are said to have died of exposure on that storm-swept Gallipoli coast.

In the evening Anson, Evans, and I were picked up by a party of R.A.M.C. (Royal Army Medical Corps) men who took us to the 1st Welch Field Ambulance on the beach. "What a wretched crowd of scarecrows we were," I wrote in my diary some days later, "all ranks huddled together, livid with cold and dressed in filthy, ragged uniforms, one man writhing and wailing on the ground." The R.A.M.C. men did their best to make us comfortable with blankets and mugs of hot tea; but the blizzard was still raging, and the cold was intense. On the following night we were put on stretchers and carried onto a lighter, which took us to one of those beautiful hospital ships we had looked at so often with longing eyes from our trenches. Our dirty clothes were removed; we were washed by tender, skillful hands, dressed in clean pajamas, and put to bed in white cots. For the first time I knew the wonderful joy of getting out of the fighting line into the peace and cleanliness of a hospital.

In the spring of 1917, after being invalided home from Egypt, I was sent with a draft from our 4th Reserve Battalion to the 19th Royal Welch Fusiliers (a newly formed "Kitchener Battalion") in France. I reached them in April, when their division (the 40th) was just moving forward in pursuit of the Germans, who were carrying out their famous strategic withdrawal from their old positions on the Somme after the bloody battles of 1916. I was lucky enough to be posted to C Company commanded by Captain "Pip" Powell, a burly, dark-haired Cambridge man who had been a schoolteacher in civilian life. The second-in-command, Hal Parry, a lean, bronzed little Welshman, had been a skipper in the merchant marine and always carried a telescope slung over his shoulder. I struck up a warm friendship with these two admirable men, who were amused by my exotic name and promptly nicknamed me Gondola. Pip was a natural leader of men, generous, humane and intelligent, and Hal had a fine, dry, salty humor that no amount of physical hardship could quench.

It was very cold and constantly raining as we advanced along the Péronne-Cambrai road. We bivouacked at night in old German trenches and dugouts but had to exercise caution because the enemy had left behind numerous booby traps. One of our men picked up an object that looked like a fountain pen. It contained a detonator which blew off several of his fingers. Our advance continued up to the ridge in front of the village of Gouzeaucourt and into the neighboring villages of Gonnelieu and La Vacquerie. Here the retreating Germans fought a rearguard action before retreating to their famous Hindenburg Line in front of Cambrai and St.-Quentin.

The official *History of the Royal Welch Fusiliers* calls this "a small affair," but an action which seems small to the military historian is often quite formidable to the troops who take part in it. By the time we reached Gouzeaucourt, we were, as I wrote in a letter to my father, "a horrible sight, unwashed, unshaven with our clothes, which we had not been able to take off for a week, sticking to us." At any rate, however, we now had "battle bowlers," or steel helmets, and also leather jerkins, which would have been a godsend in that November blizzard at Suvla Bay.

We dug ourselves in, using partly an old German trench line on the ridge in front of Gouzeaucourt, and there, one early morning, our divisional artillery and that of the Guards Division put down a tremendous barrage, which was suitably accompanied by a terrific thunderstorm. Behind this wall of flame we went into La Vacquerie where our sappers blew up a number of gun emplacements and dugouts. However, it was decided not to hold the village, and we went back to our ridge in front of Gouzeaucourt, now named in honor of our regiment "Fusilier Ridge." Three of our company commanders (fortunately not Pip) and a good many "other ranks" were killed in this "small affair." In the following weeks our division organized an elaborate trench system in front of Gouzeau-court. Through our field glasses (and Hal's telescope) we could see the sun glinting on the huge bands of wire entanglements in front of the much talked-of Hindenburg Line. Our front line was separated from that of the enemy by a wide no-man's-land of 800 to 1,000 yards.

After the action at La Vacquerie our sector became fairly quiet. "Quiet" on the western front was, of course, a relative term. There was constant desultory shelling, bursts of machine-gun fire, snipers on the lookout for unwary enemies who exposed themselves above parapets by daylight, and trench mortars lobbing their murderous missiles periodically over no-man's-land. Our brigade now spent three weeks in the line without being relieved. Very soon we were all lousy, and our webbing equipment was nibbled by the large rats which abounded in the trenches. Nevertheless, in spite of all the hardships and discomforts, I remember that spring of 1917 as a time of warmhearted comradeship both with the men of my platoon and the other company officers, and although I naturally missed my books and the amenities of civilized life, I was a good deal happier than in the comfort and security of my "nice" prewar bourgeois suburban home.

After a period of divisional rest in the devastated country near Péronne, we were back in our old sector in front of Gouzeaucourt. The bright boys on the staff were always thinking of new ways of keeping the men in the line occupied. The idea that was dominant in our division in those summer months of 1917 was the "fighting patrol." When we first established our new line in April, we used to send out small parties, consisting of two or three men with an officer or N.C.O., into no-man's-land after dark to patrol the area in front of our wire. The fighting patrol was a much more ambitious affair, consisting of fifteen to twenty men commanded by a subaltern or, sometimes, a captain. Its orders were to patrol the whole of no-man's-land up to the enemy wire and engage any enemy patrols that it might meet. The members of these patrols had their faces blackened, wore woolen cap comforters instead of battle bowlers, and had the buttons of their tunics covered or tarnished. I rather enjoyed going out on patrol. I liked the thrill of danger, the sense of escaping from the troglodyte existence of the trenches and being out in the open under the night sky. We used to creep through the long grass in no-man's-land up to the German line, and when one of the numerous German flares went up, we would stay in frozen immobility till the light faded. There was a sunken road which provided excellent cover for our return.

On the night of July 8, after completing our usual tour of no-man's-land, I led my patrol over the bank into the sunken road. It was bright moonlight, and as we dropped into the road, we found ourselves in the middle of a number of men in flat caps, obviously a German patrol. For a moment the English and the Germans stared at each other in amazement. I had my loaded revolver hung around my neck on a lanyard, and in my excitement, I raised it and fired into the mass of strangers. I certainly hit a man near me and saw him fall. Then there was a blinding flash, and I heard a tremendous roar. The next thing I remember was regaining consciousness on a stretcher in our front line with a bandage round the lower part of my face and my mouth full of blood, feeling as though my lower jaw had been blown off.

Later I learned that after I fired my revolver, a German threw one of their stick bombs, which exploded above my head and knocked me senseless. My excellent sergeant and others of our patrol then threw some Mills bombs at the Germans, who promptly scattered, and I was carried back to our front line with a field dressing tied around my bleeding mouth. I remember Pip leaning over my stretcher and saying, "Poor old Gondola. You've certainly got a Blighty one this time."[1] Actually, he was wrong. When my wound was dressed, it was found that my jaw was intact; but some teeth had been knocked out, and various pieces of bomb had been lodged in my tongue and cheek.

I was taken to a hospital run by a Harvard medical team at Étretat in Normandy, where a skillful American surgeon extracted the pieces of bomb and sewed up my perforated cheek. My healthy young body soon recovered from the injury, the hole in my cheek healed, and my swollen tongue went down to its normal size. Instead of going home, I was sent to Lady Michelham's convalescent home at Dieppe. This wealthy and generous woman had taken the two best hotels in this Norman seaside resort as a con-

---

[1] A "Blighty one" was a wound which would send you back to "Blighty," the soldier slang word for England.

valescent home for wounded British officers. One day, while enjoying a delectable fortnight in these pleasant surroundir picked up a glossy magazine which contained a poem by an au of whom I had never heard before with the resonant nam Siegfried Sassoon. It was an attractive piece of verse expressing ...c longing for beautiful things felt by many sensitive spirits amid the drabness of trench warfare:

> Return to me, colours that were my joy,
> Not in the woeful crimson of men slain
> But shining as a garden; come with streaming
> Colours of dawn, and sundown after rain.

It seemed to me that this was a poet who was to be watched. Shortly afterward, when I was at the base camp at Rouen, waiting to be sent back to my unit, I read a review of a recently published book of verse by Sassoon called *The Old Huntsman*; the reviewer quoted in full a poem of a very different kind from the mellifluous lines quoted above. It was called "Blighters," and its quality of burning sincerity made every other war poem that I had seen fade into insignificance:

> The House is crammed: tier upon tier they grin
> And cackle at the Show, while prancing ranks
> Of harlots shrill the chorus, drunk with din;
> "We're sure the Kaiser loves the dear old Tanks!"

> I'd like to see a Tank come down the stalls,
> Lurching to rag-time tunes, or "Home, sweet Home,"
> And there'd be no jokes in Music-halls
> To mock the riddled corpses round Bapaume.[2]

Here was a man who had found the supremely right words for the growing indignation of the men of the front line at the heartless vulgarity of the people at home who were enjoying "a lovely war." I cut the poem out and learned it by heart: It seemed to crystallize feelings which had been growing up obscurely in my mind ever since I saw those pathetic corpses at Suvla Bay.

When I returned to my battalion in September, they were still in the Gouzeaucourt sector, which had become much livelier. Large trench mortars were active on both sides, and Jerry (as we called the Germans)[3] had developed an unpleasant habit of bringing up captured French 75's to his front line and sniping at us at point-blank range with formidable field guns. In 1917 it was exceptional

---

2 Bapaume is a town on the Somme near Péronne where many thousands of British and German troops were slaughtered in the battles of 1916.

3 The words "Hun" and "Boche" were mainly used by armchair patriots at home.

for infantry subalterns in the line to escape wounds or death for any length of time. I was lucky. On October 27 I was hit in the right forearm by a German machine-gun bullet when I was in no-man's-land. This time my wound was a perfect "Blighty one." I was given one of the horrible anesthetics of those days at an advanced dressing station while the bullet was extracted, and it was found that the bone was splintered and the wound was septic. Very soon I found myself gliding in a hospital train into Victoria Station in London, where a lady in black offered me some cake, which I accepted, and a religious tract, which I refused. That night, lying in bed in a hospital in Camberwell, I heard the bark of antiaircraft guns and the thud of bombs. It was my first experience of an air raid on London.

My arm took longer to heal than I expected, and I was at home on sick leave at Christmas. I was now the perfect exhibit for an English middle-class family in the winter of 1917 with my conspicuous wound, my full lieutenant's uniform (I had now had my second pip) with the divisional flash on my shoulders showing that I had come from "overseas," the ribbon of the 1914–15 star and two golden wound stripes. My proud father took me on a round of visits to various friends, and I was lavishly dined and wined. These were people of the sort who always referred to the enemy as the "Hun," looked forward with glee to hanging the poor old Kaiser, and were now vociferous in denouncing the wicked Bolshevists who had "let us down" on the eastern front.

As I gulped down their champagne with a fatuous smile on my face, I felt horribly unreal, a sort of ghost from another world, the real world of the brotherhood of the front line, and, when we went to the theater to see *Chu Chin Chow* and *The Bing Boys,* as I looked at the crowded auditorium and the glittering lights, I could not help wondering whether it would not, perhaps, be a good thing if a tank should come lurching through the stalls to jolt out of their complacency all these well-fed people who were enjoying "a lovely war." Actually, the war was not quite so lovely now even for these sheltered London suburbans. There were occasional air raids, tiny affairs, indeed, compared with the blitzes of the forties, yet sufficient to cause some alarm and despondency, and the German U-boat campaign was causing a shortage of various foodstuffs, notably butter and sugar, though the better-class restaurants still continued to serve succulent meals. As soon as I was well enough to go out, I bought a copy of *The Old Huntsman,* in which, besides the poems I had already seen, I found much that was congenial to my present mood.

When I returned to the Reserve Battalion in Wales, in view of my wounds and service on two fronts, I was placed on the strength as second-in-command of a company, which meant that I should not be sent overseas again for six months unless there was an urgent need for officers in the line. Such a need arose in the spring of 1918 after the devastating offensives of Ludendorff on the Somme and at Armentières. So, on June 17, I found myself crossing the Channel once more on a crowded troopship; this time it was full of American officers, one of whom, seeing my 1914–15 ribbon, came up to me and said, "Say, Lootenant, were you at Mons?"

At the base camp at Rouen, I found that I was posted to the 25th Royal Welch Fusiliers, a battalion formed originally from an amalgamation of two dismounted Welsh yeomanry regiments, belonging to the 74th Division, which had recently come to the western front from Palestine. When I arrived at the battalion headquarters in a partly ruined chateau near Arras, I sensed an entirely different atmosphere from that of the other fighting battalions in which I had served. These men had taken part in Allenby's advance to Jerusalem. They were, for the most part, big bronzed fellows with something of the panache of victorious troops and something of the swagger of cavalrymen. Many of them had their puttees wound in the reverse way from that of infantrymen and carried their haversacks hitched up, cavalry fashion, under their arms. The divisional sign was a broken spur, and the very smart flash was a green diamond with a vertical white stripe, which I had sewn onto the shoulders of my tunic as soon as possible. The adjutant, a stout, dark man with a row of decorations, ushered me into the presence of the colonel, who said, "You're to go to A Company as second-in-command to Captain Sassoon." I pricked up my ears at these words. Could it really be that I should have the incredible luck of serving under the author of *The Old Huntsman?*

The rest of the day had an apocalyptic quality for me. A guide led me down a muddy path to A Company headquarters, a hut in front of a mass of trees silhouetted against a sky in which a fine June sunset was flaring through broken clouds. A tall figure came out of the hut to meet me. Ignoring my smart salute, he shook me by the hand.

"I suppose you're my new second-in-command. I've never had one before—"

"Yes, sir, er, are you the poet Siegfried Sassoon?"

As I blurted out these words I knew what the answer was. That splendid, erect form with the noble head, mane of dark hair, piercing black eyes, and strongly sculptured features could belong only to a poet. He took me into the hut and made me talk about myself. I tried to describe very inadequately the effect "Blighters" and Siegfried's other trench poems had had on me. In his book *Sherston's Progress,* where he calls me Velmore, he describes his new second-in-command as he appeared to him on that June evening in 1918: "a tall, dark young man who had been up at Oxford for an academic year when the outbreak of war interrupted his studies. More scholastic than soldier-like in appearance (mainly because he wore spectacles) he had the look of one who might some day occupy a professorial chair."[4]

Pip Powell had been an excellent company commander, but Siegfried was something quite different. He was what, in modern jargon, is called a charismatic personality who radiated heroic energy and generosity. He is good enough to write that when I was his second-in-command, I gave him "an extra head and a duplicate pair of eyes." The fact was that like every man in A Company, I at once became his devoted servant and, seeing that he was bored by the immense quantities of paper that descended on every company commander in 1918 from "higher up" "for necessary attention," I tried to relieve him as far as possible of this part of the work and deal with the innumerable instructions, directions, requests for returns, etc. as punctually and expeditiously as I could.

Soon after my arrival our division began to move "up North." On July 12 our battalion took over part of the line in front of St.-Floris near Armentières in the sector where the Portuguese had been pushed back in the German offensive in April. Here we found something very different from the well-organized trench systems to which I had been accustomed in 1917. The "line" here was a series of breast-high posts strung out over a wide area and connected by a shallow ditch. A little way behind the posts was an enlarged shell hole dignified by the name of company headquarters and, close by, two similar excavations occupied respectively by the company sergeant major and the signalers. No-man's-land varied from 100 to 200 yards and consisted of beautiful fields of nearly ripe wheat and barley.

There were two other subalterns besides me in A Company; but one of them soon went off to be battalion Lewis gun officer, and the other, an attractive youth called Jowitt, was sent on a short course. In these circumstances Siegfried and I decided to divide the night into two watches, during which one of us would stay at company headquarters to deal with messages while the other patrolled the posts. I found it a curious paradox that the author of *Counter Attack,* which had just been published, that volume full of bitter indignation at the hideous cruelty of modern warfare, should also

---

[4] *Sherston's Progress* (London, 1936), p. 230.

be a first-rate soldier and a most aggressive company commander. He was determined that A Company should demonstrate its superiority to the enemy as soon as possible, and he spent a large part of his nocturnal watches crawling through the deep corn in no-man's-land with a couple of bombs in his pocket and a knobkerric in his hand. On the first night after our arrival he crawled up to a German post and brought back one of their stick bombs. I implored him to be careful and told him his life was too valuable to be risked in this way.

By the middle of July the German artillery had got our range, and we were heavily shelled with their big 5.9's or crumps. After breakfast on the seventeenth, Siegfried and I were squatting together in our cubbyhole when a series of heavy thuds warned us that the crumps were getting uncomfortably near. Finally, a tremendous impact sent us flying across the mouth of the dugout, but there was no explosion; a dud had landed just behind us, and a great crack opened in the earth at the back of our hole. It looked like a huge, grinning, diabolical mouth, and we christened it "the grin of death." Most of the German shells at this time contained phosgene gas, and some of them the recently introduced and even more horrific mustard variety, so that we had to spend much of our time very uncomfortably wearing our respirators. On the night of the eighteenth, Siegfried took the second watch from midnight onward, and as usual, I begged him to be careful and do nothing foolhardy. When we stood to an hour before dawn, he had not returned. At about five thirty I began to get anxious and, leaving Company Sergeant Major Evans to hold the fort, I went up to the posts with my batman and a runner.

The first three platoons that I visited had seen nothing of Siegfried, and when I reached No. 4 Post, it was broad daylight. The corporal in charge of the section on our extreme right told me that the captain had gone into no-man's-land sometime ago. Taking this corporal with me, I was just getting through our wire when I saw Siegfried's head bobbing up in the pale yellow corn about twenty yards away. As he raised his arm to wave to me, I heard the sharp crack of a rifleshot from No. 3 Post. It came from one of our overzealous sergeants who mistook his company commander for a German. When I reached Siegfried, his face was covered with blood, and I thought for a moment that he was badly wounded; but he assured me that the bullet had only grazed his temple, and leaning on my shoulder, he was able to limp back to the post, where he fainted. He regained consciousness lying on a stretcher on which he was carried down to the dressing station. As I walked beside him I could not help saying, "O dear, Siegfried, I was afraid something like this would happen. Now you've left the ruddy company on my hands."

I was now, at the age of twenty-two, commanding a company in a rather sticky sector of the line with no officers. My second-in-command was, therefore, Sergeant Major Evans, who, I must say, was worth a half a dozen average subalterns. I decided to divide the nights with him as I had formerly divided them with Siegfried. The next morning the divisional general came to see me and asked if I thought I could carry on for another week, and I told him I would do my best. The following days were the most unpleasant and exhausting that I spent in the line. I had hardly any sleep, gas shells rained down on us continually, and we had numerous casualties. An additional pleasantry was supplied by our own artillery. They started shelling the German front line with projectiles which emitted a horrible gas that blew back onto our own posts. The staff gave me almost as much trouble as the enemy. Runners were constantly appearing with messages from "higher up" claiming "immediate attention." One of these gave me some grim amusement. It was an urgent request from divisional headquarters to let them know at once how many men in my company wanted divisional Christmas cards! I scrawled across it, "Probably none if present conditions continue."

It was a great relief to see Jowitt's cheerful face when he returned three days after Siegfried's departure. He and I promptly got to work on preparations for a daylight raid on an enemy post which Siegfried had planned before he was wounded. The raid was a complete success. We took five prisoners—a corporal and four privates. Sitting on the fire step in one of our posts, these Saxons looked very young, thin, and pale in their dirty field gray uniforms as they drank mugs of tea and smoked cigarettes that our men gave them. It seemed incredible that these young English and German soldiers who were now on such excellent terms should have been trying a short time before to slaughter each other with all sorts of diabolical instruments.

Soon after we came out of the line, a gas shell fell on my company headquarters in a ruined farmhouse and filled my lungs with phosgene. I was sent to a hospital at Étaples in a very uncomfortable condition diagnosed as "phosgene poisoning and bronchitis." After a period of light duty at Rouen, I was lucky enough to be able to rejoin my battalion just in time for the great advance in the beginning of October.

In the light of a gray, misty dawn near La Bassée we scrambled through our wire in fighting equipment with iron rations (canned meat) for three days. In front of us was a smoke barrage through which we could dimly see the shapes of tanks, and when we reached the enemy wire, we found that it had been effectively flattened by these monsters. Going gingerly for fear of booby traps, we managed to get clear of the German trench system by the late afternoon, and I shall never forget the thrill of breaking through the barrier which had resisted Allied attacks for four years and reaching the first inhabited building, a farmhouse with a light in the window, where an elderly Frenchwoman and her daughter, looking pale and ghostly in their black clothes, made us some coffee. Very early the next morning we entered Lille. As we marched through this great city, the first important town to be liberated by the Allies, with fixed bayonets and drums beating, the whole population seemed to be in the streets, on the balconies or at the windows of the houses, from which tricolors and an occasional Union Jack were flying.

There followed a period of several days during which the dream of all the generals on the western front was at last realized and we were able to take part in "open warfare." In a letter dated October 18 I wrote, "I have been walking or riding for thirty-six hours without a wash, change, sleep or anything to eat except army biscuits and an occasional cup of *ersatz* coffee supplied by the inhabitants who turn out to greet us." During the advance we had to drink quantities of this curious liquid made chiefly, I believe, from acorns and chicory. We soon crossed the Belgian frontier and reached the line of the Scheldt at Tournai, where the Germans made a stand for a few days.

On November 1, a bright autumn morning, we crossed the Scheldt on a temporary bridge erected by our sappers in place of the one that had been blown up by the retreating Germans. On entering the ancient city of Tournai, we found it almost completely intact and were surprised to notice that the provisions shops were well stocked with such luxuries as creamcakes and pastries which it would have been impossible to obtain at that time in most English and French towns. When we left Tournai, A Company, which I was now commanding again, with a detachment of cyclists, was sent forward as an advance guard.

Covering 15 to 20 miles a day, we soon left the main body of the brigade far behind. Walkie-talkies were still in the future; but my signalers had some carrier pigeons, and we sent back one of these birds every evening with the map reading of our position. Each village that we entered was adorned with Allied flags, and a malicious and probably apocryphal story was circulating that these flags had been sold to the peasants by an enterprising German businessman before the enemy left. The Belgian villagers seemed in much better shape than the inhabitants of the French liberated territory;

and we were now regaled not only with *ersatz* coffee but also with stronger liquids and cigars. I have a Brueghel-like memory picture of a kermess organized in our honor at a little inn, where we danced with strapping Flemish girls to the music of a bagpipe into the small hours.

When we halted for the night at a village on November 6, I received a visit from my brigadier. It was a dark, rainy evening, and as we squatted in a shed looking at a map by the light of my electric torch, I said, "Can I push on and take Brussels, sir?" Considering that my advance guard consisted of about 100 infantry and a few cyclists, I always regard this question as the highlight of my military career. The brigadier, however, told me to stop where I was and await the arrival of the rest of the brigade as he had information that there was a mutiny among the German troops in Brussels and we had better not get involved.

The next day the rest of the battalion caught me up, and we now continued our advance along the main road, passing hastily over the mined crossroads. The great stream of British troops moving eastward was now met by another stream going in the opposite direction. It consisted of ragged, footsore German deserters and Allied prisoners who had walked out of German prison camps, now deserted by their mutinous guards. We all knew now that German envoys were at G.H.Q. and that an armistice was imminent. On the morning of November 11 we were still being shelled and machine-gunned occasionally by German rear guards, and one of our captains was killed by a direct hit on a latrine. Our objective that day was Perquise, a village on the Tournai-Brussels road, and we were probably farther east than any other unit in the British Army.

That morning our staff captain galloped along the line of march shouting, "No firing after eleven o'clock!" We halted just outside Perquise, and at midday some German officers came and showed us where the road was mined. As we approached the village, we were met by a crowd of peasants headed by a little hunchback with an accordion who led us in triumph into Perquise playing the "Marseillaise." That evening copies of the Armistice terms roughly printed on broadsheets by the famous secret press of the *Indépendance belge* at Brussels were distributed among the troops. The weather was cold and rainy. No wine was available in the village; but I managed to obtain a chicken for the evening meal of A Company mess, and we washed it down with some rum and water. After dark, as I strolled around some farm buildings where our men were billeted, I heard a voice complaining of "the bleeding weather" and another replying, "Put a sock in it. After what we've heard today, I could sleep like a bird in a tree."

Georges Gaudy

GEORGES GAUDY was born at St.-Junien, in the department of Haute-Vienne, on February 18, 1895. He developed a taste for studying for a religious vocation, and conceived the desire to enter the seminary, but this inclination did not withstand the sound of arms in 1914.

He tried to enlist, but was turned down because he was underweight. He then set himself to eating great quantities of sugar to gain the pounds he needed. Whether the regimen worked or not, he was finally accepted, and ably participated in almost all 57th Infantry Regiment actions from January 10, 1916, through September 2, 1918.

In 1920 Gaudy published his first account of the war, L'Agonie du Mont-Renaud. "If I had to classify the war books, rank them," Albert Thibaudet has written, "I am quite sure that this is the one I would put first."

Trous d'obus de Verdun and Chemin-des-Dames en feu appeared in 1922 and 1923. In 1926, Gaudy published a social study, La Ville rouge.

Having belonged to the nationalist movement Action Française, Gaudy became editor of the daily paper of that name and began to give numerous lectures. His books continued to appear: a war novel, Les Galons noirs, a fourth volume of memoirs, Le Drame à Saconin et l'épopée sur l'Ingon in 1930, and La France cherche un homme in 1934.

Called up again as a captain in 1939 for service, in the rear, he volunteered and left for the front on December 31, and participated in rearguard actions. After the fall of France, Gaudy published Combats sans gloire at Lyons, in the free zone. In more than 310 copies given him to autograph, he reinserted—by hand—passages cut by the censors.

From July 27, 1945, to August 16, 1950, following service in Africa and Italy under General Alphonse-Pierre Juin, Gaudy was involved in the occupation of Austria, and during that period—in 1946—he published Combats libérateurs. On his return to France, he took up his profession of journalism and lecturing.

OUR OLD FRONT*

Man, in all he does in every age, will blend
Measures of music and song. That is why, my friend,
The war that moves our passions—
Noble goddess, who dwelled in our childhood dreaming regions—
Calls out the voice, before the somber marching legions,
Of the brass-throated clarions.
                    —VICTOR HUGO, *"Les Voix intérieures"*

IT WAS January 20, 1916, when I arrived at the front to join the 57th Infantry Regiment as a private.

By then, if you went through the communication trenches, you heard very different songs coming out of the hollows from those that shook the depots in August, 1914, like the "Marseillaise," the "Sambre-et-Meuse," the "Chant du départ."

The trench slaves found expression for their feelings in the repertory of wretchedness and various ballads and verses from the most deprived proletariat.

Yet they were always ready for heavy work and combat.

What struck you was the physical vigor of these poilus, washing up half-nude in the snow. Their gaze was calm, their smiles a little mocking, their faces tanned.

A strength capable of taking on the roughest battle of all time, the Battle of Verdun, had been forged in suffering—which is, mysteriously, the condition of all perfection.

This maturing of the French man of war can also be predicated of the English and the German. Like Ernst Jünger, author of *Stahlgewitter*,[1] I have observed that it took two years of trials for the front to carve the fighter's countenance. Its intensely virile expression was lit with a look broadened by the flash of shells, deepened by an inner struggle. His soul appeared in its light.

When peace returned, the survivors needed no ribbons on their jackets to recognize and greet one another with a grave smile in a crowd. Today their number is very reduced. The youngest are

---

* Translated from the French by Sally Abeles.

1 *Storm of Steel: From the Diary of a German Storm-Troop Officer on the Western Front,* tr. by Basil Creighton (Garden City, 1929) .—Tr.

seventy years of age. But from time to time I meet an eighty-two-year-old veteran in Montmartre—Berthieu, who was a lieutenant in the 57th. He goes shopping there, walking with a military step as if he were leaving for the Marne or Marengo.[2] I see another, named Éveille, who still wears a moustache, and who was the quarter-master corporal of the 11th Company in the same corps. An artist could paint him in either the busby of Napoleonic days or the helmet of 1915. It would look as though the man had deceived time and had simply changed uniform.

If February 21, 1916, had ended the conflict, instead of opening the inferno of Verdun, history would still have gathered a rich enough harvest to call this war the Great War.

The battle of the frontiers, the battles of the Marne, of the Yser, Éparges, Vieil-Armand;[3] of Artois, where Vimy, Souchez, Carency, Notre-Dame-de-Lorette, Ablain-St.-Nazaire stand out in memory; the offensive in Champagne on September 25, 1915, the matrix of the incessant struggles for Tahure, Souain, Massiges, Mesnil-les-Hurlus; and corresponding with these constantly rekindled fires, the conflagrations in the Argonne in the ever-smoking sectors of Fille Morte, La Harazée, Haute-Chevauchée, Four de Paris, Vauquois—ample scenes for illustrating dramatic pages.

The single image of Verdun presently eclipses the battles which flamed before it and which it would be unjust to veil. No Verdun would have been possible without the savage apprenticeship imposed during the preceding eighteen months.

But after World War II, a confusion of claims arose, contrasting the incomparable Battle of Verdun with the justly famous Stalingrad and Cassino campaigns.

There are degrees of hell, abysses below abysses. Even a tempest on the Ushant cliffs is not the maelstrom described by Edgar Allan Poe.

In the Stalingrad tragedy the Wehrmacht had from 220,000 to 230,000 men. The German losses at Verdun, of 325,000 killed and wounded for a similar period, were far larger than General Friedrich Paulus' total force.

I watched Cassino flame for weeks, like Vieil-Armand in the Vosges fifty years ago.

I cannot repeat here accounts from *Choses vues et vécues* at

---

[2] An Italian village where the French, under Napoleon, defeated the Austrians in June, 1800.—Tr.

[3] The name the French troops gave to the Hartmannswillerkopf spur, in the Vosges Mountains.—Tr.

Verdun,[4] but here are some typical happenings that are not spoken of there.

The first day of the German onslaught, as all our field pieces were destroyed behind the Caures Wood where Colonel Émile Driant's men hung on, only one 75 field gun remained. Dr. Voivenel heard it firing all night long, alone against the whole horde of German heavy artillery.

To the last gun and to the last man—that was characteristic of Verdun.

There were days, particularly in late June and early July, when the shadows that covered the ground, the artificial night created by the dust and smoke, made it impossible to maintain any contact or exercise any command, even at the company level. This was due to the dreadful intensity of the shelling. Germans and French found themselves mingling at several points, with the General Staffs incapable of knowing their positions and fixing their limits. Then the battle was reduced to one-to-one combat, each man fighting for his shell hole. A shell hole where one tenacious man, in a fever of anguish, his throat burning with thirst, drank the water from a hollow containing a decaying corpse, surer of fetching himself dysentery than glory. The final victory, certainly, was due to the high command, but it belonged as well to the terrified soldiers, who transformed their fear into fighting fury when the enemy rose before them.

This phenomenon can only be explained as the result of intensive training.

The Battle of the Somme, launched by British and French forces on July 1 of the same year, became particularly arduous when the Picardy plain turned into a sea of mud that sucked at men and animals.

We were arriving from rest camps when we met the Foreign Legion returning from the lines. Plastered to the ears with the sticky clay of the Santerre district, the legionnaires, like the other soldiers, had cut off the tails of their overcoats, which would have got coated with earth and would have weighed them down. As they caught sight of us, they shouted, "Hey, reinforcements for the cemetery!"

When the frost came, the guns shot slivers of clay as trenchant as steel, and we gathered up the bodies of men on watch in the front positions who had frozen to death.

In 1917 on the Chemin des Dames ridge, General Robert

---

4 *Verdun et le Chemin-des-Dames: Choses vues et vécues* (Paris, 1966).

Georges Nivelle's staff, which had replaced General J. J. C. Joffre's, believed the French forces could win and communicated this conviction to the troops.

On the eve of an offensive claimed to be the last one, the drive which was to have carried us into Belgium in four days, all the men with leave from our regiment, except one who left and didn't return, wanted to stand by so they wouldn't miss the victory blow they thought was so close, alas.

We were behind the colonials, who were to launch the breakthrough. Half an hour after the attack was launched—this was April 16, at six in the morning—we learned that the attempt had failed.

The next night we slept in a drizzle and in the snow on the Paissy plateau.

The following May 5, our Army corps, the 18th, snatched the Craonne and Vauclerc plateaus from the Prussian Guard. This terrain drank the blood of 10 of our regiment's officers and 404 men of the ranks killed and 11 officers and 461 men wounded. Though exhausted, the regiment kept its morale up.

Great was the universal disappointment caused by the collapse of excessive hopes. Agitators took advantage of this. At the end of May, I saw men at a control depot who were wearing uniforms but without any collar tabs, collecting soldiers on leave and trying to make them sing the "Internationale" and march on Paris. A people till now united could end in crisis like this. General Henri Philippe Pétain restored balance to the troops.

Two or three years before World War II the Germans were asking themselves how they could have missed the chance of profiting by this serious unrest. Ettighofer asked this question in his book *Eine Armee meutert.*

In the same period, they were examining why they had taken Verdun as an objective, a choice that strategic reasons alone could not justify.

When these publications appeared, I was scheduled to make a speech at a conference in Nîmes, which was presided over by General de Bourgon, former Chief of Staff to Verdun's military governor, General Coutanceau. De Bourgon told me that General Erich von Falkenhayn had succeeded in imposing his views at the Charleville meeting called by William II in September, 1915. His goal was to break the defense of Verdun with a blow so massive and so stunning that, he thought, French morale would collapse, the Cabinet would fall, and a separate peace could be concluded with a new government.

Then: 1918! In the spring, the sky opened, and divisions that had fought so hard for a few acres of ground were on the move again.

The storm broke on our British allies, as it would beat down on us equally effectively the following May 27.

During the night of March 20–21, Lieutenant Jünger of the Hannoverian 73d and his comrades, dizzy from the din of the explosions, whistled and struck the table in their shelter with their fists, imitating the fall and boom of the shells.

Asked to say a poem that would express the surroundings, Jünger recited the Frenchman Arthur Rimbaud's "Le Bateau ivre."

When all the figures of the war in the trenches have disappeared, there will be no one left who understands this choice. I tried to explain it in an article in the May 17, 1936, Revue de Paris.

The lines that seem the clearest are not the least obscure:

> In the tempestuous swell of the tidal sea
> I in that past winter, deafer than children's brains,
> Ran, and the peninsulas unmoored and land-free
> Have not known more sovereign brouhaha unconstrained.

The first, third, and fourth lines pose no problem. But the second?

The notion of time in life at the front, so intense, so laden with events and emotions, was not the same as derives from customary pace of life in peace.

For we would say "in the past" about episodes that had occurred the previous year.

If children's thought processes seem simple, it is because they have not yet experienced the multitude of sensations that generate images and ideas. Now, on the subject of life and death, the combatant got such a powerful initiation that he felt as though he had been born on the battlefield, especially if he were one of the younger men.

Four days after the German offensive, our battalions moved toward the enemy. And certainly no one saw any of those melancholy faces, those funereal expressions so dear to the post-1930 film makers, who thought they were representing the soldiers as they were that last springtime.

Later, in 1923, I decided to return to Ourscamp in Chiry (Oise), which was our reserve position from March 26 to May 15, 1918, during the bitter defense of Mont-Renaud.

"I hadn't left the village," a civilian told me, "when the Fifty-seventh came through. You wouldn't have thought these were fellows who'd just spent two nights in trucks and were going to their deaths. What spirit! And how they sang!"

The songs were certainly joyful, but they weren't very proper.

In September, 1936, I chanced to be in Nuremberg in the Hof-bräuhaus, sitting at the table of a Mr. Schultz, a pleasant Berliner who had commanded a light artillery battery in 1918.

"The first French troops we encountered, at the Crozat Canal, had on new outfits and fought like tigers," he said.

"They were General Brecard's cuirassiers," I explained.

"Then," Mr. Schultz continued, "we wanted to blast Mont-Renaud, which barred the way to Paris. We could have flattened the objective under a massive shelling and so won a quick victory. Nothing of the kind. You'll see on a map that a chateau tops that elevation. I was the one who fired the first shots to hit that chateau."

"And I was the one who got them," I said.

He didn't believe me. I asked for some blank paper and drew him sketches and described the timing in such detail that he was convinced.

"So there you are!" he said to the two brown-shirted storm troopers who were with him. "In 1918 we faced each other as enemies. Today we're sitting together as comrades at the Nuremberg *Parteitag*."[5]

I refrained from revealing to him that the German ambassador in Paris had refused me admission to this *Parteitag*. Mr. Schultz decided that a *Frontkamerad*, a comrade at the front, as he called me, should have one of the best places. The next day he gave me a card meant for the editor of a Berlin paper, who had been prevented from attending at the last minute.

I have often taken pleasure in meeting German soldiers. If hatred sometimes fired our words during the hostilities, it did not live in our hearts. The most dreadful violence subsided as soon as it was no longer necessary. If we felt a hearty friendship for our own, the brave conquered enemy soon inspired nothing more than pity. The most human of the combatants was the infantryman who saw the pathetic face of the man he might have killed, but the gunner and the pilot would have been even more distraught had they known the suffering of those souls. "If the artillerymen over there felt our pain," we would think at Verdun, "they would stop this cruel pounding."

The same was true for us at Mont-Renaud when we were targets for Mr. Schultz and his compatriots.

Since 1920, the date when my book *L'Agonie du Mont-Renaud*[6]

---

5 Party Day, one of a series of Nazi Party conventions at Nuremberg; the first was held in August, 1927.—Tr.

6 *L'Agonie du Mont-Renaud,* reissued (Paris, 1957) .

appeared, reverent visitors, coming alone, in groups, and sometimes even in masses, have continued to crowd that promontory closing the valley two miles to the south of Noyon. I have spoken there to 12, to 100, to 30,000 people.

There our regiment broke twenty-two attacks.

The bevel-cornered post was taken, lost, retaken twenty-six times in one hour.

More than 100 lightly wounded in this regiment alone refused to be evacuated. I was among them. I say this to counter those who know neither suffering nor death and who deny indisputable facts.

Over the duration of the hostilities, 25 officers and 545 men refused to be sent to the dressing station.

The merit of a troop complement lies more with its elite than with its body of men.

On May 27, 1918, the awesome bastions of Chemin des Dames fell before the German onslaught. The enemy's advance was rapid. Second Lieutenants Turbet-Delof and Drouault heard the news in Paris, where they were on convalescence leave, and took the train for Compiègne. But our regiment was no longer in the vicinity of that city where it had regrouped its forces. Now walking, now hitching rides on trucks, Turbet-Delof and Drouault rejoined the 57th on the Saconin plateau, southwest of Soissons.

In that battle, as Louis Madelin has put it well, the divisions thrown in to fill the breach melted like wax on white-hot metal. Turbet-Delof and Drouault, still wearing parade dress, with elegant tunics and thin-soled shoes, hurled themselves into the movement. Our battalions, cut to ribbons, quivered under the bursts of gunfire.

Jünger's observation is accurate. Yes, these were very young and inexperienced soldiers, but under leaders seasoned in combat they formed redoubtable assault troops.

The beardless young men in *feldgrau* fighting on the Saconin plateau, May 31–June 2, camouflaged their helmets with stalks of grain and rushed the French machine guns. Sergeant Major Richard and Sergeant Havard shot down seven with the Lebel rifle. Automatic guns mowed them down in clusters, point-blank. Without knowing it, they were imitating our soldiers of the Year II.[7]

After the spring losses, we in turn had companies almost entirely re-formed out of 1918 blues,[8] who had never been under fire and

---

7 Year II according to the Republican calendar, initiated by the National Convention on September 22, 1792. The reference is to the high spirit and aggressive daring of the otherwise ill-prepared French troops, which brought them their victories of 1793–94 against Prussian and Austrian units.—Tr.

8 Recruits.—Tr.

for whom we felt real tenderness. On August 28 in the Somme, I commanded two light infantry sections and a machine-gun group. There were two veterans among us: the poilu Larrieu, who had seen action everywhere since the Marne, and I. The eyes of our conscripts were big as saucers. They watched our smallest gestures with absolute trust; they took in every word as devoted and obedient young footsoldiers, intent on victory. They saw us as old hands at battle, accustomed to its surprises, conditioned to act in combat as are colliers in a mine, sailors in a storm. The flame of 1914, in this last season of the war, quickened an army which had both a willing heart and fighting experience.

We had to advance eastward under 150-millimeter percussion shells over a vast grass-grown plain north of Nesle, for a distance of about 800 yards. In 1914, half our forces would have been lost in a dangerous move like this; it cost us only 4 wounded.

But a tributary of the Somme, the Ingon, bordered with marshes, posed an obstacle to us, which we nonetheless overcame. Two bold maneuvers, one of them carried off by Second Lieutenants Fischer and Drouault, delivered the entire enemy bank into our hands. Later Drouault fell, forever, a bullet through his belly.

Initiative and daring caught fire and grew with the flush of success. Two months later, at Mennevret, two battalions of the 112th Infantry under Colonel de France formed a single column and penetrated the German position after sundown; they advanced five miles without firing a shot, and took 1,200 prisoners.

It was harder for us to take Hill 77, peppered with Prussian machine-gun nests, on September 2 and 3; we wrested it from them piece by piece. Eleven officers and 318 men killed, 17 officers and 715 men wounded—such was the price of victory.

Prouder than ever of our regiment, repeatedly celebrated through the centuries, the survivors went to sleep among the dead. The regiment, based on mutual respect and brotherhood, was a family every member wanted to honor. Where *esprit de corps* flags, there remains only a collection of individuals, without a unifying soul.

The Great War, as we have seen, was not at all uniform and homogeneous, but so varied that it was impossible for someone entering the scene for the last half of 1918 to imagine its previous seasons.

The songs, when they can be unearthed, express these differences. Napoleon's swashbuckling marchers in 1796, on the road to Milan, swelled the echoes with Fanchon's lively refrain, which the Italians would hear once again in 1944.

But the troops going up to the Verdun sectors were mute, like the men at the Moscow.[9] It was useless, Marshal Pétain observed, to question those returning. They did not answer and looked at the interlocutor without seeing him. In that hellish sector, where shot and shell had left not a leaf on the ruined trees or a scrap of green on the ground, where all the natural smells except that of the Meuse had been destroyed, the Frenchman, who laughs in adversity, joked no more. The poilus exchanged only wan smiles. If there were songs in that time, my comrades and I know nothing about them.

But during the heavy action of May 31–June 2, 1918, reinforcements swung along the base of the Soissons plateaus with a step that spoke of confidence and gallantry. A half league away, Maxims and Hotchkisses sputtered, and 105's burst in the clear sky.

Peasants who had stayed placed buckets of water at the side of the road. It was very hot. Sweat ran under the unbuttoned coats. A soldier would gulp down a good mugful and then rejoin his unit in a couple of bounds and take up the singing again:

> When the leaves appear in the spring,
> A balmy breeze comes soft as a dove,
> And lifting its crooning voice to sing,
> It tells the heart it's time to love.
>
> If Cupid knocks upon your door,
> Lovely Liz, don't hide your charms.
> For he brings joy you can't ignore.
> So then, Liz, open your arms.
>
> Here come the poilus, here come the poilus,
> Back from Verdun, from the Yser,
> Back from Hurlus.
> Choose the one for whom you care.
> Choose him, and if you love him true,
> He'll love you fair.

And the men from beyond the Rhine went to battle singing sad and melodious airs.

Minds change in our ebullient race like the wind. But combat tactics and form were modified just as often.

My account *"Les Postes de l'Armée Gouraud"*[10] reveals a scene

---

9 The Moscow River, which Napoleon's multinational and unenthusiastic forces reached but then retreated from in the unsuccessful campaign of 1812.—Tr.

10 ["The Gouraud Army Posts,"] *Revue des deux mondes* (July 15, 1929). General Henri J. E. Gouraud was commander of the French 4th Army, which attacked on the Verdun and Champagne fronts on September 26, 1918, with General Pershing's American forces, in the final Allied offensive of the war.—Tr.

that was unlike any other moment of the fighting. We seemed to be immersed in a fantastic setting, a universe devastated by some earlier cataclysm, where our units lived in the wild grass in a solitude and silence deep as death.

I commanded two of these units. Only the post commander knew that, on watch in that abandoned zone by General Pétain's orders, we would have to hold out to the last man without the slightest hope of relief. Like the fighting men of Carthage, we had no other roof but the sky. Wire entanglements barred the entrance to the shelters so that no one would give way to the very strong temptation to take refuge in them when the aggressor appeared. We lived like wild animals in old Argonne. If one of its frequent storms soaked us, we could hope only to be dried by the sun.

That was one of the happiest periods of my life. The realization that there was no one in front of us, that we were covering an opposition line running two and one-half miles, that we were the country's living shield, that an imperative mission of sacrifice, which set us apart from the others, ennobled us, filled my soul with a holy joy.

But on July 14 I went on leave. I was in a depot at Châlons-sur-Marne when the front erupted at midnight. Paris heard that nocturnal rumbling of guns.

Our train arrived. There was a high-level debate over whether we should go our way or had to be returned to the lines.

Neither I nor my fellow travelers, so willing the day before to bear the brunt of an attack as stoic soldiers, wanted to return to the lines. Finally, the locomotive whistled, and the train began to move. We felt a selfish joy.

To break the enemy's offensive, attack, counterattack—this is killing work. Far from the war in space and time, we no longer recall any but the spectacular battles, and we forget that life in the open demanded more patience than valor. Our *Grande Armée* veterans had endured forced marches like Marius' "mules," especially in 1805.[11] And like them, we slept as we marched.

There were also times of crucifying immobility. On May 8–9 we stood packed together in a passageway in Fort Vaux at Verdun for thirty-six hours, crammed in a human mass. Hardly was one of us able to squat down from time to time.

I was already familiar with these things, the evening I arrived to join the 57th. From the camp at Souge to the trench, reached two days later, we moved into a different hemisphere. I had been

---

11 The Grande Armée was Napoleon's army. Caius Marius (155–86 B.C.) was a gifted and popular Roman general.—Tr.

on duty at that point. Instead of sleeping, we worked in
rying logs soaked by the snow; they slipped through our
nds and bruised our shoulders.

slept the sleep of an animal crushed with fatigue, in the
.....ter swarming with rats, and soon I in turn was being eaten alive
by the vermin.

For two-thirds of the year in that northern land we were regularly drenched by rain, which seemed to penetrate to our bones.

We lived Goethe's description of the night of the Battle of
Valmy—September 20, 1792—on October 5, 1917. Leaving Suippes
in a twilight night, we advanced to the Souain ridge. A squall rode
the barren wastes of Champagne in a raging downpour. We had to
march the flooded road in water to our ankles. Coat, tunic, sweater,
pants, skin dripping, we stayed that way for two weeks, unable to
dry off or change clothes, seeing nothing but barbed-wire fencing
on the clay soil potted with holes filled with a liquid gray mud.

But the worst thing was the lack of sleep. In the sector where I
first served, we came down from the first line like drunks zigzagging
on the road. So Foch's battles in 1918 were fought by poilus who
were drunk on the need for sleep as if on wine.

Happy is he who knows that man is on earth not to enjoy life, but
to find his salvation.

A military vocation grows stronger in a man who never sounds a
complaint.

Sir Basil Liddell Hart

CAPTAIN SIR BASIL LIDDELL HART *was born on October 31, 1895, in Paris. After his parents' return to England, he went to St. Paul's School and then to Corpus Christi College, Cambridge, where he took the honors course in history. In 1914 he became an officer in the King's Own Yorkshire Light Infantry. After two periods of service on the western front, where he was wounded and gassed, he first made a mark in the field of military theory by evolving the battle drill system in 1917 and other new tactical ideas subsequently adopted, particularly the "expanding torrent" method of attack that became the basis of the blitzkrieg technique. In 1920, when only twenty-four, he was given the opportunity of writing the first postwar official manual on infantry training and subsequently edited the weapons manual* Small Arms Training.

Invalided to the half-pay list in 1924 (and to the retired list in 1927), he was appointed military correspondent of the Daily Telegraph *in 1925 as successor to the renowned Colonel Repington. Ten years later he moved to the* Times *in the same role and as its adviser on defense as a whole. Meanwhile, he had also been military editor of the* Encyclopaedia Britannica.

In 1927 he became personal adviser to the new War Minister, Mr. Hore-Belisha, and helped initiate a far-reaching program for the modernization of the Army. Many of the proposed reforms were achieved, but opposition continued to delay the development of the tank and antiaircraft forces. Feeling that progress was too slow compared with the imminent danger of war, Liddell Hart gave up his advisory role in the summer of 1938 in order to press the needs publicly.

Throughout the years since the First World War, he had been a leading advocate of airpower, armored forces, and amphibious strategy. Many of the foremost commanders of the Second World War called themselves his disciples and pupils—including General Guderian, the creator and leader of the panzer forces. The German encyclopedia Der Grosse Brockhaus *quotes Guderian as saying that Liddell Hart was "the creator of the theory of the conduct of mechanized war," and General Chassin of France described him as "the greatest military thinker of the twentieth century, whose ideas have revolutionized the art of war." The late President Kennedy more recently paid tribute to his revolutionary influence on "two generations."*

In all he has written some thirty books, and his writings have been trans lated into more than thirty languages. He was knighted in 1966.

FORCED TO THINK

LOOKING BACK on my experiences in what is now generally called World War I, my chief impression in retrospect is of its *amateurishness*, especially in the first year, or even two.

When Britain entered that war, in August, 1914, I was a student at Corpus Christi College, Cambridge, working for the history tripos—the honors course in history—and spending the summer vacation in Cornwall, the family part on my mother's side, where it had been since migrating there from the Scottish border in the eighteenth century. A few weeks later I received a summons to a medical board in London and there passed the still stringent eyesight test with the aid of a medical officer who was more than willing to prompt me in reading the smaller letters on the chart.

After passing the medical board, I waited more than two months for further word from the War Office, where a very inadequate staff was trying to cope with the immense flood of volunteers that Kitchener's call had produced. Meanwhile, I joined the special commissions class formed in the Cambridge O.T.C. and soon qualified as a musketry instructor—all the sooner by reconciling myself to the nonsensical fact that the veteran experts provided by the school of musketry favored a parrotlike quotation of passages in the official manual rather than any simpler explanation of their meaning.

At the beginning of December I received my commission, as second lieutenant, in the King's Own Yorkshire Light Infantry (K.O.Y.L.I.), and was sent to an officers' course of instruction at Tunbridge Wells, the headquarters of the 2d Army. Among my experiences there was one that provided an illuminating sidelight on the crustier kind of old-style general. While on weekend leave I was recalled by telegram, and on returning found myself under what the Army calls open arrest. For on the Saturday night some officers attending the course had staged a rag in the local theater, and when this was reported to the Army commander, General Stopford, he had ordered that the whole course was to be placed under arrest without discrimination. This rigid martinet was the man who, eight months later, bungled the Suvla Bay landing on Gallipoli by the rigidity of his inertia, with fatal effect to the Dardanelles expedition.

Although Stopfords were plentiful in the old Army, there were also many refreshing exceptions—and at that time there was a junior member of his staff, Captain J. F. C. Fuller, who after the war took a lead in the effort to broaden the outlook of the Army and modernize its structure. Although our friendship and cooperation in that effort did not develop until 1920, it was in a way fateful that our first link should have been the experience of serving under Stopford.

In January, after passing out of the course with good marks, I was sent to a recently formed service battalion of my regiment. By that time it was being provided with khaki uniforms to replace the makeshift blue that had been originally issued—and had made them look more like a gang of convicts than a military body—but it had still only 100 rifles for nearly 1,000 men, and these were of out-of-date pattern.

The commanding officer, a Regular, was a martinet of the better kind and was quickly producing good results—although his severity in dealing out punishments was such that it might well have caused complaint from men less enthusiastic, or less ignorant, than these eager volunteers. The two senior majors, however, were far from being as competent. One of them greatly impressed us on arrival with his three rows of medal ribbons—an array that could then only be rivaled by the Commander in Chief of the British armies in France. But comic relief was provided when he attempted to drill a company and, having ordered it to "advance in echelon," kept on ordering it to turn right, turn left, and turn about in the vain hope that he would find that it had somehow got back into line. He then began feverishly turning over the pages of a little drill guide in search of the solution, until at last he was driven, ignominiously, to call on the senior subaltern to straighten out the now breathless company. We discovered later that he had never been in action but had gathered his medals by hurrying to visit base areas, as an Intelligence officer, wherever minor campaigns took place.

Many of the dugout warrant and noncommissioned officers were no better, except as tutors in the ways of military wangling. Our company sergeant major had a habit of remembering some urgent office duty when a route march had gone as far as his feet and fatness would comfortably permit and would then hail any passing civilian motorcar with the impressive shout, "On His Majesty's service," and demand to be driven back to camp, regardless of where the driver might be going.

Further evidence of amateurishness, and in higher quarters, came after I went to France, shortly before the abortive September offensive there—the British Army's first large-scale offensive—wherein both the British and the much larger French Army suffered losses that were out of all proportion to the slight gains. During the British offensive in the Loos sector, the 21st and 24th divisions, composed of splendid human material, were thrown into the battle in a shockingly bungled way. A sequel to it was the replacement of Sir John French, as Commander in Chief of the British, by Sir Douglas Haig—whose 1st Army had actually carried out the attack.

Not only at the front but in the rear the war was conducted in a very easygoing way during 1915, whereas by the next year not only the troops but military bureaucracy were entrenched; the exhilarating "fun" of active service, brightened by a moderate spice of danger, passed away with that change to machinelike organization. In 1915 one often came across officers who, disliking conditions or superiors in their particular area, had moved themselves to another and been taken on there with little difficulty in getting their self-transfers authorized.

I had a personal experience of the prevailing casualness when sent to conduct a large draft from the Somme to the other end of the British front at Ypres, where casualties had been heavy. Marching to the railhead, Méricourt-Ribemont, the draft embarked in the usual string of boxcars, labeled CHEVAUX 8, HOMMES 40, that were used for transporting troops, and the train then meandered through the countryside at the usual pace, so slow that those who felt cramped could jump off and stretch their legs by a run without risk of getting left behind. About 11 P.M. we reached Abbeville, which had been developed into a large military rail center, and were shunted into a siding, where I was told at the R.T.O.'s (railway transport officer) office that there was no possibility of going on until the following night and advised to get a room in the town meanwhile. So after seeing the draft fed and bedded down, I followed this advice. At daybreak I went back to the station but found no sign of them on the siding where I had last seen them, and a search of the many other sidings was equally fruitless. Then I went to the R.T.O.'s office and was blandly told that the cars had been hooked on about 3 A.M. to a train that was shorter than expected. I then had to wait a further twenty-four hours until there was a train which could carry me on in the wake of the draft.

On reaching Calais, about 7 A.M. on the third day, the R.T.O. there told all on board that the train could not be sent on northward until the next morning, "so leave your kit on the train, where

I'll look after it, and spend the day in the town." When we made our way back to the station at the specified time that evening, the train had disappeared, and the R.T.O. quite cheerfully explained: "I found that I could send the train on, after all, but there will be another one this evening which you can take." Thus, I had now lost my kit as well as my draft! I recovered the former late that night from a siding at Hazebrouck, and, after spending the night in that town, went on by train to Poperinge, the railhead for Ypres, and there got a lift on a horsed limber to the battalion—where I found, to my relief, that the draft had safely arrived the day before. The commanding officer was evidently so familiar with the happy-go-lucky ways of the Railway Transport Service that he took the miscarriage as a matter of course. After a drink and a chat I started on my way back to the Somme, which turned out to be another interrupted journey. On returning, I put in a claim for four nights' "detention allowance" to cover my hotel expenses. The base paymaster returned it with a puzzled query but, on hearing the story, was so amused that he promptly approved the claim.

A little later, stricken by sudden sickness and a high fever, caused either by the fumes of a bursting shell or by something bad I had eaten, I was carted off on a stretcher to the nearest field ambulance and then to the casualty clearing station at Corbie. Next day I felt better, and my temperature was down, so I wanted to go back to the battalion—which merely convinced the doctors that I must be ill, so I was sent off, still on a stretcher, by hospital train to the base hospital at Rouen. There the same thing happened, and I had trouble in persuading the doctors to let me off being put on a hospital ship for England.

That ironical experience would seem to suggest that a would-be malingerer's best chance might lie not in feigning illness but in clamoring to be allowed to stay at the front! The tedium of a fortnight in the hospital was relieved by a visit from the King, George V, who came around the wards—a few days before the bad fall he suffered when riding Haig's horse. The King, poor man, looked more embarrassed in trying to make conversation and ask suitable questions than we were in responding.

Eventually, when allowed out on afternoon leave, I slipped down to the base headquarters at Rouen and induced a friendly staff officer there to post me to a battalion of the regiment stationed in the Ypres Salient that, after suffering heavy losses, was very short of officers. In retrospect it seems a strange choice and desire on my part—as Ypres was notoriously the worst sector of the front—but many of us at that time of inexperience had a similar desire to test ourselves by experience of the worst.

The conditions of trench warfare at Ypres have been depicted by so many pens that an addition would be superfluous. But it may be worth mentioning another illustration of the same widespread impulsion that was characteristic of that relatively early period of the war. It came when I was sent up with two weak platoons to hold a stretch of trench line which had been abandoned three months earlier after a flattening bombardment and had since fallen in more fully during the autumn rains. Two companies previously having held it, its reoccupation to cover a gap was ordered because of an expected German attack on the sector. After a reconnaissance by our senior major and a brigade staff officer, they reported that it was a "death trap" and that it would be "murder" to send anyone there, but their protests were overruled by the divisional staff, *who* had not seen it. Paradoxically, it gave me a thrill of pride to be entrusted with such a mission.

During the night I kept the men hard at work in bailing out the water and digging themselves in as far as possible, while getting news that the enemy were clearing away the barbed wire in front of their trenches in preparation for an assault and that Prussian troops were taking over from the Saxons who had been there. But the next day passed without more than frequent shelling, and it became evident that the Germans had canceled the attack. We were then withdrawn to the canal line.

I was less fortunate soon after when concussed by sandbags brought down by a shell exploding in a trench and can acutely remember how, when I was sick and vomiting, every successive shell was a shock and strain—showing how much reaction depends on physical state. This time, when carried back on a stretcher, I made no protest, but felt only relief when the doctors sent me back successively to a forward hospital at Hazebrouck, a base hospital at Le Touquet, and then by hospital ship to England.

In my memoirs I have dealt with a number of my impressions of the front, and Ypres in particular, at that time, so here am mentioning only experiences and aspects that I did not touch on there. One is that under such tiring and chilling conditions, sexual desire was not very strongly felt by most men—contrary to the picture painted in some of the war novels—and only a small minority sought the local brothels when out of the line. But many more of us missed, and felt a longing for, the sight of some attractively feminine women. That was not so much an actively sexual desire as an esthetic desire for the beauty and grace of womanhood. It was evidently realized in choosing the junior nursing staff, the V.A.D.'s, for the Duchess of Westminster's hospital at Le Touquet. The duchess herself, the quintessence of elegance, glided around the wards in a dark dress, with a faint suggestion of nursing uniform, superbly cut and molded to her figure, while adorned with a string of lovely pearls. The sight of her was a tonic in itself, and as I was there again the following year, it became stamped on my memory.

I also felt an intense desire to see plays again—more intense than ever before or since. So when I had recovered sufficiently to be allowed out of the hospital, in London, I went twice a day to the theater.

Soon afterward I renewed contact with Charles Grey, the editor of *The Aeroplane*, who told me in confidence about a new armored fighting vehicle capable of moving across shell-torn ground and breaching the enemy's trench front, which a friend of his, Lieutenant R. F. Macfie, was developing along with others in the Armoured Car Force of the Royal Naval Air Service. This was my first news of what was subsequently called the tank, to keep its nature secret, which made its battlefield debut on September 15, 1916, during the Battle of the Somme—a new instrument with which I was to be closely associated in later years.

After two months' convalescent leave, I was posted to the 3d K.O.Y.L.I., the draft-finding unit for the Regular battalions. It was then stationed at Hull. The battalion sent a detachment nightly to guard the large cluster of oil tanks on the bank of the Humber estuary near the city. It was difficult to imagine what value this guard could be, and when zeppelins were overhead it was not a comfortable thought that if one of their bombs dropped onto an oil tank, little would be left of the infantry guard. Even more uncomfortable, however, was that the only accommodation for the guard was a laundry building filled with corrugated iron sheets—the most uncomfortable form of bed that I have ever known.

Another trial followed in the form of being sent to what the subalterns called the penal settlement of Aldbrough, where a detachment was stationed to guard the coast road. It involved a long and lone walk every night to visit each of the posts along the road, which was closed to traffic. Pitch-darkness and current spy scares made the round rather eerie. The adjutant, an old-style soldier, considered that young officers who had served at the front needed "to be taken down a peg" and shown that this experience had not earned them any special consideration by prewar standards. But once I passed the kinds of tests which he deemed necessary, his attitude completely changed. Now welcomed as a suitable officer of the regiment in postwar years, I was recommended for a Regular commission with retention of my full seniority and the step in rank which I had recently been given.

Unfortunately, battalion headquarters had not received a new

Army form produced for such purpose, and the recommendation was returned by northern command headquarters with instructions that it must be submitted in triplicate on the correct form. By the time a supply was obtained, I was out in France again. Thus, the commanding officer's good intentions were temporarily frustrated, while the delay impaired my situation in the long run, since injuries suffered in the summer fighting led to a further postponement.

While I was at Aldbrough, the whole battalion had been moved out to the Yorkshire coast as a precaution against a feared invasion, and anxiety about this possibility became so marked that for three weeks we had to sleep fully dressed and equipped, standing to arms at 2 A.M., and sometimes marching from our camp to the beaches to occupy trenches dug along the seafront at Withernsea. This period of tension ended when the Irish Rising came, at Easter, and it became clear that the Germans were not going to exploit it by an invasion of England.

Meanwhile, I had gone before a medical board at Hull, where the president opened by asking me if I wished to return to France. On replying yes, I was promptly passed as fit—with a commendation that was in sharp contrast with the treatment this notorious medical board dealt out to anyone who was hesitant in giving such an answer—a senior officer in the regiment, who had amply proved his courage, was virtually accused of cowardice when he said that his wounds were still troublesome. The different attitudes of medical boards were very strange.

In my case the medical board's verdict of fit was confirmed in a better way when a week or two later, after only a few practice runs, I led the regimental team in the north of England cross-country championships—a 10-mile race over the rough ground outside the famous St. Leger course at Doncaster, which we lapped four times. After the first round I felt ghastly but by the end felt relatively fresh—a wonderful feeling. That turned out to be the last race of my brief running career—which was cut short by German gas a few months later. But in consolation the doctors told me that my lung development had helped save my life.

On returning to France in the spring of 1916, I traveled by an embarkation train to Folkestone that started from the same platform at Charing Cross as in 1915—and to which I also returned each time in the hospital train. On this occasion I was in charge of eight junior officers—five of whom were killed on July 1, the opening day of the Somme offensive, while all the remainder, including myself, were casualties by the end of that month.

Before leaving England, I had been told at the War Office that as

I was now on the list of the Regular battalions, I should go to the 2d K.O.Y.L.I.; but on reaching the base camp at Étaples, I was disappointed to hear that under a new policy of blending old and new, officers with previous experience at the front were being posted to service battalions. I was all the less happy to hear that under this ruling I would go to the 9th K.O.Y.L.I., which was in the 21st Division—one of the two that had been blamed for the autumn failure at Loos.

It was now on the Somme sector, and events were soon to show that apart from being unjustly blamed for the way it had been used when inexperienced, it had become one of the best in the field. That was due not only to the quality of the material but to the way it had been developed during the winter by Major General Claud Jacob, the future field marshal, who took over the badly shaken division after Loos. In the spring he was promoted to command a corps and succeeded by Major General David Campbell, who commanded the division in the Somme offensive and until the end of the war. I came to know him much more closely in the immediate postwar years as he took up many of my tactical ideas and became one of my best friends. It was thus an interesting coincidence that he came to the division at the same time as I did—a fact of which I, as a very junior member, was naturally more aware than he was at the time!

By another coincidence the initial task I had been given on reaching Étaples was to conduct a draft to the 18th Division, commanded by Major General Ivor Maxse, who became my other principal backer after the war and to whom I owed even more for encouragement and help. These two men were my military foster parents, and I am deeply indebted to them for the early opportunity they did so much to create.

"Amateurishness" Continues—on the Higher Levels

On returning to the Somme, I found the staggering difference between the tranquil conditions of the autumn and those now existing. Formerly quiet roads and villages behind the front were now under frequent shellfire, while the formerly shallow and weak German lines had become a web of strong trenches, with deep and well-built dugouts. By the constant raids and harassing during the winter and spring that the British high command had ordained, it had virtually driven the Germans to develop and fortify the front against which it was planning to launch its next offensive. Moreover, the chances of surprise were diminished by the all too manifest preparations for such an offensive, especially in the spread of light railways near the front, to carry up supplies as close as possible. From the amount of shelling they received, it became obvious to some of us that their portent was obvious to the Germans.

In sum, the growing experience of the troops and their still undimmed spirit were offset by continued amateurishness on the higher levels of command.

Extraordinary optimism predominated there, and even where there were doubts, these were suppressed from a misguided loyalty or desire to retain the confidence of superiors. Although Sir Harry Rawlinson, the commander of the 4th Army, which was entrusted with the main part of the offensive, seems to have felt considerable doubts, he kept them private and assured his executants that there would be no resistance after the prolonged bombardment of the enemy position, so that the infantry would only have to walk over and take possession. So infectious was such optimism, or so blinding the loyalty to superiors, that when assaulting battalions "reported that the enemy machine guns had not been silenced" and were mowing down their men, they were told by some divisional staffs, unwilling to believe the truth, that "they were scared." It does not seem to have occurred to the commanders and staffs in general that if the trenches were made untenable, the enemy machine gunners were likely to move out and occupy the shell holes, created by the bombardment, from which they could resume and maintain their fire.

The rigidity of the plan, with its insistence on strict conformity in alignment, was itself a severe handicap to success by surprise. The handicap was increased by the slow pace ordained, in order to conform with the barrage, and that in turn was enforced by the heavy load of equipment that the infantryman carried—66 pounds, which was more than half his own average body weight. Even an Army mule, the proverbial beast of burden, is not expected to carry more than a third of his own weight.

In the final preattack stage, three cavalry divisions were brought up close to the front, and Haig's instructions were that they should ride through on the first morning to Bapaume, 10 miles beyond the front. In the event, Haig's troops were still several miles short of Bapaume after nearly five months' struggle—and by then had lost more than 400,000 men.

My only sight of the cavalry was when, a couple of days before the attack, I rode back to the railhead village to visit the town major, an elderly soldier whom I had known in 1915. On reaching his office, I found a swarm of angry cavalry officers around it, seeking promised accommodation. Pushing inside, I found him too drunk to deal with anything and then found his sergeant major and his clerk similarly disabled in a bedroom and a latrine respectively. In retrospect, this comic episode of intoxication seemed a portent of the cavalry's frustration.

In the preattack period, we had a visit from Colonel "Ronnie" Campbell's bayonet fighting team, sent by G.H.Q. to instill the troops with what was called the spirit of the bayonet. Its frenzied performance may have had some effect in increasing the number of Germans who were bayoneted after surrendering, but its worse effect was in multiplying our own men's loss of life by teaching them to push on and "close with the bayonet," without firing, while the more cool-headed enemy, who did not fix their bayonets, went on shooting them down as they approached, realizing that a bullet outranges a bayonet until the bayonet-fighting attacker is within 2 yards' reach of him.

A more effective spur was produced by David Campbell, our new divisional commander, when he addressed the battalions. Known to us as the man who had won the Grand National—in 1896, when riding the Soarer—he applied a touch of whip and spur by telling them that they had to wipe out "the shame" of the division's performance at Loos. Resented at the moment, this sharp criticism impelled the troops to strive all the harder to prove that it was unjust. Although the fences were found to be much worse than anyone expected, the 21st Division penetrated half a mile deep into the German position, whereas all the divisions on its left and immediate right flank failed to make even a dent in the enemy's front and were mostly back in their own trenches that night.

The offensive was launched on the morning of July 1 at 7:30—long after dawn—by which time there was not even a morning haze to obscure the view of the German machine gunners, who were thus able to scythe down the close-packed lines of our slow-moving infantry with deadly ease. Most of our troops were dead or wounded before the parapet of the enemy's front line was even reached. The survivors on our sector, discarding their imposed formalism, soon broke up into little groups that used their initiative and worked their way from shell hole to shell hole, taking advantage of this and any other cover they could find, so that they then succeeded in penetrating more than half a mile into the lines, with relatively small loss.

Most of the men and almost all the officers had been knocked out in crossing the short distance of no-man's-land—the commanding officer and all four company commanders had been killed. I and other seconds-in-command of companies had been kept in immediate reserve, as well as a few other officers, but a call came for us as soon as the extent of the losses became known at brigade headquarters. We found the survivors in a sunken trench and took over charge. That night the leading battalions of the division's reserve brigade came up to strengthen the wedge but did not push on farther. If fresh divisions had been brought up, they might have pushed through with little opposition before the Germans had recovered their balance. But nothing was done on the second day.

On July 3, about midday, our reserve brigade mounted an attack against a small wood lying a quarter of a mile beyond our left flank and captured it after an early check, repulsing two strong counterattacks. As ammunition was running short and a further counterattack expected from reinforcements coming up from Bapaume, a lot of the prisoners were pressed into service at bayonet point as ammunition carriers—with entire disregard of the Geneva Convention!

At nightfall the division was withdrawn to rest. When we reached "Happy Valley," a sheltered hollow behind our original front line, we were revived with panniers of tea laced with rum. Of our battalion of about 800 strong, fewer than 70 men, with 4 officers, came back. On reaching the road, this remnant formed into columns of fours and moved along singing, "Pack up your troubles in your old kit bag"—just as the full battalion had done six days earlier when setting out for "the great adventure." This now ever-unforgettable marching song raised a lump in the throat at the thought of the many friends who would never sing it again. We continued on our way to entrain at "Edge Hill," a forward railhead recently built to support the advance and about 5 miles behind the front line. Here we were rejoined by a number of strays, who had missed their way during these confused days.

We soon heard that our own losses were far from being exceptional. From our own regiment, six battalions had been engaged, and hardly any had come out of action 100 strong. The total losses of the 4th Army on the first day alone were almost 60,000—the heaviest day's loss in the history of the British Army.

The burden of the attack had been borne mainly by Kitchener's New Armies, and these quondam civilians carried on the fight after suffering a percentage of loss such as no professional army in recent centuries had been deemed able to bear without breaking. Yet most of the divisions engaged in the opening assault were in action again within a fortnight.

On July 4 a train carried us back to Ailly-sur-Somme. The news of our destination filled me with keen anticipation of a good meal and bed at the chateau overlooking the village, which was the country place of my father's close friend, M. Carmichael, who had generously played a godfatherly part in my life. Both before the battle and the previous year I had seized opportunities for brief but refreshing visits to Ailly. But when we disentrained there, we were told that we had to move on to Picquigny, and by a circuitous march, as another cavalry division was moving up to the front along the main road.

That march, although only about 5 miles, was the most agonizing I ever experienced—we were so dead beat that every step became more aching, while hunger pains became acute, after living for several days mainly on biscuits and bits of chocolate. But at the end of that trek I had what is engraved on my memory as the best meal of my life, followed by the longest sleep. For after seeing the men billeted and given a hot meal, I went into a little village café and ordered for myself an *omelette pour deux*. It proved to be the size of a normal omelet for four, while accompanied by a yard-long loaf of French bread and a bowl of *café au lait*. Having finished the meal, I ordered a repeat, except for the loaf, and then two quarts of beer. After all that I had a different kind of pain in my stomach, but tumbled into bed in my billet and slept around the clock.

I managed to ride over to M. Carmichael's for dinner twice that week—and am amused to see that in a letter to my parents, which they preserved, he described how "Lt. acting as Captain arrived on His charger with his suite" and went on to say of me "Spirits excellent, even avowing a military career would be very satisfactory." I am surprised to find that I felt so fond of soldiering at that moment, after the experience of the previous weekend! A more jocular comment in his letter was: "Upon my word a Hart on horseback seems the most extraordinary thing in this war." But that obviously applied to his recollection of my father in the pulpit, for my mother had ridden a lot when young, and even bareback. My seat on a horse was far from being as firm, and having a very thin bottom, I often found it painful after a long ride.

After six days of so-called rest—which was occupied mostly in writing letters of sympathy to widows or bereaved parents and in absorbing fresh drafts from the base—we moved up to the front again, for the assault on the Germans' second line. After the repulse suffered at the start all along the northerly half of the 14-mile attack frontage, Haig had decided to abandon the attack there and concentrate his further efforts on the southerly part, where wedges had been driven into the German front and where the French, on the adjoining sector astride the Somme, had made bigger progress at much less cost. The Germans' second line position was buttressed by Bazentin-le-Petit Wood, High Wood, and Delville Wood.

The leading British troops, nibbling their way forward during the past week, were still some distance—varying from 300 to 1,000 yards—from that position. So Rawlinson decided to cross the space by a night approach and assault it at dawn on July 14, after a brief hurricane bombardment—another new feature. Haig had at first objected to this apparently hazardous experiment but eventually agreed to it.

The outcome was the capture of the German second line with comparatively light casualties. Whereas on the battlefield of July 1 the khaki-clad corpses were far more numerous than German ones, the latter outnumbered the former on the battlefield of July 14. Unfortunately, the experiment was not repeated in the months that followed or in the following year. But the sight and contrast of the two battlefields made and left a deep impression on my mind—and subsequent military thinking.

Our brigade was in close support on this occasion, the assault of the 21st Division being delivered by a newly transferred brigade. But on the third day my company was detached and sent forward as an immediate brigade reserve and then moved forward again to fill a gap in the new front line, which was now on the far side of Bazentin-le-Petit Wood. On the way I had got a puncture in my hand, but after getting the wound bandaged, I carried on, as only one other officer was left. Moreover, he was so inexperienced and jumpy that the N.C.O.'s who were commanding the platoons came to me, together, to complain that he was upsetting the men. Shortly afterward he came to show me an almost invisible prick in his skin, so I seized the chance of sending him back for medical treatment, with a note asking that he should not be returned as I could manage better without his assistance.

At midnight on the seventeenth-eighteenth my company was relieved, when reinforcements arrived, and we moved back to rejoin our battalion. Passing through Mametz Wood, we suddenly heard a lot of shells landing around us, but as they did not explode with a bang, we imagined that they must be duds—until there was a strong smell of gas. It was our first notice and warning that the enemy had begun to use a lethal gas shell, filled with phosgene and more deadly, though less painful, than the former chlorine gas that had been projected from cylinders. Coughing violently, I stayed to warn and divert the platoons that were following and then led the company back to the battalion bivouac. In the morning I went to the nearest field ambulance to get my earlier wound freshly dressed —feeling bad, but still unaware how bad. There the doctors examined my chest and promptly put me on a stretcher. From there, by stages, I was sent to King Edward VII's Hospital for Officers in London, founded and run by that dynamic and unconventional personality known as Sister Agnes, a friend of the late King.

Close to twenty years later, when visiting General Dill there, I saw how her intervention saved the life of that outstanding soldier after mistaken treatment by the Army's medical service had brought him to the verge of death. I did not myself return there as a patient until forty years later, for a major operation, when I was happy to find that her successor as matron, Miss Alice Saxby, was quite as dynamic while more knowledgeable.

Six months in the hospital or convalescent leave gave me opportunity to think over the lessons of experience.

"To Reason Why. . . ."

IN REFLECTION it gradually became clear that while the troops were growing in experience, there was something seriously wrong in the doctrines inculcated by the higher command. Among the troops the "amateurishness" of 1915 had developed into the blind but trusting obedience of 1916. By 1917 this became habitual obedience but was no longer so trusting.

"Theirs not to reason why; theirs but to do and die" had become a habit, as in the Army of the Crimean War—and to a large extent it persisted until the end of the war. But I wanted to know "the reason why" in order to teach and train the men under me. And the more I studied the question, the clearer it became that there was little or no reason in the methods we were pursuing or in the doctrines we were taught. Indeed, they were flouting the lessons of history. So I sought to think out and improve our tactics.

In January, 1917, I was returned to "light duty in an office—the Record Office at York," and then obtained an appointment as adjutant to an Australian squadron of the Royal Flying Corps—which proved to be a valuable experience in the difference between intelligent working discipline and the formal discipline that prevailed in our Army. Then in the spring I was offered the post of Regular adjutant to a battalion of the recently constituted Volunteer Force. Here the main responsibility for its training was thrown on me—a responsibility and opportunity that were very welcome. It was a challenge to think out and a chance to try out new methods.

The commanding officer, a former Regular cavalryman, often talked of how during the London season he and his brother officers only visited their regiment when it came to their turn as the officer on duty. He was a man distinguished by natural ability and charm, and his use of these gifts had been restricted by having an ample private income—which is far more often stultifying to talent than the opposite condition. On the few occasions when he came to see tactical exercises he used to ask my views privately and then repeated them verbatim as his own comment. But his absence and deficiency of professional knowledge provided me with all the fuller opportunity.

One of the early products was a battle drill that enabled any unit of infantry—platoon, company, or battalion—to be opened out or closed in varying degrees by signal, so as to avoid loss from enemy fire during the approach. The use of a simple code of signals was better than vocal and complex orders, often inaudible under fire, or slowly transmitted messages, while it also made possible quicker and more flexible control. Even when fully opened out, a commander could maneuver the whole instantaneously, like a naval flotilla. It could be used not only in the approach but subsequently whenever and wherever suitable. By trying out the system with a whole battalion on the training areas, I was able to see how and where it could be improved.

Another development of it was a progressive series of attack drills that brought out the various kinds of maneuver that could be used, which were in essence few, and could be carried out with or without live ammunition—this being used to simulate battle conditions better.

I incorporated all these forms of battle drill, along with other developments in new tactics, in a little book, *New Methods in Infantry Training,* I produced in 1918 through the Cambridge University Press. It was widely used in other units, particularly officer cadet battalions, during the last part of the war, and in 1920, when called in to rewrite the official *Infantry Training* manual, I got the battle drill accepted by the War Office and included in the manual. By that time I had also worked out a completely new form of parade ground drill based on battle drill, but this was rejected by conservative influences, particularly in the Brigade of Guards, as incompatible with ceremonial. They did not realize that the existing close-order drill was an obsolete survival of what in the eighteenth century had been designed as a tactical drill suitable for battle. It was not until the eve of the next war that the War Office sanctioned the introduction of a new drill based on modern tactics, and even then it was an unsatisfactory compromise—as all official developments tend to be.

Battle drill itself, in its two forms, was accepted and incorporated in the official manual. But as the years of peace passed, it fell gradually into disuse—until it was revived in 1940, and then largely by the efforts of younger men, many of whom were not even aware that it had been introduced and adopted a generation earlier.

The opportunity of rewriting the official manual after World

War I also enabled me to get the value of night approaches and attacks emphasized, as well as the use of other kinds of "obscurity." But these likewise became neglected in peacetime training until again strongly urged in the report of a War Office committee, of eight generals, constituted in 1932 to examine the "Lessons of the War"—a report to which I was asked to contribute. Even then its application soon lapsed, while little was done to develop my supplementary proposals for the development of artificial fog and of artificial light to aid movement and exploitation in the dark. It was only when Montgomery took command in the field in 1942 that real progress was made in these respects—he used night attacks in most of his battles from Alamein onward and used what was called artificial moonlight increasingly from 1944 on.

In the course of recasting the *Infantry Training* manual in 1920, I had evolved a method of attack that I christened the expanding torrent. It was a development of the infiltration tactics of 1918, based on the ideas of deep penetration and of maintaining the momentum by sustained pressure along the line of least resistance— through the continuous and habitual use of reserves, on each higher level successively, to back up such forward troops as were making progress, instead of reinforcing those who were held up.

In further reflection I realized that armored forces were the ideal instrument of such an attack technique, and far better than infantry for the purpose because of their capacity for faster and more prolonged movement. So from then on I became the advocate of armored forces and of their employment in this exploitation and deep penetration role.

Mobile armored and mechanized forces were likewise far superior to infantry or horsed cavalry for applying the "indirect approach"— the name I gave to the fuller development of it into a general theory of doing the "unexpected" and pursuing "the line of least expectation," strategically and tactically, that I worked out in the later 1920's and set forth in a book that has run through a series of editions and translations.

The compound idea was enthusiastically taken up by our armored forces, but unfortunately resisted by the preponderant elements in the British Army, so that the Hitlerite German Army, taking up the idea with greater energy, as well as being given ampler resources, became the one that applied it and proved its decisive value in their *blitzkriegs* of World War II. It was some consolation that the Israelis subsequently became its best exponents and have proved its continued value in three successive tests—1948, 1956, and 1967.

Paolo Monelli

PAOLO MONELLI *was born on July 15, 1894, into an old family of Crema (Lombardy), who later moved to the neighborhood of Modena, in Fiorano di Modena, at the foot of the Apennines. At the lyceum in Ancona he became a good friend of the now-famous architect Pier Luigi Nervi, and since Nervi wanted to become an artillery officer, Monelli decided to do the same, not having any definite plans for the future. But he flunked the entry exam to the Accademia Militare. Then, crying, "Down with the Army!" he registered at the law school of the University of Bologna, considering law the least difficult field of study.*

At the beginning of World War I Monelli was completing his fourth year at the university and was glad that the war gave him the opportunity to defer the choice of a profession to a later time. Drafted in 1915, he was assigned to the Alpine Corps, destined, on the whole, for mountain warfare. Captured and held as a prisoner of war 1917 to 1918, he became a member of military missions from 1919 to 1921. He was a Vienna correspondent for the Gazetta del Popolo from 1921 to 1922 and Berlin correspondent for La Stampa from 1922 to 1926, being sent on special missions to, among other places, the Near East and Spitsbergen. He was a special correspondent for Corrìere della Sera from 1926 to 1929 and with La Stampa from 1929 to 1935. In 1935 and 1936 he was a war correspondent in Ethiopia and was director of the Paris office of Corriere della Sera from 1936 to 1939. During World War II he served as a war correspondent until he was imprisoned by the Fascist government in 1943. In 1944 and 1945 he was a lieutenant colonel in the Corpo Italiano di Liberazione. After the war, he was a special correspondent for La Stampa from 1946 to 1967 and for Corriere della Sera from 1967 on.

His books Toes Up and Mussolini: Intimate Life of a Dictator, translated into English, French, and Dutch are among his best known, and Italian readers are especially familiar with such works as Io e i tedeschi (1929), Barbaro dominio (1933), Roma (1943), Naia parla (1947), Nessuna nuvola in cielo (1957), Avventura nel primo secolo (1958), Il vero bevitore (1963), and Ombre Cinesi (1965). He has won many prizes for his outstanding contributions as a journalist, including the Saint Vincent Great Prize for Journalism (1960), the Great Prize for Journalism of the Accademia della Crusca, Florence (1965). He has also received four Medaglie al valore, and the Croix de guerre Belge.

ALPINE WARFARE*

———◆———

"This war is not a gentleman's war," I was told one day in Marmarica, in 1942, by Paolo Caccia Dominioni, a lieutenant colonel in the Reserves, who later toiled for years in order to recover the bodies of the soldiers who had fallen in that campaign and gathered them mercifully in an ossuary.

That day we had eluded the solitary hunt by a lone enemy bomber of our camouflaged car, the only one crossing the desert that afternoon on the track leading to the front lines of El Alamein. The lone car must have had on the pilot the effect of a speck in the eye. He overtook us, returned at once, and zeroed in on us. Realizing his intentions, we just about had time to throw ourselves under the car when it was hit by a volley of machine-gun fire. The bomber passed over us again and again until it tired of its little game, and we were relieved to hear it rise and get away.

Both of us, stretched out flat on our faces, couldn't help thinking of the destruction brought upon cities of all nations involved in the war by such attacks from the sky, the torment inflicted on the peaceful citizens, the destruction of irreplaceable historical monuments. And naturally this led us both to compare the present war with World War I, cleansed in our minds from all horrors twenty-five years later.

Twenty more years have gone by since World War II. Other wars have followed—skirmishes and destruction in Korea, in the Near and Far East—and more and more the war of 1914–18 appears to us who have taken part in it incredible and fabulous.

Having by now come to the end of our day, looking back on our past, our youth devoured without our having had any awareness of it, the rest of our life used up in the practice of our profession, in caring for one's family, in the monotony of everyday occurrences, in the plot here and there somewhat confused in our reminiscences, the years from 1914 to 1918 stand out immutably clear, precisely outlined, never blending with the few that preceded and the many that followed them like a long, unforgettable dream beyond time.

This feeling was immediate. Two years after having returned to civilian life, upon publishing my war diary, I felt compelled to

---

* Translated from the Italian by Lucille Carasso.

advise my readers in a short introduction of how much of that past had already died in me—"that past whose ineffaceable furrows are carved in my memory like the abandoned trenches on the peaks of the mountains once again alone." Then, already looking back on my carefree and serene adolescence, I felt as if it were on the other side of an abyss that it hardly seemed possible for me to have physically crossed.

Then another phenomenon intervened, I wouldn't say to mar, but to blur the awareness of that crystal-clear intact recollection of the experience that lifted us into a new dimension, and that, when concluded, made us feel dissatisfied and dazed upon getting back to earth, as if we had returned from an interplanetary flight.

I beg the reader to forgive me if I once again talk about myself, but the editor of this volume has prevailed on me once again to take a stark look at that past. During the last months of the war, while still in uniform and vegetating in a prison camp, I mentioned, as follows, the sudden revelation of having landed in a superhuman adventure: "Dreamer, the good times are over . . . Finished are the bloom of youth, the dangers always negotiated, our humble pride, at that time still devoid of sin, that snowlike freshness capping our thoughts when life was so light, without yesterdays or tomorrows, hung on one second as on a cobweb thread shining in the dawn, appearing over the mountain."

Another phenomenon, as I say, came in time to perturb our awareness of that youthful experience. Stormy events in all parts of the globe, another war—not bloodier, but in some ways more terrible than the first one. The upset brought to our lives by impetuous technical progress, swifter than any social advancement and often in contrast with it, and new meanings in the relationships among peoples made us doubt the fairness of the motives that sustained and comforted us then. And the charge made against us by writers, politicians, thinkers of the generations that followed of complicity with the governments of those days, while unfair, provoked in us, nevertheless, a feeling of guilt.

(Alberto Moravia, who was still a child when World War I broke out, gives a concise and spiteful opinion of it. He calls it "an outbreak of collective madness, the reasons of which should be studied by the psychoanalyst rather than by the historian." He speaks of the retrospective disgust inspired in us nowadays by that ignoble slaughter. He affirms that war lacked the contrast between reason and madness, between truth and falsehood, between civilization and barbarity, which in World War II managed somehow to light up the darkness of the massacre.)

My generation, whose destiny it was to take part in World War I and World War II, tends to upset that opinion. In World War I, the contrast Moravia spoke about between truth and falsehood, between reason and madness, was obvious, whereas World War II was all barbarity—what with genocide, the concentration camps, the extermination of war prisoners and of the civilian populations. (In Italy, the civilian dead killed by aerial bombardments equaled in number the soldiers killed in battle.)

And if not exactly a sense of guilt, we feel the bitterness brought on by a useless experience—worse, by a deadly one. We Italians, those who were found good for another massacre, fought in World War II as dutiful citizens and well-disciplined soldiers, but with the anguish of an abjurer, as if we were forswearing the motives of the first war by participating in a second one from the opposite camp, while feeling that this was wrong.

Not only to us veterans is World War I that crystalline abstraction that I have tried to define. It stands as well in the fabric of history as a unique phenomenon. It was a crisis that upset humanity, forswearing century-old principles, without establishing new and valid ones for the centuries to come; it was the end of an era, without being the heartening beginning of a better one; it was an abrupt crossing from the gullible and smug Middle Ages to an iconoclastic and faithless era. None of the myths and values that made us—the very young—accept that war and the sad duty of having to take part in it is still valid today. I believe this may be said of the youth of all nations that took part in the conflict—the French were animated by a spirit of revenge, the English by the pride of their Empire, the Germans by a mystic folly of being the master race. We Italians had the certainty of fighting for a generous cause—the completion of the movement for political unity in Italy in the nineteenth century with the annexation of the two noble cities that had remained outside the country's boundaries, Trent and Trieste. Civilians, students, young professional men felt that it was good and dignified, as in the times of Horace *pro patria mori* (to die for one's country) ; we considered ourselves a select group, as opposed to those civilians who, in spite of the fact that an aviation still in its infancy would occasionally kill a few with little 50-kilogram bombs, continued to live a peaceful and well-sheltered existence. In one camp as in the other of all participating nations, everyone thought that this was going to be the last war ("a war to end all wars") and that it was, therefore, right to sacrifice oneself in order to give one's children and all humanity an everlasting peace. (It has been our bitter experience later to see how many more wars have come from that first one.) We still live today with a nightmare of a third world war's breaking out at almost any time, in which atomic weapons shall be used—weapons we do not dare use at present, so frightening is the thought of the consequences. In the meanwhile, we perfect the so-called conventional weapons to such an extent that they become only a little less terrifying. Humanity is perhaps the victim of an inexorable biological law sentenced by an obscure necessity of the species to a bloodletting of many millions of lives, almost with every generation.

I do not know in what manner other countries that took part in World War I honor their survivors. In our skeptical, practical, intolerant Italy, they have been excluded with no consideration from the mainstream of the nation. They have been reproached first for having taken part in World War I with patience and a strong sense of duty and now for not dying soon enough. About a dozen years ago they were promised a life annuity as evidence of their country's gratitude, and many proposed bills all became shelved in the offices of the Chamber of Deputies and of the Senate until this year a pension of 5,000 lire each month was at last awarded to the neediest—less than $8.50—and each man was knighted; this order was created especially for them and will end with the last survivors.

When I was drafted in the year 1915, I had the good fortune of being assigned to the Alpine Corps destined on the whole to mountain warfare. It was a war very different from the one being fought on all other fronts, and it especially deserves to be described because I don't believe one will ever again see the like of it. It could be that in wars to come—should they be inevitable—some aspects of the preceding wars may still be seen, such as pitched battles swiftly fought with armored vehicles and Commando engagements. Mountain warfare immediately appeared to be obsolete after the invention of the helicopter and the creation of the paratroopers. For example, today, when entire divisions can be transported by air and dropped into enemy territory over the most arduous natural obstacles, it appears to be absurd that in the year 1916 one thought it both necessary and convenient to mine entire mountains garrisoned by the enemy, as did the Italians and the Austrians.

But in the years from 1914 to 1918 some of the categorical imperatives dating back to the Napoleonic Wars, when a war was won only by crossing the borders and physically occupying the enemy territory, were still valid. Italy found herself having a common border with her enemies—a border about 13,000 feet high, bristling with plateaus, glaciers, snowy mountain peaks, and the ramparts of the Dolomites—and there was no alternative than to leave from there on our way to a battlefield or from there to resist the enemy onslaught.

The Alpines and, for that matter, also the Austrian and the German mountain-based troops (Kaiserjäger, Landesschützen, Alpenkorps) had a regional recruiting system that gave these soldiers, of whom exceptional performance beyond the call of duty was demanded, a strangely homey mentality. The draftees of the older classes would return to the battalion in which they had served as enlisted men only to find sons and nephews there and would live together under conditions that often were inhuman and certainly much more uncomfortable than those of other specialties; boys of twenty and men over forty would run the same risks.

The English translator of my war diary, Le Scarpe al Sole (Toes Up, New York, 1930), Orlo Williams, has described the Alpine soldier in the following terms:

Perhaps the proudest and the toughest corps engaged on any front. They labored and fought amid the grandeur of the Dolomites, their homeland, fragrant with wet rocks and pinewood; by day a sparkling world of sun and snow, by night cold starlight. In their lonely positions at the forepart of the desperate battle against superior Austrian and German artillery, their success depended on individual prowess and courage, not on machines. Hard drinkers, swearers, and champion scroungers with an immeasurable pride in themselves and their corps, they lived brutally and died heroically.

It is a rather accurate and concise judgment. I must add, however, that the Alpine battlefields were not limited to the harsh and romantic Dolomites, the desolate glaciers of the Adamello, the Ortles, the Monte Cristallo, the inhospitable plateaus on which winters were just as hard as on the mountaintops. And with regard to the definition of "hard drinkers," it was mostly wine—even the wine that on the plains below would have been considered vinegar. And it didn't take long to find out that above the 5,000-feet mark all wine is always good and has to be drunk in much larger quantities than usual before going to one's head. But graspa, too, the strong liquor of the mountaineer, a brandy made with the stalk that remains of the cluster of grapes after the grapes have been removed; it really is aqua vitae (water of life) in its most perfect essence.

More than once did I see a fatally wounded soldier on a stretcher, who having been given a glass of *graspa* in order to ease his passing, recover his senses durably after having drunk it. Anyone who does not believe me should ask Captain Somaggio of the 7th Alpine, who under Mount Tomatico, while leading the Val Cismon Battalion, was hit by a bullet that everyone, especially the doctor, considered to be an immediate send-off to greet the angels. "A sip of *graspa*," murmured the dying soldier. "Let him have it," said the doctor to the stretcher-bearer, "he will not be drinking it much longer." (Somaggio is still repeating these words today.) But as I was saying, in reference to "hard drinkers," it is not true that, according to a slanderous legend, the Alpines are formidable and incorrigible drinkers. Only when forced to live during weeks and months under the most difficult conditions, which often made it impossible for fresh supplies to reach them, did they express their longing for wine in songs—"We are Alpines; we like wine." And if I once wrote that the word "Alpine" doesn't stem from "Alps," but consists of two Greek words for "once more" and "drink," meaning, therefore, "he who is always drinking one more," I am afraid that no philologist will ever accept my etymology.

The Italians and the Germans (with this word I am referring to the Austrians, the Tyroleans, the Bavarians in the Alpenkorps) fought battles during World War I at altitudes never heard of before. Even today, in the Dolomites, anyone who has breath, good legs, and doesn't suffer from vertigo, can reach heights that would be ill suited for a bivouac of only a few hours, yet these soldiers stayed there for weeks and months, winter as well as summer. One can still see the remains of small huts hardly visible on rocky ledges, held up by ropes or dug into the rock itself, that could only be reached through a narrow rim carved out of the mountainside. Do you remember Charlie Chaplin's film *The Gold Rush,* in which a small hut was poised half on the snow and half in the empty space? Some of ours were always like that, yet we lived in them, and the sentry on duty shivering on the outside, in a temperature that could dip to 25 degrees below zero, would call AWOL those of us who stayed inside where a small stove that became red-hot in no time at all would bring the temperature up to 25 degrees above zero. Just by entering or by leaving the hut, one would experience a sudden change in temperature of about 50 degrees. But the tiny hut was often a luxury; the squadrons above us often had to be satisfied with aerial niches lined with planks or tar paper that one could reach by narrow stairs secured to the rock or by clinging to a fixed rope, and the mountain drop was so sheer on all sides that not even the snow could cling to it.

As the war went on, both sides felt more acutely the need to garrison lastingly or to conquer passes and summits always higher, always more difficult to reach, in order to expand the defenses and create a springboard for future encounters. If at first we went on the glaciers and climbed the sheerest walls of the Dolomites with small patrols of specialists, such as Alpine guides—volunteers who in peacetime were experienced mountaineers and skiers—in order to fight a surprise attack, we soon destined to lasting Alpine engagements entire battalions, in which the great majority were far from being champion climbers or skiers; the skiers were still a small minority or came from hasty training courses of one month's duration, and the climbers, too, were inexperienced. All the others were even less brilliant, but better suited to fight at altitudes above the 6,500-feet mark, and in winter at that—men born in the mountains, excellent hikers, resistant to fatigue, exceedingly strong beasts of burden, and good sharpshooters. Above all, they were men with introspective natures, especially the older ones who had matured as shepherds, woodcutters, coal miners, immigrants, laborers through a hard life, similar to life in wartime. Furthermore, thanks to their natural qualities, the self-denial of the officers, the example set by the Alpine guides, the mountaineering technicians, the desire to emulate an enemy who had confronted them with selected and exceedingly strong mountaineers and sharpshooters, they succeeded in ascending the sheerest mountain walls; they fought, spent nights in the bivouac, and securely established themselves on the glaciers. They went into exile in the wintry mountains under conditions that appeared to be prodigious.

In peacetime the Alpines used to poke fun at one another, for being by birth and tradition in such an uncomfortable (to say the least) service, for having to march during long hours over snow or stones, for carrying in their knapsacks (large as wardrobes) loads double those of the rest of the soldiers, and for going so rarely to the city. "Did you sell the cow? . . . Did you bring the butter to the mayor?" they would ask one another—because legend has it that with the proceeds from the sale of the cow, or by lavishing rustic gifts on the highest authority in the town, the young draftee could buy the coveted assignment in the Alpine battalion in which the older men in the family had served before him and in which it would have been disgraceful not to be admitted. While climbing in single file along the steep paths or going up the softened glaciers, where at each step the foot sank in the snow up to the ankle, they would often say, *"Passa parola che la monta."* These words would reach the men below still trudging along, and those who already had reached the top would bend down scoffing at them, while offering their mountain poles for them to hold onto.

In the Alpine warfare of the years 1915–18 *Passa parola che la monta* was again repeated. It started in the Alps, the high plateaus, the mountains 6,500 feet high. And there were the conquest of Monte Nero, 7,400 feet high up the precipitous rocks of a lean slope, the engagements on the Alpi Carniche (Carnic Alps), Pal Piccolo, Pal Grande, Canin, Rombó—mountains more difficult to negotiate than their heights would indicate. Battles were fought at heights of 8,000 feet and more for the conquest of the Fiemme Alps, at more than 10,000 feet in Le Tofane, which has walls that reach for the sky, *E passaggi di quarto grado* and at 11,000 feet on the Marmolada. Always higher up, closer to the stars, by paths that constantly became more precipitous. Here were the engagements on the Loccia Alta, on the Dosson di Genova (10,800 feet), the Crozzon di Lares (11,000 feet), and the Adamello (11,650 feet), occupied in the dead of winter. Then came the Corno di Cavento (11,150 feet), taken, lost, and taken again. Last, the San Matteo (11,900 feet), or let's say 12,000 in round figures). This one was, I believe, the highest battle—or I should say battles, since it was taken from the enemy with tremendous difficulty on September 1, 1917, then lost again to the enemy in spite of our desperate resistance on September 3. (Beautiful soldiers theirs, too—tenacious and reckless, Kaiserjäger and Landesschützen.) I omit mentioning the patrol engagements; the war bulletin of August 14, 1918, cites an attack by the Austrians to our advance posts in the high valley of Zebrù at 12,680 feet.

Someone defined those aerial fighters as the madmen of the mountain, probably believing this would please them. The expression was wrong and hyperbolic; these were not mad, but very wise, men. (Less wise, perhaps, were the orders emanating from the supreme command which they were forced to execute.) Never were plans studied in greater detail or carried out with more wisdom than those on the glaciers or up the breathtaking paths amid showers of falling stones. Such adventures were not made in a spirit of bravado or for the fun of it all. One who can take the staircase will not enter someone else's house through the wall, but on the staircase the enemy was on the lookout. That's why we would send decoys on one side exposing them as targets, while the rest of us would go up the other side cautiously and unsuspected. In this manner we took the Corno di Cavento (11,150 feet above sea level, a large, tangled rock springing up from the glacier), while the skiers on it exposed themselves to machine-gun fire, and the Austrians laughed at those idiots who expected to reach the top from such a low altitude in spite of their well-equipped positions. The climbers of the Val Baltea Battalion, climbing over a rock so sheer that it would have been sufficient for a sentry to look down and release a stone in order to make them all tumble into the valley below, set foot on the summit. Most of the time an engagement was preceded by weeks of careful and minute preparation: escalades by specialists testing ropes fastened to the most precipitous spots or chiseling steps in the rock. The chronicle of that war doesn't limit itself to aerial battles fought over snowcapped mountaintops, to escalades over impervious granite ramparts, or to surprise attacks in a storm—the storm being protector and enemy at the same time. (That is how San Matteo was conquered, during an unexpected blizzard; many were killed by lightning.) That war was, above all, a matter of great patience. "When these mountains shall turn to plains, I will go home," written—in the guest book of the Milan hut in one of those moments of dejection not too rare among good soldiers, when one no longer believes the war will ever end—by the corporal commanding the patrol that occupied it.

During the winter months the engagements were few, almost as if only in order to stretch oneself out a bit, to surprise an outpost, or to mock the opponent. The most frightening enemy was nature itself; stormy and icy days were followed by periods of rain, winds from the southeast triggered the fall of avalanches, other avalanches of softened snow came cascading down the mountain, and powdery snow was whipped around the mountain slopes by hurricane winds that often blew the men away like twigs even before knocking them down. Mountain batteries with mules and cannons, huts, entire platoons were hit, smothered, buried without a trace, without a cry, with no other sound than the one made by that gigantic white mass itself. The first winter, 1915–16, was especially horrible because we hadn't as yet mastered the art of living at such supreme heights in places, until then precluded from all human experience. More men died under avalanches and by freezing than by gunfire in the summer.

Each and every one of nature's obstacles or the defenses prepared by the enemy would have appeared to be a sufficient deterrent to any action; all around us the enemy was almost always above us. Because of the mania of our commanding officers in keeping the front-line defenders in contact with the adversary, instead of placing them on an equal footing on the opposite mountaintop, the difficulty of finding shelter and of keeping our supply lines open compounded the problem. It was extremely hard to tow up to the summits Da 149 cannons to counter the 305 of the Austrians. Long lines of men tugging at the ropes would drag up with difficulty the cannon placed on a sled, while others armed with poles would keep it from sliding to the right or the left of the track and fall to the valley below. It took seventy-seven days to carry up to the Veneró-colo Pass a venerable piece, "Da 149G" (the G stands for *ghisa,* or cast iron). One day we succeeded in hoisting with enormous difficulty a small mountain cannon on the Tofána di Roces (10,590 feet). The first shot had just been fired, and we were observing with great interest the damage it had done, when the cannon quietly began sliding backward and tumbled 3,000 feet below, where it remained until the end of the war. And we had also to contend with the shifty and treacherous snow that could in any season start falling precisely where the mountain experts would swear this could never happen and where avalanches were considered an impossibility, as were the stone and rock landslides held together only by overnight freezing, but very dangerous if walked on when the sun was shining.

The battle was always the fulfillment, possibly with a feeling of relief at that, of many months of waiting, of monotonous excavation and other careful preparations. The real battle would start the moment the peace-loving Alpine removed the knapsack from his shoulders and began to enjoy the spot he had reached. In order to get there, he had traveled during endless hours over stony or icy paths, climbing during the night, carrying the load of a mule (machine guns, bombs, and provisions), pausing occasionally while waiting for the advance patrol to prepare the way with fixed ropes or nails driven into the mountain wall. And when at last he had arrived just below the top's rim, the mortal combat would begin.

Naturally intelligent, when tired of such a life, the good soldier often hoped to get hit—but not on a path barely traced on a perpendicular mountain wall where the first dizzy spell would have landed him in the chasm below. However, when all went well and one was picked up by the stretcher-bearer, it could happen that, as in the dizzy Tofane, one would be placed in a sack, gaping wound and all, and thus lowered on a rope along the side of the mountain, often banging against it, to the snowy field below. Upon arrival the stretcher-bearer had to take a good look to make sure no entrails had escaped from the wound and gotten lost at the bottom of the sack.

I said earlier that in possible wars of the future we shall never again see that medieval kind of warfare so often waged with mines with equal stubbornness on the part of both the Italians and the Austrians during the years from 1916 to 1918, whose first innocent victims were the mountains themselves, savagely hit and mutilated for all eternity.

A harsh peak in the Dolomites (9,160 feet high), the Piccolo Legazuoi, was hit four times by three successive Austrian and one Italian mines; the second explosion caused a bold side of that mountain to come crashing down. Even now, the tourist climbing from Cortina d'Ampezzo to the Falzárego Pass, looking up to the mountain at his right, can identify the new texture of the lighter rock next to the century-old folds of the Punta Berrino, and can see, over a narrow plateau—the Cengia Martini—where the Alpines of the Val Chisone Battalion and the ones from a company of the Belluno lived together, holding onto a narrow ledge.

The ledge and the plateau were considered the hardest positions on the entire Dolomite front. They were bare, inhospitable rocks exposed to direct gunfire and to showers of bombs from above, the highest peaks being in enemy hands. Plagued in the winter by terrible blizzards, they could be reached only by ropes stretched out across ravines and crevasses.

Although aware of the fact that the enemy was excavating a tunnel under their positions in order to blow them up, the Alpines wore themselves out for months in those horrible outposts, so irksome to the enemy, since it was from there that the accesses to their own outposts could be hit directly.

During several weeks, the unmarried officers of that battalion took hourly turns inspecting a certain cave where a Geophone was placed in order to determine whether the enemy's drilling apparatus preparing the detonation chamber was still at work.

It was an uneasy time, with the constant prospect of being trapped like a mouse, since there was always a possibility that the Austrians would keep their machine going once the job had been done in order to delude the Italians into believing that it still had to be completed. At the end of every man's tour of duty, even the dizzy plateau on which one emerged, so exposed to cannon and gunfire, looked like paradise.

News that the explosion was imminent finally came from our garrison in the nearby Col di Lana—it, too, the victim of a ruinous explosion that exposed the reverse of the enemy lines. Our men informed us that the rubble had been cleared away, which meant that the detonation chamber was ready. We, therefore, stopped spying and waited with bated breath for the explosion to take place.

Now can the reader imagine the dismay of the enemy, near and far, when during the night of May 23, 1917, the mine exploded, and when, no sooner had the roar and the echoes died down, he heard the never-dreamed-of and extraordinarily out-of-place sound of a fanfare of bugles, cornets, and basses coming from the exact spot which was to have been blown off the map? This is what had, instead, taken place. In the imminence of the detonation, the company at the rear had leaped to the counterattack while the sparks, the rocks, and the stones were still cascading down to the Falzárego Valley, repelling the enemy who was advancing in order to take possession of that ruin.

Adding insult to injury, the battalion's commanding officer had summoned the fanfare and kept it in readiness; it now broke out in a stirring march, indicating the immediate return of the Alpines to what had remained of the plateau.

During those three years, similar engagements took place frequently in several parts of the Alpine front. The job of digging a tunnel often proceeded simultaneously on both sides, as a sort of competition that would determine who was going to be the first one to detonate the mine.

One of the first and most powerful ones exploded on the Castelletto (8,700 feet high) and called by the Germans *Schreckenstein* or Rock of Terror. It was a formidable rock with almost vertical walls, crowned by fantastic pinnacles barring any attempt of advance in the Dolomites, separated by narrow crevasses from the walls of other mountains dominating it on all sides.

Those passes were equally well policed by experienced German and Austrian mountain troops of the Kaiserjäger and of the Alpenkorps. Since the winter of 1915, the Italian command had proposed eliminating that natural barrier and to that effect had mined some of its higher spires. At the beginning of February, 1916, those Alpines patiently started to dig a tunnel more than 1,600 feet in length, in the heart of the mountain; work in the detonation chamber proper got under way at the end of March with two gasoline-powered drills. The enemy soon got wind of the menace and started at once to dig a countermine. Ten weeks went by, during which both sides worked feverishly, each one trying to spy on the enemy and annoy him in every possible way; selected sharpshooters were lowered on a rope, and from that precarious position they shot at enemy outposts 1,300 and even 2,000 feet away. It was agonizingly difficult for both sides to get supplies and machinery through under the frequent fire of the enemy's artillery.

The detonation was later described as follows by the major of the Kaiserjäger, Carl von Raschin, in his *Skizze über die Tofána-Kämpfe, im Jahre 1916:*

On July 11, 1916, at 3:20 A.M., the long explosion of the Castelletto took place. In a huge blaze the entire south side of the mountain came crashing down with an ominous and sinister sound. The earth shook, as if hit by a cataclysm, tremendous boulders were hurled into space—as high up as two and one-half miles. Rocky walls crumbled amid dense clouds of gas and a thick rain of debris. The center of the explosion was exactly where we had expected, and therefore destroyed a hut in which, in spite of the prohibition, twenty men had just then sought refuge. They, plus two sentries and two more men, were killed while trying to escape the boulders cascading all around them. They were the immediate victims of that explosion. The rest of the garrison (about 100 men) had been felled by gas, but they were soon revived by their comrades and by the medics summoned for this purpose.

Everything had been prepared for a struggle, though no longer in the pre-established positions; they, too, were upset by the frightening earthquake. Everyone was possessed by a belligerent ardor and eagerness to fight. The explosion was accompanied by an unbelievably intense artillery fire from the Italians, and the entire region shook under it during the next five hours.

On our side, however, the situation was even worse. Fumes from the explosion frustrated all attempts of the 77th Alpine Company to get over the gap it had created in just a few short leaps. Men were falling one on top of the other, hit by the mephitic gas that found no outlet. It became imperative to save the men that were being asphyxiated before doing anything else. The soldiers that found themselves at the entrance to the tunnel were ordered to reenter it, holding their breath (on that front we still had no gas masks), get the inanimate bodies of their buddies, and quickly carry them out into the open.

During the next two days the tunnel remained an insurmountable obstacle. The definitive conquest of that wounded mountain cost the Alpines three days of incredibly hard battles against an enemy determined not to let them reap the fruits of that explosion. Only on July 14, at noon, did the defenders give up, and the officer in charge of that campaign could finally inform his superiors that he had placed two cannons on the top of Castelletto.

I have always spoken of the Alpines, in this reminiscence of mountain warfare, meaning, of course, also the soldiers in charge of the Alpine artillery. But I must add that they were often joined by courageous and efficient infantry brigades not always composed of people from the north of Italy or from the region of the Apennines. Yet these men adapted readily and good-naturedly to surroundings that were especially hostile to them.

I remember Alpine battalions that were often destined to fight in places other than the high mountains—on the last hilly bulwarks of the Po Valley against which the 1916 Strafe expedition was crushed; on the Isonzo front where they vigorously resisted the overpowering German offensive, eventually retreating to new positions; in the valleys; and up the sides of the Montello; and over the Grappa massif—in their victorious counterattack.

Thus, on one hand, we celebrate Alpine patrol and squadron engagements in which each individual stands out in sharp contrast with his comrades, each with his primitive virtues, his dignity, and his pride; on the other, pitched battles, the most tragic being the one fought on the Ortigara, in June, 1917.

It was a barren rampart with three peaks on the edge of the Asiago Plateau, at the point where it drops perpendicularly to the Val Sugana, similar to a gigantic Carso (Karst) —parched, lonely, desolate, with not a single river, road, or house to cross or dot the landscape, where, at certain points, the mountain reached heights of 6,500 feet.

This battle lasted twenty hellish days and cost the Austrians their selected battalions of the celebrated 3d Army Corps, the "Iron Corps." (In a report from the Austrian headquarters one can read, "The battalions who have returned from the Ortigara Inferno are dross.")

We lost two infantry brigades, a regiment of sharpshooters, twenty-six Alpine battalions, some which had been hastily regrouped after having been destroyed a first time and driven back up to be annihilated a second time. Mountain batteries rushed to the front lines to shoot with cannons as if they had been guns.

The mountain itself was also hit, turned upside down, destroyed, as were the most severely hit points on the Carso front. In an incredibly narrow space, men by the tens of thousands were nailed to the rock under artillery fire hitting them from every inch on the horizon, and under avalanches of fire, clouds of gas, and torrents of *liquidi infiammati,* the three peaks were won, lost, retaken, and finally abandoned when we no longer had a single battalion with which to continue the struggle.

I returned, after long years had gone by, to the field of the 10,000 dead. It was somber, forbidding, doomed to barrenness for eternity, still looking as it had appeared during a battle when a sudden lull took place—those deceitful lulls, during which we would find ourselves emerging from the tumult bewildered in the silence that surrounded us and pervaded by a feeling of loneliness and abandonment, in view of the serene, faraway mountains, looming under an endless sky without light and with God.

Visions of my beloved comrades still alive, wrecks burned by deadly fumes, wary and bent during an assault, flashed through my mind. I heard the awkward echoing of metal against the rock, messtins, sword sheaths, gas mask containers. I saw the crushed battalions bearing the good old names of home, the men I had known and whose deaths I had witnessed, and the countless others that had been for me nothing more than a gray veil over the mountain—men with the hard and absent look of combat on their faces; only the eyes appeared somewhat dazed because they were dead, all the dead reenacting for my hallucination the deadly game of half a century ago.

But these facts are not relevant to the story I am relating. In conclusion, as an example of those engagements in which individual men appeared to be waging an assault on the sky itself (as H. G. Wells wrote when he was war correspondent on the Dolomite front), I will cite an episode of July, 1915, in which Sepp Innerkofler, the most famous guide in the Dolomites and a volunteer in the Landesschützen, lost his life.

The Alpines had occupied the forks on both sides of Mount Paterno (9,000 feet high), a tremendously bold pinnacle near the Tre Cime di Lavaredo, where they were holding a small outpost at the top, which could be reached only by steps in the rock and fixed ropes. The Austrian headquarters ordered that important position retaken. The episode is related as follows in a book written by a medical officer in the Alpine Corps, who from the Lavaredo fork witnessed it through his binoculars:

There are six, all volunteers, of which three are over fifty years of age, renowned guides in the Val di Sesto (Sepp Innerkofler, Hans Forcher, Andreas Piller). They have received the order to climb the Paterno and occupy its top. Armed with rifles and hand grenades, they leave a hut near the Dreizinnenhütte. With them is a patrol consisting of thirty Kaisersschützen and a few military engineers led by Christl, who is Sepp's brother. They set out on a gravel path descending from the Forcella del Camoscio, and proceed slowly and stealthily, being careful not to displace any stone that might arouse the enemy's suspicion. Christl and his platoon stop at the top of the path, waiting for things to start happening. The six put on their hiking boots and start up the wall of the Paterno. With complete assurance they climb under cover of darkness; the way is known as the northwest passage, the same one Sepp was the first man to ascend in 1896, and had climbed countless times since. One hour later they reach the top in the dim light of dawn. From Monte Rudo the Austrians start to shoot at once. Then twice again the roar and the hiss of the cannons are heard from a lower altitude; a fourth roar brings down a hail of shattered rocks—then a silence. The six men keep on climbing in single file along the edge of the peak. From Forcella di Pian di Cengia, the Alpines can clearly see them looming against the red sky. That is the awaited signal, and while the six climb toward the west, the Italians open fire from Lavaredo. Immediately the Austrians respond, bringing their own machine guns into action. Over the din one can hear the cannons on Monte Rudo, a mortar from Sasso di Sesto, a 105 Howitzer shooting without let up toward the Forcella di Pian di Cengia from the Torre degli Scarperi. And the six are still climbing, cautiously, in spurts, hiding in every hollow. A fragment of grenade hits Sepp on his forehead. Blood comes streaking down his face and covers his eyeglasses; yet he continues to climb. A rock hits Forcher, also on the forehead; he bleeds, but he, too, continues to climb —they have almost reached the top. Suddenly, as if by a pre-arranged signal, an eerie quiet succeeds the racket. A silence of death spreads through the valley, over the mountaintops, on all sides of the trenches. At this precise moment, slowly, and clearly visible, one man alone begins to ascend. Ten steps below the top he crosses himself and with a sweeping motion hurls a grenade over the wall of the outpost above—then a second, and a third one.

Suddenly, his face still bleeding from the effects of the first bomb, his figure sharply etched against the incredibly terse sky, an Alpine soldier appears, standing over the wall; he holds a rock high over his head. He throws it, and Sepp is fatally hit. Raising his arms toward the sky, he falls on his back and drops into a crevasse. On the mountaintop, the Alpine who saved the Paterno is still standing upright; he is Piero de Luca of the Val Piave Battalion.

I later read in an Austrian report that the Italian Alpines had lowered themselves to the bottom of the crevasse, in spite of untold difficulties, returning Sepp's body to the top. There they buried him, inscribing a reverent epitaph on the grave of their valiant opponent.

The Men of 1914

R. C. Sherriff

R. C. SHERRIFF *joined the Army on leaving school in 1914 and served as an infantry officer on the western front until wounded at Passchendaele in 1917.*

On demobilization as a captain he joined the staff of a London insurance office and wrote plays as a hobby for a local amateur dramatic club. After the professional production of Journey's End *(1929), about which Stark Young wrote, "The most striking thing about this English play is this underlying poetic feeling, not a poetry of the imagination so much, but rather a poetry of human concern," he went to Oxford to read history at New College and subsequently made writing his career. There were 594 performances of* Journey's End *at the Savoy Theater in London and 485 at the Henry Miller Theater on Broadway. It was produced in all parts of the world in twenty-seven different foreign translations.*

Mr. Sherriff's novels, including The Fortnight in September, Greengates, *and* The Hopkins Manuscript, *have been widely translated and published abroad, and several of his plays had long runs in West End theaters. He has done much work in Hollywood, writing the scripts for numerous films, including* Goodbye Mr. Chips, The Invisible Man, *and* Lady Hamilton.

Now living in the country, he is interested in farming, archeology, and rowing. He was captain for some years of the Kingston Rowing Club, for whose members he wrote several plays in his amateur days.

He is a Fellow of the Royal Society of Literature and a member of the Athenaeum.

THE ENGLISH PUBLIC SCHOOLS
IN THE WAR

———◆———

WHEN MY WAR PLAY *Journey's End* was first performed, some people said there was too much of the English public schools about it. Some thought it glorified them without good reason; others that it discredited them unfairly. It depended on the way they thought about these schools.

For my own part I had no ax to grind one way or the other. I didn't go to a public school myself. I was at my small hometown grammar school, and in those days the gulf between a local school and a public school was so wide that the boys lived practically in different worlds. I hardly ever met a public school boy until I joined the Army. As a junior officer, I lived among them. Almost every young officer was a public school boy, and if I had cut them out of *Journey's End,* there wouldn't have been a play at all.

As they have no counterpart in any other country, it is worth saying something here about the way they came into existence and how they attained their unique prestige and influence.

It must first be said that an English public school isn't public. On the contrary, it is private and exclusive. Nobody seems to know how it got the misleading name. It is a mystery buried in the past.

No two of them are alike. All have their own distinct character and traditions. All are quite independent of one another, and all grew up in a casual, haphazard way, without a thought of the glamorous future in store for them.

They began in a small way: mostly town schools for the sons of local tradesmen. Some were founded by charitable men as "free schools" for destitute boys. A lot of them never got any further. They remain to this day the schools for local boys. The ones that broke loose from their local anchorage and achieved wide recognition did so mainly by luck and chance.

Sometimes an outstanding headmaster would build up a reputation for scholarship among his boys. The news would get around among well-to-do men living at a distance from the school. They would send their sons to the school as boarders, and once the school had secured a wealthy clientele, it was on its way to fame and fortune. Old boys, proud of the school, would send their sons to it. In due time the sons would send their sons, and generations of a family would become associated. It would be taken for granted that their boys would go there, even if by then the parents were living in the farthest corners of England. Most boys would remain loyal to their old schools all their lives. Handsome legacies were made by will. Treasuring old traditions, the governors of these schools would never pull down their ancient buildings, but as money came in, they would renovate them, enlarge them, and add wide playing fields. Some of the best medieval and Tudor architecture in England survives in these old school buildings.

It was difficult for a man to get his sons into these successful schools unless his family had past associations with them. There would be a waiting list, and the headmaster could pick and choose. There were no open scholarships for boys from the lower classes. Intellectual ability was less important than that the boy should be the "right sort." A good family background meant more than good brains, but by and large these two distinctions went together. The schools in a position to demand them would charge high fees. This enabled them to employ good masters, and good masters produced good scholars.

Until about 1860 no formal link existed between these schools. They plowed their own furrows and went their own ways. They developed independently along the lines that suited them.

Then one day about half a dozen headmasters of the leading schools got together and decided that it would be a good thing to establish some sort of organization through which they could meet on regular occasions to exchange views on education—to discuss their problems and debate various ways and means for expanding the scope of their teaching to embrace new aspects of scientific knowledge. It was an excellent idea, and they all stood to gain from it.

And so the Headmasters' Conference was established.

At first it was like a small, exclusive club consisting only of the founder members. But to make the enterprise more effective, it was decided to bring in other schools that had the prestige to qualify them for membership.

There were no defined rules. It didn't depend on the age or the size of the school. The founder members were a law unto themselves and invited only the schools they liked the look of. That meant, of course, the elite: the schools with firmly established reputations that only took the best type of boy and aimed at the highest standards of scholarship and behavior.

And so it grew up. Headmasters were proud to be invited. It gave their schools an uplift and placed them among the best in the land. They became known as the public schools.

It was a valued, exclusive trademark that schools outside the Headmasters' Conference would not presume to use. It was a scholastic aristocracy, and the pupils of these schools were proud to call themselves public school boys.

There was more to it than pride and snobbery. Professional and business firms would always prefer a boy from a public school. It opened the gates to many fields denied the boys from lesser schools.

I knew nothing about all this when I was a boy myself. I had never heard of the Headmasters' Conference, and it would have mattered little if I had.

We were happy enough in our small local grammar school. It was an ugly old place in the main street of the town. We had no playing fields of our own and had to play our games on the public recreation ground, but we had our own little built-in pride. Our parents had to pay ten pounds a term for our education, and the boys with parents who couldn't or wouldn't pay went to what were known as board schools. We at the grammar school wore scarlet caps, with the crest of the school sewn on them, and gray flannel jackets with scarlet trimmings. The board school boys wore any old clothes, which made us feel superior. It gave us "class," and that was everything. It gave us self-respect and a pride in our school, and I was grateful to my father for sending me to it. He had very little money and had to pinch to pay the fees, but he was as happy as I was that his son should be a grammar school boy with such a good start in life.

The shock came when the war began in the summer of 1914.

I had just left school and started work in a London office.

It was announced that a volunteer army was to be enlisted to reinforce the hard-pressed Regular Army in France: Kitchener's Army it was called, and they wanted 100,000 men.

It was also announced that suitable young men were required for training as officers.

I was excited, enthusiastic. It would be far more interesting to be an officer than a man in the ranks. An officer, I realized, had to be a bit above the others, but I had had a sound education at the grammar school and could speak good English. I had had some experience of responsibility. I had been captain of games at school. I was fit and strong. I was surely one of the "suitable young men" they were calling for.

I put on my best suit and went to the headquarters of our county regiment.

I was sent to a room where about a dozen young men like myself were waiting to be interviewed.

The adjutant came in. He sorted out some papers on his table and called for the first applicant to come forward.

"School?" inquired the adjutant.

"Winchester," replied the boy.

"Good," said the adjutant. There was no more to say. Winchester was one of the most renowned schools in England. He filled in a few details on a form and told the boy to report to the medical officer for routine examination. He was practically an officer. In a few days his appointment would come through.

The next applicant was from another famous public school. He too sailed through triumphantly.

My turn came.

"School?" inquired the adjutant. I told him, and his face fell. He took up a printed list from his desk and searched through it.

"I'm sorry," he said, "but I'm afraid it isn't a public school."

I was mystified. Until that moment I knew nothing about these strange distinctions. I told him that my school, though small, was a very old and good one—founded, I said, by Queen Elizabeth in 1567.

The adjutant was not impressed. He had lost all interest in me. "I'm sorry," he repeated. "But our instructions are that all applicants for commissions must be selected from the recognized public schools, and yours is not among them."

And that was that. I was told to go to another room where a sergeant major was enlisting recruits for the ranks, and it was a long, hard pull before I was at last accepted as an officer. Only then because the prodigious loss of officers in France had forced the authorities to lower their sights and accept young men outside the exclusive circle of the public schools.

It seemed to me at the time a silly way to go about things. To say that no young man was suitable to be an officer unless he was public school was humiliating and unfair, but looking back on those confused and difficult days, I can see the common sense and reason in it.

Britain was not a military nation. Napoleon called it a nation of shopkeepers, and the Kaiser described its armed forces as a contemptible little army. Both were no doubt right. An island nation with no frontiers to defend had small need for soldiers. All it wanted was a strong navy to guard its shores and a small, highly trained and disciplined army to protect its empire.

It numbered about 250,000 men, and it had an elite officer class.

Sandhurst was the chief military academy for infantry officers, and in those days the infantry predominated.

When a young man entered Sandhurst, it was almost like entering a monastery. He would never be in touch again with the civilians outside the Army. His life would be spent principally on service with his regiment abroad. When on duty at home, he would live in Army camps. His friends, apart from his own family, would nearly all be from his regiment. Even when he retired, he tended to live in select little communities of old officers with interests and memories of the only sort of life they knew about.

He was devoted to his profession. He was proud of it and had good reason to be. An officer was expected to live up to the highest standards of personal and professional integrity. If he fell short, if he discredited his regiment in any way, he was quickly hounded out by his fellow officers, even if he wasn't told officially to go. "An officer and a gentleman" were bywords.

Until the Great War the Regular Army had always been able to look after itself. In the comparatively small campaigns of the past the losses were easily made good from its own resources. There were plenty of good men willing to take the King's shilling and join the ranks, plenty of eager young officers coming out of the military academies, well prepared and fully trained. The officer class remained elite, remote, inviolate.

Now suddenly the Army command was up against a problem it had never had to face before.

In the first few months in France the Army lost more officers than in all the wars of the previous 100 years put together.

It was a shock to the people, a humiliating shock to the Army itself that it could no longer defend the nation as it had done in the past and had to call in the civilians to help them.

There was no problem about recruits for the ranks. They were lining up in crowds at every recruiting station in the land. The first 100,000 were enlisted in a few days.

But officers were the problem. That first Volunteer Army would need at least 5,000 officers, but where were they to come from?

The men at the top—the generals at the War Office from Lord Kitchener downward—were bred in the old traditions. It was difficult for them to envisage an officer who had not qualified through the long and arduous training at a military academy. But Sandhurst could barely supply replacements for the losses in the Regular Army. It would need a dozen Sandhursts to train the officers now required.

Naturally the authorities wanted the new officers to be men with the same background and character as those of the Regular Army, with a dedication to their duty that was ingrained in a Sandhurst cadet long before he was considered fit to join a regiment.

Undoubtedly there were men of the officer type among those unwieldy crowds who were pouring into the recruiting offices, but there was no time to sort them out, no existing tribunals to examine them individually and separate the wheat from the chaff.

But the need was pressing. Officers had to be made quickly, with the least possible trouble. The Army command had to find some sort of yardstick, and naturally they turned to the public schools.

Most of the generals had been public school boys before they went to military academies. They knew from firsthand experience that a public school gave something to its boys that had the ingredients of leadership. They had a good background. They came from good homes. At school they gained self-confidence, the beginnings of responsibility through being prefects over younger boys. Pride in their schools would easily translate into pride for a regiment. Above all, without conceit or snobbery, they were conscious of a personal superiority that placed on their shoulders an obligation toward those less privileged than themselves. All this, together with the ability to speak good English, carried the public school boy a considerable way toward the ideals that the generals aimed at for good officers. And so the edict went out that all young men selected for training as officers in the New Army must come from the public schools.

It was a rough method of selection, a demarcation line hewn out with a blunt ax; but it was the only way in the face of a desperate emergency, and as things turned out, it worked.

It worked in a way that could scarcely have been envisaged at the time. The generals naturally assumed that under their experienced leadership the public schools boys would mature into officers of the old traditional type and lead their men to victory in the old traditional way that the generals had learned so thoroughly from their textbooks.

But these young men never turned into officers of the old traditional type. By hard experience they became leaders in a totally different way and, through their patience and courage and endurance, carried the Army to victory after the generals had brought it within a hairsbreadth of defeat.

These hapless generals have received such torrents of condemnation from young historians in recent years that they at least deserve a few extenuating words of sympathy.

For the most part they were men in their middle fifties, some around sixty, all near retirement age, and they had spent their best years in an army that had mainly been at peace. Their whole training had been for a type of open warfare that served well in years gone by: the Boer War and the Afghan War, campaigns against hostile tribes around the frontiers of the Empire. Many of these campaigns had needed skill and courage, and they had acquitted themselves well.

Now suddenly, as elderly men, they were confronted with a totally different sort of war. The Army had fought valiantly at Mons and in the retreating engagements that followed. It played a decisive part in stemming the German hordes and to its honor well nigh destroyed itself in the process.

To that point the generals had fought a war of tactics and maneuver that they understood. In a bigger way it was like the wars they had fought in the past and were competent to manage.

But when the stalemate came, when the armies entrenched themselves in a line of impenetrable fortifications from the sea to Switzerland, the old sort of war was over, and a new and totally different one began. It needed men with resilient, imaginative minds who could discard all the old outdated methods and adapt themselves to new ones.

But you can't teach an old dog new tricks, and that went for the generals.

It is reasonable to say that when the initial assault of the Germans was defeated, when they failed to take Paris and were forced back to a line of defensive trenches, the Allies had them beaten.

The Germans had been bent on quick victory by attack. The Allies' main purpose was defense. They had won the first and vital round. If they had then thrown all their resources into building a line of fortifications and had garrisoned it with their ample supplies of men, they could obviously have denied the enemy all hope of victory, and the end would eventually have come, as it did in fact come, through the starvation of the German homeland through blockade. By that means victory would have come with a negligible loss of men instead of through the slaughter and maiming of a generation.

But the generals saw things in a different way. It wasn't war to dig oneself in behind a line of impregnable fortifications. It was demoralizing, humiliating, a confession that you had sacrificed the initiative and lost your fighting spirit.

Most of them had won medals for open warfare in campaigns gone by, and they wanted to get back to the sort of fighting they were good at. Trench warfare, in fact, gave them nothing to do, no opportunity to display their prowess. The trenches, they admitted, were a tiresome necessity until they had mobilized enough men to break through into the open country behind the enemy lines. Once that was achieved, they could show their mettle. By bold maneuver, brilliant strategy and tactics they could soon have the Germans beaten. In that they were probably right. They all had experience of active warfare abroad, and the German generals had none. They hadn't fought a war since 1870, nearly fifty years before.

The British generals had every justification in believing that once they had broken through those German trenches, a brilliant and decisive victory lay ahead.

And so began the long and ghastly sequence of offensives.

The first was an attack that became known as the Battle of Loos. It was a historic occasion in the sense that for the first time the civilian Army fought beside the Regulars. The first contingent of Kitchener's Army went into the assault together with battalions of the Territorials, who were voluntary "weekend" soldiers in peacetime.

By then a good supply of ammunition had arrived from the new munitions factories in England. The generals began by plastering the German positions with shells. It was, of course, an obvious advertisement to the enemy that an attack was pending and gave them valuable time to make their preparations.

At zero hour the infantry advanced, and the carnage began. They were caught in the wire entanglements and mowed down by German machine guns. In the end a small dent had been made in the enemy lines—a few miles wide and a few miles deep. The territory gained had no strategic value.

The Germans fortified the edges of the gap, and the thing was over. For the gain of a few square miles of useless land the generals had sacrificed thousands of men.

For this they could be forgiven. It was the first trial of strength against a new sort of military barrier, and the only way to test its effectiveness was to attack it. The attack might have succeeded. The German line might have collapsed and left the way clear for the open warfare that the British generals yearned for.

The reasons for the failure were clear enough to every soldier who came out of it alive.

The first was that you can't destroy barbed-wire entanglements with shellfire. The more you shell them, the worse they get. The generals apparently hoped that the shells would blow the wire away and leave a clear passage for the advancing infantry. But I saw barbed-wire entanglements after days of intensive shellfire. The stakes supporting them were blown out of the ground, but the wire was still there—all twisted and distorted and more difficult to get through than when it was taut and straight.

The second lesson taught by that abortive attack was that land churned up by a massive bombardment of shells was impossible for the rapid advance of infantry. They had to pick a slow and arduous way around the craters, at the mercy of enemy machine guns.

The third and final lesson was that the Germans had built deep dugouts impervious to shellfire. Most of them were more than 20 feet deep, strutted with stout pit props. The defenders could remain down there in safety while the enemy artillery churned the ground above them. When the barrage lifted for the attackers to advance, the Germans would come out with their machine guns and mow them down.

If these obvious lessons had been taken to heart the terrible losses in the Battle of Loos could almost have been justified.

But they made no impression on the generals. They decided that all they needed was another and more copious supply of men and a larger quantity of ammunition.

They planned the Battle of the Somme upon an epic scale, but with no new weapons, no new ideas. It was the same old scheme that had failed at Loos—horribly magnified.

Massive reinforcements had poured in from England. Mainly hastily trained volunteers. The P.B.I. they called themselves: the poor bloody infantry. The more cynical label was cannon fodder.

There was a tremendous bombardment. The attack was launched, and by the end of the first day the Army had lost 60,000 men. They were lost for the reasons that had made themselves plain a year before at Loos: unbroken wire, ground made impassable by shell craters, enemy machine gunners protected by deep shelters until the barrage had been lifted for the infantry to advance as easy targets.

The generals were undeterred, and the slaughter went on for weeks. The final result was another dent in the German lines, a few miles wide and a few miles deep. Nothing had been gained. The captured ground had no strategic value, and the total British casualties amounted to 250,000 men.

Passchendaele, 1917, was the final, crowning misery. I was in it myself and can speak from personal, unforgettable experience.

One of the difficulties of a junior officer was that nobody ever told him what these attacks were intended to achieve.

In the Second World War the generals would brief their officers before an attack. They would get them together and give them a clear preview. The officers would go back and explain things to their men, and every soldier would go into the attack as well informed as the generals in command.

Nothing like that happened in the First World War. The Army commander briefed his division and brigade commanders, who in turn passed on the information to the colonels of battalions. But it never got to the junior officers, who were to lead the men. Secrecy appeared to be the watchword, and you just waited and did what you were told when the time arrived.

I never knew a thing about the Battle of Passchendaele except that I was in it. I only discovered what it was about years later when I read a history of the war.

The Ypres Salient had always been a thorn in the side of the Germany Army. It was a narrow wedge jutting into the German lines around the town of Ypres. For them it was the gateway to the Channel ports. For the British it was the gateway back to Belgium. The British had held on desperately and beaten off every German attack, but the salient was hell on earth for British battalions that held the trenches there. Our own battalion had done its spell of duty. We had held the trenches at Zillebeke for several weeks. The Germans held the high ground all around the salient, and you were shot at from three sides.

The idea of this new offensive was to burst open the German lines around the salient with a massive blow that would open the way to the Belgian coast and turn the northern flank of the German line. Among the plums that were to fall into our hands were some of the ports from which the Germans operated their U-boats, and the British Navy would cooperate.

It was an excellent idea on paper. Planning it all at Army headquarters down to the last detail, the generals must have believed that the war was practically won. All that they didn't take into account were the tiresome realities.

Our battalion was holding some trenches at the southern end of the British line when one night, without warning, we were replaced by another battalion and marched back to a village a few miles behind. This in itself was ominous. If they took you out for a rest, it usually meant that you were for it in the near future.

After a few days, during which the battalion was brought up to strength with drafts from England, we were ordered to parade and set out for an unknown destination. The way of our march was to the north, and that meant back to the Ypres Salient. Rumors were already drifting around that something big was brewing up there, but we junior officers were told nothing officially. We had to depend on cookhouse rumors, which usually turned out to be right.

We marched about 20 miles a day in the sweltering summer heat, and it took three days to reach the assembly area behind Ypres. One of the factors overlooked by the Army command was the condition of the men they were sending into battle. Most of ours had been serving in the trenches for the past few months and were quite unfit to face those long forced marches. In the trenches they got no physical exercise. They lived crouched up in sentry posts and slept beneath flimsy shelters roofed with corrugated iron. They slept in their uniforms and were not allowed to take their boots off. Most of their food came out of tins with no fresh vegetables or fruit. If they got bound up inside, the doctor would give them a pill, called a number nine, that purged them, then left them bound up again. They suffered from skin eruptures through ill-balanced food, and foot blisters would frequently turn septic.

As a lieutenant, I was in charge of about thirty men. Some were old friends, who had served with me since I joined the battalion a year before, but most of the newcomers were conscripts, often around forty years of age.

At the end of each day's march there would be a "foot parade." The men would take off their boots and socks and sit in a row in the barn where they were to sleep the night on straw.

Some of the feet were horrible to look at: raw skin and bleeding blisters and big, angry sores. Their Army boots rarely fitted comfortably. They were made in a few standard sizes, and a man was lucky if he got a pair that were neither too big nor too small. To march all day in them with blistered feet must have been a torment. The Army socks were hard and filthy through wearing them night and day. There was nothing you could do for these poor men but get the medical orderly to give them some ointment to rub in. Most of them needed at least a week of careful attention, but we had passed the point of no return. The medical officer could send a man down only if he had completely collapsed and could no longer stand.

There was no mechanical transport in those days. A few mule-drawn wagons carried the cooking utensils and spare equipment, but the men marched like beasts of burden with heavy packs on their backs, rifles and bandoliers of ammunition slung across their shoulders.

Sometimes they would break into a marching song to ease the misery, but now and then, as I marched at the head of my platoon, I would hear a clatter behind me and turn to see a man lying prostrate in the road.

The sergeants were instructed to prod them and order them to get up. There was always the possibility that the man had decided that he had taken as much as he could bear and had staged his collapse to get out of it. But most of them were genuine—down-and-out.

We arrived at last at a cluster of tin huts that was to be our camp until we went into the attack.

The great preliminary bombardment had begun. We were surrounded by batteries of artillery, and for three nights it was bedlam. It had now begun to rain. Some people said that the artillery fire brought down the rain, but it was probably just bad luck. The generals had planned the attack for August and naturally reckoned that the weather would be good. But for three nights and days it rained incessantly, and the ground became a quagmire.

Living conditions in our camp were sordid beyond belief. The cookhouse was flooded, and most of the food was uneatable. There was nothing but sodden biscuits and cold stew. The cooks tried to supply bacon for breakfast, but the men complained that it "smelled like dead men."

The latrines consisted of buckets with wet planks for the men to sit on, but there weren't enough of them. Something had given the men diarrhea. They would grope out of their shelters, flounder helplessly in the mud, and relieve themselves anywhere. Some of the older men, worn out by the long marching and wretched food, were sick. They would come groping out of their shelters, lean their heads against the corrugated iron walls, and stand there retching and vomiting and groaning. Then they would go back to their huts and lie on the damp straw with their canvas packs for pillows.

These were the men who were to break through the German lines, advance into Belgium, and win the war.

In contrast with this human misery, there was something grand and awe-inspiring in that tremendous cannonade of guns. If you stood out there at night, you would see the whole surrounding country lit with thousands of red stabs of flame as salvo after salvo went screaming overhead.

By the end of the third day of ceaseless rain everything in reason and humanity called for the attack to be postponed. It was an effort to walk around among our huts. At every step you went up to your ankles in mud. What it would be like in the forward battle area we dared not think.

Our one hope, until the last, was that the attack would be called off. But the generals went on.

At dawn on the morning of the attack the battalion assembled in the mud outside the huts. I lined up my platoon and went through the necessary inspection. Some of the men looked terribly ill: gray, worn faces in the dawn, unshaved and dirty because there was no clean water. I saw that characteristic shrugging of their shoulders that I knew so well. They hadn't had their clothes off for weeks, and their shirts were full of lice.

Our battalion was to be in the second wave of the attack. The first wave, we understood, was to go over soon after dawn and advance to certain defined positions. We were to follow, move through their positions, and capture the next objective about a half mile farther on. A third wave was to follow us and so on.

It must have looked fine in the planning room at Army head-quarters, but unfortunately, we had been told nothing at all. The officers had been served out with maps that covered a wide area of Belgian towns and villages miles behind the German lines, but as things turned out, we got only about 500 yards.

Our progress to the battle area was slow and difficult. We had to move forward in single file along duckboard tracks that were loose and slimy. If you slipped off, you went up to your knees in mud.

During that walk the great bombardment from the British guns fell silent. For days it had wracked our nerves and destroyed our sleep. The sudden silence was uncanny. A sort of stagnant empti-ness surrounded us. Your ears still sang from the incessant uproar, but now your mouth went dry. As an orchestral overture dies away in a theater as the curtain rises, so the great bombardment faded into silence as the infantry went into the attack. We knew now that the first wave had left the British front-line trenches, that we were soon to follow.

When we reached the old, deserted front line, the battalion was deployed along it.

Ahead of us was what had been the no-man's-land between the two contending armies: a horrible desert of twisted wire and churned-up mud.

The newspapers, to keep up morale at home, would describe the moment of attack in dramatic, inspiring words: a line of stalwart, resolute soldiers, burning to go like greyhounds on the leash, impatient for the word to leap out of the trenches and charge forward with a cheer.

It wasn't quite like that with our exhausted, dejected men. All of us, I knew, had one despairing hope in mind: that we should be lucky enough to be wounded, not fatally, but severely enough to take us out of this loathsome ordeal and get us home. But when we looked out across that awful slough ahead of us, even the thought of a wound was best forgotten. If you were badly hit, unable to move, what hope was there of being carried out of it? The stretcher-bearers were valiant men; but there were far too few of them, and no stretcher-bearers could carry wounded men across that shell-churned mud.

The order came to advance. There was no dramatic leap out of the trenches. The sandbags on the parapet were so slimy with rain and rotten with age that they fell apart when you tried to grip them. You had to crawl out through a slough of mud. Some of the older men, less athletic than the others, had to be heaved out bodily.

From then the whole thing became a drawn-out nightmare. There were no tree stumps or ruined buildings ahead to help you keep direction. The shelling had destroyed everything. As far as you could see, it was like an ocean of thick brown porridge. The wire entanglements had sunk into the mud, and frequently, when you went in up to the knees, your legs would come out with strands of barbed wire clinging to them, and your hands were torn and bleeding through the struggle to drag them off.

The enemy began to send over heavy shells called coalboxes. Fired from away behind the German lines, they came down almost perpendicularly and exploded with a thunderous crash and a huge cloud of thick black smoke.

All this area had been desperately fought over in the earlier battles of Ypres. Many of the dead had been buried where they fell, and the shells were unearthing and tossing up the decayed bodies. You would see them flying through the air and disintegrating. It was a warm, humid day, and the stench was horrible.

We began to see the relics of the first wave of the attack. It had apparently been caught in machine-gun fire. Most of the dead men had rolled down into the waterlogged shell holes and lay grotesquely sprawled like broken wax dolls, drained of blood by the stagnant water.

We came to the shattered trenches of the German front line. According to plan, the first attacking wave should by now have reached its objective about half a mile ahead, but it was soon clear that barely a remnant of that doomed first wave had got there.

In the old German trench we came upon a long line of men, some lolling on the fire step, some sprawled on the ground, some standing upright, leaning against the trench wall. They were British soldiers—all dead or dying. Their medical officer had set up a first-aid station here, and these wounded men had crawled to the trench for his help. But the doctor and his orderlies had been killed by a shell that had wrecked his station, and the wounded men could only sit or lie there and die. There was no conceivable hope of carrying them away.

We came at last to some of the survivors of the first wave. They had reached what had once been the German support line, still short of their objective. An officer said, "I've got about fifteen men here. I started with a hundred. I don't know where the Germans are." . . . He pointed vaguely out across the land ahead. "They're somewhere out there. They've got machine guns, and you can see those masses of unbroken wire. It's useless to go on. The best you can do is to bring your men in and hold this line with us."

The plans laid down for the attack had apparently made no allowance for a setback or emergency. They were based on the assumption that when a general pressed a button, the whole thing would go like clockwork. The first men who land on the moon will undoubtedly be in better touch with the men on earth than we were with the generals who had sent us into this catastrophe. In theory the engineers were to lay telegraph wires through which Morse signals could be transmitted, but the engineers had got bogged down or killed. We were completely isolated. The only communication with the rear was to scribble messages in notebooks and give them to orderlies to take back. But the orderlies wouldn't have the faintest idea where the nearest command post was, even if they survived.

We found an old German shelter and brought into it all our wounded that we could find. We carried pocket first-aid dressings, but the small pads and bandages were useless on great gaping wounds. You did what you could, but it was mainly a matter of watching them slowly bleed to death. Even if there had been stretcher-bearers, it would have been impossible to carry them to safety.

It came to an end for me sometime that afternoon. For an hour or more we waited in that old German trench. Sometimes a burst of machine-gun bullets whistled overhead, as if the Germans were saying, "Come on if you dare."

Our company commander had made his headquarters under a few sheets of twisted corrugated iron.

"I want you to explore along this trench," he said to me, "and see whether you can find B Company. They started off on our right flank, but I haven't seen anything of them since. If you can find them, we can link up together and get some sort of order into things."

So I set off with my runner. It was like exploring the mountains

of the moon. We followed the old trench as best we could but ha.
to crawl across the blown in gaps. There were small concrete block-
houses here and there called pillboxes that the Germans built when
the swampy country prevented dugouts.

The Germans were now shelling us with whizbangs—light shells
fired at comparatively short range with a low trajectory. It was a
soldier's legend that you never heard the shell coming that was
going to hit you, but I know from firsthand experience that you
did. We heard the report of it being fired, and we heard the thin
whistle of its approach, rising to a shriek. It landed on top of a
concrete pillbox that we were passing, barely five yards away. A few
yards farther, and it would have been the end of us. The crash was
deafening. My runner let out a yell of pain. I didn't yell so far as I
know because I was half-stunned. I remember putting my hand to
the right side of my face and feeling nothing; to my horror I
thought that the whole side had been blown away.

Afterward, with time to think in the hospital, I pieced the thing
together. The light shell, hitting the solid concrete top of the
pillbox had sent its splinters upward, mercifully above our heads;
but it had sent a ferocious spattering of pulverized concrete in all
directions, and that was what we got.

How badly we were wounded we didn't know. We were covered
with blood and mud. All that mattered was that we were still on
our feet, with our wits about us, and we stumbled back the way we
had come. The company commander took one look at us and said,
"Get back as best you can, and find a dressing station."

We began the long trek back, floundering through the mud,
through the stench and black smoke of the coalboxes that were still
coming over. Here and there were other walking wounded, mainly
in pairs, supporting themselves pitifully with arms around each
other's shoulders. Many were so badly wounded that they could
barely drag themselves along, but to save themselves was their only
hope. There was no one else to save them. How many survived I
didn't know. We saw some fall and lie prostrate in the mud. We
could only hope that they went on again when they had rested.

It seemed hours before we reached a dressing station, then only
by a lucky chance. It was a ramshackle tin shelter amid a dump of
sandbags that once had been a gun emplacement.

The doctor was treating anybody who managed to find his way
there. A lot of men were lying around, and some stretcher-bearers
were sorting out the living from the dead. The doctor swabbed the
wounds on our hands and faces and tried to see through the holes in

s where pieces had gone in. "You don't seem to have
very deep," he said. "Can you go on?"

practically down-and-out, from exhaustion as much as
wounds. But anything was better than staying in that
arnage. We said we could, and he told us the way to the
ld hospital—another mile or more beyond. It was nearly
n we saw at last the subdued glimmer of lights in the tents
where the wounded were receiving their first proper attention. It
must have been six hours since we were hit. We had come on our
feet at least 5 miles, but we were among the lucky ones.

Back at the base hospital, with the aid of probes and tweezers, a
doctor took fifty-two pieces of concrete out of me—all about the size
of beans or peas. "Fifty-two pieces," he said, "one for every week of
the year!" He wrapped them in a piece of lint and gave them to me
as a souvenir.

I needed no souvenir to remind me of the monstrous disgrace of
Passchendaele. It was proof, if proof were needed, that the generals
had lost all touch with reality.

Passchendaele was the fruit of more than two years of experience
that had shown beyond all doubt that you couldn't break through
the German defenses with the weapons available or with the tactics
employed.

But even after that dreadful start the generals went on with it for
weeks, losing about 10,000 men a day. And all they had to show for
it was another dent in the German line that didn't get them
anywhere.

But I have to tell about the public school boy officers and the part
they played.

The offensives staged by the generals were like the spasmodic
eruptions of a volcano that smoldered on in the long months
between.

It smoldered in the trenches, and it was there that the foundations were laid for the final victory.

The trenches were the bulwark. Even when the big attacks were
on, the whole line had to be garrisoned and held, and the British
Army was responsible for more than 100 miles of it.

The winters were merciless, but trench life in summer and good
weather was tolerable if the generals left us alone. All you needed
in this garrison work was endurance, patience, and a ceaseless
watchfulness, protecting the men from unnecessary risk and exposure.

But the generals couldn't see it that way. They were obsessed
with the idea that we should keep up the "offensive spirit." We

always had to be firing mortar shells or rifle grenades at the German trenches that were usually not more than 100 yards away across no-man's-land. The Germans were prepared to live and let live and kept quiet if we kept quiet, but naturally, if we fired at them, they fired back. They had a more destructive mortar shell than ours—a huge missile called a *Minenwerfer*. It was shot high into the air and came down with sparks spluttering out the back. If it fell in the trench, it would blow a crater about 10 yards wide, and hours would be spent in repairing it. If it hit a shelter where men were sleeping, it would blow them to pieces, and we rarely came out of our spell in the front line without the loss of several good men.

This business of keeping up the offensive spirit in static trench garrison work was senseless and wasteful. In those four years along 100 miles of trenches we must have lost thousands of men for no purpose at all.

We lost, I am sure, far more men than the Germans did. The German command had organized the structure of deep dugouts in which the men off duty could rest in peace and safety. But the British command had no use for deep dugouts. They considered them contrary to the offensive spirit, that the men would grow soft and enervated and think too much of safety, rather than attack.

So we had to spend our time off duty in shelters dug out of the sides of the trenches—nothing but a few corrugated iron sheets above us, with a single covering of sandbags. The only times we could rest with any assurance of safety was when we held trenches that had been captured from the Germans and could benefit from their fine, deep dugouts.

The trouble was that trench warfare bored the British high command. It wasn't warfare as they had been trained to understand it. It gave them no opportunity to exercise their skill in tactics and maneuver, from which they had gained distinction in African and Indian campaigns gone by. Trench warfare was a tiresome, but unavoidable, necessity when they were planning their next big offensive, and they took as little personal interest in it as possible.

I was in and out of the front-line trenches for a year and saw a general only once. That was on a day when the divisional commander came around. It happened that we had been through a bad night of continuous shell and mortar fire. We were very tired and dirty, and there was something incongruous, almost ludicrous, in the sight of that extraordinary old man, beautifully spruced up in his well-cut tunic, riding breeches, and immaculately polished boots. He had rows of medal ribbons from past campaigns, a light blue armlet, and the emblem of his rank emblazoned upon his polished tin hat. He looked like a man on his way to a fancy dress party.

He stopped and glared fiercely at me. I remember he had a lot of hairs bristling in his nostrils. He fixed me with his eyes as if to instill a bit more offensive spirit in me and went on without a word. He complained to our colonel that some of the men looked dirty and unshaved and went on his way, never to be seen by us again.

Such episodes like this built up in the minds of the fighting soldiers a conviction that the generals cared nothing about the war that the rank and file were fighting and were running their own exclusive war of fantasy, dragging in the fighting men as pawns and cannon fodder.

There had been widespread mutinies in the French Army that suffered, it seemed, from generals no better than ours, and it may be wondered why there was never a murmur of revolt among the British infantry in the face of such indifference and disregard for their well-being and their lives.

Without raising the public school boy officers onto a pedestal it can be said with certainty that it was they who played the vital part in keeping the men good-humored and obedient in the face of their interminable ill treatment and well-nigh insufferable ordeals.

The colonels of battalions were mainly professional soldiers, survivors of the old Regular Army. They were good men who shared the hardships of the fighting soldier. But the junior officers— the commanders of companies and lieutenants in charge of platoons —were predominantly from the public schools, and it was they who lived in close personal touch with the soldiers in the ranks. They led them, not through military skill, for no military skill was needed. They led them from personal example, from their reserves of patience and good humor and endurance. They won the trust and respect of their men, not merely through their willingness to share the physical privations, but through an understanding of their spiritual loneliness. Many of the younger ones had never been away from home before. Their lives had been spent in a simple and secluded way with their parents, young brothers and sisters, a few intimate friends from the neighborhood who shared their interests and recreations, including perhaps the girl they were courting. They knew little or nothing of the world beyond, and they found no true comradeship with the strange men that the war had chosen for them to serve with. They were desperately homesick, with a pathetic yearning for their own people in the towns and villages of England.

These boys were only happy, perhaps, when they were on sentry duty alone, with the moon and the stars for their companions. It was the duty of the officer on watch to visit these sentry posts. If you could break through their shyness, they would sometimes talk to you of their homes, and you could lead them on to tell you of their work and small achievements, their hopes and ambitions if, one day, they returned. You might be able to help them see a glimmer of light at the end of the dark tunnel that enclosed them.

It was on such quiet nights of communion between man and officer that the foundations of final victory were laid, not in the planning rooms at Army headquarters. And it was in this way that the public school boy officer could play so true a part.

When a man surrendered himself to the Army machine, his individuality was exchanged for a number. When he put on his uniform and wrapped up his civilian clothes, he wrapped up with them his personal initiative and the right to think. "Think!" shouted a sergeant to a recruit who had had the effrontery to use the word. "For a common soldier it's mutiny to think!"

But the common soldier naturally expected something in return for all that he surrendered. He expected leadership, an officer who thought for him—better still, an officer who thought with him.

The general had lost all personal touch with the common soldier. He lived in a remote French chateau miles behind the line. The soldiers never saw him, never even knew his name. If some of them had come around the trenches, talked to the men in their dugouts, made the men realize that they all were in it together, then they might have become legendary heroes, as men like Montgomery and Alexander became to the soldiers of the Second World War. As it was, the generals gave nothing to the common soldier to gain his respect or affection. They were a menace lurking in the background, always concocting a new devil's brew with the same old poisonous ingredients.

And so the common soldier turned instinctively to his own company officers for the leadership that he required, to the young officers who lived with him and talked to him as a human being like themselves and helped him hold onto a shred of pride and self-respect.

Fortunately, the great majority of these young officers were worthy of the trust imposed on them. If they had behaved, in miniature, as the generals behaved, then God knows what would have happened in the end.

In those days, in England, there were class distinctions that everyone recognized and accepted without resentment so long as they were not abused. In civilian life the humble workman was content to obey a foreman who had risen from his own class so long as the boss was socially a cut above the foreman.

By the same token, a common soldier would obey the sergeants and the sergeants major who had risen from the ranks, but when it came to his officer, commissioned by the King, he expected something more. What it was he could never have defined in words. But if the officer had it, then the soldier instinctively recognized it, and that indefinable something was what was instilled into a boy at the public school.

It had nothing to do with wealth or privilege. Very few of the public school boys came from the landed gentry or distinguished families. For the most part they came from modest homes, the sons of local lawyers, doctors, or schoolmasters—hardworking professional men. Some were the sons of country clergymen who lived on the verge of poverty and sold their precious family heirlooms for the money to send their boy to a public school.

Too often the sacrifice was in vain. The Army ordained that officers should wear distinctive tunics, cut differently from the private soldier. When they led an attack, this made it easy for the Germans to pick them out and shoot them down before they turned their attention to the men. At the Battle of the Somme, thirty young officers went in with our battalion, and only four survived.

These public school boy officers were not soldiers in the ordinary meaning of the word. Very few of them would have wanted to stay on in the Army when the war was done. They only wanted to get the thing over and return to the jobs they had planned to do. But while the thing was on, they did their best, not realizing at the time what a vital part they were playing. The common soldier liked them because they were "young swells," and with few exceptions the young swells delivered the goods.

Charles Edmund Carrington

CHARLES EDMUND CARRINGTON, *born in England but brought up in New Zealand, ran away from school and joined Kitchener's army. He was a volunteer from the first month to the last in both world wars. After graduating from Oxford, he was for some years a schoolmaster; then, removing to Cambridge, he spent his professional career as a publisher, on the staff of the University Press. His first book,* A Subaltern's War *(1929), appeared under the pen name of Charles Edmonds. A reaction against the modish pacifism of that time, it was more extensively reviewed than sold. Thirty years later, using his own name, he rewrote and enlarged it with the title* Soldier from the Wars Returning.

He traveled widely, for business and pleasure, especially in the countries of the British Commonwealth, on which he has written much. His British Overseas *came out in 1950. He contributed to Lord Hailey's* African Survey, *to the* Cambridge History of the British Empire, *to the Chatham House Surveys of International Affairs, and to other such works. He wrote the authorized biography of Kipling, reviewed for the* Times Literary Supplement, *and lectured in many countries for the British Council. For seven years he was a research professor at Chatham House, the Royal Institute of International Affairs, and he has also been a visiting professor in America. His only indisputable best seller is a school history of England.*

Describing himself as the "unpropagandable" man, he is frequently found on the unfashionable side in public controversies. Happily married, he lives, retired, in London.

SOME SOLDIERS

A YEAR OR TWO AGO, my wife and I fell into a motoring mis-
adventure when driving through Sicily. It was no great matter, and
it was a relief to find that the gesticulating crowd of Italians who
surrounded us were on our side, taking the view that the other
driver had been at fault. While I was trying to justify myself in
tourist phrases, I heard someone who seemed to be saying, "Send for
Giuseppe. He speaks English." There came out of a shop a man of
my own age, with square shoulders and a look in his eye that I
understood. "You're an old soldier, I think," said I; and then, in a
louder voice, "Sono combattente della prima guerra, io, sull' Altipi-
ano di Asiago." It may not have been good Italian, but it was
enough. The name of the Asiago Plateau worked like a charm,
softening his face into smiles, and I knew that I had made a friend.
He took my affairs in hand, settled with the other driver, placated
the police, and would not let us go until he had regaled us in a
wineshop.

Why do the battles of the First World War evoke such sentiments? Why did this common memory form so immediate a bond
between me and this elderly Italian, in a society that has—very
reasonably—forgotten the battles of Asiago? Of course, this is not a
new factor in history, which abounds with evidence of old bores
talking about old fights. In this instance it is a universal phenomenon to be observed in the whole generation of Western men
who were young between 1914 and 1918, so widespread that to this
day some of my contemporaries are a little ashamed to admit that
they were not in the trenches, even if they had an adequate excuse.
There is no tradition like this from the Second World War, when
no one knew who was on active service. In 1944 the man in uniform
might be a clerk, living in comfort and safety, while the man, or
woman, in civilian clothes might be a hero of the Resistance or the
Blitz. But among survivors of the earlier war, you were either in it
or out of it, and the password—Asiago, for example—will quickly
reveal your genuine status.

We may bore you with our anecdotage, but we don't bore one
another. If an outsider should crash one of our reunions, his

imposture is revealed as soon as the conversation moves into the jargon of names and half-hints and allusions which cannot be counterfeited, which defy the interpretations given by young historians when they write about the First World War today. We are still an initiate generation, possessing a secret that can never be communicated.

We have not suffered more than other men; we have not been struck harder blows by fate; we have not been more self-sacrificing; and are not more bloodthirsty. Our characteristic is that we were all put to the same test; all exposed our strength and weakness to the same public gaze; all, when young, rejected the illusions about life and death that some men nourish in old age. Twenty million of us, of whom perhaps 2,000,000 are still alive, shared the experience with one another but with no one else, and are what we are because, in that war, we were soldiers. There are many such dedicated societies in the world, but no other, so far as I know, which comprises a whole age group of the able-bodied men, while excluding other age groups and the other sex. Why else, after fifty years, have we written this book?

I never meet an "old sweat," as we liked to describe ourselves, who accepts or enjoys the figure in which we are now presented, though it is useless—undignified—to protest. Just smile and make an old soldier's wry joke when you see yourself on the television screen, agonized and woebegone, trudging from disaster to disaster, knee-deep in moral as well as physical mud, hesitant about your purpose, submissive to a harsh, irrelevant discipline, mistrustful of your commanders. Is it any use to assert that I was not like that, and my dead friends were not like that, and the old cronies that I meet at reunions are not like that? But as for what they were and are, I'm sorry, I can't explain. Is it worthwhile to write once more about a subject on which a later generation has made up its mind? Let me try to reconstruct some portraits of soldiers, in the figure they cut, fifty years ago, when I was young and impressionable, and let me begin at the top.

Kitchener meant as much to the British in 1914 as Churchill meant in 1940, and his direct achievement was greater. No account has yet been written of the complete revolution in the national life which he carried out almost single-handed. In his first month of office, with no precedents, no staff, no political machine behind him, no authority over organized labor, no national registration, no tradition of compulsory service, but, on the other hand, a deep-rooted suspicion of militarism to overcome, Kitchener envisaged and planned the recruiting, officering, arming, equipping, and training, of a new army of thirty divisions. At the same time, he doubled the strength of the Regular Army in France, doubled the Territorial Army so that half of it could be released for service abroad, and mustered the armies from the Dominions. After a year of war he had forty British divisions in action, most of them new formations. The Americans, with all the British experience to improve upon, had only managed to get one Regular Army division into battle at the end of their first year of war.

Kitchener has been ill served by his biographers, who concentrate on the political intrigues in which he became enmeshed at the end of his life and say little of this creative task which has no parallel in British history, perhaps none in any history. Inevitably, he made mistakes, but as he used to say, "No one has ever made war who has not made mistakes." All Kitchener's men were volunteers and had been warned by him at the beginning that the war would be long and hard—three years at least. Neither he nor they nourished illusions about what they were in for. No doubt, when we were young, we indulged in fantasies about this father figure, nor need we be surprised when a maturer knowledge reveals that, like you or me, he had weaknesses and inconsistencies. When he died, and the whole Army went into mourning, we felt the loss. Has any general accomplished greater things? But no legend can make him a lovable figure, as Churchill was. We never supposed that it could.

Kitchener's army was our university; never again have I experienced such enthusiasm, so firm an impulse to overcome obstacles and improvise substitutes when every military requirement was lacking, to persevere with our training for the crusade, having no desire so strong as that of forcing our way overseas and into it. Meanwhile, leave all else to Kitchener, who would provide everything in due course—as Kitchener did.

No great knowledge of the world was needed to appreciate that his 3,000,000 volunteers included as high a proportion of pretentious, corrupt, and silly rogues and fools as any other random group of 3,000,000 human beings or that some of the least deserving would quickly ensconce themselves in places where they could exploit their talent for imposing upon simpler and better men. But I never came across a glorification of war; I heard no bloodthirsty sermons by militant clergy; I remember no invocations of the joys of battle; I was never in the company of Regular soldiers who talked, as French soldiers did, of *la Gloire* and *la Patrie*. All that would have been called "damned bad form" in the British Army. We were deadly serious about our assignment, without finding a necessity of often saying so, and there seemed no reason why we should not have fun when off duty, since we expected to die tomorrow.

If I had studied military matters I should have known, in 1914, that Sir Douglas Haig had been already selected by Haldane, the most able War Minister Britain has ever known, as the general with a future, our most thoughtful and proficient soldier. His chronicler has done his reputation no good by publishing extracts from his private diaries which reveal a grudging, critical, streak in his nature. A self-effacing man, he never supposed that the course of action to which he stubbornly devoted himself would be advanced by a display of exhibitionism. Perhaps his cold logistic theory of command needed the corrective that was applied in the next war, by such flamboyant generals as Patton and Montgomery. So confident was Haig, so assured of his professional mastery, that his mind, once made up, moved slowly. He lacked that brilliant, imaginative coup d'oeil which distinguishes genius from mere talent, and the plain fact that he was no Napoleon obscures what should be equally plain, that his tactics, appalling as they seem, won the war. In the dreadful campaigns of attrition, Haig at last achieved his object, whereas the German generals, who planned similar battles, could never reach a decisive victory, even when they had all the material advantages. Battles are won by margins, and there was a marginal quantum lacking in the German high command. Haig's superiority was the moral factor which always prevails in war.

It is hard to forgive him for not going to examine the battlefield of Passchendaele for himself, but it was his stated policy to leave tactical decisions to the man on the spot. I myself saw Haig in a front-line village on the Somme and was mightily impressed to know that he had made my sector his personal concern; it was not his custom. We all knew that at Ypres in 1914 he had ridden forward through the Menin Gate to take command at the crisis of the battle, but he was then a corps commander, and we knew other corps commanders who had lamentably failed at such crises.

Civilians misunderstand the ribaldry of soldiers, who commonly rail against their commanders, as the Continental Army did against Washington, and make scurrilous songs about them as the legions did about Caesar. Since all war is a chaotic improvisation, a continuous process of trial and error, in which the forfeits are paid with blood, generals must speculate with men's lives and cannot expect to be thanked for their lost wagers. Wellington once said (though he never lost a battle) that a victory is the greatest tragedy in the world except a defeat.

As I remember, the corps commander, whom we sometimes saw at a safe distance, and the divisional commander, whom we often saw, lived in a cold shower of critical comment, blamed for everything that went wrong. Haig's name, somehow, was not vilified, and if it had been, his army would not have survived to win the hardfought Battle of the Hindenburg Line, the tactical blow that brought Germany to its knees, in September, 1918.

I saw Haig lead the victory procession in London, through cheering crowds who left no doubt that he was still their hero. The anti-Haig reaction sprang up at a later date, mostly among the postwar generation.

Bless my soul! I could tell you some tales about bad generals, while trying to allow for the fact that neither you nor I have any experience of the strains to which generals are exposed. It will make a change to write about a good general—good, that is, as generals go.

Sir Robert Fanshawe commanded the 48th Division throughout the three campaigns that I served in it. He was about as unlike as one could be to that bloated figure, so dear to the funny men, the stereotype of a British general. A thin sandy-haired little fellow in his fifties, with a quiet pleasant voice, he often reminded me of Chaucer's Knight. We called him Fanny, "and in his port he meek was as a maid"; but a soldier from an Army family, he had fought in Africa and India, and his recreations were given in the books of reference as fox hunting and pigsticking. He always "gave tongue" at staff conferences, he once told me, and was no sooner allotted a command than he pestered G.H.Q. to allow him to attack. His plan was duly pigeonholed by the staff as "Fanny's First Play," since they knew their man. He spent more days in the front line than any man in his command and always followed up the attack behind the leading troops, assuring questioners that it was the safest place in battle. He would drift unobtrusively into a trench, wearing an old raincoat over his decorations, would ply the sentry with chocolate or beef cubes, and would listen to complaints before making his comment. "You say you are uncomfortable here. The Germans over there have very good dugouts. You can go and take them as soon as you like." But he never set his men impossible tasks, never fell into the classic error of generals in all armies of those days, the tendency to press on with an attack long after the opportunity of victory had slipped away. He and his brother, also a general, were knighted by the King on the field of battle, side by side, something that hadn't happened since the Middle Ages.

Colonel Sladen was a big-game hunter from East Africa, the best-dressed man in the regiment, and my hero. Once, in Kenya, he came on three lions over a kill; bagged two of them with a right and left; dropped his rifle; and photographed the third as it ran away. I thought well of that. I was with him twice in situations of real combat, learning to rely on his instant decisions. One cold night I came in late to report at his headquarters, with a fighting patrol, wet through and exhausted.

"See that your men get their rum ration," said the colonel.

"Sorry, sir, there's no rum ration."

He thought for a moment, then called his servant, who brought out a case of whisky, obtained with no little bother for his own mess. It was precious as molten gold.

"How many men? Fifty? Share six bottles among them."

Soldiers never forget a thing like that.

But, then, I have to think of Jim Aldridge, a quiet sensible efficient man. "Higher Authority," that formidable phantom, had decreed that neglect of rifles and rifle shooting was the bane of the Army and must be rigorously punished, a doctrine that no one held more firmly than the colonel.

I was young and knew no better, not even that Jim Aldridge was an exemplary soldier. I "crimed" him for having a dirty rifle on sentry duty and, though the sergeant swore it was an unheard-of event, the colonel was liverish, that morning, and inflicted a savage sentence of field punishment. The horror of this was that Jim, who had already been a year in France, lost his turn for home leave. His name went down to the bottom of the list and did not come up again for nine months, when he joined the last batch of men who for one reason or another had been held back. As they left the trenches, on their way home after so long a delay, Jim Aldridge was killed by a chance shot. I still feel bad about this, though he never seemed to bear me any malice.

For about nine months, Captain Edward Hawke (or that is what I shall call him) commanded the company, and I was his second-in-command. One or the other of us would be detached for special duty sometimes or allowed on leave for a spell, but mainly, we lived together, eating at the same rough board and sleeping in a hut or cave, smaller than a convict's cell, with two or three others who came and went, after a short trench life. We were jolly, as a rule, smoked too much, played cards, drank a little—if there was anything to drink—and often quarreled furiously. Though, by the laws of probability, one or both of us should have been killed, we're very much alive today. He was a year or two older than I, perhaps twenty-one, and—as I now see—was a great deal less silly. (What children we were! I don't set much store by the wisdom of the teen-agers.) I learned how to keep him sweet, chiefly by finding in the canteen the brand of marmalade he liked for breakfast. And what I remember best of that long winter in the trenches is snuggling round a charcoal stove in the dugout, singing. We had a large repertoire of drawing-room ballads, "nigger minstrel" songs, musical numbers from the revues then playing in London, folk songs, and the bawdy old soldier's catches that run right back to the eighteenth-century wars. Then a noise would break out or a sweating runner would arrive in the trench with a message from headquarters, and the fun would stop. "Sorry, it's your turn, Carrie," Hawke would say—this was long before the day of easy Christian naming. "You've got to take a patrol out from the Z Hedge, and find out if there are any Boches in the Sixteen Poplars."

What a jab at the solar plexus, but neither he nor I must show the strain we were under, by a twitch of the lip or flicker of the eye. To release the slightest sign of emotion was to lose a point in the game we played, all day and all night. He was a better player than I was. Once, I remember—dare I say it even now—I quite broke down under shellfire, yammered and shook, till Hawke, just as frightened as I was, but a shade tougher, quieted my hysterics with one sharp word.

I first took note of him in a trench raid at Gommecourt Wood, shortly before the Somme, my first action. I had volunteered for the storming party and enjoyed the experience, though the raid was a bloody failure. Why else remember it or write about it now? In front of us, the demolition party blew a hole through the first belt of barbed wire with explosives, then tried to clip their way through the second belt of barbed wire with wire cutters. Behind them, Hawke and I lay, side by side in the gap, ready to rush in and kill as many Germans as we could find in the trench, before bringing back one or two live prisoners—not too many—as specimens to be examined by Intelligence. We never got through. After twenty minutes the wire was still impassable, while their guns were pounding the trench from which we had started, and a line of Germans was firing at us from 30 or 40 yards away. On one side of me a man, shot through the groin, was lugged away screaming, while his sergeant shouted at him to be quiet. As we were getting ready to retire, I saw a bullet strike Hawke's helmet with a shower of sparks, not 2 feet away from me. "Dead!" I thought, but he jumped up and ran back to our lines, bleeding and blaspheming. "They've shot my bloody ear off!" They had indeed. Somehow this seemed more like comedy

than tragedy, and we treated it as a joke when he came back to du
with no lobe to his ear. War was a rough game to be relished, if one
was young enough, in those days, and as the man shot through the
groin never came back, we soon forgot him.

Little Tich Bashford was the smallest man in the regiment, and
one of the most willing. How he got past the recruiting sergeant at
2 inches below the minimum height was as much a puzzle as how
some of us got past at two years below the minimum age. He didn't
say much, and he rarely smiled, but regarded me with a cold sus-
picious eye and silently did the same amount of work as men twice
his size. On one dark wet summer night, when we were digging a
communication trench up to the Thiepval Skyline, on the Somme,
we noticed that he was making slow progress. It was not the 8-inch
shells, falling at regular intervals that deterred him; it was the
tough, murky, malodorous task. Then someone showed a hooded
light that revealed his obstacle. He had dug his way resolutely
through a buried corpse, decapitating it with his spade. Even then
he had no words for his discovery.

I killed Tich Bashford, the only man I'm sure I've killed. Of
course, I've tried hard; I've charged with the bayonet and been the
first man in the trench, used a revolver once or twice, point-blank,
thrown half a dozen bombs in action, fired a machine gun, now and
then, at a distant target; but I was never a good shot. With Tich it
was different. When we attacked at Passchendaele, I chose four good
orderlies to stand by me and lost them all. One simply vanished and
was heard of no more; then there were three. We were stopped by a
group of Germans, shooting coolly from a shell hole, and when I
looked back for comfort, I saw another of my band lying gray-faced
and dead; only two left now, Tich Bashford and my servant,
Bradley, who was brandishing his bayonet and urging me, "Come
on, sir, let's go for the buggers." "No," say I, "get down and open
fire." Too late. Bashford is shot through the chest and staggers
about, roaring like a bull. (Little men often have big voices.) Then
Bradley falls, shot through the head. What can I do now? I can
think of nothing but relieving—and silencing—Bashford. I had a
tube of morphine tablets, bought from some shabby chemist in
Amiens, and, holding Bashford down, I gave him—one—two—three
—until, suddenly, he died under my hand. Then a supporting
platoon came up, and we got on with the battle.

We were searching the dugouts in a captured trench when the
first bomb landed in the fire bay above me. Did I run up from the
rabbit hole? I put my skates on. Away and back. "Get out of my
road, bayonet man, and let them run that can run." Back to the

ere grim old Corporal Patterson sat behind a barri-
e Rock of Gibraltar, with his hand clenched upon a
, my platoon could advance no farther, and here we
ppointed spot, our final objective. I distributed my
nd holes, choosing for myself the one with the best
there was already someone in possession.

ly German soldier I can now clearly visualize, among
some dozens of whom I caught a scared glimpse in battle, and the
only remembered corpse, among hundreds from which I turned
disdainfully away. After spending three or four tense hours in his
company, I had got to know him well, a tall, pale, plump, blond,
young Teuton of my own age or a little more. He lay as he had
fallen, in an attitude of running, struck by three shrapnel bullets in
the back—not running away but carrying a message, for in his hand
was a dirty scrap of paper on which three words were scribbled:
"die Engländer kommen." His gray eyes were open, and his mouth
showed strong white teeth. I looked on him and loved him. There
was no hostility between us, as there had been no malice when he
was alive. When the time came for us to withdraw, it was as if I had
lost a friend. I covered his face and—which seems hard to explain—I
brought away his Iron Cross ribbon for a memento. Robert Graves
had not yet introduced me to the notion of combat as a love-hate
relation.

From these sentiments I was distracted by Corporal Patterson,
who was in some physical trouble, which he unwillingly revealed.
All afternoon he had been gripping the safety lever of his bomb,
since he had pulled out the pin and couldn't get it back. White-
knuckled and with shaking fingers, he could hold no longer and
dared not throw the bomb which would "give away our position" to
the enemy. "Throw and be damned," I said. "We're off."

The return journey in the dusk was down 2 miles of battered
trench, under enemy observation and gunfire. Shellburst after
shellburst followed us along the valley, till something struck me a
blow on the shoulder and knocked me down. "I've got one," I said.
But Patterson felt me all over and pronounced me unhurt; it was
no more than a clod of earth that had numbed my right arm. We
staggered at last into what we thought a safe trench, where I had
time to total up the day's account.

"Why, it's Sunday," I said. "What a way to spend a Sunday!"

"Only lost one man from my section," said Corporal Patterson.
"It's enough to mak a mon believe in releegion."

The only live enemy I ever loved was an Austrian journalist,
Richard Bermann, who wrote novels under the name of Arnold

Höllriegel. He was through the war from beginning to end, on the eastern and western fronts, mostly as a reporter for the *Berliner Tageblatt*. When we met in later times, we never disagreed on politics or on the anomalies of a soldier's life, and his sardonic tales about staff officers were just like mine. Whatever was the nature of the trap we had been caught in, it was the same trap, and the Germans had endured it with the same rough humor. (Not at all like that unreal civilian's fantasy of the back areas, *All Quiet on the Western Front*.)

A young soldier friend of Bermann's was lying wounded in hospital when the sergeant came round with a clerk to complete the records. "Name? Regimental number? Profession in civil life?" What was he to say, having left school, like me, to join the Army?

"Philosopher," he suggested.

"What's that?"

"Philosopher."

The sergeant looked fiercely at the hesitant clerk. "Yes. Philosopher. There is such a thing. Write it down."

My philosophy, and the young German's, which did not probe deeper than an Epicurean acceptance of our world as it was, generated no self-pity.

Richard Bermann was a little older than us and much more worldly. He told me many tales of the trenches from the other side, which he regarded with a sophisticated eye, having known the upper world as well as our underworld. He had seen the funeral of the Emperor Franz Joseph; and had suffered the indignities heaped on the delegates of the defeated powers at Versailles; and had watched two regiments of Polish patriots, one fighting on the Austrian, the other on the Russian side, march into action against each other, both singing the same Polish national song. His romantic tales of cavalry skirmishes by moonlight in the Rumanian snows and his cynical account of Austrian archdukes served to round out my picture of a world that was dying. I had no doubts, in those days, that to wrench Central Europe into the twentieth century by force was a justifiable war aim. But this picturesque absurdity was to give way to something worse. I cannot bear to let my mind rest on Richard Bermann, that tubby, comical, little man, who looked more Jewish than he was. He died in Auschwitz, by tortures that I would rather not imagine.

On the old war memorials one sometimes read the words *"dulce et decorum est pro patria mori."* Once in the war, when I had nothing better to do, I thought of brushing up an interrupted

even to the extent of trying to read Latin, since Horace,
ser, had interested me at fifteen years old. What did he
his famous tag? How far was his tongue stuck in his cheek?
or one's country brings delight as well as honor." Well!
rooke had said much the same to my own generation. I

> dulce et decorum est pro patria mori
> mors et fugacem persequitur virum,
> nec parcit imebllis iuventae
> poplitibus timidove tergo.

I have been trying to translate these verses for nearly sixty years.
That second line can hardly come into less than two of English:

> He who fights and runs away
> Lives to die another day.

How feeble a rendering of *fugacem virum,* for the blond German,
struck dead while running. Horace had a word for him, and having
disposed of the brave soldiers and the cowards with a right- and left-
hander, he dismissed the pacifists with a kick on the arse, the
"trembling backside." Let me put it more politely.

> In the cause of your country you die with delight,
> But Death's still at your heels if you run from the fight;
> Even pacifist youngsters no mercy will find,
> When shamefully stricken by Death from behind.

Read on again. We have not yet come to the end.

> est et fideli tuta silentio
> merces. . . .

Heroes and cowards die the same death, and the literary men who
agonize about one or the other sort die after them. Perhaps silence
is best. "And," says Horace (who ran away from the Battle of
Philippi) , "and, honest silence brings a sure reward." "Blab," says
Horace, "and you shan't step into the same boat as me. Tell no
more about the blood-soaked earth. Reveal its secrets and you
expose only your own folly."

René Naegelen

RENÉ NAEGELEN, who is married and has three children, was born at Belfort in eastern France, on August 27, 1894. His father and mother were natives of Alsace, but they left their village in order to escape the German occupation. The youngest in a family of seven, René Naegelen was compelled to leave school at the age of fourteen. His parents then decided that he should be apprenticed as a pastry cook. When he was still a sensitive boy, he saw in his father's bakery housewives buying their daily bread on credit. He also saw workmen in wooden shoes going to the local mills before daybreak and not leaving work until night. He saw families reduced to misery by disease, and he was aware of the harshness of working conditions in France at the turn of the century. From his early adolescence his observation of social inequalities prompted him to join labor unions and the Socialist movement. His whole life has been devoted to the cause of the underdog. As early as 1913 he was already recognized as the leader of the Belfort branch of the Socialists.

In August, 1914, when the Kaiser's Germany triggered off the First World War, France called on all her sons. Twice wounded and seven times mentioned in dispatches, Sergeant Naegelen, who had been awarded the Médaille militaire (Military Cross), came back from the bloodbath more of a pacifist than ever, with the strong determination to defend his ideals. He founded a printing house, a newspaper, and a literary magazine and fought passionately against the abuses of capitalism. His revolutionary mystique led him to a four months' stay in Soviet Russia. There he met Lenin and Trotsky, interviewed the famous writer Maxim Gorky, and came into close contact with the Russian people.

He was bitterly disappointed when he came back from Moscow; the police dictatorship of the Soviets appeared to him a betrayal of Socialism, a form of bondage for the working classes, not the intended emancipation. From then on, René Naegelen was to oppose Communist despotism, as well as social conservatism.

He received as he gave. Being at once the owner of a pastry shop, a journalist, a writer, and a militant left-winger, René Naegelen meant to remain free in a free world. Therefore, he did not accept the fall of France in 1940; he joined the anti-Nazi underground, playing a dangerous and important role, *miraculously avoiding the clutches of the Gestapo. Made an officer of the Legion of Honor, he received the following statement of recognition from General Eisenhower: "The name of René Naegelen has been placed on record at the Supreme Headquarters of the Allied Expeditionary Force as being commended for brave conduct while acting under my orders in the liberation of his country, 1944–45."*

In 1946 he was elected to the French parliament on a Socialist ticket in the Belfort constituency. He resigned, however, to devote himself exclusively to journalism. From 1948 until 1965 he was the managing editor of Populaire de Paris, the Socialist Party daily paper. He considered the trust and affection placed in him by the prestigious President Léon Blum as the greatest honor in his life.

René Naegelen has written Les Suppliciés, an account of his own experiences in World War I, which was a best seller in 1927, Les Vacances du courage, and Cette Vie que j'aime (in three volumes), all of which attracted notice for their racy style and frankness. He was awarded the Louis Pergaud Prize and a prize from the Académie Française.

RECOLLECTIONS*

November 11, 1918. O God, fifty years have passed, half a century! On November 11, 1918, at 11 A.M. after five years of uninterrupted fighting, the last shell was fired, the last man was shot. Then our church bells chimed in unison, for peace was restored.

The First World War, which was to be the last of all wars, had been won! 1,400,000 of our men had perished. How many of our allies? And of the enemy?

Twenty years later, Poland, after Austria and Czechoslovakia, fell under the claws of demented Hitlerism; the sons of those who had fought in 1914–18, the sons of those who survived and of those who died, set out on a new war—five years again, and an even more frightful slaughter.

Having fallen in 1940, France was unfortunately to give up the fight, shrouded in her own defeat. If the free world overcame at all a form of barbarity incredible in our age, it was thanks to the almost desperate doggedness of Great Britain; thanks to the United

---

* Translated from the French by Hélène and François Marchessou.

States of America, whose colossal industry provided the "weapons for democracy" before she sailed across the Atlantic infested with enemy submarines and laid the lives of her boys down for our country; thanks also to the courage of the indomitable soldiers of Soviet Russia.

Since I have the honor of contributing to this commemoration of the first worldwide tragedy, I consider it my duty to call up the infantrymen, those outcasts in every war, laboring under exhaustion and affliction, and I feel the urge to spin the yarn of their ever disappointed hopes, of their fits of dejection and despair. Eager never to swerve from the realities through which I have lived, I feel bound to use the hated "I," so that I may retrace, stage by stage, the long Calvary.

September 24, 1915. On the eve of the great Champagne offensive, my regiment in parade order listened to the intoxicating words delivered to the troops on that day by the commander in chief. The brass instruments and the cymbals gave the tone. The colonel's voice carried well: "Soldiers of the Republic: The hour has come to attack and to win. In the wake of a hurricane of iron and fire, you will storm forward together! Your onslaught won't be resisted. Its first wave will carry you to the enemy's batteries, behind the fortified area from which they are opposing us. You will fight them relentlessly until victory is yours. Fight wholeheartedly for the liberation of your country, for the triumph of Justice and Liberty!"

On that day—however incredible it may seem—I would not have changed places with anyone, not even for an empire!

We advanced only 4 miles, sustaining heavy losses, then digging trenches into the chalky soil of Champagne, burrowing our way into the ground during the long months of a dismally trying war.

February, 1916. Verdun! The Kaiser's Germany also hoped for the end of the conflict. Verdun! The famous battle was to last six months, without achieving any other result than the deaths of 370,000 men, Germans and French together.

"Stand your ground!" was General Pétain's order. "No retreat! Meet death on the field! Let survivors launch counterattacks!"

Having been lost, recaptured, and lost again—sixteen times in the case of a village called Fleury—our positions ultimately remained in the enemy's hands; the breakthrough did not take place.

In June, 1916, my regiment went up to Verdun.

The front line lay ahead of us, concentric and incandescent, its thousands of artillery batteries belching out fire.

That night believers and unbelievers alike prayed to God, "Lord, let me come back. I am not guilty. Protect me!"

Were they already marked, the men who were to lie in that charnel house? Would I ever say, "I was at Verdun," or would others say of me, "He was killed at Verdun"?

All loaded up and harnessed like pack mules, we set out at dusk in order to reach the front line before daybreak, stumbling in the shell holes, panting, running, stamping, harassedly ducking under the blasts of explosions. The night seemed to proceed toward some monstrous collective crime.

May I tell you my most horrible experience? We were facing the famous Fort de Vaux. Dawn laid bare the harrowed ground. The stench of half-putrescent corpses in the process of being shredded by shells made the air fouler still. Overcoat sleeves flapped in the air. A mass of flaccid flesh fell on me; I used my entrenching tool to throw away this remnant of a soldier which stained my uniform.

Three of us were crouching in a hole under the barrage of artillery fire. Then a flame, a blast; then darkness and smoke, the acrid smell of gunpowder. Was I killed or wounded? I cautiously moved my arms and legs. Nothing. My two friends, however, lying one upon the other, were bleeding. The bowels of one were oozing out. The other had a broken leg; there was a red spot spreading on his breast, and he was rolling his panic-stricken eyes. He looked at me silently, imploringly; then unconsciously he unbuttoned his trousers and died urinating upon the gaping wound of his comrade.

Horrified, I fled from their unbearable presence. I looked for shelter, any shelter from the gunfire. But the dead filled all the available craters and drove me away: yesterday's corpses with their features contorted in painful agony or composed after a merciful end, swollen, gray corpses, corpses almost liquefied and alive with worms and flies.

Ten days of deadly thirst in the blazing June sunshine.

Such was the battlefield at Verdun.

November, 1916. Our fall offensive, which had been launched on September 25, was breathing its last on the plains of the Somme. It had not stopped raining for days: a fine, cold, penetrating rain. The enemy line was 200 yards away from ours, but our makeshift trenches, dug with small portable tools, had become inhospitable ditches filled with ice-cold yellowish water. On each side the men would lie down on the bare ground or walk to and fro in the open. There were no more horizon-blue or *feldgrau* (field gray) great-coats: The wheatland, whose acres had cost so many lives, had

become our common uniform. We could and ought to have frater-
nized since not a single shot was fired, but French and Germans
alike seemed to be in a daze, knowing they were no longer foes and
yet failing to realize they were brothers in misfortune.

After so many days, so many sleepless nights, drenched to the
skin, bespattered with mud from head to foot, shivering and shaking with cold, stiff all over, the gallant infantrymen—the heroes—
were worn out.

My friend Sergeant Anguenot, formerly so brave, so full of life
and humor, came to me, his arms dangling.

"Look at me! I wish you could have a look at yourself. Jesus
Christ, just look at me! Mud on my neck, mud on my shoulders,
and the water dripping down my ass. On my hands, and yours, just
look! What the hell are we doing? Can you tell me?"

"The relief party should arrive tonight or tomorrow."

"The relief party!" he jeered at me. "The relief party, you bet,
will save us for cannon fodder." He shook me like a madman. "Let's
die as soon as possible."

He dropped to the ground dejectedly. I squatted down beside
him. "Come on, boy, the men are watching us. Get up for their
sake."

"The men, the men . . . there are no more men!"

He shrieked again: "Bullshit! Fuck them all! If only I could get a
shell in the belly!"

"Come on, come on."

He wiped his hands on the short grass, nodding. "You get all
covered with mud with these damn paws."

He saw the tears in my eyes; to hold back his own, he overdid it
and said, "Now listen, I'll walk straight across toward those on the
other side, and I'll bawl, 'Now shoot at me, you bastards!' "

We walked for quite a long time under the overcast sky, but
there was nothing I could do for a man who was broken and defeated.

The same night we were relieved by riflemen who were already
bespattered and dispirited.

Sergeant Anguenot was a long way from the front line when a
shell seeking out a convoy hit him directly, fulfilling his desperate
wish.

April, 1917. We thought we were immune from brainwashing.
We were wrong! Once more without any previous flourish we fell
prey to the subtle game of so-called indiscretions whispered around;
besides, we had been eyewitnesses. Once again, we thought, victory

lay near at hand after a mighty assault. Consequently, we acquiesced in the "ultimate" effort. We accepted death.

During the severe winter of 1916–17, we had been sent to a quiet
sector in the Aisne: so quiet as to remain undisturbed by shells,
bullets, or alarms. The war was fast asleep, and yet in that very
district, on a front line of about 60 miles, a tragedy was to be
enacted in the spring.

I knew it, for there was every indication that it was going to take
place. On the clear January nights, under a magnificent sky, I
would take the watch. It was beastly cold—15 degrees below zero.
The steel of the gun was biting my bare hand, the frozen mud had
cemented the loose duckboards together, the north wind kept
sighing softly in the barbed-wire entanglements, and the whole
universe seemed to be deserted.

While the man on lookout stood on the fire steps, I walked the
whole length of the company frontage, leaning back at times against
the parapet, staring and listening. At first I was overwhelmed by a
gravelike stillness, but my ears were attuned to the least perceptible
sounds: the muffled rumbling of the trunks; rails squeaking on the
narrow-gauge line that carried ammunition; the occasional calls of
the supply men. In the propitious night a whole body of men were
busily carrying out their tasks.

A machine gunner who stood motionless by his weapon, concentrating as much as I did upon the faraway hum, whispered to me,
"Life'll be no picnic out here this spring!"

When we came off duty for a short while or went back to the
trenches, we saw the pyramid-shaped stacks of shells, the engineers
who were installing side tracks on the railway lines for the heavy
pieces of ordnance, territorial soldiers carrying huge torpedoes on
their backs, others paving the roads and lanes, and huts being
erected with gigantic red crosses on their roofs.

In February and March false stories were being spread:

"Nivelle said to Poincaré [then President of the French Repub-
lic] that he would break through the lines of the Huns, that his
troops would spend their first night at Laon. I am positive. I have it
on good authority. And then, old sport, it'll be open warfare, and
everyone'll be home for Christmas."

"As for artillery, there'll be no lack of that. Almost as many guns
as men on the front line, not only the regular 75's but heavy ones:
155's, 240's, 360's, and even 400's. Have you seen our torpedoes?"

"Renault is turning out hundreds of tanks, and armored tanks at
that, complete with heavy guns and machine guns and all! I know a

lot about it, I tell you. My brother works on the assembly line at the Renault plant."

"The English will launch an attack on the same day somewhere in the north. The Huns won't know which way to turn."

March 16. In the very sector where we planned to attack, the enemy fell back about 20 miles.

"You see, they're making off before we fired a single shot."

In fact, Ludendorff had foreseen the offensive and ordered his army to withdraw to the heavily fortified Siegfried Line. He was setting a trap, and we fell into it blindly.

April 10. My captain entrusted me with the first platoon of the assault wave. Most of my men were young recruits who had been drafted in 1916 and 1917. Those boys of twenty, who had lived neither through the disaster in Champagne nor through the excruciating days at Verdun nor through the mud and cold on the Somme, would fight better than their seniors. The seductions of danger, the pride arising from the risks incurred, acted as a venomous magic. We had been elected. So many thousands of factory hands had toiled for us. So many engineers, gunners, and airmen were working for us, the infantrymen, forgetful of our sore feet and vulnerable flesh. Tomorrow the eyes of the nation will be upon us!

April 16. Six o'clock. We went over the parapet. Our captain shouted, "For France, forward! For France!"

A surprising lull had replaced the roar of artillery, now lengthening its range. A blue haze hovered over the enemy trenches. A smell of chemicals rose from the plowed soil.

To the right and to the left, the assault waves unfolded, rifles raised; all of a sudden I caught a fleeting glimpse of the whole French Army spread out over miles and miles.

Had we covered 100 yards, or was it more? Unexpectedly, grenades started bursting all about us; at short range a howling machine gun discharged its rounds and forced us all to the ground. The captain lay a few yards away, cruelly hit, mortally wounded. Above the deafening din I could hear screams of pain and calls for help. My thigh was smarting; I had been hit. I felt apprehensively into my trousers; my fingers reached a superficial wound and emerged red: a splinter from a grenade, a mere trifle. If I had attempted, even on all fours, to reach a dressing station, I would certainly have been shot.

Secure in a strong pillbox, the bastards fired at everything that moved. Two of our men, somehow sheltered by a collapsing trench, were firing with an automatic rifle; others hurled their grenades. At last, one after the other, the Germans stealthily crept out of their positions. How many men in my platoon, how many in my company, escaped unhurt?

I found out later that several units and regiments had managed to overrun the front lines of the enemy but had failed at the second.

Sixty French divisions brought into action from Soissons to Rheims, over a distance of 20 miles, lost 45,000 men in no time at all. They captured 22,000 prisoners, seized 180 cannon, and advanced a few miles. So what? The battle for the breakthrough, for the deliverance, was to be lost within its first hour.

If only the General Staff had stopped there! Nivelle must have been insane when he hoped for a success and issued orders for further attacks on April 16–20 and on May 5, 6, and 10, throwing the Reserve Army, without adequate shelling experience, into an assault on the Chemin des Dames. General Hirschauer, however, refused to send his men to this absurd death: "I would rather give up my sword than sacrifice the blood of my soldiers!"

If one general had this exceptional courage, there were many others who kept at a safe distance from the front lines while they sent their troops to the slaughter. The figure of 110,000 men killed or disabled was often mentioned. It caused a stir in official circles. France was to go through a dreadful tragedy.

The first rebellious acts took place on May 4, 1917. On the tenth my regiment, among others, agreed to return to the front, provided that it should remain on the defensive. A company refused to attack the mill at Laffaux. Insubordination spread and became open rebellion. Upon returning from the battle of April 16, the survivors argued in the barns, while rumors were abroad, concerning a new onset. Voices rose in excitement. There would not be enough gendarmes, those hated gendarmes, to compel the soldiers to return to the slaughterhouse. Gatherings took place in the billets. Regimental officers secretly sympathized with their men. At Coeuvres a whole battalion found shelter in a wood, disarmed its officers without violence, and set up defensive positions.

The April mutinies affected whole divisions, including 113 infantry regiments, colonial units, riflemen, and 17 batteries. Was the French Army about to crack, the French nation about to collapse? The answer was no. On the very front line, at the Chemin des Dames, not a single body of soldiers, not a single man, failed to perform what national defense required, because General Pétain, who had succeeded Nivelle, gave orders to stop the offensives.

But before the appointment of the man who thus managed to quell the mutiny, a sly and dark repressive force, all of whose crimes will never be known, sent to the firing squad "as an example" many innocent, brave, and experienced soldiers.

As for me, I heard of the death of my brother Joseph, who was killed at Craonne on April 17, 1917. Joseph had been entrusted with my father's bakery; he was my senior and had two very young children. My parents had four sons and a son-in-law serving in the infantry. I was conscious of their heartrending sorrow and of their apprehensions concerning my brothers and myself. We were "in for it, all of us." That's what my friend Sergeant Anguenot told me, just before he died.

I was perfectly aware, however, that the United States, fortunately enough, had just declared war on the Central Powers. The *Army Bulletin* and the newspapers printed President Wilson's address to Congress under huge headlines. I still have the text, but in order to call up the past, I would rather trust my memory. Phrases flared up inside me, lofty phrases: "We shall draw the sword and fight for Justice, Civilization, Freedom, and Peace, giving our lives, our fortunes, everything we have. . . ."

I knew that victory was a certainty, although not in the near future. And yet I was also aware that the United States had little more than sporting guns and that it would take them months and months of training before they would be able to come and help us. Friends from over there, all our hopes rested with you, just as twenty-five years later, in the dark night of the Nazi occupation, we expected you, we implored you silently, even humbly, from the recesses of our wounded hearts.

Victory! And yet we had to hold on. If we did so, it was thanks to the authority of a chief who was no military genius, but a great man.

Entrusted with the supreme command, Philippe Pétain, the Victor of Verdun—let us not cavil at the title, for his glory lies elsewhere—was at the head of a seriously ill army. He knew the origin of the disease and behaved as a good physician, not as a venturesome captain. His first step was to put an end to the repression and let bygones be bygones. He reintroduced leave periods, made them more frequent, ordered the demoralized divisions to be assigned to quiet sectors, being hard only on officers and N.C.O.'s and kind toward privates. He multiplied his instructions that the soldiers be treated humanely and respectfully, that their food be improved. We felt confident that he would put an end to large-scale offensives—futile battles and slaughters.

Within a few weeks he worked a miracle, breathing new life into the French Army.

We acknowledged him as an authoritative father, wise and kind, concerned about the physical and moral health of his men and unwilling to shed their blood in vain. It never occurred to a soldier to make fun of him. The earnest look on his face encouraged us to trust him. This is why in 1940, 1941, and 1942, the veterans, nonplussed and astounded by an amazing defeat, and the French population as a whole, welcomed back Philippe Pétain, a marshal of France, as the head of the French state. It was the return of the father in the days of distress. I do not mean to recall the inconsistencies, the weaknesses, the errors that were his in 1943 and 1944, when he was eighty-seven.

We held our ground despite the defection of Soviet Russia in October, 1917, despite the Italian rout at Caporetto and the furious onslaughts of the enemy eager to bring things to an end before the arrival of the American divisions.

In the north, in the vulnerable sector of our front, where the French and British armies met, Ludendorff, who had secretly gathered sixty divisions supported by 7,000 pieces of ordnance, launched them on March 21. They hustled the English out of their positions, ran after them, and headed for Amiens.

The road to the sea, the road to Paris, lay open.

We hastily managed to consolidate the breach. The Germans' progress was stopped in view of Amiens and Noyon. Thus, they failed to carry out the expected breakthrough.

On April 9 the enemy had another try at it farther north but went no farther than pushing forward a new bulge.

Things reached such a critical stage that the British finally accepted the idea of a unified command entrusted to General Foch.

Now on French soil, 400,000 American soldiers, fresh from the boat, were undergoing indispensable training. Ludendorff had no more time to lose.

He finally decided on the Chemin des Dames.

On May 27, after a lightninglike shelling, his troops rushed upon reputedly impregnable positions. Thanks to bold, hitherto unheard-of tactics, their success was crushing; they crossed the Vesle the very same night, entered Soissons on the following day, and reached the Marne a few days later. They would soon be no farther than 40 miles from Paris.

They captured 65,000 men and their headquarters, along with aviation and artillery depots, as well as vast quantities of equipment and supplies.

Germany thought that victory was at hand, but France, her leaders and her soldiers, refused to accept defeat.

Our last remaining reserves, the very last, were thrown into the heat of battle, reconstituting the front and paralyzing an enemy weakened by long marches. It should be said that in the quiet sectors American units relieved ours and made the transfer possible.

Georges Clemenceau made an appeal to the whole nation: "I am waging war." France summoned all her strength. So did Germany.

In Champagne, Ludendorff attempted what he had not been able to do on March 21 and 27. It was meant as the final battle, the Kaiser's battle! William II himself was going to the front in order to encourage his troops; such was his intention at least. The Germans believed they were clever when they chose the evening of our national day for their attack. They thought our soldiers would be sleeping off their wine. They were mistaken. On such occasions our lady bountiful, the Army Service Corps, did triple the rations of wine and brandy, with a liberal allowance of champagne. In war, men often get tight while in billets. It is something of a ritual among the soldiers of all nations, but on the front line, everyone, believe me, remains clearheaded.

On July 13 a French patrol chanced to capture a *Feldwebel* (sergeant) who knew the exact time of the attack. The French command proved more farsighted than usual as it ordered the front trenches to be evacuated after adjusting the range of the artillery on the second line, which had also been cleared for the occasion.

The astounded Germans ran across empty trenches, got their feet caught in barbed-wire entanglements, under the heavy pounding of our 75's. Those of their units who had been entrusted with the exploitation of success became mixed with the first assault waves. It was complete chaos, a failure.

At noon, the order to move forward reached my division, hitherto placed on the reserve line, for a possible counterattack.

All danger had vanished from the Champagne front. Germany had played her last stake in a few hours.

Trucks drove us westward and dropped us somewhere in the vicinity of Meaux.

On July 18 General Mangin's army launched an attack in the Aisne Valley. Without any preparatory shelling but with the support of 300 tanks, they obliterated the bulge at Château-Thierry, quite by surprise.

From then on we kept the initiative of joint operations involving the French, the British, and the Americans, under the respective commands of Generals Pétain, Haig, and Pershing.

Foch dealt out sporadic blows, repeatedly ramming a wedge in one sector, then in another, luring the enemy reinforcements, then striking elsewhere, confusing the opponents, dislocating their defenses, compelling them to withdraw irremediably.

My division was brought into action on August 2. One of the great events concerning me took place on August 27, my twenty-fourth birthday. After twenty-five days of fighting—brief skirmishes, advances, and retreats—of sleepless nights with our bowels torn by epidemic dysentery, we were about to die of thirst. Nobody cared, since we were moving forward. The Germans deftly fell back at nightfall. They withdrew so as to give us a warm welcome in their new positions. The German infantrymen fought desperately, courageously, commanding both our anger and our admiration. The prisoners we picked up were underfed and even more exhausted than we were.

On August 8 a heavy shell fell flat on our group. My captain, Louis, a Reservist, fell never to rise again. Two of my dearest friends never rose again either. With shaking hands I collected each of their wretched legacies: a wallet, a watch, a few coins, some letters and photographs—trifles I would send to their parents. Then leaving their mangled bodies on the field, I joined my company, which had dwindled to a mere eighty. I gave vent to my sorrow in tears.

Where did we stand on August 27? In front of the Vesle. Our miserable company occupied an unassuming crest on the counter-slope. Experience had taught us how to choose the counterslope and remain motionless in the daytime. For lack of breath, the battle had come to a halt. We wondered whether the Germans would come out of their hiding places to recover the ground we had conquered.

Our front stretched roughly over 300 yards. The men, therefore, were crouching at a distance from each other in their dugouts. Everything was still, but all of a sudden heads and shoulders briefly popped out: "Pass it on: We'll be relieved tonight, pass it on. . . ." The magic whisper ran along the whole line.

We would be relieved that night. The war, my war, would be over that night. For a couple of weeks my ailing stomach could no longer stand canned food or wine. I had survived on a hunk of bread and water—when I happened to find some.

The lieutenant broke the news that Americans were going to replace us. Americans! He was to pass on the orders to their officers. Concerning my own platoon, he left it to me to do the same with the N.C.O.'s.

I saw you at dusk, as you came to us, brothers from beyond the

sea. You were dauntless boys who ignored the shelters of our dugouts. From one end of the sector to the other, you fell into line, as
if on parade, exposing yourselves to the vigilant eye of German
balloons. You stood erect and undismayed at the very moment when
a battery of 150's caught us under its fortunately misdirected fire.

We shook hands and waved good-bye and good luck. An American unit had taken the place of a French one.

While we waited for the crippled, the battalion gathered in a
small clump of trees. Then we watched ambulances speeding up to
the front: "Gee! They've got guts, those Americans! They're big
guys. Never saw one of our cars venturing to the front line to pick
up the wounded."

In a nondescript village a military surgeon called to my "bed-
side" found me lying hiccuping on the rotten straw of a country
barn with a high fever and pinned the red clearance slip on my
greatcoat.

A whole month in a lousy place of a hospital; then a two months'
sick leave; then at last my dear old bed in my father's house—and
my mother's cooking!

Pampered and relaxed, I ate ravenously and picked up again. It
could be seen every day, according to my mother. The war was
going on for my buddies. How I followed on the map the progress
of operations, the march of the armies toward victory and peace!
Years later on one of my many pilgrimages to the battlefields I once
climbed the 225 steps of the monument erected on the hill at
Montfaucon in commemoration of a major victory of the U.S. 1st
Army. On September 12, 1918, you alone stormed the St.-Mihiel
salient and captured 18,000 prisoners. I also made a point of visiting your huge cemetery at Romagne-sous-Montfaucon, where
14,000 of your boys lie buried beneath 14,000 white marble crosses.
With a heavy heart, unable to hold back my tears—but who could
have?—I walked slowly along the shady lanes of the soul-stirring city
of the dead over which flies the Stars and Stripes.

November 11, 1918. "Why don't you put on your Military
Cross?" my mother asked. "You really should pin it on today."

All the houses were decked with flags; everybody—women, men,
and children—was in the street. My parents were not a little proud
to walk beside me, and I did not object to displaying my military
uniform and medals on such a day.

There was a crowd on the central square at Belfort, where the
local brass band played appropriate tunes. At 11 A.M. the bells of St.
Christopher's rang out to peace, the sole venerable cannon of the

citadel fired the twenty-one-gun salute, and the national anthem was heard.

The war was over!

My father and mother kissed me, hugged me, and sobbed. The women, young and old alike, clapped their hands at this touching sight and kissed me in their turn. How many kisses were exchanged! There was much kissing going around; indeed people no longer knew how else to give vent to their emotions. The boys put their arms around the girls' waists, and the girls did not object. I was carried away by the popular rejoicing as by a heady wine. I fancied myself bearing on my shoulders the awesome glory of the victors, the triumphant glory of those who survived.

At the same time, however, an inner voice made itself heard: "I wish you could see what a fool you look. You are walking with such martial strides—chin up, chest thrown out—that your parents can hardly keep up with you. If you dared, you'd hold up that hand of yours which once wielded a rifle and launched grenades. A murderous hand perhaps. . . . And you would shout, 'I was at Verdun!' Of course you are a hero, the hero of the day. Revel in the fulsome flattery, dear fool! It does not stop war from being a filthy trick. You can't help it!"

Finally, we had to return home. In the family dining room everybody resumed his accustomed seat, weary in soul and body. A fourth guest sneaked in. On the mantelpiece, in his gilded frame, Joseph, the most vulnerable of my parents' five sons, stared at us with a frozen smile. He lay out there beneath his wooden cross. His comrades dug a bed for him and, to prevent the earth from hurting his eyes, put over his face the battered tin plate which was in his haversack. That's how they found him. We all turned our eyes toward the photograph that time would turn yellow.

How sad my mother looked! She painfully tore herself away from her armchair and broke the silence: "I don't feel up to anything, but still I have to prepare your dinner."

From the street rose the strains of "La Madelon," that stupid refrain, a blatant lie which the infantrymen never sang.

"We've won the war."

"Look! we fixed them!"

"They're drunk," I said.

My mother stopped her ears: "I can't take it anymore."

I closed the shutters and shut out the world, its cruel joys, and light.

On November 11, 1918, in so many bereaved homes. . . .

To those who asked, "What was the worst trial?" I would answer,

"Lice, the invincible lice, thirst, the fear of being atrociously maimed, of losing an arm or a leg, of being emasculated. . . ." And the memory of the few minutes before the attack at Grivesne, in April, 1918, when I rested under a budding apple tree, the promise of blossoms and fruit, which was no longer meant for me. I was twenty, and I had never embraced a woman; I had never felt her warm, naked skin against my eager body; I thought I would die on the very threshold of my wretched life with an empty heart and empty hands.

As men of the free world, twice, and each time for five years, we risked our young lives for the sake of justice and civilization.

I wish I knew where civilization lies. Certainly not in scientific progress and technical improvements: cars, television, and the rest—junk and gadgets.

Civilization lies in spiritual achievements, in culture, in the arts, in harmony and justice.

The celebrated writer Georges Duhamel, the author of *Vie des Martyrs* has written: "Civilization lies in the hearts of men. If it is not to be found there, it is nowhere."

That's where it lies—the promise of greatness.

Sir Geoffrey Keynes

"I was born in Cambridge on March 25, 1887, the younger son of Dr. John Neville Keynes, later registrary of the university, and Florence Ada Brown, afterward mayor of Cambridge and chairman of the National Council of Women. My brother, four years older, was John Maynard, later Lord Keynes of Tilton, the economist, who married the Russian ballerina, Lydia Lopokova, in 1925. My sister, born in 1885, is Mrs. Margaret Hill, C.B.E. (Commander of the British Empire), wife of A. V. Hill, C.H. (Companion of Honor), F.R.S. (Fellow of the Royal Society), physiologist, and Nobel prizewinner.

"I was educated at a private school in Cambridge, at Rugby School and at Pembroke College, Cambridge, where I was a foundation scholar. In 1910 I went to St. Bartholomew's Hospital, London, as a medical student, qualified in 1913, and was then appointed house surgeon at my hospital. I served in Flanders and France in the Royal Army Medical Corps throughout the First World War, becoming a surgical specialist with the rank of major. While on leave in 1917, I married Margaret Darwin, younger daughter of Professor Sir George Darwin, K.C.B. (Knight Commander of the Bath), F.R.S., and we have four sons. After being demobilized in 1919, I became chief assistant to Professor George Gask at St. Bartholomew's and was elected surgeon to the hospital in 1929. In 1939 I was appointed senior consulting surgeon to the Royal Air Force, in which I served for six years, reaching the rank of air vice marshal. I received a knighthood as a surgeon in 1955 and in 1956 was appointed Sir Arthur Sims Commonwealth Professor, in this capacity visiting all the medical schools in Africa and Canada. I hold the degree of Doctor of Medicine of Cambridge University and am a fellow of the three Royal Colleges: Physicians, Surgeons, and Gynecologists and Obstetricians. In 1922 I published the first English textbook on Blood Transfusion and have made numerous contributions to medical journals and books, relating chiefly to blood transfusion, hernia, cancer of the breast, the thyroid gland, and the thymus gland.

"While an undergraduate at Cambridge, I developed an interest in literature and bibliography, publishing my first book on John Donne in 1914. I have subsequently published many other bibliographies and have edited the works of William Blake, Sir Thomas Browne, Rupert Brooke, and others. I have received honorary doctorates in literature from the universities of Oxford, Cambridge, Edinburgh, Sheffield, Birmingham, and Reading. I served as trustee of the National Portrait Gallery from 1942 to 1966, being chairman of the board from 1958. I retired from active surgery in 1957, but have continued working as a writer, publishing a full-length Life of William Harvey in 1966 and a catalogue of my library in 1964.

"I have visited the United States of America several times and am an honorary fellow of the American Association of Surgeons, an honorary member of the Grolier Club of New York, and an honorary member of the Modern Language Association of America."

A DOCTOR'S WAR

———◆◆◆———

IN AUGUST, 1914, I was halfway through my twenty-seventh year. Young people of my age had lived through the late Victorian and Edwardian times with a sense of complete physical security, and most of us had never given a thought to the possibility of our being involved in a European war. On August 4 I was enjoying a holiday from my work as a senior house surgeon at St. Bartholomew's Hospital, London, camping with a group of friends on the Cornish coast at Manaccan, a village on the south side of Falmouth Bay. We received the news of the declaration of war with Germany with astonishment almost amounting to incredulity but soon had to face the fact, and everyone arranged to return at once to his home. I went back to St. Bartholomew's and decided without hesitation to offer myself to the War Office for enrollment as a junior officer in the Royal Army Medical Corps. The decision was influenced partly by my not being happy with my chief, but more by a conviction that Great Britain would win the war, that it would not last long, and that the experience must not be missed. Since medical officers were noncombatants, there was no element of heroism in volunteering for the Army. "War" did not suggest unnamed horrors but to a young surgeon meant useful employment in his own profession while doing his bounden duty for his country.

Formalities at the War Office were soon completed, and on August 16 I reported with the rank of lieutenant R.A.M.C. to my unit, a base hospital at Woolwich. Some equipment still had to be

bought in London, and on August 18 I chanced to meet my friend
Rupert Brooke near my rooms in Bloomsbury. He gazed at my
uniform with envy and almost with despair. Like many other young
men, he was having great difficulty in deciding in what capacity he
ought to serve. For me the decision had been quick and easy. My
military inexperience was almost total—a week in camp at Alder-
shot in the Rugby School cadet corps a few years earlier had not
encouraged a military outlook, yet it was not difficult to fit into the
framework of an Army medical unit, where everyone but a few
senior officers was as innocent as myself. My brief diary tells me that
on August 20 the Germans occupied Brussels and that I (fortunately) failed to buy a sword in London. Active service was held to
have automatically abolished most ceremony, and even details of
uniform could be decided by each individual. In common with my
close friend Maurice Perrin from St. Bartholomew's I decided to
have a tunic of khaki drill, corduroy riding breeches, and skiing
boots reaching to just below the knee, thus getting rid of the
constant nuisance of winding on and unwinding puttees, though
these were the regulation wear.

On August 22 the unit left Woolwich, by train, for Southampton
Docks and embarked the next day on a dirty cargo boat bound for
Le Havre and Rouen. The ship's progress up the Seine was enlivened from the banks by cheering crowds composed entirely of
women, children, and old men, to whom our troops responded with
songs and countercheers. The ship docked at Rouen on the evening
of August 24, twenty days after the declaration of war, and our
equipment was unloaded with a view to the hospital's being established in tents near the town. Casualties were arriving by train in
large numbers by August 28 but were taken to other units. On the
following day I was detailed to superintend the digging of latrines,
a foretaste of the realities of war, but next morning it was reported
that the Germans were marching on Paris. We were instructed to
reload everything onto the ship as quickly as possible and to return
down the Seine to Le Havre. We knew little of what was happening
at the front, so could live only for the moment and obey orders.
One of the Regular officers tried to frighten us by assuring us that
the ship would be "peppered with bullets" on our way down the
river, but our eventual retreat was very much like our arrival,
though there was noticeably less enthusiasm on the riverbanks. The
ship did not, in fact, leave Rouen until early on September 2, when
the Germans were (erroneously) reported to have reached Amiens.
We spent the next day steaming round Cape Finistère out of sight
of land, while many of the officers and troops became patients with

violent gastroenteritis. On September 4 we found ourselves near St.-Nazaire in the estuary of the Loire, and it was several days before we knew where we were to go. Meanwhile, our equipment had been unloaded onto the quay, and time was occupied by taking parties of men down to the sea for bathing, where they surprisingly attempted to observe the conventions with underpants, handkerchiefs, or even puttees. For several nights I slept under the stars or, when it rained, under a small groundsheet. On September 10 our equipment was hopefully loaded onto a train, and next day definite orders were received to proceed to Versailles. This sounded improbable after the rumors that had reached us in the previous week; but it turned out to be true, and by the evening of September 13 we knew that we were to establish our hospital at Versailles in the Hotel Trianon Palace. After so many nights spent on the iron decks of a ship, on the ground, or in luggage wagons, the news seemed improbably good; but it proved true, and so ended the prelude to a doctor's war.

The hotel, situated just outside the gates of the Palace of Versailles, could easily be adapted for use as a hospital, the large *salons* forming admirable wards. For two days I was busy planning and fitting up an operating theater (room), until on September 16 two patients were admitted. One of them, under my care with a compound fracture of the leg, died the next day, the first indication of the lethal nature of wounds received on the richly manured ground of northern France and Flanders. We had been instructed not to interfere with apparently clean bullet wounds, experience of the South African War at the turn of the century being the only evidence available to the senior R.A.M.C. officers of how to deal with penetrating wounds. We soon learned, however, of the difference between wounds sustained on the clean South African veldt and those contaminated by European mud. Anaerobic bacteria lurking in the soil were responsible for the gas gangrene which proved to be one of the chief causes of death among those men who reached a base hospital alive. By September 17, patients were arriving in hundreds, many of them having spent several days on the way from the battlefield of Mons. Hospital trains had been improvised from French *fourgons,* or cattle trucks, and the condition of the men posed many problems to our inexperienced judgment. Common sense was the best guide, but "doing our best" was often distressingly inadequate while we learned the lessons of war surgery by trial and error.

For the next four months I worked at Versailles, steadily gaining experience of how to deal with the wounds of modern warfare. The question of amputating limbs raised the most perplexing and frequent of all problems. Reluctance to perform a mutilating operation, when nonperformance might cost the patient's life, created a difficult situation for a young surgeon. His seniors could give little help. The officers' ward was put in my charge, though the responsibility was no greater than if the patients had been private soldiers. The conditions were the same for all. The work was uneven in intensity, the arrival of ambulance trains from the front naturally increasing the pressure for a time. Always a large proportion of the patients could be sent on to England after a short stay in hospital or returned to duty. Consequently there were leisured periods when we could visit Paris, explore the beauties of the palace and the Petit Trianon, go riding in the park, or, best of all, make friends with the French pilots at the neighboring airfields of Buc and St.-Cyr. All my early experience of flying was gained in this way, my first flight being in a Blériot monoplane. Later flights were in the primitive Farman biplane, where one sat exposed in a sort of open-sided basket, and in the more advanced Caudrons and Moranes. I even enjoyed coming down from 5,000 meters in a spiral descent on edge, followed by an almost vertical dive. It all seemed safe enough, even in the aeronautical dawn of 1914. One of these visits provided the additional satisfaction of taking a salute from Georges Carpentier, the greatest pugilist of his day, though his face was the flattened image of his profession rather than the handsome hero of popular legend. More than once I met my brother Maynard in Paris, where he was investigating French finances.

The proximity of the hospital to Paris naturally brought many interesting visitors. Not only were there official visits from the surgical consultants such as Sir George Makins and Sir Anthony Bowlby—the latter from the staff of my hospital and so particularly welcome—but also from unofficial visitors such as Lord Robert Cecil, Sir Frederick Treves, Prince Arthur of Connaught, and, of most interest to me, the great Élie Metchnikoff, pioneer in the study of rejuvenation by surgical operation and of the prevention of aging by the ingestion of the Bulgarian bacillus in clotted milk.

There were thus many amenities, and life was far too comfortable to constitute real experience of war. It was, therefore, not too unpleasant to learn on February 6, 1915 that I had been detailed by the C.O. for duty on an ambulance train. I accordingly left next day for Boulogne, having enjoyed a last evening in Paris at a revue, *Paris quand même,* at the Folies Bergères. For nearly six months I was to endure the peculiar conditions of life with two other officers on a constantly moving hospital. My bed-sitting room was an ordinary first-class compartment in a train composed mainly of second- and third-class carriages for sitting patients and of *fourgons* adapted for stretchers to carry those more seriously ill or wounded. Headquarters were at Boulogne, but we had to be ready to move at a moment's notice to any part of the front in France or Flanders. Often orders came during the night, and the first question to ask on waking in the morning was: "Where are we?" So I became familiar with many railway stations—there was seldom time to investigate the towns or countryside around them. The number of patients carried on each journey varied between 100 and 400. During my turn of duty in the train we carried nearly 19,000 patients. Medical duties were usually restricted to ensuring that the wounded men, who had already been attended in a field ambulance or casualty clearing station, traveled as comfortably as possible with the help of sedative and analgesic drugs. Frequently they had to suffer violent jolts during shunting operations, occasionally so violent that couplings were smashed. Sometimes the engine driver was placed under arrest when he seemed to have been guilty of extremes of negligence or incompetence. We feared that men with fractured limbs would be subjected to unjustifiable pain or risks by the antics of callous drivers.

Usually the patients had been fully cared for before being sent on by train to the base hospitals, but on one occasion (March 12, 1915), during the Battle of Neuve-Chapelle, the train was ordered to go close to the front line near Armentières and take on casualties who had barely received first aid. The journey to Boulogne was spent working under great difficulties, even the coaches meant for lightly wounded men having to be filled with patients who had to lie down, many of them desperately ill. Several died during the journey or even before the train started to move. This was a distressing introduction to dealing with casualties coming straight from the battlefield. Yet on the whole, life on an ambulance train was fairly easy once we were used to the extreme irregularity of our existence. More than ever we lived in the moment and were largely unaware of what was happening beyond our limited horizon. On April 27, I had news of the death of Rupert Brooke three days earlier in the Aegean, and I began to be more aware of the fate which was to kill the majority of the friends of my generation at Rugby School and Cambridge University.

On July 24, having worked all night with a complement of 364 patients, I received the news at Boulogne that I was ordered to join the 7th Field Ambulance in the 3d Division. After a day spent at

Boulogne with my future brother-in-law, Lieutenant Charles Darwin, I left for Bailleul in a supply train. The next morning a London bus helped me on the road in a search for divisional headquarters, and I finally found my new unit in a field near Poperinge. The town was under intermittent bombardment, though on July 29 ten of fourteen shells failed to explode. I was now more definitely at the front than hitherto and found myself going about my duties on horseback, though I had seldom ridden before. My posting to the 7th Field Ambulance proved, however, to be only a brief interlude, my real destination being the 23d Brigade of the Royal Field Artillery, which I joined on August 5. A year had passed since the declaration of war, but it was only now, while engaged at close quarters with the enemy, that I realized how gently I had been let down into the caldron of war. The 23d Brigade, R.F.A., was stationed in the Ypres Salient, the gun emplacements being in front of the walls of the town beyond the Lille Gate. The area was under constant shellfire from three directions. The brigade H.Q. was in small dugouts in a field near Kruisstraat on the south side of Ypres, about half a mile from the walls. Every hedge was occupied by guns, large and small. The ground was pitted with shell holes, and several shells exploded in the field close behind us during the first evening; but the situation was regarded as fairly peaceful by my four companions, the colonel, the adjutant, the orderly officer, and the interpreter, a son of the governor of Calais. As medical officer, I found to my astonishment that I was attended by a batman, a medical orderly, a groom, and three horses. The animals lived in the wagon lines, some distance farther back, but were brought up to headquarters whenever I had to go anywhere other than the three batteries. At other times, when we were out in a rest area or moving to a fresh station, they were essential, and I found that my life was spent largely on horseback, a totally unexpected experience and most enjoyable. Though quite uninstructed in riding, I fell off only once, when my horse fell in attempting to jump a wide ditch from a slippery takeoff, giving me a severe concussion. When we were in action, I took sick parades at H.Q. and at each of the batteries, doing my rounds on foot along the walls of Ypres. I often rode off to the wagon lines and the ammunition column, where I saw sick parades in my consulting room (a converted pigsty) and ensured that general sanitation was adequate.

Ten days after my joining the brigade, my posting was confirmed, so it seemed that I would do, and this gave me immense satisfaction. Not only were my nerves unruffled by the exceedingly dangerous position in which we lived, but also I was becoming closely attached to my companions, who received me as their equal in spite of my utterly unmilitary outlook—so obviously that of a civilian in uniform and a noncombatant. On one of my visits to a battery I sat in a dugout on the edge of a railway embankment with the major in command, while shells were thudding into the other side of the embankment. I noticed to my surprise that the major was trembling and dripping with sweat. Shellbursts were my daily lot, but none of the shells seemed to be meant for me. Frequently they would burst 100 yards beyond our dugouts among some empty gun emplacements, and occasionally it seemed sensible to dodge behind a tree when we heard them coming; but usually we took no notice. If the enemy chose to bombard an adandoned gun position, it was none of our business. One of my favorite entertainments was going to watch the 17-inch shells roaring into Ypres with a noise like an express train and making huge craters among the ruins. This nonchalance was natural but was not to be confused with courage. It was plain inexperience. My friend, the sweating major, knew more about it than I did, as I subsequently discovered.

Occasionally there was a quiet day, and on one of these (August 24, 1915) I walked into Ypres and straight through to the central square. Every house was in ruins, but the streets had been swept clear of debris. At the time, in midmorning, it was completely deserted except for an occasional messenger on a bicycle hurrying through as though pursued by a ghost. The lovely medieval Cloth Hall was fearfully battered, but the walls remained with one brave little pinnacle of the central tower still standing. Frescoes on the walls of the upper floors were hanging in space. The neighboring cathedral was even more devastated, though the tower was still erect, surrounded by huge shell craters. The bones of the last ten centuries were sticking out of the ground and a charnel house odor filled the air. I took two blue Flemish tiles from a fireplace in one of the houses in the square as a memento. A few days later, when the mail had just arrived, I was enjoying the perusal of a new *Bibliography of Dr. Samuel Johnson*, sent from Oxford by a kind friend (Sir William Osler) , when I heard a shell coming. I looked up to see the last turret of the Cloth Hall actually falling after a direct hit. Even this did not suggest to my mind the idea of a personal missile with my name on it. That came on the next day, September 12. German airplanes had been active overhead for two days, and we had certainly been very careless about getting under cover when they were around. About 10 A.M. several shells came over as usual to the end of the next field, and we took no notice, though the last two did come nearer. At lunchtime we were thinking of our usual

alfresco meal, when we heard another shell coming and realized
from the different sound that it was going to land among us. It was
too late to move, and I turned to watch it hit the ground 10 yards
away. It was an 8-inch shell, and by all the rules I was instantly
killed. Instead, I saw a fountain of mud and debris shooting up into
the air and attempted to hide under a wooden ledge fixed to a tree
as a sort of sideboard, hoping to escape the mud as it came raining
down again. No one was hurt, for the ground was so soft that the
whole force of the explosion was dissipated upward while the
fragments were buried in the soil. The enemy had, in fact, ranged
accurately on our headquarters, and it was time to run to some
neighboring dugouts, where we crouched until the shelling
stopped. Orders had been given to all ranks to evacuate the site, but
soon I was summoned to the telephonists' dugout, where three men
had chosen to remain. A direct hit had been the price of disobedience, and every trace of the bodies of the men above their waists
had vanished. It seemed in a way foolish to worry about what
remained; but it was felt that their legs had to be given decent
burial, and so I carefully extracted as much as I could and summoned the padre to perform his part. In those few minutes I had
learned my lesson. I was no longer a civilian in uniform but was
suddenly almost a soldier, though very much afraid.

On August 23 a German airplane dropped a typewritten message
near us in a bag weighted with sand:

An das 16 Flying-Corps (Poperinge)
Nachdem wie aus der von Ihnen abgeworfenen Meldung zu ersehen
ist, unsere erste Meldung leider nicht in ihren Besitz gelangt ist, ver-
suchen wir nun zum zweiten Mal Sie über Kapitän Pike zu benachrich-
tigen.
Pike wurde am 9.8 von einem unserer Flügzeuge im Luftkampf
heruntergeschossen, und ist kurz nach der Landung seiner Verwundung
erlegen. Er hat also einen schönen Fliegertod gefunden und wurde mit
allen militärischen Ehren auf einem Kirchhof hinter unserer Linie
*beigesetzt.**

At this date the courtesies of civilized warfare were still being
observed, though we usually referred to the enemy as the Huns,

---

* After we had seen the message dropped by you, our first message unfortunately
failed to reach you; we now try for the second time to inform you about Captain Pike.
  Pike was shot down in air battle by one of our aircraft on August 9 and, soon after
reaching the ground, died of his wounds. So he met with a fine airman's death and
was buried with full military honors in a churchyard behind our lines.

without much feeling of personal enmity in spite of experiencing narrow escapes from death many times each day.

Near the end of September, 1915, I was given fourteen days' leave in England, returning to the daily round in the salient on October 6. A fortnight later the brigade moved back to a rest area. The casualties in our brigade had not been serious during my three months in the front line, but there could be no question of the wisdom of giving the troops a prolonged rest from the continual tension of static warfare in an extremely hot corner of the front. On November 30, I was provided with a new medical orderly in the person of an ex-cotton master who had worked with 800 men under him in Russia. He was able to help greatly in the organization of my medical inspections and sick parades, and I began to take lessons in Russian. Meanwhile, there was more free time, and I rode widely around the country, visiting friends in other units and learning something of what was happening on other fronts beyond our own. Our rest was to last until just after Christmas, and on December 16 I rode to Dickebush Lake, only 2 miles from Ypres, which was to be the next station for our brigade.

Three days later, after the sound of very heavy firing at the front line, we became conscious of a strong smell of chlorine. The Germans had made their first gas attack north of Ypres, the discharge lasting one and a half hours, but it had failed, even though followed up by a heavy bombardment with gas shells. We were under orders to stand by, but as few Germans were able to leave their own trenches, no reinforcement had been necessary. We were provided with ludicrously inadequate gas masks—just a pad of cotton wool wrapped in muslin—so it was fortunate that the concentration of gas proved to be so light.

On December 20, while still on my rounds, I found that my horse was being followed by a magnificent deerhound, which appeared to think I was his owner. Indeed, I proudly assumed the part and astonished the officers at the next battery headquarters by appearing with this retinue. The battery major possessed a small terrier bitch, and my magnificent gentleman immediately did the honors by lifting his immense hind leg and saluting the top of the officers' mess table with a generous flow of urine. This was taken in good part, and my deerhound followed me home, sharing my bed for that night. This glory could not last, and next day a messenger came from the mayor of Poperinge to collect the Earl of Feversham's dog.

Christmas was celebrated with the customary dinner, for which a remarkable collection of bottles had been assembled, yet no one was noticeably drunk, perhaps because no one had forgotten that we were to move into our new action stations at Dickebush next day. Two days later the relief of the 40th Brigade, R.F.A., had been completed, and I was able to take stock of my new surroundings in the *brasserie* (brewery), a large building close to the lake, around whose banks the gun emplacements had been fixed. The building was so large that it must have been visible from the German lines and could have been easily destroyed by gunfire. We were convinced that its survival was due to the fact that the owner was in communication with the enemy, though there was never any proof of the truth of this uncharitable belief. Nevertheless, we were thankful that our winter quarters provided a sound roof overhead, and we chose to forget that it might have been at any moment destroyed with ourselves inside.

Though more than fifty years have passed, the name Dickebush still stirs memories of events as vivid and moving as anything that has ever happened to me. After four months I was beginning to realize how deeply my life was bound up with the welfare of the officers and men of the brigade. It had been difficult to feel much personal devotion to a hospital temporarily situated in a French hotel or to an ambulance train with its perpetually changing load of patients. The relation of a medical officer to an artillery brigade in the front line was intensely personal—a noncombatant sharing all the dangers and interests of an Army unit which on active service knew nothing of spit and polish, but was rich in the qualities of courage, friendship and determination. I could not really enjoy the music hall songs they perpetually played on the gramophone in the officers' mess; after my long academic training at the university and hospital I had innumerable interests which none of them could share, but their fine humanity under the conditions we all had to endure was irresistible.

The position of our gun emplacements and headquarters at Dickebush were much nearer the trenches than they had been in the Ypres Salient. We were overlooked by captive balloons and airplanes and might even be seen from lookout posts on the ground. Except that the enemy refrained from destroying our great *brasserie,* life was made more frightening by the frequency of shell-bursts. I had to give up Russian lessons with my medical corporal; it was impossible to concentrate on the unaccustomed alphabet and syllables with constant speculation at the back of my mind: "Where will the next one fall?" For six and a half months the tension was unbroken for me except for a brief spell of leave in England. Occasionally a small shell, or whizbang, hit the *brasserie,* one falling while some troops were in the divisonal baths established in one end of the capacious building. All the men ran out naked but soon preferred to risk the arrival of another shell inside—it was March 25, 1916. There were many other excitements. Mines were sprung under neighboring trenches, local battles swayed to and fro, and it was sometimes satisfactory to see a few hundred prisoners being escorted to our rear. There were frequent dogfights in the air over our heads, fifteen or twenty machines sometimes taking part. Antiaircraft fire was usually ineffectual, the technique of ranging on moving targets being undeveloped. Occasionally a machine was seen to crash, with cheers from the ground if it was thought to be German. Falling fragments of antiaircraft shells were another frequent hazard, though it was seldom that any injury resulted. Although the individual batteries were often shelled, the German gunners were inaccurate, and our casualties were not very heavy. Often I would notice that the enemy was ranging on one of our batteries and would watch from behind a tree to see if my help was likely to be needed.

On one occasion, when I happened to be in my dressing station near the *brasserie,* a message came that a gunner had been wounded and was lying beside his gun at the edge of the lake. Would I, please, come at once? I then experienced a feeling which it is hard to describe. It was my duty to walk immediately with stretcher-bearers from a position of comparative safety to a gun pit, which was being accurately shelled every few minutes. I ordered my legs to take me there, but at first they refused to move. My mind was equal to the ordeal, but another part of my brain declined to pass on the necessary instructions. I soon succeeded in reaching the position, having fallen flat several times on the way when shells were heard approaching. It was only about 200 yards to go, but the cerebral conflict involved in doing anything so contrary to nature caused a most strange sensation. Was this "cowardice"? When I reached the gun pit, the gunner was almost dead, and nothing could have been done to save him.

Earlier in the year I had recorded January 25 as "a bright but terrible day." A German airplane came over about ten o'clock to range a gun firing at one of our batteries with 8-inch shells. Eleven times it came over, dropped a starlight signal, and returned to report, always keeping about 500 yards beyond the range of the nearest antiaircraft gun. About two o'clock the shells were falling faster around the battery, and finally one landed in the middle of a group of officers standing outside the billet where they lived. This shell killed five men altogether, including the major in command

and the French interpreter, whose father, the governor of Calais, had visited the unit only an hour earlier. I attended as best I could to each of them, but all were terribly mutilated and were dead or dying. I felt it my duty to report at once to the colonel. I found him walking in the garden of the *brasserie* and went through the motions of a clumsy salute—I was never able to achieve the smartness of a proper military salute. Though hardly able to speak, I told him that he had lost five men, including the finest soldier in the brigade, the battery commander. He said nothing. We were both on the point of tears, and it was hard to maintain the stiff upper lip proper to the occasion. Far greater tragedies were happening elsewhere all the time. The long, drawn-out horrors of Passchendaele were to take place not far away; but the pattern of war is shaped in the individual mind by small individual experiences, and I can see these things as clearly today as if they had just happened, down to the body of the major's terrier bitch (the same that had been saluted by the deerhound) lying near her master.

During the second week in February, 1916, the brigade was to move back to a rest area 20 miles from Boulogne, and I was given a few days' leave. Less than a month later the brigade returned to Dickebush to find various buildings in the neighborhood had been destroyed, though the *brasserie* was still only slightly damaged. Life at Dickebush continued on an ascending scale of terror. We suffered many casualties, and it was a great relief to be allowed to go again to a rest area on April 15 for a fortnight. Soon afterward rearrangements in the divisional artillery deprived our brigade of all three batteries, so that for a short time I was almost unemployed. It seemed to me to be an appropriate moment to apply for a posting to a casualty clearing station—that is, a tented hospital, at a suitable distance from the front line, able to give full surgical and medical treatment to men brought in by the field ambulances. Patients could sometimes be landed safely in hospital within an hour of being wounded. The brigade, as I had known it for so many months, was disintegrating owing to reorganization, half the officers with whom I had been most friendly had been killed, and I longed to be doing a more professionally useful job. First aid and sick parades were all that a medical officer in the front line could expect to find ready to his hand, and this could not satisfy for very long a young man who knew that his vocation lay in some branch of major surgery.

The reorganized artillery remained in Flanders for another two months, but toward the end of June rumors ran strongly that we were soon to move south into France to take part in the great Battle of the Somme. Our move began on July 1, and six days later we had reached the Ancre, a tributary of the Somme. On the way I had seized the opportunity of visiting a C.C.S. (casualty clearing station) at Heilly, where a surgeon from St. Bartholomew's was working, and had arranged with him that Sir Anthony Bowlby should be asked to have me posted to this unit. As so often happens in real life, it is knowing the right people that counts, and it was this that now provided the key to the actual beginning of my career in surgery. This could not, however, happen at once, and early on July 7 I was watching from the ridge near Carnoy one of the many attempts to capture the notorious Mametz Wood. I can still see the little black figures advancing toward the blasted trees. Later in the day I watched similar figures, this time running in the other direction while shells fell among them. These were probably prisoners being rounded up after the capture of Contalmaison, but, as usual, we, being on the spot, knew little of what was actually happening. While eating breakfast that day, I was hit on the shoulder by the only missile that actually found me throughout the war, but it was a spent shrapnel bullet, which failed even to penetrate my raincoat.

We were now living under very different conditions from those we had endured for so long in Flanders. We were in the middle of one of the great battles of the war, and armies were in movement. We found ourselves on the crest of a ridge in a line of what had been German trenches with very little food and no shelter. Deep dugouts were there in plenty; but they were occupied by German corpses, and we had to do the best we could on the surface of the ground. It was a good vantage point for watching the line of battle, but the noise of guns of every kind firing over our heads and from all sides was distracting; premature bursts caused some casualties. Three divisions of cavalry were at hand, ready to go through the anticipated breach in the enemy line. On July 12 a German prisoner told us that they were beginning to realize that the game was lost but thought that they would still put up a good fight—as indeed they did. Gradually our artillery moved forward, and on July 17 we were in Montauban Alley, a trench just in front of the village of Montauban with a view from Mametz to Delville Wood of evil memory. At nine thirty that evening we had just finished our supper of bully beef, when suddenly small shells began whistling over our heads at the rate of thirty or forty a minute, making no detonation as they hit the ground. Our gunners were at first completely mystified; but presently a shell fell near us, and it became apparent that these were a new form of gas shell. We were in a shallow trench, and while the other officers were putting on their gas masks, I thought it better to climb up into the open air, where the concentration of gas was much lighter, and so escaped with only a mouthful of gas. One man was badly gassed, and I had to carry him half a mile to a collecting post. By then I was so exhausted that I had to rest there for two hours. When I returned to my unit, it was getting light and raining, but the shelling continued until after four thirty. We reckoned that at least 30,000 shells had been used and began to look around to see what effect they had had. My first unpleasant impression was that only by a miracle had I escaped stepping during the night on one of the many German dead bodies, which lay about in the long grass where they had been for several days, their faces pitch-black and decomposing. It appeared that the bombardment had been aimed at a neighboring crossroad, where we found the way blocked by dead mules and horses, some disemboweled by direct hits. I noticed one of our men sitting at the roadside; he was bolt upright but had no head, again the result of a direct hit. As a gas attack, however, it had been a failure in spite of the enormous expenditure of material. Larger shells now began to fall very close, and I rigged up a tiny shelter in a trench with a roof of corrugated iron and sandbags. The protection was mainly of psychological value, for I was only 200 yards from the crossroad. One shell fell within 10 yards of my flimsy hiding place. There were more and larger gas shells, so that I became thoroughly gassed and almost incapacitated, though there was little I could do in any case. Meanwhile, battles in the air were occurring at frequent intervals and provided exciting interludes. On July 22 we moved forward again, our headquarters being situated between two 6-inch howitzer batteries, with another close behind. It would be difficult to imagine a more unpleasant situation or a more likely target for the German guns. I spent the afternoon preparing some sort of dugout which would provide a pretense of safety. Then at last came the message that I was to join a C.C.S. forthwith at Heilly, and it was with profound relief that I made my way to Carnoy and so by stages during the night to Heilly.

I had been in the front line for a year all but a few days, for most of the time in one of the hottest sections of the trench warfare in Flanders. I was spiritually and physically exhausted and felt that I had earned at least a spell of more creative work away from the front line. I learned later that the colonel of my artillery unit had recommended me for a Military Cross, at that time the most coveted decoration a young officer could be given. I did not get it—no doubt there were many others who deserved it more—but the recommendation was enough by itself to assure me that nothing had been shirked, so that I could concentrate for the future with a good conscience on my professional work, while living in comparative safety and fair comfort.

For the remainder of the war I was able to practice surgery on a huge scale in casualty clearing stations in France. From my first day at Heilly I was allowed to perform abdominal operations under the supervision of my future chief, George Gask, who, after the war, initiated at St. Bartholomew's the first professorial surgical unit in London. I began to feel that I had achieved my life's ambition, though I had not anticipated that it would be under the abnormal conditions of a world war.

After a month at Heilly I was instructed to rejoin the artillery in the front line and actually left for Amiens and Doullens, but fortunately my surgery had made a sufficiently good impression to earn a reversal of the order, and I was now told to join a C.C.S. at Edgehill, near Dernancourt, a ridge overlooking the town of Albert with the well-known "hanging Virgin"; the effigy on the cathedral had been damaged by a shell and left projecting horizontally from the roof, where it remained, a bizarre landmark, for two years or more. The operating theaters were in tents where a vast amount of lifesaving surgery was performed on those men too severely wounded for immediate dispatch to the base hospitals. Those who remained in the C.C.S. were kept only as long as was needed to make them capable of transfer to the base. Many died and got no further. The survivors formed a constantly changing population in our wards, surgical success being measured not only by survival but also by the shortness of their necessary stay under our care. Work was continuous, but naturally varied in intensity according to the sequence of events at the front line. The hospital was too far from the front line to be in danger from enemy shells, but the sound of the guns was the incessant background of our lives, and we could often anticipate the arrival of casualties by noting the increased intensity of the bombardment; this sometimes reached a level that had to be heard to be believed. While there were days of comparative inactivity, at other times the surgical teams had to work for an indefinite stretch of time, limited only by the number of patients to be attended. I have vivid memories of one occasion during a major battle when I was working. After three hours' sleep I had to operate continuously for another twenty-one hours. That night I happened to be orderly officer and was called up after only three more hours' sleep. My physical state was such that I was at first unable to stand, and it took some little time before I could collect my faculties in order to carry out my immediate duties.

Meanwhile, the newly developed technique of blood transfusion was being increasingly used. I learned more than one method during a visit to an American C.C.S. from Harvard University and thereafter applied these, using chiefly the technique based on the use of sodium citrate to prevent coagulation of the donor's blood. The donors were chosen by preliminary blood grouping of both patient and prospective donor, a procedure which was still a novelty. Official encouragement took the form of allowing a fort-night's extra leave in "Blighty" (England) to the donors chosen from among the lightly wounded men. Potential donors lined up eagerly for the test—rejection was regarded almost as a slur on their integrity, the scientific aspect being incomprehensible to the aver-age soldier. Transfusion provided an incomparable extension of the possibilities of lifesaving surgery. Trained anesthetists were scarce, and often I dispensed with their services. A preliminary transfusion followed by a spinal analgesic enabled me to do a major amputation single-handed. A second transfusion then established the patient so firmly on the road to recovery that he could be dismissed to the ward without further anxiety. At other times I was greatly dis-tressed by the state of affairs in one large tent known as the moribund ward. This contained all the patients regarded by a responsible officer as being probably past surgical aid, since it was our duty to operate where there was reasonable hope of recovery, rather than to waste effort where there seemed to be none. The possibility of blood transfusion now raised hopes where formerly there had not been any, and I made it my business during any lull in the work to steal into the moribund ward, choose a patient who was still breathing and had a perceptible pulse, transfuse him, and carry out the necessary operation. Most of them were suffering primarily from shock and loss of blood, and in this way I had the satisfaction of pulling many men back from the jaws of death.

The necessity for this rather surreptitious work on my part and the intermittent activity of such intensity that the standard of treatment would obviously be lowered argued that there was some lack of organization. The whole medical service had inevitably been improvised at the start of the war on a scale previously unknown, and it took some time to adjust the available skill to suit the circumstances. During the year 1917 this adjustment was taking shape, and presently the medical higher command was warned of impending battles, and surgical teams, consisting of operating sur-geon, unqualified assistant, and anesthetist, were assembled at the clearing stations likely to be most heavily involved. Eight-hour shifts of duty could then be instituted by day and night, thus avoiding the extremes of exhaustion previously experienced. I was sent on many of these expeditions, taking with me the transfusion apparatus which I had evolved. This worked so well that it became the standard apparatus in Great Britain for twenty years after the war—though it is now to be seen only in medical museums.

For eighteen months I was engaged in this exciting and often rewarding work, gaining extraordinary surgical experience from thousands of operations of all types from minor injuries and fractures to abdominal, thoracic, cranial, and even cardiac emergencies. The training was in a way unsatisfactory, since it was easy to slip into bad technical habits through the urgency demanded by the work. Sheer physical and mental tiredness must have taken its toll, though it was hard to admit this form of shortcoming. Novel problems constantly presented themselves, mostly surgical, but sometimes of quite a different kind. One of these was the admission to the ward under my care of Prince Friedrich Karl of Prussia, a second cousin of the Kaiser Wilhelm and a nephew of the Kaiserin. He had been shot down in an airplane, a bullet passing through his abdomen and out through his back, perforating the intestine and injuring lumbar arteries and nerves on its way. The intestinal injury was operated on by a consulting surgeon, and the prince seemed to be making a good recovery for several days. He was an embarrassment to the authorities, being related to the English royal family. His cousin, Prince Arthur of Connaught, was sent to visit him, though he came with obvious reluctance. The Intelligence Department thought this might be an opportunity to extract important information from the German prince. Accordingly, a bilingual British officer was disguised as a wounded German and placed in the bed next to the prince so that he could engage him in conversation. It thus became my duty to carry out each day behind a screen an imaginary dressing of the bogus German officer. I resented this attempted deception being practiced on my patient. He was a fine-looking young man with the brilliant blue eyes peculiar to the royal families of Great Britain and Germany. It was impossible not to admire him and to regret that he should be treated so dishonestly, and I have to admit that I was pleased to learn that nothing whatever of military value had been extracted from him by our spy. He was sent on to the base, after about ten days, apparently well, but died soon after from a secondary hemorrhage from the injured lumbar vessels.

The area behind Albert was, as I have said, relatively quiet, but there were alarms at night from enemy activity in the air. Almost every evening soon after dark several German Goliaths would become audible. These were large bombers immediately recognizable by the peculiar beat heard in the roar of their two engines. They dropped their bombs with impunity, since night flying by our fighters was impracticable, until one memorable night when we at last heard a fighter coming to our defense. We saw his tracer bullets ripping into one of the Goliaths, which fell in flames. All the other Goliaths within sight or hearing immediately fled back to their bases, and we heard no more of them for some time.

Our minds and hands were so fully occupied with our work that we hardly ever thought about the end of the war. War, more or less static, had become a normal state of affairs until on March 21, 1918, rumors came to us that the enemy had effected a wide breach in the Allied lines to the south and that our forces were swinging around in retreat. To me, at any rate, the idea that the Allies might be defeated had never presented itself. Ultimate victory was certain, even though the conflict might continue well into a fifth year. Now suddenly the air was full of doubts. On the next day two German fighters, Messerschmitts, appeared out of the clouds and sprayed our camp with bullets from only 200 or 300 feet over our heads. No one was hurt, but it was clear that the incredible had happened.

For many months I had been receiving antiquarian booksellers' catalogues from England and had often had books sent over to me in France. I still have a copy of Sir Thomas Browne's *Pseudodoxia Epidemica*, 1669, containing the note: "Sent off from Edgehill, Dernancourt, near Albert 21 March 1918, the day of the great German offensive. It passed through Albert on 22 March, the last day on which the post could be sent that way." We were instructed the same day to evacuate all our patients immediately by ambulance train to the base and to make ready for our own departure. We left our camp on foot on the evening of March 25, and I spent the night of my thirtieth birthday tramping across country toward Doullens. Another officer and I were detailed to make sure that none of our hospital staff dropped by the wayside. Many of the men were in the C-3 category—that is, unfit for active service—and so enlisted as hospital orderlies. It was with great difficulty that we persuaded some of them not to sit down in their tracks, though somehow all of them did reach their destination. It was galling to be sternly rebuked in the middle of the night by a red-tabbed staff officer on horseback for not keeping our men in proper ranks. He did not understand that many of them could barely walk, and I did not attempt to enlighten him. So we trailed into the citadel at Doullens next morning. I was utterly exhausted and collapsed onto a stretcher to sleep for nearly eighteen hours.

Fortunately the German offensive proved to be the final effort of despair. It reached its natural term with a large salient denting our lines, but with the Allied defenses not seriously broken. Our hospital on the Dernancourt ridge became the front line soon after we left, but we were already getting to work again, with such material as we had managed to salvage, in the citadel at Doullens, a fortress of such strength that no bomb could penetrate into the dungeons where we labored. Casualties poured in, and there was no time to wonder what was happening elsewhere. One day I was operating on a man whose genitals had been mangled by a fragment of shell when I became aware that I was being watched intently by a visitor. I looked up and saw it was King George V; I tactfully gave no sign of recognition and concentrated again on what I was doing.

The succeeding months saw the closing phases of the war with the Allies advancing relentlessly to victory. Soon after the episode at Doullens I was transferred to another C.C.S. as a fully fledged surgical specialist with the rank of major. In these days pneumonic influenza was killing thousands of men who had come safely through the hazards of war; I can never forget the sight of our mortuary tents with the pathetic rows of bodies of the men killed by one of the most lethal epidemics ever known.

On Armistice Day, November 11, 1918, I was with a surgical team at a C.C.S. near Cambrai. A close friend and former rock-climbing companion, George Leigh Mallory, then in charge of a railway gun, was visiting me and shared my tent for the night. Together we witnessed that extraordinary scene, when the whole front in France seemed to be occupied by maniacs, letting off flares, Very lights, and every other form of demonstration they could lay their hands on. Engines whistled and hooted. Discipline had temporarily vanished. We all thought we had seen the last of war. I could not foresee that twenty-one years later I should again put on uniform, this time blue instead of khaki, and spend six years as consulting surgeon to the Royal Air Force.

R. H. Mottram

RALPH HALE MOTTRAM *was born on October 30, 1883, in Norwich, in the house in which Gurney's Bank was founded in 1786. The ground floor formed the offices, in which previous generations of Mottrams had lived, as chief clerks, since the Quaker Gurneys, becoming wealthy, moved out into the country.*

He joined the staff of the bank in 1900, just after their amalgamation with the intermarried Barclay cousins, of Lombard Street and elsewhere, all of Quaker origin. But he himself wished to become an author and was much encouraged by the friendship of the late John Galsworthy, which continued until the death of the latter in 1933.

The outbreak of war in 1914 cut across all such interests. His essay shows how he enlisted, was commissioned, and sent to Flanders in 1915. By a series of coincidences, all connected with the sudden and never anticipated expansion of the armed forces to embrace the whole manhood of the nation, Mottram served in many minor capacities, ending up, sidetracked, in administration. He was thus forced to see, not strategy or adventure, but the daily life men must live to fight. On demobilization he wrote The Spanish Farm *about this existence. Galsworthy liked it and wrote a preface. It was chosen by the committee which governs the Hawthornden Prize for the award of 1924. Encouraged by this, he gave up the bank and became a professional writer.*

"STAND TO!"

"Stand to!"

That command, in a voice hoarse from damp, compelling from urgency, was repeated a few fire bays to the left. It could not be heard much farther off; it was drowned in a rising clamor made up of the earsplitting whiplash crack of rifle fire, the continuous mechanical stuttering of machine guns, sporadic, unpredictable, less staccato explosions of grenades and mines flung through the air. On many a daybreak, during three and a half years, from the first time I heard it, until November, 1918, it was not often punctured by artillery fire, unless some active operation across the trench line was in progress, or contemplated. The order "Stand to!" may have sounded in such daily circumstances, some 1,200 times, in French or English, Flemish or Portuguese, anywhere between La Panne, just east of Dunkirk, and the Swiss border, say, 400 miles. Fortunately, on that autumn morning when I first heard it, we were spared any calculation of that kind. I was busy, thankful to be in bodily activity, that gradually dispelled the wet chill unavoidable when one has slept in a ditch in a Flemish beet field, on wet sandbags, more or less propped over one by a desultory framework of wood. This was what became known as a dugout, a term that had more reality farther south, in France proper, where such shelters could be dug deeper. My business was to see that the men of my platoon were alert, if huddled, on the fire steps, but with their heads below the ragged and sodden parapet, through which they peered at the enemy, a few yards away, across two belts of barbed-wire entanglements, ours (dilapidated), theirs (much better), rifles at the ready, bayonets fixed. Gradually, the noise subsided. On most mornings, movement became possible, with care. The company commander came wading back from making contact with our "next on the left," to ensure the strung-out defense was intact. He paused and removed his rubber waders (four per company), emptied them, and handed them over:

"I hope you'll be so busy you'll make the water in them boil!"

"Here's the brigadier."

He came, bending cautiously, his red-banded cap crumpled in his pocket, visiting his (nominally) 4,000 men who defended his sector, in turns of duty. He glanced around at us and our plight, but spoke in a voice firm as could be expected:

"You understand, Mottram, this line must be held at all costs!" To less enthusiastic volunteers, it might sound like a death warrant.

"Yes, sir!" one responded.

He did his best to encourage: "You can ask for artillery support, if necessary!"

I try to make this record, in as few words as I hope may be vivid, to recall that scene of fifty years ago. I seek to relive the impact on the senses it made, the deafening noise of two immense armies in static collision, the odor of beet field, liberal disinfectant, and odd whiffs of flowerlike fragrance, a last reminder that poison gas had been used on that site six months before. The daylight gradually strengthened. There was nothing to see but wet fields, at which one squinted between sandbags. To expose one's head or even hand was to court wounds. I hope I have shown how lucky a few of us are to have survived. I have already used terms which mean nothing to those who did not witness what I have tried to describe.

The emergency passed. My company skipper said, as the fusillade diminished: "Stand down, now. See they get breakfast!"

I hurried along to find that in their several holes (they were nothing more) the men of my platoon were already trying to boil water, from their bottles, if they had had forethought to bring with them, next to their skin, the only "dry" place, inflammable wood, paper, and matches to ignite the coke they had lugged through the mud. A week earlier, when we had been in support (as I shall show), one of them said to me: "There's lovely taters in the garden of that blown-down cottage. Can we have them?"

"Yes," I told him. "How will you boil them?"

He gave a sheepish grin: "We found a pot. What mother keeps under the bed!"

Let me try to explain words I have used in this strange recital.

Stand-to happened also at dusk, but with less emphasis. Dawn was the dangerous moment at which some attack might be expected, though surprise became rare in that continuous battle. As it grew dark, both sides would be waiting for their rations, food, ammunition, supplies to be brought up, by horse-drawn limbers, to the dump some hundreds of yards to the rear, from which they were distributed by hand. It was just folly, committed only at the height of "great offensives" (always futile) to goad the enemy (or he, us) by shooting up his (or he, our) supper or other "meals." Stand-to is now an evocative paragraph heading in any eyewitness account of what I have tried to describe. It happened twice a day, for all those years, along all those miles, in half a dozen languages. Why? Let me offer a brief reminder to at least half the readers of these words, who were not participants in these scenes but to whom they constitute history, if only unofficial.

In 1914 Germany was the foremost nation in the world, an empire created in seventy years from some scores of principalities and dukedoms. She justified it by her lead in philosophy and education, manufacturing for export, music, and, above all, her rigid military discipline. Inherited from Frederick the Great, it was based in the twentieth century on the threat: "The French will use their black troops; the Russians will unleash their Asiatic hordes." For, in 1870, Germany, newly united, had defeated France and taken from her the title Empire. She had no less taken from her Austrian partner, the mantle of Charlemagne and Hapsburg under its aging, frequently bereaved hereditary head, the old Emperor. Austria, also an amalgamation of duchies, had a core of German language and habit surrounded by non- and even anti-German races and was competing with Russia for the leadership of those largely Slavic elements in southeastern Europe that had, before 1914, thrown off the centuries-old Turkish regime. A German railway had reached Istanbul.

Germany might well have continued to lead the twentieth century, had there not been the detonating fuse of ill-will between William of Hohenzollern, third Kaiser of the German Reich, and his uncle Edward VII, pleasure-loving, easygoing, who preferred French life and outlook to German. The actual explosion, as anyone can read, came through the assassination of an Austrian imperial heir, while he was visiting what was then Serbia. It was all so remote from Britain, in 1914. Edward VII is credited with having created an *entente*, after years of mistrust, with France. Queen Victoria, the aged little German grandma, was dead. A vaguely progressive political upheaval had given us a so-called liberal government, committed, as various factions that composed it thought, to Home Rule for Ireland, advances in education, housing, wage earning: Even theology blinked an eye. What possible interest had we in the rivalry of Russia and Austria? We were alone, and regarded by both opposing groups as being treacherously alone, in our island. To France we were dubiously, not allied, but in *entente*, whatever that was. Did it extend to her ally Russia, so long a threat to our hold on India? None knew, least of all ourselves, preoccupied with home politics. *"Ils vont nous lâcher,"* M. Cambon lamented. It looked so. To Germany we were the century-old naval obstacle to her aspiration for overseas colonies. To America, socially attractive, but, as it now seems, even then incredibly remote, if no longer antagonistic. Of that August, one quality has outlasted half a century: sheer astonishment. While, in a week or two, immense armies mobilized, we were debating other, nearer matters.

But there was, occasionally remembered, the crowning "treachery" of all. We were parties to "guaranteeing Belgium." The cynical amusement this caused leaped to murderous hatred. "Of course," said the Germans, "if we don't outflank France there, France will outflank us! It is obvious. Will Britain fight?" "Great Britain guarantees only that no other European power shall hold Flushing." "It is obvious!" said the French. "Will Britain fight?" To us, only a signature, years before, on a treaty, was obvious. By the narrowest margin, members of our Cabinet dissenting, the rest of us, as if walking in our sleep, stood by the hardly known treaty, and fell into, rather than made, war.

We didn't nationally mobilize. We couldn't. The idea was anathema. We had the Navy, forbidden to disperse as it concluded its annual maneuvers. We had our professional Army, so accurately described by the Kaiser, from his point of view, as "contemptible." It was 120,000 strong, located in India and Ireland. We got it home in record time, without interference, and sent five divisions to join the French. We had our Territorial Army, "Saturday afternoon soldiers" for "Home Service only." They went to the coast, unless asked (politely) if they would mind serving abroad. (A few did so, at once.)

"Not so long as I can get home at nights," one replied. I heard him.

We had Kitchener, who had defended Egypt from the Mahdi's conquest and subdued the South African republics. He called for 100,000 men to enlist, above those already engaged, for three years or "Duration of the War." No one knew when that would be. He got them and asked for another 100,000. While Russia and Austria, France and Germany were locked in some of the greatest battles of history, these "Kitchener's men" and scores who otherwise couldn't push into the recruiting offices and went to the Territorial battalions were gradually sworn in, given one silver shilling to "serve the King." Our pay was one (shilling) and twopence a day (twopence for Brasso to shine buttons). By Christmas, when the Continental armies were fought to a standstill, we were clothed, billeted, armed, some with rifles from Japan, light as toys, drilled, and organized.

How did I fit into this unique, rabidly individualistic lack of preparation? I was then thirty-one, with aging parents to care for and a job one couldn't just abandon. I managed to "enlist," with difficulty on account of the crowd. Barclay's Bank, in which I was employed, promised to give us back our places in it, when "Duration" permitted. I was no soldier. Under the influence of my friend Galsworthy, I wanted to write poetry. But by the early weeks of 1915 the old regular ex-sergeant major who drilled us at Lowestoft was saying: "You young men with education ought to take commissions."

I applied, was gazetted on April 1 (ominous date), little knowing that this alacrity to make me an officer was caused by the casualties we had suffered. Even so I had months of trying to train even less trained enlistments. I heard about various expeditions to Antwerp, the eastern Mediterranean, and Asia. By September, Kitchener's first 100,000 and his second, some Territorials, and the Regular Army were launched on their first major offensive in Flanders, the Battle of Loos. Magnificently gallant, it just failed. The Germans, startled, were preparing to evacuate Lille.

I now have to record a series of strokes of good fortune so personal that I cannot claim I deserved them. They must be what are called coincidences. They are these:

I was given my embarkation orders to join the 9th Battalion of the Norfolk Regiment. I found these troops outside the Belgian horse-coping town of Poperinge, railhead of the Ypres sector of the British-held line of defense. Shattered and hastily re-formed, they were billeted in farmhouses as the bombardment of Loos died down. I found a "mess" of what were the unwounded survivors. There were only 8 out of 32 officers. I was hardly surprised, having threaded my way through the evening hate, long-distance bombardment at stand-to. We were relics of K 3, Kitchener's third 100,000. It did not take me long to discover what this extemporization lacked. There were just no more trained experienced officers. Had the confusion been less, I myself might have been dragged into Loos and killed out of hand. Instead, I was sent in the morning to interview the brigadier, an ex-professional soldier.

"Can you ride a horse?"

"Yes, sir!" (I could sit on one without falling off.)

"Can you use a motorcycle?" from the staff captain.

"Yes, sir!" (I had had one of an early type.)

"Can you speak foreign languages?" (He was thinking of Indian dialects probably.)

"Yes, sir!" (French fluent, some German, Flemish seldom written.)

"You'll have to do Intelligence!" He did not say that the real Intelligence officer had been killed.

"We take over the line tomorrow. Report at the Furnes Canal Bank at stand-down."

I was given a lift. From ancient picturesque Ypres, already largely rubble, within 100 yards of the line, the canal to the North Sea soon ran into inundations that preserved that tip of our defenses on to the beach, for four years. The spoil bank had already been thoroughly honeycombed with more elaborate dugouts than were possible behind the fire steps. I was bidden to sit down with the brigadier (a great privilege), his brigade major (deputy, for Operations), and staff captain (administration), all professional soldiers.

What was this line of defense into which the earlier combats of 1915 had stagnated?

I have said it ran continuously for 400 miles. It was triple. Facing the enemy were the fire steps from which we watched. Some hundred yards west (*i.e.*, on our side) was the support line the various units exchanged for the fire steps at intervals of (we hoped) a week. That was about as much as men could stand of being wet and missing sleep. More hundred yards farther back at the reserve line, where the dump for rations lay, one could walk about, at that distance, just out of bullet range. Thence stretched back toward Poperinge and the railway, some 11 kilometers, a view of ruined Ypres, abandoned farms, tracks in the mud, avoiding roads which the enemy was liable to snipe. I tried walking along one and was pursued by field gun shells. The troops in this situation were formed (in all armies of that period) into infantry divisions. Ours consisted of three brigades of infantry, of four battalions of approximately 1,000 bayonets each, three brigades of artillery called gunners (18-pounder field guns, 4-inch field howitzers), three companies of Engineers (called sappers), four field ambulances (called all sorts of names, but gladly resorted to), and supply and transport details, perhaps, in theory, some 20,000 men commanded by a major general. Owing to some reorganization after Loos, we had been shunted into the 6th Division, largely of Regular professional troops, which had joined the first five divisions of the British Expeditionary Force after Mons. The 7th and 8th divisions accounted for the rest of what had been the old prewar Army. Those numbered 9th to 14th were Kitchener's first 100,000, Scottish, Irish, northern, and so on according to their districts of enlistment. The 15th to the 20th were the second 100,000. K 3 was never so clearly identifiable; there were just no more volunteers, and units were raised where they could be. The divisions numbered 30th onward were formed of the Territorial Army and eventually ran up to the 70th. Cavalry were seldom seen except as individuals. The air was the element left to the Royal Flying Corps, newly formed.

Divisions held the line for varying periods of weeks, brigades alternating and then (until active operations occurred) went back some miles to rest (reinforcements and renewals). This rough description begs at once the question: This town of English-speaking near soldiers, strung out for all those miles, had to be housed (a whole fringe in the open), clothed, fed, sanitated, cared for in wounds and sickness, transported, and kept in fighting trim. For years. How? One element at least, was our divisional "Follies," an amateur music hall entertainment held in a concert hall at Poperinge. If the enemy bombarded, the actor next to sing would say, "The town major wishes to evacuate the theater." This was greeted by howls of derision by members of the audience who had been under much closer bombardment for weeks. This entertainment was unofficial, but it played its part, in the morale of volunteer conscripts. In 1918 they were more homogeneous, less restive than any other army. All the others, save the Americans of 1918, collapsed and disintegrated; even the French Army had critical moments of disruption. The British, for only a few days. I saw their final parade at Lille in 1918. Tired, battered, disillusioned, the slow-tempered, compromising British lasted best. But mark one element of this dryasdust paper view. Men were being killed all the time. Miraculously, I wasn't.

But to resume my account of my reception at brigade headquarters. I was given a wire netting mattress under the telephone. The others disappeared. I was rather pleased to feel I was, apparently, of some use. That didn't last long. Shortly, there was a crescendo in the continual firing just ahead. Field guns joined in. Then our 9-inch.

What on earth was I supposed to do? Wake the brigadier? Ring the artillery? I had just no guidance. Fortunately I did nothing. Gradually the noise died down. I suppose I drowsed. Months later I heard an explanation. The first enlisted Canadian troops wrote home describing the conditions on troopships (cattle boats strewn with straw). This adversely affected recruiting. The authorities (can they have been so intelligent?) said: "Very well. Plutocratic young Canadians can book their own passages and enlist at Liverpool."

When this news (Canadian pay was a dollar, not one shilling

twopence) reached Reservists who had not been called up, they discovered relatives in Canada and went to Liverpool to enlist. The authorities were delighted. No longer would a Canadian colonel have to greet his parade: "See here boys. An English general is coming around. Stand up straight in line, and quit spitting, and for Christ's sake don't call me Alf."

The Canadian formation we were relieving had thus become sprinkled with old soldiers. Told, that night, that they were going to march back to camps near Poperinge, they knew better than to carry 120 rounds they had been issued and emptied their pouches into the enemy. The Germans, still very nervous, responded, but not for long. They wanted to be relieved, too. Luckily I didn't wake the brigadier. Did he guess? But Intelligence was a farce. Then and for years after there was little information you couldn't gather from air scouting. I did odd clerical jobs for the staff captain and rode his horse. He was busy. In about a week the brigadier said: "Your company commander is short of officers. He wants you back." I was rather pleased to go. I was wrong.

Trench warfare, someone said, consisted of boredom relieved by moments of terror. I took part in the endless round of fire step, support, reserve, company reserve, brigade reserve (that meant going up at night to dig). The days of the week meant nothing. There was nothing to do but prop up our dissolving piles of wet sandbags, which might be useless any moment when we got the order to go forward, and clear the enemy out of Belgium. We were getting more guns, even more shells. Rations did come up. We were not seriously attacked. The enemy was busy with the Russians. But there were always fewer men, never enough or better ones.

With one's feet in the snow and one's head and shoulders meagerly sheltered, one wrote to relatives of casualties: "Dear——, I regret to say your son is posted missing. I cannot say what happened, but will let you have any news of him I can gather. He was liked by his comrades and did his duty courageously." Sometimes we were able to mumble, crouching over dead bodies, as much of the burial service as we could recall. There was sickness, of course. There were "schools" to attend when one could be spared for riding, bombing, machine gun, the Mills grenade, and the Lewis gun as they eventually appeared. To what purpose, we wondered. Then amid such routine, among so many wartime lives, something did happen. Apparently irrelevant, it happened to me.

In the darkness of those nights, wading through a spatter of bullets, a runner brought a pink message form: "Officers having knowledge of foreign languages are to report to divisional headquarters."

By the light of a flickering candle, crouching in the company commander's shelter, we read it over. He said:

"This is IT. We are going to break through at last. We shall see what your French and German are worth. You'd better report." He kindly added: "We shall miss you!"

I dodged along to the dump and got a lift. It was an instructive ride. Behind me was the flicker of star shells fired by nervous foes. All around, in gun positions and hideouts, revealed by cracks of light or snatches of talk and song, was that vast "town" of an army in position, waiting for (we hoped) a spring offensive, the dream of successive years. I was decanted at POP (Poperinge) and found divisional headquarters in the *Salle des Mariages* of the town hall. An elderly, tired, disgusted ex-Indian officer grasped, at length, why I had appeared.

"Look at this," he demanded. "Can you deal with it?"

"This" was a pile of blue forms, printed in French, filled up by people more used to hoes than pens. The title was *Réclamations pour les dégâts occasionés par les troupes britanniques*. There was voluminous detail.

"You'd better have a look in the morning." He wanted to get away. I didn't want to stop him, dumped my pack in a corner, and proceeded to loosen my belts.

"Get someone to find you a billet," interposed he, horrified at the idea of my trying to sleep in his "office." It was, in fact, drier, safer, and quieter than I had been for some weeks. A night-duty signaler found me a mattress. At stand-to, the junior staff captain put me right.

What had happened was this: At the Second Battle of Ypres, in April, 1915, the Germans had endeavored, by the first use of poison gas, to reach the Channel ports. Canadian troops, directed by "Old Plum" (General Plumer, the only Army commander with any understanding of the use of infantry in an essentially static infantry battle; the others were of cavalry training), had narrowly fought off the attack. The line had been pushed back to the walls of Ypres; the inhabitants fled, leaving half-cooked meals and beds unmade. British cavalry, coming up to restore the situation, found theselves in (wartime) clover. They ate the food, slept in beds (beds!), used chairs, or shelves, any dry wood, to light fires. In that hop-growing district, in which vines are trained on great poles, we were said subsequently to have burned a million of these. All this didn't matter, until, in a few days, the Germans were obliged to fall back. The inhabitants returned and found what use had been made of the houses they had so prematurely abandoned. Now the French are used to nationwide army maneuvers and their national interruption of civil life. Householders, farmers, and tradesmen, under French law, were entitled to claim for such depredations, hedges gapped, broken windows, endless disagreeable demands of soldiers practicing their trade.

When the inhabitants of the Flemish border found what had been done (with all the exaggerations of real war conditions by *British* troops), they made a first-class row in the Chamber of Deputies. To appease French opinion and keep them in active participation, these special forms were printed and circulated to the British armies concerned. South of Plumer's 2d Army at Ypres, Horne's 1st Army extended, then, or shortly, to Arras, and the 3d and 4th eventually took over, later down to St.-Quentin. But the most continuous occupation was in the Département du Nord, and that was what the H.Q. of the 6th Division wanted me to deal with. It was the sort of job no real soldier liked and, in fact, resented. It was interference of the "natives" (that was how staff colonels and majors thought of the inhabitants) in the business of war. It was no glorious project of a breakthrough. It was a tedious, repulsive business they were determined to shift onto other shoulders. Mine were apparently appropriate. It was all part, little realized at times, of a war that went on too long, in closely populated, civilized country, not the wastes of Indian frontier or African veldt, where there was nothing to destroy. I was given a desk in the corner of the office of the deputy assistant adjutant and quartermaster general, the Q or "Admin." office, out of the way of the real staff officers "busy fighting the war," and told to get on with it. To me, it was not only safer than anything I had known for months. It was something TO DO, other than the futile business of propping up an ever-demolished parapet and enduring extreme discomfort, if not actual wounds.

The real staff officers were very cordial, once I was installed. I saved them trouble. They willingly lent me their horses they had no time to ride, gave me a brief booklet edited by the War Office, and put me in G Mess with the vet., the medical officers, and to my great pleasure, Comte Sanche de Gramont (junior branch of the family) and Baron de Wynck. These were the French and Belgian liaison officers. Often with them, by any transport available, I set to work. De Gramont was a handsome, educated fellow, speaking excellent English his Scots nanny had taught him in infancy. Like most Frenchmen of his kind, he expected adequate catering from life, war or no war. When our messing was not good enough for him, he just said, often effectively, "Change the cook." When his young woman of the moment disappointed him (they had many counter-attractions with the British Army), he changed her for another. I am not criticizing him. He left his comfortable, easy job to join the French Flying Corps and was soon killed. De Wynck was less spectacular. But as the ominous news leaked out that the Germans were taking advantage of the Russian winter to mount a massive onslaught on Verdun, De Gramont was likely to say: "When are your people going to do something, Mottram?"

About that time, in fact, we were coming to the end of our volunteers. Various national service expedients were tried. The 6th Division, after months, was moved out, reinforced, and prepared for what we dimly heard of as a great offensive, in the Somme district, miles to the south. I was so busy it meant little to me. I was getting about to the various farms and hamlets to which the blue forms *"Réclamations pour les dégâts"* related. Some I satisfied with a small payment in lieu of rent they had been deprived of. Sometimes it was a question of persuading the unit billeted not to tether their horses to the destruction of enclosures. Sometimes it was a new road through a pasture. At others, an airdrome, then demanding 80 yards' runway, absorbed a whole field. If the old farmer (all the men of military age were gone) spoke only Flemish, he usually had a daughter or wife who had learned French and, as time went on, some English. The glad news that something was being done about damage in billets ensured that there were always more fresh claims to be dealt with. The news of the Irish Rebellion hardly stirred our consciousness, occupied by more immediate risks.

I recall queer incidents. The Guards Division relieved us. I was bidden (I had become general utility man) to hand over various trench stores, tents, latrine buckets, I forget what else. I was left in our camp, my horse tied up, until a nice-looking young officer in a raincoat (no badges) appeared.

"You're dashed late," I told him. "My division has been gone for hours. Sign for this stuff. I want to get off!"

To my surprise he beckoned a senior near him, who signed for him. Outside, as I mounted, I noticed an unusual number of military police about. I then realized I had been addressing someone who is now known as the Duke of Windsor. I caught up with the division, but there was no rest for me. "Tell Mottram to do it" was applied to all sorts of odd jobs. Eventually I got a lift in De Gramont's car. We went south, by ever more crowded roads. We overtook a marching unit. I recognized the cap badges and waved. It was the last I saw of my own battalion, the men I had commanded, or indeed of the division in which I had served. I suppose it was something to do with the Somme battle. Apparently someone had felt the need for an overall direction that constantly shifting infantry divisions couldn't provide. All I know is that I was (at some length necessary to any official organization) removed from the division and placed under a commission presided over by a general. I found later that the same sort of thing happened to the officer in charge of laundries (imagine organizing the washing of a million shirts a week! If they became lousy, that meant typhus, as in many another army before or since). It might be trench tramways (another specialist job). It might be fire fighting (billets were always liable to be carelessly handled). It might be water supply (great canvas tanks drenched with chlorine). Roads (the French second-class roads were quite inadequate, though Napoleon's granite-paved military main roads were excellent, so far as they went—*i.e.*, from one center to another). I was allotted to an area. It happened to be not the Somme, but Ypres-Messines. I had to ease the installation of all the troops that, after months of mining and countermining, blew up the whole ridge shielding Lille. Was it a diversion to succeed the Somme? Lloyd George thought it had shortened the war! But not by much. It may have caused the great retreat of the enemy, who drew back some miles. That was far more impressive to us than the dim rumor of a revolution in Russia:

"Good thing, too," someone said; "perhaps that'll shake them up."

We hardly listened. I was out all day and every day, by whatever means I could secure, trying to fit more and more troops into my area, from which was to be launched what is now known to history as the Battle of Passchendaele. I forget what number of guns was employed. I do not forget (there are photographs now to show) the effect. It turned a wide belt of wet Flemish farmland into a sea of over-knee-deep mud.

When, at length, this failure, like all the other failures of those years, was abandoned, people as preoccupied as I had been had leisure to read the papers. We learned that the much discussed Russian armies had made peace. This had set free an extra sixty German divisions to forestall the American armies that the conduct of total war had called into being. But when would they be ready?

The outlook was so bleak that I obtained eight days' leave and had just time to be married. It was January 1, 1918. Not a very auspicious day.

The Germans did their best to prevent me. It is all history, now, that on March 21 they attacked and shattered the southernmost sectors of the British-held line. They just failed to break through. Their second stroke fell on April 11, on the edge of my area in the

Lys Valley. The salient of Armentières was pinched off. My last view of the rich farmlands in which I had helped to find some respite, I hope, for thousands of tired, dispirited, decimated troops, was taken from an automobile I commandeered. I had been as far as Bailleul, shelled to the ground. I had seen a whole civil population walking, with what they could carry on their backs, to what they hoped was safety. As it grew dark, star shells hung over Estaires and Merville, Locre and Kemmel Hill, familiar places where I had so often smoothed over the *"occupation par troupes britanniques"* with small doles from an imprest account. *"Mais vous êtes si riches!"* was the hopeful protest. On that night a whole countryside was in flight. I met no one. Shuttered houses were empty and silent.

That was forty-nine years ago, almost to a week, as I record it. There is something in tenacity, Galsworthy's favorite virtue. "Old Plum" never relinquished Ypres. The magnificent American armies of General Pershing were in France. Ominous enough at the moment, that exhausting day proved to be the peak of the enemy effort. After weeks of hasty readjustment, the old 2d Army front sagged but held fast. A few weeks later, calling on French troops that had been brought up to support us, I saw the weary old liaison officer in their divisional headquarters, moving the little flags on the Operations office wall map FORWARD. I nearly corrected him. But a few days later, a British brigadier asked me to arrange a maneuver area for him, as he took over.

"You can't have it there, sir," I pointed out; "that's in enemy occupation now."

"No, it isn't. He's gone. My patrols can't find him!"

It was true. The victorious German Army had overreached itself. It melted away. My next orders were to arrange for the return of civilians to the area that had been fought over. They had sown their potatoes and wanted to harvest them, so brief had been the recoil of the 2d Army. The magnificent American Army was in France. Even so, it was almost too late. When the Armistice came it was nearly an anticlimax. The war of those days (they call it conventional warfare now) had gone on too long, demanded too much. Demobilization, so eagerly looked for, became a hardly bearable strain. It was haunted by the same astonishment as in 1914. No one had ever demobilized 1,000,000 British men from overseas or knew how. It was five years, when I returned to my desk in Barclay's Bank, since I quit it to enlist. It was occupied by girls. However, I was reinstated. I felt numb but thankful. Many a man had had worse luck than I.

Recovering gradually, I tried to make amends. I, at least, knew what I was fighting for, and how that old frontier, from Dunkirk down to Cambrai, had been fought over again and again, down the centuries. By the series of coincidences, I saw and handled the British who fought and the civilians on the spot who made summary room for them. Many a man must have been marched up to some half-destroyed village and killed there not knowing where it was or why. The most striking features of that landscape were great solid old farmhouses, we knew as billets, many of them called *Ferme l'espagnole,* the Spanish farm, because they had been built as block-houses, in the sixteenth century, to accommodate Spanish troops of the medieval Austro-Spanish Empire to keep back the French. We were facing the other way, but the ghost of half-forgotten conflicts haunted that area, and the anxieties of the women who braved life, the courage of men like De Gramont, gave me a theme and I wrote of it all as *The Spanish Farm.*

It is, of course, the wrong sort of book of the war. It is not about military triumphs or political results. It is about the uneasy alliance or *entente* that barely outlasted five years of British or French history. Galsworthy liked it, and wrote a preface to say why. That, perhaps, persuaded the committee who choose the award of the Hawthornden Prize to bestow it on me in 1924. Galsworthy is now enjoying a posthumous boom, and that may be why I am asked to recall my "experiences in or understanding of the Great War." The letters we exchanged while we served encouraged me to do as I am now asked.

If my book gives an intimate picture of the daily course of the war, fought between English-speaking men, scattered among French and Flemish borderers, it must be in the last scene, in which a "stranger" goes back to survey one of the 2,000 graveyards in which British dead are marked by memorial crosses. He finds the names of those he had commanded "properly at ease," beneath their little crosses.

Edwin Erich Dwinger

"I was born in Kiel on April 23, 1898. My father was an Imperial Marine officer from Holstein, and my mother, Russian by birth, was from the Tula district. I went to school in Kiel, but spent every free hour on horseback. My father's home, an estate in Holstein, bred splendid riding horses.

"In the spring of 1920, after my return home from Russia, I was found to be highly tubercular. Staying first in an Alpine sanatorium, I soon managed to become the owner of a small estate, dividing my time between the breeding of horses and the writing of novels. My first book, Korsakoff, appeared the very next year, and I wrote usually a novel a year. Army Behind Barbed Wire (1929) and Between White and Red (1930) were translated into twelve languages.

"I spent World War II with the 10th Tank Division, whose staff officers Klammroth and Hargan procured the bombs for the intended assassination of Hitler. They were my friends; thus, in the summer of 1943 Himmler confined me under heavy guard on my estate.

"Since World War II, I have written five books, and I have traveled all over the world."

THE FIRST CIVIL WAR
OF THE WEST*

◆━◆━◆

I SHALL NEVER forget the first of August, 1914, a Saturday. Suddenly, up from the street, came drumbeats and the shrill signals of two trumpeters. I ran down, and saw two drummers, an officer behind them, and back of him the trumpeters. The officer read in a

---

* Translated from the German by Herbert Schaumann.

far-carrying voice: "His Majesty has ordered a general mobilization. Starting the first of August. . . ."

The small group marched down the street. At the next intersection they assumed the identical formation. Again the drums rattled, the trumpets brayed, and the officer's sharp voice proclaimed: "His Majesty has ordered. . . ."

The days immediately following were charged with a turbulence of which I would not miss an hour. From dawn to night I roamed the streets, happy that our summer vacation from school was still in force. Every soldier in his new gray field uniform was heartily being cheered, troops on their way to the station were pelted with flowers, and the liveliest hubbub rocked taverns and cafés, where, with hardly a pause, bands kept up the playing of patriotic tunes. Till their voices gave out in utter hoarseness, all rose to share in the singing of *"Deutschland über Alles," "Die Wacht am Rhein"* and *"O Deutschland, hoch in Ehren."*

It is impossible to convey to anyone nowadays the genuine enthusiasm that animated us and our absolute conviction of a real danger. Perhaps I might now falter in my description of this "rise of a nation," but I have as a co-witness the report of Carl Zuckmayer in his splendid book *Als wär's ein Stück von mir (A Piece of Me)*. No one, surely, will charge Zuckmayer with nationalism, and with him I reassert unequivocally: The German people felt that they had been unjustly attacked; they genuinely believed that they had to beat off an encircling aggression. They fought not to conquer, but to save their very lives.

I had just turned sixteen, but I knew, of course, I would enlist. Getting hold of a picture atlas of regiments of cavalry, I wrote that same day to a dozen garrisons. Naturally, I chose regiments by their uniform: Cuirassiers, Uhlans, and Hussars—in that order. I did not bother about Dragoons. Were their uniforms at all fit to ride in?

Never will I forget the painful morning that brought the first batch of replies. The very envelopes enthralled me. "The 3d Pomeranian Cuirassiers," "The 2d Uhlans of Brandenburg," "The 1st Silesian Hussars." At last I had opened them all, and my proud head was bowed. Every one of the regiments was packed to bursting. They no longer accepted volunteers.

At once I became more modest, choosing less illustrious outfits. In place of the Cuirassiers, for instance, I tried the Hunters on Horseback, whose uniform, if not their fame, resembled the Cuirassiers'. Of late His Majesty had authorized them as the alternative to the Cuirassiers, to accommodate the sons of rich industrialists. This creation of the regiment explained its derogatory epithet: "Shopkeepers' Cavalry."

My second try yielded three affirmative replies. They were terse. I was to report for an examination in the business offices of the regiments. I traveled from regiment to regiment. The verdict, in each case, after a glance, was: much too young, admissible perhaps in a year. . . . I was to come back in a year? But then the war would be over.

My modesty now had sunk to the point where on my way home I made the rounds of all cavalry garrisons, even the Dragoons, "the Black Parchimer" and the "Red Ludwigsluster." I begged, I implored them, and they laughed in my face, the heartless sergeants. They were only Dragoons, I consoled myself, a common outfit. But they kept up their song: As yet we have enough seventeen-year-olds. There is not a chance for anyone born in ninety-eight.

Again I was back in the Hamburg railway station, when I chanced to hear of a regiment of Dragoons lately shifted to Wadsbeck owing to the evacuation of Alsace-Lorraine. Instantly I rode out to Wadsbeck, my last chance. I completely disregarded the old saying,

> Dragoons, part man and partly cattle,
> Are infantry thrown on a saddle.

Bold-faced, I set all on one card, answering the decisive question: "I'm seventeen. . . ."

This, at least, got me as far as the examination. I was declared fit. Proudly, I again presented myself at the business office of the regiment, and I was admitted into the presence of a benevolent major. He once more asked me my age. I could not lie to so fatherly a gentleman, and shyly, like a young girl, I whispered, "Sixteen." He was about to dismiss me, when I was seized with the courage of a steeplechase rider facing his topmost hurdle. "Is it then," I piped up in my most manly manner, "a question purely of age, without regard to suitability?"

With a laugh, he grasped both my shoulders. "All right, you're in."

The very next day we got our uniforms. They were fifth-hand, of course, each item being too large by at least three sizes. The dark blue trousers, stiff with patches, could stand up by themselves, the sky blue tunics were the merest threadbare semblance of the original fabric, and the white cuffs and white trim appeared never to have been white at all.

Our first days passed in emptying with our hands the stables of horse manure. Polishing of gear, luckily, soon was added, though for a long time not a word was breathed about any of us mounting a horse. That day, too, arrived, and each of us got his very own "critter." They were easily the worst. We called them bargains. They were conscripted nags, in all stages of the life of the animal, newly come from pulling a milk cart, or beer barrels, or a plow, or a gypsy caravan. Mine, a veritable elephant, was called Valkyrie. I could scarcely see across its withers. In time I managed the beast, but only by drilling her for hours in the stable during every one of my night watches.

There followed, a few weeks later, the first exercises in the open. How wildly our hearts beat whenever the staff trumpeter galloped past our platoon. He held the trumpet flush with his horse's neck, and the braying metal screamed as though the sound were torn from the throat of the animal. And how handsome the signals were: staccato for trot and a melodiously rocking interval to start the gallop. At other moments, if the sergeant caught us crampedly seating our mount, we had to walk the next evolution, pacing at a long-legged gallop alongside our horse, while the hoofbeats of the next row of riders all but drummed up the length of our spine. Still, no one, though it is now fashionable, should speak here of military chicanery. We were young, and the hard training, far from hurting us, later saved our lives. How else could we learn to mount with lungs heaving from exhaustion, the mouth fighting for breath, and the heart about to burst?

After another four weeks we were handed what we had been waiting for uneasily, yet with a secret pride: the lance. It sounds like the Middle Ages. Yet I actually wielded a lance, and this very moment I could perform its manual: "Thrust to the ground." "Thrust backward." And the chief command: "Lances lowered for the attack."

The lance not only necessitated our managing the horse with one hand, but at the thrust one had to bend deep down to the earth. We had to learn to shift the lance and, finally, to twirl it at a gallop above our heads. The lance taught us to ride.

I never will forget the spring evening we passed through Hamburg in our gray field uniforms, headed for the freight terminal and our shipment to Russia. At the head of our horses nodded flowers, and flowers were stuck in our carbines and tied to the tips of our lances. The reins lay knotted at the horses' necks, for our hands were held by girls walking on either side of our mounts. Eternally in force, despite all wars, continues the ancient saying: horses—riders—girls.

We arrived directly in Kurland (a former Russian province on the Baltic Sea, now a part of the Latvian S.S.R.), and we were fed into the great advance, the last victorious ride of divisions of cavalry. And we faced cavalry, Dragoons from Petersburg, royal Hussars from Moscow, and Cossacks, countless like the hordes of Genghis Khan. We had to ride—ride—ride.

The pine forests churned with heat, the rosin heavy with a fragrance as of burning. The sand stirred dustily, and the fens sucking our horses' hooves made a smacking sound. We passed the spot where our regiment had ridden an attack in the grand style, a ride that was history. Learning of it and knowing that half the men of my outfit had died in that charge, a Mars-la-Tour of our times, reconciled me completely to being a Dragoon. I no longer felt sorry for myself. Rather, I considered myself lucky in having hit on a regiment whose fame, outlasting that of all others, shall remain.

One fact dawned on me even then: This was to be the last war using cavalry. Technology was about to obviate the horse; machines would take its place. With the passing of the horse, all noblesse of warfare would die. The laws would cease to be honored that so far had cast wars in a knightly mold. I was a part of the last military engagements embodying a higher tradition.

And another fact not only reconciled me to my place with the Dragoons, but filled me with a heady pride: My commander was Count Holck, the greatest steeplechase rider of the century. I recalled his having worn our regimental uniform over the hurdles in Kiel. Rarely did he enter a race without winning it. Light blue and white were his colors. What could exceed the thrill of riding under such a man?

The attack I finally rode was not in the grand historical manner or under Count Holck. I was simply another young ensign in a small patrol. It was premature, this last attack of mine, and the occasion of my being shot down, off my horse, and of my dear comrade, little Nil, being shot, and of my capture by the Cossacks.

I was hit the very instant I was waving my naked sword to flash to my platoon the signal for the attack. "Attack. . . . Lances lowered," I was about to call, and "At—" was all I could get out. My sector sprang apart like a puddle hit by a fist. Little Nil straightened in the saddle, stiff as a candle, wavered, and fell over backward. This was the end of our rocking rides with lances hip-high. This ended the war of noble knights.

Of course, I should have cried, "Mother," but instead I called, "My God, why have You forsaken me?" Professor Schwartz in Biblical studies had singled out this cry as "strikingly indicative of the humanity of the Son of God," and at this moment it spontaneously rose to my lips. I was, after all, only seventeen.

I awoke with a sense of someone sawing off my legs. My mouth was full of earthy crumbs, for in my pain I had bitten into a plowed field. My hand blindly fingered for my sword, but I had been robbed clean. My telescope, my watch, my revolver, the small bag I carried on a string around my neck—all were gone. "I'm a prisoner," a small voice kept screeching, and the realization hit me worse than a bullet, dead center inside my skull.

Can I possibly save myself? My legs are lamed, my back is rigid, and I can't even shift my weight. A fire rages between my thighs as though they clasped burning coals. I open the trouser fly and insert a hand. To the right, along the inside, four of my fingers slip into a gaping hole. To the left, farther down, close above the knee, only one finger finds room in a wound.

"I shall bleed to death." The recognition scarcely pains me. Already I have lost too much blood to be strongly affected. Death, after all, might be preferable to captivity. Gazing up into the blue sky, I strain my head toward a wind-whipped flapping. It is one of our lances. Its wimple, black and white, tugs at the staff in a call for help.

Some Cossacks eventually ride by. They have tied our subaltern to a stirrup. His face is white as chalk, and he is limping. Being hurried past breathlessly at a distance of about five steps, he sees that I am still alive, and he points my way. Two Cossacks jump from their horses and come strutting toward me, bow-legged. One of them looks at my bloody belly and motions as if to say, it's no use. . . .

But they do not prevent Schmidt II from stripping down my pants to bandage me. Tensely I watch my right thigh. If it now gushes, then I've had it; but if it merely wells, gently. . . . "It merely wells," says Schmidt II, reading my thoughts. About me lie a few of the dead of my troop, and passing among them, Schmidt appropriates their small packets of bandages. With a groan he lowers himself to his knees and starts bandaging and bandaging. "What a stinking mess," he says darkly; "it keeps oozing through."

At last they button my tunic, and supporting my back, they lift me. With my right arm around Schmidt's shoulder and my left hugging a Cossack's neck, my legs dangle jointless like a puppet's filled with excelsior. "Get going," the Cossacks call, swinging themselves into their saddles with a metallic clatter.

At the next field station I am being properly bandaged. With other wounded in a small Cossack cart I am driven to Mitau, then to Riga, and finally to Moscow. Here in the quarters of the Gruditzki Regiment, transformed into a military hospital, I look down from my window on all the Kremlin.

After about four weeks I am told that my once chance for

survival lies in amputation. My right leg will have to go. "But," I groan, "then I couldn't ride. What's the use of living if I can't ride?"

At the very last moment, Bruno von Brehm, the Austrian writer who later will gain fame with his book *Apis and Este,* chances to pass my bed. At the time he is a young cavalry officer with the Artillery. He does not cease his efforts until he locates a professor who saves my leg. I owe him not only my life, but all my hours on horseback that were yet to come.

That autumn suddenly we were chucked from our beds, and in a march on crutches through all Moscow we were led to the Ugrieschkaja Station for the transport to Totskoye. This prison camp turned out to be the worst in Russia, though it lay in the European part of the empire. Typhoid here in one winter killed 17,000 out of 20,000 men.

In justice it must be said that the disaster of Totskoye genuinely moved the Russian people. At the time of the highest daily losses, Delegate Gladisch delivered in the Duma an unpitying accusation that made the other delegates blush with shame.

"These horrors," he said, "are perhaps the worst of all time, because this senseless destruction of thousands of young people was caused not by primitive men, but by beings on a higher stage of their development. Only last year a sanitary commission categorically declared these barracks unsuitable, being infested with typhoid. The interdict did not keep us from piling into them twenty thousand men, and the epidemic, of course, followed. But since this billeting had been carried through against the express order of the sanitary commission, the disaster assiduously was kept from the authorities. Hence its uncontrollable proportions: no one dared request medicines for a camp that had never been listed." The representative closed his speech with a reminder of the pyramids of human skulls raised by Genghis Khan. He called these less degrading than the pyramids of human corpses achieved by the twentieth century at Totskoye.

So great a panic seized the guards at the height of our dying that they and their horses were about to take flight, leaving the camp to its fate in the steppes. But then appeared the governor of Orenburg, General von Sacharow. "I have heard," he said, addressing the officers of Totskoye, "that this camp is to be left to its fate since its inmates apparently are past help. Yet since five thousand are still alive, I order all men and officers back to their posts. As for my issuing this order from a safe distance, I shall take quarters here for the duration."

True to his word, General von Sacharow moved into the barracks. He caught typhoid. In a few weeks he died on his voluntary post.

Some statistics may be in order here. Of 170,000 German prisoners of war in Russia, only 90,000 returned home. This means that nearly every second man perished. In combat only every eighth soldier was a casualty. The probability of losing one's life was four times larger in captivity than in the field. And more would have perished except for the good offices of Elsa Brändström, the daughter of the Swedish ambassador in Petersburg. She with other women of the Red Cross brought trainloads of help to almost every prison camp in Siberia.

In spring, Siberia was our destination. The survivors were shipped a month's journey by boxcar, to Camp Dauria in the Transbaikal. This camp lay in the midst of a frontier garrison of Cossacks near the Chinese border. The Cossacks here wore the same yellow stripes down their trouser seams as those who had taken me prisoner in Kurland. This, in a sense, made them old acquaintances. For two years I lived here near the Gobi Desert. The next station on our railway line was Manchuria. We built a camp theater, where I performed as an "actress." Epidemics now claimed only a few victims.

During the Kerenski revolt in February and in the six months following, all went well, for we had befriended many Kerenski officers. But the regime was toppled in October, and Red Guards entered the Transbaikal. At the time we cheered them, for they embodied, or so we thought, a national upheaval engaging our deepest sympathies. We turned from them after their atrocities committed on our friends, the Kerenski officers. These horrors inwardly enlisted us on the side of the counterrevolution, which was about to reconquer all Siberia. We hardly resisted Admiral Kolchak's call to join his White Army. We were promised our instant return home after the conquest of Moscow, and we joined the Whites with easy hearts. At the time they were on a victorious sweep westward.

With a few officer comrades I was part of the Cossack Corps of General Kappel, the best general in Kolchak's service. The last chief-in-command of our army was a Lieutenant General von Sacharow. Having to report to him, I expected to meet Governor von Sacharow from Orenburg. "That," he said with a smile, "was my father." This was the second Sacharow I met in Russia. A third one was to follow, and I would like to mention him briefly, though my dealings with him relate to World War II. I met this Sacharow while I, with General Wlassow of the Soviet Union, was in process of forming an army of liberation, to fight on our side in the over-throw of Bolshevism. The Sacharow I met on this occasion was a fine captain of infantry, the son of my former chief-in-command. Like his father, he became my friend. The general, until he died, had been a frequent guest in my home. The third Sacharow is every inch worthy of his grandfather who, as a White Russian, perished under the Soviets.

Our victorious advance on Moscow faltered in the late summer of 1919. It turned into the riotous flight east, which really had been expected. The nearer Moscow, the more our troops melted away. Our reinforcements had to negotiate 12,000 kilometers and Red partisans who, having been left behind, infested the forests every-where. The congested Red Army of Trotsky, ebbing backward at last, instantly and in many places pushed through our thinned ranks.

Our renewed trek all the way back to the Transbaikal—the *Anabasis* of modern history—left 1,000,000 dead in the snows of Siberia. In Atschinsk alone died in one night 40,000 horses, and a whole row of towns perished of epidemics in the wake of our passing. General Kappel, who had been wounded, froze to death in crossing the frozen Baikal, but General von Sacharow, with the last of his faithful followers, managed to reach Chita.

The Red Guard caught up with us, the remnant of Kappel's corps, in the center of the blue ice of the enormous Baikal Lake. I succeeded in dressing in the uniform of a dead Red Guard, and I appropriated his papers. Later I identified myself as a certain Trossmann, a German prisoner of war forcibly abducted by White Russians.

For the third time I entered a prisoner-of-war camp, this time near Irkutsk, but I soon escaped its barbed wire. Pretending to be a Red Guard out of service, I traveled west, chiefly in trains, which once again were running. For the fourth time I managed the distance of 10,000 kilometers, posing as a Red Guard in districts run by Reds and presenting papers provided by a Swedish delegate in the few dispersed sectors still held by White Russians. With the help of Swedish delegates I also saved nearly all my notes which underlie my books *Army Behind Barbed Wire* and *Between White and Red*.

In 1920, long after the war, I finally made it back to Germany. I bought a small estate, and again I was on horseback. The breeding of noble strains of horses is still my passion. Looking back from this height of life to World War I, I repeatedly reach the conclusion that it was the first civil war of the West.

Cyril Falls

"I was born on March 2, 1888, at a nursing home in Dublin, my parents then living in County Longford. I have no memory of this phase because, before I was a year old, we moved to County Fermanagh, where we took a handsome late Georgian house, Killyreagh, some 3 miles from Enniskillen. My schooling began at a dame school in the London suburb of Norwood, chosen because it was near my maternal grandfather's house, continued at Bradfield College, Berkshire, and concluded at Portora Royal School, Enniskillen. I was a somewhat unsatisfactory pupil, except in history.

"My first book of any importance was a study of Rudyard Kipling, the proofs being corrected in a tent early in the First World War.

"Having published a history of the 36th (Ulster) Division, in which I had finally served as general staff officer (G.S.O.) 3 (my material coming from the office in which the official histories were compiled), the director liked it well enough to appoint me to write several of the volumes. This made me sufficiently known for the London Times to take me as military correspondent to succeed Liddell Hart at the beginning of the Second World War.

"Soon after this war I was appointed Chichele Professor of the History of War and Fellow of All Souls College, Oxford, both appointments coming to an end in 1953. Since then I have been a free-lance writer and have published a number of books, one a best seller, entitled The First World War in England and The Great War in the United States.

"I was married on leave in 1915 and we have two daughters with large families, one married to a lieutenant colonel in the Royal Marines, the other to a former lieutenant in the Coldstream Guards and now representing in London a big firm of New York brokers."

THE BEST OF MY WAR

I. LIAISON WITH THE FRENCH

MY EARLY SERVICE in the First World War was with my regiment as what is known as G.S.O. 3, a junior officer on the Operations staff of my division. I shall begin recounting my experiences with 1918, when I was appointed a liaison officer with a French division. I owed this great pleasure to one of our staff who had been appointed to G.H.Q. and, when more liaison officers were needed because a British corps was serving under French command on the Chemin des Dames, mentioned that I spoke good French.

I was, of course, delighted because this would be an interesting job and would give me an opportunity to see what the French had left in them after the terrible defeats they had undergone. The journey, in three successive cars, was somewhat farcical because no one had heard about my appointment—not even the French Mission at the headquarters of our 4th Army, or even the French corps to which my division belonged.

When I arrived at corps headquarters, the laison officer, Romer Williams, well known as a hard rider to hounds, told me I must stay for dinner and for the night. Then I was initiated into the game of keeping one's end up. The next day the corps commander was entertaining the *commandant d'armes* of Amiens, now nearly deserted, and the Chief of Staff said I must lunch with the junior staff officers. Williams said that if so, he would do the like, a good riposte because he was a favorite with the corps commander. So it came about that we all sat elbow to elbow and had an excellent luncheon.

That afternoon Colonel Lister, the liaison officer with the French 1st Army, came over and we three drove to the headquarters of the 37th Division. On the way he improved the occasion by giving fatherly advice. My chief task would be to "create an atmosphere" and keep the French and the Australians on their left on good terms. There would be little office work. I would have a car and a British driver, a very rare amenity for one of my status in those days.

When I was left amid a babble of French, my own seemed rusty. The divisional commander, Garnier Duplessis, patted my shoulder and said he hoped I would be happy and must complain to him if I were not. The headquarters, in a chalk quarry, consisted of two big huts, one for the staff, the other for the artillery headquarters, and everyone slept in saps cut into the chalk. It looked comfortless, but that night's dinner was far better than in our messes. Only the general had even a minute room to himself, and the rest slept in bunks—calling up memories of decent trenches in a warm spring or summer. The next day I looked into a little cottage across the road and found it empty, but undamaged. On asking why, I heard that the general had forbidden anyone to sleep outside after there had been some bombing at night. Later on I ventured to move in with all my possessions, including canvas bath and bed. I believe he was the only one unaware of my disobedience.

I saw a very different background when I visited the 3d Australian Division soon afterward. There they had comfortable huts in a valley and kept their dugouts for emergency. A day or two later I paid my first visit to the front line, accompanied by my opposite number with the Australian right division. Villers-Bretonneaux, in the front line, had been captured by the Germans and retaken by the British. We found officers of both nationalities playing poker, and the Australians complained jocularly that a fat French company commander, known as Captain "Pinard" for his pleasure in the ration wine, was cleaning them out.

This sounds as though it were an extremely quiet front, which it was not. The Germans fired quite heavy bombardments from time to time and made some raids. The Australians were first-class raiders, but the French division, the infantry being half Zouaves— now largely made up of Parisians, the capital city having no regiments of its own because most revolutions had started there—and two Algerian Tirailleurs did not gain much success.

The enemy also made great use of mustard gas. It has been said that this was a disgusting weapon, but in fact, even those fairly close to the explosions suffered no pain and indeed often remained with their units. The horror came when the burst was so close that the victim was splashed. Then, indeed, he suffered agony, was sometimes returned to civil life, and occasionally died.

I got a shock when I discovered that Garnier-Duplessis *never* visited the front line. Had he been a British divisional commander and had this been discovered, he would have been sent home immediately and at best given some job such as a civilian could have undertaken. Yet the Frenchman was one of the ablest soldiers of his grade in his country's army. From first to last he treated me with great kindness. The staff officers did visit the line, but much less often than ours.

It may seem absurd that, though it was obviously desirable for Australian and French staff officers to do so together, it was not easy to arrange this, though I occasionally managed to do so and acted as interpreter. The Frenchman stood at a table, sometimes as early as 6:30, drank coffee or chocolate, and perhaps ate a piece of toast. The Australian breakfasted a good deal later, and heavily. He did not care what time he got back, whereas the Frenchman felt he had to do so by 11:30 for *déjeuner,* his main meal of the day. It may be a slight exaggeration to say that he was almost as liable to reproof as a British officer on a guest-night in time of peace, but that was how it struck me.

However, there was eventually a change. Garnier-Duplessis was promoted to the command of a corps, to be succeeded by Simon, till now commanding one of the brigades. Intellectually he was not the equal of his predecessor; but he went up often, and I, of course, always accompanied him if he was visiting the junction with the Australians. One occasion sticks in my mind. Though there was some shelling, occasionally nearer than I liked, he insisted on entering an unpleasant advance post, where he fell and cut his hand badly on broken glass. To our shame, neither of us had the bandage or the disinfectant everyone was supposed to carry. An Australian private insisted on using his and tied up the wound. What grand men they were! In the line their discipline was first-class, but it was sometimes free and easy when they were not.

One serious offense, very amusing in its way, was related to me by a medical officer. An Australian private had reported to him that he had been peppered in the back by shrapnel. On examining the wounds, he realized that they had been inflicted by something much smaller and, when the man refused to come clean, gave him a jag that hurt. The Australian then confessed that he had entered a farmyard far behind the front and stolen a sucking pig. As he reached the gate, an old farmer in nightshirt and nightcap had fired at him with a shotgun from his bedroom window.

There had been some speculation on whether the enemy would launch yet another offensive and that it would cover our front; but this soon passed, and Lister said there was nothing to stop my going on leave. My wife and I had a pleasant time, first in London, then at the seaside. About ten days after my return, when I was visiting the Australian corps headquarters, the brigadier general, Thomas Blamey—famous in the next great war and dying a field marshal— kept me to luncheon and told me that my division was to be relieved by Canadians and that I would move to the next French division. This suggested to me that it was not the enemy who were going to take the offensive. Thenceforward I had a series of visits to make and interpreter's jobs to do.

There were some comic incidents. For instance, when I returned from escorting several officers from G.H.Q. and army headquarters "to see the strength of our defenses," I told Simon that they had examined the crossings of the Luce River, almost in the front line. He grinned and said this seemed unnecessarily far forward. I gathered that he knew by now what was really brewing, a major Allied offensive, before which his division would be relieved by a Canadian—though Blamey had said I must not tell him so—leaving a few Australians in the front line in case of a raid.

Champagne was served in my honor, and the general made a delightful farewell speech, ending with a toast. When I rose to reply, I stammered—I do not think my French failed me, but a lump in my throat made me pause and stutter. "If the French do not like you," Lister had said soon after my arrival, "they can be poisonous; if they do like you, there's no limit to their kindness." I decided, I hope with gratitude and no conceit, that these Frenchmen must like me.

On August 2 I drove to the headquarters of the 42d Division, humble beside what I had left. General Deville sat at the head of the table in a shabby tunic and served the soup himself. At first sight he seemed to me a mass of nerves. Then I recalled having heard that the division, in which he had served in the Battle of the Marne as a brigadier and never left, had a high reputation. Two days later Simon arrived with Beauregard, both very smart now that their division was temporarily out of the line, for a conference. Before departing, he asked Deville if he could spare me for luncheon the next day, at which he smiled and said he would try.

What a morning! Everyone was busy, but after about half an hour the general appeared. *"Mon cher Falls, on vous à fait attendre. Vous aller mourir de faim. Mais avant de nous mettre à table j'ai un mot à vous dire."* He got out a piece of paper and read the following: *"Chargé d'assurer un service de liaison, s'est porté a maintes reprises, pour l'accomplissement de cette mission, jusqu'aux postes les plus avancées et les plus exposées. N'a cessé de faire preuve d'entrain, de bonne humeur, de sang-froid, et de bravoure."* Then: *"Je vous remets votre Croix de guerre,"* and it was pinned on. After that we sat down to the happiest of luncheons.

On the fifth I took the French orders to my fellow Ulsterman, Major General Lipsett, commanding the 3d Canadian Division, and got a copy of his, after which he kept me for dinner. Not long afterward I was sad to hear that this good soldier and charming man had been killed when commanding a British division.

During the afternoon before the assault we moved to an advanced post. I had to face various crises, inevitable on such occasions. It seemed that I had hardly got to sleep when an orderly shook my arm, and I got up to find it still dark and very foggy. After our *petit déjeuner* we were handed sandwiches, and our water bottles were filled with wine. We soon moved up to a dugout in the old front line, where I found the general talking in quite good German to a group of officer prisoners, who addressed him as *Eure Exzellenz*.

He began to fidget about the lack of news from the left, but all I could get from the Canadians was that things were going very well. However, the visit was made worthwhile by what I saw on the main Roye-Amiens road. A long column of prisoners was approaching, those at the head carrying wounded of both sides on stretchers. In front of all was a magnificent young Canadian, carried shoulder high by four Germans, lying on his stomach with his chin propped on his forearms, obviously enjoying his position and making me think of a victorious Roman general in a triumph.

I now said I would try to cross the trenches in my car, memories of former offensives having prevented our horses, just what we now wanted, from being brought up. The trenches were being filled in by troops of the oldest classes, and the car lurched over easily enough. The German proved worse, and we should not have got over had not the *pépères*, as these men were called, heaved the car across. I got a fair amount of news and witnessed the rout of a German counterattack by a French column which formed line as if on parade and swept the enemy away with light machine-gun and rifle fire. On my return I found Deville, who had also been out, in the highest spirits. *"Nous avons indiqué à nos troupes leurs objectifs avec notre canne, avec cette canne là,"* he cried. A change after sitting at a telephone and perhaps finding that the troops were back in their old front line!

The next day I transferred to the 126th Division, commanded by General Mathieu. I was driving through our new headquarters when I heard a voice shouting: *"Monsieur le capitaine Falls!"* It was General Deville. He said he had cited me in his divisional orders, which meant that I had got the *Croix de guerre* twice in four days and was entitled to wear two stars on the ribbon. A great day, and my joy kept me going, though I had had only seven hours' sleep in the last two nights.

Now came an unhappy affair. The 126th Division was to make a dawn attack, but the British 32d, rushed up from reserve to the Canadian Corps, would be unable to do so until 7 A.M. Romer Williams telephoned that he had been unable to get either the French or the Canadian corps to see reason. I stayed up till I learned that orders had been changed for the better. At 4:30 A.M. Aublin, my French opposite number, arrived in a fury with new orders: The 32d would not attack until 9:30. Mathieu picked up the telephone to stop our assault but had hardly begun to speak when we heard the roar of our artillery. The French, thus starting alone, made fine progress but were driven back by a counterattack on their open flank, and the British division was later repulsed with heavy loss.

On August 12 a crack division of Chasseurs, the 47th relieved the 126th, and I finally discovered why the British did not want to push on. Haig was determined to break off the attack and set his 3d and 1st armies, reinforced by the Canadian Corps, going, while Foch wanted to continue on our front. The generalissimo finally gave way and agreed that it should be released for the new offensive.

I pass over some of my worst days of the war until the early hours of the eighteenth, when the telephone woke me and I learned that General Rawlinson, who commanded the 4th Army, had issued orders that all liaison officers were to be replaced and that I was to report at G.H.Q. The speaker, Lister's successor, said that everyone in the liaison knew I had done my best and had said so, but Rawlinson would listen to no explanation. Lister had left a note mentioning my *Croix de guerre* and added that he had meant to put my name forward for a further honor, which could only have been the Military Cross.

Dillemain said he would gladly give me a good-conduct mark, and Mathieu, who had somehow got my news, offered to write to our G.H.Q. to say that I was in no way to blame for the misfortune of his division. I was deeply touched, though I did not feel that their kindly intervention would do much good.

After about a week at corps headquarters, helping Lister's busy successor, I drove to G.H.Q. at Montreuil. There I was told that I was not to return to regimental duty because there was a shortage of trained staff officers. The officer concerned asked if I would like to visit the United States to talk about Intelligence staff duties. This was a fascinating opportunity, but I said I would rather see things through. He then told me that until a vacancy occurred, I was to go to 6th Corps headquarters for attachment, and he then sent me off by car. There I picked up useful lessons but became bored by having no responsibility. I had to wait with what patience I could

muster until October 8, when I joined the 62d Division, commanded by General Sir Robert Whigham—and lived happily ever
after.

II. WHIGHAM AND THE 62D DIVISION

WHIGHAM was by far the best of the three British divisional commanders whom I served. He had recently returned to France after a
long spell at the War Office and refused the command of a corps
because during his absence the type of warfare had so greatly
changed. He demanded a great deal of his staff, but the only time I
saw him lose his temper was when our capable signals officer was for
once remiss.

Soon after my arrival we ran into trouble. The G.S.O. 1, a
gunner officer with an excellent record, had no previous staff
experience and proved unsatisfactory. On a vacancy occurring in
one of our artillery brigades, he was sent to fill it and did so well.
His successor, a very senior officer for the grade, also proved indifferent, but it was impossible to swap horses again. The consequence was embarrassing because the general virtually always dealt
with our brilliant G.S.O. 2, "Mouse" Bissett, who took charge with
such aid as I could give him.

On the day I arrived, a great attack was launched by the 3d and
2d Divisions, and the Guards made ready to go through. It will be
seen that we were in excellent company, but the 62d deserved to be
in it. It had come out late, as all second-line Territorials did, and
gone too soon into the horrible Bullecourt affair, to suffer crippling
casualties. Its commander, Major General Braithwaite, had pulled
the survivors together, and it had been joined by three crack
battalions from Palestine, one to each brigade, to replace Yorkshire
battalions broken up. Everyone was delighted that he had been
promoted to the command of a corps because this expunged the
blot on his scutcheon created by the fact that he was considered to
have been a failure as Chief of Staff at Gallipoli.

The attack was generally a great success, but at the junction
between our corps and that on our left the enemy made a damaging
counterattack with five captured British tanks. I wrote in my diary:
"Our infantry cannot face them any more than can the Germans.
How would the war have ended had Germany been first in the field
with tanks? I am afraid there is only one answer, even though she
probably has not had, anyhow since 1917, the industrial resources to
develop them as we have."

On the morning of October 9 we moved up to the neighborhood

of Flesquières, of evil memory because of the repulse suffered there on the first day of the Battle of Cambrai. The next morning it appeared certain that the Germans would make their next stand on the Selle River, running northward to the Sensée at Denain, and that our turn had come.

When we were given our objective, we realized that our task would be difficult because the enemy had dammed that river by blowing up the railway bridge at Solesmes, so that we could not cross it on our own front but would have to do so on the fronts of the flanking divisions and then turn inward. There was another complication: The corps orders said that though many civilians were known to be in the town, there should be a heavy bombardment. Whigham showed himself at his best here. We knew that even though there were plenty of strong cellars, many of them would be smashed by high explosive, whereas those taking refuge in them would be safe if only shrapnel were used. On the other hand, if the enemy launched counterattacks against our flanks, he would not be stopped by shrapnel. Yet Whigham decided to take the risk and proved right, since there was no flanking counterattack.

Our assault was launched at 2 A.M. on the twentieth and was so successful that nothing more need be said of it. I went forward after daylight and met a lightly wounded private coming up from Solesmes, who called to me: "There's kissing going on down there, and a bit more than kissing, with Jerry shelling like hell all the time." I questioned civilians regarding any signs of a new line of defense, but they knew of none, though they said the country became close a little farther on. I gave the children the biscuits in my pocket, to their great delight. In all, I was about for twenty-four hours without feeling very tired. The wine of victory is stimulating.

Shelling continued to be very heavy the next day; but there was good shelter, and the 3d Division was about to pass through us. I rode into a village ahead hoping to acquire information about the Ecaillon. The villagers did not think it formidable, though they said there was now a good flow of water. They insisted on my drinking a cup of their very small store of coffee, and I had to wipe away a tear or two created by their plight. This time I had filled my pockets with biscuits and earned popularity by kissing a golden-haired beauty of six on a comparatively clean spot.

On October 30 we learned that we were to relieve part of the 2d Division and found good billets and a good house for headquarters in Solesmes. November opened with grinding work, but I found some relief in riding to get information about the enemy, especially his battery positions. I was given remarkable aid by an extremely intelligent priest about the little towns of Gommagies and Fresnoy, as likely to be obstacles. Then I returned to give such aid as I could to Bissett. He now excelled his best hitherto, remaining as cool as a cucumber, however hot the pace. I never heard a grumble from the brigade commanders from the time I joined the division. The next day I compiled a list headed "What to Look For," giving such information as I had picked up about fences and hedges, with map coordinates of all known German batteries, many of which had escaped in this open warfare simply because the troops had not known where they were. I had fifty copies sent out.

On the night of the third I drove up to synchronize the watches of the brigade concerned in the first phase, leaving the car outside the village because it was pretty close to the front line. It was pitch-dark, and I had hard work finding the headquarters. Suddenly there was a series of crashes, and a salvo—heavy stuff—fell unpleasantly near. The whole business did not last more than a minute, but it was a very unpleasant one. Not given to prayer, I found myself repeating a school mnemonic for Latin adverbs, beginning: *"Ante, apud, ad, adversus."* The shooting over, I eventually found the headquarters, had a chat, and set watches for the morrow's "zero."

November 4 was a great day, that of the launch of an offensive on the front of three British armies, everywhere successful. Our brigade crossed the Rhonelle, a tributary of the Ecaillon, and captured Fresnoy. We took more than 700 prisoners for some 500 casualties, a high proportion wounded because the German artillery was either quickly silenced or pulled out. The next day saw another big advance but few prisoners. We could not realize that this would be the pattern until the end of hostilities, the enemy never making a strong stand but handling machine guns and a few batteries very cleverly. To our delight we kept neck and neck with the Guards Division, which took some doing. Whigman jumped into open warfare as though he had experienced it for the last four years, and Mathieson, commanding the Guards, was equally good. On the whole front the British took about 400 guns, but the Germans did well as regards the number they got away. On November 5 we reached the outskirts of the famous Forest of Mormal side by side with the New Zealand Division on our right.

The next day we found that every captured or evacuated position had a little mound of empty cartridge cases, as Whigham rubbed into corps headquarters when it suggested we might get on a little faster. Some of our supply column lorries were on the roads from sixteen to twenty hours of the twenty-four. Another handicap was that the Germans had left a number of hidden delayed-action explosives on the railway, which went off days or even a week after being laid. However, we reached our objective, neck and neck with the Guards.

On we went again on the seventh, but advanced only 3,000 yards, good in the old days but not now up to expectations. Whigham and my seniors pushed on to establish a new headquarters, leaving me in a fairly responsible position for some two hours. When I moved on in the dark with the clerks who had remained with me, the car stuck in a ditch in pitch-darkness, and I had to tell the driver he must wait for a lorry to pull it out. By road it was nearly 2 miles to the new headquarters; but on studying my map with a torch I found that directly through the Forest of Mormal, it was only about 600 yards, so I bade the doubting clerks follow me and set off down a ride. That soon ended, and we plunged into the forest at its thickest—the clerks angry because they thought we were lost. Next, we heard a car running its engine, which meant a road ahead. On we went, to find it was the engine of the headquarters electric light set, running in its lorry. Honor was saved.

Great news came in that night. German *parlementaires* came through the lines near Guise, with a pioneer company to repair the road. We picked up a plaintive message on the wireless beseeching the French to stop shelling in order to let them through and later learned that they were to meet Foch on the morrow.

The next day I ran into a horrible incident. An old man, one of a party helping us fill in a crater, mumbled that a girl had been murdered by a German. I went with him to a cottage, and the parents told me the story. When our foremost troops drew near, the girl, aged sixteen, called exultantly to a German who was making off: *Courés vite! Voici les anglais!"* The brute swung around and shot her dead. I sent in a formal report, knowing that it was useless because the family did not know the man's name.

November 10 was quiet, so that I could ride round Maubeuge and its splendid Vauban fortress. November 11 was one of the most famous days in history, when the Armistice began and hostilities ceased at 11 A.M. I give the opening of an article I wrote in the *Times* for the fortieth anniversary:

Just before 11 A.M. on November 11, 1918, many British batteries fired defiant last salvos, carefully ranged as ever. Then silence fell. The gunners' gesture was not a sign of excitement. There was little of that. Many doubtless thought of lost kinsmen and friends, but the prevailing mood seemed to be a groping effort to realize that all was over. At night, however, some bonfires were lit. Very lights and coloured rockets streamed into skies illuminated by a sickle moon entering her first quarter. This was 40 years ago to-morrow. Many thousands of the youngest soldiers in this Armistice scene are now grandfathers.

I myself felt that vile as the war had been, it had been so vast, such a mad upheaval of the greater part of Europe, that survivors would always feel they had played a part in one of the most curious events in world history. That night came exciting news: We were to form part of the Army of Occupation. This was a tremendous honor for a second-line Territorial division, and we were the only ones to enjoy it. Many men, including the dead, had contributed to our standard, but it would not have reached this without Whigham's leadership. This was still tested because the Territorial officers, who had become excellent leaders in battle, could not induce the rank and file to think of anything but demobilization, as Regulars would have contrived to do.

From now on I had to do a great deal of riding, because in picking up knowledge of the country ahead, I had to take short cuts along lanes so muddy and churned up by the Germans that they might have put a car out of action. The Germans had supplied location lists of unexploded delayed-action mines on the railways, but these had been so well hidden that they could not always be found even with this information. The officers responsible were sent for to find them and, as might be expected from engineers, showed as much courage in extracting them as they had in laying them.

For brigade and divisional headquarters the slow march through the Ardennes was fun. The latter stayed at several chateaus of great antiquity and beauty, but the longest stop was at a modern one. We gave a big dance there, fetching most of the ladies in warm and comfortable ambulance wagons. When the guests departed I pushed the French liaison officer, Polignac, member of a famous family, into one unlit inside. He was good-looking and said to be a terror to the opposite sex, but they faced the terror unflinchingly.

I pass on to our arrival at the little town of Schleiden, in the pleasant but primitive Eifel, inhabited by primitive people. In some villages they had not seen a car for years and did not know whether we were German, English, or French. There we had a happy Christmas dinner.

Some of the troops not having behaved quite like little gentlemen, I was hardly surprised when a man was charged with rape. The officer defending him asked the girl three questions. "Where and when did this take place?" Answer: "Outside the stables about seven P.M." "How long had you been talking to this man when it happened?" Answer: "Not more than half an hour." "Now [loudly and impressively] tell me whether the same thing happened the previous night." Answer (with tears) : "Yes." The court: "The case is dismissed."

We ended the year with a great binge in B Mess. After dinner there were tugs-of-war, cockfights, juggling, and songs. Just before midnight there was banging on the street door. We ran out to find A Mess, headed by Whigham, standing in the snow. In they came, and he was saluted with "For He's a Jolly Good Fellow," to which he replied that we all were jolly good fellows. Soon afterward the headquarters moved to Düren, where there was an excellent theater and a good permanent company, equally at home with plays and opera. There was a ban on fraternization, but this did not affect me because, as G.S.O. 3, I was responsible for arranging these affairs and concerts. The German players and singers might almost have been described as neutrals, devoted only to their art. The prima donna was something more. A big military car often called for her after the show and took her to Cologne to spend the night in presumably fairly senior British company. Those of us who enjoyed opera also went there from time to time, and I have seldom attended one more delightful.

Before I returned to England, I witnessed Germany's sufferings at their worst. I came on a big party of boys seated at the roadside lunching off leeks and thick slices of dry bread. I mustered enough German to ask the supervisor who they were. He told me they came from an orphanage—90 percent war orphans—and were working on the repair of the road. They were chatting as boys do, but distressingly emaciated. It took days to get the memory out of my mind. These poor youths were not criminals; they were paying for what the country's leaders had done in starting the war.

By May I had to think seriously about my future. I knew I should enjoy the Army in peace but would almost certainly be reduced to the rank of lieutenant, a prospect I did not relish as a married man. I am sure I took the right course when I decided to return to civil life.

Sir Compton Mackenzie

SIR EDWARD MONTAGUE COMPTON MACKENZIE *was born on January 17, 1883. His father was Edward Compton (Mackenzie), who for more than thirty years kept old English comedy alive in Great Britain and in Ireland. His mother was Virginia Bateman, the third daughter of H. L. Bateman, the first American impresario to invade England. He discovered the genius of Henry Irving.*

Compton Mackenzie was educated at St. Paul's School and at Magdalen College, Oxford. He started and edited a paper called The Oxford Point of View *and was a leading figure in the Oxford University Dramatic Society. He took a second class in history.*

His first book was a volume of Poems *published in 1907. His first play was* The Gentleman in Grey, *produced in that year. His first novel,* The Passionate Elopement, *was published by Martin Secker in 1911 after having been refused by many publishers. This was the first of more than forty novels and fifty works of autobiography, history, memories, belles lettres, etc.*

During World War I he served with the Royal Naval Division at Gallipoli and, after being invalided out, was military control officer in Athens and director of the Aegean Intelligence Service in Syra. He received the O.B.E. (Order of the British Empire) and was a Chevalier of the Legion of Honor and of the Redeemer (Greece). In 1923 he founded and edited The Gramophone. *He first broadcast in 1923 and is still broadcasting. He made his first appearance on television in 1938. In 1931 he was elected Lord Rector of Glasgow University as the candidate of the Scottish Nationalists.*

In 1946 he was commissioned by the Indian government to write the history of the Indian Army's achievement in the Second World War and spent more than eighteen months traveling all over the East. He is LL.D. (Glasgow and St. Francis Xavier, Antigonish), Hon. R.S.A., F.R.S.L., and a Knight Commander of the Royal Order of the Phoenix (Greece). He was knighted by Queen Elizabeth II in 1952.

FROM NAPLES TO CALAIS

ON NOVEMBER 11, 1968, the end of the First World War will have happened fifty years ago. Am I being extravagant when I surmise that if television had existed then in its condition today the First World War would not have happened? When I look back to 1914, I am hardly able to believe that the outbreak of that war came as it did.

In June, 1914, I was in Capri working hard at the second volume of my novel *Sinister Street,* the first volume of which had been published the previous autumn. It was growing very hot, and I felt that a little holiday would help my progress with the book. Three days but not a minute more could be spared: three full days of sun and seawater and laziness. Vincenzo, my boatman, had relatives in Nerano, a village on the far side of the Sorrentine Peninsula, and he knew of a house, right on the beach of Cantone below, a tumbledown old *palazzo* where we could spend as many nights as we liked. On the third evening Vincenzo had gone up to Nerano to get the evening's provisions and newspapers. I see him now coming down with them through the dusky olive grove above the beach.

"What news?" I asked.

"No news," he said; "some Austrian duke has been killed somewhere. *Ecco il giornale!*"

It was too dark by now to read even the headlines, but in the candlelight of that tumbledown *palazzo* by the sea's edge I read how the Archduke Francis Ferdinand had been assassinated at Sarajevo. I must have had a moment's illumination of the future, for I declared that this murder would mean a European war.

Vincenzo smiled. *"O signor scherza,"* he said politely. All believed that I was joking.

Four months later, when we met again, he would be reproaching himself for being such a fool as to think I was joking on that fateful June evening.

I decided that my wife and I must get back to England as soon as possible. That journey from Naples to Calais has remained in my memory as the end of an epoch. As the train runs northward through France, the names of the stations we passed—like Verdun— seem printed in blood. Yet the head steward of the restaurant car, a German with a fair Kaiserish moustache, was so courteous and attentive that on our way north I began to think we might have been premature in hurrying home so quickly. Michael Arlen came along and made himself known to us. When I told him we were hurrying home in case war was on its way, he smiled indulgently at my overheated fancy.

It was in the middle of July when we got back to London, and I went off to Lords to see Oxford beat Cambridge at the university match.

Various friends I met asked what had suddenly brought me back from Capri.

"I'm worried about this war," I told them.

"This Irish business? Oh, that'll be all over presently."

"I don't mean civil war in Ireland. I mean a European war."

"Of course, you would have to work out for yourself something improbable."

That state of mind could not exist today in similar circumstances, thanks to television.

Nobody I met would consider a European war even a remote possibility. On the posters advertising that infernal paper, *John Bull*, at the tail end of the omnibuses was TO HELL WITH SERVIA.

Convinced as I was of the imminence of war, I was in a fever to finish *Sinister Street*. My wife and I went to stay in the country where I would often be writing and revising all night and going to bed at seven o'clock in the morning. The book was being set up as I wrote it, so that revision had to be meticulous.

For the rest of that July I was obsessed with the fear that we were going to let France down if things came to the worst. In the air race from London to Paris and back, two out of the six starters finished, taking about three and a half hours each way. The Home Rule Conference failed, and the Ulster Volunteers had obtained from Germany 35,000 rifles and 3,000,000 cartridges in the spring without any attempt being made to stop them. No wonder the Germans supposed that we were too preoccupied with Irish affairs to pay any attention to Europe.

When Austria-Hungary declared war on what we were told should be called Serbia, not Servia, Russia began to mobilize. Desperate last-minute efforts were made to prevent the conflict's extending (that pompous neologism "escalating" was not found necessary in 1914) into a European war. It was too late. Next day Germany declared war on France and Russia. We still abstained. I believe that if Germany had not violated Belgium's neutrality, we should not have entered the war.

I was writing away through that Tuesday evening of August 3, the countryside hushed. When midnight struck, that hushed countryside was filled with the rumble of trains running southward. All night, while I was writing, that rumble continued, and when I leaned out of the window to drink in the morning air before going to bed, the rumble of the trains bearing equipment and munitions and stores to the south coast could still be heard.

I went up to London that afternoon to consult a soldier friend at the War Office about a commission.

He smiled indulgently.

"We don't want married subalterns of thirty-one."

"But I did hold a commission in the Volunteers fourteen years ago."

"I daresay, and if you were still eighteen, I would do all I could to put you in the way of a commission today. But you are thirty-one. Your job is to keep us amused by writing books. You'll be much more use to your country that way than as a subaltern on active service."

I decided to finish *Sinister Street* somehow and after that somehow to get into the war. The manuscript of that second volume is now in the Bodleian at Oxford, and from time to time on the opposite sheet are the names of the cities and towns falling before the German advance—Namur, Liège, Valenciennes, and the rest of them. I do not know how I managed to concentrate on *Sinister Street,* so much was I longing to be in the war. This longing was not inspired by any lofty sentiments of patriotism or even by sympathy with "plucky little Belgium." It was inspired by the realization that this was the greatest moment in the history of my time and that somehow I must be sharing in the excitement of it.

Most people in that autumn of 1914 were still incapable of appreciating how utterly this war was going to change their world; it is difficult to believe now that in the shop windows of London there were placards with BUSINESS AS USUAL, to which some shopkeepers added THOUGH THERE'S A WAR ON. At the same time too many Londoners were wondering why others had not enlisted, and too many idiotic young women were handing white feathers to boyfriends they were tired of.

All that autumn I tried hard to get into the war, but without success. I hear now Henry Newbolt consoling me for my failure:

"From what I hear the whole business will be over by February at latest. That's the general feeling among those who know."

"Kitchener doesn't seem to think that. He asks for three-year volunteers for his army."

"Ah, well, Kitchener's a cautious chap," Newbolt said with a smile.

"I don't believe Winston thinks the war will be over by February," I argued.

Newbolt smiled again.

"Winston is enjoying himself too much to think that."

"I wanted to get into his naval division, but I wouldn't have a chance to get through a medical. I'll have to go somewhere with a fairly decent winter climate."

By the end of October, still with no prospect of getting into the war, I decided to return to Italy. The desperate Battle of Ypres was at its height when my wife and I crossed the Channel. On the boat I saw my War Office friend in khaki and told him I was going to Capri to write a book.

"The best thing you could do," he assured me.

"I was hoping for some kind of obscure staff job in Egypt."

"My dear man, the last people we want on the staff are charming amateurs like yourself. And anyway, this business of diverting to Egypt troops we require in France will have to stop. The only place where anybody is any use at all just now is over there."

He pointed to the misty outline of the French coast beyond that ashen autumnal sea. I felt apologetically superfluous among that crowd of mixed uniforms on the quay at Boulogne. Even that little fellow with the face of a provincial comedian, in a uniform between the Salvation Army and the Church Lads' Brigade, who was going to hand out tracts and toffee somehow or other behind the lines, was living life as it ought to be lived, not as I proposed to live it presently in Capri, writing one more unnecessary novel. I waved my War Office friend good-bye in the blusterous chill of late October and enviously watched him like a senior schoolboy greeting other and important seniors at the beginning of a new term.

The peace of Capri in that cloudless November made me feel even more guilty about inaction when things were so desperate in France and Flanders. I was thankful when I was asked to write an article on behalf of the Commission for Relief in Belgium.

I felt a little less guilty about my inaction when Mr. Hoover, who was doing such a superb job for the Belgian refugees and was to become President of the United States one day, wrote to tell me I had described the work of the commission "in a manner which reaches an absolute ideal."

Nevertheless, I was still set on getting into the war. When I sat down to write my novel *Guy and Pauline* (called *Plasher's Mead* in the United States), I had debated with myself for a long time whether I had a right to draw on the emotion of my own experience over a broken engagement. Finally I decided that if I were destined to be killed in the war in which I believed I should somehow succeed in playing an active part, it was my duty to put into what might be the last book I should ever write the most poignant experience of my life, while at the same time changing all the externals of the real story into a work of imagination.

My belief that I should manage to get into the war was justified. When I was three-quarters of the way through my novel, a letter came from an old friend written on board the R.M.S. *Franconia*:

"I am writing to you by order of Sir Ian Hamilton, Commander-in-Chief of the Mediterranean Expeditionary Force. I'm cipher-officer on his staff. . . . I noticed a day or two ago that he had bought Vol. II of *Sinister Street* to read. . . . I told him I knew you, etc., and that you had tried for a commission in Egypt without success. He said at once, 'Write to him and tell him to get into communication with Eddie Marsh [the late Sir Edward Marsh was Winston Churchill's private secretary] and get sent out to me as a Marine, and I'll find him a job of some kind. . . .' The possibilities of this show are romantic to a degree."

So that is how I reached the Dardanelles and was to play my part in what would officially be known as the Great War for Civilization.

That last remark in my friend's letter may suggest that we all thought of ourselves as romantic figures. When Rupert Brooke wrote his sonnet, he was not romanticizing himself consciously. He did not join the Royal Naval Division as a patriotic duty but because it was likely to provide the most familiar companionship in the exciting days ahead.

In the 1920's it became the fashion to sneer at Rupert Brooke's poetry. When in 1928 a fountain memorial in memory of the dead of the Royal Naval Division was unveiled by Winston Churchill, there were sneers at the sonnet by Rupert Brooke engraved upon it. I wrote in *G. K's Weekly*:

Mr. Winston Churchill's noble words will probably strike as mere rhetoric in the ears of the devitalized young intellectuals by whom Rupert Brooke's sonnet is no longer regarded as poetry. The war was not many months old before the humanitarian press was inveighing against the romantics who were to arise after it was over and glorify the beastly thing. They have not yet appeared. They lie in Flanders—those romantics. Their dust is mingled with the tawny soil of Hellas.

The mighty cone of Athos observes their tombs. They went early to the fight, those romantics; conscription does not breed martial apologists.

The real lesson to be gained from the last war, as it seems to me, is that never again shall we wage war as we waged it in Flanders and France. Yet, the bitterest supporter of the Western school of tactics was the humanitarian *Nation,* which shed as many crocodile tears as would have set the Nile in flood over the waste of the world's youth, rather than forget its vendetta against Mr. Lloyd George and admit that the Eastern school of strategy was right. Better the bloody mess of Passchendaele than the romantic side-show; better that thousands of conscripts should be slain than that those romantic volunteers should have taken Constantinople.

In reading through once again the sonnet of Rupert Brooke that is carved upon the mermaid fountain, we may find it untouched by time. . . . To pretend that Rupert Brooke is not a figure on which the imaginative mind may dwell with greater exaltation than on some pale and trembling junket of a creature in a book or a play is mere wantonness.

When my friend wrote about the romantic possibilities before the Mediterranean Expeditionary Force in 1915, he was thinking of the fall of Constantinople and of the British and the French marching on across the plains of Hungary to attack Germany from the northeast, which had only one great fortress, Breslau. If the British and French high command on the western front had not been so fearful of the war's being decided on an eastern front and therefore had not done all that was possible to make Gallipoli a failure, if Kitchener and Fisher had stood firmly behind Winston Churchill, if the Conservatives out of office had not concentrated on forming a coalition government with the excuse of getting on with the war, Constantinople would have fallen and the war would have been over by the autumn of 1916 at latest, possibly even by the end of 1915.

I recall sitting from midnight until 4 A.M. waiting for news of the Suvla landing on that August night. When without the news we had hoped for at G.H.Q. I was on the way to my tent, the thin slip of the waning moon was rising over Asia. I remember as if it were last night, not fifty-three years ago, my sudden realization that if we were going to win the war, we should have to become as ungentlemanly as Germans to do so.

If the war had ended in that autumn of 1915, the sacrifice which so many contemporaries of mine had made would hardly have been appreciated. It was not until the material discomfort of the war began to affect the civilian population that there was induced a

246] PROMISE OF GREATNESS

state of mind which was to respond to the obscene horrors of postwar books written with a self-pity that expressed the self-pity of their readers. Those who volunteered to give their lives and gave them without complaint were not praised in such books, lest a hint of admiration should render to war one tattered shred of the glory that was once believed to enfold it. There may have been nothing heroic in the readiness of those young men of 1914 and 1915 to volunteer. There may have been nothing behind that impulse except a desire to do the right thing. However, since none of them considered himself a hero and none of them made a book about his sufferings, those still alive in the "twittering twenties" might have spared them at least as much respect as they gave to writers by whose sufferings some of us might have felt more pitifully moved if they did not seem to have lavished all the pity in the world on themselves.

I must quickly add that I was lucky enough to escape the protracted misery of the western front and, therefore, was never tempted to be sorry for myself. Instead, I was employed in Intelligence and so discovered paradoxically how low the level of human intelligence can sink. If I were asked what I considered the most injurious legacy of what was officially called the Great War for Civilization, I might vote first for the habit of inhaling the smoke of cigarettes. It is difficult to believe now that by 1917 one was offered a cigarette with an apology because it was a "gasper." The gasper of 1917 is the cigarette inhaled all over the world today, and when one is offered any other kind of cigarette, it is with an apology. However, the damage done by swallowing cigarette smoke is a personal risk. A far more injurious legacy of the First World War is the mania for what is called security. The millions of pounds and dollars and rubles being wasted on this idol fifty years after the First World War came to an end makes one wonder why humanity is set on reaching the moon when lunacy is so widely spread on earth.

Espionage in time of war may be inevitable, but in the world today such espionage has nothing like the importance it had in Old Testament days or in ancient Rome or even as late as in the American Civil War. Nevertheless, espionage is still inevitable. It was to counter espionage that the passport system under which we suffer today was invented. I reflect with sorrow that I was much involved in the creation of that passport system. I did not realize that something necessary in time of war would become a lucrative profession after the war. In my third volume of war memories, published in 1932, I related how the Passport Department of the British Legation was the center of our Intelligence work. For revealing this, I was prosecuted under the Official Secrets Act, although by 1932 every embassy, legation, and consulate all over the world used information about passports as the cover for Intelligence.

When the case was over, I wrote a skit on the Secret Service called *Water on the Brain* to contribute something to what the case had cost me. After the Second World War, *Water on the Brain* was reissued as a paperback. I received a letter from a doctor in San Francisco telling me that during the war the O.S.S. in Cairo had found a copy of the original edition, of which they had made more than a hundred photostat copies. These were given to young American Intelligence officers to teach them their job. I thought my correspondent was pulling my leg, but the next day I had a letter from Cleveland, Ohio, telling me the same story. So I told the story in print both in the U.S.A. and in England. It was not contradicted. I think I may be forgiven for wondering whether the millions of pounds, dollars, and rubles spent on "security" is money well spent or wasted.

I wish that President Roosevelt had included freedom of travel among his freedoms. I do not waste emotion on regrets for the past, but I still sigh sometimes for the time before the Great War for Civilization when one could decide to go anywhere in Europe at a moment's notice, though one was advised that it would be prudent to carry a passport in Russia, Turkey, or Spain.

It can be argued that the First World War hastened material progress. That may be true, but material progress without corresponding mental progress is like giving children elaborate toys they are not yet capable of appreciating. Undoubtedly the development of the airplane was due to the First War, and the infernal triumph of air warfare in the Second War made the prospect of a third war as appalling as once upon a time was doomsday.

Thankfully I reflect that to plunge into a third world war as we plunged into that First War without the faintest conception of how it was going to affect the world is no longer imaginable. We drifted into the Second World War because owing to the loss of the flower of our youth, there were too many second-rate careerists in politics. When I look back on so many contemporaries of mine who were killed, I know that their loss was one of the causes of the Second World War. We were lucky, of course, in not having any apprehension of the First World War, because we enjoyed our youth to the full. To the young people of today the Edwardian decade appears the way the Regency appeared to those of us who were feeling oppressed by the tail end of Victorianism.

It could be argued that her country might have benefited if Queen Victoria had left it not long after her golden jubilee, because the Prince of Wales would not have had to spend what were thirteen years of frustration before he ascended the throne.

If Edward VII had begun his reign in 1888, changes that the First World War brought about might already have begun. Women would have had the vote. The lot of the poorer classes would have been ameliorated. Ireland would have had Home Rule. Friendship with France might have led to a triple alliance with France and Russia. At the time of the Entente Cordiale in 1904 I pleaded for that alliance in the paper I edited at Oxford and used to speak in favor of it at college debates, always in a small minority. Such a triple alliance would have made a European war at least unlikely.

Naturally the war affected me as much as it affected other writers about my age. There had been bother with the circulating libraries over the first volume of *Sinister Street*. That was in September, 1913. When the second volume was published in November, 1914, the libraries circulated it without a blush. When I sat down to write *Sylvia Scarlett* while on sick leave in Capri, I found it impossible to recapture the leisurely and decorated style of my first novels. During the two years when I was working in Athens and afterward in the Cyclades in Intelligence, I must have written not less than 5,000 telegrams, many of them of great length. At more than a shilling a word I could not afford to indulge in adjectives, and I had to say what I had to say as briefly as possible. In Athens I had read for the first time Stendhal's *Chartreuse de Parme*. I had tried to read it when I was an undergraduate, but without success. Now with the experience of life in a small country with a court that resembled the small Italian courts of the eighteenth century and the very early nineteenth century, I was able to realize what a master of his art Stendhal was. He spoke of the Code Napoleon as a model for style. I found the writing of telegrams an equally good model for telling a tale as directly as possible.

My experience in Greece had been so wide and exciting that later I felt I should be wise to withdraw from the center of things in order to escape from the prevailing belief of some of my juniors that art and literature had not begun to exist until the twenties. So I withdrew to a small island in the Channel and deliberately wrote against the mood of the moment.

I recall Logan Pearsall Smith's saying after the Great War for Civilization that the continuity of culture had been broken. That is even more evident after the Second World War. I find in my old age that I am becoming less and less hopeful of that break's ever being mended. The past is increasingly despised and ignored; the present is being acclaimed by too many as of almost religious significance, probably because young people today have always at the back of their minds the dark shape of a third world war.

One advantage they enjoy over the young people of 1914: They will not be plunged into war as abruptly as their predecessors. Television and international sport, particularly football, are pacifying influences. Of course, there is always the chance that some lunatic affected by the rays of the moon will drop the bomb. We can only pray that this will not happen.

Pax Britannica! There is something to be said for it when we look at the state of Africa and Asia today. But *Pax Britannica* vanished after the Great War for Civilization.

L. P. Hartley

"I was born in Whittlesey, a small town in the Cambridgeshire fens, whose church has the loveliest spire in England. My father was a solicitor there; he also practiced in the cathedral city of Peterborough, a few miles away, to which we moved in 1900, when I was four. My father did not believe in sending his children (I have two sisters, one older and one younger than myself, and both unmarried, as I am) to boarding school, early; he was a man of culture, and at least half of my education was due to him.

"Eventually, in 1910, I went to Harrow School, and after an interval in the Army, during which I did not see service abroad, I returned to Balliol College, Oxford, where I held an exhibition. I stayed there until 1922 and then got a job as fiction reviewer for The Spectator. A book of short stories (Night Fears) and a nouvelle (Simonetta Perkins) brought me only twelve pounds each, so I concentrated on reviewing until about 1942, when I finished a novel I had begun about twenty years before—The Shrimp and the Anemone. This was a success, and I gave up reviewing and have written fiction more or less successfully (The Go-Between was my best effort) ever since.

"I now live chiefly in London, but I have a house in Bath on the River Avon, where I have a boat and find much relaxation in rowing it."

THREE WARS

PEOPLE sometimes ask me—people much younger than I—what it felt like to be living in England before the First World War. Was the "atmosphere," the spirit of the age, the *Zeitgeist*, different from what it is now?

It was different, but I find it hard to define the difference. To say it was the difference between feeling that life was then a boon, but is now a menace, does partly describe it; in those days hope took for granted what in these days fear takes for granted. The idea of a general catastrophe, which may annihilate us all and which is somehow more terrifying and life-destroying than the thought of one's own death, didn't exist: Indeed it didn't come into being until after the Second World War. The First World War shook one's belief in the essential goodness of humanity—the belief that all's for the best in the best of all possible worlds that, with many conspicuous exceptions, had dominated Victorian thought. But one felt that it was a "war to end war," that experience teaches, and that humanity had learned its lesson. The period between the wars was one of uneasy hope, compared with now, when we all are, consciously or not, in dread of some nuclear catastrophe which will nullify whatever aims we have.

Such a state of mind was unthinkable before 1914, for although philosophers like Schopenhauer and novelists like Thomas Hardy had taken a gloomy view of the human lot, they were pessimists and not misanthropes: they put the blame on fate, not on man. The old saying *homo homini lupus* did not occur to them and might, indeed, have shocked them.

Boarding school was such an arduous experience that I, for one, was often unaware of what was taking place outside the microcosm. But at that time, and indeed for many years, I had been learning to play the piano, and in 1912, or thereabouts, I was suddenly confronted by the new phenomenon of jazz music, "Hitchy-Koo," and so on. I disliked it very much, and all the more because, as a pianist, I couldn't manage the syncopation.

"Never mind," I thought, "it is one of these new crazes, those songs that catch the public ear, like 'A Grasshopper Sat on a Railroad Track,' and it will soon be forgotten," but it wasn't, and hasn't been. Somebody said that "the rot started with Beethoven"; I think it started with jazz and the indifference to sense, and morality, and genuine emotion that goes with jazz, which in any case has to be sung slightly out of tune. Perhaps the world has been slightly out of tune ever since.

In the summer of 1914 I was still at school, at Harrow-on-the-Hill, and there was an epidemic of mumps. At Harrow nearly all the boys had rooms to themselves, and if any of them fell ill, not so seriously ill as to be taken to the sanatorium, but seriously enough to keep other boys out, the matron would fix on the door a card labeled NO ADMITTANCE which allowed the invalid to rest in peace. I did not expect to catch mumps, nor had I caught them when the school broke up for the summer holidays. But the incubation period of mumps is longer than that of any other of the ordinary infectious illnesses—twenty-six days, I think. On the night of August 3, while I was at home, I realized that I had the symptoms. I got out of bed and pinned a notice on the door, NO ADMITTANCE, MUMPS IN HERE!

I don't know if I imagined that no one, my mother or anyone else, would take the risk of visiting me, but I felt that, medically speaking, I was a pariah. The next day it was announced that we were at war with Germany.

The old dispensation had come to an end. I was not aware of this; I was aware only of high fever and a pain in my neck. By comparison, the political situation meant nothing to me. Fever always brings a kind of schizophrenia, and it did then. NO ADMITTANCE, MUMPS IN HERE!

But, of course, the world is not to be kept out by a warning on one's door. When mumps had subsided, I went back to school. I was at an age to have joined up. I didn't, because I didn't want to. I was utterly unbelligerent and hated the thought of fighting, in however good a cause. But I was obliged to join the school corps.

In prewar days I had always held out against joining the corps, preferring lessons to field days, although I quite enjoyed practicing at the rifle range—an exercise which was compulsory, though I never excelled at it. Before 1914 I think that in England warfare was envisaged in terms of the Boer War, a gallant enterprise in which none but self-chosen heroes, with a vocation for arms, took part. It didn't affect the majority of the population, whose role was to look on and admire. And admire I did, at the age of four or five, in spite of the fact that my father, who was a Volunteer, and must to some extent have enjoyed military training, was also by conviction a pro-Boer, an unpopular thing to be. I enjoyed singing, or hearing sung (for I doubt if, at that tender age, I could have sung a tune), such martial ditties as "The soldiers of the Queen, my lad, have been, my lad, have seen, my lad, have fought for England's glory, lad," etc. and, more poignant:

> Goodbye Dolly, I must leave you
> Though it breaks my heart to go;
> Something tells me I am needed
> At the front to fight the foe.

And one of my earliest and most recurrent memories is of the night of the relief of Ladysmith, when the whole of the little town in

which we lived (Sir Harry Smith's birthplace) went mad with
excitement. The noise in the streets still lingers in my mind like a
great red blur. It terrified me, and I remember that my mother told
me afterward that I cried, "I don't like the jum-jums," meaning the
drums which reverberated under our windows.

But I also thrilled to the excitement and the patriotic fervor, and
even my father would recite Kipling's "Absent-minded Beggar,"
with its refrain:

> So pass your hat for your credit's sake,
> And pay, pay, pay!

I was never sure, and still am not, whether the "beggar" was just
any man, a "bloke" as people would say now, or someone who was
actively soliciting alms for the war effort, as in 1914 it came to be
called.

But in those days I was only an infant spectator of that national,
very limited conflict and never dreamed that anything of the sort
could ever affect me. I laughed heartily at the answer to the riddle
"Why does Kruger wear thick boots?" "To Keep De Wet from
defeat." South Africa was so far away, and what happened there was
only, for me, a stimulus for emotion and romantic excitement, with
heroism, not death, as its leading motif.

In a way, my wartime attack of mumps was symbolical. I had to
accept it, just as I had to accept the war; but I couldn't and
wouldn't regard the war as belonging to the natural course of
events, any more than I could regard a state of fever as life advanced
to a higher power, although some might argue that it is.

Unfortunately for me, the war lasted much longer than my attack
of mumps. For many in England and the United States and other
countries its duration was all too short. We bow the head but do not
understand.

The rifle regiment to which we were affiliated at school had
differences in drill from other infantry regiments—e.g., such words
of command as "carry arms" and "trail arms." These nuances of
training in weapon warfare meant nothing to me, nor did I mind
being cursed by the sergeant major or the drill sergeant, for my
clumsy efforts to comply. Neither of them treated us anything as
severely as recruits in the Regular Army were treated. We were not
subjected to a fusillade of four-letter words, nor were doubts cast on
our paternity or maternity.

In any case, public school life in those days had inured us to a
good deal of verbal and physical unpleasantness. I remember how,
in the Second World War, a friend of mine who was too old to fight

joined the local fire brigade. The other firemen complained bitterly of their lot, their hardships of one sort and another, and they said to him, "Why don't *you* complain?" He replied, "Because I was at school at Eton, a much tougher upbringing than any of you have had." Which was true, for the children of the well-to-do, in those days, had a harder time than the children of the underprivileged. They had to eat what was put before them, however nauseating, whereas the children of the less fortunate members of the community were allowed to refuse any dish they didn't like, just as animals do.

In the autumn of 1915 I went to Balliol College, Oxford, where I had been given an exhibition. I expected, as I believe many of my fellow countrymen did, a recrudescence of the Boer War spirit in 1914, and for a while—a little while—it did come back, with the poems of Rupert Brooke and the famous poster of Kitchener, one of the heroes of the Boer War, pointing an accusing finger above the slogan, "Your King and your Country Need YOU!" In those early days, the romance of war did stage a comeback. The whole country was electrified. But not for long. When the casualty lists began to pile up and it was gradually realized that the war was not for a few professional soldiers—a football team fighting on our behalf—but a catastrophe that might go on for years and involve millions of people, including myself, the climate of opinion began to change, and mine changed with it. War was not a kind of play to be enacted before an enthusiastic but detached audience: It was something that affected everyone and would change their lives. Wartime was a different kind of life from peacetime, nor have we in England ever recovered the pre-1914 feeling. At least that is my opinion.

It is not only that crime has grown steadily with the growth of material prosperity, so that the English, instead of being one of the most honest people in the world, are now not noted for honesty; it is the loss of confidence in human nature, the general feeling that the other fellow will do you down if he can—and, doing so, will have the sympathy of the community at large, implicit if not expressed. This moral deterioration can be laid at the door of the state, which, in 1914, so grossly increased its powers. Power corrupts, as we have often been told, and absolute power corrupts absolutely.

I was brought up on the theories of John Stuart Mill to believe that the state is the great enemy because it takes man's moral responsibility out of his own hands and imposes its decisions on him, which have come to be accepted as fatalistically as if they were laws of God—more so, indeed, for they have thrived on the decline of the belief in God as the supreme lawgiver, to whom man is responsible for his acts and who is the only keeper of his conscience. The laws of God depend on faith; the laws of the state depend on fact: In the material and to some extent in the moral sphere, the state can make you do what it likes, whereas God cannot; the state has usurped the kingdom, the power, and the glory. The individual has been devalued: He takes his orders from the state.

Herbert Spencer wrote a book called *The Man Versus the State*, whose very title thrilled me, but when I went to Oxford in 1915, before I joined the Army, I had to listen to the then master of Balliol, A. L. Smith, giving his famous series of lectures, "From Hobbes to Maine," in which he argued that the state, as an embodiment of the community, could make the individual dance to its tune, however unjust, in the eyes of the individuals who composed it, its commands and demands were.

While I listened, my blood boiled, for had not these doctrines of Hobbes, Locke, Rousseau, Bosanquet, etc., with their insistence on the omnipotence of the state, made the Four Years' War possible? Not quite in the same way as it made possible the Six Years' War, for the Four Years' War was for King and Country and inspired to some extent by the patriotism that was a legacy from the Boer War. The country, remembering those glamorous days, went into it with songs on their lips. Whereas the Six Years' War was a war against Hitler; it was a war of resistance, and though it ended in victory, it produced no poetry.

I stayed at Balliol for two terms and then joined the Army as a gunner in a regiment called the Royal Garrison Artillery. I doubt if it exists now, but they thought I should be suitable for it, because of my academic leanings. Actually I was not, because such gifts as I had inclined to the humanities, whereas the Royal Garrison Artillery demanded a certain mathematical aptitude for the use of the slide rule, for calculating trajectories, and the whole mystique of gunfire, which I simply didn't possess. When inspecting officers came around, I was sometimes pointed out to them, almost with awe, as a man from Balliol, but when the time for examinations came, I did not live up to my legendary reputation.

Being medically unfit for active service, I was then transferred to an infantry regiment where ballistics was not required, and I served as camp postman in an enormous camp called Catterick Bridge in Yorkshire. So large was it that it had a railway of its own, with two stops between each end, and was facetiously called the Catterick Bridge Express.

On my way to Catterick I remember seeing a poster from *John*

Bull, Horatio Bottomley's popular paper, saying, "Why so many suicides at Catterick?"

The November of 1916 was bitterly cold. Our hut had a central stove, which sometimes got red-hot, so that one could hardly get near it, while beyond the radius of its influence the temperature was almost freezing.

But apart from the cold, I wasn't altogether unhappy at Catterick (a beautiful place, seen from a tourist's eye). I read Montaigne's *Essays* and the *Apology* of Raymonde Sebonde, and I delivered the letters. As Christmas drew near, a great many parcels were added to the letters, and although the "Catterick Express" was a help, I had to do most of my rounds on foot, carrying a sack on my back, which grew heavier every day. But the job had its compensations, for never have I been made so welcome as I was then. Whenever I approached the lighted door of a hut (it always seemed to be dark outside, whatever the time of day), I was greeted with frantic cheers from the inmates, whether I had a missive for them or not.

At last, and most unexpectedly, I received a summons to attend an O.T.C. (Officers Training Corps). No one was more surprised than I, for I had shown so little military ability! But some high-up from my old school had tracked me down and wangled (as we used to say) this promotion for me.

I remember the corporal in charge of our hut saying to me—it touched me then and still does—"We always knew you were a gentleman," and I remember a fellow gunner (Redfern his name was) advising me, "If you talked more, you'd get on better."

The O.T.C. was housed in Sidney Sussex College, Cambridge. There we slept 4 in a room—instead of 30, as at Catterick, and 250, as in my first camp. I studied the infantry regulations and learned, more or less, how to behave as an officer. But owing to some physical disability, I could never, marching, quite keep in step, and I remember our sergeant major walking alongside of me and pointing out this defect. But unlike what sergeants major are supposed to be, and often are, he was a kindhearted man, and I owe it to him (I'm nearly sure) that I was never called on to drill the battalion, a feat of which, from nerves and other reasons (*e.g.,* lack of a resonant voice), I should never have been capable of, although the test was part of our schedule.

So having passed or avoided these various pitfalls, I became Second Lieutenant Hartley, fit only for Home Service, which in my case meant defending the coast of East Anglia from possible German invasion.

My life then became, materially and in all ways, much easier. At

Colchester, where I was stationed in the Meeanee Barracks (Mee-anee must have been the scene of some British victory in India), the officers were given V.I.P. treatment, and my greatest hardship was being sent, as a contact, to an isolation hospital for infectious diseases. It was so cold (March, 1917) that my hands swelled up to double their size with chilblains, and I remember my batman saying to a doctor who came to inspect us, "I have three officers here, frozen to dead."

However, we weren't dead, and the war went on peacefully for me until I had an attack of bronchopneumonia, after which I spent two months at the Third London General Hospital. Neither my heart nor my lungs were thought to be in good order. Eventually I went before a medical board. While I was waiting for my turn to come, an orderly said to me, "You ought to drink some black coffee." "Why?" I asked. "Because it plays your heart up," he said.

Perhaps there wasn't time for me to take his advice; at any rate I didn't. The president of the board was a benign old gentleman called Sir Frederick Treves, who many years before had had the honor and responsibility of taking out King Edward VII's appendix. Throughout my war service I had felt that authority was, or would be, against me. Even as an officer, I envisaged, Kafka-like, officers above me who would call me to account. Suddenly all this was changed. The orderly was right when he told me that this medical board was "a good crowd." No doubt I stood to attention and saluted; but after that all the multiple obligations of discipline faded away, and I was an equal, except insofar as I was an object of pity. "My poor boy," Sir Frederick said, "you have done your utmost for your King and Country."

It wasn't true, but after the harshness of Army life, underlying or apparent, it was a soothing and gratifying thing to hear.

In August, 1918, I was discharged and could wear "civvy" clothes if I wanted to. I was advised to go to a health resort to recuperate. My mother took me to Mundesley on the Norfolk coast, where there was a hospital for tuberculous patients nearby. No sooner had we settled down in lodgings than we heard that the little town was stricken with Spanish influenza: More coffins were being carried out than there were visitors coming in. In these plague-ridden conditions I hardly noticed the Armistice on November 11, any more than, thanks to mumps, I had noticed the outbreak of war more than four years before.

The Second World War came, and we, who could remember the First, had no illusions as to what it would be like—it was a grim task that we set ourselves. There was resolution and determination in it, but in spite of Churchill's inspiring speeches, there was little of the enthusiasm and almost joyful acquiescence in self-sacrifice which gave a romantic panache to the First War, which had been the war of Rupert Brooke—something to glory in—until it became the war of Siegfried Sassoon and Wilfrid Owen—something to shudder at.

"Thou hast multiplied the nations and not increased the joy." How true are those words of Isaiah, and nothing has been more of a killjoy than the two world wars. The first did indeed leave behind the reaction of a brittle, evanescent gaiety: The "bright young people" made merry, as far as they could, now that the threat of extinction had been (as they thought) permanently banished. Sentiment and emotion lived on, as witness the hold that Armistice Day, November 11, 1918, still keeps on the public mind. Whereas the conclusions, or inconclusions, of the Second World War brought no such elation, only a dreary sense of relief, for who but a few can recall the dates of V day and VJ day?

It will be many years, if ever, before we recover the pre-1914 *joie de vivre* and confidence in life.

Sir Charles Petrie

SIR CHARLES PETRIE *was born in Liverpool, Lancashire, in 1895 of an Irish father and a Scottish mother. He was thus eighteen years of age at the beginning of the First World War. At its conclusion he returned to Corpus Christi College, Oxford, where he had been studying when it began, and took his degree in modern history in 1920.*

Since then he has devoted himself to authorship and journalism and more recently to the radio and television. Between the wars he traveled widely on the continent of Europe, and for his historical work he has been decorated by the governments of Greece, Italy, and Spain. During the Second World War he was an official lecturer to the British forces. In 1957 he was made a Commander of the Order of the British Empire, and in 1965 he was the recipient of an honorary degree at the University of Valladolid.

Sir Charles has so far paid only one visit to the United States, and that was in 1953, when he was in New York, Boston, and Princeton. Recently his activities have been confined to Ireland and Spain, for he is both the president of the Military History Society of Ireland and a corresponding member of the Royal Academy of the History of Spain.

For some years Sir Charles was in publishing, and he is a regular contributor to the Illustrated London News, *as well as editor of the* Household Brigade Magazine. *His latest book is* Don John of Austria.

FIGHTING THE FIRST WORLD WAR
IN LONDON

THE OUTBREAK of the First World War found me at the age of eighteen residing with my parents in Liverpool and about to go up to Oxford. After vainly trying to get into the Army and being rejected on account of my eyesight, I went into residence at Corpus Christi College and remained there for twelve months. By the autumn of 1915 the military authorities were not so particular, and as I had had a year's training in the Oxford University Officers Training Corps, I was given a commission in the Royal Garrison Artillery.

I was posted to Tynemouth, and a very bleak spot it was. My quarters were in the castle, which had been built in the reign of Henry VIII and which appeared to have remained unchanged ever since. The first night I was there, my bedroom window blew in. Sometimes the wind was so strong that a rope had to be put across the barracks square to enable the men to get from one side to the other, and on more than one occasion a parade had to be dismissed because it was impossible to preserve any sort of formation. Such discomforts, however, were amply compensated for by the unfailing kindness of the people of Northumberland, and by the beauty of the scenery on the upper Tyne. After I had been some months at Tynemouth, the medical authorities decided that my sight was not good enough to allow me to be sent overseas, so the military powers-that-be somewhat paradoxically decided that I should go to anti-aircraft. Accordingly, I was sent for a course to Shoeburyness, where I remained for a month, and at the end of this period I was sent to gun stations at, successively, Halifax, Rugby, and Banbury. While I was at Shoeburyness, the Easter Rising took place in Dublin, but those of us who had relatives in Ireland were allowed to opt out of service there so far as possible against the republicans.

My men were mostly Reservists from Cork and Kerry, and my feelings on first taking command were somewhat akin to those of Parnesius, in Kipling's *Puck of Pook's Hill,* when he led his detachment out of Anderida. However, my own Irish background soon enabled us to understand one another, and all went well. In a typical English countryside there were, all the same, some awkward moments. At Christmas, 1916, we were outside Rugby, and the local inhabitants got up a concert for us. The day before it was due to take place the sergeant major asked me whether the national anthem was going to be sung. On my replying that this would certainly be the case, he told me that the men would refuse to sing it. No ordinary argument would have been of the least avail, so I decided to appeal to the innate courtesy of the Irish. When I had all the men collected in the barracks room, I asked them if they would join in "God Save the King" out of compliment to their English hosts if "The Wearing of the Green" were also sung. To a man they said they would, and so it was settled, after I had assured those who

were arranging the concert that far from having a political significance, "The Wearing of the Green" was just a sentimental tune
which would remind the men of home.

In those days antiaircraft was still very much in its infancy, and
the enemy was the zeppelin rather than the airplane. At Shoeburyness we were trained on a variety of guns, both fixed and mobile,
and there were not a few accidents owing to the different lengths of
the recoil, which varied from 45 inches in the case of the 13-
pounder to 11 inches in that of the 3-inch naval gun. All these guns
were converted, and many of them left a good deal to be desired.
For nearly a year I had a 6-pounder Nordenfelt, which I am glad to
say I never had a chance to fire. The only time a zeppelin came
within range we had no ammunition and were constrained to
admire her beauty in the moonlight. Perhaps, however, the lack of
shells did not matter so much as we imagined at the time, for when
they did arrive, they were filled with only salt. Indeed, the position
of many gun stations seemed to be dictated by political, rather than
by military, considerations. Lack of ammunition was the rule rather
than the exception, but all the same, officers and men had to
pretend that the guns were ready for action, presumably to impress
the civilian population, and each night we were compelled to stand
by as if we were in a position to open fire. It was a sorry and
somewhat demoralizing piece of make-believe.

What made antiaircraft so onerous was not the amount of work
there was to do but the necessity of being at call on short notice, as
they say in the City. For twelve months I had no other officer with
me and no leave at all: Once a week I was allowed to be away from
the gun station for three hours, but the rest of the time I had to be
within ten minutes' reach by day, while by night it was forbidden to
leave the compound. The men were in no better plight: They got
one late pass every ten days or fortnight, though in defiance of the
regulations, I used to allow those on duty to go one at a time to the
village pub for a "quick one."

To those of us at home the war seemed a distant affair. From time
to time there were scares of invasion, but outside the War Office no
one took them seriously, and we had our daily routine. The men
had little to do off parade, and they were often profoundly bored.
The war seemed to have always been going on, and there appeared
to be no likelihood that it would ever cease. We were mere pieces in
a game, and we moved about the board for no apparent reason. No
initiative of any sort was required of us, and the result was that the
most important event made little impression on minds which were

half-atrophied. Had it not been for the unfailing kindness of the local inhabitants at all levels, life would have been intolerable.

In the spring of 1917 an event occurred which made me a Hispanophile for life. The Conde de Romanones, the Prime Minister of Spain, was strongly pro-Ally, and the British government came to the conclusion that he was going to follow the example of President Wilson and bring his country into the war. Accordingly, one day at Banbury we received orders to send in a list of all officers who could speak Spanish. I knew a few words, so I sent in my name and then rushed off to Oxford for a phrase book, from which I proceeded to acquire some sentences of "the-pen-of-my-aunt-is-in-the-garden" variety. In due course orders came for me to report to a certain room at the War Office for an interview. When I got there, not a word was said to me about Spain or Spanish, but I was asked if I could ride a horse and told to translate aloud the opening lines of the second book of the *Iliad*. I then went back to Banbury and a week or two afterward was told to report at King's College, Strand, for a three months' course of Spanish.

I had always been interested in foreign affairs, and Spain had a special attraction for me, but my selection for this course definitely decided my vocation. There were about twenty-five of us, drawn from all arms of the service, and no instruction could have been more thorough than that which we received: We were taught not only the language, but also the literature, history, and customs of the country, presumably with the idea of fitting us to become liaison officers should Spain join the Allies. I write "presumably," because neither then nor at any other time were we told why we had been sent for the course. Those were the days of the daylight air raids on London. So novel were they that during the one on July 7, I was riding in Hyde Park and somewhat optimistically pulled up under a tree until the enemy had passed. As soon as the course was over, we all were returned to duty, and not a word did any of us ever hear on the subject of it again. It is true that Spain did not enter the war, but one would have thought that somewhere in the government service, use might have been made of men who had been trained with so much care and at such expense.

Autumn found me back at antiaircraft on the outer defenses of London at Much Hadham in Hertfordshire. The raids during the summer had galvanized the authorities into action, and the whole of the A.A. (antiaircraft) services were on a much more business-like footing than had been the case earlier in the year. The zeppelin was being defeated with comparative ease, though its real Waterloo did not come until this same autumn, when of eleven airships that came over on one raid, only four returned safely to Germany. It was clear that no country could stand losses at that rate. The airplane was another matter. At Much Hadham we had two of the then new 3-inch guns, and during moonlight raids at the end of September, 1917, we were in action nearly every evening. It was a curious change to be having tea at Rumpelmeyers at five in a relatively carefree London and to be in the middle of a battle only 25 miles away three hours later.

It was rarely that we could see our target, and mostly we were employed on barrage work, when we used to fire something like 30 rounds a minute from each gun. Anything up to 200 rounds a gun an evening was the normal procedure. Of course, height and direction were in those days largely a matter of guesswork, but we managed to keep the enemy up to over 10,000 feet, and in the First World War accurate bombing at that height was impossible. One night a German plane shut off its engines, glided under the barrage, and machine-gunned us: At first we thought the patter of bullets on the fallen leaves betokened a thunderstorm, but we were soon undeceived. We had no tin hats; but fortunately the enemy did not persist in his attack, and our only casualty was one man slightly wounded in the arm.

As will have been gathered, while I was on antiaircraft I moved about England a good deal. The countryside during the First World War was very much more like what it must have been in the eighties or nineties than what it was to be during the next conflict. The private motorcar was never seen, but that was no great hardship since the horse had not been driven from the roads by August, 1914. For instance, I remember once having to go to Chelmsford in a hurry from a camp near Chipping Ongar, and the only method of doing so was to hire a dogcart: I did this without difficulty and drove myself over, though it now seems in passing strange to be living in this space age, and yet to have driven into the yard of the Saracen's Head at Chelmsford, and to have called for the ostler to take one's horse. Official cars there were in plenty for the staff, but the ordinary regimental officer had to get across country as best he could, using horses, bicycles, the slowest of trains, and his own feet in the process. It was often a nuisance at the time, but one realizes now that one was seeing the last of Victorian England, the England of Trollope and Whyte-Melville.

The autumn of 1917 saw me away at last from antiaircraft, for which the badness of my sight had never really fitted me, and at a desk in the R.G.A. (Royal Garrison Artillery) Record Office at Dover. The office was on the seafront, and as I lived in the castle, I got plenty of exercise walking to or from my work four times a day. The mess was a pleasant enough place, though this was in no way due to the C.R.A. (Commander of the Royal Artillery), who was a typical field officer of an earlier day. On one occasion he came to the conclusion that too much whisky was being consumed, which, as far as some half dozen officers were concerned, was true. Accordingly he gave orders that no officer was to have more than two doubles a day. The only result, however, was that the consumers of whisky drank more than ever, for they "borrowed" the two doubles from those—the vast majority—who did not drink whisky, and settled up when the mess bill came in. Such is often the fate of ill-conceived sumptuary legislation. From time to time, I may add, the scene was enlivened by bombs from the air or shells from the sea, though not to anything like the extent that was to be the case in the next war.

My experience in a long mess like that at Dover led me to the conclusion that, at any rate at home, there was less camaraderie in the First World War than there was to be in its successor, nor is this surprising in view of the fact that English society as a whole was much more formal in 1914 than it became as a result of the struggle against Hohenzollern Germany. The senior officers in the main were very stiff toward their juniors, who were given the impression that try as they might they would never become soldiers in any real sense. The "spit and polish" brigade was firmly entrenched in the seat of the mighty, and those who had not been in the Army before the war were too often regarded as "temporary gentlemen," irrespective of their personal character and social background. This has always been my impression, and it was confirmed in the autumn of 1940, when I was lecturing to the Australians on Salisbury Plain, for those who had fought in the First World War all commented on the increased friendliness among both soldiers and civilians. A good many of the pre-1914 regular officers had never seen a shot fired in anger, as the saying goes, and they were inclined to regard the Army as their own special preserve from which intruders should be barred or, if this was impossible, admitted only on sufferance. The dividing line between Regulars, Special Reservists, Territorials, and New Army also strengthened the centrifugal influences in military circles.

In the spring of 1918 I was, to my great satisfaction, attached to the Historical Section of the War Cabinet, of which the offices, long since pulled down, were in Whitehall Gardens. They constituted a veritable rabbit warren, for they spread over several large houses, and during the whole twelve months I was there, the only part of the labyrinth with which I was thoroughly acquainted was the way from the entrance to the room in which I worked. The staff was small—half a dozen of us in all—and we were generally regarded by politicians and soldiers alike as an encyclopedia on all that had hitherto happened in the war, our main job being to keep such information up-to-date. A great many people of note came in and out of the office, not least Austen Chamberlain, whose official biography I was to write in later years.

The latest joined member of the Historical Section was made responsible for what were known in the office as the three beasts— black, pink, and red. The black beast contained the minutes of earlier Cabinet meetings, while the pink and red beasts were fort- nightly publications giving the disposition of troops at home and abroad respectively. All three were highly confidential. They were kept in a most imposing safe, whose key was locked in a smaller safe; the key of the second safe was kept in a drawer, whose key, in its turn, was placed each evening in an ornament on the mantelpiece, because, as the custodian was brightly informed, "The Hun will never think of looking for it there. He'll think you've got it on you, so that he may cut your throat when you're in bed, but he won't find the key." There were also secret papers, respectively termed P. and W.C., for which the same luckless officer was responsible: they were private and War Cabinet papers.

Once during my time at Whitehall Gardens I saw the "Purple Emperor" himself, namely Lord Curzon, then Lord President of the Council. I had to take some document to the Persia Committee, over which he was presiding, but all I remember of the incident was that although I had to remain in the room for an hour, he never had the courtesy to offer me a chair. It is to be feared that such treatment of those whom he considered to be his inferiors was typical, not exceptional, and it explains his widespread unpopu- larity.

A good deal has been written about the number of incompetent people who, owing to social or political influence, were in high places in those days. All I can say is that during the time I was at the War Cabinet Office, I did not come across them, though whether they had been weeded out earlier or whether they never existed I do not profess to know. There were a few obvious misfits, but that was all. The incompetents were numerous enough lower down at depots, training centers, and the like, but certainly by 1918 they were not in Whitehall.

This was my second experience of wartime London, and there can be no doubt that the lot of the capital in the First World War was far happier than it was to be in its successor. There were, it is true, air raids, but they were relatively insignificant. Then the difficulty was to find accommodation of any sort, and money flowed into London from all over the kingdom: Civil servants, far from being evacuated to Blackpool, were recruited from the provinces to staff the new government departments which came into being owing to the needs of the war or the whims of the politicians. Indeed, the period of the First World War is one of the most important in the recent history of the capital, for the pressure lasted not only throughout the conflict, but after its conclusion, partly owing to the short-lived boom, but chiefly owing to the continued presence of large numbers of demobilized officers and men who regarded London as the best center from which to reenter civil life. The capital, too, largely escaped the subsequent slump, and it did not begin visibly to be affected by the international situation until the Munich crisis. In the period of which I am writing the chief centers of attraction for the officer off duty or on leave were the Berkeley, Hatchett's, and the Piccadilly Grill. That was the heyday of the revues, and of those that stick in the memory the best known were *The Bing Boys* (with George Robey and Violet Loraine), *Theodore and Co.,* and *Cheep.* Also, there was always *Chu Chin Chow.* To London flocked in the thousands the relatives and friends of men on leave, and never can any city have been so thronged with men and women solely intent on enjoying themselves as was the capital during the First World War.

What is often forgotten about that war is how unexpectedly it ended. In the middle of July, 1918, the Central Powers were spread all over the map, Russia and Rumania were out of the fight, and the Allies were everywhere on the defensive; yet by the middle of November the Allied troops were in Cologne, and Austria-Hungary had ceased to exist. We know now that Ludendorff had prophesied disaster at the beginning of the year, but all we saw then were the apparently invincible German armies, flushed with the series of offensives which had begun in March. When a secret report came into the office to the effect that the apparent might of Germany was a mere façade, behind which was a growing chaos and despair, we dismissed it as what a later generation would have called wishful thinking, for the wish seemed not merely father to the thought, but its whole ancestry.

Even when Turkey and Bulgaria had collapsed, the belief of those best qualified to express an opinion was that the war would last well into 1919, and men talked gloomily of the Germans desperately defending every hill, river, and town all the way back to Berlin. There had been so many disappointments and disillusionments that we no longer dared to hope, and it was not until the middle of October that we became convinced that the great military machine, which had been the wonder and terror of Europe for nearly fifty years, was really on the verge of collapse.

Such being the case, I settled down at the War Cabinet Office in the expectation of remaining there for a year or two. One of my jobs was to keep in touch with the Italian and Serbian military missions and with the Russian exiles, whose headquarters were at Whitehall Court, at the back of the War Office. There was a speciousness about the Russians which the Italians and Serbs lacked, but they were much more difficult to deal with, for they themselves did not know what they wanted, whereas the others knew only too well. Much undeserved ridicule has been poured on these Russian exiles trying to earn a living as taxi drivers or by selling their bodies and their jewelry, but the real tragedy of Imperial Russia was that by the time the breaking point came, she had lost her best. Admittedly, the attitude of her government on the eve of war was disingenuous in the extreme, and the Czar could hardly have been weaker, but what is not always remembered is that those who might have saved the situation at the time of the revolution were killed in the early days of hostilities during that invasion of East Prussia which was made very largely for the purpose of easing the pressure on the Allies in the West: So I felt that we owed their surviving friends and relatives something more than the sneer which was only too often their lot. Furthermore, I had been in Russia as a boy, and one year when we were spending a holiday at Samaden, in Switzerland, my father used to play golf with the Grand Duke Nicholas, the future Russian commander in chief, and Guchkov, the Octobrist leader, was more than once a guest at our house. So I had seen something of Russians elsewhere than in exile at Whitehall Court, and I did not get on with them too badly; anyhow I much preferred being sent to interview the Russians than the Serbs or the Italians.

There were many disillusionments to be experienced by a young man at the War Cabinet Office in those days, and not the least was contained in a box file labeled THE WAR AIMS OF THE ALLIES. One evening when we were on late duty with nothing much to do, a colleague and I got this file out, took a few blank maps, and set about tracing on them these war aims. We had not, however, gone very far before we discovered that vast areas, particularly in the Near East, had been promised to at least two separate powers, so we put the cards back in their box, tore up the maps, and returned to our normal work sadder, if wiser, men.

As September passed into October and it became clear that the collapse of Germany was imminent, the one subject of conversation in Whitehall was what sort of peace we were likely to have. Although those of us who worked at the War Cabinet Office had naturally more idea of the real situation than had the general public, even we imagined that the government had some plan for a final settlement other than the above-mentioned contradictory promises which had been made to various allies: In these circumstances it is hardly surprising that we should have been wildly out in our forecasts. Also, until a few days before the Armistice, it was never anticipated that there would be an internal revolution of any magnitude in Germany. What was expected was that the Kaiser would be forced to agree to a much more democratic constitution which would bring the Army under the control of the Reichstag and that the influence of Prussia in the Reich would be greatly weakened. Perhaps had these somewhat modest expectations been fulfilled, the future of Europe might have been happier.

What none of us anticipated was that the Allies, in opposition to their own interests, would carry the work of Bismarck to its logical conclusion and complete the unification of Germany, thereby paving the way for Hitler and the Third Reich. The strongest centrifugal force lay in the dynasties which ruled the various kingdoms and duchies, and which were always restive under the tutelage of Berlin; yet the German people were deliberately encouraged to overthrow their ruling houses, to many of which they were deeply attached, as the price of peace, and so the last obstacle to a unified Reich was removed by those concerned in its retention. Once the dynasties had gone, there was no reason for the continued existence of their former dominions as separate units, and so the path was cleared for that complete Prussianization of Germany which was to be the outstanding accomplishment of the Nazi regime.

Few voices were raised at the time against this mistaken policy, but now that fifty years have elapsed, it is difficult to disagree with the late Jacques Bainville that the war was lost in the first clause of the peace treaty, in that the settlement should not have been made with Germany as a whole, but rather that there should have been separate treaties with Prussia, Bavaria, Saxony, and the other states which had composed the Hohenzollern empire. Unhappily, the French were so determined to reverse the verdict of 1870 that they forgot that this in its turn had been rendered possible only by the victory of Prussia over Austria four years before, while the British government does not appear to have thought about the matter at all, having drifted into peace almost as inconsequently as it had drifted into war.

With the arrival of November events began to move so fast that their effect was numbing. The Kaiser's flight into Holland was the only incident of itself to strike the imagination, for it seemed inconceivable until it had happened, since at that time we knew nothing of the drama that had been enacted at Spa: For the rest one heard, almost without grasping its significance, the daily list of places captured by the advancing Allies—places that only a week or two before seemed outside the scope of any offensive possible until the following year at the earliest. Then the rumor began to go round that if the Germans delayed signing the Armistice, preparations had been made for the bombing of Berlin, for that city had hitherto been too remote a target for the airplanes of those days, and such was the prevailing climate of public opinion that most people hoped this would take place.

The actual events of November 11, 1918, must always remain fresh in the memory of any who were in London at the time. The day began in the normal way, and people went to their work as usual. As eleven o'clock approached, it was as if the population of the capital were coming out of a trance—a trance that had lasted for more than four years. The war was nearly over: In a few moments the last shot would have been fired. The moment for which millions had been waiting and which had been so long delayed that they had almost ceased to hope for it had arrived. Soon all pretense at work was abandoned, and in the West End a great crowd surged into Downing Street to salute the architect of the victory. Mr. Lloyd George duly appeared and said a few words, chiefly to the effect that the time had come to relax, after which there was a stampede to Buckingham Palace, where a very remarkable demonstration of loyalty took place toward the monarch who had played his part so well in the conflict that was now at an end. As the crowd cheered itself hoarse, it was impossible not to reflect on that other monarch, the Hohenzollern, fleeing from the people to whom he had so recently been little less than a god. Thus ended what we now know to have been the Peloponnesian War of modern Europe.

Few Londoners, however, were in a mood that morning for abstract questions of national psychology or political science, and the scene was soon transformed into something reminiscent of the Roman Saturnalia. In the main streets wheeled traffic eventually became impossible, but before this was the case, taxis by the dozen carried excited patriots on their roofs up and down Piccadilly and the Strand, while east of Temple Bar the magnates of the City were dancing on the tables in the restaurants. By one o'clock it was only with the greatest difficulty that one could get a drink anywhere. As the afternoon progressed, the disorder grew worse, but the King and Queen received an ovation as they drove through the packed streets. Older people recalled Mafeking night. The lights were on again, and that in itself was an inducement to come into the streets. In Trafalgar Square a huge bonfire was started at the foot of the Nelson Column and was fed with the notice boards from the buses. An old gentleman asked a policeman the quickest way to Charing Cross Hospital. "Call for three cheers for the Kaiser," was the immediate reply. I went to the Savoy that evening, and the first thing I saw was a girl in evening dress being sick in the gutter in Savoy Court. Nobody minded or appeared to think it odd. Inside the hotel a number of young officers were trying to burn a German flag in spite of the protests of the management. As I was going home on the District Railway, a rather drunken workman got into the carriage and kept on repeating, "We've won the bloody war, but we'll lose the bloody peace: You see if we don't." *In vino veritas?*

For two or three nights the authorities very wisely tolerated a good deal of rowdyism, and then it was stopped; after that there was a reaction, and people began to wonder just what the victory really meant. There were some major excitements, such as the surrender of the German Fleet, which I should have witnessed but for an inopportune attack of measles, the visit to London of Foch and Clemenceau, and one or two minor events, such as a general election, in which, however, no one took much interest. The war was over, and the one desire of officers and men alike was to get back to civil life. Few stopped to realize that there was no magician's wand to put everything back where it had been in July, 1914, and the government, with slogans such as "A land fit for heroes to live in," did nothing to dispel the illusion that the golden age was at hand. No hint was ever dropped that the period of adjustment after the war was likely to be at least as difficult to win through as had been the war itself. People were definitely encouraged to believe that without any effort on their part all would soon be for the best in the best of all possible worlds.

The fact was that the government, both at home and abroad, was, as I have already suggested, as unprepared for peace in 1918 as it had been for war in 1914, and it was heartrending to see the rapid dissipation of all those centrifugal forces that had contributed so much to the winning of the war. In their place grew up a spirit of envy and malice, an attitude of every man for himself, which boded ill for the future and which characterized every class of the community. . . . But that is another story, and the spring of 1919 saw me back at my studies at Corpus Christi College, Oxford.

Awakening

Henri Massis

HENRI MASSIS *has written some of the most significant works of our time
and received many honors, including the Grand Prix de Littérature of the
Académie Française in 1929 and the Grand Prix Osiris in 1966. Born in Paris
on March 21, 1886, he entered the Condorcet Lyceum where, in 1903, he
studied philosophy for a year in the class of Alain-Fournier, who, like André
Maurois, inspired him. Later he prepared for his degree at the Sorbonne.*

*During the years 1905–7 Massis frequented the home of Anatole France, to
whom he dedicated* Le Puits de Pyrrhon. *Then he fell under the influence of
Maurice Barrès, who "properly engendered spirit into life." He was also influ-
enced by Henri Bergson, under whom he studied at the Collège de France.
The grandson of Renan, Ernest Psichari (1883–1914), who was killed in
World War I, was for Massis a companion and a guide in spiritual growth.*

*Having gone through a period of religious doubt and searching, Massis
returned to the Roman Catholic faith in May, 1913, striving through his
writing to illuminate the mind by faith. He had already begun to publish his
critical essays on Renan, on France, on Gide, when World War I broke out.
He joined the 152 Infantry Regiment.*

In May, 1923, Massis published the first volume of his Jugements (*on
Renan, France, Barrès*), *dedicated to Jacques Maritain "in testimony of their
common hope in the metaphysical restoration." In January, 1924, he brought
out the second series of* Jugements (*on André Gide, Romain Rolland, Georges
Duhamel, Julien Benda, etc.*)

Massis published in 1941 at Lyon Les Idées restent, *wherein he reassembled
his ideas on art, literature, morals, politics, and history, not as an anthology,
but as a summary of the essential realities of which his work is a defense and
an illustration.*

In 1948 a definitive edition of his essays was published: D'André Gide à
Marcel Proust. *The following year he wrote* L'Allemagne d'hier et d'après-
demain. *In 1951 he published* Charles Maurras et notre temps, *wherein an
epoch is relived around a great figure. His whole life, he felt, was a preparation
for* De l'Homme à Dieu (*1959*). *In the period between these two he wrote*
L'Occident et son destin, Visages des Idées, *and* L'Europe en question.

Elected to the Académie Française on May 19, 1960, Massis published in

1962 Barrès et nous, *followed by an edited correspondence. In 1967 he wrote* Au long d'une vie, *in which he traces the various stages of his spiritual journey.*

THE WAR WE FOUGHT*

I COULD NOT give a historic opinion on the war of 1914–18 in the evening of my life. For me, the whole war is contained in a corner of land and a few hours, hours and land like all the others where the living and the dead stand together, and nothing seems to me more suited to evoking that war than the notes I scribbled in the trenches. Better than general observations, they seem to my mind to give an image of the event as a lived truth and, by their power of applying generally, to show the thoughts that moved us then. I transcribe them without any changes.

January 8, 1915. It will be six days tomorrow that the 3d Battalion has quartered at Noeux-les-Mines. A short breather, a bit of rest when in the movement of an almost ordinary life the will relaxes, yields to former habits, when the mind lingers on what we have just suffered and lived through. . . .

All the men drift into similar thoughts. I know just what they are saying in those letters the post orderly will carry off this evening; these long letters written in camp are less strained than the cards written in pencil the other week in the front lines; the courage they show will be no less steadfast, but there is a break, and perhaps a few weary words will slip out, the weariness that makes us seek distractions and pleasure in the moment. . . .

How dismal the last days of the year were! Yes, for weeks, though death is always on the prowl, invisible, permanent, wandering in all directions, though it never gives us respite, we have had a kind of tranquillity. Anyhow, what action could we attempt in this mud that coats our burdened troops with clay, that makes the ground treacherous, this ground churned by shells, sown with blood, and

---

* Translated from the French by Sally Abeles.

that increases the anguish of the nights in which we move toward
our lairs like blind shadows?

Oh, those cold December nights, when we huddled in our disgusting ditches, phantoms with cheeks as dark as bark, in the great
black silence, deeper yet from being pierced with solitary spaced
shots. . . .

. . . Well, there is the secret of our weariness: we are not yet up
to this war which makes a man disown himself in going to ground,
which makes courage useless, which makes heroism seem to be
nothing anymore, unless it has changed from an exalted state into a
steady and humble attitude.

But the war seems to us to be first a dreadful resignation, a
renunciation, a humiliation; there is no place for pleasurable sensation in it, and you don't understand immediately the grandeur of
the beauty of the asceticism it forces on us, of the punishment it lays
on the fighting man. . . .

If for a few days, shaking off the coat of mud our last retreat to
the trenches has covered us with, we want gentler human pleasures,
it is because after four months we have not yet relinquished our
will to act. You feel the same impatience among the men, among
our officers; this is the source of their melancholy and weariness. We
had to be put in our soil to defend it, but the hour is still far away
when our feet will sound on the ground, when it will become hard
like a road again. . . .

In this village, where our troops are staying to rest, we are learning to live again.

Tranquillity for a few hours; momentary, but in war never total
numbness. You drink, you read, you sing; everybody seeks out his
pleasure, takes refuge in what consoles him for the moment, but
with a weird sense of discomfiture and as if it were forbidden! The
soul does not demobilize at all, and in this instant of abandon, it
always has this sober vision present, this tragic vision of the reality
which tomorrow will perhaps lead it back to. . . . A presence you
expect a sign from. . . .

Also, in this diversion, it keeps alive a murmur of the talk passing
around: "It looks as if we'll attack around the fifteenth. . . ." "No,
we'll be in the second line, and we won't do anything before
spring."

Alternating fears, hopes, with everyone trying to find out what is
going to happen. . . .

January 9. By what mysterious signal are all our men crowding
into this exact church in Bouvigny where a mass was said for our

battalion? . . . Do they know that for many of us this will be the
last Sunday and the last blessing?

Their fervor in praying, a virile, military fervor, has something
about it that grips the heart. In this meditative silence, they feel
that the coming week will not be a waste, that things will come out,
and they are thinking about it already: The priest and the soldier
bow before the sacrifice. They have regained confidence and gravity, which you feel in the fever of the preparations; you eat hastily,
you get ready, the companies assemble, and the dark column of
footsoldiers advances through the villages, collected and cheerful.

January 10. Our company has laid up at Marles; the others have
left for the rear area. We will go on up day after tomorrow; two
days there, in the Bouvigny woods; two days, here again, quartered
on alert, at Ditch 3; then two more days in the trenches, and we
return to Hersin-Coupigny, which draws us with the memory of
peaceful hours.

Those are the orders: So this week, too, will pass without incident, dreary, muddy, indifferent, just like the others. Come now,
let's learn to endure these rough winter quarters! . . .

By the light of a candle this evening in the devastated trench,
Ducollet[1] read to several of us comrades from a comedy by Musset.
And we didn't get back to our barn until midnight. How lovely the
night is, and how sweet life! . . . We carry back *Fantasio*'s dreams,
and they are killing each other 800 meters away, behind the black
hill. . . .

January 12. A day of waiting. This morning an inspection of the
men, equipment, and arms. Barracks work. At noon a liaison officer
comes bringing orders. All companies fall in; we are shifting sectors.
We are going to relieve the 21st Infantry at Ablain-St.-Nazaire,
where our battalion fought before, in November. So sudden a decision, the puzzlement over such a decision and the memory among
the veterans of recent engagements suddenly bring down a slightly
weary quiet, in which we slide away.

Five o'clock. . . . In column by twos, we leave. . . . Our whole
being is mobilized within, and the sober file, silent, enters the dark,
damp communication trenches. Stray bullets whistle over our
heads: orders are passed *sotto voce* that everyone repeats to himself.
We step in one another's footprints, so acute is our fear of getting
lost. Then, jumping a mud-filled ditch, where many fall and sink in

---

[1] A young Comédie Française actor. (The play was Alfred de Musset's *Fantasio*.
—Tr.)

up to the neck, we are in the open, on the flank of a hill. A sergeant from the 21st serves as our guide: movements and muffled voices. . . . We go into the unknown, lurching, anxious. Over there, impatient with another impatience, those we will relieve are waiting. . . .

Finally, here is the trench we are to occupy: a commonplace hummock, but its intertwined pattern of communicating trenches and paths make it a secret thing, a labyrinth full of mystery and danger. It must be reconnoitered, men must be placed. . . . Several times before dawn, we move through this black and sticky path inhabited by shadows. . . .

The sentries have taken their places in the lookout posts; behind them their comrades, crouching and curled up, sink into the embankment like vines and blend with it. And around us, the ghastly night: The shots pace the anguished hours; there is the poignant melancholy of those nights in which death lives; the heart stays suspended in terror; dreams grow feverish when overtired limbs do not bring sleep to these stiff, heaped bodies. . . .

But day breaks, reviving all these phantoms, and restores confidence. You can see before you. . . . *They* are there, 15 meters away, behind that fringe of roiled land. And for two days the eyes will be riveted, hypnotized, on that knoll, that fold of ground, that curve of landscape, that ridge, that clump of trees, that short stretch of horizon which will be the last view of the earth for some. . . .

All day there is clumsy stirring about in this scruffy ditch; the air is wet and cold. They are firing, on this side and the other. . . . Some bombs loosen the dirt of the parapet. They pack it back. . . . Soldiers without pleasure in warring, they wait. For what? Nothing and everything, for death can bury them here during this desolate assignment, without their testing their strength against it; death is as if oblivious, mindless. It does not even want their courage, at least what used to be meant by courage, for in this war it demands a harder virtue: It wants to be waited for, at every hour, with patience. It is not at all the adventure of a heroic moment, the exalted passage of the hero into eternity, the sublime vocation of the warrior. It is less solemn: It takes whom it will, when it will, in the most humble posture, always imposing its ceaseless presence, requiring us to be always ready. . . .

This is how it went after you at the front, innocent child whom we laid in a corner of our mud prison at the end of this sad and useless day. You hadn't ever seen the enemy yet: You made your bloody sacrifice in ignorance, and it is not less beautiful. . . .

Grieved by this death, which made our inactivity lie heavy, we saw night fall again. . . . Yet another day just like this one; then others will replace us here, and we will lay down, for a few hours, this anguish that cleaves the soul like a sword.

January 13. This evening we will be relieved. . . . Everybody is waiting for this as for a deliverance. We are dogged by fatigue, insomnia; it is cold. . . . The hours pass, and always that fold of earth, that curve of landscape, that ridge, motionless but concealing such tragic, invisible life.

We will never again be able to contemplate the French countryside without peopling it with these bloody realities. Behind its vistas, so delightful, so similar, we will put the abundant tombs of our actions, which will give it a deeper beauty from dawn to dark, and the stack of perishable sheafs, which will rise where we have bled, will produce the imperishable bread of memory. . . .

More firing. . . . Nothing happens. It is four o'clock. More than two hours. In our command post, Knoertzer, Meunier, and I are reading Stendhal's *Rouge*[2] to one another. . . . The liaison officer brings letters and an order for Lieutenant Knoertzer.

"The company commander wants me," he tells us. "I'll be back for the relief."

A half hour later he returns, his face set, and the seriousness of our young chief makes us shiver before he has said a word. We are alone. . . .

"Well, here it is," he tells us. "We attack tomorrow evening at six o'clock. Our mission is to take the two lines of German trenches in front of us—the first one fifteen meters away; the second twenty meters behind it. Two platoons will charge the trench facing ours with bayonets; a platoon of First Company will rake the second line, while the platoon now at the far end of our trench will give us fire cover on the left.

"We will be supported by seventy-fives and nineties, which will prevent the formation of reinforcements in the village of Ablain. So that's it; I'm telling you, but I won't notify the men till tomorrow, a couple of hours before the attack. . . ."

Deep silence in the narrow hut, lighted by a meager candle set on the cross section of a bayonet. We looked at one another worriedly, saying nothing, but we saw into the depths of one another's breathless souls; you could have heard our heartbeats, and if we did not speak, it was so they would not make our voices tremble.

---

2 The nineteenth-century novel *Le Rouge et le noir* (*The Red and the Black*).
—Tr.

"God doesn't give courage, he only lends it," said D'Aubigné,[3] and after this admission by the great captain, who would hesitate to say that he shook before danger for a moment? It is true: For several minutes my body was shaken by a violent trembling in spite of me. What did my two companions feel? I do not know, but I know that all three of us judged this attack so perilous that we were certain it would bring us death. The Germans 15 meters away—we would be slaughtered as we left the trench. . . .

This certainty agitated in us during the long night as side by side we tried to sleep—a savage night like a hallucination, when our willpower flagged with our fatigue and we did not know whether it was the cold or horror that shook us—and this delay the action gave us aggravated the instinctive agitation of our being.

As we get up, as we escape from these nightmares that roll out all our past life, we say to one another almost joyfully, "It's eight o'clock; it'll all be over in ten hours! We've got to get ready, study this attack a little." We sketch out the positions on a piece of paper and comment on the order given the day before. The same certainty still possesses us, is even augmented by the study we are making. But it is no longer a question of us, and this necessity we have to get out of ourselves frees us of anguish.

We summon the platoon leaders to our command post right away; we explain the maneuver, the orders to them. Quietly we assure them of success—"We've got to succeed"—and now our whole being inspires confidence. . . . In a while, when they leave, we will destroy our private papers and make our final arrangements with the same interior peacefulness. Each of us draws up letters for his people that seem written from the same dictation:

"We are going into attack this evening at six o'clock; it'll be a particularly rough business. If these words come to you, it will be because I will have fallen. . . ."

"Still, it's hard," says Knoertzer in a low voice. . . .

A final moment of weakness, a final look cast behind, regrets suppressed that already have a note of resolution about them. . . .

We eat; you have to eat. . . .

Noon. Let's go notify our men. . . . We move out into the trench. The men, dazed with fatigue and hoping to hear the order to fall back for rest, accept the one to attack without flinching; a light glimmers in the eyes of these groups in clay, living sculptures carved from the narrow trench. We comment on the coming attack

---

3 Théodore Agrippa d'Aubigné, 1552-1630, a writer and companion in arms of Henri IV.—Tr.

to almost every one of them, for our men like to know what they are doing; they ask for details; we give them to them. . . .

Now they know; they get to work. With their shovels they make grooves in the outer wall, prepare steps to use for leaping out of the furrow. . . . A single will drives them; then they exchange hasty confidences, similar promises. Some embrace. . . .

A magnificent moment when man puts his trust in man, gives himself simply; incomparable human friendship, communion whose memory will light our souls until death. And in this warmth they work, clean their guns, load them, adjust their bayonets. . . . We tend to the final preparations.

Some who know that Lieutenant Meunier is a priest go to confession to him; hastily he gives absolution. Besides, it will be given to the whole company before it moves to the assault, and the great divine mystery of war passes over us, the superhuman reality for which our feeble explanations fail, the inconceivable sacrament that we will receive in a while in the frenzy of battle. . . .

Five o'clock. Night is coming. A feverish muffled murmur runs through the whole trench. Here comes Sergeant Vanier's platoon. Explanations exchanged in low voices; then the stretcher-bearers, who are put in the rear communication trench. . . . Deep silence over the countryside, where a thick, cold fog is falling; occasional gunshots. . . . Our men are no longer firing. . . .

A few minutes to go. . . . We wait for the signal from the chief. . . . Your whole being is miraculously calm; nothing except a hot forehead. . . . Lieutenant Knoertzer is to our left; I am beside him with the liaison officer. A smothered voice: "Ask Lieutenant Meunier if he is ready. . . . Pass it on. . . ."

And you hear the question pass from mouth to mouth, then fade away. . . . But before the reply comes back to us, the black cyclone of the artillery soughs overhead. . . . An instant of hesitation, during which it seems to us that a battle is already raging beyond the impenetrable horizon.

Spurred suddenly by a mad force, we leap into the night. . . . All of a sudden a flare bursts in an ashen green glare, weird, fantastic, and we jerk about in it like outsize shadows. . . . Around us the heavy boom of the 90's sounding like a bass to the inexorable song of the 75's, and distinct from them the stuttering of the machine guns; over there, the night crisscrossed with flashes. . . . Is it this sight that holds us poised, immobile, a step away from the German trench, or astonishment at being there alive?

"Advance, advance, damn it!" Knoertzer howls. "Jump, we've got 'em. . . ."

Is it possible? We *have* their first line: A few shots, and they've run. . . . We fling ourselves into the communication trench leading to the second line, which Sergeant Gérard's platoon has already occupied. We shout wildly, *"Victory! Victory!"* It's the rallying cry.

Exhausted, Knoertzer shouts his orders. We call out to one another; we run in all directions; we find them in their huts, hands up, pale, trembling, crying, *"Kamerad! Kamerad! . . ."* More than 20,000 prisoners are evacuated to the rear. . . . Salvos in the air: It's over! . . . We have possession of the area.

On the opposite ridge the infantrymen have come out of their trench, and under the livid glow of the sky we see their shadows hailing us. "Joy, joy, tears of joy." This is the same kind of mystical illumination. . . . To have been able to live to taste such a joy is enough to make you faint with happiness. . . . How magnificent it is! How magnificent! . . . Our group leads a strange saraband in the night. Mighty shouts resound with the rhythm of a chant: "Bravo! Victory!" . . .

A beautiful night, with the beauty of a festival. . . . The last shots cast their red light. . . . The din of the artillery stops suddenly; the sky turns black again.

Midnight. We expect the enemy to counterattack at daybreak. Can 2d Company, exhausted from lack of sleep and hunger, shattered by the emotions of this fight, make this new effort? The company commander doesn't think so: he will have it relieved in an hour. Only the platoon leaders will stay. . . . More than a few minutes. . . . Muffled steps, much stirring of shadows returning to our old line. Crossing it, my foot is fractured. . . .

Hardly have we left the area taken the evening before than the enemy crosses the way in the sooty dawn, then deploys suddenly, reoccupies his original position, throws back into their trench those of our men who haven't yet got there. . . . A platoon from 4th Company has already replaced the 2d and is there. . . .

At only eight in the morning, Lieutenant Knoertzer receives the order to report to Commander Mademin's H.Q. "For the honor of the 3d Battalion," they've decided to launch a new attack. . . . It will begin at noon. . . .

Our men have barely got a leg over the parapet before a machine-gun fusillade drops them in a line on the lip of the trench. . . . Knoertzer, who is leading them, falls, hit in the hand. I hoist myself to him, drag him by his overcoat to get him back to our lines. . . . Then I'm conscious of nothing anymore. . . . The attack is broken. . . . It's over. . . .

Knoertzer and I make it to the rear, through the lateral connect-
ing trench filled with dredging mud, in which we push along flat on
our bellies. . . . The two of us are alone, groping our way, our
straining bodies sinking into the oozing ground. . . . The sheer
effort of pulling ourselves free of its suction. . . . I claw the
slippery sides of the ditch we are submerged in. . . . My coat has
turned to clay. . . . I can no longer lift my feet, a chunk of muck
imbedded in the viscous slime. . . .

Evening is falling already. . . . Solitary spaced shots ricochet
through the copse we are trying to reach, cutting branches. . . .
An exploding shell wounds me in my left hand, and I fall again, my
head in the mud, to drag along again on my belly. . . . Knoertzer
is still in front of me; I grab his arm, which stiffens and sags with an
exhausted movement. . . . Where do all these detours lead?
Which is the way out? What is in front of us? To the right, the left?
It seems as though there is nothing anymore. . . .

The farther we get from danger, the more we are overtaken by an
unutterable dread. . . . Night is falling. . . . Are we making any
headway? We feel as though we haven't gained an inch. . . . Ah,
there, behind that knoll covered with a clump of trees, we glimpse
something. . . . Yes, we're approaching the H.Q. . . . But here's
the battalion ambulance looking for us. They take us out and lift us
into a transport, on stretchers. . . . And suddenly I hear, "Are you
there, fellow? Are you there?" A fraternal voice has come through
the dimness. . . . Drouot, my dear Drouot! Before I can take the
hand he is holding out to me, the ambulance has departed into the
night. . . . Will I ever see him again?[4]

January 17. Here I am in the hospital in Tours on the Rue
Descartes, with the Sisters of Perpetual Adoration; I was evacuated
from the front and brought here. . . .

I spend part of my days rereading the notes I wrote up there, and
what strikes me is the nature of this war, which is asking a man for

---

4 Paul Drouot, who would have been one of the great poets of his generation, was
killed on June 9, 1915. Before leaving on August 2, 1914, Drouot wrote this will: "I
do not want to leave a trace. Everything is useless here below, you see, everything
except the soul. . . . I leave nothing that is worthy of publication. I ask that all my
papers, notes, drafts, beginnings of poems or isolated verses be destroyed—which will
hardly change them. A work must be finished. I thank those who have so indulgently
given me credit on the appearances. I would have liked to prove them right sometime. A thousand concerns have prevented me till now, and at the present hour,
nothing is important anymore except great issues, the country's, the soul's. We have
to go off on crusade, the mind free of vanity and the heart wholly devoted to its
business of being a heart. I wouldn't want to mouth phrases. I embrace my two
masters, Élémir Bourges, the great poet of *"La Nef,"* and Henri de Régnier. I pray
my friends, if I do not see them again in this world, to lift their minds to God when
the memory of me touches them. My trust is henceforth in Him."

virtues that no army in any period has required. No tangible satisfaction: Everything about it is done within, in the ground, in a
man. The whole of a man is involved in it, not only the conqueror
or the businessman, the man fighting for domination or gain; it is a
man in his entirety who is taking up his country's cause, it goes
without saying, since it is with all his soul and all that has formed it
for him. But in return a man expects the renewal of his soul from it,
a means to an inner perfecting. This is the unexpected thing. Never
had these spiritual elements been incorporated into war to the
point of dominating it. Never had men heard a like call to moral
notions to live this event. Never had the fighter's feelings reached
such a depth. . . .

I remember something one of my men said in my hearing as we
went to the trenches: "We are all here for misery." A sublime
acceptance, a recognition of a necessity deeper than any other. This
man gave misery the right to exist; he experienced it in his exact
understanding of what it demands and consented to everything. A
dedicated victim, he knew that the hour had come to carry the
whole weight of human suffering, without tiring, without giving
way. Whether he chooses the pick that digs up the soil or the shovel
that throws it aside, everyone hollows out his grave. Then what can
be the hope that lifts the eyes above the furrow choked with human
wreckage? If he assents, it is because he feels obscurely that when
the end comes, all suffering is fulfilled in glory and salvation, and
that "All suffering which serves a purpose, all suffering which can
serve a purpose, is the daughter of the suffering of God." This is a
kind of grace, the outpouring of a faithful heart that suffers in
silence.

But out of the depths of its silence a voice rises from this Army
dripping with its native earth. And it is the voice of its eternal
vocation, which Paul Claudel makes us hear in his *"Nuit de Noël
de 1914"* (Christmas Night, 1914) ; I read this page of it yesterday
to my comrades in the hospital:

What we are defending with our wealth, with the acre in which our
right and our destiny vest, what we are defending is God Himself who
has put Himself in our keeping, is that decent place in our heart where
He is, is the infinitely weak all-powerful, is that lowly breath in our
heart that has made us all upright!

It is God we are defending, even those who do not know His name.
For each people is born for itself, but France has been born for the
whole universe, in order to bring it joy!

It is not only her body she is defending, it is her soul, which belongs to the whole universe; it is not only her life she is defending, it is the word of God to the whole universe, which is eternal joy, in eternal freedom.

This is what we believed.

Even now, in the evening of our life, how deep is the echo of the cry that Georges Bernanos flung us from the heart of that past, ten years after the war of 1914–18: "Old friends of the heights battered by the wind, companions of raging nights, solid band, inflexible band . . . who one day took the burning spurt of the enemy's artery and all his heart's blood full in the face, oh, boys! November 11 we drank the last cup from our vines. November 11 we broke the black bread baked for us."

Yes, the war was the home of our youth. We were born of the war, the war was immediately upon us, and in truth we have never done anything else. . . . After an armistice of some years, war led us back up there, to those regions we never departed, which guard our deepest secrets, where we have left our souls with the bodies of our friends. Twenty years it had not stopped holding us under its law, for the most serious, the most decisive of wars is perhaps the one fought when we are no longer battling one another. It has left us with "such a wrinkle of hurt at the corners of the mouth" that death alone can relax that line marking our faces. But it has also given us Hope, a Hope that has consumed us ever since, a Hope that itself is invincible, even in death. Yes, "the divine gaze rested on us," that gaze "so steady, so tender" which still stirred Bernanos when, in 1919, returning from the war, that war we withstood, were really able to withstand, he said: "In that sheath of instincts, of acquired or hereditary habits, in the flesh and the blood, something has awakened, has moved once and for all, irreversibly. It is done. We can no longer be mistaken about ourselves now. We must make ourselves free or die!"

The war would never cease to mark our work and our days.

L. Wyn Griffith

"I was born in 1890, the eldest son of a village schoolmaster in Wales. Some years later, married and with three children, my father scraped his way through University college, Bangor, took an honors degree, and for many years was headmaster of Dolgellau Grammar School. There, after years in village schools, I was educated until I was nineteen, when I entered the civil service as an assistant surveyor of taxes. In 1914 I enlisted in the Royal Welch Fusiliers and went to France in 1915 as an infantry captain, became a staff officer, and was demobilized in 1919. I was married in 1915, and my eldest son was killed in action in 1942.

"For me, writing has always been a spare-time activity, shared with serving on committees concerned with Wales and with the arts. Most of my books deal with Wales, two of them novels, one a war book, Up to Mametz, one an account of my childhood called Spring of Youth, the others being various attempts to interpret the life of my country to those who cannot speak its language. I was privileged to spend eleven years as vice-chairman of the Arts Council of Great Britain, after being chairman of its Welsh Committee. I have been broadcasting regularly, in Welsh and in English, for more than thirty years, and I am a vice-president of the London Center of P.E.N., chairman of the Council of the Honourable Society of Cymmrodorion, a Welsh society now in its third century. I have never been at a loss for something to do and have enjoyed doing it."

THE PATTERN OF
ONE MAN'S REMEMBERING

Reach back to years I spent, to men I knew,
to days I drank each minute dry,
give tongue to want: I must not die
mere wisdom-bound because the hurt
grew great and this my loss is loss of men.

Reach hand to touch rough-coated arm,
let none dismiss with pity grief
this company of ghosts about my heart,
they were my youth, the sorrow mine.
I bought this peace but paid no price
so great as theirs.

I HAVE QUOTED the beginning of a long poem about the war that I
wrote twenty years after it ended, for several reasons, none of which
is concerned with its merits or demerits as verse. It would have
extended the powers of a great poet to measure up to the greatness
of the occasion and the intention, and such powers were never
mine. Nevertheless, it expresses something I had never succeeded in
putting into prose, although I had written a book about the war
that was well received by the generation involved in it.

The processes, emotional and intellectual, attached to a concern
about reliving and rethinking so tremendous an event in the life of
an individual are not without interest, and if I recall them, it is
because they may not be familiar to many and because, fifty years
later, it is possible to do so with detachment.

When war broke out in 1914, I was twenty-four years old,
employed in the service of the government, and forbidden to join
the armed forces because the work on which I was engaged was
considered important. Flattering, you might think. But no: I was a
Welshman, and my contemporaries were enlisting in the Royal
Welch Fusiliers. They were escaping from offices, shops, farms, and
factories, from the humdrum duties of civilian life to which I was
condemned. I cannot remember that I ever thought of soldiering as
anything but a better way of life than sitting at a desk: Killing or

being killed was something that might happen to someone else. None of my contemporaries thought that there was anything "noble" about joining the armed forces. It was what your friends were doing, and it was only natural that you should do the same, if you could. By devious ways, I succeeded in joining them and became a mere "number" clad in uniform—became in fact, uniform, undistinguishable, responsible for nothing more than obeying orders and keeping clean and tidy myself and an obsolete weapon.

This is what happened to many millions of men in many countries. But if, as I do, you belong to a small nation, with its own language, Welsh, surrounded by a large nation speaking English, you enter into a double life. English is the language of the Army, Welsh the language of friendship and companionship, "ours" against "theirs." There is, inside you, a citadel which cannot be stormed by force, but which can be entered with the key of language. And when you find yourself in the company of your fellow countrymen, private soldiers with a private language with which to escape from this new world of drill and parade and discipline, a language belonging exclusively to a way of life in which you were nurtured and from which you are now exiled, companionship brings a new kind of intimacy. A new bond is created, a sense of being a community within a community, which intensifies the very meaning of comradeship.

I was in the Army for four and a half years, three of them on active service in France as an infantry officer, a company commander, and finally as a general staff officer on what was called Operations (to distinguish it from Intelligence!) , so that I had to undergo a number of transformations of body and mind. This involved a series of apprenticeships, and now, fifty years later, I can recognize a succession of events that remain in my memory and bring with them a resurgence of emotions, pleasant and unpleasant, associated with learning the various trades.

Associated also with another kind of adjustment, I have referred to the dichotomy brought about by this matter of language, of living in Welsh and in English. My regiment, the Royal Welch Fusiliers, consisted mostly of Welsh-speaking Welshmen whose background was similar to my own. In Welsh, we could talk freely, officers and men alike and with each other, without impinging in any way on matters of military protocol that seemed to belong exclusively to the world of English. This created a bond of unity, that sense of being an enclave within a community. This was the regiment in which Robert Graves, Siegfried Sassoon, David Jones, and Frank Richards served, authors of the best of the war books. But they did not speak Welsh, and so there was a world into which they could not enter. This does not detract from the value of their books, but it impoverished them at the time. And now, for me, it complicates this matter of "remembering," bringing in a range of emotions that do not depend on the hazards of war for their potency. Though I write in English, I have only to think or speak in Welsh, and they spring to life. These "men I knew" were of my own kin because we spoke the same language, the one we had inherited, not the one we used as we learned our trade of soldiering.

Let me give an instance of what I mean. The scene is the canal bank near Ypres, on a dark winter night in 1916: some desultory shelling, an occasional rattle of machine-gun fire, a Very light shooting up into the blackness and falling to make it even darker. A company waiting to go up into the trenches on relief, waiting, "always bloody well waiting," for the order to move up the communication trenches to the front line. They start singing, in harmony, being Welsh, a fine old Welsh hymn tune in a minor key. The brigadier general asks me, "Why do they always sing these mournful hymns? Most depressing—bad for morale. Why can't they sing something cheerful, like the other battalions?"

I try to explain to him that what they are singing now is what they sang as children, as I did, in chapel, in the world to which they really belong. They are being themselves, not men in uniform. They are back at home, with their families, in their villages. But he does not understand. Nor can he, with his background. I do not think I "understand" it myself; but the facts were there, and they still are. While they sang, they, and I, were in another country.

There have been, and there will be, other wars, and men will sit down to remember them and to write about them. It would be foolish to try to generalize about the way in which they will do so, but it is at least possible and permissible for one writer to recount the various processes of remembering that time brought with it and the different impulses which he experienced at successive periods and how all this took shape in the written word.

Back, then, to 1919 when I was demobilized and went back to my wife and my job and to an orgy of reading, making up for lost time. The cares and the pleasures of living drove away all thoughts of war. I did not dream about it. It was something that had happened to someone else. I had a house and a garden, and the business of life was to grow children and to succeed in my work. My colleagues in the office had not been allowed to join the forces, and I rarely met any fellow soldiers. I was living in England, away from my countrymen, out of contact with men who spoke my own language. This was a new life, unrelated to the past.

Some two or three years later, I made a brief record of my share of the war, a mere account of events, some 1,500 words in all, because I thought it might interest my sons when they grew up. I put it in a drawer and forgot all about it. It was quite impersonal, and as I had not kept a proper diary, it all came from what I can only call the top layer of my memory: a mere chronology, and incomplete at that. It has now disappeared, and no one is any the poorer for its loss.

However, some three years later, in one of those domestic upheavals called spring cleaning, it came out of a pile of papers, and I sat down to read it. I can still remember the shock I received, saying to myself, "Well, if this is all you can say about the biggest experience of your life, of years of hazardous living, it would be better to say nothing than to be proved incapable of writing an account of it." So I tore it up. However, the matter would not rest there, for there was an implied challenge, and inside me there seemed to be an upsurge of remembering that brought back the war that I thought I had overlaid with the day-to-day business of living.

I accepted the challenge, and set out to put on paper all I felt and saw and did on one day in February, 1916, when I was in the trenches opposite Givenchy in Flanders. It was an unpleasant occasion, and I began to relive the days and nights that followed, in all their terror and discomfort, with the stench of mud and chloride of lime and the smell of bacon frying on a mess-tin lid in the early morning. I can only call it a kind of emotional explosion inside me, and under its impetus I wrote on and on until I came toward a kind of climax, the Battle of Mametz Wood in July, 1916, where so many of my countrymen, including my own brother, were killed. There I stopped, because I was afraid of my own memories and dreaded their coming to life. So I turned back and wrote about the way from Winchester to Givenchy, so as to give some shape to the account. I found that I had given some kind of picture of the war as I had seen it, and in doing so, I had become accustomed, even reconciled, to remembering. My sons might even learn something about me, as well as about the war. I had no thought that anyone else would share this knowledge.

But the challenge was still there, in Mametz Wood, and I found that there was no peace within me until I had faced and recorded this high point of the war where for me and so many other Welshmen the tragedy reached its culmination. The words had to be torn out of me, hurt as it must. The events are mere history, to be found in many books, but my own reactions, as I recorded them, turned remembering into a surgical operation. And, as happens with the body, there came afterward a kind of peace within. I had spent my emotional capital, in this detailed recovery of what I thought to have been buried beneath years of happiness, and I was left in what I can only call a neutral state. This kind of remembering had done its work, and I was purged of the pain of war, untroubled, confident that I had nothing more to fear from its recurrence in the years ahead.

But the mind has its own timetable in these matters, and later on, looking back on what I had written, I found that though I had had some measure of success in recording what I felt and did and saw during a period of six months in the trenches, it had become a minor fragment of written history. The thoughts and emotions that went into the making of it were now no longer those of the living author. There was a change in the nature of day-to-day remembering, a fusion between the event and wisdom-after-the-event, an impulse to achieve something more general in character. Something that might, perhaps, if it succeeded, reflect what was universal in an experience that was personal. And here, I now can see, I became once more the inheritor of generations of Welsh peasants who had been conditioned by years of long sermons, of Sunday school, of moralizing, of life in a community where there was a "lesson to be learnt" from even the most insignificant of daily happenings. This belongs to a world that has now vanished, but it was relevant at the time, and certainly potent in 1914, so that it was not irrelevant in the 1930's when one was thinking about the war.

And so it came about that the next phase of remembering was harnessed to a search for something I had failed to say in prose. If I could find it, it could be true of others besides myself. The upshot took the form of a long poem in blank verse. It was not a good poem, because I was not a good poet, but the discipline of writing it compelled a sharpening of the mind, a concentration of thought, a paring down of vague emotions, and a sharpening of their expression, as well as an attempt to expand the particular into the general. In one sense, it was an effort at greater objectivity: Memories of sheer delight, of undiluted pleasure, forced themselves into it. Long days of marching in the autumn through all the colors of the woodlands in the Vale of Severn as well as long nights of standing in the mud of the trenches, a feather bed in a billet, as well as a duckboard on the fire step in the front line.

This was a move toward a greater honesty, but it was only partly successful. There was more self-pity in it than pity, and overelaboration of the obvious emotional response. Its importance to me lay in the fact that this indulgence in remembering began a process that continued over the years, a kind of dehydration of sentiment, bringing about at the same time a growth of anger, as well as a tendency to dwell on the happier memories. War has its joys and its agonies, and to think of it otherwise, in retrospect is to be dishonest. And anger, while it lasts, neutralizes sorrow.

The long poem—it was called "The Fading Years," and for its motto I wrote out the words and music of the old Welsh hymn tune sung on the canal bank at Ypres—had done its work for me, and that was the end of it. Some years later it was reborn, in a different shape, harsher in form, truer to its time and to the ears of a new generation; under the title " 'Tis Not the Song They Wish to Hear," it had a measure of currency, and it marked the end of all I wished to say about the war. Or so I thought. But in 1945 I was asked to write a program in verse to be broadcast to celebrate the end of another war, some of it to be spoken, some set to music, and I found that in it I was still remembering the 1914–18 war, the only war I knew. I can recall nothing of it except one line—"Great companies of men who answer not their names"—and two lines of a chorus sung by women:

> The world is waiting for the grace of love,
> And in our pity lies our power.

If these have stayed in my memory, it can only be because they epitomize two ways of responding to the phenomenon of war: of saying farewell to the sorrow that had lived with me for so long, for thirty years.

Since then the memories that come unbidden to the mind are of incidents that have not been recorded in any of the many books and histories, and they are pleasant ones. The others have evaporated and are no longer troublesome: They were part of the burden of another man, younger and perhaps better able to bear them.

We reached Mons the day after the Armistice and began to learn what the years of enemy occupation had meant to the ordinary men, women, and children of Belgium. As it drew toward Christmastime, General Godley (who went on to command the Army of the Rhine) called together his staff one morning and said, "We must do something for the children of this town. Some of them have never known a proper Christmas. How much money is there in the canteen fund?" Plenty, he was told. "We'll throw a children's party. Ask the mayor for the use of the town hall." Someone pointed out that you couldn't get all the children into it. "The party will last three days then. That ought to be enough. Send some lorries to Paris to get oranges and apples and toys, if there are any, and plenty of buns. We'll fill them up with buns and biscuits."

I do not know how many thousands of children of all ages and sizes came to the party or how often they came. Some of the smaller ones had never seen an orange before. They ate their buns at the party—they could not wait—and they took buns home with them. Nobody cried; they all looked starry-eyed in wonder at this profusion. And towering above them stood General Godley, six feet six inches in height, as happy as any child at the party.

Another unrecorded incident is still vivid in memory. It was April, 1918, at the height of the battle which was to determine the fate of the Channel ports, with the German thrust forward at its peak. General Godley was in command of some eight or nine divisions hurriedly sent to fill the gap and block the way. As a rule corps headquarters was some distance away from the scene of battle, for obvious reasons, the chief of which was the necessity of maintaining communication forward and back. There was no radio in those days. Godley said, "I can't fight a battle from here. Find me a signal office as far forward as you can." Eventually I found a signalers' dugout, well forward, but in contact with divisions and with the army headquarters so long as shelling did not cut the lines. Godley and his chief of staff, General Gwynn, came there with their maps and operation orders. There were two telephones, and my job was to listen to everything and keep a record. I was privileged to watch a general fighting a battle. It might have been the Napoleonic Wars. He moved brigades and battalions and batteries to meet the varying hazards and opportunities. And when it became apparent that the defense was assured and a signal came to say that the 2d French Cavalry Corps was coming to our aid, he said to me, "Go to meet them and tell them to stay where they are. There's no room for them."

I set off and met General Robillot, who commanded the corps. In my best French I tried to explain that the roads forward were so congested that it would be impossible for him to advance. He bridled and said they were cavalry and did not depend on roads. "But your transport and artillery do," I replied. He was forced to agree. I then asked him whether it was true that his corps had traveled all these miles in two days, that we could not believe it possible, that no one but the French could have done it. The butter did its work, I was asked to lunch, and the French corps stayed where it was.

An empty house in Bailleul in June, 1917, just before the Battle of Messines. I had been sent to the 2d Anzac Corps, as what was called a learner, an infantry captain who had been allowed to absorb some of the wisdom and experience of the staff at the headquarters of a brigade of infantry and who was more aware of his shortcomings than of his knowledge. The day after I got there, the general staff officer, third grade, was wounded on a visit to the front line. Contrary to general belief, junior staff officers were often in the front line. As I was on the spot, I was appointed to succeed him. I can think of no better reason. I put on my red tabs, very proudly, as soon as I could get them. When I went to that house in Bailleul where I was to join the mess, I heard a gramophone: The record was *En Bâteau*, by Debussy, the orchestral version. Suddenly I seemed to have come home; I was in my own country. And when David Liddell put on the next record, of the first two movements of Bach's *Concerto for Two Violins*, the war seemed to have ended. I was back in 1914. The third movement has always come as a surprise to me ever since. And as I listen to the concerto nowadays, I am back in 1917, in a small town in Flanders, with lorries and guns thundering over the *pavé* toward the opening stages of the Battle of Messines. But only for a moment. The music conquers the memory and lives on in its own right, as it should.

The flow of the years has eroded the power of response to the stimuli of fear, anger, sorrow that were once so potent. Events in retrospect have died into words on the printed page, incapable of producing anything but a "Yes, that was how it was" by way of reaction. No more dreams of being involved. And as it all recedes, almost beyond recall, it has become something impersonal, as remote as the Trojan War. The sorrow of losing comrades who did not survive the war has turned into the sorrow of losing those who did survive it and whom I have outlived.

This, then, is a record of the impact of the war upon my life after the Armistice, so far as it has been made manifest to me. I cannot say what the unrevealed effects are, what unnoticed modulations have taken place, and it may well be that these have proved more powerful than my attempted rational explanations of matters that are, after all, a blend of thought and feeling, difficult to bring within the net of words. The knowledge that the Somme and Passchendaele had more than decimated the youth of Wales, had almost destroyed a generation of my countrymen, may have brought me closer to my own country and helped to make me devote myself to playing a part in some kind of reconstruction of what we regarded as our national culture. But, on the other hand, it may only have been the pull of generations of my forebears. The strands are too closely knit for me to unravel, and all that matters is that it happened, and that it continues, with some measure of achievement.

I have reason to be grateful. I escaped physical hurt and financial loss, I emerged capable of dealing with daily life, fortified by the steadfast love of a wife who suffered torments of suspense for four years of war. My reward is that when I think of the war, the elements of fear, of real and imagined danger, of discomfort and of deprivation, of filth and of repulsiveness, of anger and hate, of contempt for the ignorance above which insisted on the continuance of Passchendaele have lost their strength. They have been overlaid by the memory of men I can no longer speak to, by the incidents of escape into short spells of life in a cottage overlooking the River Dee:

> Noon is a silence, dusk a candlelight
> On rough walls slanting.
> Heap wood upon the fire: no evil in this flame.
> Would I were done with all but love
> And in the morning grey smoke curling.

It must be one of the few rewards of growing old that fifty years have proved long enough to turn hate into acceptance. And that is the pattern of one man's remembering.

Montgomery Belgion

MONTGOMERY BELGION *was born in Paris of English parents in 1892. Thus, at the age of twenty-one, he had to exercise an option to be either French or British. He chose British. Paris is where he went to school, and he was still there when Europe went to war in August, 1914. During the early stages of World War I he was ill, but on being passed by the doctor, he went to London as a volunteer and in January, 1916, was elected to the Honourable Artillery Company, in which he became an infantryman and saw service in France in that same year. Invalided home, he was commissioned in the Dorsetshire Regiment and went to France again for the closing battles. He was at the front on Armistice Day. In World War II he again volunteered and became a captain in the Royal Engineers, Movement Control, part of the railways branch of the British Army. He was in France till June 1940. He was taken prisoner in Greece in 1941 and exchanged in 1944.*

For some years Mr. Belgion was a newspaperman. He has twice lived in New York. In 1921 and 1922 he was successively on the New York Daily News *and on the now extinct New York* World. *He has contributed to the* Sewanee Review, Southern Review, Hound and Horn, *the* Saturday Review, *etc. From 1925 to 1929 he was with Harcourt, Brace, publishers.*

His books cover a wide range: Our Present Philosophy of Life, The Human Parrot, News of the French, Reading for Profit, *and* Victors' Justice. *Awaiting publication is his* Megalopolitics, *and he is completing a book of memoirs. His* Reading for Profit *sold 100,000 copies and has been translated into French.*

In 1945 he married Gladys Helen Mattock, and they live in the country in England.

A REMINISCENCE AND
A MEDITATION

I. THE REMINISCENCE

AT THE TIME THE SHOOTING, shelling, and bombing stopped in
France in November, 1918, I commanded an infantry platoon in
the 3d British Army (General Byng). We did not in that army
march forward into Germany. The moment the Armistice was in
force we were on our way to the neighborhood of the Channel
coast. We were then far from being a battalion 1,000 strong. Some
companies were commanded by subalterns, some platoons by sergeants. The sections were about half their proper number, the men
barely adult and under the height of the peacetime regular foot-
slogger. But before we set out to cross what were called the devastated regions, we were richly reinforced. Other ranks poured out
from England—sleek, well-fed officers from the north of Ireland.
With insufficient appreciation of the rot wrought in Germany by
the blockade, the high-ups in London expected the war to go on
into the spring of 1919, and they were husbanding their personnel
so that it might last out that long despite front-line casualties. Our
company commander, a Canadian lieutenant five feet high, handed
us over to an upstanding, bridge-playing captain of distinctly higher
social status.

The latter described to us Armistice Day in London. From
Piccadilly Circus and the adjoining streets anything on wheels had
been banished by the size of the delirious crowd. The beer and
spirits merchants did a feverish trade. The verb "to maffick" came
into its own again. Girls gave kisses to any man in khaki within
sight. It was a great time. Out in France it had been different.

On the day before, Sunday, the tenth of November, in a village
southeast of Maubeuge and almost in Belgium, I awoke to an
unwonted quiet. We were in support. The front, if front there was
still as the retreating enemy seemed to dissolve, was some distance
ahead. The sun was shining. The day contrasted with the rain,
noise, and confusion of the night before. We had been marching we
did not know whither. In the rain the muddy *pavé* had to be

disputed step by step with the vehicles and men coming the other way. Ahead of us was an occasional gun flash, but it hardly lit up the dead horses and mules that lined our road. A Gustave Doré would have been needed to do pictorial justice to the scene. Abruptly we were brought to a halt. The men were glad to fall out in the right-hand ditch and to slip off their equipment. The pause was just long enough for us to look forward to relaxing. We were fallen in facing the other way. We retraced our steps. We asked ourselves the idiotic question: Had we been brought forward by mistake? Soon we saw that we were being taken back only a short distance. We had taken the wrong turning, and now we had to go straight on, to the right instead of, as we had done, to the left. The rain stopped. We shambled on, and at last, still in the dark, we reached the village where I was to awake next morning. We were put into billets, the men in a barn and I on the tiled floor of a house. After our nightmarish march it was Eden.

That Sunday morning was still no respecter of persons. The senior subaltern of C Company was walking up the road that led forward out of the village when he was hit in the thigh by a shell splinter. Very likely he would lose his leg. I, too, went up that road, I forget why, but undisturbed. I came upon a solitary private half-sitting, half-crouching in his equipment on the verge close to the hedge. He seemed to be waiting and looked as lifelike as any figure in the waxworks. But, of course, he was dead. Later I passed him a second time, and now he was in his socks. His ammunition boots had vanished—no doubt into the thrifty possession of a French peasant. In his socks he figured death more strikingly than would a grinning skull.

We had no newspapers. Wireless was reserved for ships. Yet we knew that events were impending. I was in too great a suspense to keep still. The Canadian company commander I have already mentioned agreed that I might go off in the afternoon in search of news. I borrowed his horse and reached the outskirts of Berlaimont, aware of my unhappy seat. I failed to synchronize my own rise and fall with that of the animal that bore me. My good humor was unaffected. I felt that the news I wanted was only waiting to be learned. But when outside Berlaimont I sought out the divisional D.A.A.G., he was circumspect. All he would say was: "Tomorrow you will hear something of interest. Till then you'll have to wait." Such was the message I took back to my company commander. It was enough to fill me with a secret glee.

The little man suggested we should go to the movies. The marquee which exhibited them was in an adjoining field. When we came out, it was dark. We heard the unmistakable drone of an airplane. A couple of distant explosions followed. After our peaceful day the sound was intrusive. How appalling to be killed or wounded by a stray bomb splinter at this stage, I thought. But already the dark sky had regained its silence.

Next morning, sure enough, the D.A.A.G.'s promise was fulfilled. It was Monday, the eleventh of November, an unforgettable day in my life. Across the wide village street from my billet was the inn. It had an external balcony that ran the length of its front one floor above the ground. About nine o'clock we were fallen in by platoons and companies facing this balcony, and the colonel appeared on it and told us what I had been waiting to hear. At eleven—in under two hours—the Great War would be over. At last!

Compared with the relief and joy in my heart, our cheers sounded perfunctory. Our feelings were too deep for expression.

That day we did not march back any farther than Berlaimont. We were there by midday. On account of my familiarity with French, I was detached to find billets. How wonderful it was! No precautions need be taken against enemy hostility. For my own shelter I went to the *juge de paix*. He was elderly and dignified. He said he had had a German officer quartered upon him, who had behaved well. I could have his room. I said, "I expect you have a few bottles of wine buried in your garden. Perhaps you'll let me have one on such a day as this?" He agreed.

I brought the bottle to the company mess for dinner. I thought I should have to share it with three other officers. I found the company commander and a subaltern had excused themselves. I was left alone with a young man, who, when I offered him a glass of the wine, remarked, "I'd rather have a glass of sherbet." As soon as he had finished his meal, he left me with the bottle. It was a pleasant wine, not meant to be savored in solitude.

II. The Meditation

SUCH WAS my last day of World War I. Looking over its events across an interval of nearly half a century, I wonder how far it may be made to sum up the whole war—particularly for those to whom that war was, in the words of D. H. Lawrence, "tawdry and vain." I had never believed in the war. I did not believe that Germans were wicked. I did not believe that Germany had plotted the destruction of the West. I did not see why any Frenchman or Englishman should die or be irretrievably damaged so that a moribund Russia might a little longer simulate life and lay a palsied grip upon Constantinople. Above all, I was sure that Germans (who were nearly all strangers to me) were not really any different from Frenchmen (whom I knew well). Perhaps I was too young to realize the vital importance for Europe and Western civilization of a compromise peace, a negotiated peace, but I was already predisposed to such a solution. All that matters in a war is not victory, but escaping defeat.

I did not believe in the war, but nevertheless, I was a volunteer. I need never have donned uniform. I was living in Paris. For much of the early part of the war I was unfit. In about November, 1915, the doctor having now passed me, I went over to London and tried to persuade a Captain Douglas at the War Office to get me commissioned in the Army Service Corps, Mechanical Transport. He suggested I should content myself with driving an ambulance for either the American or the British Hospital in Paris. But this did not satisfy me. The time had come when I felt I could no longer stand aside while most young and fit Englishmen were offering up their lives and facing fear, dirt, and danger for the sake of country or for some cause such as the extermination of Prussian militarism, which, so it was alleged, the war was being waged in order to accomplish.

I admit that in principle I did not feel bound to join the P.B.I. (poor bloody infantry). Normally a volunteer chooses his arm of the service. The siege artillery would have been attractive, and in 1917 I knocked in vain at the door of the Intelligence Corps, in 1918 at the door of the room in which personnel was being selected for the Murmansk expedition. I should not have minded beginning as an officer. I vaguely thought of some specialist job in which I could be of real use. When I came over to London a second time, at the beginning of 1916, Arnold Bennett gave me a note to Ian Malcolm, the Undersecretary for War, but Malcolm advised me to follow the example of a cousin of his and begin in the ranks. I had given up my livelihood in Paris, with which, anyhow, I was dissatisfied. I could not turn back. So I offered myself for election to the Honourable Artillery Company, which had vacancies only in its infantry section.

It was hardly a passport to longevity. I made three friends in the H.A.C.: Crosby was killed on the Somme while still a private; Handyside, who had come from Brazil to volunteer, did not long survive obtaining a commission; and if Hammond, like myself, was unscathed at the armistice, it was, I feel, thanks to getting commissioned early in his military career in the Army Service Corps, Mechanical Transport. I was a private in the 2d Battalion of the

H.A.C. when at the beginning of October, 1916, it marched from the Tower of London to Waterloo Station with fixed bayonets, as it was entitled to do. We went first into the trenches at a reputedly quiet spot, just beyond the woods at Ploegsteert ("Plugstreet"), and when we pulled out of these after a week or so, it was to march to the Somme. On the way I had influenza and was sent to hospital, No. 10 General at St.-Omer. There it was noticed that I had a rupture, and the rupture took me back to England in a hospital ship. Nearly a year's light duty followed my operation, and then I was eight months at cadet school. I graduated at the end of July, 1918. By then I had been away from the front in France for twenty-two months. I had entirely missed Passchendaele and the like.

Moreover, the cadet school was providing officers for the Tank Corps, and had I, as thus designed, gone into the tanks, I should have seen no more warfare in France. Newly commissioned tank officers were sent to some place in the center of that country. But when I graduated, the Tank Corps was full, and I and my contemporaries were advised to apply for infantry commissions. That is how I came to be in the Dorsets. It seems I could have persisted and got into the tanks after all. But I and two cronies gave up our striving. At the end of September, 1918, we were, all three, sent out to reinforce the Dorsets in France, and two of us were posted to the same battalion of the New Army. The war was to go on for only another six weeks. It was long enough for me to be in two major battles. I came out of both without a scratch. I was lucky.

I do not mean I did not have some narrow escapes, and not every one of them from the evil intent of the enemy. We had begun the battle for the Forest of Mormal early in the morning. By the afternoon we had made much headway when we were ordered to lie prone. I can still remember spent German bullets hitting the pebbles just ahead of me as I lay in that position. Before the Second Battle of Neuvilly—my first experience of open warfare—we had done a turn and were relieved in the dark. I had brought my platoon almost to the road that would take us back to rest in Caudry as, just ahead of us, three whizzbangs burst incandescently in a row on the road itself. We took to the grassy hillside and so ran into our guns, so numerous as to be side by side. In the actual battle, two nights later, my platoon reached its allotted objective, and men of another battalion passed through us. A panicky lad in this second wave suddenly pushed his bayonet against the gas mask across my chest and cried, "Hands up, you German bastard!" Instead of obeying, I snatched the rifle barrel away. "Don't be a damned little fool," I said in some indignation. "Can't you see I've got on an English tin hat?"

After the battle a subaltern in the same battalion as myself told our fire-eating brigadier that he had killed no fewer than five Germans. The brigadier put him in for the M.C. (Military Cross), and he was duly awarded this decoration. He neglected to tell the brigadier that the Germans he said he had shot were disarmed prisoners being led to the rear by a corporal from another battalion. The same man, whom I shall call Kerr, took a dislike to me; he warned the company commander that if I stayed in the same company with him, he would bump me off from behind next time we went over the top. So I was transferred to D Company, and at first I was puzzled to understand why. About Christmastime we were in billets near the coast of Artois, and one night Kerr further tried to push me into a village pond, again from behind. Altogether a choice specimen—a farmer's boy, it was said.

It is only fair to add that the officers of my battalion were told before that particular battle not to take prisoners. Evidently that was not the order given to the battalion which took the prisoners that Kerr shot. It should also be noted that in World War I, as I found out when, after the Armistice, I joined divisional staff, decorations came up with the rations, and it only remained to dish them out. For instance, the divisional French interpreter received the M.C. although he had not unduly exposed himself.

To return to my lot as an infantryman, I had been let off lightly. I was never in a raid when, usually with blackened faces, a small party went out at night into no-man's-land and, keeping stock-still whenever a Very light went up, tried to get through the barbed wire, invade a German trench, and bring back one or two prisoners. A raid was held to give adventure to trench life. It was not an exercise in which I should have excelled. Again, I never had to take part in withstanding a counterattack, which meant, according to the book, that the defenders were to wait till they saw the whites of the attackers' eyes before firing at them. Many times in England I had rehearsed the final assault course; never while in France did I meet an armed German face to face and have to plunge my bayonet into him as I had into the swaying sack back at home.

Had I not missed all that kind of thing, the chances of losing my life or of being crippled and handicapped (so that I should have been left with only half a life) would have been very much greater. It needed but to stay out at the front long enough, it seems to me in retrospect, and, as I have already indicated, death or mutilation was assured. In my last battles I took the precaution of carrying the blade of my entrenching tool across my private parts. In attacking the Passchendaele ridge in 1917 and in keeping communication across the intervening sea of mud, British casualties mounted to

400,000. Haig attacked at Passchendaele in the vain expectation of a breakthrough. His persistence in shelling for days before each attack broke up the ground and made movement on foot difficult.

> (They called it Passchendaele) ; my wound was slight,
> And I was hobbling back, and then a shell
> Burst slick upon the duck-boards; so I fell
> Into the bottomless mud, and lost the light.

Thousands shared the grave of mud. In defending Verdun the year before the casualties numbered 362,000. And Verdun, as the late General Fuller once explained to me, had to be denied to the Germans for political and not tactical reasons. If it had fallen, the line would have been improved for the French. But with the fall of Verdun the French government of the day would have fallen too. By the end of 1915 the French had suffered 1,001,271 killed or missing. In December, 1917, the French forces were wasting at the rate of 40,000 a month. The offensives of General Nivelle in the previous April had brought the French Army to a state of collapse. It was only a matter of time, and nobody could fail to have been wounded or killed. The subaltern in the Dorsets who had a shell splinter in his thigh on November 10, 1918, had been through Passchendaele and survived only to be hit, as I have told, on the Armistice eve.

Moreover, a soldier could deliberately take risks and be unhurt. More often than not, one would be struck down by chance, not only in an attack or opposing a counterattack, but either going up to the front from rest or coming away from it, while on the way to the latrine or in it. We had a Sergeant Potter at Plugstreet who was killed while lying in his dugout in the woods while we were in support. He was sorting the contents of his pack. The danger was constantly lurking, and the blow, when it fell, came unheralded, unseen. If you heard a shell coming, it was not for you; the one with your name on it you never heard. You might not duck low enough as you passed the spot on which the enemy sniper had trained his sights. You might be done in (from behind) by one of your own comrades-in-arms.

These conditions of the war affected the nature of martial valor. If you took an enemy trench single-handed, you certainly risked your life. Siegfried Sassoon was awarded the M.C. for doing this. In the 1st H.A.C. we had a Captain Pritchard who received the V.C. (Victoria Cross) for a similar feat. Both survived, but some soldiers might be killed on leave; some civilians, while doing no more than cross the street in the blackout. A soldier in France was equally exposed while engaged in a deed of derring-do as he was in coming simply within range. To crawl out into no-man's-land and bring in a wounded comrade, or to go out there and bury a dead one, might not be as spectacular as taking a trench single-handed, and yet it was indisputably as heroic—perhaps more so, for the capture of a trench would very likely be done in a mood of exaltation; crawling out to retrieve the wounded or the dead had to be in cold blood.

A soldier in World War I, however brave or foolhardy, could not deliberately die as a hero; he could only live as one. He could give dignity to enduring an ever-present but, most often, hidden menace. Some men and women have been carried kicking and screaming to the scaffold, and yet it is only the man who knows he is under sentence of death who can die violently, if he is equal to it, in the grand manner. Other violent deaths are fortuitous. But the condemned can be heroic to the last. There have been the Christian martyrs. Take a man who accepted execution rather than deny the ecclesiastical supremacy of the Pope in 1535—St. Thomas More. How dignified his end! What a model! But what did More really die for? He was beatified in 1935 as one who preferred to lose life itself rather than recognize his secular King as entitled to proclaim himself head of the Church of England and therefore independent of Rome. In fact, of course, he was simply insisting that he was right and that his King and the King's advisers were wrong. That is what all martyrs do. They die for the sake of maintaining that they themselves cannot be mistaken.

To find an instance of execution nobly suffered when it is not on account of present belief, but owing to previous acts, we have to go to the French reprisals in World War II upon men of Vichy. The victims of such reprisals could, if they had the necessary self-possession, die nobly, while aware, of course, that their demeanor would be described to posterity. Such a death was that of the Frenchman Pierre Pucheu at Algiers in 1944.

The son of a suburban tailor and a woman bookkeeper, Pucheu was trained as a secondary schoolmaster, but he swiftly turned into a financial wizard, such as a bank puts at the head of affairs in a firm whose overdraft seems to be rising too high. Born in 1899, he never engaged in politics till the Vichy government, set up in France when the Germans had overrun the country, was six months old. Then, in February, 1941, he was appointed Vichy Secretary of State for Industrial Production, and from July, 1941, to April, 1942, he was Minister of the Interior. With Laval's return to power in the spring of 1942, Pucheu grew disappointed with the Vichy government and wished to join the new military forces being employed against the Germans in North Africa. He had met General Giraud when the latter returned to France after making a sensational escape from a prisoner-of-war camp in Germany. Now the general was in Algiers, and Pucheu wrote to him, proposing to come to Algeria, and asking for modest military employment. He was ready to serve, if need be, in the ranks. Giraud replied that in North Africa Pucheu would meet with much hostility, owing to his Vichy past, but that if nevertheless he came over under an alias, he would be found a job with the troops. Three days after he had reported to a unit in Morocco, he read in the newspaper that he was being put under house arrest farther south. He wrote several protests to General Giraud against this treatment, and one to General de Gaulle, once the latter was in Algeria also. In August, 1943, Pucheu was imprisoned at Meknès, and in March, 1944, he was tried in Algiers and sentenced to death.

If I am to make my point about the manner in which Pucheu died, so much had first to be set out. I need hardly say that he felt he had been poorly done by, and he was, and is, not alone in this respect. He was convinced that he was the victim of a judicial murder. As M. Robert Aron shows,* Pucheu was merely the first to suffer in a series of reprisals which the men who had declared a provisional French government at Algiers, and in particular General de Gaulle, were determined to inflict on men of Vichy so as to brand them as usurpers and hence to reinforce their own claim to office and power.

On March 20, 1944, Pucheu was awakened in his cell at four thirty in the morning. He would understand at once why he was being called so early. He heard mass. Next, he declared that he intended to command the firing squad himself. Consulted by telephone, a well-known French politician, Le Troquer, who was then Minister of Defense in the Algiers provisional administration, agreed. Pucheu was told that three generals proposed to attend his execution. He insisted that they must go away. General Cochet, who had been one of his three military judges, persisted in staying. Pucheu, on catching sight of him, said, "Out with you, sir. Go away. I don't want to see you. You might have remembered that it was I who had you freed from prison, and that but for me God knows where you would be now. Get out!" A little before six o'clock he reached the execution ground. He asked for the colonel in charge. He wanted the warrant officer introduced. He shook hands with him. "What regiment?" "The guards." "Sir, I'm taking your place.

---

* *Histoire de l'épuration,* I (Paris, 1967), pp. 202–36.

I shall give the words of command. What is usual?" "Ready! Aim! Fire!" "You will present your men to me. I want to shake hands with them." He went up to the squad. "Gentlemen, I pardon you in advance. You are obeying orders. You are not involved in this political murder; I have nothing against you." One by one the soldiers were presented, and with each he shook hands.

He then took off his overcoat. The chaplain held out a crucifix. He kissed it. He embraced the chaplain. He turned to one of his two counsels and embraced him. He then embraced the other.

He stood erect in front of the stake and faced the squad. The soldiers stepped forward to within seven yards. He folded his arms across his chest. "Gentlemen, are you ready?" He raised his right arm. "Aim!" He dropped his right arm. "Fire!" The rifles spoke together. He was dead. Several of the soldiers wept.

We owe the account of how Pierre Pucheu died to his senior counsel, Maître Buttin. It makes my point that no soldier in action, and indeed no soldier exposed to shell or bomb or aircraft machine gun in the immediate theater of operations, can die in that way by his own decision. In World War I there were, of course, not only brave Frenchmen, not only brave Englishmen, not only brave Americans. There were also brave Germans. Ernst Jünger has contended that the flower of German youth answered the call to the colors in August, 1914, as though going to a bridal union with Death.

> If I must die,
> I will encounter darkness as a bride,
> And hug it in mine arms.

But, in fact, that was impossible. Pucheu died a victim of war, but not while soldiering. Of course, he knew that the world would be told how he died, as the world was told of the sacrifice at Thermopylae. He was showing what he could do. I am sure it was beyond the reach of most men. Few would have been equal to his self-possession and his ready ascendancy over his executioners. By his display of self-possession he showed that only the condemned can die with nobility. A soldier in action may be fatally wounded, and then he may be granted time to muster human dignity before his end. But for most soldiers in World War I to be wounded was to be knocked insensible without warning or to be thrown into so much pain and anguish as to be lost to directing one's actions. So the modern soldier cannot in action strike an attitude. He can no more die like Antony or Cleopatra than he can die like Socrates.

A soldier goes to help another under fire. He surprises a whole party of the enemy and takes them prisoner, single-handed. By his cool daring he exposes himself and yet succeeds in bringing a number through danger to comparative safety. The order comes to climb out of the trenches and advance in the attack: the soldier, officer or man, who has the self-mastery to keep cool and to steady his fellows will perhaps steer clear of the most obvious perils. All decorations are awarded in theory for that kind of action. But in World War I death or mutilation had less and less relation to bravery. You were as likely to be hit if you cowered as if you moved resolutely and openly.

Hence, in World War I the real heroism, the true greatness of the soldier, was shown, I submit, not in his daring, not in his bravery on occasion, but in his steady endurance. From his first moment in the firing line he was in danger, and nearly always it was a danger he could not ward off. He might duck to escape snipers; he might take cover from shrapnel. He could not counter the chance shot, the chance shell splinter, the bursting whizbang, and it was usually the chance blow that was going to get him. So long as he was unhit, he was in peril, and he might pose as indifferent; but he knew it, day after day, week after week, till he was actually hit or he went on leave.

No wonder the endurance sometimes broke. That was how in 1917, after Verdun and after Nivelle, the mutinies broke out in the French Army, and France was saved by Marshal Pétain. I have never read a full account of those mutinies. We know that French privates simply walked away from the front line. But when on leave in Paris in 1918, I heard from a French colonial soldier of at least one battalion also having to be surrounded by loyal troops as it was marched to the station from barracks in Lyons. In 1918 the 1st H.A.C. had to restore discipline among a rebellious unit in Étaples. The war strained endurance to the breaking point.

Therefore, when the Dorsets marched back on November 11, 1918, not only were we assured that our lives once again lay before us; we were released from that steady, nagging compulsion to stick it. Since 1914 masses of men, many of them humble, simple men, had shown what they could endure and for how long they could endure. By comparison, what mattered a preference for sherbet over a beaker full of the warm south, full of the true, the blushful Hippocrene? The need for endurance was over.

Francis Foster

Successively ordinand, soldier, author and literary critic, and priest, Major the Reverend Reginald Francis Foster (pen name, Francis Foster) was born in 1896, a scion of a long line of Sussex landowners. He was trained for Anglican holy orders but enlisted in the British Army in early 1915 and, later commissioned, served in France till he was wounded, when he was granted a permanent commission in the Indian Army, spending the rest of the war on the Palestine front. He was with his regiment in Egypt for two years thereafter and later served in the Waziristan campaigns of 1919–21 and 1921–24.

He resigned his commission in order to enter the literary world, in which he had already gained a footing. Deeply interested in esoteric religion, he was ordained priest by a Syro-Chaldean Church bishop in 1933 and acted as a missionary in England, though he continued to earn his living by writing. When, in 1940, a German invasion of England seemed inevitable, he volunteered and was accepted for combatant service in the British Army.

Since the end of the 1939–45 war he has devoted himself exclusively to writing. Some thirty books (novels, an autobiography, belles lettres, and technical works on fiction writing and punctuation) and several hundred short stories, essays, etc. of his have been published, and his two plays have been broadcast by the B.B.C. He has just completed what he regards as his *magnum opus*, entitled The Perennial Religion.

He is married to Joan Elizabeth, daughter of Sir A. Harold Bibby, Bart., D.S.O. (Distinguished Service Order), the ship owner, and Lady Bibby, and has three sons and three daughters.

HOLY GROUND

DURING what in Britain was officially termed the Great War, full conscription did not come into force till 1917, though a modified form of it was authorized by Parliament during the previous year, before which the armed forces had had to rely on voluntary enlistment for recruits. It may be assumed that most of those who joined the Army or Navy during the first few months following the declaration of war in August, 1914, were motivated less by recognition of the country's peril (for the general belief was that Germany would be defeated by the end of that first year) than by fervent patriotism or the spirit of adventure. I was not one of them, though, having reached the age of eighteen in April, 1914, I was old enough to enlist.

By the beginning of 1915, however, most people were forced by stark facts to realize that Lord Kitchener's forecast that hostilities would last at least three years was justified. Yet still I remained a civilian, though I was perfectly healthy. The plain truth is that a recent experience had convinced me that I was a coward. It occurred during the late summer of 1914. I was returning home from a convivial evening spent with artist friends in Chelsea when I heard an uproar outside a tavern whose doors had just been closed for the night. A small crowd of cheering people surrounded a man who held a woman's head in chancery (a stranglehold) and was vigorously punching her face. I stopped, horrified, and shouted indignantly, "Let her go, you brute!" whereat, to my surprise, the man released the woman. She stumbled toward me, waving her arms and crying, "Go away, mister! 'E'll murder you if 'e gits 'old of you!"

The man, a hulking fellow of less than middle age, was obviously fighting drunk. Rubbing sweat from his eyes, he lurched toward me, the spectators enthusiastically urging him on. For a few seconds I stood my ground; then I turned and fled incontinently. To say that I was deeply ashamed of my cowardice is a wholly inadequate description, for indeed I felt utterly despicable. I did not reason to myself that what I had witnessed was common outside many public houses on Saturday nights and that anyone who tried to intervene was a fool.

When at length I sought my bed, I lay awake reflecting unhappily on what had occurred and imagining various different
endings of the episode, and at last falling asleep, I dreamed continuously on similar lines. Next morning, full of self-contempt—
though I did not recognize my feeling as that—my one desire was to
avoid other people, even though my own company was so disturbing.

About a month later recruiting sergeants began to appear on the
streets of London, and invariably when I saw one in the distance, I
would cross the road to avoid his solicitations. Though nobody
reproached me for still being a civilian, I gradually became sure
that I was an object of other people's scorn. It was precisely this that
caused me, in May, 1915—nine months after the beginning of the
war—to enlist in the Artists' Rifles, which is to say that I became a
soldier only because I feared to be deemed the coward that I believed I was.

Later I discovered that the 2d Battalion that I had joined had
recently become an Officers Training Corps and that conditions in
it were considerably more unpleasant than those prevailing in
ordinary infantry units: We had to sleep on bare ground or hard
floors; our rations were of poor quality and badly cooked by
amateurs; leave was rarely granted; training was rigorous and intensive. But once my body became inured to these hardships, I
welcomed the long hours of work and the general discomfort
because they staved off the dreadful anticipation of eventually
going into the firing line.

I must have managed to impress my superiors, for the following
November, with five other private soldiers, I was paraded before a
visiting lieutenant colonel whose purpose was to choose two of us to
be granted commissions and posted to his battalion. I was one of the
men selected. A fortnight or so later my name was listed in the
London *Gazette* as a second lieutenant, and later I received an
order to join a battalion of the East Lancashire Regiment.

During the year of intensive training that followed, I gained two
first-class certificates at courses on musketry and bombing, the effect
being that I became somewhat more self-confident. Nevertheless,
the prospect of eventually going on active service continued to fill
me with apprehension. When, therefore, the division in which my
battalion was included received orders to join the Expeditionary
Force in France, my only happiness derived from the fact that at
last the monotonous training was at an end. When I returned from
embarkation leave, I was informed that I and my platoon sergeant,
together with one officer and one sergeant from each of the other
three companies, were to form an advance party and proceed to

France, with similar parties from other units in the division, our purpose being to learn the ropes in the part of the line that the division would eventually take over.

Four days later the advance party was in Boulogne, and thence, after some delay, we entrained for an unspecified destination. After many hours of excruciatingly slow travel we reached Béthune. Thence the contingents of the brigade that included my battalion marched along the towpath of the La Bassée Canal, halting at length to consume a brief meal. As the winter dusk was beginning to fall, we resumed our journey, and soon the thudding of big guns and the occasional stutter of a machine gun could be heard. Eventually my battalion party was detached from the rest of the column and allotted one of a number of soldier guides, who had apparently been waiting for us at this point. He would, he told us, conduct us to our destination.

I was ready to drop from extreme fatigue when at length the guide announced that we had reached "Windy Corner." He responded to a sentry's challenge and then, turning, remarked to me, "The N.C.O.'s are to remain here, sir, and you are to report to battalion H.Q. It's down here, sir."

I went gingerly forward in the intense darkness and found that the man was holding back something that had been apparently covering the entrance to what seemed to be a hole in the ground but proved to be a cellar—next morning I found it was all that was left, apart from rubble, of a sizable house. We officers descended a flight of steps, at the bottom of which, in an underground room, we were greeted by a young captain, who told us he was the adjutant. He had been seated at an improvised table on which stood a field telephone set. A couple of wax candles stuck in beer bottles provided illumination.

"You chaps are to be detailed one per each of our companies, so you'd better toss up to decide who goes to which," the adjutant informed us.

We decided the issue accordingly, and I was told that C Company, to which I was to proceed, was in the close support line, "just along the road." Another guide was summoned from a neighboring cellar, and following in his wake, I climbed up the steps into the darkness again. My destination was not far away, and it, too, proved to be a cellar, which was occupied by a single subaltern, huddled in a greatcoat.

"Been waiting for you," he greeted me, grinning in a friendly manner. "You're late. Expect you'd like some grub. My name's Bunch, by the way. You won't see the O.C. [officer commanding] till the morning. He's gone to bed. So have the others."

I was provided with bully beef (corned beef) and bread for supper and invited to make free with a bottle of whisky. I began my meal while Bunch produced a brier pipe, which he filled from an oilskin pouch. When the tobacco was burning to his satisfaction, he remarked, "This is a very quiet part of the line nowadays. We were sent here two months back for a rest—we'd had a rather hot time on the Somme earlier. Captain Bill—that's the O.C., and Bill's his surname, by the way—is the only surviving original officer in this company. I'm the next oldest, for the other subalterns haven't been with us more than a few months."

"Why is it so quiet here?" I ventured.

"Because in the winter the front in this section is just a quagmire—the water in the trenches is knee-deep mostly. Apart from an occasional gun battle, there's very little doing."

The "bedroom" allotted to me proved to be a corner of the neighboring cellar that had been partitioned off by means of blankets suspended from the ceiling. The bed was a wooden frame across which wire netting had been stretched and nailed. I was so weary by the time I lay down that I fell asleep instantly and did not awake till I was roused next morning by an orderly who brought me a mug of "gunfire" (early morning tea). My watch told me that the hour was half past five o'clock.

While, a little later, I was shaving, a heavy thud caused the candle flame to be suddenly extinguished. The orderly produced an electric torch and switched it on. "No good relighting the candle," he explained. "The usual morning hate [bombardment] has begun and—" He paused as another heavy thud sounded. "That's one of our six-inch howitzers back at Gorre. Jerry'll start up shortly, you'll find."

His ears were so experienced that he was able to differentiate between British and German gunfire, for after about a dozen rounds had been fired by the battery he had referred to, he assured me when the next thud occurred that it was from Jerry cannon; since he had no reason to lie about the matter, I accepted his words. I was gratified to find that the bombardment caused me no undue alarm, though I was glad when it ended.

When I later went for breakfast in the neighboring cellar, a tall captain was seated at an improvised table, eating, and Bunch presented me to him. He was Bill. I liked him on sight; later I was to find that he was a very prince among men. After the meal he took me sightseeing. I had already learned that the village was Festubert, the scene of very heavy fighting earlier in the war. The support line ran through it, and the front-line trenches were only about half a mile distant. Houses and church in the single street were mere heaps of rubble, and every tree had been reduced to a pathetic stump. In the churchyard, coffins, some of them gaping open, were exposed as a result of gunfire. What astonished me was the fact that though at certain phases of our stroll streams of machine-gun bullets whined unpleasantly nearby, Bill did not take cover; I myself was horribly scared, but fear of revealing what I felt prevented my taking any action. At length I ventured a request for an explanation, and his answer was a laconic, "You don't hear the bullet that hits you!"

That evening, while dusk was falling, the company was mustered and afterward proceeded, platoon by platoon, to a store from which thigh boots were issued to each man. Having donned them and left our ammunition [regular Army] boots behind, we went forward to relieve the company in the front line, proceeding thither by way of communication trenches, through which we waded knee-deep and more in filthy water. The O.C. had directed me to join Bunch's platoon, and when we arrived at our destination, I watched interestedly the routine of taking over from the outgoing garrison. The Germans seemed to be aware that something was afoot in our trench, for they constantly put up flares till just after the take-over was completed. At length Bunch showed me the officer's funk hole that had been dug out of the side of the parapet—the front wall of the trench—and which I was to share with him. He explained that it was not possible to excavate proper dugouts in this sector because of the waterlogged condition of the trenches. The German line, I learned, was 250 yards distant across no-man's-land.

The month was December, and the night cold was intense. At about half past eleven Bunch suggested my going to bed till an hour before dawn, when everyone would have to stand to on the fire step because it was during that period (and also during the evening hour before full darkness) that an attack was most likely to be made. I crawled into the funk hole, therefore, and, huddled in my greatcoat, lay down, my head pillowed on my haversack. For some minutes I listened to distant gunfire; then, falling asleep, I did not wake up till Bunch summoned me for the dawn stand-to. When the hour's vigil ended, breakfast was brought to the men from the support line, and they were each given an issue of rum. Bunch told me that he and I would feed at company H.Q. and that though he would conduct me there on this first occasion, in the future I should have to go alone and relieve him on my return.

To reach company headquarters involved our wading along a communication trench to the close support line. Captain Bill was in high spirits when we arrived. "Enjoying life?" he asked me, and trying to match his gaiety, I replied, "It's endurable, anyhow."

The day passed quietly, though a constant rumble of distant gunfire came from the east, where, Bunch told me, a "bit of a battle" was in progress. A little before sunset Captain Bill appeared in the front trench with his sergeant major. Bunch was absent, being asleep in the funk hole. "Lovely evening," Bill commented cheerfully when he joined me alongside a sentry who, standing on the duckboards on the trench bottom, was peering through a periscope at no-man's-land in order to be able to spot any sign of enemy activity. Then, to my astonishment, Bill mounted the fire step (which, I knew, was contrary to routine orders regarding daytime procedure) and, his head above the top of the parapet, began to survey the wasteland beyond. Half a minute later he beckoned me to mount beside him. After a little hesitation, wondering whether he was daring me, I climbed up fearfully beside him.

I could see through the British wire fronting our trench and approximately halfway between us and the German wire the pathetic stumps of several trees. Feeling sure that our exposed heads must be clearly visible to the enemy, for we were silhouetted against the sunset behind us, I was expecting a rain of bullets, but no shot was fired.

"Let's go stretch our legs for a bit," Bill suggested, and without waiting for a reply, he put the palms of his hands on the parapet and heaved himself over the top. I wondered whether he had become insane. He stood there grinning down at me. I glanced back at the sergeant major. His face was enigmatic. What had I expected of him, in any case? I asked myself, feeling quite desperate because of the position in which I was placed. Then, deeply reluctant, I slowly clambered up beside Bill, who now turned to the wire and began to search for one of the usual gaps that was left to make access to no-man's-land beyond possible. Meanwhile, I waited motionless, my pulses racing and bile in my throat.

Finding at length what he sought, Bill turned to me again and beckoned. His expression was now semiserious. It invited confidence. The sickness in my throat subsided, and I went to him, following him afterward through the gap in the first belt of wire and zigzagging behind him through gaps in later belts. Finally, we emerged into open ground. Bill now headed as straight for the clump of blasted trees as the many waterlogged shell holes would allow, I close behind him and feeling that I was dreaming. He neither paused nor hesitated till he reached the remains of what (I could see now) must once have been willows, and arriving there at length, I at his heels, he seated himself on one of the stumps and calmly lighted a cigarette. I could see the German wire defenses quite clearly, for they were now little more than 100 yards distant. From somewhere close and to the left came the detonation of mortar bombs or artillery shells; my insufficiently experienced ears were not yet able to differentiate between the two.

We did not speak. At length Bill threw his cigarette end away. "Ah, well," he said laconically, "I suppose we'd better be getting back." He rose to his feet.

The sunset glow was beginning to fade from the western sky. Side by side now, we began to saunter back. Because I was now no longer fearful, elation filled me. But I could not understand what had caused the transformation. It was as though I had become another person altogether or, rather, as though I had entered another life. When at length I clambered after Bill into our familiar trench, I was even regretting that the expedition had ended.

Waving a hand to me, Bill set off back to his headquarters. Before following in his wake, the sergeant major saluted me smartly, giving me a prodigious wink the while. And when I was alone with the sentry again, I knew that during the last half hour I had undergone the most momentous experience of my life.

Some five weeks later I was again in the line, but this time with men of my own battalion, which had meanwhile arrived in France and taken over this sector of the front from the battalion of the Warwickshire Regiment in which I had been initiated into trench warfare. I, with my platoon, was ordered to occupy "Death or Glory" sap, alongside the La Bassée Canal. As the name implies, this was a trench that had been dug forward of the rest of the front line, the distance between its head and that of a similar sap in the German line being less than 150 yards. Earlier in the war this had been the scene of particularly violent fighting, but now conditions were very quiet.

Ever since my expedition with Captain Bill into no-man's-land, I had been aware of a profound mental change in myself. Now it seemed to me essential that both to prove its realness and to complete the metamorphosis, I must venture into the wasteland again, and this time alone. But I knew that here there was no dead ground between the lines, so to go out in daylight would be altogether indefensible. After stand-down on the second evening, therefore, I told my sergeant that I was going over the top to examine our wire entanglements. He expostulated, but bidding him warn the platoon that I should be out in front, I clambered onto the parapet and crossed to the wire. The moonlight being bright, I found the first gap without difficulty, and passing through it, I made my way forward till I was in open ground. Now I could see the German wire vaguely in the moonlight, and realizing that I might be visible to sentries in the enemy line, I got down on my hands and knees and began to crawl toward it.

It must have been more than half an hour later when I returned to the sap, feeling extraordinarily exhilarated. My sergeant helped me down from the parapet and then began to protest vehemently on account of what I had done. "All right," I told him; "next time you and I shall go out together," to which he returned, "Even so, there'd probably be a stink if the O.C. learned about it, so I'll have to warn the men not to talk about it—even among themselves." The following night, therefore, he accompanied me on my next exploratory tour, and thereafter we were constantly out in front at night. Sometimes, however, I would receive an order to take out an armed patrol of several men to investigate the state of the German wire following a bombardment or to discover whether pumps were clearing waterlogged enemy trenches or to effect liaison with a similar patrol operating on our left—our right was, of course, flanked by the canal.

On one such occasion of the last kind my patrol was near the German wire when one of the men, stumbling into a shell hole, accidentally discharged his rifle. At once flares rose from the enemy line. All but one of us dropped to the ground to avoid being detected, the exception being a man whose tunic had become caught up on the German wire. Then a machine gun began to chatter, and bullets whined about us, the man who was still standing being hit in the forearm. A corporal and I tore him from the wire, and making him lie down, I roughly bandaged his wound with my khaki handkerchief. Then I passed word to the others that they were to crawl in my wake, and I set off, heading for a derelict trench that I had discovered several nights earlier. Luckily I found it soon, for there was now continuous firing from the enemy line.

In a short while the stutter of machine guns began to subside, and only an occasional flare was put up. Presently, as I was rounding a traverse, I bumped into something that yielded and let out a grunt. The man behind me collided with me as I halted, for here in the old trench it was difficult to see clearly. I had already taken my pistol from its holster and was crouching when, looking up and forward, I discerned the unmistakable shape of a German helmet. I guessed that we had run into an enemy patrol that was sheltering from gunfire in the trench. Aiming just under the helmet, I fired. I heard the bullet strike metal; then followed a veritable shriek, and several forms heaved themselves out of the trench and began to run toward the German line. Since dawn was now not far off, I decided that we should get back to "Death or Glory" sap without delay, so I ordered my men out of the old trench, and we set off at a run for "home."

Because I am intent not on recording all or even the outstanding episodes in which I played a part during the Great War but on achieving a special purpose that may already have become evident, I shall now pass to what happened some months later when, in early May, 1917, just after my twenty-first birthday, I became a casualty and my service in France ended. On an occasion when the lieutenant colonel commanding the battalion paid a routine visit to the front line, he invited me to volunteer to lead my platoon on a night raid on the enemy trench opposite. I had not the least inclination to do so, for it was commonly believed that the officer in command of such an operation was invariably killed, but refusal, of course, being impossible, when the battalion returned in due course to rest billets, I was directed to take my platoon to a chateau near Gorre, where we should undergo a week's special training.

The raid was planned by the divisional staff. Zero hour would be at 2300 on the night of May 14. At zero minus thirty minutes an artillery barrage would be put on the trench we were to raid; at zero minus fifteen my platoon would go over the top, and meanwhile the barrage would gradually creep back to the German support line to prevent reinforcements from going forward. Two sappers of the Royal Engineers would accompany the raiding party, carrying a Bangalore torpedo to blow a gap in the enemy wire. This device consisted of a number of lengths of tubing filled with high explosive. The first section being pushed under the wire; another would be screwed to it; this was thrust forward; then a third was attached; and so on till the wire was fully penetrated. The torpedo was operated by turning a cock on the end section that ignited a fuse which, five seconds later, would detonate the charge. The cock was to be turned precisely at zero hour, and the gap being made, my men would pass through it, enter the enemy trench, killing all its occupants except two, who were to be brought back to our own line for interrogation. At zero plus twenty minutes a bugler stationed in the middle of no-man's-land would sound the familiar cookhouse call to signal the withdrawal.

On the night of the raid everything went according to plan— except that while we lay waiting alongside the wire, one of the sappers crawled to me and reported that the cock on the torpedo was apparently jammed. Scrambling to my feet, I ran forward, intending to try to operate the thing myself. No sooner did I touch it, however, than the torpedo detonated; the other sapper must himself have succeeded in turning it in his mate's absence. The ensuing blast rocked me back on my feet, but I seemed not to have been injured except that, despite the illumination from many flares in the air above, I could see nothing whatever. My men were already running through the new-made gap, and the press of their bodies carried me some distance with them. Then they all were past me. By now I had realized that I was blind. I could do nothing but stand where I was and hope that my officerless men would be able to carry on. Meanwhile, hand grenades thrown by enemy survivors were falling all about me. One at length fell on my foot. I kicked lustily. It exploded in the air before me, and my right arm suddenly jerked back as a fragment had hit it. There was no immediate pain, but I could feel blood soaking into my right trouser leg. Able, I found, to raise the injured arm, I put it across my body, pushing the hand into my tunic.

The piercing call of a bugle signaling the withdrawal sounded above the clamor of the gunfire. A few seconds later my men were returning through the gap. I shouted to attract attention and tried to grasp at one of them. Then they all were past me. By now enemy guns were also in action, but the detonations of shells fired by our own enabled me to distinguish between them. I turned, and keeping my back to the sound of the explosions and my good hand out-stretched to encounter possible obstacles, I contrived to get clear of the wire. Then followed a seemingly endless nightmare journey back across the wasteland, feeling forward with each foot before every step. Four times I fell into shell holes, and soon my clothing reeked of foul water.

Despite continuous machine-gun and rifle fire, I was miraculously not hit. At last my left hand outstretched before me touched wire— our own, I knew, for the barbs were not so long as those on German wire. Knowing that it was impossible to find my way through the echeloned gaps in the various belts, I shouted, "Help! Wounded British officer!" repeatedly. Fortunately the gunfire was already subsiding, and flares were now comparatively few. I heard a noise nearby at length; then a voice called clearly, "Here he is, Tom," and a hand touched me. I explained my condition, and one of my two rescuers told me he would lead if I kept hold of his shoulder and his companion would follow me. A little while later I was lifted over the parapet into the trench. Thence I was carried on a stretcher for a considerable distance, and when it was finally set down, I heard the voice of our battalion's medical officer.

He examined and bandaged my wounded forearm, telling me that a fragment of bomb was imbedded deeply in it and that an operation would be needed for its extraction. He was greatly concerned about my blindness, which, however, later proved not to be permanent, for when at length I was put to bed in a field hospital, I found that I could see dimly with one eye, which eventually became nearly normal, whereas I regained only partial sight in the other.

When, some months later, I was discharged from the hospital in England I was posted to the reserve battalion in Yorkshire. Several weeks afterward volunteers for permanent commissions in the Indian Army were called for to replace heavy British officer casualties in Mesopotamia, and because I had discovered that I enjoyed soldiering, I responded, was accepted, and in due course was dispatched to India. Three weeks after I joined my new regiment there, it was ordered to proceed to Palestine to join General Allenby's army. Now a captain, I did not become a casualty again till, in August, 1918, I succumbed to amoebic dysentery. It was not till just after the Armistice, three months later, that I was discharged from the hospital in Alexandria, Egypt.

The fact that the transformation that I have recorded must have been experienced, though not, of course, in exactly similar circumstances, by very many civilian soldiers in the new armies during the major wars of this century should suffice to acquit me of egoism in writing autobiographically on the subject. The problem that I now have to solve concerns the precise cause of the change.

The genesis of the affair obviously occurred on that memorable occasion when Captain Bill invited me to go for a stroll with him in no-man's-land. Since he was a veteran soldier and well acquainted with the Festubert sector, he must have been well aware that, some of the area between the opposed lines being in "dead" ground, to venture out there even in daylight was reasonably safe. But I myself knew nothing of local conditions, so it is just possible that in inviting me to share his seemingly dangerous project, he was testing my courage or even daring me; nevertheless, I am convinced that he merely wanted a congenial companion to accompany him while he stretched his legs out of the waterlogged trenches.

While I stood trembling in apprehension on the parapet, watching him search for the first gap in the wire, I recalled that I had had to force myself to climb out of the trench—that I had acted as though I were two persons, I and also *myself*. And in a flash the memory came to me of the incident outside a London tavern in the late summer of 1914 when I was menaced by a drunken man, and I realized simultaneously that on that occasion I had similarly visualized myself objectively and, moreover, not as I was at that moment but as I imagined I should be shortly, and as a consequence I had fled in panic. Then Bill found the gap and, turning, beckoned to me. Inevitably I was now regarding him, not the Germans, as my enemy, for he was virtually forcing me to do something that I dreaded. But I liked and admired him enormously and wanted to emulate him and win his esteem, so to regard him as an enemy was irrational. Very reluctantly I followed as he zigzagged through the gaps in successive belts of barbed wire. Then, as I emerged from the last into the open and saw him calmly surveying the clearly visible German wire defenses, it was as though a veil had been lifted from my eyes. If I was in peril, so was he; we were sharing a common danger. For the first time in my life I stopped visualizing myself and was suddenly tranquil. When Bill began to stroll forward, I followed in complete confidence.

Not till more than six months later in a military hospital in England, when one night I lay sleepless because of pain in my wounded arm, did I gain full comprehension of what had happened to me. I realized that originally, while I had been in the habit of visualizing what I feared would shortly occur, I was irrationally splitting myself in two so that I was both the subject (the thinking *I*) and the object (the *me*) of my contemplation and, moreover, that I was projecting myself into an imaginary future. The habit had been conquered on the occasion that I forced myself to accompany Captain Bill on that excursion into no-man's-land, the genesis of the change in myself occurring when I became aware that he and I were sharing a common peril and that though I had met him only thirty-six hours earlier, I already esteemed him and regarded him as my friend. It was this thought that put an end to anxiety on my own behalf and hence began the process of extinguishing the love I bore my objectified self.

While we proceeded toward the clump of stricken trees, I became sure that if I could abandon forever the old and evil habit of visualizing myself in danger and anticipating an imaginary future—if I could destroy completely my objectified self with whom I had become so familiar and so much loved—I should become an effective fighting soldier. When we reached our objective and Bill nonchalantly lighted a cigarette, I was as calm as he was, and I became certain that the transformation was already complete.

Five weeks later, when I ventured out alone from "Death or Glory" sap into no-man's-land to test my courage and at length lay alongside the enemy wire, listening to Germans talking among themselves, I knew that the reason why I was completely unafraid was that as a result of having destroyed my imaginary objective self, I had become fully integrated, which is to say that I had gained integrity, and that in future I should invariably live—and live fully—in the present time, leaving the future to take care of itself.

In view of the circumstances in which I discovered the cause of my believed cravenheartedness—when, that is, the fear of seeming to be fearful forced me to accompany Captain Bill on a stroll toward the German trenches—I have always since then regarded the no-man's-land of the Great War, blood-soaked, ravished and ravaged by shellfire, strewn with the debris of earlier battles, and stinking of unburied corpses though it was, as holy ground. Indeed, to me it resembles the Gethsemane in which Christ prayed that He might be relieved of the necessity for immolating Himself and then, in communion with God, discovered the peace that is the fruit of negating the objective self.

The truth is that to think of, and thus objectify, oneself is the root cause of all the evil that mankind commits.

Basil Willey

BASIL WILLEY, *the only child of William Herbert Willey and Alice Ann Le Gros (of Jersey), was born in London on July 25, 1897. He was educated at University College School, London, and Peterhouse, Cambridge. During World War I he was a lieutenant in the West Yorkshire Regiment in France (1917–18).*

In 1915 he was awarded a history scholarship at Peterhouse, where he was graduated with first class honors in history (1920) and first class honors in English (1921). He was a Hugo de Balsham Student at Peterhouse and won the university Le Bas Prize (1922) with the essay "Tendencies in Renaissance Literary Theory." In 1923 he became a lecturer in English at Cambridge, and in 1935 he was made a fellow of Pembroke College. From 1946 to 1964 he was King Edward VII Professor of English at Cambridge, succeeding Sir Arthur Quiller-Couch. He was a visiting professor at Columbia University from 1948 to 1949 and at Cornell in 1953. From 1958 to 1964 he was president of Pembroke College, and in 1964 he was made an honorary fellow of Pembroke. In 1959 he was a Hibbert lecturer and in 1964 a Ballard Matthews lecturer (Bangor, North Wales). He was made a Fellow of the Royal Society of Literature in 1950 and an Ho.Litt.D. (Manchester) in 1948. He is also a Fellow of the British Academy.

His published works include The Seventeenth Century Background (1934), The Eighteenth Century Background (1940), Nineteenth Century Studies (1949), Christianity Past and Present (1952), More Nineteenth Century Studies (1956), The English Moralists (1964), *and* Spots of Time, A Retrospect [1897–1920] (1965). *His literary approach is summarized in the Foreword to* The Seventeenth Century Background: *"When speaking of philosophical matters I have supposed myself to be addressing, not professional philosophers, but students of literature, and not professed students merely, but all to whom poetry, and religion, and their relation to the business of living, are matters of importance."*

In 1923 he married Zélie Murlis Ricks. They have two sons and two daughters.

A SCHOOLBOY IN THE WAR

I SIT DOWN to begin this chapter in the garden of my Lakeland cottage, once the home of Wordsworth's daughter Dora Quillinan. The April sun shines warmly, the wind roars through the bare trees on Loughrigg Fell, and a beck from the hilltop tinkles at my side. The Great War of 1914–18 seems remote and unreal indeed. And yet just now I read in my *Times* that yesterday in France the Canadians were celebrating the fiftieth anniversary of the Battle of Vimy Ridge. The correspondent who described the occasion spoke of "the immense and melancholy plain between Arras and Lens, dominated by Vimy Ridge," and this phrase caused a lost pulse of feeling to stir in me again, for it was on that plain, soon after the Vimy battle, that I had my first experience of trench warfare. And in that sector I was in and out of the line with my battalion (the 18th West Yorkshire Regiment, and later the 15th) for about a twelvemonth. Now, in my seventieth year, as I look back across that half century to myself at twenty, "some inward agitations thence are brought," and do they "impregnate and elevate the mind"? Yes, in spite of the brutality and filth and fear, they do in a way. And this is because I was then living at a pitch of physical and imaginative excitement never since equaled, so that to recall that time sets the spirit working again among the embers.

The *Times* correspondent goes on to say that "nature has clothed the sea of mud and shell-holes in a decent mantle of green; but the trees have not had time to age, and the villages of sad, unmellowed brick have not recaptured their shattered personalities. . . . Time," he adds, "has moved more slowly here than on the Normandy battlefields" of the Second Great War. It had certainly moved but slowly on the only occasion that I revisited Vimy (just before the Second War), and if the same is still true, it can surely be allowed some symbolic meaning. Symbolic, for Englishmen of my generation at least (and perhaps for history, too), of the prepotency of the First War over the Second. It may be that this does not apply to some other nations—nations which in the Second War suffered disasters from which they have never recovered. But for Western Europe, and above all for us Britons in our island sanctuary, 1914 fell like a thunderbolt from a blue sky, and no subsequent event could ever appall and shake us as that did. Here, as always, I speak for my own generation—for those of us who were born under Queen Victoria and began to grow up under Edward VII and George V. Elder statesmen even then had premonitions of things to come, but for the young (and well-to-do) it was bliss to be alive. Those were the halcyon days when birds of calm sat brooding on the charmèd wave (waves which, to the world's great benefit, were ruled by Britannia), and when anyone who, like the young Churchill, longed for military honors, had to seek them at the ends of the earth: the North-West Frontier, Cuba, the Sudan, or South Africa. Throughout the nineteenth century after Waterloo, it was possible for Englishmen, despite the Crimea and other people's wars, to feel that the *Pax Britannica* had come to stay, and liberal optimism looked forward to ever-widening international friendship based on commerce and reason. Had there not been the Great Exhibition? Had not the laureate prophesied the Parliament of Man, the Federation of the world?

It was from this deep security—if you like, this fools' paradise— that we who were too young to know better were suddenly pitch-forked into the holocaust. We, the heirs of all the ages in the foremost files of time, had to behold and take part in the collapse of the most imposing and seemingly permanent structure of civiliza-tion ever known, and watch it melt into blood and mud. It was not like this in 1939. Terrible as the Second War was, it lacked this contrasting background, since for the preceding decade there had been a hardening of hearts, a rattling of sabers, and an ever-growing spirit of violence and unreason.

I do not want to repeat overmuch what I wrote in *Spots of Time,* but I should like to say that I tried there to convey the feeling of this irruption of evil into our paradise under the symbol of the bugle call I heard in childhood, sounding across the tranquil Brent Valley (still virgin countryside then) from the Mill Hill barracks. At an upper window of our house, which overlooked open country on the northern fringe of London, I used (for I was an only child) to spend blissful hours, especially on June evenings, gazing out upon the quiet scene and identifying myself with the afterglow in the northern sky, the ivy-covered Seller's Hall with its cedar silhou-etted against yellow, and the unseen owls tu-whitting in the twi-light. And from time to time, breaking the hush and trance, the pert, brassy bugle would insult the ear, fit emblem of the military mind—too insensitive to move outside its narrow diatonic groove or to be aware of its own limitations. I instinctively loathed this alien sound, long before I knew that it meant the loss of my Eden. And not only *my* Eden, but everybody else's too, including the Rupert Brookes who went gaily "forth into God."

In 1914 I was only seventeen and did not think I should ever be in the war. I was, therefore, not involved in that wave of patriotic idealism which sent the flower of our young manhood, with a song in the heart, to its destruction. But as the years went by, and Marne was succeeded by Givenchy, Ypres, and Somme, it became obvious that I should be called up. So I joined my school O.T.C. and went straight from that, in July, 1916, to an officer cadet battalion to be trained for a commission. Although war and soldiering were so remote from my real life and inner world that I could never feel I had anything to do with them, it did not occur to me to take the pacifist line. I simply faced the inevitable, perhaps not with a very good grace, and certainly without any flourish, but without question. I knew that I could not object for conscience's sake because I had no firm convictions, religious or other, and had not examined the theoretic grounds for such a position. Moreover, in my own way I was, as I still am, intensely patriotic. I loved England with all my heart and soul, but abominated the British Army. For me, there was absolutely nothing—no pride, pomp and circumstance of glorious war, no desire to excel in smartness or efficiency, no eagerness for promotion, honorable mention, or medals—just nothing whatever to mitigate the loathsomeness of military training with its routines of drill, the foulmouthed sergeants, the chlorinated gas masks, the bayonet practice where we were incited to blood lust, the musketry, and perhaps worst of all the insolence of the officers, with their "brows villainous low."

I am trying to describe how it all felt to live through, not to justify my own attitude on abstract grounds. Naturally I now see certain merits in military discipline to which I was then blind, and even before I had done with soldiering I had outgrown my callow reluctances and distastes and come to think most other men better fellows than myself. But it was harder for me to learn this lesson, I think I may truly and humbly say, than it was for many—perhaps most—others, because I was the only child of a very sheltered, pure, and religious home and had never been to a boarding school. More fearful to me than bullets or shells or sudden death was the experience of being snatched away from what I now know to have been a way of life exceptional in its Christian innocence and unworldliness and plunged straight into what then seemed to me a sink of all iniquities. In the cadet battalion I was one of only a very few who had come straight from school; nearly all the others had seen active service as privates or N.C.O.'s in France or elsewhere and had done well enough to be recommended for commissions. Never having had the normal boarding-school contacts with vice, prurience, snobbery, brutality, and worldliness, I was aghast at the sort of men these seemed and at the things they said and thought and did. Music had always shared, with the beauty of landscape, my heart's allegiance, but the songs these men sang on the march (in George Fox's phrase) "struck at my life." All this nauseated me so much that my "psyche" revolted, and I actually succumbed to a bad attack of jaundice during the training period.

I soon began to see that my horror of these men would not do, that, in fact, I was wrong in judging them to be merely immoral, brutal, and bloody-minded. They *were* all those things, but then they were also kind, brave, self-forgetful, heroic, and gay to a degree far beyond my reach. To be a good soldier, I thought and continued to think throughout, meant to have many qualities the reverse of those recommended by the Christian religion. But then I found that most of these men excelled me not only in soldierly qualities, but in the best human virtues, too. In my puritan priggishness, I was like the man who thought his whole platoon out of step but himself; it was I who was the oddity, the exception, the odd man out. My comrades were simply average specimens of a species I had never before met: *l'homme moyen sensuel.* All I could claim were the negative, the pharisaic virtues of not smoking and not drinking, not swearing and not whoring. It also came to me that perhaps even the hated bugle had been the appointed summons (it might have come in some other form, but it came in this) to bid me emerge from the womblike insulation in which I had tarried too long. Life inflicts this trauma upon us all in due season, but what a price my generation had to pay for such "deliverance"!

In France the lessons continued in a new guise. In the cadet battalion, which was in Cambridge, I had had a billet almost to myself; it was, in fact, by what may or may not have been pure chance, a room in my own college. But in France, as a second lieutenant, I was perforce a member of an officers' mess, sometimes in rest billets and sometimes in the line. Privacy ceased to exist, and my fellow officers, as well as the men of my platoon (nearly all of them Yorkshiremen), were at first as strange to me as foreigners. They spoke an alien dialect, and when I could understand what they said, it was generally bawdry. Long winter evenings spent huddled with them in billets or dugouts, they smoking and drinking and playing cards and telling dirty stories, and I trying to read a serious book as though I were at home—these things at first nearly broke me down. However, a certain native adaptability and (thank God) a sense of humor kept me going, and though I stuck to my guns and remained myself, I learned tolerance and humility. I was, of course, mercilessly mocked and derided for my puritanism by everyone from the colonel downward, but as I very soon found, they were fine and magnanimous fellows and managed to put up with me as a harmless oddity. But it did amaze me that they should think my sort so very queer and exceptional.

To me these were the real issues; machine guns and whizbangs and 5.9's almost irrelevant sideshows. As I look back, I seem to see myself trying to live my own sort of life as if there were no war on and as if I expected to survive it (a very unlikely thing for a subaltern in those days). My letters home and my diaries were filled with descriptions, in the distilled language of literary youth, of places and buildings, of sunsets and scenery, and occasionally of people, and with "great thoughts" about life and destiny. The letters must have been highly unsatisfactory to my parents (to whom nearly all were addressed), and they did once plead for something more down-to-earth, something more human, about everyday doings. But they understood, what some reviewers of *Spots of Time* missed, that I was deliberately playing down the horrors of war for their benefit, and giving them a *couleur de rose* view to allay their gnawing anxiety about their (unworthy but sole) offspring. Even when I was in the trenches, I would try to interest them in the amenities of our dugout or the humors of a front-line dinner with the C.O. and make no mention of the time when the Germans pinpointed the dugout with 5.9 shells and blew to smithereens an observer who had just gone out after reporting to us.

Some of my experiences were of a kind new and valuable to me, not because I was a soldier but because I had lived most of my life on the outskirts of London. For instance, I had never before lived in a country house in midwinter. When I joined my battalion in January, 1917, Europe was in the grip of one of this century's most arctic winters. My unit had just come out of the line for a month's rest, and the officers of my company were billeted for a time in the *mairie* of a village called Le Meillard. That lovely eighteenth-century mansion, with its farmhouse smells of woodsmoke and stored fodder, its pigeons, and especially its kind and cultivated inhabitants (who cannot fail to have thought the English barbarians, though they did not show it), remains associated forever with the searing cold of that January and mitigates the memory of it. Nor, again, had I ever before spent the month of May in a nightingale-haunted village beside a turreted castle—as I did later that same year. This was when I was sent on a course to be trained as a signal officer, and never before or since have I seen the glories of that loveliest of months more lavishly displayed. No doubt the beauty of it was heightened and made more poignant by the sound of the distant guns—the guns of the battle at Gavrelle in which half my battalion was wiped out. Another such experience was the week's route march (for there was little mechanized transport in those days) from the Somme to Béthume in early spring. Each day's march, though exhausting on account of the weight of equipment, was enjoyable because it took us through an undevastated rolling countryside not unlike Buckinghamshire and ended each night with a feast of new-laid eggs in a picturesque, if stercoraceous, farmhouse. The change in the scenery, as we came down from the uplands into the northern plains and saw coal mines far away on the horizon, was exciting.

It is on scenes like these that I prefer now, as I did then, to dwell; they permanently enrich the memory and remain as vivid as ever, while the images of shell holes, trenches, barbed wire, corpses, and tragic ruins have worn thin and spectral. I could have said more about such things—about lice and mud and stench and the spasms of fear—but I see no reason for it. Battlefields and the stark facts of the actual fighting have been described with incomparable power, in prose and verse, by writers, some of whom are contributors to the present volume. Moreover, I saw much less of these things than men like Blunden, Sassoon, or Graves, who were in the thick of them and have given us classic accounts of them. Twice when my battalion went over the top, I was away on courses of training, and later in 1917 our parts of the line (in front of Vimy Ridge and Arras) were, shelling apart, relatively quiet. It is almost true to say that the first German soldier I saw was the one who took me prisoner on March 27, 1918, at Moyenneville near Albert. It is literally true that I never set eyes on a single German until, in March, 1918, our division was rushed to the Somme to try to stop the enemy breakthrough of that month. At that critical time and in that sector, the trench system had been left far behind and the fighting was more of the traditional kind, in open country. I remember well the incredulity with which I first saw, swarming toward us over a hill about half a mile away, a lot of men in gray, accompanied by others on horseback. Hitherto I had thought of the territory behind the German barbed wire as a tabooed and malignant region in which danger lurked and out of which death, impersonally, might at any moment spring on us. It was a new realization, though not new knowledge, to find that it contained real men.

Every night for about a week in that month of March, we retired before the German advance, presumably with a view to consolidating a defensible position farther back. Nobody seemed to know quite what was going on or what to do; the staff may have known, but our colonel certainly didn't. (When later I read Tolstoy's *War and Peace* I recognized in his big battle scene the authentic notes of vagueness and confusion.) It was my duty as signal officer to walk back each night under cover of dark to find a new battalion headquarters. The sleeplessness and bewilderment of that week and the final battle in which many of us were taken prisoner have left an ineffaceable memory, with a dark emotional coloring peculiar to itself. On the day of that battle, March 27, I saw more horrific sights than in all the rest of my military days put together. For years afterward I was never safe from the recurring vision (one of several) of a young officer I had known and liked, stumbling toward the dressing station with a gaping wound in his abdomen and whispering, "Oh, Doctor, is there any hope?" Or the sound made by the prone figure beside me, the private soldier with a bullet through his head, whose body went on breathing stertorously, it seemed forever, after the death of his mind.

I myself had a bullet wound, but it was only through the thigh, and I was a walking case for the first few days behind the German lines. Later, in a lazaret at Mons, the wound began to suppurate, and at Antwerp (where I had become a stretcher case) blood poisoning caused fever and semidelirium. However, a sudden improvement began on the hospital train to Hamburg, when the suppuration discharged of its own accord. But I was in the hospital in Hamburg for nearly three months. At last, on my twenty-first birthday, July 25, 1918, I was sent under military guard, but by a civilian train, to the distributing camp at Rastatt in Baden. I was there for more than a month, and then, just as the German regime began to crack, I was with the party which was sent right across to Kamstigall-bei-Pillau, a remote East Prussian seaport on the Baltic Frisches Haff. The three-day train journey from Rastatt to Kamstigall was the second worst I have known; it was in fourth-class carriages with bare wooden seats and no corridor amenities. We were detrained from time to time at the bigger railway stations (Halle, Berlin, etc.) to receive our ration of soup—generally ersatz macaroni and dried pears with sour rye bread. We passed through some fine mountain scenery at one point, but here I learned something new (new to me then, though I found it later in one of Coleridge's letters from the Harz country) about the landscape emotion. I found to my surprise that it depended on associations and memories. These German mountains were of the sort which, had they been in England, would have made my heart leap up. But here, they were only protuberances in an alien and hostile land: faceless, expressionless, and blank. I called this my second worst train journey; the worst of all was between Cambrai and Mons, when, as a walking-wounded case, I was put with others like me into a truck lined with straw, of the *Hommes 40 Chevaux 8* type so familiar to the troops in France.

I have given a full account in *Spots of Time* of my eight months as a *Kriegsgefangener,* and perhaps in any case it would be out of place to enlarge upon them here. During those last months in East Prussia it was obvious that Germany was on the point of collapse, and the German troops in charge of the camp became openly friendly. In fact I came across very little hostile feeling or arrogance toward our side during my whole time in Germany; from the day of capture onward the usual approach to "Tommee" was a cigarette and a handshake. But now it was all brotherliness and to hell with the Kaiser. On Armistice Day, November 11, 1918, the red flag was hoisted over the camp, and the private soldier who had been the interpreter announced himself as president of the local soviet ("Workers' and Soldiers' Council") and commandant of the camp in place of the (deposed) Prussian general. He courteously threw open the camp gates and invited us to walk wherever we liked. However, this was wisely vetoed by our own senior officer (a brigadier), and in due time (it seemed endless to our impatience) we sailed from Danzig to Leith in a Danish ship.

Those final weeks, when the smell of victory and liberation was in the air, set flowing in our veins a current of expectancy and exultation which would have been still more eager if we all had not been laid low, for weeks, by the grippe or influenza which swept the Continent that autumn. If we arrived home, as most of us did, looking like skeletons, that was due to the virus, not to starvation. The wretched Germans were, indeed, starving and used to beg us to spare them things from the food parcels which kept us going at a higher standard than their own and which nevertheless were never looted in transit. The streets of Danzig were placarded with FRIEDE UND BROT, and crowds (mostly of pale and ragged children) shouted, "Englishman!" to us as our ship prepared to sail, holding up their hands for the crusts we threw to them.

A heroes' welcome awaited us at Leith, and there was cheering and waving along the line southward. But the shouting and the jubilation died down, as such things must, and my return to my old home in north London, late on a December evening, was outwardly an anticlimax. My parents awaited me with hearts too full for much speaking, and I could see that the years of anxiety—so much more corrosive for them than for me—had worn and weakened them, my mother especially.

Within a month I was back at my Cambridge college, where but for the war I should by now at twenty-two have been a third-year man. I was still in uniform for a while, but a real undergraduate at last reading history. In those immediate postwar days the students fell into three fairly self-contained groups: the freshmen straight from school, who to us seemed little boys; the small group of men who through unfitness or other cause had been up at college all the time; and last—by far the largest—the returned warriors. We of the veteran group felt that the place belonged to us and that the university curricula must be adapted to our needs. The founding of the Cambridge English School was symbolical of this. It is perhaps not generally known that the first tripos (i.e., honors) examination in English, as an independent subject, was held in 1919. The founding fathers, H. M. Chadwick, Sir Arthur Quiller-Couch, and the Reverend H. F. Stewart, who during the war years had been making the blueprints, knew that as soon as peace came, there would be an influx of mature and experienced men who would stand for no nonsense and who would demand something more modern and more relevant than the classics, yet something which would mediate the same humane values as classics had done. It was to meet this expected demand that Cambridge English was started. Sure enough, the demand came, and English got off to a spectacular start. True, it was viewed with grave suspicion by the academic old guard, and it long remained a Cinderella subject. When in 1920 I switched over from history to English, my college shook its head sadly and sent me to a tutor of the old school who prophesied disaster for the new subject and unemployment for me or anyone else deluded enough to take it. Yet it was in those years, and for many to come, that "Q," the main propagandist for English, was drawing audiences unexampled in Cambridge history, and soon I. A. Richards was to begin those lectures which revolutionized the approach to literature and founded the New Criticism.

But it would be quite wrong to give the impression that winds of change began to blow immediately after the war. It is true that we of the new English school felt that the future was on our side, and we were glad and proud to be in at the start of so promising an experiment. But the feeling which overrode all others was a deep longing to pick up the old threads again and return to the *status quo ante bellum*. And here I am speaking not only of the university, but of the whole nation. It was a good world into which the monstrous horror had broken, and we must build it up again, into something better, if possible, than we had before, but on the old principles and the old assumptions. Above all, never, never again could there be, never must there be, another war.

It was in that sort of spirit that we resumed our normal lives in the early twenties, those years which are so often said to have been disillusioned, but which in reality were innocent and auroral—the years when liberalism and romanticism seemed still unchallenged, the years before the east winds really did begin to rise. The nineteenth century might have been the biggest casualty of the war, but the fact was not yet generally known.

Alec Waugh

ALEC WAUGH was born in London in July, 1898, the son of Arthur Waugh, a distinguished man of letters who directed for many years the fortunes of Chapman & Hall, the house that first published Dickens. He was educated at Sherborne School and at the Royal Military College, Sandhurst. Gazetted to the Dorsetshire Regiment, he served in France as a machine-gun officer from July, 1917, until he was taken prisoner in the big retreat in March, 1918. In July, 1917, he published his first novel, written when he was seventeen, The Loom of Youth—a realistic story of public school life that was sufficiently realistic to cause Sherborne to remove not only his name but his father's from the old boys' society.

The first number of the United States Celebrity Register says of him: "His first book was too localized to enjoy success in America. It was not until eight years later, in 1925, that with the publication of Kept, a story of London Post-War Society, he reached an American public. Its success enabled him to begin his extensive travels. The South Seas, the Far East and the West Indies have provided material for many of his novels as well as his later histories. Since 1927 he has been a frequent visitor to the United States and for over thirty years New York's Hotel Algonquin has been his second home. . . . Not so humorous in his writings as his brother Evelyn, he has a keen wit in person. . . . He has friends all over the world."

He has written more than forty books, of which his West Indian novel, Island in the Sun, an international best seller, is both the best and the most successful.

His brother, Evelyn, was by five and a quarter years his junior.

A LIGHT RAIN FALLING

MY SIXTEENTH BIRTHDAY fell in July, 1914. I was then in the sixth form at Sherborne School. That summer I had, as a cricketer, got into the first eleven. The previous term I had earned my house colors at football. Literature was opening its wide doors for me. My father, Arthur Waugh, the managing director of Chapman & Hall, the publishing house that had launched Charles Dickens, was a prominent man of letters; he had won the Newdigate Prize Poem at Oxford; he had contributed to the first number of *The Yellow Book*; he had published several books of criticism. He and I were very close. In the holidays he read me poetry every evening; my essays were peppered with quotations. My love of literature was being fostered as warmly and as wisely at school as it was at home. I was singularly lucky in my schoolmasters. My headmaster was Nowell Charles Smith, a distinguished Wordsworthian; the sixth-form tutor was H. T. Wade-Gery, to whom many references are made in C. M. Bowra's *Memories*. My special tutor was S. P. B. Mais, the erratic rebel whose entry in *Who's Who* is probably as long as any in the volume. I was pouring out reams of Byronic verse. Life was roseate with promise.

To nearly everyone the outbreak of war was utterly unexpected. School broke up on the last Tuesday in July. The headmaster in his farewell speech on the previous evening had referred to the bad news in the morning papers. I thought he was referring to the threat of civil war in Ulster. Myself, I was concerned with the cricket championship. My county, Middlesex, was lying close behind the leaders, Kent and Surrey, which were playing each other at Blackheath at the end of the week. The result of that match would improve Middlesex's chances against one or other of its adversaries. I had spent half a morning working out in terms of percentages which result would best suit Middlesex. It appeared that a draw, with Surrey getting points for a first innings lead, would be the most satisfactory. My father had promised to take me out to watch the game on the last day—Saturday, August 1.

When that Saturday came, war had become inevitable. Yet we went out to the Rectory Field all the same. So did several thousand others. It was a warm, sunny morning. We sat with Philip Trevor, the *Daily Telegraph* cricket correspondent. "I'll write a report of this," he said, "but it will never be printed. Monday's paper won't have room for anything but war news." During the morning telegrams were brought out to two of the fieldsmen. "Calling up orders, I suppose," said Trevor.

The game followed its course; it was fairly exciting, up till teatime, with a chance of Surrey winning, but the Kent tail held firm. The sky clouded over; rain began to fall, and soon after five o'clock, play was abandoned. It was the conclusion I had hoped for, five days earlier—a draw, with Surrey taking points for a first innings lead. Now I could not have cared less. In retrospect, that game petering out into a draw, with a light rain falling, became symbolic of the extinction of a way of life.

On the next day, Sunday, I went down in the evening to my old preparatory school at Haslemere, where my former headmaster had arranged a cricket match for the August bank holiday. We found a small crowd of some thirty people gathered round the entrance to the station. "Any news?" they asked. There was no radio then; there were no evening papers on a Sunday. They had gathered by ones and twos independently to meet the trains in the hope that someone from London could tell them something.

How different was the start of the Second War. In September, 1939, there was that gray, tired voice announcing over the air the failure of his policy of appeasement, and next morning the billboards were covered with security posters—"Careless talk costs lives" —a symbol of the period of gray repression on which the country was entering. In contrast, in August, 1914, there had been a stirring call to arms, with the posters of Kitchener's pointing finger, "Your King and your Country Need YOU!"

There was no conscription till 1916, and there was a gallantry to "the taking of the King's shilling." The recruit was treated as a hero. The spirit of the hour was caught by Rupert Brooke's sonnet "Now, God be thanked, who has matched us with his hour." All my friends were hurrying to enlist or were applying for commissions, and I was furious at being under age. Boys who had failed to get their house colors the term before were now in khaki. Had I not proved that I was physically fitter than they were? Was I not higher placed in form? Why should I have to return to school to mark time for another year at least?

That, I think, was how everyone of my age who had my kind of public school upbringing felt. We were all impatient to be in it. We were afraid that the war would be over before we could "get across." When I read in August, 1915, of the fall of Warsaw, I could not resist thinking with part of my mind, "That's bound to mean

another year of war. For certain I'll be in it." I question if any teen-
ager had that feeling in the Second War. We went where we were
sent. We were resolved to do our utmost. But with the end of the
voluntary system of enlistment, there was no longer the challenge to
oneself to take one's place beside one's friends in battle.

It is inevitable that a young man of vitality and ambition should
be in his early years self-absorbed. No one of my age could have
failed to see the First War other than as a background to himself.
Whatever happened to me, the fifty-two months following my
sixteenth birthday could not have failed to be crowded, colored,
and dramatic. They were no less so because they were set within the
framework of a war. When as a schoolboy I had looked ahead
during the long summer evenings of 1914, I had pictured myself in
the autumn of 1918 as starting my second year at Oxford; actually I
was to find myself in an officers' prisoner-of-war camp on the Rhine;
but I was not only a lieutenant in confinement, I was the author of
a realistic story of school life that, published in July, 1917, was the
center of violent controversy and that is still in print. I was also
engaged to be married.

I have heard people say, "I would not be eighteen again," or, "I
wouldn't be twenty-two again," as though each age had its special
intrinsic disability. That has not been my experience. I have had
my share of bad years, but they have not been bad because I
happened to be eighteen, twenty-one, thirty-four, or fifty-four, but
because the conditions of my life irrespective of my age happened at
that moment to be unsatisfactory. My eighteenth year did happen
to be such a year, because as a private in the Inns of Court Officers
Training Corps, I found myself with a group of men much older
than myself, from backgrounds that were unfamiliar to me, whom I
found uncongenial. Yet it was during that year that I wrote the
novel that "made my name," and I should be grateful to it.

I had a lucky war. I was unwounded; my health was not impaired
by gas. Most men, if they have enjoyed good health, if they have
been reasonably successful in their undertakings, can look back
gratefully on their years between sixteen and twenty. Certainly I can.

Those years were marked out for me in a series of defined sections, separate and distinct: I had another year at school. I left in
the summer of 1915 to join the Inns of Court O.T.C., in the belief
that I should be gazetted shortly to the Dorsets, but the age limit for
a commission was raised from seventeen to eighteen and a half; so to
fill in the time I went to Sandhurst, to the Royal Military College,
and I was not gazetted until April, 1917. I did not, however, join
the Dorsets. At Sandhurst my rough and cumbersome tactics on the
football field had earned me the nickname Tank, so that when a

notice was put on the company board asking for applications to join
the heavy-machine-gun corps (Tanks), my friends insisted on
entering my name on it. I found, however, the training for it longer
than I had expected, and being anxious to get to France as soon as
possible, I broke it off halfway, settling for the Machine Gun Corps
tout simple, so that it was as a machine-gun officer that I sailed for
France in July, to be attached to the 3d Division, to fight in the
battles of Passchendaele and Cambrai, and to be taken prisoner in
the big retreat south of Arras on March 28, 1918.

"The Lost Generation" is a cliché: it has been claimed that
Gertrude Stein used it first in reference to Hemingway and Scott
Fitzgerald, but it was in general currency earlier than that. I met it
myself for the first time in 1920, when Douglas Jerrold, for many
years a prominent London journalist and the author of several
substantial books, in particular his autobiography, *Georgian Adventure*, offered Chapman & Hall a novel with that title. There was
a very small market then for war books. Jerrold's novel was not
particularly good, and we declined it. As far as I know, it never
found a publisher. All that I can remember about it is the title.

There were, in fact, a number of lost generations, each being lost
in a different way. I belonged to the generation that had had no
adult life before the war, that grew up during the war and, if it was
lost at all, was lost in this, that it never became a generation. A
generation is formed when a group of young contemporaries, on the
brink of their careers, meet and exchange ideas either on a college
campus or in a sidewalk café. Myself, I never had that. By the time
the war was over, I was launched on a literary career. I was also
engaged to be married. For me to go up to Oxford seemed a putting
back of the clock. But only a portion of my generation found itself
in that position. Sir Maurice Bowra, for instance, who is my exact
contemporary and who in March, 1918, was engaged in the same
campaign around Arras that I was, but who was a scholar, whereas I
was not, went up to Oxford and became one of the most significant
figures in a significant generation. I am sure that he would not
think of himself as belonging to a lost generation, nor for that
matter do I.

Apart from my one year in the Inns of Court, I enjoyed Army
life—its comradeship, its open-air routine, the buoyant consciousness of being supremely fit. I should be well content to relive my
nine months at Sandhurst. My fellow cadets were in a high degree
congenial. The training was interesting. There was a day-to-day
eventfulness about the progress that one made; there was an urgency about everything one did—a need to get one's commission
quickly, to get out to France as soon as possible. There was the

excitement of the last exams with one's marks coming through. Then there was the "passing out" parade, mercifully on a warm late April morning, with the adjutant riding up the steps of the Old Building on his horse; the final handing in of one's equipment; the prospect of two weeks' leave and the opening of one's first bank account; having money that one had earned oneself. And it was exciting at that to become an officer, to wear a Sam Browne belt, to be saluted in the streets.

I think that the First War was more exciting than the Second; or am I only thinking that it is more exciting to be eighteen than forty-two? The First War was a grimmer one. The casualties were much higher. Of the forty-four boys who went to Sherborne on the same day that I did in September, 1911, only half lived to see their fortieth birthday. About as many Shirburnians fell during the Second War as in the First, but the numbers of the school were twice as big in 1939 as they had been in 1914. The western desert was not squalid in the way that the western front was, and the First War did not offer the opportunities that the Second did, for the "Renaissance man" of enterprise and courage who performed spectacular raids in the Commandos. But the Second War was dreary, because it was a total war, because the periods of training were so lengthy, because for so long nothing happened or appeared likely to happen. Recruits of 1939 did not, many of them, see fighting until the D-day landings in 1944. My brother has given in *Brideshead Revisited* a vivid account of the boredom that descended on a unit that had been kept in training long after it was fully trained. There was none of that waiting around in the First War. But the real difference lay in this: Civilian life was drab during the Second War. I myself was posted to the Middle East in September, 1941, so that I was spared the most depressing period. But when I returned to England in the summer of 1945, I could appreciate what had happened in the intervening forty months. There had been the blackout; there had been the bombing; there had been rationing of food and gasoline; there had been restrictions of every kind: The country had become a dormitory for our allies' troops. Everyone was overworked; everyone was slightly undernourished: My friends were either drawn, lined, and thin or unhealthily obese through an excess of starchy foods—bread, potatoes, and macaroni. Nobody had much fun.

But in the First War private life went on, in large part undisturbed. If you read Arnold Bennett's journals, you will see that he and his friends were living very much as they had been four years before; only their day-to-day living was given a sense of added urgency by the war across the water. England was never in any danger, but after June, 1940, for the next fifteen months England was in very actual danger. There was a definite threat of invasion. In the First War there was some kind of defense organization, of men in fancy uniform who drilled on Hampstead Heath. My father at the age of fifty never considered enrolling in it, but I am quite certain that if he had been fifty in 1940, he would have enrolled in the Home Guard. In the summer of 1940 it was difficult for a civilian to continue his private business with any enthusiasm, unless through that business he was making a contribution to what was called the war effort. Personal ambition, the demands of a personal career were meaningless. It was not like that in the First War. The men who were not eligible for military service went on with their private lives.

London was very gay during the First War. Such bombing as there was was negligible; so was the blackout: The tops of the streetlamps were blackened, so that cones of light were thrown on the pavement. The streets were romantic with short-skirted women on the arms of khaki escorts emerging from and vanishing into the darkness.

Until 1944 the actual fighting took place far away, in the Far East and the Middle East; there was no such thing as a fortnight's leave. When a man sailed for Suez and beyond, he went for keeps. In the first War, soldiers were constantly coming back on leave, expecting to be amused and with money in their pockets, anxious to spend it on their friends. London was, in fact, a sustained, continuous party, even when the war news was at its worst. I have few more thrilling memories than that of the February morning in 1918 when I was sitting in my dugout checking the figures of a machine-gun barrage and expecting the day ahead to be an exact replica of its predecessor and of its successors, but a runner arrived from details with the news that I was to report immediately at company headquarters and proceed that night on two weeks' U.K. leave.

There was nothing exceptional about my war record—except that I had the good luck to come through unscathed, and I felt about the war very much as my contemporaries did: My feelings toward it changed with the recognition of what modern war—or, rather, what that kind of modern war—involved.

In every country in Europe, war was welcomed not only with enthusiasm but with exultation, particularly so in Britain, which had not been involved in a major war for a hundred years. The country felt restored, rejuvenated: "like a swimmer into cleanness leaping" was Rupert Brooke's phrase for it. We saw war in terms of

Agincourt and Crécy, of battles won in a day, "of bannered broidery." But within three years that first heady excitement had been replaced by Siegfried Sassoon's savage satires:

> To-day he's in the pink, but soon he'll die
> And still the war goes on, he don't know why.

In part this change of temper was due to the deadlock that lasted on the western front for three and a half years. There it stretched between Switzerland and the sea, that long line of shell holes and barbed-wire entanglements, week after week, month after month, with the flags on the maps scarcely moving. Every few months there would be an offensive that would be hailed as a titanic victory. A few weeks later it would be recognized that only a few yards of swamp had been acquired at the cost of many thousands of lives and at a great expenditure of bullion. Loos, Verdun, the Somme, the Chemin des Dames, Passchendaele, Cambrai—one by one they came and went with the same result, the same absence of result. In the late autumn of 1917 Lord Lansdowne wrote a long letter to the *Times,* arguing that the war was ceasing to serve any purpose, that the time had come to call a halt. Many were in agreement with him. The thing had gone on too long.

At the beginning an attempt had been made to whip up hatred of the Germans, as in Germany there were slogans of *Gott Straffe England.* There was a recital of atrocities, but that spirit of hatred did not last for long. It was hard for soldiers in the line to feel any hatred for the poor devils who a few yards away were in the same mess as they. It was impossible not to regard them as fellow victims in a shared calamity.

The apparent pointlessness of the war on the western front bred a feeling of resentment against the governments who were responsible for it and for the generals who carried out or failed to carry out their orders. There was talk of bad faith and of mismanagement in high places. Sassoon's poem "The General" was read with chuckles. A general was described as greeting heartily a regiment on its way to battle:

> "He's a cheery old card," grunted Harry to Jack
> As they slogged up to Arras with rifle and pack. . . .
> But he did for them both by his plan of attack.

In no other war—unless the current campaign in Vietnam provides a parallel—was there such a prolonged period of stagnation where nothing seemed to be done, where nothing seemed to be achieved. Because of the immobility of the line, the higher commands were completely cut off from the men they led. The staff at divisional headquarters lived in comfort and in safety behind the lines. They were immune from attack; bombing had not been highly developed; they were very rarely shelled. Though their troops might be only a few miles away, they were virtually out of reach. During the eight months that I was in the line, I did not see a single senior officer over the rank of lieutenant colonel. A machine gunner's position was to a certain extent exceptional, in that he occupied a series of isolated posts and was not, when he was out of the line, involved in divisional or corps maneuvers, where he would have been exposed to exhortations from "brass hats," but the fact remains that I did not see "red flannel" for eight months.

Much has been written for and against the strategy of Passchendaele. The attack was launched in 1917 at the end of July at a time of year when there was more likely to be rain than not in an area where the low-lying ground with a water system only a few feet below the surface was certain to be churned into mud very quickly. By the end of the first week it was clear that the primary objectives had not been reached, that sustained bombardment would reduce the mud into a quagmire. There was no longer any possibility of the planned-for breakthrough; yet the attack was continued into November.

The defense of Haig's strategy has been that the continued assault aided a general campaign of attrition and also relieved pressure on the French. Such arguments could no doubt be maintained effectively in a debate, and we do not know what would have happened had Haig not continued his attack. He might have given the Germans the breathing space they needed, and the attack that they launched in March, 1918, might have proved irresistible. That is as it may be; of one thing we can be certain: The fighting man was convinced that Haig had no idea what he was doing, that he had not seen with his own eyes—how could he have?—the terrain over which he was ordering his men to advance, that he had to rely on second- and third-hand reports, often from interested parties who were anxious to report smooth things. He was operating in the dark. There was no equivalent for this situation in the Second War, which was a war of movement, and it should not be forgotten that the generals of the Second War had been the subalterns of the First. They had learned a lesson. On both sides of the line they shared the dangers and discomforts of the men they led, and they retained their trust and confidence.

The First War generals forfeited that trust. Before the Battle of the Somme the troops had been assured that the artillery would put down a barrage that no living object could survive; yet the moment the barrage had lifted, the Germans came up from their deep dug-outs, mounted their machine guns on the parapets, and mowed down the advancing troops.

The fighting man in the First War felt that he was being lied to; he also felt that he was being lied about. He felt that the "people at home" had no idea of the ordeal he was enduring.

If the static conditions of fighting on the western front bred a resentment against and distrust of the staff officers at the rear, far more did it create a resentment against civilians. Civilians were very little affected by the war; there was rationing during the last months, but housekeeping was far less difficult than it was to be during the austerity years after the Second War; the blackout was mild; there were no unemployed; a great deal of money was being made. It used to be said, "This war is not likely to end; too many people are doing well out of it." There was special animosity against the politicians whose positions depended on the continuance of the war, who could not afford to admit that they had made mistakes, who had to maintain the public's enthusiasm for "the sacred cause." It infuriated the soldier. In the autumn of 1916, after the slaughter of the Somme, the men in public life were mouthing the same platitudes that they had on recruiting drives two years before. It had been all right to call war the great game when regiments had gone over the top dribbling a football and colonels had led their men brandishing a hunting crop. But it was not like that any longer.

It was in the Battle of the Somme that the majority of Kitchener's 1914 recruits first saw real fighting, and that autumn constituted a watershed for the soldier's attitude toward the war. He fully realized then for the first time the squalor and horror of a modern battlefield.

In a novel, *The Balliols,* that I published in 1934, I tried to explain what it was that he discovered. I described the hero of the story:

. . . leaning against the parapet of a narrow trench while the shells crashed round him. . . . He tried to find, in a desperate attempt to occupy his mind, a simile that would explain the contrast between this war and war as he had seen it during the trench routine of the winter months.

He found a simile.

He thought of sickness as the ordinary healthy man pictures it. There are headaches, there are bilious attacks, there are colds, there are epidemics of influenza, with ricocheting temperatures and a night or two of anxiety. . . . It was in such terms that the average healthy man saw sickness. And then one day he is taken round a hospital. He sees what sickness is for those who are really ill. The operating tables, the rubber gloves, the knives, the chloroform, the antiseptic bandages, the suppurating wounds, the injections of morphia and strychnine. He thinks "Is this what sickness really is?"

The simile held true. Trench routine bore the same routine to the warfare of the battlefield that the casual sickness of the healthy man bore to the illness of the mortally stricken invalid; that headaches and feverish colds bore to organic ailment. In trench routine there were the discomforts of cold, exposure, lack of sleep; there was the unending friction of exhausted nerves; there was at night the sharp ping of bullets, the occasional direct hit with a shell, when a dugout would be blown to pieces and casualties rushed to a field dressing station. It was this that the eminent visitors to the line were shown; the publicists, politicians and priests who went home imagining that they had been shown war.

But *this:* the desolate carnage of the battlefield: this was an altogether other thing—the long unending plain of mudholes, waterfilled, precariously lined by duckboard tracks; the bombardments during which it was impossible to make one's voice carry beyond a traverse; when the shells hailed down so fast that you could not distinguish individual trajectories when there would be a roar at one side or another; and a fountain of earth and iron tossed in a high cascade; when the stretcher bearers were fewer than their tasks, when not only No Man's land but the long stretch of reclaimed land over which the tide of field grey uniforms had receded slowly, was littered with the bodies of distorted and unburied men.

A new note now entered into the writing about the war. There was a resolve on the part of the soldier to present war as the ugly thing it was, to do with words what painters like C. R. W. Nevinson had done on canvas. From France came Henri Barbusse's novel *Under Fire (Le feu)*, and in England there was Siegfried Sassoon's satires. The refrain line "Mustn't the dear old Kaiser love the tanks" was followed by the quatrain:

> I'd like to see a tank come down the stalls
> Lurching to ragtime ditties and "home sweet home"
> And there'd be no more jokes in music halls,
> To mock the riddled corpses in Bapaume.

Simultaneously for many young soldiers, certainly for me, there came a newly awakened social consciousness. Up till now the average public school boy had been automatically a Conservative. His father had voted Tory, and he was resolved to do the same when he was old enough. He was trained to think of himself as a leader. He was a privileged person, and privilege entailed its own responsibilities. He might have sponsored a program of government for the people, but government by the people was quite another thing.

The young officer began to feel differently about the men he led in action. What voice had they had in determining their present fate? They had been taken from their homes and jobs; a gun had been put into their hands, and they had been told to kill Germans with it. What were they getting out of it? Had any government the right to do this to them? Many young officers carried back with them to civilian life a number of unanswered questions.

Many of us returned, too, in a spirit of crusade, resolved to ensure that the crime of war would never be reenacted. The world must be convinced of the horror and the waste of war; power must be taken from those in whose interests, in the defense of whose property and privileges, in the acquisition of whose wealth and powers, wars were begun and waged. Wars never brought anything but misery and deprivation to the proletariat. We reminded ourselves that the I.L.P. (Independent Labour Party) alone had protested against the continuation of the fighting long after it had ceased to be a war of self-defense. There was a big swing to the left, and within a year or two Oxford University had elected as the president of its Union a member of the Labour Party, Kenneth Lindsay, later to be a member of Ramsay MacDonald's Ministry.

What happened to that spirit of crusade? Most of us too soon were caught up by the problems of civilian life: There were livings to be earned; there was the relief that the war was over; there was the exhaustion that follows the completion of a sustained effort, as runners collapse when the tape is breasted. The old men were firmly in their saddles. By the time we had recovered our breath, it was too late, and we realized that far from learning the lessons that the war should have taught, the world was busily repeating its mistakes and that "the war that will end war" (H. G. Wells' phrase) was being followed by "the peace that will end peace." We shrugged. There did not seem a thing to do about it. Anyhow it was a long way off. We had the present, and we had our youth. Our health was unimpaired. Let us enjoy ourselves while we could, so we embarked on the frivolities and excesses of the period of "the bright young people" whose spirit was expressed in Scott Fitzgerald's stories and my brother's *Vile Bodies* and *A Handful of Dust*. It was in the main an outburst of high spirits, but it had an undercurrent of despair: the making the most of the sunlight while it lasted. 1939 was still a long way off.

Amos Wilder

AMOS NIVEN WILDER *was born in Madison, Wisconsin, on September 18, 1895, the son of Amos Parker Wilder, then editor of the* Wisconsin State Journal *and later Consul General in Hong Kong and Shanghai. He prepared for college at the Thacher School, Ojai, California, spent two years at Oberlin College, transferred to Yale, and after his junior year there went to France in the fall of 1916. After a winter with the Paris section he joined Section 2 of the American Field Service in February, 1917, and then Section 3 in Serbia in July. When the United States Army took over the ambulance sections, he enlisted in Paris in the United States Field Artillery in November, 1917. He served as a corporal in the 17th Field Artillery of the 2d Division and was discharged in France in June, 1919.*

He took his B.A. at Yale in 1920, his B.D. in 1924 (after three years' study at Brussels and Oxford), and his Ph.D. in 1933, also at Yale. He was ordained to the ministry of the Congregational Churches (now the United Church of Christ) in 1926 and served as minister of the Congregational Church in North Conway, New Hampshire for three years. He taught first at Hamilton College (1930–33) and then as professor of the New Testament at Andover Newton Theological School (1933–43), the Chicago Theological Seminary and the Federated Theological Faculty of the University of Chicago (1943–54), and the Harvard Divinity School, from which he retired in 1963 as Hollis Professor of Divinity, Emeritus.

Amos Wilder has been a Fellow of the Belgian-American and the Guggenheim foundations, a visiting professor at the University of Frankfort, editor of the Journal of Religion, *a member of the editorial board of* Christianity and Crisis, *a member of the Yale Corporation, and president of the Society of Biblical Literature. He has received honorary degrees from Hamilton, Oberlin, and the universities of Chicago, Yale, and Basel. His publications include works on the New Testament and on contemporary literature. His first volume of poetry was entitled* Battle-Retrospect and Other Poems, *published in 1923 in the Yale Series of Younger Poets.*

AT THE NETHERMOST PIERS
OF HISTORY
World War I, A View from the Ranks
For Jules Deschamps

———◆———

THE FIGURE of the old soldier reminiscing about his battles has often been disparaged in life and letters. New generations have other interests, and the grandchildren are restive, as guests are when they are confronted with a travelogue even though enlivened by homemade movies. When veterans forgather, of course, the situation is different. Old cronies will evoke common memories and even get out their maps and souvenirs. But outside the guild all such rehearsals carry the suspicion of parade. There have been too many examples of those who have traded on their exploits like the old rascal in O'Neill's *Touch of the Poet* who had gone so far as to fictionalize his martial disgraces into honors. There is also, of course, the impulse of the combatant to draw the veil upon the atrocious and to say good-bye to all that. In our period, moreover, the taboo on sentiment, rhetoric, and, worst of all, idealization works as a final check on any annals save the most austere.

It is at this last point, however, that I make bold to demur and to take all the risks, with the further excuse, indeed, of the editor's invitation. However it be with World War II and more recently, one cannot properly evoke service in World War I without according a place to sentiment and ideals, and not only as a recognition of regrettable illusions. So far as concerns America's part in that war, I write as an unreconstructed Wilsonian. One thing that specially engages my interest in these annals after so many years is precisely the ambiguity of those ideals as they animated so many of us, the rights and wrongs of our crusading impulse and rhetoric, the fine distinction between truth and propaganda, between historical mission and manufactured inducements, between authentic hopes and deceptive, apocalyptic anticipations.

A related matter that impels my fascinated scrutiny, also in its ambiguous character, is that of the war experience in its dramatic aspect, in its dimension of myth, the resonances of the sensibility and imagination of youth in its confrontation with the prodigious, and the strange postwar sense of anticlimax and disillusionment that accompanied the return to civilian life defined as normalcy.

Many college men of my generation volunteered in the American Field Service before America entered the war. Our motives were varied. The main idea, as with the Lafayette Escadrille, was to be where things were going on, and with this was mixed the romance of adventure. The urge of the Francophile played no small part. An early appeal of the Field Service for volunteers began with the words of Joffre: "The United States of America have not forgotten that the first page of the history of their independence was written with a little of the blood of France." There was an increasing sentiment, moreover, that America should be in the war. I had been on a Y.M.C.A. staff at a boys' Plattsburg (or training) Camp at Fort Terry (Plum Island, off New London, Connecticut) in the summer of 1916 and had heard Theodore Roosevelt fulminate to the ranks of teen-agers on the disgrace of our delay.

More significant to me as one concerned with the issues of pacifism and the moral aspects of the war was my experience as a student at Oberlin College in 1914–15. President Henry Churchill King in his large Sunday Bible class dealt for many months with the origins of the war, with an analysis of Prussianism, traditional Christian views of church and state, and the Christian attitude to war. The upshot was in effect a justification of American participation with the Allies. No doubt King did not know some of the things that were brought out later by men like Sidney Fay about the origins of the war. In any case the lurid tales of German atrocities were not part of the argument. King, like myself, was a Congregationalist and with Oberlin as a whole represented the tradition of the abolitionists and of the New England theocrats, according to which the church associates itself with the moral responsibility of the state. It was the same Calvinist tradition which led Woodrow Wilson later to select the term "covenant" used by John Calvin for the ordering of Geneva (not to mention the Scotch and English Covenanters) for the instrument of the League of Nations. In the spring of 1919 when the Army of Occupation in Germany released many college men to attend French and British universities, I was in the Army School Detachment at the University of Toulouse. Several of us interested in the Christian ministry were assigned to the old French Huguenot seminary at Montauban. The dean, Émile Doumergue (close relative of the later President of France, Paul Doumergue), was the greatest Calvin scholar of the time. He took immense delight in recognizing this link between the Geneva of John Calvin and the political and international idealism of Woodrow Wilson, son of a Presbyterian manse.

Americans who were in Europe before our declaration of war encountered bitterness over our delay. Passing through London on my way to the Continent in October, 1916, I heard the following *réplique* on the stage of a music hall. One comedian observed that George Washington "never let a lie slip through his teeth." "Yes," was the answer, "because like all Americans he spoke through his nose." But the disparagement, at least of American civilians, continued after the war in France, and sometimes for good reasons. In his *Chant funèbre pour les morts de Verdun*[1] Henry de Montherlant exclaims at the sacrilege of the first American tourists of the Verdun battlefields who carried off skulls in the trunks of their cars. "Peoples without a past need souvenirs. Already Washington used to exhibit piously one of the supposed keys to the Bastille, which actually were fabricated at Paris by the dozen."[2] But the American vanguard in France was honored, often in embarrassing ways. Arriving from the front with soiled uniform and, no doubt, marks of fatigue, I was offered a seat by a Frenchwoman in the crowded *métro*. The irritations that are perennial between the Americans and the French at the superficial levels of politics and tourism do not touch the deep confraternity in arms of the anonymous combatants in the ranks.

On the fourth of July, 1917, I was in Paris on the way from the French front to join an ambulance section with the French in Serbia. Thus, it came about that I was present at the Picpus cemetery where Pershing went that day to visit the grave of Lafayette. It has often served me as warning to the historian that though I was an eyewitness within hearing, I long told the story of hearing Pershing say, "Lafayette, we are here." I learned later that the words were spoken by a Colonel Stanton. One sometimes hears it said that the whole episode was a myth. This is going too far, but such are the perils of firsthand reminiscence. In any case I can remember accurately the day in April of that year when we saw the official French *affiche* at Ste.-Menehould announcing the American declaration of war and the emotion it aroused in the army zone among the French poilus and the few Americans already in service.

For the purposes of this chronicle I have disinterred from old trunks and cartons the letters I wrote home from France and Serbia, not looked at for fifty years. Most of them were written on the

1 Paris, 1924.
2 *Ibid.,* p. 38.

cheap lined sheets picked up in a village *papeterie*. Correspondence
from the Field Service includes the official French postcard designated *Correspondence militaire* and sometimes carries the sur-
charge *Contrôle postal militaire*. One envelope was stamped
RECEIVED WITHOUT CONTENTS. N.Y.P.O., PENN. TERM. STA. One illegi-
ble letter received in France had the written annotation *accident de
mer*. After I transferred to the U.S. Army the letterhead of the
Y.M.C.A. often appears with its red triangle and ON SERVICE WITH
THE AMERICAN EXPEDITIONARY FORCES or that of the Knights of
Columbus with its emblem and the American flag in color. From
this time on each letter was censored: thus, "John Smith, Lt. 17th
F.A." The envelopes carry the seals U.S. ARMY POSTAL SERVICE and
A.E.F. PASSED AS CENSORED, again with the signature, which after all
these years reminds me of the names of the several officers of my
battery.

Army letters were often written in a dugout at night by the light
of the little lamps which like our briquettes the French had taught
us to improvise. With a small can and gasoline parleyed from a
camion driver, supplemented by a strip of cloth for a wick and a
sawed-off cartridge, one had a flare that would burn for hours.
Books could not be sent through Army mail to the front, but my
family tore the covers off them and sent them rolled up like
magazines. My letters carry a running comment on classics thus
available.

Besides the letters other survivals came to light: a receipt for $25
from a New Haven garage for a "Course in automobile repair and
driving"; a Paris driving license, November 28, 1916 (my driving
test was on the Champs Élysées) ; every kind of identity card,
permis de séjour, ordre de mouvement—including the tour de force
of red tape overcome for permission to spend a week's leave in the
Lake District, wangled from both civil and military authorities,
French and British, as well as the American Embassy in Paris. Here
is a receipt from "Lloyd & Co., High Class English Tailors," Place
de la Madeleine, for my ambulance uniform, "tunic, breeches and
insignia"; an inventory of equipment received when enlisting in
the Field Artillery; a penciled plan of a small French village indicating billeting arrangements for A Battery: officers, men, picket
lines, infirmary, pumps for drinking water. A printed set of rules
handed to men on leave in Paris included as No. 7: "The Military
Police have been ordered to take the names and report all ranks,
including Militarized Civilians, who permit themselves to be so-
licited on the streets."

Even the most trifling of such items gratify by their concreteness.

The past swims less in the vague. So the historian cherishes his papyri fragments, coins, and graffiti. Sometimes such archives have more importance. I found the original of a traced firing mission for batteries of our regiment indicating the successive advances of a creeping barrage, by minutes, in the area of Belleau Wood (duly deposited with the historical section of the 2d Division) .

More of the order of minor graffiti is my on-the-spot notation of the humor and profanity of doughboys loading terrified horses by a ramp into a French boxcar (eight *chevaux*—twenty *hommes*) . The first horses driven in plunge, kick out, and fall down.

"Bang! Bang! They're making a noise like a dozen batteries. There won't be anything left of this sawed-off freight car."

"Whoa! Whoa! Tie the S.O.B.'s in here before they trample me to death."

"Put a little straw up to 'em. A horse will come out of delirium tremens for a wisp of hay."

"As soon as they get done with it, though, they begin to see things."

Two men come out of the menagerie, pale and limping. "That's the way it goes. I was drunk as a cuckoo when I joined this man's army."

Singing: "Why didn't we wait to be drafted?" "Whoa there, you——brutes! Shut the door on them. They'll all be dead when we open it again, anyhow."

"There gotta be three men stay in there with 'em, too."

The Field Service had had its origins in the activities already initiated by Americans in 1914 under the auspices of the antebellum American Hospital in Neuilly. Before going to Section 2 in the Argonne, I served three months in the Paris section, our cars being stationed at the large new Lycée Pasteur, which had been converted to a hospital. We met the long hospital trains that came from the front into the Gare de la Chapelle. From Neuilly we would go across Paris to this station behind the Gare du Nord in a convoy of twenty or thirty heavy Buick ambulances. The Paris taxi drivers were already at this date a legend and were looked on as our only rivals in the skills of the road. They were not supposed to cut through our convoys, and if they so presumed, they were fair game for reprisal. Some of our soldier-of-fortune drivers boasted of neatly taking a wheel off one or more of these intruders. We took our loads of stretcher cases to hospitals in and around Paris often in the small hours of the night and made it a point of honor to know our way without the aid of the gendarme-guides provided.

I have lately been reminded that it is precisely to this Paris of
1916 that Proust brings back his narrator in the last part of his great
work. Marcel observes the city in wartime. Referring to the duels in
the sky, the searchlights, and the sirens, he invokes the Walküre of
Wagner and the *Götterdämmerung*. He plays with the analogy of
Pompeii and Herculaneum and, with his own scrutiny in mind,
thinks of how "the frivolity of an epoch, when ten centuries have
passed over it, becomes the matter of a grave erudition." He evokes
the "august" or "supernatural" aspect of the combatants on leave
from the front who in a few hours have exchanged the fabulous
world of the lines for the world of the boulevards. He speaks of the
touching charm of the young poilus: *"le petit Parigot . . . avec
son air dessalé, sa mine éveillée et drôle—quelle finesse, quel bon
sens!"* And *"les gars de province, comme ils sont amusants et gentils
avec leur roulement d'r et leur jargon patoiseur!"*[3]

Speaking of the slang phrases of the war, *"passeront pas," "poilus," "on les aura,"* Proust finds his teeth set on edge by the vul-
garisms, but then finds them sanctified. His sentiment about the
warriors in faded blue brings back something of the mood and piety
of the time:

> But if you saw all this world, especially those of humble lot, the
> workmen, the small tradesmen, who had no idea of their hidden
> capacities for heroism and who would have died in bed without ever
> suspecting it, if you had seen them run through the fire to assist a
> comrade, to carry off a wounded officer, and when themselves hit
> smile at the moment of death when the army surgeon says that the
> trench has been recaptured from the enemy, I assure you . . . that
> one gets a worthy idea of the French and one can appreciate better
> the epochs of the past which in our school days struck us as some-
> what overdrawn.[4]

The French combatant writers of the time—Duhamel, Dorgelès,
Montherlant—all disparage the city and the civilian in contrast with
the tenor of the front. In the novel, by Philippe Barrès, *La Guerre a
vingt ans*,[5] Alain, the soldier on leave, attends a dance hall with a
companion and is made aware of the abyss between. One could lend
oneself, he reflects, to the fiction of a dance on the edge of the
volcano. But the affair was flat and gross. The joy with which he
had begun his leave from the front, "as one who had escaped from

---

3 *À la recherche du temps perdu,* III (Paris, 1954) , pp. 806–7.

4 *Ibid.,* pp. 752–53.

5 Paris, 1924.

among the dead," is suddenly deflated. "We alone, in our Gehenna, know the value of the world's marvels." Looking about him at these men and women who do not love what he loves or hate what he hates, he would like to "blow up the ceiling of the hall and let them see suddenly, as they lay trembling on the floor, the sky where the sooty cloud of the shell expands like a tragic poem."[6]

During the spring of 1917 I was with Section 2 of the Field Service in the Argonne. This sector was relatively quiet at this time, though at night we witnessed the appalling flashes, star shells, rockets, and glare and heard the interminable hammering of the inferno of the Champagne attacks on our left. Driving to and from the dressing stations in the lines without lights, the ditches on either side of the road masked by the snow in the darkness of the forest; evacuating besides the usual cases now and then a wounded prisoner, and once shut in for the trip with a distracted poilu; running the gauntlet of shelled roads—all this was the common experience of the service. I have lately noted that Dos Passos refers to one of these same posts and shelling at its approaches in his account of ambulance driving, *First Encounter*,[7] the post at the monastery-church of La Chalade, reached, as he notes, from Les Islettes on the east-west road through the Argonne.

The terrain, topography, place-names associated with the incommensurable drama of war took on, especially for the fresh sensibility of youth, a mythic character. Moving up to the front was like entering a preternatural landscape. The soldier in the twentieth century felt himself enveloped as it were by archaic spells. Especially as one moved into the calcined desolation of the forward trenches, a kind of electric alertness metamorphosed all perception. The peculiar feature of so much of World War I, with its relatively stable lines and no-man's-land, meant that the advanced trenches were like the frontier of chaos, charged with the passion of the world.

When this area was convulsed by barrages, mortars, attacks, while the hinterland teemed with supporting units, and laboring gun crews and harassed convoys of supplies, batteries, tanks, cars, ambulances, the whole experience took on a legendary character. Montherlant's war novel *Le Songe*[8] operates with a continuous counterpointing of the experiences of 1917–18 with motifs drawn from the *Iliad*, Plutarch, and other ancient fables like the *Song of Roland*. The drama is caught up into a timeless epic. "The ancient realm

---

6 *Ibid.*, p. 257.
7 New York, 1945. Republication of *One Man's Initiation*, 1919.
8 Paris, 1922.

and the modern, the realm of phantasms and the realm of things, were confounded in a fantastic universe which no longer threatened him."[9] The night-shrouded camion carrying the casqued men to battle is *Argo*. The eve of battle with its omens and hallucinations is described in a chapter entitled "Noctium Phantasmata." Strains of music are heard in the heavens, and Plutarch is recalled and his account of the strange harmonies of instruments and voices that were heard overhead by the armies in the middle of the night that preceded the decisive battle between Antony and Octavius. "Once again at the right moment the great life of antiquity imparted to its exiled child what little was required . . . ; the great tomb opened and a swallow or an eagle flew to him bearing its omens." And noting that this tormented night ushered in the decisive victories of July, 1918, the narrator hails the "fabulous concordance" with the eve of that battle in which the Roman order and the world's weal were born in the victory of Octavius.[10]

I recognize that readers today may be puzzled, if not scandalized, by this theme of the prestige of the war experience and its imaginative overtones. I can only quote again from Montherlant, in this case from his *Chant funèbre pour les morts de Verdun:* "One would prefer that nothing resulted from war except evil. Many problems would thus be simplified. But this violin bow, spotted with blood, draws profound accents from man which it alone can evoke from him."[11] One can illustrate further from the related mystique of the fraternity of the combatants over against the civilian world and their disenchantment with and alienation from the postwar world. The then young French writers, Joseph Kessel, Philippe Barrès, Montherlant, focus their early war novels (*L'Équipage, La Guerre a vingt ans,* and *Le Songe,* respectively) on the gulf between the solidarity of combatants on the one hand and the relative insipidity of all civilian relationships. These first testimonies reflected the shared experience of an incommensurable action and passion and the bonds of fealty to the dead, as also in the greater works of Georges Duhamel. Montherlant cites[12] three similar passages from the novels in question:

[The war] altogether a somber and sublime universe in which the spirit drew near to the depth of things.

P. Barrès

---

9 *Ibid.,* p. 183.
10 *Ibid.,* p. 182.
11 *Op. cit.,* p. 109.
12 *Ibid.,* pp. 21–22.

Now that he emerged from the kingdom of shades and of naked souls, he knew.

J. Kessel

Now he knew what counted and what did not count.

H. de Montherlant

From July to October, 1917, I was with one of the two ambulance sections in the Balkans. Evacuating French casualties and victims of malaria from Monastir most of the time, we were also confronted in this colorful theater of the war with Serbian, British, Annamite, Greek, and even Russian troops—the latter vituperated as they lay down their arms in consequence of the revolution. Returning to France and enlisting in Paris in the U.S. Field Artillery as a private in November, 1917, I was assigned to a battery in the 17th F.A. and so served in the ranks through the rest of the war in the 2d, or Indian Head, Division.

I cite passages from two letters written in this period which, naïve as they are, may be taken as firsthand documentation of the men in the ranks, the American doughboy: "One hundred years—five hundred years from now, what idea will the historian or the average American have of the men who fought his second War of Independence[13] for him? They have the soldier's vices—wine, women and dice. What are their virtues? The men are so young. Their qualities are all condensed in the one great quality of zest for life. That overflowing consciousness of being alive is the basis of any amount of generosity and lavishness of power which makes the French love us so much. And add to this something which the 'bossy' American is not accustomed to in his imperial days of peace—the pause that comes before a revelation of the *épouvantable,* the appalling, in life, as I have seen it show in eye and cheek after the first experiences of shelling—and you get a malleability, a disposable enthusiasm, that overrides all the vices. The shock of war tempers the bravado, recklessness and insubordination of this human type which are nevertheless admirable traits. They have such surpluses of vigor that they take their zest as a witness against the possibility of their doing or taking harm. That's exactly what I mean to say: they feel like kings and the king can do no wrong."

Again, in a letter from a replacement camp in September, 1918, I describe the ethnic variety and savor and unexpected talents that abounded in the ranks. Here was a corporal among these casuals

---

13 No doubt what I had in mind by this curious designation was that America was now again finding its identity in the world of nations, as was not the case in the Civil War.

who had mined in Kentucky and in the Andes and who, though like most he had never been to college, had his own curiosities: He was an expert on the Cherokee Indians and on the habits of spiders. Here was a Swede who had run away from home in Sweden to go to sea, been shipwrecked on his own coast, and had eventually become a foreman in Colorado. He was a gifted narrator and talked among other things about Socialism among the workers in Denver. Here was a Galveston longshoreman who told a kind of Eugene O'Neill story about proving himself on the docks against his father's veto. "What an amount of fine raw-material is going into the war in the ranks. Unschooled, coarse often, disrespectful, but variously disciplined by home memories—a stern but just father, a worn-down but unflinching mother—or by a long pull in the first years of bread-winning, or by some schoolboy romance, or by some unknown grade-school teacher, or childhood imagination captured by some forgotten Decoration Day ceremony. Most of this is pretty well submerged by the recklessness that they like to put on. And there is a tendency to assume a crowd spirit with much grumbling and sometimes worse. But getting at each man alone, or getting the crowd in good spirits, you have a promise for America that is immeasurable."

The deeper currents of history and its meaning are better sensed among the anonymous many or the common soldiers than in loftier quarters. By the same token the professional historian writes at two removes from the dense reality of events and from those who carry the burden of time and who are exposed to its hidden intentions and secret omens. Even the writer or artist is disqualified to the extent that his vocation separates him from the mass or makes him a nonpolitical being. It was unfortunate that our best-known World War I American writers as a rule (in contrast with such French writers as I have named) were not fully immersed in the war and in the ranks.[14] We had no Duhamel, and none with the human-politi-

---

14 E. E. Cummings served in an ambulance unit, not the Field Service, until his unpardonable arrest and mistreatment by French authorities. After his release and return to the States the war ended before his enlistment in the Army could return him to France. John Dos Passos notes in data supplied to a reference work that he served in several ambulance units, again not the Field Service, and the U.S. Medical Corps. Hemingway, who sought active service but was rejected because of his eyes, served in Italy in ambulance and canteen service briefly before he was wounded in the summer of 1918 and then returned to the same service for a few weeks before the Armistice. He did not serve in the elite corps of the Italian *arditi*, as is sometimes stated, but with them. Nothing could be further from my thought here than to question their courage or motives or to lack appreciation for their talent. It is simply a question of the narrow base of experience in this war which lay behind their writings.

cal commitment of a Charles Péguy. The soldier characters of our American writers go A.W.O.L. like Dos Passos' artist-hero, John Andrews; or are affronted by the unwonted austerity of discipline, sometimes indeed excessive as in E. E. Cummings' *Enormous Room*; or make an esthetic separate peace, as in Hemingway. The prestige of such writers has done much to encourage a foreshortened view of the American role in the war, something less than honor to its dead, and misjudgment as to the instincts of the nation in that juncture as they came to expression and to temporary frustration in the tragic drama of Woodrow Wilson and our relapse into normalcy.

As one who served in the ranks in a Regular Army division that was among the first in the field, I take this occasion to testify that our indeed inarticulate common soldiers so far from their native ground had, nevertheless, a sense of being willing actors in a necessary drama and one inseparably linked with the meaning of the American story. The core of the matter was not some engineered hatred of the "Hun," or sentiment for France, or the jeopardy of Britain, or unlimited submarine warfare and the honor of the flag, but an instinct for civil order and due political authority among the peoples. Though the United States had had a short history, its Roman and Calvinist heritages from the founders, together with its experience with lawlessness on the frontier, had conferred on us a sense of the life-and-death urgency of public authority, the a priori necessity of law and its sanctions over against human veracities, and dikes against anarchy and mania. This issue explains the stubbornness with which Wilson linked the peace treaties with the League of Nations. This issue, more general than that of who started the war and deeper than that of democracy and self-determination, was obscurely recognized by the American soldier. And it was in this context that we construed the apocalyptic overtones of the war and of such actions as the attack at dawn on July 18, 1918, in the forest of Villers-Cotterêts or that of November 1 in the Argonne.

Three days afterward I described the bombardment which preceded the latter attack in a letter which for all its ingenuousness suggests the sensitivities in question: "I went outside when it started, and as far as one could see either way there were the continuous flashes and roar, which went on hour after hour until light and then on until midday. When one lay down indoors the guns sounded like the sucking and ebbing and swirling of a great whirlpool. At such times one feels with uncomfortable clearness that sense of awe towards the future. History making itself now,

now, at this ordinary night and day and in this ordinary gray landscape. One comes close to the Plan and sees Castor and Pollux fighting over the Romans palpably."

At another angle, as of any war, the aspect of this war was loathsome and atrocious. It is not surprising that any inducements to Americans to participate in it would appear fraudulent. I choose one example among many and cite a discussion of the war by soldiers in various of the Allied armies as presented in John Dos Passos' *First Encounter*.[15] Here, in Chapter IX, there is a long diatribe against "the lies, the phrases, the press" that brought America into the war, seen as "a tragedy," and as "goin' back on our only excuse for existin'! Who shall ever know what dark forces bought and bought until we should be ready to go blinded and gagged to war? . . . People seem to so love to be fooled. . . . We are slaves of bought intellect, willing slaves."[16] In the context the speakers identify themselves as "merely intellectuals" over against "the stupid average working-people who have the power." The Americans, it is explained to the Europeans, "are like children. They believe everything they are told, you see; they have no experience in international affairs, like you Europeans."[17]

This reaction to the enormity of war on the part of the more emancipated artists and intellectuals in the Army was understandable. But it was superficial. The artists have their own admirable personal codes—for example, the heroic code of Hemingway—or their iconoclastic enthusiasms: Dos Passos' group in the passage in question unite in the hope of an eventual revolutionary Socialism. It is relevant to cite here as representative for many of the artists and writers of the period André Gide's statement that he "regretted that under Mallarmé's influence he had long been unpolitical."[18] Dos Passos himself, writing an introduction to the 1945 reprinting of his book (*First Encounter* was first published as *One Man's Initiation* in 1919), calls attention to the impact of the war of 1914–18 on Americans as "a horrible monstrosity, outside of the normal order of things," as compared with World War II.[19] And he has presented a radically different picture of the earlier war and its issues in his recent work *Mr. Wilson's War* (1962).

The Americans in the ranks were certainly less sophisticated and articulate, but they had an obscure sense of the meaning or inevita-

---

15 *Op. cit.*
16 *Ibid.*, p. 144.
17 *Ibid.*, p. 141.
18 Van Meter Ames, *André Gide* (New York, 1947), p. 162.
19 *Op. cit.*, p. 8.

bility of the war. Woodrow Wilson expressed it after an imperfect fashion, and his personal tragedy was an index of the same impasse and resistances that determined the ordeal of the soldier. No doubt there was sentimentality and utopianism in the idea that this was the war to end war. But such intensity of hope when all is at stake is not unfamiliar, nor was it silly in analogous periods, like those of the English Puritans or the founders of New England, not to mention the beginnings of Christianity. Certainly the goals of Wilson were less sentimental than those of the contemporary Marxists, and he was more realistic than those who sought a vindictive peace and the several forms of national aggrandizement or those Americans who failed to recognize that the time had come for committing the nation to responsible international structures.

At the conclusion of his massive work on this war the French historian Pierre Renouvin notes that though Wilson was only the final compiler-editor of the many elements that went into the Covenant of the League of Nations, yet "it remains true that without him, his tenacity, his faith, the new conception of international relations would not have been made the foundation of the peace treaties of 1919–20."[20]

Yet if at this remove in time one still defends America's participation in the war and insists on the core of truth in the high-flown rhetoric of promise, one can do so only in full recognition of the abomination of the slaughter: the ghastly and protracted carnage which understandably motivated the revulsion and even the cynicism of many interpreters. This consideration excludes any rational justification of the war. What we are pointed to is the kind of historical fate or linkage of events which Lincoln dealt with in the categories of offense and judgment with respect to the Civil War. We are pointed to the human condition itself whose cure exacts these kinds of fates which transpire over our heads and which are wiser than any of those who either protest or serve them.

---

[20] *La Crise européenne et la première guerre mondiale* (Paris, 1962) , p. 663.

Frederick A. Pottle

"I was born in 1897, grew up on a farm in Maine, attended the local schools, and graduated from Colby College in 1917. My major was in chemistry, but in my senior year I came upon Shelley, suffered a violent conversion, and proclaimed myself a poet. After teaching a few months at Hebron Academy, I enlisted in the Medical Corps, was assigned to Evacuation Hospital No. 8, and went overseas in the spring of 1918. Our outfit was established first at Juilly, near Meaux, during Belleau Wood and the summer offensives, and then at Petit Maujouy, near Verdun, during the St.-Mihiel and Meuse-Argonne actions. I worked in the operating room as private first class with the rating of surgical assistant. In the spring of 1919 I left my outfit, then functioning as a post hospital in Mayen, near Coblenz, to teach chemistry at the A.E.F. University at Beaune, in Burgundy. I came home as a casual and was discharged in July, 1919.

"After teaching high school for a year in Portland, Maine, I entered the Yale Graduate School and happily embraced a career of scholarship and teaching. Except for two years at the University of New Hampshire (1921–23), I have been at Yale ever since, retiring in June, 1966, as Sterling Professor of English, emeritus.

"My book Stretchers, the Story of a Hospital Unit on the Western Front, was published in 1929. I gave the Messenger lectures at Cornell in 1941, publishing them that same year as The Idiom of Poetry (revised and enlarged edition, 1946). My teaching at Yale was principally in the Romantics, but my research has mainly centered on Boswell, of whose private papers I have edited many volumes, both alone and in collaboration. My magnum opus, James Boswell, The Earlier Years, 1740–1769, was published in 1966."

CREED NOT ANNULLED

SOME WEEKS AGO, as I was sitting in a college dining room filled
with undergraduates—it was about the time of the march on Washington to protest the war in Vietnam—I said to a faculty friend
considerably younger than myself, "It makes me sad to think that so
many of those boys are unknowingly depriving themselves of a
valuable experience. What would they say if I told them that I
seriously considered my Army service the best-invested years of my
life?" His reply was probably not unlike what theirs would have
been: "All that blood and suffering so that you could think better
of yourself!" The reproof waked old echoes. It brought back power-
fully the feelings I had when I first got to France in 1918, not
feelings that war was essentially and always evil; oh, no. Feelings
rather of shame and regret that I had not got more deeply immersed
in the war. "What right," I then kept saying to myself, "what right
have I to be safe and enjoying these memorable experiences while
other men are being maimed and killed?"

What memorable experiences? Such as being for the first time in
a foreign country, of strolling greedily through sun-drenched old
villages in the Seine-et-Marne, its enchanting landscapes impressing
themselves on my memory by a heightening of consciousness such as
I had never felt before and have not felt since. The joy of frank,
unreserved male friendship found at last by me, who all through
college never had a real chum. The French soldier of my own age,
four years a veteran, who gave me his *croix de guerre*. The woman
at Domrémy who said, "*Vous américains, vous êtes la Jeanne d'Arc
des alliés.*" That moment on July 4, 1918, as the band was playing
"*La Marseillaise,*" when the wind swirled our flag completely
around the French flag. Such as the wounded boys lying patiently in
the old courtyard waiting their turn in the operating room. In a
sunset thrilling with larks, the row of raw mounds and open graves
under the wall of the old cemetery. Me, light-headed with tonsil-
litis, embracing the trunk of an oak tree and cursing feebly as the
bomb goes off 100 yards away. Me, working hours and hours and
hours on wounded men, till my knees won't bend and thigh cramps
bring me up moaning when at last I can stretch out on a litter.

And other gains as regards what I hope it will not be thought priggish to call my character and morals. It was in the Army, not in college, that I acquired such a modicum of manliness as I have been able to attain to. It was the Army that taught me my limitations. I am ambitious, and I wanted promotion—not, of course, a commission, for to be an officer in the Medical Corps one must be a Doctor of Medicine, but a mere sergeancy. Time after time after time, in company formation, I heard the names of the chosen read out with keen disappointment and then, at the very end, the fighting over for months, was awarded a ridiculous corporalcy, the last promotion, I fancy, made in the outfit. But by that time I had sincerely come to prefer my status as private because promotion would have cost me my best friends, and I was no longer disposed to think myself unjustly treated. In World War I there were no technical ratings conferring rank, and corporalcies and sergeancies implied a power of command. The Army taught me that I did not possess powers of command and that the only areas in which I could certainly excel were scholarship and writing. It was a painful lesson, but it was useful to learn it at the age of twenty-one and in an interim employment.

And another lesson only slightly less useful. What I have been saying may seem like a eulogy of the Army system as such, but it isn't. I still subscribe to all the expressed and implied criticism of the Army I put my name to almost forty years ago. I deplore and resent the Army's ingrained anti-intellectualism, its distrust and dislike of book learning. I despise martinet discipline, the theory that you must break a man's will before he is any good as a soldier. I repudiate indignantly the practical assumption, so contrary to the facts and to all American political theory, that officers are a social elite and enlisted men canaille. I loathe the pervasive dishonest "soldiering" practice of the Army, the elaborate pretense of keeping men usefully employed when in fact they and their noncoms are hiding under the barracks. But out of the official inefficiency, stupidity, injustice, brutality, and (worst of all) boredom of the Army, no less than from its terrors, pains, degradations, and exhaustions, I learned that anything, literally anything, can be endured. The cries of hysteria and despair that have rung in my ears for close on to forty years now have seldom come from men who saw service in either world war. We don't believe that the human race is going to kill itself off. We know that man is tough and resourceful. The prospect of the future is bleak, but we shall squeak through.

But to return to what I was saying earlier. I felt guilty about being safe in a countryside where the guns only muttered; when I looked at those mangled young bodies, I didn't feel so much that war was evil as that in decency I ought to lose a hand or a leg. I'm afraid that to this day I'd rather have a Purple Heart (that decoration wasn't conferred in 1917–18) than any other honor or decoration whatever. But gradually the feeling of unworthiness wore off as I found that the wounded men themselves, the men who had unarguable proof that they had really been at the real front, had no scorn for any soldier who was doing his job anywhere, even if it happened to be behind the lines. They were skeptical and cynical like young men now—when do you think the word "profiteer" was invented?—and they would have returned you a ribald answer if you had asked them if they were fighting to make the world safe for democracy. But they sincerely thought they were, all the same, and they counted us their partners in the task. We thought so, too, and I think that most of us now, in spite of the disillusionment of fifty violent years, in spite of our shyness at even thinking such old-fashioned language, believe that our cause was just and, well, heroic. It is because of that that I feel no shame in saying that the war was for me personally a most valuable experience. Life is not fulfilled without intimations of the heroic; nothing else brings a man fully alive. I do not say that one must go to war to receive intimations of the heroic; I do report that the only memories I have that reflect even a gleam of the heroic are of my war years.

I was not engaged in any way in World War II, but I taught a great many veterans of that war, and I found that they went far beyond my generation in their inability to speak the unqualified language of martial valor. They would not tolerate Churchill's patriotic rhetoric, and they would not tolerate any patriotic poetry as quickly as possible. Yet there was something very positive in their whatever. Unlike us, they would not even let themselves *think* that they had fought to make the world safe for democracy. To them the war was a dirty, hateful, incomprehensible job that had to be done attitude: dirty and distasteful as the job seemed to them, and impatient as they were at any attempt to glorify it, they never doubted that it was a *necessary* job. And this unvoiced, unacknowledged acknowledgment of the call of duty (again those naked, embarrassing, old-fashioned words) substituted to a considerable extent for the glimpses of glory we experienced. Though my veterans of World War II spent three, four, even five years in service as compared with my scant nineteen months, I am sure that many of them would agree with me that no years of their life had been better invested.

As regards Korea and especially Vietnam, I would wish to speak very tentatively and uncertainly, for the situation rouses passionate feelings and I have access to no special source of wisdom. Certainly, many of our people now are denying both the heroism of the present conflict and the duty of any man to engage in it, and they would as certainly be very impatient with anyone who said he thought a man who went to Vietnam as a soldier would be making a good investment of his time. That angry impatience, that sense of intolerable frustration ready to flash into violence, makes one suspect something less than clear conviction, makes one wonder whether most of the people who feel themselves opposed to the war in Vietnam really know the fundamental cause of their opposition. The war in Vietnam, I would suggest, is mainly unpopular because it is a war with limited aims, a police action, and Americans do not identify with the police. Yet it is precisely in having achieved these unpopular limited wars—police actions—that many men of my age feel that the world has taken its first tottering steps out of an inveterate anarchy. Few of us were so saintly or so silly as to suppose that our war would end wars all by itself: it would end world wars as it caused the nations to scale down their armaments radically and combine to set up an effective international police force. If looting and arson start instantly in the cities of the United States when police power is withdrawn, it is fairly obvious that the international equivalent of looting and arson is going to occur in the absence of an international police force. And it is equally clear that the presently fumbling but incalculably precious idea of responsible international police action can be kept alive in our time only if the United States assumes the responsibility of furnishing most of the soldiers required for the next fifty years or so. The young in the United States today respond readily enough to a call to serve humanity which they recognize as such—witness the Peace Corps— but it is going to take a powerful surge of the will to make service in Vietnam seem to them service to humanity. The young men of World War II were spared this painful exertion; their dirty mess was dumped on them in the bombs at Pearl Harbor. Our young men of today must force themselves against instinct to take up this dangerous and distasteful job for the benefit of humanity, and they must do it unexalted by glimpses of the heroic and unconfirmed by the sense of responding to duty. But they can without shame expect that the years they spend at the job will be deeply rewarding.

Vera Brittain

"I was born when the nineteenth century was passing into the twentieth, and can just remember the war songs which the slouch-hatted soldiers sang as they marched to their deaths at Spion Kop or Magersfontein. Never, I suppose, has a generation of children been so heavily shrouded by the shadow of future events or so serenely unaware of its impending fate.

"I came from a typically unambitious Staffordshire family, the only daughter of a Midland small-town manufacturer with no interest in literature or learning. The ambition to go to college, which I developed while still at school, appeared to my family and neighbors to be extremely revolutionary. My provincial contemporaries wanted only to have a good time and marry early; their demands on their parents did not include the expenses of higher education. Eventually I was largely self-educated, went in for and passed the necessary examinations, and even landed an exhibition at Somerville College, then, as now, the most learned and intimidating of the Oxford women's colleges.

"Marriage in 1925 took me even further from my background, for when we met, my husband, Professor George Catlin, was assistant professor of politics at Cornell University and himself an exhibitioner of New College, Oxford. He was an early instance of the brain drain, for his subject was not then taught at his own university. His teaching at Cornell meant that our lives have been divided between England and the United States.

"Our son, John, has followed the family tradition by going in for business, but our daughter, Shirley, broke new ground by becoming a politician. Like myself, she took the Somerville College scholarship examination and became a history scholar. In 1948 she won a Smith-Mundt Fellowship at Columbia University and, on returning to England, immediately began to stand for Parliament. After fighting one by-election and two general elections, she became Labour M.P. in 1964 for the Hitchin Division of Hertfordshire. In 1966 she won the seat again with a 10,000 majority.

"That long step ahead of me was characteristic of our relationship, for—as my essay reveals—I belong to the 'breakthrough generation' of women who have transformed a track to the future into a highway for our successors to tread. My writings, especially the Testaments of Youth, Friendship, and Experience, describe this great creative adventure."

WAR SERVICE IN PERSPECTIVE

SINCE THE FIFTIETH ANNIVERSARY of the outbreak of the First World War, I have kept a pile of newspaper clippings beside me in a big folder. What do these clippings, collected from a large number of papers and magazines, emphasize from the impressions of numerous contributors?

First, I find a long section on the weapons of war, showing many varieties of protective device, from the gas masks developed out of the primitive protection of a wet handkerchief to elaborate helmets resembling a Martian face mask dreamed of in a science-fiction story by H. G. Wells. The clippings go on to give pictures of different types of shells, designs for experimental airplanes, and plans for the vulnerable zeppelins. Then come photographs of the terrifying tanks, which at first overwhelmed Britain's enemies by their strange monstrosity. Finally, by way of an anticlimax, we see pictures of London's terra-cotta-colored B type buses which proved ideal for the transport of troops in France.

Another bundle of clippings is devoted to the assorted war posters by means of which truth—"the first casualty in war-time"— gradually lost its integrity. This was achieved through the undermining of mental independence by emotional appeals which varied from representations of the Kaiser as an inventor of ingenious atrocities to the sentimental pictures of white-haired mothers urging their sons to fight. There followed a series of grotesque legends, which began with the story of the corpse factory in which the bodies of dead soldiers were said to be converted into explosives and went on to the tale of the entirely fictitious *Lusitania* Medal reported to have been struck at the Kaiser's suggestion and bestowed on the crew of the submarine which sank the *Lusitania* in 1915.

I still recall the contemporary reactions, including my own, to these crude but graphic appeals. Even in the eyes of an ingenuous girl recently out of school, most of them seemed just plain silly. Kitchener's finger pointing from numerous hoardings left me quite unmoved by its hysterical monotony. Though I was about to become a college highbrow, my responses to pressure, so untypical in most ways of the society in which I was brought up, were, I think, characteristic of the nation as a whole. Before the Second World War the patient work of such political research workers as Arthur Ponsonby—a founder of the Union of Democratic Control and Foreign Secretary in Britain's first Labour government, whose classic *Falsehood in Wartime* was published in 1928—had unmasked the most extravagant stories. These investigations left the British people imbued with a healthy skepticism which even the newer forms of propaganda, such as radio and television, failed to undermine. A comment made to me by a London workingwoman on the consequences of an air raid in 1944 must have been typical of many others: "I heard it on the B.B.C., so it can't be true."

From graphic examples of propaganda, my collection moves on to the numerous portraits of British war leaders—Haig, Plumer, Herbert Lawrence, William Robertson, all of whom looked well fed, substantial, and complacent. They make a gruesome contrast to the fragile wraith of bedridden Private George Oakley of the Middlesex Regiment, who enlisted at the age of eighteen and, when his picture was published, had spent forty-eight years in the Star and Garter Home for ex-servicemen at Richmond, Surrey. He was one of 28,000,000 men, wounded on both sides of the struggle, many of whom are still living a hidden death-in-life existence in servicemen's hospitals.

Other pictures show the gruesome litter of war amid the forests of black crosses in a German cemetery. One newspaper sent a special correspondent to travel round the former battlefronts and photograph whatever items of surviving debris seemed most worthy of record after fifty years. He came back with pictures, among many other things, of bent bayonets protruding from the earth at Verdun—a reminder of the men buried alive by bombardment as they waited to go over the top.

On the slope of what was once Hill 60 the breech of a machine gun lies slowly rusting away. In a private wood near Albert in Picardy, the ground is still thick with remnants of war: helmets and old boots, barbed wire and beer bottles, which lie undisturbed amid branches and brambles where they were left by departing British soldiers half a century ago.

From the nature study of war's somber remains, we move on to the special supplement of a historically minded editor who chose to commemorate the fiftieth anniversary of the war by pictures of the Archduke Franz Ferdinand and his family—a mild and well-intentioned man who did not deserve his fate of identification with the tragedy that sparked off four years of atrocity and mutilation. One cracked picture shows him with a brisk handlebar moustache in a bright blue uniform which seems to reflect the limpid color of the unferocious, philosophical Hapsburg eyes.

A "family portrait" brings back to life the plain, Teutonic Duchess Sophie and the three morganatic children—the handsome Maximilian, their elder son, who was mayor of Artstetten until his death in 1962; the second son, Ernst, who was sent to Dachau for five years by the Nazis and who died after his release; and Sophie, Franz Ferdinand's only daughter, an amiable-looking *Hausfrau* who is now the Countess von Nostitz-Rieneck and lives with her husband in a small villa at Salzburg.

As though by intentional contrast, the same magazine shows a grimacing art student in Munich listening to the proclamation of war from the midst of the crowd. It is Adolf Hitler, whose words from *Mein Kampf* are quoted:

My own attitude towards the conflict was both simple and clear. In my eyes it was not Austria fighting to get a little satisfaction out of Serbia but Germany fighting for her life, the German nation for its "to be or not to be," its freedom and future. It would have to follow in Bismarck's footsteps; young Germany must again defend what the fathers had heroically fought for from Weissenburg to Sedan and Paris. But if the struggle was to be a victorious one, our people would by their own force take their place again among the great nations, and then the German Reich could stand as a mighty guardian of peace, without the necessity to curtail its children's daily bread for the sake of this peace.

On the Third of August I addressed a petition to His Majesty King Ludwig III to be allowed to serve in a Bavarian regiment. The Cabinet Office during those days certainly had its hands pretty full, and my joy was all the greater when my petition was granted the same day.

Now began for me, as for every German, the greatest and most unforgettable period of my life on earth. Compared with the events of that mighty struggle, all the past fell into empty oblivion. I think with pride and sorrow of those days and back to the weeks of the beginning of our nation's heroic fight, in which kind fortune allowed me to take part.

Finally, I turned amid my press clippings to the reviews of some of the war books which recorded those years and were published between thirty and forty years ago. They bring back the names of some still-living authors whose work seems likely to endure, such as Edmund Blunden and Robert Graves. Among them I find an anniversary article in the London *Times* by no less a personality than its former editor, Sir William Haley.

Writing as Oliver Edwards, the pseudonym that he adopted for the literary articles that he contributed to the columns of his paper, he included an assessment of the books which were, in his view, the most memorable to come out of the First World War. In this article he described *Testament of Youth*, published by Victor Gollancz in London in August, 1933, and by the Macmillan companies of New York and Toronto shortly afterward, as "the war book of the Women of England."

This was not, perhaps, quite the tribute that it might have appeared, for relatively few women played an active part in the First World War. They were, on the whole, merely aides operating behind the various fronts. Such roles as they did fulfill were modest, subsidiary, and insignificant. War was a man's business. In 1914 the women who volunteered to serve as nurses with the Scottish Women's Hospitals in areas where qualified women of any description were extremely scarce were told by the Establishment to "go home and keep quiet." This was, it seemed, in masculine opinion the only useful thing that women could do.

Even after the war was over, women of relevant age were not regarded as having had any real contact with its realities. Some years after my own direct experience had ended, I came to know a cultured and critical young man named Roy Randall who wrote for several highbrow weeklies. His literary ambitions were unlimited, and he liked to discuss them with me. Occasionally, out of politeness, he referred to the modest free-lance journalism by which I was struggling to find a foothold in the writing world.

One day, much to my embarrassment, he asked me what work I hoped to undertake in the near future. I had then published two short novels and three unimportant little volumes of nonfiction and was living largely on the meager proceeds of my free-lance articles and book reviews. After three or four years of intimidated and spasmodic endeavor, I was also trying to draft the outline of *Testament of Youth* and did not want to disclose the ambitious character of this effort, which I knew that my companion would regard as extremely presumptuous. So when Roy pressed me for an answer, I replied vaguely that I was trying to do "a kind of autobiography."

His contemptuous reply was even more devastating than I had foreseen:

"An autobiography! But I shouldn't have thought that anything in *your* life was worth recording!"

This shattering judgment, though it shook my equilibrium, did not put me off my project. At that time I had served for four grueling years in London, France, and the Mediterranean and had seen my nearest and dearest contemporaries—lover, brother, and

two much-loved friends—hounded to death in the holocaust of a
male generation. But knowing that my appearance still suggested
that of a half-fledged university student I did not protest but merely
resolved with the more determination to record while light lasted
the events that I remembered.

When I related this conversation at a dinner with my near
contemporary Rebecca West and her husband, Henry Andrews,
Henry seemed disposed to agree with the skeptical Roy, but Rebecca, echoing my private thoughts, turned on him and said: "You
mean she's not a field marshal? But it's the psychological kind of
autobiography that succeeds nowadays, not the old dull kind."

The idea of a war book had come with the publication of
memoirs by some of the few male literary contemporaries who had
survived the war. It was also provoked by sheer perversity. I knew
well that no one expected a woman to understand anything about
war, much less to try to record it. But it must have come into my
mind soon after the first performance of R. C. Sherriff's *Journey's
End*—that famous swallow that was to make a summer—which I saw
with Winifred Holtby, the author of *South Riding*, when we realized that an electric atmosphere of reminiscent emotion had replaced the mere *succès d'estime* which we had both expected.

Soon after seeing the play and reading the too poignant published memoirs, I began to ask myself: "Why should these young
men have the war to themselves? Didn't women have their war as
well? They weren't all, as these men make them out to be, only
suffering wives and mothers, or callous parasites, or mercenary
prostitutes. Does no one remember the women who began their war
service with such high ideals or how grimly they carried on when
that flaming faith had crumbled into the gray ashes of disillusion?
Who will write the epic of the women who went to the war, and
came back leaving the bones of their men in the trampled fields of
France and amid the gray rocks of the Asiago Plateau?"

Could I, who had done nothing important yet, carry through
such a massive undertaking? With scientific precision, I studied the
memoirs of Blunden, Sassoon, and Graves. Surely, I thought, my
story is as interesting as theirs. Besides, I see things other than they
have seen, and some of the things they perceived, I see differently.

The kind of memoir that could be written only by a prime
minister or an ambassador, I believed with Rebecca West, was
ceasing to have much appeal. A new type of autobiography was
coming into fashion, which would represent the ordinary people of
the world upon whom wars were imposed. I wanted to make my
own story as truthful as history but as readable as fiction, and in it I

intended to speak, not for those in high places, but for my own generation of obscure young women.

Inspired by blind faith and the urgent need for reconciliation with the past, I began to collect and reread letters and memoirs and to try to assess the significance of my own adventures which Roy Randall had thought so trivial. I soon realized how typical they were—not so much in terms of women's experience, as of that of an entire generation. The details of our lives had naturally differed; there was clearly a great contrast at that date between the stories of men and women. But we all had experienced the tremendous revolution—one of the greatest in history—which carried the nineteenth century into the twentieth. It became my intention to attempt to estimate the apocalyptic quality of these changes which transformed forever the world into which my contemporaries and I were born.

A woman could perceive the picture as clearly as a man—perhaps more clearly, owing to the inevitably greater detachment which a woman's wartime insignificance gave her. Gradually now I began to perceive my "war book" as a vehicle for the picture of a vast age of transition, slowly becoming evident through the illuminating details which changed as each disastrous, tragic, and dramatic epoch merged into another.

Midway between the beginning and end of the war I had written to my brother in the trenches about the quality of our age. He was then on the Italian front and, though only twenty-one, was the kind of correspondent who understands everything. Such individuals are so rare that I have missed him all my life and still wish that I could refer to him some of the problems that I now have to face.

About the summer of 1917 I wrote to him: "I think that 'Before' and 'After' this war will make the same kind of division in human history as 'B.C.' and 'A.D.'" At the time this seemed an extravagant and even absurd assessment, but after half a century it does not seem to me that I was so far wrong in my estimate of that tremendous perspective.

The quality of the two titanic revolutions was, of course, quite different. The transition from the pagan to the Christian world meant a vast spiritual change affecting all human lives from the first century onward; it challenged existing values irrespective of whether those challenged understood the issues involved.

The changes created by the events of 1914 and the years immediately afterward were social and political, but they, too, were apocalyptic and fundamental. Mankind was never the same again after 1914, any more than it was ever the same again after the Crucifixion. Only those who recall, however dimly, the vanishing sunset splendor of the final Victorian years can estimate in their personal histories the quality of the transformation which the events of 1914 created for the much battered human race.

The normal experience of mortal life has been one of war and catastrophe. This was a fact very difficult to realize by the young of my generation. In spite of the tragedies and errors of the South African War—which are only now fully reaching realization in the spiritual bankruptcy of *apartheid*—our earliest memories, especially if we came from the ever-growing middle classes, are of prosperity and security. These ultimately proved as ephemeral as most varieties of good fortune, giving rise to such cynical obiter dicta as "Life is the predicament that precedes death." But at the time they seemed permanent—a fact that explains the contrast between the poets of the two war generations. The work of Sassoon and his near contemporaries was one long cry of protest precisely because they were the products of an exceptionally fortunate social era. When their Second War successors reached adulthood, the world had reverted to the normal human experience of frustration and disappointment, and the horrors of war casualties offered a less emphatic contrast with preceding events.

In the verses entitled "The War Generation: Ave," with which I opened Chapter 1 of *Testament of Youth*, I endeavored to put into words the innocent contentment of late Victorian childhood, especially among those born far from the influence of formative political events.

> In cities and in hamlets we were born,
> And little towns behind the van of time;
> A closing era mocked our guileless dawn
> With jingles of a military rhyme.
> But in that song we heard no warning chime,
> Nor visualized in hours benign and sweet
> The threatening woe that our adventurous feet
> Would starkly meet.

> Thus we began, amid the echoes blown
> Across our childhood from an earlier war,
> Too dim, too soon forgotten, to dethrone
> Those dreams of happiness we thought secure;
> While, imminent and fierce outside the door,
> Watching a generation grow to flower,
> The fate that held our youth within its power
> Waited its hour.

The belief that individuals were entitled to expect peace and happiness as their normal fate took so long to die that remnants of it still came to life even when the First War had been over for years. In 1939, when I took my son, then a boy of twelve, to his preparatory school for his first term, I happened to make a conventional comment to his headmaster about the misfortune for a child of having to begin his schooldays in a year when the unhappy history of my own generation was about to repeat itself in a series of dire events. The headmaster, a grave Quaker, mildly reprimanded me for the lack of historical perspective of which I seemed to him to be guilty.

"Think what it must have meant to start your education at the beginning of the Thirty Years' War!"

But for all its problems which affected our children as those of the First War did not, I have never been able to feel that September 3, 1939, presented a comparable cataclysm to that of August 4, 1914. The second date had been long foreseen, and though it heralded more and worse disasters which were to come closer to the comfortable British people than the cross-Channel terrors of the First World War, it lacked the same quality of shock. It was that sense of shock which, as it came into perspective, eclipsed all the other and more recent memories.

What does that date, August 4, 1914, immediately bring back to me? Not, certainly, the recollection of gunrunning in Ulster which so oddly preceded much greater anxieties, or yet the assassination of the Archduke Franz Ferdinand, though it was soon associated with macabre rumors that blood had been seen on the sun and moon. The immediate memories are purely personal and do not concern the statistics of world transformation, though I was to give so much attention to them later. The huge figures of the war casualties and the cost of war expenditure vanish in a phantasmagoria of human scenes and sounds. I think, instead, of names, places, and individuals and hear, above all, the echo of a boy's laughing voice on a school playing field in that golden summer.

And gradually the voice becomes one of many; the sound of the Uppingham School choir marching up the chapel for the Speech Day service in July, 1914, and singing the Commemoration hymn:

O Merciful and Holy
Who once by ways unknown
In simple hearts and lowly
Dost build Thy loftiest throne,
As Thou of old wast near us

To bless our Founder's care,
Bow down Thine ear and hear us
In this, Thy house of prayer.

There was a thrilling, a poignant quality in those boys' voices, as though they were singing their own requiem—as indeed many of them were. Among these were my brother, Edward, and his best friend, the prizewinning Roland Leighton, who had hoped to marry me and become a *Times* leader (editorial) writer, but instead found a lowly grave amid the white crosses which marked the Somme even before the great battles of 1916 were fought. But when the personal memories are, with difficulty, banished, it is the suddenness and shock of the whole event which remains with me longest.

Many years before the Great War, George Eliot, though she lived in one of history's calmest centuries, had prophetically visualized the situation of the war generation in her novel *Daniel Deronda:*

There comes a terrible moment to many souls when the great movements of the world, the larger destinies of mankind, which have lain aloof in newspapers and other neglected reading, enter like an earthquake into their own lives—when the slow urgency of growing generations turns into the tread of an invading army or the dire clash of civil war. Then it is that the submission of the soul to the Highest is tested and . . . life looks out from the scene of human struggle with the awful face of duty.

That "awful face of duty" sent the generation which had known no major war since their grandparents had fought in the Crimea into the interminable miles of trenches which stretched from the Ardennes to the North Sea or took them in the ships, great and small, which when they were sunk carried hundreds of young men— many of them midshipmen barely in their teens—into a cold anonymous grave without hope of rescue or the least understanding of the issue for which they had sacrificed their lives. They belonged to a sheltered human vintage for which occasional disasters, such as the sinking of the *Titanic* in 1912, were isolated reminders that tragedy existed. But no one, before 1914, expected it to come nearer, for smooth events had established the conviction that human happiness was normal and disaster exceptional; those to whom it happened were thought to be particularly unlucky.

To us, with our cheerful confidence in the benignity of fate, war was something remote, unimaginable, its monstrous destructions and distresses safely shut up, like the Black Death and the Great Fire, between the covers of history books. In spite of the efforts of a few percipient teachers who taught a generation of schoolchildren unaccustomed to read the newspapers to take an interest in at least the headlines, "current events" had remained unimportant just because they were national; they represented "subjects" that were habitually taught in classrooms but would never, conceivably, have to be lived.

What really mattered were not these public issues, but the absorbing incidents of our private lives—our careers, ambitions, friendships, and love affairs. And now, with the suddenness that George Eliot had described, the one had impinged on the other, and public issues and private lives had become bewilderingly inseparable. The significance of these events did not become clear until those who had suffered them began to write about them— which meant that they had to think about them. In some cases, as in my own, the thinking process lasted for years before it was decanted into words. And part of the process showed that *anyone* whom those years concerned was entitled to assess them—young or old, men or women. War was a human event, not a happening which affected one age or sex rather than another.

Yet if the whole comfortable generation had felt sheltered and secure, its women seemed to be especially cut off from reality. Their subservience was not a matter for discussion except by a handful of wild fanatics who had begun to make extravagant claims to equality and opportunity. The inferiority of women was accepted as part of the natural order of creation. The suffragettes, to the amusement of the unthinking public, began to make their vehement demands, less than a decade before the world changed forever.

As I was to realize many years later when, at long last, the war insisted on being put into words, the very detachment of women from the most direct forms of active service impressed on me once and for all the domination by war between 1914 and 1919 of even the most trivial aspects of everyday life. The war could not be escaped even by the most skillfully devised plays, books, and concerts. It permeated the arts; in my first year at Oxford the Bath Choir, which I had joined, gave a moving performance of the Verdi *Requiem* which haunts me to this day, and I still remember listening at Southwark Cathedral in July, 1916, to the Brahms *Requiem* which so poignantly coincided with the first day of the tremendous Somme battle. Even today the First War atmosphere is immediately brought back to me by the plaintive notes of Cowper's hymn "God moves in a mysterious way," so often sung at church services by congregations growing ever more anxious to be consoled and reassured.

The wearing anxiety of waiting for letters probably made all noncombatants feel more distracted than anything else in that sustained nightmare. Even when the letters came, they were at least four days old; the writers after sending them would have had time to die many times. This particular form of painful suspense, which had to be ignored on duty with as much resolution as the individual could muster, began for me when Roland Leighton went to the front as a boy barely twenty in March, 1915, and ended for me only in June, 1918, when my brother's death after that of Roland and our two dearest friends left me with no one else for whom to feel anxiety.

During the periods of waiting, especially when the newspapers, with inevitable vagueness, reported the imminence of a "great push," ordinary household sounds became a torment. The striking of a clock, marking off each hour of dread, broke into the immobility of tension with the shattering effect of a thunderclap. Every ring at the bell suggested a telegram, the only method of conveying urgent news before the days of radio and television; every telephone call implied a long-distance message giving bad news.

The extent of this torment naturally varied with both the quality of individual imagination and the measure of personal involvement. Probably I should never have been the only woman to contribute to this symposium had not my own involvement been so deep and so continuous. Even today, after fifty years, it still seems to me almost incredible that during those four years there actually were women who had no friends or relatives in the trenches or on the perilous seas, who were not perpetually waiting for messages of disaster. It is not surprising that many women developed an anxiety neurosis which lasted until the end of their lives.

To this constant dread was added, as the end of the fighting moved ever onward into an incalculable future, a new fear that the war would come between the men at the front and the women who loved them. Between 1914 and 1919 the war always did, putting a barrier of indescribable experience between the two sexes, thrusting horror deeper and deeper inward, linking the dread of spiritual death to the apprehension of physical disaster. When one of two dear friends was blinded at Arras in 1917 and sent to England to die in a London military hospital, I went to his funeral in Sussex, where his family lived. More bitter even than the sorrow of his death was my acute consciousness of England's uncomprehending remoteness from the tragic, profound freemasonry which united the men and, very rarely, the women who accepted death together overseas.

The women who served or only waited in the Second World

War, though they experienced fresh horrors and many other dangers, such as the V-1's and V-2's with their incalculable descents on undefended targets, were at least spared this fear of estrangement due to ignorance, for in this second onslaught of fate men and women alike shared the perils that threatened both sexes. In some countries, such as Germany, which endured the terror of saturation raids by British and American bombers, women faced greater risks than their men, who had at least better protection in the forces than in the barely defended small towns and villages in or near the major target areas, such as Kiel and Hamburg, and the vulnerable closely packed cities of the Ruhr.

I recall reading in a German newspaper quoted in England about 1944 of the distress experienced by a group of servicemen traveling on leave from the Russian front to their homes in Hamburg, then virtually extinguished by the merciless raids on civilian areas of 1942–44. Standing in the corridor of their train, these soldiers, who had been out of Germany for two or three years, were rendered almost speechless by seeing the ruins of their homes and "bowing before the sacrifice."

This meant that the experiences of the women of the First World War were, in fact, unique and probably could not now be duplicated by any woman in any war—irrespective of the certainty that no woman and no man would be likely to survive a major conflict at all. In such a conflict, as Shakespeare wrote in *The Tempest:*

> The cloud-capp'd towers, the gorgeous palaces,
> The solemn temples, the great globe itself,
> Yea, all which it inherit, shall dissolve;
> And, like this insubstantial pageant faded,
> Leave not a rack behind.

Assuming, meanwhile, that the menaced human race can count on a few more years of life on its insecure planet, the two wars, surprisingly, went far to solve the problems involved by women's social and political status, a matter with which I have always been deeply concerned. The myth of female inferiority has always been rooted in the contention that men die for their country but women do not. Now neither sex, except in very primitive societies, can do this with any expectation that their efforts will be effective against the colossal amoralities of dominant science. If any of us is to have a future on this earth, it must depend on man's ability to reconquer his power over the machine, which he yielded in the First World War.

When I finally went down in 1921 from the Oxford that, in spite of parental skepticism, I had first tried to enter in 1914 (winning an exhibition to everybody's astonishment, including my own), I was just in time to take part in the struggle for degrees for women, which Oxford granted twenty-seven years before Cambridge.

The war was often said to be responsible for the immediate postwar feminist reforms in Britain, and indeed it helped, in the sense that it did give women the opportunity to show that they could do what they had long claimed. These results would not, however, have achieved their purpose without the preliminary years of feminist spadework, ending in the spectacular protests of the suffragettes, who put the women's cause on the map.

But in a much deeper sense the two wars made the sexes equal, not merely because women proved that they could do the work of men (as they did), but because they could, and did, die the deaths of men. Thus, they shared the "supreme sacrifice," which made them equals in death as in life.

The implications of this immense social fact have still to be worked out in this second half of the twentieth century, which has sent so many women into key positions in public life and given them an equal share of such human experience as any of us alive today can hope to achieve.

Social-Historical Perspectives

Esmé Wingfield-Stratford

"*I was born on September 20, 1882. My father was Brigadier General C. V. Wingfield-Stratford, C.B. [Companion of the Bath]. I was educated at Eton and King's College, Cambridge, where I studied history under Oscar Browning, and in 1904 I took a research scholarship at the London School of Economics. In 1907 I was elected to a fellowship of King's, which I held till 1913. in which year I became a D.Sc. (Econ.) of London University. In September, 1914, I received a commission in the Q.O. Royal West Kent Regiment—which in the following month was sent out to India and in which I became a captain.*

"*In December, 1915, Miss Barbara Errington, daughter of Colonel and the Honorable Mrs. Errington, came out and married me in Bombay. We had one daughter, Roshnard, now Mrs. Norman Johnstone. When at the holy city of Multra, I was fortunate enough to be able to study the inner side of Hindu philosophy and religion under the auspices of Pundit Rai Bahadur Radhakrishna, not only one of the greatest of Brahmans but also a leading authority in archeology and all things Indian. I returned to England in 1919 and have ever since resided at Berkhampsted, pursuing my calling of author and historian.*

"*Between 1908 and 1964 I wrote thirty-six books—ten of history, including* The History of British Civilization *and my Victorian trilogy; five of biography, including my Charles I trilogy; one of autobiography; three on psychology; twelve on various aspects of political and social philosophy; two of poetry; and three novels. I am a believer in liberty raised to that highest plane on which it is identified with God's service; I am allergic to every sort and kind of ism from existential to Marx; I am a humble patriot of the Anglo-American Commonwealth of Free Nations; in theory I am a skeptic, and in practice I aspire to be a Christian.*"

WHAT REALLY HAPPENED

THE HIGH SUMMER of 1914 was to all outward appearance a time
of unprecedented and mounting prosperity for the nations of Europe. The replacement of animal by mechanized power was paying
fatter and fatter dividends to its human beneficiaries on the sole,
and what might have seemed the obvious, condition that it should
be directed to their common benefit and not to their mutual destruction; in other words, that the peace that had been kept for
forty-three years to the advantage of everyone concerned should
continue to be kept.

And yet, as they can testify who are old enough to remember that
glorious July, there brooded over Europe the same sort of almost
intolerable tension on the mental, as one gets on the physical plane
in the East before the monsoon clouds that have been packing the
sky more and more thickly from day to day discharge themselves
in deluge and thunder on the parched earth. It was no longer a
question of *whether* but of *when*. Those best qualified to judge
were surest that the unspeakable event was ripe, like a time bomb,
to detonate—old Admiral Fisher had even fixed the date for September, and his calculation might well have proved correct had
not a couple of shots fired in a remote Balkan town had the effect
of short-circuiting the mechanism.

But though the newspaper-reading public had been properly
shocked on hearing that the heir to the rickety Austrian throne
had got what he had been asking for, in the course of what appeared
to be a deliberately provocative visit to a notorious Balkan trouble
center,* he was not the sort of person likely to be missed by anyone,
least of all his senile and imperial uncle. It was a nine days' wonder
soon forgotten by those not actually in the know. None of the
ostensible danger signals was up. As in the days before the Flood,
ordinary folk went about their peaceful avocations until, without
warning, the thing happened, and these same people, with no
quarrel against each other or conceivable interest in the fate of
the ill-starred archduke, were rushing to arms in their millions as

---

* Though, as a matter of fact, it was with no more sinister object than that of
giving his poor morganatic wife a treat by allowing her to function as a real royalty.

if bitten by a common impulse of mutual extermination. And one asks why—need it have happened?

To answer that, we shall need to go back to another August just forty-four years previously, when the shabby adventurer who had jockeyed himself into the quasi-dictatorship of France was himself jockeyed by his Spanish wife and the Paris mob into picking a reckless quarrel with the new power that was in process of amalgamation in the center of Europe, under the iron rule of the Prussian Hohenzollerns, directed with consummate skill and economy of means by their Chancellor Bismarck.

Reckless most of all because it presented the Prussian commander Moltke, who had recently disposed of the Imperial Army of Austria in a matter of seven weeks, the opportunity to repeat the performance by a sort of fool's mate. For the French armies, hopelessly inferior in every respect, were strung out in what was in effect a fatal salient, which enabled Moltke to attack not from east to west but from north to south and, having overwhelmed the French force nearest the Rhine, to execute a gigantic right wheel, pivoting round the great fortress of Metz and presenting the main French Army with the choice of being shut up in it or getting out in time, which latter it attempted to do just too late. There was then nothing that the unhappy emperor, with his throne at stake, could do but march to its relief with the scratch force that was all that was left to him, and this Moltke, completing his wheel, duly rounded up against the Belgian frontier at Sedan. Thus, practically the whole French Regular Army had been effectually accounted for, and there was nothing that the new republican government could—or indeed wanted to—do but sue for peace on terms that would have put paid to any chance of outside interference with the formation and stability of the new Prussianized Reich. Had these been granted, this second Seven Weeks' War would have set the seal on a consummate triumph of military and diplomatic genius, a European peace that might well have lasted to this day.

Had the master diplomat only retained the artistry in dealing with fallen France that he had shown in dealing with Austria four years previously, when he had gone to the verge of resignation and even suicide to prevent the King and generals from turning a defeated opponent into a permanent enemy! Had he known then, as he did on every other occasion, when to stop! But whether he lacked the strength to stand out a second time or whether for this once he succumbed to the incurable Prussian itch for grabbing everything in reach regardless of consequences, he stooped to what his only comparable rival in the same field would have described as not only a crime but a blunder, in refusing to grant peace at any lesser price than that of tearing from the body of France the very two provinces that had constituted the fatal salient, thus not only prolonging the war by months of accumulating expense and hatred and planting a malignant tumor of irredentism in the body of his new Reich, but depriving Germany, in the now eventually inevitable second war, of the winning advantage she had enjoyed in the first.

It seems incredible that Moltke, of all people, who, backed by the rest of the military chiefs, had been the prime agent in insisting on this, should not have realized what a blunder—and a military blunder—they were perpetrating. But the inheritor of his post and tradition at the turn of the century, Count von Schlieffen, to whom war was as purely a matter of inhuman calculation as chess, rightly appreciated that France, no longer out on a limb as she had been in the last war, could now stand on a comparatively straight and heavily fortified defensive line that an invader would have to force by direct frontal attack, which was clearly contrary to the Moltkean strategy of envelopment. The problem was, therefore, to find a way around, and there being no such way *through* French territory, the count drew the logical conclusion that it would have to be through that of Belgium, an unoffending neutral whose neutrality had been explicitly guaranteed by Prussia. But in working out chess problems, one does not concern oneself with the sanctity of bishops or the honor of knights. The plan was accordingly docketed in the pigeonholes of the General Staff, which was incapable of thinking up any alternative, so that Germany was irrevocably, though secretly, committed to it in the event of war on one or more probably two fronts. Whether these purely technical calculations would ever have to be translated into action was a matter with which the count and the staff were in no way concerned—that would be for the supreme war lord and his ministers to decide.

But it was just about the time of Schlieffen's retirement that a gradual and fatal change began from the conditional to the imperative mood. As long as there had been a firm civilian hand on the controls of state, there had been no danger of their passing into those of the military. Bismarck had been no warmonger. It had been his object, once he had established his new Reich, to maintain it as a center of European gravity, a power, though inviolate, yet, as he put it, "saturated" and capable of imposing its peace on the whole system.

But after the neuropathic William II had gratified his power or inferiority complex by getting rid of him, his place was filled by a succession of mediocrities and charlatans, who were incapable of maintaining his policy or indeed of pursuing any consistent line of policy whatever. First, the liaison with Russia was allowed to lapse, and not content with France's having thus been presented with this incongruous ally, the Kaiser, backed by an easily inflamed Anglophobiac chauvinism, must needs be drawn into the suicidal folly of challenging the sea power of a Britain that desired nothing better than to cooperate with him in maintaining the Bismarckian peace. And thus, between bombast and jitters, Germany began to believe the self-created legend of her own encirclement, and the staff to base its plans on the assumption of not a hypothetical but an inevitable war, whose date it was, therefore, essential to fix at the moment of maximum relative strength, which, for a variety of reasons, would be not far from the late summer of 1914.

The archduke's murder, therefore, provided an ideal excuse for precipitating the desired event at the desired moment, and the royalty-obsessed Kaiser, by going into one of his periodical brainstorms and firing off hysterical messages that were taken only too seriously by a fribble of a Foreign Minister and a fire-eating Chief of Staff (in collusion with his own) at Vienna, had set in motion a European avalanche that it was beyond his, or any other ruler's, power to control. The plans for the mobilization and launching of the vast conscript armies began to function automatically, and even the staffs themselves, though capable of overriding their own governments, were powerless to modify or even to apply the brake to them. Too late did the supreme war lord, in a state of dithering despair at the prospect of the catastrophe he himself had precipitated, exchange frantic telegrams with the equally helpless autocrat of all the Russians. The Czar's order, and promise to Germany, to limit the extent of his mobilization was simply disregarded, and when the Kaiser pleaded with his own commander in chief at least to delay the transition from mobilization to actual hostilities, he was brusquely notified that the Schlieffen plan had got to run to its predetermined timetable, because the staff, having spent years in working it out to the last detail, could do no other.

That this included the rape of Belgium and thus a direct challenge to Britain on the plainest moral and political grounds formed no deterrent. Her military power, by German calculations, could be ruled out as negligible, and her sea power, as far as the land-minded staff planners appreciated it at all, they believed could be circumvented by the slight inconvenience of refraining from marching across Dutch, as well as Belgian, soil, thus leaving open a passage for German trade, impervious to British blockade. As for the moral aspect of this wrong that in the words of their own Chancellor they were doing, such considerations no more troubled them than they had their much belauded sage Nietzsche, who had proclaimed in one of his more lucid ebullitions that it is the good war—and not vice versa—that sanctifies every cause. But to Britain this aspect made the decisive difference. No one who remembers that time will forget the surge of horror and wrath that swept the country to the support of what was then spoken of as "Little Belgium," and an otherwise almost invincibly pacific majority in Cabinet and Parliament along with it, into a conflict in which there was never, for all its unforeseen length and agonies, to be the least question of letting up till that wrong at least had been righted.

It had been assumed by the experts who planned it, and was taken for granted by the propaganda-drunken masses, that this was going to be a war of battles and decisions in the old style, over, like the European ones of the mid-nineteenth century, in a matter of weeks or months. The military mind, whose nature it is always to think of the present in terms of the past, had utterly failed to appreciate the revolutionary change in the nature of warfare that a Polish banker called Bloch, at the *fin de siècle*, had accurately foretold, whether or not he had fully diagnosed its underlying causes.

War was, in fact, like industry, advancing at an accelerating pace toward a goal of total mechanization. Up to the present century it had been waged on a two-dimensional surface, and on land the mobile and, therefore, potentially decisive arm had been, as at Cannae and Blenheim, the mounted one, counterbalanced in various degrees by the mass and missile power of the footslogging infantryman. But in the new European conditions the horse had become a useless encumbrance, maintained at enormous expense of manpower and resources by commanders brought up in the cavalry tradition, always hoping for the chance that never came for it to resume its decisive function of mobility. But this, until a mechanized substitute could be created, was to reduce war to a tactical stalemate and a long drawn-out agony of attrition, since the man on two legs, if a smaller target than the beast on four, was another unmechanized anachronism, capable of being mowed down in such disproportionate quantities by the mechanized firepower of a properly entrenched enemy as to put any attacking force at a murderous disadvantage.

Had the military chiefs been capable of perceiving what had been so plainly set forth by a civilian financier, it is probable that the hordes of Germans, with their unmechanized transport and cavalry screen trudging the dusty August roads, could have been held up, and the Schlieffen plan stalemated, sufficiently near the frontier to make it possible for both sides, without loss of face, to cry quits and come to the conference table. But the French command, obsessed with notions dating from the third or even the first Napoleon, had thought up its own recipe for a quick victory, out-Schlieffening Schlieffen's, of a counteroffensive in Lorraine, in which hundreds of thousands of recently mobilized conscripts were driven forward to be as easily and cheaply exterminated as the Dervish masses had recently been in front of Kitchener's lines before Omdurman. This at least enabled a German supreme commander, whose only qualification for the post was that his name happened to be Moltke, to carry out the plan, which he was so little capable of understanding as fatally to compromise by depleting (in the teeth of its author's dying entreaty) its vital right wing, until it came up against the obstacle of fortified Paris. Here the Army commander on that flank, finding himself too weak to sweep round, according to program, swerved inward, throwing the whole vast enveloping movement out of gear. It was in vain that a motorized staff colonel went careening about behind the lines in the attempt to infuse some sort of order into this chaos of milling armies.

It was now the turn for the stolid French generalissimo, who had at least kept his nerve, to hurl all the remaining Allied forces he had been able to rally or rush up on the now exhausted and bewildered invaders, in a confused counteroffensive that caused them to recoil from the line of the Marne to that of the Aisne, on which they had the sense to dig themselves in and present their pursuer with the *ne plus ultra* of a mechanized defensive. It now only remained, in a mutual outflanking competition, to prolong the double line of entrenchments to a point on the seacoast as far forward as possible from each combatant's point of view, in the course of which the British Regular Army, in a heroic and successful attempt to keep this to the east of the Channel ports, came not far short of annihilation.

Such was the upshot of the so-called Battle of the Marne, hailed at the time, as it has been ever since, as a great and decisive Allied victory, which it may have been in the sense of averting the complete knockout of France envisaged by Schlieffen and actually brought off under Hitler's auspices in 1940. But the plan had all the same scored a win on points that might easily have meant a decisive balance of advantage, in the long run, for the invaders. For the double trench line from Switzerland to the sea had been so drawn as to leave behind it on the German side practically the whole of Belgium and the most highly industrialized region of France.

So the fatal but foreseen competition was set of bleeding to death behind the lines for as many years as it would take for the first of the multinational leviathans to reach the point of total collapse. In the west the Germans had only to sit tight on their gains to compel the Allies to waste their manpower and resources in a series of disproportionately bloody attempts to dislodge them, while in the east they were free to match their incomparably superior mechanical weapons against the vast superiority of Russian manpower, backed by the invasion-swallowing spaces into which the still unbroken lines were pushed back in an agony of expansive, instead of comparatively static, attrition. This war of the trench line was plainly developing into the most prolonged and massive exercise in collective suicide on human record up to that date.

And yet what might have seemed the obvious idea of saving millions of lives, by desisting from a course so plainly fraught with loss and misery beyond computation to all parties concerned and concluding a peace on the basis of the *status quo ante* with perhaps a few commonsense mutual adjustments of outstanding grievances, was hardly broached. Even the suggestion would have been accounted treasonable. The Germans were more even than in 1870 obsessed by the doctrine of "what I grab I hold"—or do not let go without a multiple *quid pro quo*. The French, after a slight initial penetration, were almost equally obsessed with the desire to recover their lost provinces, while with England the righting of the wrong done to "Little Belgium" had become more of a moral imperative than ever.

So by common consent this agony of the trench lines and of the populations behind them was to go on as interminably as the hell it was. A vast literature has been produced in the attempt to bring it into line with other wars by highlighting its so-called battles by such impressive names as Loos, Verdun, the Somme, and Passchendaele, and a fashion has been set of blaming it all on the Allied commanders—the catchphrase being one attributed to Ludendorff of "lions led by donkeys"—though hardly, on the same reckoning, such colossal superdonkeys as its author. But granted that imaginative genius is not—and certainly was not then—a quality fostered by military training, it is hard to suggest what genius itself could have done to break the deadlock on the western front, while for the Allies just to have given up trying and sat pretty in their trenches would have left the Germans free to concentrate all their resources on a Russia that, even before the war, had been so ripe for revolution that it has been plausibly asserted that only the war could have postponed it as long as it did.

The inexorable fact of the situation, as it was in 1914, was that until a mechanized substitute could be evolved for the obsolete cavalry and the obsolescent infantry, the defensive, under such conditions as those on the western front, could take a disproportionate and murderous toll of any direct attack—and on that front no other sort of attack was possible.

It was a facile lead to urge that the alternative to forcing a way through was to find a way around, by striking a dislocating blow at some point away from the main European fronts. What seemed the most promising of several attempts to find such a short cut to victory was sponsored by the First Lord of the Admiralty, Winston Churchill, a man conspicuously endowed with the creative energy that is the essential of genius, but less so with that coolness of judgment that Napoleon desiderated as the first quality in a commander.

His idea was to knock out of the war Germany's latest ally, Turkey, which might never have come into it had not the Admiralty in the first instance allowed one of the most up-to-date enemy warships to slip through its fingers and get to Constantinople. To force the maritime approach to that city through the Dardanelles by a combined naval and military coup, while the Turk was off his guard and his main forces otherwise engaged, would have been almost certainly feasible, though that this would have led to the fall of Constantinople, or even to the collapse of Turkey, or have enabled the Allies to have averted that of Russia by supplying her armies with the munitions of which they themselves were notoriously short for their own armies, is mere wishful assumption. But it would doubtless have been a point in the game worth scoring.

But it is one thing to think up an idea in the abstract, and another to apply the necessary means of realizing it, and an operation that, if undertaken at all, demanded the utmost speed, secrecy, and all-out concentration stands on record as a supreme example of their exact opposite. It was made the subject of prolonged debate between civilian ministers, of dispute between rival commanders, and friction between allies, ending in that most fatal of all martial solutions—a compromise, and the almost insane one at that, of trying to force a collection of obsolete warships through the bottleneck of the strait, without breaking the neck of the bottle with the comparatively small number of troops that would then have been required to occupy their enclosing shores. Under these circumstances it was perhaps fortunate that an unswept minefield sent four of these expendible crocks to the bottom, thus preventing the rest from achieving the success of the lobster in thrusting himself into the pot.

It was then that the British command bethought itself of saving face by the use of troops, and a scratch force of such units as could be spared was got together in Egypt, and this, even when it at last got to sea, had to put back to port because the improvised staff had so bungled the loading of the equipment that the whole job had to be done again. By this time even the tardy Turk had turned the Gallipoli Peninsula into an almost impregnable fortress, and it was only by a miracle of heroism that such as survived of the attackers managed to obtain a precarious lodgment on the beaches, leaving the Turks ensconced on the heights above them, and themselves, instead of bypassing the agony of the trenches, stuck fast in another and worse one.

The culminating act in this tragedy of blunders was that when, at long last, fresh forces were sent out to surprise the unoccupied heights behind the Turkish position and had made an unopposed landing, the men were turned loose to disport themselves in the waters of the blue Aegean, while their amiable, but unblooded, commander remained on board for his afternoon siesta, and the future dictator, Kemal, was rushing up every man he could lay hands on to secure the heights that might have been had that afternoon for the British asking. Next morning it was too late, and another force was added to those stuck fast on the beaches. The only success achieved in the whole miserable business, which brought down the last Liberal government and seemed likely to end the career of its still undiscouraged promoter, was the unexpectedly bloodless evacuation that wound it up, though only after it had cost some half a million futile casualties.

The war was now fixed inexorably in its predicted deadlock of attrition, and to that of bloodletting was added starvation, as the stranglehold of sea power came cumulatively into play. Britain's rule of the waves, or rather the surface of them, was confirmed only after a major fleet action in which the German Fleet, having scored most of the ostensible points and having got back to port unintercepted by an overwhelmingly superior British one, remained there as effectively immobilized as if it had been sent to the bottom or worse, as the idle crews became ripe for the mutiny that precipitated the final collapse.

But in the old two-dimensional war, and even after such a decision as Trafalgar, blockade had been a two-way process, and now the idea had dawned on the Germans of conducting it in three dimensions, by the employment of submarines. This was the most deadly threat that Britain had ever experienced, as with her ruined agriculture and disproportionately urbanized population, she was utterly dependent for her daily bread on supplies from overseas.

And the German submarines, continuously reinforced, had taken to haunting the trade routes and coming up to the surface to torpedo the ships that were bringing it. This presented at the same time a dazzling prospect of Germany's starving Britain out of the war and a temptation for her suicidally to overplay her hand by bringing an even mightier antagonist into it.

It was only the pachydermatous obtuseness of her Prussianized power complex that could have led Germany into the colossal blunder of forcing on Britain a conflict that could hardly fail, eventually, to involve all those white communities who shared her heritage of language and tradition, irrespective of membership in her grotesquely misnamed Empire. It needed such a shock to put into reverse—even for the "duration"—the indurated habit of the two chief of these regarding one another as alien and potentially hostile powers, instead of partners in defense of a common and evolving tradition of liberty which transcended all national differences and upon whose maintenance, in face of the total sublimation of the will to power that threatened to engulf it, the future and even the survival of human civilization depended.

It was all a question of whether, at this hour of supreme crisis, Britain and the United States would sink their differences in the realization of this overmastering unity and common trusteeship. The idea that Britain could have remained in even formal association with her transatlantic colonies during the conquest, development, and repeopling of their vast hinterland is fantastic. One service, even if the war of mutual independence had never been fought, could she have been capable of rendering, and that she did when, in the early 1820's, she called—in the words of the greatest of her Foreign Ministers (Canning) —"the new world into existence to redress the balance of the old" by interposing the veto of her then unchallenged sea power between the two hemispheres, thus denying the Western to imperialist exploitation, and giving the basis of permanency to the doctrine that would otherwise have passed for no more than a gesture of rhetorical bravado by a somewhat dim American President.

This effect of a sea power, which America would in due course be able to provide for herself, was what it had been on Britain in the critical phase of *her* development: It made her for all practical purposes an invasion-proof island, free to shape her destinies in her own way of constitutional freedom. Not all the accompaniments of that process were the most edifying, but they did not include the tyranny of autocratic or imperial discipline which is the lot of those who are conditioned to a struggle for existence over open land frontiers. America's isolationism was not only a product but a sublimation of British insularity, and it was but natural that her almost unanimous belief should have been that it was incumbent on her to hold aloof from, and make such profit as she could out of, a war between the contending military and imperial powers of the Old World, among whom owing to an agelong accumulation of bitter memories and misunderstandings, she did not hesitate to include Britain.

For a time it worked. Neutrality not only satisfied her moral consciousness, but rewarded virtue by even more satisfactory dividends. So long as British overseas assets lasted, they were mopped up by American industry in a spending orgy, and when these ran out and the creditor became the debtor nation, the process was continued by dint of ever-mounting loans that it was plain to see gave the lender a vital stake in the solvency and, therefore, the survival of the debtor, whom defeat would plainly turn into a total defaulter. Thus, the effect of Britain's control of the sea routes was to harness the gigantic resources of American industry to her own war effort, which in a war of attrition had all the effect of an alliance short of actual belligerency. Not that American industry would have been loath to double its profits by supplying both combatants impartially with the means to destroy each other, but this, in spite of the bottleneck, so conveniently left open, of neutral Holland, the British blockade, applying America's own Civil War doctrine of the continuous voyage, was geared up to prevent. And to her inevitable and formidably worded protests, Britain continued to react, as tactfully as might be, to the principle that "sticks and stones may break my bones, but words can never hurt me." For indeed the deep heart of American public opinion was already being penetrated by the certainty that, however desirable it might be to keep out of the war, to throw her weight into it *against* Britain would spell moral even more than material suicide. And they judged but superficially who imagined her to be solely swayed by the cult of the dollar, and ignored the deeper impulse of moral idealism that was embodied in no one more representatively than her own President, Woodrow Wilson, though he, like that other idealist avatar Mahatma Gandhi was a more mixed human product than either his fans or debunkers have given him credit for, his idealism being tempered by unpredictable infusions of professorial donnishness and party gamesmanship.

But the genuine and not ignoble desire to keep the United States in proud and peaceful detachment from the jarring imperialisms and power politics of the Old World was frustrated by an irresistible propaganda applied with Teutonic thoroughness by Germany.

From the first, she lost no opportunity of rubbing it in that she stood for everything that the American nature most hated. The stopping and searching of American cargoes bound for neutral ports might be irritating to the last degree, but not shocking and horrifying like the rape of Belgium and the shooting of a British nurse—consoled in her last moments by an American chaplain. Such imponderables could not fail to build up a highly unflattering image of the Kaiser-christened Hun—but when it came to what was regarded as the cold-blooded murder of American citizens on the high seas and the deliberate restaging of the tragedy of the *Titanic* in that of the *Lusitania*, with the loss of 112 American lives, the patience of Wilson himself became strained to the verge of breaking point, and despite some hardly plausible verbiage about being too proud to fight, he did put his foot down with sufficient firmness to extract an undertaking that the sinking of unarmed ships by submarines should be stopped from now on.

But for *how* long in face of the perennial Prussian practice of grab all and concede nothing and the virtually uninhibited sway that the military command had acquired over the civil power? The agony of the trench lines had risen to a climax to which there seemed to be no prospect of a denouement. Bigger and bloodier offensives continued to be mounted in which the flower of European youth suffered itself to be immolated in the exchange of a few acres of churned mud. Behind the lines the hundreds of thousands of war-horses continued to munch their fodder, and only a mild sensation was caused by the appearance of a few British units of mechanized cavalry, inappropriately called tanks, in such scanty numbers and to so little effect as to excite the easily aroused contempt of the hard-bitten German commanders. But behind the lines the strain of not only bloodshed but privation was beginning to tell even upon the patient populace of the fatherland. The stranglehold of sea power was gradual, but cumulative, in its effects. And patience was not the strong suit of the Hindenburg-Ludendorff combination that had now come, in an aura of fanatical hero worship, to embody the German will to victory. Though landsmen, they had convinced themselves that their submarine blockade was capable of throttling Britain in a matter of weeks if applied with out-and-out rigor and that the unmilitary Americans, in the doubtful event of their ever getting from words to deeds, could be brushed aside with as much contempt as the tanks. They, therefore, decided to take the plunge of causing Germany to announce in effect that she would repudiate her promise to Wilson and send every American ship and citizen that her submarines could come by to Davy Jones.

This would have seemed the limit of provocation, but it would have taken nothing short of the Prussianized mentality to think up the colossal *gaffe* of sending a message, which the British Intelligence duly intercepted and publicized, to the Mexican, of all governments, offering German backing for grabbing back those portions of her territory that had been embodied in the United States in the middle of the previous century. A ludicrously impracticable suggestion in itself, but the plainest possible intimation that in the event of a German victory and the consequent annihilation of British sea power, the Monroe Doctrine would go up in hot air, and German ambition, having triumphed in Europe, would extend its talons westward to make nonsense of any dream of a New World safer for democracy than the Old.

For indeed the German war lords had done, just in time for their enemies, what they were incapable of doing for themselves. They had gambled, and gambled against an eventual certainty. They had torpedoed not the last British food ship, but the last hesitation even of President Wilson about putting the full force of American belligerency behind the Allied war effort. And in so doing, they had exchanged what, if they had only had the self-restraint to bank on it, was not far short of a winning advantage in a European war for the almost certainty of defeat in a world war.

For in the war of attrition it was becoming more and more of a probability that it was Britain's European allies who would come to the breaking point before Germany. The series of holocaust offensives that they were practically compelled to launch as long as the enemy remained entrenched on their soil, though the comparative figures are to this day widely disputed, must, by their very nature and pending the advent of a mechanized mobile army, be more prodigal of blood to the attacking party. All were feeling the strain to the verge of the mortal limit, but the first to break under it was not Germany, though the gamble of her neutral-drowning blockade had failed, by the narrowest of margins, to come off. For not only did Lloyd George, a far more capable war leader—though of very different moral caliber from Wilson—who had jockeyed himself into the premiership, force the winning card of the convoy system on the British admirals, as he had previously forced a sufficiency of machine guns on the generals; but with America no longer too proud to fight, there was no more nonsense about the freedom of the seas. The blockade was applied with a ruthlessness that made strange reading of her previous notes of protest. Not only was her grip tightening mortally on Germany's throat—or rather stomach— but her aid and comfort were now extended to the full relief of Britain's necessity, both naval and economic.

It was high time. For hardly had America come into the war than the event happened that ought, by all previous reckonings, to have tipped the scales decisively in Germany's favor. The revolutionary forces that had been gathering beneath the surface of Russian life now erupted with spontaneous violence and swallowed up the bedlam autocracy of the unhappy Nicholas II. The event was hailed at first with joy by her allies as a sort of democratic rebirth—but the removal even of the craziest keystone from its supporting arch was fatal to the structure of imperial authority on which the Russian war effort depended. The patient Ivan Ivanovich, deprived of his Little Father, was no longer content to be driven, in his millions, to the slaughter. Authority had departed from the administration, and fighting spirit from the Army. And the Germans, little realizing the nemesis they were invoking on themselves, clinched the matter by smuggling into Russia an agitator of genius, who in due course, under a smokescreen of ideological verbiage, set up in his own person a Red czardom more ruthless than the White had been since the days of Ivan the Terrible and who had not the least idea of honoring Russia's pledges to either allies or creditors. Thus, her seemingly inexhaustible resources of manpower, which, on a count of heads, had made up more than half the Allied war potential, were wiped off the slate.

Nor was this all, for in this same year, 1917, the French Army missed by the narrowest of margins going the way of the Russian. A new offensive by a new general, who had an infallible recipe for effecting the long deferred breakthrough, was launched with every circumstance of suicidal publicity and petered out in the usual bloody fiasco. The French Army, paralyzed by mutiny, was on the point of going the same way as the Russian. But it was Hindenburg and Ludendorff, of all people, who let slip their supreme opportunity, and a French commander, who was subsequently to die in confinement as a traitor to France, stopped the rot, thereby rendering her no less a service than Joan of Arc. And as if that were not enough, the Italian Army, which having come into the alliance as the result of Italy's having put up her services to auction and launched the usual series of fruitless offensives on the Austrians, turned tail on the appearance among them of a few German divisions and was only rallied on the Piave by the rushing up of Anglo-French supports that could be ill spared from their own front.

By the beginning of 1918 the military forces of the original alliance seemed plainly incapable of driving the Germans off their soil or of getting them to discuss any terms of less abject surrender than those that they had already demanded from Russia and that

the wily Lenin had not hesitated to concede in all their preposterous totality, leaving the Prussian Gargantua to expand to
bursting point in the effort to digest his vast meal of annexed
territory—a process that used up the greater part of the forces that
would have been otherwise available to be switched over to his now
only remaining militant front.

Even so a sufficiently formidable addition was expected in the
spring to convince Ludendorff that he had only to go over to an all-
out offensive to make the Allied western front go the way of the
eastern, before the half-baked American forces could arrive—if they
did at all—in sufficient numbers to intervene. The French morale
was, to say the least of it, doubtful, and though, to the eternal honor
of the British soldier, his had shown no signs of wilting after the
cruelest of all the offensive holocausts in Flanders mud, which
would have broken the spirit of any other army. But the murder-
ously thinned British lines were stretched still thinner by the need
for taking over yet another sector of the joint front from their
almost exhausted allies.

It was here that Ludendorff struck with all the gathered might of
his reinforced armies, using the element of surprise that had been so
strangely neglected in previous offensives. Germany, her internal
economy strained nearer and nearer to collapse by the blockade,
was out for the kill, and as blow followed blow, the Allied lines
went reeling backward in what by all previous standards would
have counted for a shattering series of defeats. At one point, when
the objective was a hill supposed to be of vital strategic importance,
Field Marshal Haig made his historic appeal to the defenders to put
their backs against the wall and fight to the last, which even so did
not prevent the enemy from accomplishing the feat ascribed to the
Grand Old Duke of York of marching up the hill.

All through the spring and into the height of the summer the
devastating process continued, and what Ludendorff had accomplished was precisely this—he had caused his victorious hordes to
quit their almost impregnable lines, and get themselves killed at
last on a scale proper to the offensive, in a gigantic battle of the
bulge that never bulged quite far enough to cover any objective of
strategic significance but caused them to extend their new lines like
stretched elastic nearer and nearer to snapping, while behind, their
communications ran over a conquered wilderness of mud and ruins.
And still Ludendorff went on, confident that every new blow would
be the last, or the last but one.

And then, as he drove his weary infantry on to punch a fresh dent
into the bulge, he was struck in the flank by a charge of the new

mechanized cavalry that the French Army had at last acquired. And—what was of even more ominous significance—American troops, the first of millions to follow, took an active and enthusiastic part in the proceedings. Ludendorff, sent reeling back, re-formed his front, confident that he had a winning card up his sleeve in a knockout offensive on the already sorely tried British. But the British got in first with the new arm, to such effect that Ludendorff himself spoke of the "black day of the German Army" and felt in his heart that its game was up. So from the opposite point of view did Haig, who, alone among the Allied high commanders, believed that the way was open to victory before the end of the year. A way not of massed breakthroughs, but of swift concentrated attacks on one part of the enemy line after the other, each pressed just far enough to gain the full advantage of the initiative, and no farther. As one black day for the German Army followed another, and as the new army out of the west swept in ever-mounting strength into the Allied counteroffensive, the subconscious foundations of German morale became impalpably undermined. Their armies fought on with a desperation that was no longer quickened by hope. And Haig, who had sustained such bloody frustration in previous offensives, but now seemed to have found the inspired touch, judged that the moment had come for an all-out frontal assault on the enemy's strongest position, the famous Hindenburg Line, and, with his new mechanized arm employed to the limit, succeeded in forcing it.

That was the decision. There was even now no breakthrough, no pursuit in the old pattern. It could be argued that the Germans were capable of standing indefinitely on a shorter line and holding up the now exhausted Allies *sine die*. But, in boxing parlance, this latest blow had knocked the stuffing out of them. It had already been knocked out of their allies, who anticipated them by collapsing one after another—even the poor old horse had his last martial gallop in pursuit of the once unbudgeable Turk. Under these circumstances even Ludendorff lost his nerve and began to talk of seeking terms, and though he wanted to return to his former intransigence, the spell—like the spellbinder—was broken.

The ordinary German, whatever else he was, was no fool. He could read the writing on the wall as plainly as any man. Even if he could hold out till next spring, his family would be sinking to deeper and deeper extremes of misery, and next year he would be invaded from all sides, and with the American Army swollen to millions his collapse would be certain. Whereas, as matters stood, the soil of the fatherland was, unlike that of the countries he had ravaged, intact, and the permanent damage it had sustained was proportionately less. And now terms were offered him, not such as he had, and would have, imposed on a defeated enemy or even such as his European enemies would have imposed on him, but based on principles of philosophic impartiality formulated by the American President, who spoke with a voice of sufficient authority to obtain at least the formal subscription of his cobelligerents. What it plainly amounted to was that Germany had only to lay down the arms that rendered her a universal menace, set free the peoples she had enslaved, make good as much as possible of the damage she had wantonly perpetrated, and retire within her natural frontiers to cultivate her garden in peace. This was better than the whipped, but unrepentant, German had dared to hope for. Nothing could stop him now—first his fleet mutinied; then all his extravagantly belauded ruling caste of emperor, kings, princes, and panjandrums of all sorts of fantastic designations were consigned, by one sweep of the revolutionary broom, to the rubbish bin. The terms of surrender that Marshal Foch demanded and that even Haig had feared would prove too tough a morsel were greedily swallowed, and the German Army quietly dissolved, in the proud conviction that it had never been beaten, but only, somehow, betrayed—it would in due course be apprised by whom.

That this almost unhoped-for victory should have been greeted by the civilian populations of the winning side with orgies of hysterical jubilation was no more than human; but how much of a victory it would prove to be, and for how long, would depend on whether the victors could show a wisdom in framing a peace proportionate to their valor in winning the power to frame it.

The principles on which that peace was to be framed, and to which the honor of the victors was explicitly committed, Wilson had defined with an explicitness befitting the most outstanding example of a philosopher-statesman since Marcus Aurelius, and its objective he had sufficiently indicated as that of "a world safe for democracy," coupled, perhaps, with the phrase coined by the English Premier of "a war to end war." And had they and their peoples been capable of rising to the height of their all too fleeting opportunity, who can say that even this might not have been attained and safeguarded for as long as could have been humanly foreseen?

But Lloyd George, at that moment, had other fish to fry and was stumping the country whipping up the basest passions of the victory-drunken mob in order to secure his triumph at the general election he had lost no time in precipitating, and Wilson had already fatally compromised the hero's part for which he had cast himself in the tragic drama of world peacemaking by doubling it with that of political gamester, thereby alienating, instead of drawing into the common effort, the bosses of the rival faction in a contest that was itself a product and symbol of American isolationism and had hardly more basis of intelligible principle than that of the blues and greens in the circus of Byzantium.

He came to Europe—the first reigning President to do so—amid the thunder of a hero's ovation of record-eclipsing expectancy. After which preliminary flourish the delegates of the victor powers settled down to the practical task of formulating the terms to be imposed on the vanquished, and the tragedy moved with Sophoclean inevitability to its denouement.

The visionary idealist was, by the very integrity of his pursuit of a reformed world order, no match at their own game for the hard-bitten realists of nationalist diplomacy; but he clung with invincible persistence to his vital point of a supernational League, though at the price of abandoning one after another of the points and principles which he had so meticulously formulated and on the strength of which the enemy had laid down his arms. But he had at least obtained the consent of the French to drop Marshal Foch's demand for the permanent occupation of the Rhine line as a *sine qua non* of national security by pledging America and England to guarantee the now restored French frontier of 1870. He clung with a pathetic faith to the belief not only that he had averted the danger of a second world conflict but that, when the passions inflamed by the first had had time to cool, the League, enlarged by degrees to world-wide dimensions, would be capable of smoothing out the disproportions and injustices of the only peace that, *faute de mieux,* he could get agreed to by the Allies and imposed on an enemy now hardly less ready to sign the most outrageous demands on the dotted line. Thus, the steadfast President had got his way on his main point of an American-imposed, and what no one doubted to be an American-guaranteed, United States of the World, with the power to perpetuate its own peace.

There had been a textbook of comparative politics prescribed in at least one English university at the beginning of the century and designated by the name of its author, Woodrow Wilson, from which it might have been gathered—what its author seems to have forgotten—that an American President has power only to conclude a treaty, subject to its endorsement by two-thirds of the Senate. And now that body, swayed by the faction that Wilson had gone out of his way to alienate and subordinating all other considerations to the party game, lost no time in jettisoning the whole treaty, League and all, and returning to its vomit of prewar "normalcy." Wilson, holding fast to his own integrity and with tragic confidence in his power to carry the people over the heads of the politicians, broke under the strain and lingered on as a paralyzed and slowly dying invalid—even so fated to survive the bewildered nonentity who, as his successor, was to serve as figurehead and victim of a saturnalia of graft and corruption eclipsing all previous records.

In the atmosphere of victory-drunken intoxication which was the equivalent of normalcy among America's now deserted allies, no one was specially bothered by this latest ebullition of transatlantic cussedness or appreciated its real and fatal significance of another and worse war in the next generation, renewed under circumstances incomparably less favorable than those of 1914. Germany, though down and out for the moment, was still substantially intact, and nothing had been done to get Prussia off her back—or perhaps could have been, short of wiping Prussia off the map, by exterminating and expelling part of her population and enslaving the rest, an idea that would have excited incredulous horror *then*, but might not always.

The American action had, in fact, not only prepared the way for the next war, but ensured the worst of all possible peaces. The French rightly felt themselves double-crossed, now that the guarantee of their frontier, which they had purchased at so great a price, had gone up in smoke, and were determined to stick at nothing to recoup themselves. The Germans had been no less defrauded in the terms of a peace bearing no relation to the terms on which they had been induced to surrender. Even Britain, bilked of the vast sums she had advanced to her European allies, was held by her American ex-ally to the uttermost farthing that in the hour of her need had been advanced to her. "They hired the money, didn't they?"

Those whom God wishes to destroy He first makes mad, and this is not the place to describe the utter blindness to reality that was to render the story of the interwar years, with its alternation of blind hopes and paralyzed impotence, a case history of collective lunacy. Those who had just emerged from the war were too much in a state resembling shell shock to bother about the future.

Typical, it might have been thought, of these was one humble member of the German Army who had ended up a half-blinded casualty. A good soldier, but a modest and singularly unambitious one, to judge from his having gained the highest distinctions for valor without ever rising above the rank of corporal. A model soldier, indeed, of incorruptible austerity and a freedom from the common human weaknesses that have characterized not a few budding saints. His father had been called Schicklgruber but had changed his name for that of Hitler.

George E. G. Catlin

One of the most influential political theorists of the modern age, George E. G. Catlin was born on July 29, 1896, the son of the late Reverend George E. G. Catlin, sometime Vicar of St. Luke's, Kew Gardens, Surrey, and of the late Mrs. Catlin, née Orton. He was educated at St. Paul's School and at New College, Oxford, where he was an exhibitioner in modern history in 1914. Graduating from the Oxford Modern History School cum laude, he received the Lothian Prize in 1920 and went on to be a Gladstone Prizeman and a Matthew Arnold Memorial Prizeman at Oxford in 1921. In 1925 he married Vera Brittain. From 1924 to 1936 he was professor of politics at Cornell University, and became acting head of the department in 1928. He was Bronman Professor of Political Science at McGill University from 1956 to 1960.

A lecturer at universities on three continents, Mr. Catlin has been a Goethe Bicentenary lecturer at Heidelberg University; lecturer in the Peking, Cologne, and Bologna universities; Weil lecturer (University of North Carolina); and Walker Ames lecturer (University of Washington). He is also vice-president of the World Academy of Art and Science (Israel). Among his honors bestowed by many countries are Commander, Grand Cross Order of Merit (Germany); Miembre de Honor, Instituto de Estudios Politicos (Spain); medalist, Societé à l'Encouragement au Progrès (France). His publications include The Science and Methods of Politics, The Principles of Politics, The Story of Political Philosophers, *and* Systematic Politics. *Of his autobiography,* Campaign, *C. A. Ralph has written that the author can "lay his hand on his heart and say that he has done as much as any man writing to try to bring the English and American peoples together."*

"MONSTROUSLY UNNECESSARY"?

THIS TERRESTRIAL GLOBE has endured many millions of years, indeed above 10 billion, and man, in some recognizable form, for more than 1,000,000. There is, hence, no intrinsic reason why the world and man should not endure for many million more years. There are wide-open reaches of time for slow social improvement. Why hurry? Why rage? Indeed few thoughts are more startling and yet more sobering than the reflections upon the hundreds of thousands of years that men have been around in this globe, compared with the mere decades or few centuries of high civilization as yet, with—if all goes well—millions of years of that civilization still to go, during which time civilized man does—what?

We may feverishly challenge this notion of continuity by saying, with Lewis Mumford, that man used to attempt the conquest of nature with his muscles, whereas now, in an utterly new era, we have the "megamachine." This is inaccurate. The sail and the windmill and the horse and wheel are not extensions of human muscle. And however much efficiency fanatics may seek to turn men into ant machines, the computer is controlled by the same human intelligence as before.

There is one dark cloud that spreads over the face of this reasonable optimism. What if the change, the technical change, the scientific invention, brought no such human improvement as was hoped and the wrong priorities were chosen? It is the historian A. J. P. Taylor who suggests that the probable future of mankind will be "to blow itself up." If not Aristotle, then Darwin and Freud have surely taught us enough of the malice or original sin in man for us to realize that this is fully possible. Moreover, this does not require a million or so years to bring it to pass. If mankind has no decent respect for its own future, if it remains obsessed with power and with the rhetoric of freedom (which is the reverse side of the coin of power), it can bring this apocalypse about within a few years. This general incineration is fully technically possible, and so many physical scientists and men ambitious for reputation are waiting in the wings and ready to help forward the destruction. The feckless or greedy exhaustion of irreplaceable natural resources and the fall of the water level; that gross overpopulation to which almost all animal species are occasionally liable; and indiscriminatory atomic war—these are the prime threats to mankind, having clear priority before all considerations of forms of government, liberty, and welfare, considerations often subjective in character. Even democracy we have to make safe for all the world, and to make justice compatible with survival.

The globe itself, then, and the primitive human race have been around for a long time. What, however, is quite pathethically recent, in the time scale, is recorded history and all that we call civilization, a fleeting matter of a few seconds in geological time. One can visit Neolithic temples in Malta, as I have done, and marvel both how "recent" they are and how frighteningly blood-stained and primitive. But a brief jet-plane flight, and we can also discover the primitive beside us today. We need not even go as far as Haiti. In *Palinurus* Cyril Connolly writes: "Civilization is maintained by a very few people in a small number of places. . . . The civilized are those who get more out of life than the uncivilized; and for this we are not likely to be forgiven." Here the second clause may be guilty of too much *aristocratisme,* even if it has not a Sybarite touch. What finally matters is not "getting more out of life" for the individual, but physically maintaining and over all improving the human species. But Connolly's first clause is valid enough. So is the story of the Tower of Babel. Civilization is a very fragile thing and newborn. In the words of André Malraux, it has a concern for "the images which creativity has opposed to time." It is opposed by anarchism, by fashionable "trendism," and what Lionel Trilling classes "the anti-culture." Power is morally neutral, but high civilization demands power for its protection. It demands protection against its enemies, among whom I count our uncontrolled and amoral scientists, technologists, and production-obsessed profit grubbers, who corrupt our democracies for gain, demolish our aristocracies, and pervert our education. The Great War was allegedly—or so we were told at the time—fought "for the defense of civilization." Was it?

The Great War, which was the First World War and another of those civil wars which has destroyed European power, a power which developed since Marathon and has declined since Port Arthur, began on August 4, 1914. A few days before its outbreak I recall seeing in London the placard of a popular journal of those days, *John Bull.* It read: TO HELL WITH SERVIA. It voiced the unwillingness of the mass of Englishmen to spill blood on behalf of a little, remote country—it is a liberal error that little countries are always more moral than big—ruled by a contemptible and murderous dynasty and infested by Pan-Slav conspirators, who had only recently organized the assassination of the Archduke Franz Ferdinand. The only fault of this worthy man was that he wanted such reform as would benefit the political condition of the Slav subjects of that Austro-Hungarian Empire which advantageously held the Danubian area together. In the eyes of the Pan-Slavs the fault was unforgivable, the hope something to be extinguished. It was intolerable that the typecast villain should behave like a reformer.

At the same time, in France, Jean Jaurès, patriot but pacifist, was protesting against the plunge of France into war. "The workers of the world" in fact did not unite—or strike. In practice the theory of the general strike for peace collapsed. The majority of the French Assembly, in 1914, were in fact anxious for a pacific policy in foreign relations. They were, however, much more obsessed with a secularist program of anticlericalism. But for the very purposes of getting that program through, they had reached compromises. They got their priorities wrong. They left the shaping of foreign policy to that section of the assembly which was by no means so peace-minded, which found its voice in Delcassé and its most acute memories in recollections of Sedan. As a result, the Germans crossed the Belgian border, and as M. Mitterun has recently pointed out, the French crossed the German border.

In 1935, traveling in a train to Moscow which was carrying Sir Anthony Eden, I remarked to Lord Cranborne (now Lord Salisbury) that I hoped that Hitler and his associates would be given such a clear declaration of our policy as the Kaiser should have received before 1914. The trouble, however, here was that no unambiguous declaration of support for France could have been given in 1914 in the British Parliament since the Liberal majority in Parliament and country alike would have denounced it. That majority was pacific but escapist. Pledges, "in the spirit of the *Entente Cordiale*," had indeed been given, and Anglo-French staff talks had taken place—and, even more secret, an Anglo-Russian naval agreement—but only the Prime Minister and his Foreign Secretary, Grey, knew the full extent of the commitments which French Ambassador Cambon was to recall. No wonder the Union for Democratic Control—democratic control of foreign policy—received later some measure of support. Lord Morley of Blackburn —"Honest John Morley"—insisted that although a member of the Cabinet, he had never been informed of these commitments. A Cabinet memorandum was produced with his own signature on it.

It seems as if "Honest John" had not attended quite closely enough to his homework. As for Lloyd George, he switched after the Germans crossed the Belgian frontier. Of the original Anglo-French Entente for amity, progress, and peace the ex-Liberal Premier Lord Rosebery had prophetically remarked that it was "much more likely to lead to complications than to peace." It was a policy pushed over on an unsuspecting nation, innocent of the implications.

The common people and even keen party politicians knew little of these things. It might too late emerge that not only the good Hamburg merchants but the Kaiser himself had neither wanted nor expected war. They merely wanted to support Austrian "pressure" in the Austro-Russian balance of power in the wild Balkans. Leon Trotsky places the prime blame for the war on the Russian government—and this may indeed have had its own motives for distracting attention from domestic affairs to foreign. But here, too, "Nicky"—Czar Nicholas II—was of two minds, wanting peace but going through the motions that led to war. What the people did hear was that German foreign policy was expansive and aggressive, like the Germany economy, seeking "a place in the sun"; that the German Navy and Army chiefs were noisily demanding the fulfill-ment of this policy, with sinister plans (even if in pigeonholes) for a strategic sweep; and that the German military was capable of infinite psychological blunders as at Zabern. The result was a condition of suspicion and even of public alarm. Lord Roberts of Kandahar, "Bobs," roused the complacent people.

A bright schoolboy, like the young Denis Brogan, might note the movement of naval craft on the Clyde, and others might remark the excessively large orders in Oxford for Cooper's Marmalade. A few, in the know, might be aware of detailed train schedules France-ward and even just where the troops would take coffee. These were yet plans and not decisions. It remained true that the vast mass of Liberals, not least the intelligent, and the mass of the country, after a century since Napoleon and the admirable Conference of Vienna, so long a summer of peace, could not believe that enlightenment could be followed by a major war. After all, the Franco-German War had been localized, and the Crimean War (not to speak of innumerable bush wars) had been in remote theaters. Similarly Voltaire had persuaded himself, just before the French Revolu-tionary Wars and Napoleon, that enlightenment had reached a point where no great wars would take place. He did not allow for Danton and for the people's capacity for impassioned folly.

Hence, when the war was about to come, there was a profound trauma for the Liberal consciousness. Was it not truly a great illusion? Could there not be "peaceful change"? The very trauma issued, as immediate consequence, in a hysteria of righteous rage. The "Huns" (the overweening Kaiser's own term) must be veritable devils, unspeakable in their antiliberal wickedness. People who had never read Nietzsche heard all about Nietzsche, whose volumes it was assumed that every German schoolchild read. When a solitary zeppelin, in 1916, appeared over Paris, there were shrieks of press protest against these "sky murderers," who indiscriminately killed even women and children. Since those days, of course, not only are soldiers burned by napalm in Jordan and Sinai, but women and children (many of them refugees) have been burned wholesale in Guernica, Lidice, Hamburg, and Dresden. So, aided by moral popular passion, civilization degenerates. ("Popular"? What majority supported Hitler and Stalin? About 90 percent.)

Was, then, the war of 1914–18 "that monstrously unnecessary war," as Leonard Woolf says in his autobiography, *Downhill All the Way?*[1] (Was that of 1939–45 the same?) It is relevant here to quote the words of two men who knew perhaps more about it than anybody else, the two major statesmen most deeply involved—Lloyd George and Winston Churchill. In his *War Memoirs,*[2] Lloyd George wrote:

In looking back upon the incidents of those few eventful days one feels like recalling a nightmare; and, after reading most of the literature explaining why the nations went to war, and who was responsible, the impression left in my mind is one of utter chaos, confusion, feebleness and futility, especially of a stubborn refusal to look at the rapidly approaching cataclysm. The nations backed their machinery over the precipice. . . . The elder statesmen did their feckless best to prevent war, whilst the youth of the rival countries were howling impatiently at their doors for immediate war.

(So much for the beneficial effects of giving youth, Komsomols, Hitlerjunge, Red Guards, the vote. In Sparta they prudently gave the vote at thirty and remained a great military people.)

Winston Churchill, in 1929, in *The World Crisis,*[3] wrote: "One rises from the study of the causes of the Great War with a prevailing sense of the defective control of individuals upon war fortunes." In a later volume, *Aftermath,* he added that "the prevention of another great war" should be "the main preoccupation of mankind." So it was. Pacifists and collective security men battled over the issue.

---

[1] London, 1967, p. 225.

[2] London, 1930, vol. 1, pp. 52, 60.

[3] London, 1929, vol. I, p. 13.

"Appeasement" for a while was an honorable word. But the Second
World War came.

When the Great War broke in 1914, there were journalists,
soldiers, and politicians confident that the war would be won by the
Entente in six weeks. However, there were Germans equally confident of a German victory in the same time. Anyone who chooses to
read the New York *Herald Tribune* reports of the war communiqués of the time, with never a suggestion of other than Entente
advance—even the Russian Revolution, it was stated, would "prove
helpful"—can only be surprised that the Entente troops were not in
Berlin within six months. (Some war communiqués from Saigon
show here a family resemblance.) The military realities were, for
others, the realities of the Somme and Passchendaele. By 1916 the
French troops were mutinous and had to be stiffened, Pétain's great
achievement. In my recollection the black day which produced
gloom among the general British public came, in 1917, with the
death of Kitchener of Khartoum, drowned with the sinking of
H.M.S. *Hampshire*. Ironically, it was yet almost a good fortune
since, once a totem, his military skill had declined and his power of
direction was impaired. Few, however, knew this. It is important
not to be misled about public opinion by the currents in the small
world of letters. It is quite true that the lyric romanticism of
Rupert Brooke, and the ambiguous revival of William Blake, gave
way to the melancholy gloom of the work (still then unpublished)
of Wilfred Owen and Siegfried Sassoon. At the highest levels the
suggestions for peace of Lansdowne, ex-Foreign Secretary, Sixte
Bourbon, and Pope Benedict XV might come to the surface in
1916–17. But they were finally to be checked by Haig—and by, of
all people, our old Boer enemy, Field Marshal Jan Smuts, member
of the Empire War Cabinet.

The great mass of the people did not hesitate until the unexpected success of the German offensive of the spring of 1918.
There were indeed British military mutinies—but not until the war
was won and troops, new and old, insisted (unwisely) on massive
and instant demobilization. There were indeed local demands—*e.g.*,
by Welsh miners for better conditions—met by troop *démarches en
force,* route marches through the areas, in which I myself took part.
But it was not until the spring of 1918, the March offensive, that
there was a public sense that "it was all touch-and-go." Young men
registered as "totally rejected"—I was one—were suddenly called up.

I heard of the abdication of the Kaiser in Rouen. At 11 A.M. on
the eleventh day of November, the eleventh month, the Armistice
was declared, although it was not certain for the troops that this also

meant the immediate end of the war. In Britain, on the heels of victory, Lloyd George called for the delayed general election—the first since 1911—the Khaki Election, which turned on the vote of the troops. In the canteens and *estaminets* of Flanders and Hainaut we discussed it. The Fourteen Points of Woodrow Wilson, regarded by many as almost a messiah, were discussed by the troops with skepticism but with benevolence.

In 1945 many people at the highest levels expected a result similar to that gained by Lloyd George in 1918. Winston Churchill, despite test polls by his own party, was among them. Max Beaver-brook persuaded him that he would win massively. They forgot that, in 1940–45, the opposition was itself an active member of the coalition. Indeed Churchill had himself written his own epitaph: The best statesman for war is not, therefore, he wrote, the best statesman for peace. In the 1914–18 war the opposition was not in coalition but a small, noncooperating, pacifist minority, led by Ramsay MacDonald. I did not myself so much vote for MacDonald as for Woodrow Wilson. I did not myself so much vote against Lloyd George, the tricky Welsh attorney, as against Clemenceau and against his British supporters, not least of them the Harms-worth press, "the wicked uncles," with their announced policy of a victory of revenge.

In winter quarters near Mons, in that hard winter of 1918–19, awaiting demobilization, I spent my time writing notes and, not least, upon the basic causes of war and the conditions of stable peace. It is a work which actually has steadily engaged me from that time for the rest of my life. Much turns upon whether despite the comfortable skeptics and the temperamental obstructionists and defeatists, the dogmatic "no men," we can produce a genuine political science and an authentic scientific analysis of these causes. At that time there was nothing of the kind. The philosophers changed with the wind of fashion, and the historians floundered as usual in the morass of irrelevant detail, forever believing that a fact about how offered an explanation of why.

René Descartes, in winter quarters with the French Army in Bavaria, had written his *Discours de la méthode*. Descartes' quarters in Bavaria, we are told, were "warm"; mine were not. As a school-boy, I had become acquainted with his work. (The sociologist Durkheim also wrote on method, and I got his work translated.) I, too, was concerned with method, with finding analytically the real causes of war, knowledge of which could avert their recurrence, and with the human uses of history. Marx indeed offered fundamental explanations, and Spengler and Toynbee later were to do so. None of them seemed to me satisfactory. I had indeed written a school prize essay on "Cosmopolitanism" and a university entrance examination paper on "The Causes of War." I was not ignorant of history; I was indeed perhaps too erudite in it. But was study of the superficies of historical facts enough? My preoccupation absorbed my later days at Oxford, at Sheffield, and my first days at Cornell. The fruit of the meditations was my Cornell doctoral thesis of 1924, later published in 1927 as *The Science and Method of Politics*. Forty years later it has just been republished.

I had noted in my reading that Aristotle, "the Master of Them That Know," was not only a political philosopher but also a political scientist. In discussing revolutions, he was not concerned to ask whether they were good or bad, but what factors brought them about and what means were adjusted to what ends. Also, his concern was with the web of society and not with any sovereign states. The great work of Machiavelli was based on Livy's *History* and on the conviction that the fundamental motivations of human nature do not change. Hence, where the circumstances were pragmatically equivalent, the same causes would produce, *mutatis mutandis*, the same results. And, finally, in the same mood as Spinoza, Thomas Hobbes had maintained that politics was a science with clear patterns to be observed in human behavior. Also, Hobbes had basically concerned himself, as I was concerned, with the issue of peace, civil peace, himself writing against the experience of two wars, English and French civil wars. My concern was with international peace against the experience of world war. Nevertheless, although Hobbes significantly based himself on a psychology, that psychology was so crassly egoistic and materialist that it could no longer be maintained to hold water. Hobbes was among the earliest psychologists, but his psychology was crude. My own interest was in following the clue of power—of being the student of power as means.

The twenties was the period when psychoanalysis, developed earlier in Vienna, became fashionable, although the major universities regarded even orthodox psychology with a disinterest verging on contempt and the connected philosophy of William James as fallacious. However, amid the more pretentious systems of Freud and Jung, the clinical work of Alfred Adler provided interesting confirmation of Hobbes' thesis of human preoccupation with power, illuminating the political arena, and gave a new precision and correctness to terms. Even the conservative Bryce had indicated the study of psychology as basic in political analysis, while such men as Rivers made their own contribution and Graham Wallas illustrated, almost anecdotally, the story of local government by psychological comment on the "human nature" of those involved. The systematic work of such an Austrian sociologist as Ratzenhofer should not be overlooked, or the more dubious and biased themes of Pareto.

Economics rests on a psychological hypothesis concerning the pursuit of wealth and of the control of property, so massively discussed by Marx. It deliberately avails itself, in this hypothesis, of abstractions and working models. The question was whether politics could do the same. At last, with the concurrent work of Bentley, Merriam, and Lasswell, a systematic conceptual scheme was worked out, which gave a new dimension to political studies. Owing much to Aristotle, Machiavelli, and Hobbes, my scheme was not merely a regurgitation of, or scholarly gloss upon, these ideas. However, the system, articulating experimentally the lines of control of political power, also returns to its own origins. The study began, for me, in observation of practice in war and ended in conclusions in practice about war. And unlike Marxism, it was competent to cope with insurgent problems such as those of nationalism. It comes to grips with Immanuel Kant's old problem of lasting peace.

At the Rome Conference, in 1965, of the Einstein-inspired World Academy of Art and Science, I put forward specific proposals for a study of conflict, peace, and war, not only economic, anthropological, and biological—and the study of animal behavior is of extreme relevance—but psychological and political. There are various local institutes already engaged in these studies, and it has been my suggestion that one in India might appropriately take the form of a memorial to Gandhi. Anyhow we have work in progress.

It was an observation of my revered sometime colleague Carl L. Becker that "all politics is power politics." It was a remark which, properly understood—and it must be borne in mind that cooperative political control can be as effective as, and even more effective realistically than, dominative control—remains true, even if it confuses or dismays many.

The problem of war and the control of power become intolerably immediate as well-intentioned attempts at securing the non-dissemination of nuclear weapons fail and as not only the United States and the U.S.S.R., not only Britain, France, and China, not only Israel and the U.A.R., have or develop nuclear weapons, but they can be expected to fall into the hands of the fanatic fringe of humanity. It is an issue not theoretical and academic, but intensely urgent and most practical.

It has to be faced that fed on slogans and doped with emotion, some peoples prefer suicide to accommodation, called surrender. In their own eyes, they are heroes. After a rebellious and stiff-necked Jerusalem was literally demolished by the massive might of the 10th Legion under Vespasian and Titus, the Zealots made their suicidal choice at Masada. Likewise, in recent years, Islamic fanaticism inspired the followers of the megalomaniac Mahdi to pursue through to their final destruction in the Sudan. The Hobbesian thesis here applies. Sympathy is wasted on such ill-proportioned fanaticism, and as Hobbes says, they have to be persuaded to peace by terror. Wrong, "objectively" evil, potentially enemies of the whole human race, if hydrogen bombs are to fall, the proper target for bombs is themselves. In the alternative, world war resumes—this time, atomic war.

Incidentally, there is an interesting rider to this argument. If the major powers, with nuclear arms, hold the use of these arms to be unthinkable, then the balance of power reverts to being the role of conventional armies and navies, with air power or, alternatively, to the highly unconventional and in the last resort anarchist power of guerrilla groups, operating outside the so-called laws of war.

It may be thought that, in the interest of peace, I am here advocating the restoration of the Roman Empire. The idea is as old as Dante and indeed demands consideration. If, as Tacitus said, the Romans "made a desolation" in rebel areas, at least they provided the imperial peace, maintained, in the words of the Code of Justinian, *armis et legibus*. Nor would I regard any consideration of forms of government or chatter about some anticivilized "liberty" as of equal importance. Liberty is that freedom which a civil society thinks it right to confer. Humanity has to confront the plain issue of whether armed and enforced peace, as stated here, an objective and not a subjective theory, is a first political priority or whether it is not. The goal agreed, the means can be assessed. How many men we should be prepared to kill for the sake of our subjective or ideological or fanatical notions about subjective freedom or justice or national glory is another story. My own answer is: very few.

Despite the judgment, which demands respect, of one of the greatest of the world's historians, Edward Gibbon, to the effect that in no other time would he have preferred to live, the government of the Roman Empire even under the Antonines was by no means perfect, and during long periods, even if primarily government by the civil service, it was markedly imperfect. Today we tend, if anything, to underestimate the role of reason. Nevertheless, rational men cling to the hope that the twentieth century can improve upon the rule of the Caesars—not to speak of Kaiser, Czar, Kaisar-i-Hind, and Turkish Kaisar-i-Rum which, being merely local, do not answer our problem. All one can say is that to base the structure of peace on the proposition that most men are rational and would seek peace is a fairly reckless optimism, contradicted by most of history, and that the record of democracy since the days of Athens and Syracuse is no better than other systems. Indeed, precisely clinging to local community loyalties broke the Hellenic power to resist Macedon. A democracy is resistant to going into a war but, when at war, is no less resistant to forgetting emotion and discussing a peace. Likewise, clinging to our pleasant local habits and freedoms and what some psychologists may call (and others would not) our natural rights—better, "natural claims"—may, in fact, prove obstacles to the rule of law.

The conclusion of Hobbes on this problem is unambiguous: strong government. Actually the settlement reached in England was not entirely his prescription. It was a firm Hanoverian Establishment compromise. It is too facile to say that the conclusion in today's international field must be a strong international authority prepared and willing to pressure and even bomb the rebels. We may logically want a world gendarme. We cannot so readily get one.

It can be suggested that a quite other policy is possible, far more humanitarian, pleasant and sweet. It is that outlined by the pacifists. It also appeals to the anarchists and "flower people." The theme is well known: that, if everybody abjured war, there would be no war. Those who do not abjure are to be met by sit-down resistance. It is, of course, entirely true that moods and fashions of violence (as in Sicily and Corsica) have to be educationally replaced by moods of valuation of civil peace as such. It is further true and commonplace that the civil peace is actually maintained, in daily life, not by a quite limited, if skilled and sometimes armed, police force but by the law-abiding sentiment of the great mass of the citizen population. The same position may be expected to be true in the international world. However, to accept this is assuredly not to say that criminals and aggressors will, therefore, go out of business or that a universal masochism is to be approved. As for the civil peace, it used for a while to come near to being the case in the city of Chicago that the underworld ruled. Too many "peaceful citizens" displayed timidity, cynicism, disinterestedness, sheer lack of civic spirit, so that the forces of order were losing their fight to those of anarchy. Recent sociological studies have shown that most of the public is pretty "disinterested" i.e., cowardly. "Aren't the police paid to do the job?" By vigor and imagination at the top, this situation has been so far redressed that Chicago has become here a model studied by others throughout the world. The same comment applies in the international world. "Patriotism is not enough or pacifism either."

If the recognition of a world authority, holding the scales and the bomb and willing to use the latter against all rebels against its sole sovereign authority, is unfortunately not practicable for the present, what feasible alternatives have we? It is seldom indeed that I find myself in agreement with Mr. V. M. Molotov, but here I hold that his judgment expressed at the San Franciso Conference of 1945 is correct. The politics of the future must necessarily be the politics of the major powers—the two (or maybe three) major powers. This system is called duopoly. Its chief opponent is traditional tribalism, such as flourishes today in Africa—but not there alone—and which flourishes in what G. Lowes Dickinson used to call "the International Anarchy." The major exponent today of this atavism is M. de Gaulle.

To clarify matters, let us turn for a moment to a slightly different issue, although one most directly relevant to this essay. Leonard Woolf, in his autobiography *Downhill All the Way,* speaks (as I have said) of the Great War as "monstrously unnecessary." In view of the blood and treasure spent, the millions of lives lost, these are—and it is an understatement—challenging words.

Without discounting the ill-considered (although no unprovoked) character of the Austro-Hungarian ultimatum to a deplorable little Balkan country or the aggressive militancy of a Prussian-dominated Germany, it can be argued that even Edward Grey, the most high-minded, liberal, and "noble" of the statesmen involved, was like a locomotive driver who is more concerned to observe the strict rule of the railroad and to be "correct" than actually to avert a collision. He was a liberal Francophile at a time when France was not guiltless of nursing an egoistic spirit of revenge.

Again, it is arguable that Lloyd George, who at least considered it, should have actually pushed through in 1916 negotiations— something Winston Churchill also considered in 1940—despite the Army under Haig, the King, and Smuts. It is true that this would have spelled negotiation with the Kaiser, still in possession of almost all Belgium and much of France. That Germany would have retained German-speaking Alsace, earlier stolen by Louis XIV, would not have been so serious as a "nonchange." In retrospect it may yet seem that "change," even if not "peaceful," and a redistribution of power would have been veritable paradise compared with the problems which in fact eventuated from "victory." Twice Russia was brought in and placated in order to "wage war for democracy," and twice Russia dominated the historical scene, under Lenin by uproar and under Stalin by sheer power.

In the issue five empires fell—unfortunately, in the case of the Austrian and Turkish, and including the British. England, as a direct consequence of the two wars, was so far economically weakened that it is busy at this moment, with ignominy, in abandoning its world role and in endeavoring to placate the arrogance of "the Constable of France." Only a neutral and neuterized Sweden and a Switzerland, of which John Foster Dulles said that it was "neutral between good and evil," were left happy. Perhaps Leonard Woolf is right. A small, perhaps united, but protectionist so-called Europe (*i.e.*, Northwestern Europe) , divisive of the West, is not likely to be of much weight. The sole thing that emerges from the record that is encouraging is the rise of American power. Whether, granted this power, the United States will be able to enter into such pragmatic agreement with the Soviet Union (which, under the present archaic system of voting by tribal patches called sovereign states, may yet make a take-over bid for the United Nations) as can enforce peace on the ambitious and insurgent has yet to be proved.

What, however, emerged also from the Great War was the theory of self-determination and the actual encouragement of nationalism. They connect with the rise of America because both were made by Woodrow Wilson the almost sacred bases of his liberal policy. What President Wilson failed to recognize was the double incompatibility (a) between self-determination, as any absolute principle, and nationalism itself, and (b) the even more patent hostility between nationalism, as an absolute, and the rule of international law which he affirmed. Strategic considerations of security apart, majority Canadian nationalism and self-determination in Quebec do not necessarily run in harness; or nationalism and self-determination in Czechoslovakia, as the Czechs found to their cost; or in drawing the frontiers in Palestine; or in Nigeria; or in the counties of Ulster. What *is* the community unit?

The problem of nationalism (which, in much of Africa, is a thinly disguised ancestral tribalism) is far more grave. Since the days of Cleisthenes the clash between the smaller community and the larger has been recognized as a menace. After the centuries of the Roman Empire in some form or other, even if only acknowledged as a principle of government—from the eighteenth century and the French Revolution on—the epidemic of nationalism spread over Europe. Abating in Europe in the twentieth century, it rages in Asia and Africa, as a disease of social adolescence. Today in Europe itself the optimistic see a distinction being drawn between local patriotism, cooperative and capable of stressing interdependence, and a chauvinism of which the slogan is strict "independence," except where, successful, it takes side-glances at empire. Nationalism in the early sense, it may be thought, is passing away in the West, to yield to enthusiasm for some political union of Europe. However, I speak of this as being optimistic, since it seems to underestimate the contemporary force of the phenomenon of Gaullism.

I have said elsewhere, in my autobiography, *Campaign*,[4] that I regard General de Gaulle as a greater threat to the future of peace than Nikita Khrushchev ever was. By this I mean that Khrushchev was able, as in Cuba and elsewhere, to make a correct estimate of the realities of power. De Gaulle lives in a world not so much of power as of hitherto successful bluff. Khrushchev as a Marxist, even if on narrow nineteenth-century lines of antagonism of class, is yet an internationalist in spirit. De Gaulle is not. He is obsessed by an archaic and atavistic mood which looks back to the epoch of Louis XIV, and he stirs the embers of chauvinist nationalism. He is dedicated to an anti-American policy. I am not saying that he is not *un grand homme*. I can think of some countries that could benefit by a De Gaulle. But success can produce its own nemesis. I tremble at the thought of some proximate German De Gaulle. We shall be back in 1914 again. The crime of General de Gaulle is that he sits back and seeks to reverse that tide of authentic internationalism which was one of the few entirely good consequences of the Great War. A revenant from another age, he is a danger to the present one.

The fear of M. de Gaulle is of a great power, and specifically of an American, hegemony. The message, however, of 1914–18 is that of the danger of uncontrolled, competitive ramifications, Balkan or otherwise. Insofar as the pragmatic mutual understanding and executive cooperation of the two great powers is the best guarantee, short of any world authority, for the maintenance of peace against anarchy, his fear is misplaced. However, it also rests on a misunderstanding. Rational Western policy does not involve, and it is historically preposterous to suppose that it involves, some political or military or even technical dictatorship from Washington, which rather aspires to interdependence and consensus. On the contrary, what is a more grave matter for consideration is the withdrawal of

---

4 New York, 1968.

some European countries from contributing their full cooperative measure of responsibility for world problems and from taking any world role. The correct picture of the future is of an Atlantic community, not dominated exclusively by one power, but, while led by the stronger, yet consisting of a group of powers, each able to share the common burden.

It may be argued that this is today impossible owing to economic weaknesses. The victories of 1918 and 1945 were more "Dead Sea fruit." It is indeed one of the merits of M. de Gaulle's policy that he has consistently and successfully put political considerations (however wrongheaded) before economic considerations. "The politics of France is not decided on the Bourse." It is he who lands in North America from the *Colbert*, as the destroyer of France and as, in her own person, deliberate demonstration of power and influence.

The reply may be that it is the needs of the welfare state which require the running down of defense to a level dangerously comparable to the weaknesses of 1936–39, with consequences we all recall. It is represented as an economic necessity. It has yet been suggested by Professor Kenneth Galbraith that it is a misfortune of our Western civilization that we spend our time thrusting goods on the consumer, often unwanted until the advertiser gets to work, stuffing the unhappy citizen like a Strasbourg goose, all in homage to the fetish of more and more production, for home market or export. A nation, such as Britain, dependent on exports to pay for food for a swollen population may be excused, although in the long run it must find its cure in a new species of larger integrated or "home" market—which need not be exclusively European and could be an Atlantic free trade area.

Everywhere this feverish stress on competitive production, while increasing present profits (and future complications), does yet provide employment for labor. However, a smaller labor market and a reduced population could be assured of full employment and high wages. Here is an alternative. One of the most startling changes in the whole eventful twentieth century has just been initiated in India, although its revolutionary importance has not yet been adequately grasped. It is far more radical than any legislation for semipermissive abortion or proposals for indiscriminate and nonselective (and hence dysgenic) birth control. For the moment it also is indiscriminate and nonselective as between genius and the recidivist criminal, but this can be changed. It is the proposed Indian legislation for the compulsory sterilization—presumably not compulsory but voluntary for the moral citizen who volunteers—of all males, who are fathers of three children or more. Once started and the initial shock overcome, it will become a world program. It cuts far deeper than present schemes for the building of larger schools and hospitals and for welfare work for the alleviation of poverty and unemployment. It is outside the scope of this essay to pursue further these speculations here. But the program would leave money available, not in terms just of use for massive untrained manpower as in China, for that defense which, whether we like it or not, is the prime concern of any political society pending world organization. It would also end the disappearance of sound economies, aid, and seed corn into the sands of unlimited fecundity.

To revert to the position of the United Kingdom, it cannot be supposed that a country, with such a history as Britain's, will continue supinely and ignominiously to abdicate from all effectiveness in power. This will be true whatever may be the temporary position of some political party leaders. Edward Heath, indeed like Richard Nixon, may have tried, but failed, to reach success in a policy—in Mr. Heath's case a policy of entry into Europe by accommodation with M. de Gaulle. Thanks to views of the general which were amply on the record, in *e.g., Le Fils de l'épée,* but which few people chose to study, this attempt reached an impasse. Much of the contemporary trouble arises from an unwillingness to admit that effective peace must rest in the hands of the great powers and, hence, that support for great power diplomacy, as against overswollen nationalist ambitions and rhetoric, is the route of progress and peace. One may talk of hegemony if one chooses, but an integrated Atlantic community, such as N.A.T.O. somewhat narrowly sought to provide, has the character of a great power in a fashion to which even a United Europe cannot aspire—and should not aspire.

We may not choose to say that the core of power is to be found in the Anglo-Saxon world—*les pouvoirs anglo-saxens.* But that core can be found, as Senator Jacob Javits and David Rockefeller have said, in a special relationship (including Canada) and in an Atlantic free trade area, which yet can, in due course, include Western Europe. It can be found in a policy, not defeatist, which turns away from the memories of 1914–18 with distaste, but affirmative. The object of an effective peace policy should be, if experience counts for anything, the concentration of massive power and a pragmatic understanding between Washington and the Kremlin.

In this essay I have sought to draw upon the traumatic experience of two wars to reach some comment on the politically and humanly prime problem of peace. It is both usual and polite to pursue, for the answers, liberal, pacifist, even Quaker recommendations. Indeed some young people, without any claims to special study, have appropriated to themselves the sole right to give the answers. The answers given here are in terms of the study of power and of support of great power controls, against national divisiveness and "the International Anarchy." Rather than this last I would prefer the restoration of the Roman Empire and the Code of Justinian.

My own thought on the subject, as I have said, began in the practical and, after moving through the arch of theory, has ended in the practical. It began in December, 1918. One of the most forceful of all political theorists, Hobbes, built his work, which was primarily concerned with the establishment of civil peace, even if by terror, on his personal experience of two civil wars—the Puritan Revolution and the Fronde. Our experience, in confronting without evasion the problem of international peace, is based on two world wars, culminating in the terror of the hydrogen bomb. We shall be unimaginative in experience and dull of wit, indeed, if we can draw no conclusions.

Trevor Wilson

TREVOR GORDON WILSON *was born in December, 1928, in Auckland, New Zealand. He was educated at Auckland University, where he received an M.A. with first-class honors. He won a New Zealand traveling scholarship in 1955 and went to Oxford, where he received the degree of Doctor of Philosophy. He held a research post at Manchester University 1957–59, then in 1960 took up a history lectureship at the University of Adelaide, South Australia.*

In 1965 he was awarded the Higby Prize by the American Historical Association for an article on the British general election of 1918. In 1966 he published The Downfall of the Liberal Party, 1914–1935. *He is at present engaged in editing the diaries of C. P. Scott, newspaper editor and friend of Lloyd George and Winston Churchill.*

In January, 1968, he succeeded George Rudé as professor of history at Adelaide University.

He is married and has two daughters.

BRITISH LIBERALISM AND THE
FIRST WORLD WAR

ON AUGUST 1, 1914, the radical British weekly *The Nation* wrote:

It is safe to say that there has been no crisis in which the public opinion of the English people has been so definitely opposed to war as it is at this moment. . . . [It] is everywhere recognised that a Minister who led this country into war would be responsible for a war as causeless and unpopular as any war in history, and that he would cease to lead the Liberal Party.

A week later the same journal stated: "the feeling is unanimous that the struggle must now be carried on with the utmost energy . . . until a German aggression is defeated and German militarism broken."

The oscillations of *The Nation* did not end here. By 1917 it had become disenchanted with the prospects of the conflict and was demanding a negotiated peace. Indeed, the Prime Minister, Lloyd George—admittedly no stickler for accuracy—accused the journal of being run by a "pacifist directorate" and said that its foreign circulation had been banned because some of its articles were "an encouragement to the enemy." Yet when the Germans launched their massive offensive against the British lines in March, 1918, *The Nation* rallied unflinchingly to the national cause. "In the full brunt of the German assault on France, the true character of the war stands revealed . . . not as a war of adventure but morally and physically as a war of defence. . . . The war was not for colonies, Imperial ambitions, or a balance of power. It was to teach militarism a lesson of restraint."

This ambivalence toward the conflict was not confined to *The Nation*. The Liberal editor C. P. Scott warned a Cabinet minister on July 27, 1914, that if the government led Britain into the war, "there would be an end of the existing Liberal combination." And a week later he related to a friend: "I was working desperately all Saturday & Sunday to work up opposition to the War . . . but events moved too fast for us & it was all in vain. It reminded me terribly of all that went before the Boer War." Yet the following May he told an antiwar Liberal that "the aggressive imperialism of Germany had to be resisted," and his newspaper declared that it could imagine no event more disastrous to civilization than a definite victory for Germany.[1]

These sharply alternating opinions point to the cruel dilemma in which Liberals were placed by the war. It would be easy to say, as did a small but important section of the party, that a Liberal government ought never to have become involved in the struggle and that by doing so it had violated Liberal ideals. The classic Liberal foreign policy was aloofness from affairs on the Continent

---

[1] Quotations are from C. P. Scott's diary, July 27, 1914; Scott to L. T. Hobhouse, August 4, 1914; and Scott to Francis Hirst, May 24, 1915.

and abstention from entangling relations with foreign powers. Had not Gladstone said that in foreign affairs all nations must be treated as equals? It seemed that the Asquith government had abandoned this principle in the years before the war, by becoming involved in an arms race, secret diplomacy, and international crises. Hence Britain found itself in August, 1914, caught up in the destinies of other countries—including the hated Czarist regime in Russia.

This was one side of the Liberals' dilemma: that by going to war they seemed to be violating Liberal principles. The other side was that, had they refused to go to war, they would have equally betrayed Liberal ideals. The party was a victim of the classic tragic conflict. Britain was the greatest of European democracies. Germany was the most potent—because the most efficient, ruthless, and successful—menace to democracy. If Britain stood aside, German militarism would sweep across Western Europe. Democracy there would never recover. The invasion of Belgium crystallized this issue. The right of small countries to survive unmolested, the right of separate nationalities to self-government, the sanctity of treaties, the rule of law in relations between states—all were great Liberal principles, and all were being trampled underfoot by the German military machine. The duty of Liberals to defend them was clear. Yet, as has been said, to do so meant violating other sacred principles: international conciliation, disarmament, equal treatment for all nations. It is little wonder that Liberals became distracted as they saw one set of beliefs being submerged so that the other might survive.

Nor was this all. Whichever course they followed would involve them in further dilemmas of principle. As they decided on war, the dilemma was how to reconcile its successful conduct with the ideals of a free, democratic society. To begin with, they hoped to evade this issue. The war would be "over by Christmas," and meanwhile, the nation would conduct "business as usual"—which, in addition, meant a free press, freedom of movement, free recruiting, and freedom for aliens, all as usual. But the nature of the war, with its fearful rate of casualties and its Europe-wide stalemate, ended all this. It became impossible for the nation to continue along Liberal paths while a small section of freely enlisted fighting men attended to the business of war. Free trade had to give way to the exigencies of blockading the enemy and producing goods once supplied by Germany. When the *Times* and *Daily Mail* printed information about French troop movements valuable to the enemy, even a Liberal editor like Scott admitted that censorship was necessary. (Within a few months, however, he was recording with dismay that the censor was also trying to suppress information about the Vatican's appeal for peace.) When the public became obsessed about spies roaming the land and took reprisal for the sinking of passenger ships by wrecking shops owned by people of German origin, it became necessary to restrict movement in the country and to intern aliens. When the production of shells and the recruitment of soldiers fell short of the pace at which both were being consumed, further inroads into freedom became necessary. The country could not afford to wait on private enterprise and personal decision for its munitions and soldiers. Industry had to be organized, trade-union restrictions curtailed, men fetched for the Army. The Liberal doctrines of free trade, free expression, and free service retreated before the demands of a central authority.

Once more, Liberals were caught. If it was necessary to withstand Germany, ought they to quibble about the methods employed? Were trade-union liberties more important than the production of munitions? When men were called on to risk their lives in the national cause, why should some (offering no ground of conscience) be allowed to refuse? Fiscal policy was also called in question. If free trade must be submerged for the duration, what about afterward? In the event of the Kaiser's regime's surviving the war, were Liberals—knowing what they now knew about it—prepared to throw wide the doors of trade to it? Even that eminent Liberal fundamentalist J. M. Robertson admitted: "I hae ma doots."

There was a broader issue involved. What was the Liberal attitude to the state? Once Liberals had sought to restrict its action at every turn. But in recent years they had extended the sphere of government against a particular evil. That evil was poverty. To combat it, the prewar Liberal government had introduced anti-sweating legislation, old-age pensions, and state insurance against sickness and unemployment. Liberals—notwithstanding the presence of charming relics in their midst—were no longer people who resisted government direction in all circumstances.

This was all very well. But a nation in which the government could censor what people read, could punish aliens, not for any offenses committed, but on account of their national origin, could maintain a large Army and drive individuals into it, and could use trade discrimination as an instrument of national policy was not a Liberal state any longer. It was a Conservative state. Tariffs, conscription, restrictions on free expression, discrimination against minorities, were seen by Liberals as fundamental to the conservative outlook. And once they had been admitted, where would they end? The Conservatives, in Liberal eyes, had on the very eve of war been using the Army to suborn the supremacy of Parliament, much as James II had tried to do in the seventeenth century. Their object had been to sabotage the Liberals' proposals for Irish Home Rule, and the consequence had been that the British Army would probably have refused to obey orders to suppress an Ulster revolt against the measure. With a much larger Army, drilled into subservience like other conscript forces, what use would the Conservatives make of it after the war? One Liberal thought he knew: Its purpose was "to discipline & enslave the working classes & to keep down Ireland."[2]

So at every turn Liberals felt themselves trapped. Their leaders did not help. Nearly all of them became involved, to some extent, in deviations from liberalism during the war—sometimes, as in their treatment of Ireland, quite wanton deviations. Asquith, the party leader (and Prime Minister until 1916), committed these breaches of principle with many signs of reluctance, but often with the appearance of surrendering to political expediency. Lloyd George, the party's most brilliant wartime figure, seemed by contrast positively zestful in throwing off many Liberal trammels. Neither attitude brought comfort to the harassed Liberal rank and file.

This conflict of principle and uncertainty of mind destroyed the party as an organized political force. Some of its members abandoned Liberal principles and turned to the Conservatives, whose devotion to nationalism as an ideal and to state compulsion as the means of applying it seemed more appropriate in wartime. Others retained the principles but defected to Labour, where they believed the ideals of Liberalism were being upheld in a purer, unsullied form. Their defection was made easier by the enhanced status of the Labour Party and the trade unions in wartime and by the readier acceptance in war conditions of state intervention in the economy— a practice which Labour adherents had generally been prepared to carry further than Liberals. Those who remained in the Liberal ranks were torn between opposing leaders and fatally unsure of their position or their party's destiny. Loss of faith in itself became the party's distinguishing feature by 1918. In 1914 it had governed the country. Four years later it was not even offering itself as a potential government—or for that matter as a potential opposition. The role of governing party had passed to the Conservatives (though with a group of secessionist Liberals under Lloyd George as their allies). The role of opposition had passed to Labour. The Liberal Party had no role. At a general election a month after the war ended the Liberal leader—so recently leader of the nation— suffered political annihilation.

---

2 Francis Hirst to Scott, May 28, 1915.

Many Liberal principles went with him. Liberties which had been surrendered "for the duration" never returned. The passport and all the restrictions on movement which it implied had come to stay. Legislation controlling aliens persisted even after Englishmen stopped wanting to ill-treat Germans. Laws against espionage and sedition and the panoply of interference in the privacy of individuals needed to enforce them continued into peacetime. Only today (*i.e.*, July, 1967) are Englishmen becoming aware of some of these legacies of World War I: that all cables passing in and out of the country, though theoretically private, are subject to government scrutiny and that press censorship continues in the form of D notices—warnings to newspapers against revealing information on defense matters whose publication is deemed "not in the public interest."[3]

Yet clearly this is an incomplete picture. For one thing, many intrusions into personal liberty have persisted, not because of the war, but because of one of its most potent consequences: the triumph of Bolshevism in Russia and its presumed challenge to stability in Britain. For another, although liberty has suffered considerable inroads since 1914, these have not gone so far as to destroy confidence in the existence of liberty. Englishmen still believe themselves to be free to say pretty much what they please, free above all to criticize the government of the day and to advocate its overthrow by constitutional means.

Further, although the Liberal Party ceased to be an effective force after 1918, many of its leading principles were adopted by one or both of the other major parties. Wartime innovations which Liberals had feared would never be discarded disappeared promptly with the coming of peace, even under Conservative-dominated governments. The most striking case was conscription. No standing Army was maintained in Britain to "enslave the working classes" or even (after a brief but deplorable period) to "keep down Ireland." Instead the antimilitarist traditions of England rapidly reasserted themselves.

Other Liberal causes prospered after 1918. Ireland ultimately received a measure of self-government wider than any proposed before the war (except for the exclusion of Ulster, itself something of a triumph for self-determination). India also progressed toward self-government. At home the franchise was made more democratic, and the supremacy of the House of Commons over both monarchy

---

3 See David Williams, *Not in the Public Interest* (London, 1965). I am grateful to Mr. Williams for drawing my attention to many intrusions into liberty which are legacies of the First World War and for letting me see the manuscript of the relevant parts of his forthcoming book *Keeping the Peace*.

and House of Lords was preserved. Moreover, the decade after the war, far from being an era of tariffs, was the Indian summer of free trade. The Conservatives held office, but only on the understanding that they did not introduce tariffs. When they tried to, at the end of 1923, they were rudely voted out of power. The first Labour government to hold office in Britain, in 1924, had a clear mandate for only one thing: the preservation of free trade. Its Chancellor of the Exchequer, Philip Snowden, wanted nothing more.

Admittedly, after 1930 the situation changed. Free trade (along with the gold standard) disappeared. But this was not primarily because Englishmen willed it. Rather, it was their desperate response to economic collapse abroad and Britain's decline as a world economic power—a decline which itself may have been in part caused by the war, but only in part. Even so, it is generally true that as long as Englishmen felt they had any real choice in the matter, they clung to Liberal economic principles.

The same applies to another great Liberal doctrine which had fallen in the dust in 1914: international conciliation. From about 1924 Conservative and Labour governments vied with each other in the quest for peace and disarmament. Indeed, the Conservative regimes of the 1930's were so anxious to avoid war that they suffered rebuffs and humiliations at the hands of Germany which the prewar Liberal government would never have tolerated. One needs only to contrast Neville Chamberlain's performance at Munich in 1938 with Lloyd George's Mansion House speech in 1911 to recognize that the Conservatives, far from rejecting Liberal principles, had embraced some of them not wisely but too well.

This argument can be carried too far. The Conservatives, it is true, put up with free trade in the 1920's and shunned rearmament in the 1930's. Yet this hardly proves that they were imbued with the spirit of prewar Liberalism. Rather, it suggests that they had been seared by the experiences of the First World War. They lacked the vigor to apply their own principles in face of criticism and fell easily into well-tried Liberal grooves. To change the fiscal basis of the economy, to enforce British rule on Ireland and India, to withstand a renascent and aggressive Germany—all required great effort. Governments after 1918 proved incapable of great effort. Hence they acquiesced in traditional economic customs. Hence, at least in some measure, they capitulated to the justifiable demands of Ireland and the wanton demands of the European dictators. Their actions reflected less the positive spirit of Liberalism than a negative spirit of inertia and failure of grip. The First World War appeared to have made the difference.

Yet this is too strong a note on which to end. There seems to have been a sharp break in British history between the great exertions of 1905–18 and the ineffectualness of 1919–39, with the war as its most obvious cause. Yet in a longer perspective there is also continuity. The Liberal government before 1914 had sought to attain certain objectives: to assuage the misery caused by sickness and unemployment; to assert the primacy of a democratically elected House of Commons; to foster self-government and self-determination overseas. In the fifty years since that government fell, there has been a steady, if irregular, advance toward these goals. The First World War may have affected the tempo of advance. It scarcely affected their attainment.

The twists and turns of the foregoing argument suggest that there can be no final assessment of the effects of the war on Liberalism. They also show why: because one is trying to measure intangibles. Nevertheless, two points of importance have emerged clearly enough: First, the war dealt heavy and irreparable blows to the party calling itself Liberal and made permanent inroads into the liberties of the individual. But, second, it did not overthrow the Liberal state, if by this we mean a state in which free speech and free elections are accepted as a matter of course, in which the direst effects of poverty are in the course of being mitigated and in which the urge to dominate and intimidate other peoples is held in check. We may even wonder at how many of these features of British life survived the war, as they have since survived Britain's steady decline as an international force and the rejection of these values through a growing part of the world.

C. A. W. Manning

Except for wartime occupations (1939–43), C. A. W. Manning has been in university teaching since 1923, when he was elected into a fellowship at New College. His ensuing Oxford period included an absence, as Rockefeller fellow, at Harvard, where he extended his reading and encountered Roscoe Pound. Roman law, jurisprudence, and international law—in which at times he deputized for J. L. Brierly—were among his teaching subjects. His international interests derived from a Geneva interlude, first with the International Labor Office, then as personal assistant to the Secretary-General of the League. Frequently, in the summers between 1925 and 1937, he lectured, and tutored the law group, in Sir Alfred Zimmern's famous Geneva School. In 1930 he moved, as professor of international relations, to London, where, though emeritus since 1962, he continues to lecture on the philosophical aspects of the subject. His contribution is epitomized in The Nature of International Society *(1962), an inquiry into the texture of the "social cosmos," the context, comprehensively conceived, of the life of political man.*

Born in 1894 of English, Scotch, and French Huguenot stock, Manning was educated in South Africa and at Brasenose College, Oxford, where (1919–22) he took degrees in philosophy and in law.

His reexamination of John Austin appeared in Modern Theories of Law *(ed. W. Ivor Jennings, 1933). Each year from 1932 to 1938 he participated in the International Studies Conference. His report, for UNESCO, on the university teaching of international relations in six representative countries was published in 1954. In 1963 and in 1964, lecturing on South Africa, he toured Canada and the United States. In 1965 he testified on the self-determination of peoples in the South-West Africa case at The Hague.*

"EMPIRE" INTO
"COMMONWEALTH"

WHEN, on August 4, 1914, Britain's Foreign Secretary spoke in the House of Commons on the probability of war, he ended on a note of confidence in the sources, popular and parliamentary, from which his government would be looking for support. However, he made no mention of British colonies—such as Canada and Australia —beyond the seas. There was, of course, no question of their formal noninvolvement. That for them in those days would, in British eyes, have been constitutionally inconceivable. But what in practice was he assuming they would do? It is perhaps reasonable to suppose that he found it best to wait and see. He can hardly have been wholly unmindful of the Empire.

For a British Empire then indeed there was, on whose long road into dissolution the war years would mark a stage. The United States, thirteen of them, had formerly been in it. And in it, still, was the country, South Africa, which is mine.

The tale of British decolonization has yet to be told. But the plot and its principles are familiar. In well-known instances subject peoples contributed toward their emancipation with their blood, waging war against their British "oppressors." But others, more propitiously, won freedom by making war at Britain's side. The transition to sovereign statehood of Canada, Australia, South Africa, and New Zealand would surely in any case have come, but it was expedited by the war.

For—as present-day Americans are in so good a position to know— there is nothing like having its loved ones fighting on a faraway front, for feeding a people's consciousness of its involvement in international affairs and its need to bring them within the purview of its constant concern. And an England so dependent on and sensible of the sacrifices in men and money that the Dominions were so resolutely accepting, in a conflict not immediately their own, would not have been very well situated, even had she wanted to, for resisting any suggestions that their wartime leaders might choose to offer on the subject of constitutional reform. Nor would she in any case be very likely to have wanted to.

Years ago I heard one Sunday a sermon in celebration of American independence. My companion, as we left the church, asked if I, as a Britisher, had felt *de trop*. This was, I may say, in one of the Carolinas, on the one hundred and fiftieth anniversary of the famous Declaration. "Not at all," I replied; "I was thinking of what people like you had accomplished for people like me." Freedom had been ours virtually for the asking.

Elsewhere the pattern was somewhat other. In at least three ways the process in Britain's Asian and African possessions has differed from that in "her" Dominions a generation before. Her acquiescence in the coming-of-age was not, in our earlier case, much influenced by third-party, notably American, opinion; there was not in 1917, in the shape of a world assembly, a floodlit platform to excite the narcissistic ambitions of the newly fledged, and our advance, if impressive at the time, was not yet a leap into full independence. All we had aspired to was a hand on the tiller of the family boat. And theretofore we had wanted hardly even that. Self-determination? I, for one, had never heard of it.

My father, a civil servant, had taught me no politics. But he had admonished me not to underestimate the Boers—"a fine people, an indomitable little nation," which had held at bay the mighty British Empire for two and a half years. He insisted that I study their Dutch language, not as yet then locally an "official" language, to the neglect of my tenuous French.

With my parent's occupational displacement, after Union in 1910, from Cape Town to Pretoria, I came to experience the neighborly kindness, at his Irene home, of General Jan Christiaan Smuts. I thus early became Smuts-conscious and was pleased, when subsequently enrolled in "his" new defense force in 1913, to be serving, in a sense, under him. Years later, in July, 1919, I was to find myself his fellow passenger when sailing from Southampton for home. And so at Cape Town I witnessed, on the quay, his reunion with General Botha, on whose death, within the month, he was to inherit the premiership of the Union. Two outstanding characters and great South Africans.

From London in May, 1917, Smuts had written to his wife: "A big movement to take me into the Cabinet, but I shall prefer to return to my little country and nation, otherwise people will entirely forget me and I shall perhaps be regarded as English."[1]

Many saw in Botha the greater of the two, as he was certainly the better loved. Of him, when he died, the *Round Table* wrote:

---

[1] *Smuts Papers,* Vol. III, p. 498.

A modern Plutarch would write for us the Parallel Lives of General Washington and General Botha. He would find the link between them less in the outward circumstances of their lives—though there it is sufficiently striking; both, though men of peace at heart, first won distinction and influence in the field, both were called from military to political leadership—than in an inward harmony of character. A strong sense of duty, the love of all that was honorable, and a certain serene wisdom were the distinguishing qualities of General Botha as of Washington.[2]

South Africa's is a checkered story. From Europe in the early 1600's there had migrated to North America people who made no attempt to form there, along with the indigenous communities, a single, hybrid society. Instead, they established a replica of Europe. Almost contemporaneously, Dutchmen settled at what is now the Cape. There were thenceforth two societies—we, the "Europeans," they, the "Natives." The British, gaining control in the Napoleonic upheaval, thought to impose other, equalitarian standards. Many of the Dutch, *alias* Boers, *alias* Afrikaners, trekked away, to found new little Europes in the north. At the turn of the century Britain subdued the Boer republics, and in 1910 she combined them, with the Cape and Natal, into the Union of South Africa, under a system of white oligarchical rule. ("Under certain conditions," writes Robert MacIver, "the only possible form of government is some kind of oligarchy."[3])

Though not all of Britain's constitutional creations have endured, this one most definitely did. For lads like me had understood that our "first step towards being a citizen of the Empire" was "to be a citizen of South Africa" and that "the only condition" on which South Africa could remain a member of the Empire was that "British and Dutch South Africans must be able to work out a common basis of citizenship."[4] And this we tried, and still are trying, to do.

Of the ruling minority, the Boers form some 60 percent, and under the Westminster type of constitution a party representing Afrikaner nationalism has since 1948 been in control. In 1914 this party, then small, stood, as in 1939 it would again, for neutrality. "We are not pro-German, but anti-British."[5] "I see," wrote Smuts in May, 1917, "Hertzog has just made another embittered attack on the Government because we have not stayed out of the European complications! He is really quite mad, although there are many

---

[2] *Round Table*, X, p. 98.
[3] Robert M. MacIver, *The Web of Government*, New York, 1947, p. 191.
[4] *Round Table*, IX, p. 626.
[5] *Ibid.*, p. 626.

who are mad with him. Wilson also wanted, oh so much, to stay out of it, and what has happened? In the end almost no nation in the world will stay out of it."[6]

Hertzog, who had left the Botha Ministry in 1912 and was in 1924 to replace Smuts in the premiership, was already becoming a power in the land. I, as a youngster, had met him, too, and been told of how, having first thought to study, as did Smuts, at Cambridge, he had, on a disagreeable first impression there of undergraduate deportment, switched instead to Holland. On what trifles does man's history turn!

The part played in the war and at the peace table by Botha and Smuts, so recently Britain's adversaries in the field, was often to be cited as vindication for the methods of British Liberalism in the years between. But not by everybody. When in 1922 Irish leaders were being cast in Whitehall for a comparable role, it befell me at a luncheon table to hear the views of him whose style, in negotiation with Kruger in 1899 and as ruler of the ex-republics on the morrow of their defeat, had left scars on the susceptibilities of the Boers. He, Lord Milner, and Smuts and Botha had twice been peacemakers together, in 1902 on opposite sides, in 1919 on the same side, of the table. Britain's experience, he now advised us, with those two men, was in his opinion "a most *im*moral lesson." Not necessarily always would trustful policies elicit from erstwhile enemies such loyalty and magnanimity as from these.

And, he might have added, such cooperation. When in 1914 Britain conceived as a first wartime objective the elimination from South-West Africa of German power and proposed to Botha that he assume the task, this was not, of course, with any pretension to dictate. It was simply a matter of moral suasion. While South Africans, myself included, might indeed have grown up seeing South-West as the possible source of future attacks on the Union, the thought of becoming the attackers there was something different and had little local appeal. Even so, Botha deferred to Asquith's urging and, to commend his policy to the public, decided personally to command South Africa's forces in the campaign. But for the Rhodes scholarship which was now heading me for Oxford, I might well have been there with him.

As it was, that August had found me in Switzerland, where my grandmother then resided. For three weeks, during French mobilization, trains for returning British tourists could not run. But eventually the ways were cleared, and we, *les anglais*, encumbered

---

6 *Smuts Papers*, Vol. III, p. 498.

with too much hand luggage, *plus* magnums of Montreux water, bade farewell to the pleasant, neutral lakeside scene. We were to be fifty-nine hours on the journey and to cross over not, as planned, from Boulogne, now on the point of being abandoned, but Dieppe.

At Geneva we changed trains, with crashings of dropped bottles by the way. Soon we were once more on the move. Someone scribbled copies of a supposed verse of *"La Marseillaise,"* and in France, at the larger stops, we would line up and sing it, to the apparent consolation of the harassed townsfolk. *"Vive la France! Vive l'Angleterre!"* It was all very pre-De Gaulle.

It was in late June that the Sarajevo killings had occurred. To the South African schoolboy—for I was scarcely more—the news meant little. But the Paris *Daily Mail* saw something in it, as did the *Feuille d'Avis* of Montreux, before whose windows one stood for postings of the latest information.

My granny, whose memories included the accession of Queen Victoria, was confident, from her experience, that "the Powers" would "find a way." And even should they fail and England be involved, Lord Kitchener would be sent for, so all would be well. And when he duly was, there appeared, in tiny print in the usual window, an item on his calling for 100,000 men.

There was nothing particularly theatrical about my motivations, on reaching London, in joining up. His Majesty was at war, and I was his faithful subject.

Sometimes I have wondered what proportion of those phlegmatic volunteers, representing England's cream, along with whom I queued to be recruited, will have seen a thirtieth birthday. Physically, they might have come from California!

We paraded, our first fortnight, in the park. There one morning we were reviewed, nonofficially, by a horseman in a trilby hat, with a cigar. First Lord, not for the only time, of the Admiralty Mr. Churchill was returning, when our officer intercepted him, from a canter in the Row.

No one, then or ever, saw anything out of the ordinary in the presence of a boy from Cape Town in a British unit. Even when, in autumn, 1918, I was for six unforgettable days to be a guest with the British Fleet, it was always as "soldier" that they addressed me, never as "you from overseas."

It was indeed unforgettable, the spectacle of those immense ships, more than fifty of them, with a Yankee squadron—*Arkansas, Wyoming,* and a couple more—steaming magnificently, yet modestly behind. Had the Hun then put to sea, as was thought at that stage not unlikely, it was Beatty's considered policy this time to brave, not evade, the torpedoes—so there could soon have been gaps, in the fighting formation, for Britain's associates to fill.

I had not anticipated seeing there those naval Americans. True, I had, during a convalescence in London a year before, applauded the marching, past the palace and afterward the War Office—where from a balcony the Cabinet looked pensively on—of the first portentous contingent, technicians I gathered, of the burgeoning new armies of the United States. These men were mostly from homes not more remote from the war than mine, but it was, I knew, as natural that their advent should be thus belated as that mine should have been the earlier, in the operational zone.

How welcome they were, at that stressful juncture, with their promise of victory by and by! With what relish did I not appreciate the Bruce Bairnsfather cartoon: "Another two million men just arrived from the base, Colonel." "All right, give 'em tea, Sergeant." I would gladly have given 'em more than tea.

As natural, I said, for me. It is perhaps worth further considering what it was that had brought the quick response of colonial Britishers in England's day of need. Reasoned explanations are offered. Recently I suggested one. With what feelings had the young men made themselves available "in what was for them their own cause only in so far as it was Britain's cause"? What would surely have counted for something, I wrote, "in the minds at least of many, was the confidence that should they themselves or their country be at some future time in trouble the mighty hand of Britain would be there to see them through. . . . If tomorrow it could be for others to render help, it happened to be their turn now."

But since then, in paging the *Round Table,* I have come upon a phrase, "the instinct of Imperial solidarity," and on reflection I believe that with those of us who were bred as little colonials, conditioned to reverence a queen and then a king and to think in idealistic imagery of the old country, the impulse to rally round rose from something deeper within us than any rational judgment. That something—brought up in England, I might possibly not have had it. Whereas, albeit an alien now in Britain, I have traces of it still. Hence the sharpness of my latter-day disenchantment. Hence the false bravado of lines I indited, that bleak, sunny morning of May 31, 1961,[7] in my determination not to care. "The break with Britain—what is that to me? The England of my dreams so far has died. So much my early vision is belied by what in practice she has proved to be." Sour grapes?

---

[7] The day South Africa's loss of Commonwealth membership became effective.

But then, with that amiable sentiment off my chest, I went on more authentically: "The Commonwealth, by contrast, that indeed it is for me a tragedy to quit: so much my life was all bound up in it, its values so embedded in my creed." However, here, too, there had been change. "Those values, with their lessons for the wise in how extremes in peace may coexist, outmoded are: the Afro-Asianist shatters the air with shouts of 'Ostracize!' "

It was partly, I suspect, in appreciation of the seemingly instinctual nature of the Empire's wartime cohesion that its assembled leaders, challenged in those anxious days to visualize the future of their association and urged by the proponents of federation to seize what they saw as the psychological moment for a decisive advance, found refuge in an agreed postponement of the issue. Call it an act of official faith, call it a cynical subterfuge, a sophisticated maneuver, call it a confidence trick, an exercise in diplomatic stalling—in retrospect, that resolution of 1917 stands out as a feat of collective statecraft, a blessed alternative to the untimely admission that, in academic logic, the federation-mongers were only too unanswerably right. Sooner or later, they were showing, it must be either federation or else separation into independent sovereign states. This, for the *Round Table*, was the essential question—"are we determined that come what may the Empire shall endure?"[8]

Granted, however, that the conditions of 1914 must never be suffered to recur, that there must be some change, what hope was there at that untranquil moment of easy agreement on its nature? Let the matter therefore be examined by a conference after the war, and first, let the war be won. Thus, in unity of spirit and in singleness of belligerent purpose, but with the constitutional issue unresolved, the Commonwealth soldiered on.

Federation. Who was it that had obliterated that particular cock robin? To a meeting in late 1919 at Victoria West, Smuts explained: "When I went to England I found that there was a totally wrong movement afoot, a movement to establish an Imperial Federation. . . . I made it perfectly clear to the English that the system was absolutely impossible. . . . Largely as a result of my attitude in England, that view of Empire . . . has been given up. . . ."[9]

While throughout the war South Africa thus partnered Canada in the leadership for Dominion equality and freedom, their preoccupations in the matter were not, therefore, necessarily the same.

---

8 *Round Table*, Vol. VI, p. 706.
9 *Ibid.*, Vol. X, 199–200.

Smuts' paramount interest was in promoting fuller acceptance in his country of its status and future in the Commonwealth. "I want very much," he wrote to Mrs. Smuts, "to see that in future our position in the Dominions is improved. I cannot and never shall forget that we were free republics." He believed he could influence his colleagues of the other Dominions "in the right direction."[10]

Looking back, one now may wonder, though I certainly did not do so at the time, with how much confidence those Empire statesmen can have reckoned on an eventual solving of their problem, after the war. Smuts, it is true, with a facility all too typical of his tongue, declared in Edinburgh: "The spirit of comradeship which is the only basis of union is there, and on that basis I am sure we shall find a solution of our constitutional relations in future."[11]

The supposition that when two or more nations, differently situated, their leaders responsible to electorates differing in traditions and outlook, are gathered together in unity's name, a spirit of comradeship will suffice to bridge the divergences and dissolve the conflicts between them is attractive, but irrational. The affecting of such a belief may serve a public purpose. But if, in fact, those Robert Bordens, Lloyd Georges, and the rest did indeed have so much faith in what one may call the myth of the diplomatic indivisibility of the Commonwealth as a formula for the strategic future, this will surely have been the classic instance of the triumph of courage over dubiety, if not of hope over experience.

But that resolution did indeed serve their turn. Innocents like myself were content to believe in that spirit of comradeship and its sufficiency to the Commonwealth's need. *Our* Empire was basically a single system, with a single situation and, at moments of crisis, a single interest, to be reflected, after discussion, in a single stance. Professor Mazrui, of Makerere, has remarked dryly on the proneness of the late Lord Lugard to posit as axiomatic a community of interest between the Empire and its several parts.[12] I own that when young, I, too, took this for granted. And so indeed, one might have inferred, did Smuts: "If your foreign policy is going to rest, not only on the basis of your Cabinet here, but finally on the whole of the British Empire, it will have to be a simpler and more intelligible policy, which will, I am sure, lead in the end to less friction, and the greater safety of the Empire."[13] "And why not?" I might have commented. Yet it all turned on that enormous "if." Brave

---

10 *Smuts Papers*, Vol. III, p. 474.
11 *Ibid.*, p. 506.
12 Ali A. Mazrui, *Towards a Pax Africana*. Chicago, 1967, p. 149.
13 H. Duncan Hall, *The British Commonwealth of Nations*, p. 320.

words, but how breezily unrealistic. Could anyone seriously imagine that, merely because it might be more convenient, it would, therefore, be easier in the future than in the past for Britain's policy to be made simple and intelligible? Not a hint here of how exactly that policy was to be caused to rest "on the whole of the British Empire." As well might the decisions of the United States be required to rest on the whole of the North Atlantic alliance.

And as for that postulated spirit of comradeship. Were the Commonwealth leaders not the spokesmen of dynamic democracies, all with opponents eager to supersede them in the seats of power—possibly with different views? Current between the wars and nourished further by the events of 1939 were suggestions of a theory that whereas in the League of Nations the members, though having sworn solidarity, found excuses when put to the test, in the Commonwealth, by contrast, the members, pledging nothing in advance, were as one when any of their number was in trouble. When the late Leo Amery once developed this idea to me, I was uncouth enough to retort that it was, on the contrary, rather as in a horse race, where the starter's special concern was to give the signal only when all were just ready to go. Why no war in 1938? Partly because Britain must play for time, till the Commonwealth, too, would be likely to come in. At this, Mr. Amery fell silent, then chose another topic.

As Duncan Hall had put it, "The core of the problem of Dominion status" was "how to reconcile the '*absolute* equality of nationhood,' and the constitutional independence demanded by the Dominions, with the maintenance of the formal unity of the Empire, which is equally desired by them."[14] In his own remarkable view, the British Commonwealth would "in the last resort . . . rely upon the force of public opinion throughout the group to bring a recalcitrant state into line with the others."[15] So, too, Lord Milner: "Anything like dissension between different British States in the Councils of the League would be so overwhelmingly condemned by public opinion in all of them that it should be an easy task for statesmanship to avoid it."[16] Easy? Whose pliability was here being presupposed? Some problems are not to be solved by simply dismissing them, in words. Had Smuts not written, in 1917: "The British Empire must be based on freedom or go down?"[17] One is reminded of the *Round Table*, June, 1916: "The British

---

14 *Ibid.*, p. 3.
15 *Ibid.*, p. 314.
16 *Ibid.*, p. 344.
17 *Smuts Papers*, Vol. III, 498.

Commonwealth is often misunderstood by shallow minds. . . ."[18]
And also, it would seem, by minds by no means shallow!

How about this one, for a misunderstanding? It concerns the historical dating of Dominion independence. In current controversy over Rhodesia, South Africa is not infrequently referred to as a warning of what may happen if a colony is given its independence before the introduction of majority rule. This, in a way, is doubtless fair enough. But when did the alleged procedural blunder occur? Early, it is implied. By the Colin Legums, South Africa's independence is antedated to 1910![19] Yet in 1915 the *Round Table* was still at most foreseeing that Canada would "clearly be content hereafter, like Scotland [*sic*], with making a distinctive national contribution to a broader Commonwealth."[20] Like Scotland—goodness me! And even Smuts, expatiating in 1919 on the improved position of the Dominions, on how their "status of complete nationhood" had now received international recognition, and on how "as members of the Britannic League" they would "henceforth go forward on terms of equal brotherhood with the other nations on the great paths of the world,"[21] forbore to say "with other sovereign states." No Dominion, in 1919, had thought as yet to provide itself with a department of external affairs.

But the image that its members had of the Commonwealth and of themselves would never cease to change. "We are not," Smuts had said, "an Empire, but a system of nations . . . not only a static system, a stationary system, but a dynamic system, growing, evolving all the time towards new destinies."[22] And this, after all, was not anything very new. "What was really happening," Duncan Hall was to write, of a somewhat earlier period, "was that the colonists were in fact ceasing to be citizens of England and were becoming citizens of Massachusetts or Virginia."[23] "In 1914," the same writer pointed out, "the term 'British Empire' signified a central government surrounded by a number of more or less dependent states: in 1919 it signified a new type of political association, namely a group of autonomous states organized on a basis of complete constitutional equality under a common Crown."[24]

At what precise point in their evolution do nations become just

---

18 *Round Table*, Vol. VI, 117.
19 Colin and Margaret Legum, *South Africa: Crisis for the West.* New York, 1964, pp. 7, 146.
20 *Round Table*, Vol. VI, p. 156.
21 Hall, *op. cit.*, p. 338.
22 *Smuts Papers*, Vol. III, p. 510.
23 Hall, *op. cit.*, p. 9.
24 *Ibid.*, p. 195.

that? It seems wisest to reply that this is first and foremost a question of a specific mode of emerging collective self-awareness. It seems agreed, for instance, that in 1867, when Canada was constituted, there existed as yet no Canadian nation, whereas in 1900 it was an Australian nation already in being which created for itself a national government. "It may be," reflected the *Round Table*, December, 1915, "that the Canadian nation was born on the battlefield of St. Julien. . . . On the morning of Monday, April 26th . . . the general sorrow was more than neutralized by pride in the heroism of the dead."[25]

And what then of my own South Africa? Of her must, I fear, be conceded rather what Prime Minister Ileo, in 1961, said of his likewise complex country: "The Congo is not a people. It is a collection of large ethnic groups and each of them is a people."[26] Nevertheless the personified South Africa, the "country" of my mystic, sentimental attachment, was for me a reality even before the South Africa of my present-day citizenship left the runway. For had "she" not shown herself a worthy match for England—at cricket in 1905, at rugby football in 1906? With a small *n*, I was already a South African nationalist, sportswise, when the Union was at most but a project in the mind. Who knows? Had Canada long since, like Australia and South Africa, sent her cricketers to Lord's, it might not have required a costly battle to imbue her scattered citizenry with a common pride, in the performance of their "boys over there."

In the war years all the Empire had its boys over there. And already in early 1915 the British Colonial Secretary was announcing his government's intention to consult the Dominions on the framing of the eventual peace. Moreover, "since 1916," it was subsequently said, "every Dominion has been fully informed both by cable and despatch on all aspects of the foreign policy of the Empire."[27] Yet when Mr. Churchill in 1940 was asked about this sharing of cabled information, he minuted: "While . . . there is no change in principle, there should be considerable soft-pedalling in practice."[28] One may wonder if there will ever, in practice, have been a total nonemployment of the pedal.

Meanwhile, when at last the war had ended, it was no longer just a question of shared information or consultation. On the insistence more especially of Canada, with Lloyd George's backing, and in

---

25 *Round Table*, Vol. VI, 156.
26 New York *Times*, February 12, 1961.
27 *Round Table*, Vol. XIII, p. 19.
28 Winston S. Churchill, *The Second World War*. Boston, 1949, Vol. II, p. 631.

face of stiff, but not unlimited, resistance from puzzled friendly powers, the Dominions, albeit anomalously, were present, if not as parties, then at least as signatories, to the treaty.

The truth seems to be that the changes wrought in the imperial structure by the pressures of the war should be measured, as it were, on more levels than one. Sociologically speaking, the progress was considerable. Constitutionally, there was at most an irreversible shift of emphasis as between legal and conventional points of view. And at the level of formal recognition there was the demonstration, quiet but unequivocal, of a type of participating personality new to the council rooms and corridors of diplomacy. The arrangement here in question was said to be designed not to give the British Empire any undue recognition, but "to recognize the position of the Dominions in the Empire and assure to the overseas British countries equal authority with the smaller nations many of whom had made no sacrifices in the long struggle for freedom and civilisation. . . ."[29]

Nevertheless, as though by necessary consequence of their mere presence at the table, the Dominions got included, as members individually, in Woodrow Wilson's League. Individually, as members, but not yet, therefore, as sovereign states. Was not India, too, a member, being not even a Dominion?

Even so, once members of the League, the Dominions were, as persons in their own right, performers, as never previously, in the international drama. It could be only a matter of time and circumstances—we now may feel—before they would stand forth on their unchallengeable own as sovereign states. Was all this then foreseen? Not explicitly, at the time. Sensible men, if asked, would doubtless have endorsed Sir Robert Borden: "It is unwise, having regard to the lessons of the past, for any of us to predict absolutely the developments of the future."[30]

---

[29] Hall, *op cit.*, p. 154.
[30] *Ibid.*, p. 167.

Pierre Renouvin

PIERRE RENOUVIN, *historian and president of the Fondation Nationale des Sciences Politiques* (National Foundation of Political Science), *was born on January 9, 1893, at Paris. His father was a manufacturer; his mother belonged to an academic family. Having finished his secondary education at the Lycée Louis-le-Grand, he began to study for a degree at the Faculté de Droit* (Law School) *and concurrently for a degree in history at the Sorbonne. At nineteen and a half, Renouvin passed the examination in history, and the following year he won his degree in law.*

The First World War intervened, and it marked him deeply. Wounded twice, he had to have his left arm amputated in April, 1917. He received the Croix de guerre of the Legion of Honor for military service.

Professor at the Sorbonne (since 1933) *and at the Institut d'Études Politiques* (Institute of Political Studies), *he has taught generations of students, focusing in his courses on the problem of nationhood, relations among the great powers in the nineteenth and twentieth centuries, methods of European expansion, and the question of the Far East.*

As a historian, he has written vast syntheses in L'Histoire des relations internationales (The History of International Relations), *which he edited. He was also the editor of the* Revue d'histoire de la Guerre Mondiale (Journal of the History of the World War) *until 1939, and has directed the* Revue historique *since 1942. He is the author of more than sixty articles published in various magazines and newspapers. Among his published books are* Les Formes du gouvernement de guerre (1924), Les Origines immédiates de la guerre (1925), *and* La Crise européenne et la Grande Guerre (1934). *In this third book Renouvin discussed not only the military and political events of the war, but entered into the study of the economic and moral forces behind the conflict, an approach for which he has since become famous.*

Along with his research and writing, Renouvin has performed official duties; he has been a member of the Institut d'Études Politiques since 1946, president of the Fondation Nationale des Sciences Politiques, dean of the Faculté des Lettres (School of Humanities) *in Paris from 1955 to 1958, and a member of the University Council from 1952 to 1958.*

Renouvin holds the grand cross of the Legion of Honor.

THE ROLE OF PUBLIC OPINION, 1914–18*

————◆◆◆————

IN A "TOTAL" WAR, to which the belligerent states commit all their might without limitation, not only is victory the outcome of the collision of arms, but it also depends on the state's capacity for organization and endurance in the realm of economic resources and, above all, on the moral cohesion of its populace. For govern-ments to be able to devote all their efforts to conducting the war, they must feel they are supported by public opinion. Knowing the state of the public mind in their own country is thus one of their major concerns, and it is no less important for them to know what the adversary's is; each watches for signs of weakening.

But how can one get a real knowledge of public opinion? The government is aware of currents of opinion in the legislature, if not from the floor (for in time of war speakers hesitate to express their thoughts publicly), then from conversations held in the corridors and in committee meetings. It knows what opinions are being expressed in the press and, more significantly, those that would have been expressed but could not break through the wall of censorship. But it fully realizes that journalists' appraisals of events never give an exact idea of their readers' state of mind; it realizes also that some opinion trends develop independently of any written cover-age. Hence, it seeks to learn through its agents about the exchanges that occur in the midst of opinion groups or professional associa-tions, particularly in trade unions. It often has soundings taken in letters—civilians' as well as soldiers'—and has attitude reports drawn up by the inspectors. Finally, it inquires of local administrative chiefs and police departments, who are in a position to give an overall impression without reference to specific documentation and who can indicate the diffuse trends expressed in conversations, particularly among the peasants.

When these records are preserved, the materials at the disposal of historical investigators are abundant. The history of public opinion has hardly begun to be studied. At present, it is possible to draw

* Translated from the French by Sally Abeles.

only a simple sketch of it, which nonetheless allows us to point up some essential lines and to answer the question that demands attention: What part did public opinion trends play in the confrontation of the forces which contended from 1914 to 1918? At what points were these trends determining?

What share in the immediate origins of the conflict should be accorded to opinion trends? In Serbia, directly threatened by the Austro-Hungarian Army, and in Belgium, whose neutrality was violated by the German invasion, the people were obviously almost unanimous in their protest against the aggression. But these positions were consequent on the event; they were in no wise causative. Was it otherwise in the major states that took up arms in August, 1914?

In large measure, public opinion seems to have accepted government policies, which were dominated by a concern for security and prestige. At Berlin on July 29, 1914, the Social Democratic Party promised the government not to interfere with its decisions, and the French Socialist Party was then led to take the same stance. The International Socialist Bureau, which at the beginning of the diplomatic crisis had asked all Socialist parties to demonstrate against war, quickly abandoned this attempt. In France, as in Germany, after a few brief demonstrations on the evening of July 28, in Paris and in Berlin, the masses of workers discarded the notion of proletarian solidarity that the International Socialist congresses had continuously expressed over the previous ten years and brought national interests to the fore.

The governments proclaimed the *union sacrée*. In England, the left wing of the Labour Party with Ramsay MacDonald and a few scattered members of the Liberal Party refused to vote war allocations, but these independents found no support in the trade-union movement. In Austria-Hungary, the Socialist newspapers clearly expressed the wish to safeguard the peace but made not the slightest gesture of resistance. Only in Russia did an antiwar movement appear among the Socialists, through a strike of the metalworkers. Minister of the Interior Maklakov expressed anguish when he was summoned to put his signature on the order for general mobilization on July 30; it seemed to him that the Russian masses were readier to hear a call to revolution than a call to national defense. Yet at no time did the Socialist opposition present a serious obstacle to government decisions. Basically, public opinion in the belligerent states was very largely resigned, doubtless because it had grown accustomed to the idea of war over ten years of repeated diplomatic crises. And this assent confirmed the governments in the path of resoluteness.

But it seems that nowhere did this state of the public mind act as a *stimulus*. In Austria-Hungary, where opposition between national groups excluded the possibility of a broad current of opinion, the newspapers which endorsed a policy of force were expressing the views of only the high officials, the diplomatic corps, or the military General Staffs. In Russia, some liberal bourgeois circles and intellectuals joined in a nationalistic trend, but in July, 1914, according to all the evidence, the spokesmen of this nationalism had no influence over political action. In Great Britain, public opinion was slow to awaken; it remained hesitant and divided until the news of the German ultimatum to Belgium, whereas the Prime Minister and the majority of the Cabinet had already decided twenty-four hours earlier to intervene in the war. In France and Germany, it is true, expressions of opinion in favor of the war were more vigorous; but these were not very widespread, and they were late. In Paris, street processions (three columns of demonstrators, numbering no more than 7,000 people in all) formed only on August 2, *after* the publication of the general mobilization order. Local officials in the provinces reported the populace calm and unexcited and confident, the draftees spirited; but only in the Midi, at Nice and Toulon, where the people are more exuberant, did they record "enthusiasm."

In sum—and this is the essential point—at no time did currents of opinion *determine* the decisions of the governments, but they did show officialdom that it could envisage the eventuality of war without danger to the country's internal stability; once the decisions were taken, public opinion approved them.

These peoples who gave their consent to war in August, 1914, following a long period of peace, were only vaguely aware of the trials and sufferings they would have to face. On the contrary, those who entered the conflict later knew through the press the nature of the conflict and the magnitude of the losses in human life, and yet they too were willing to take part in it. Were they resigned, or cooperative, or enthusiastic?

In the Balkan states, the mass of the people, who were rural, had no political education and had hardly any opportunity to exercise seriously the right to vote; political decisions were the affair of a few men, leaders of cliques rather than parties; the legislative institutions were at the mercy of the powers-that-were. The restricted circles which shared in the decision making were divided on the question of launching the country into the venture of war. At

Constantinople, Enver Pasha's policy, leading Turkey to enter the conflict on the side of Germany, was fought by Talaat Bey. At Sofia in September–October, 1915, parliamentary opposition to the policy of King Ferdinand and his Prime Minister, Vasil Radoslavov, was vehement; the leaders of this opposition warned the King they would make him personally responsible for the consequences of his policy, but their efforts were in vain. At Bucharest on August 27, 1916, when the Royal Council was presented with the decision made by the King and the President of the Council, the policy of intervention ran afoul of some criticism, in one case vehement. But it would be quite excessive to think that these displays expressed an opinion trend; these were the reactions of some political "professionals" whose concepts of the national interest were divergent but who were not concerned with the behavior of the masses.

In the case of Italy's intervention, the situation is entirely different. After conducting negotiations with the two groups of belligerents simultaneously, the Italian government ended by signing the Pact of London with the Entente states on April 26, 1915. While this government was seeking its course, the public openly discussed the possible solutions; it divided into two currents, which split open the ranks of the political parties: On the one hand were the proponents of intervention—a few Socialists, grouped around Benito Mussolini, and some trade unionists joined together with Christian Democrats and a segment of the liberal bourgeoisie and on the other, neutrality—but a "paying" neutrality—was preached by the leader of the Liberal Party, Giovanni Giolitti, and was wanted by almost all the Socialists and most of the Catholics. Here, then, were real currents of opinion.

Now, when the government was preparing to sign the Pact of London and to ask the Parliament to vote war appropriations, the majority of the deputies (320 out of 508) showed themselves adherents to Giolitti's policy. On May 13 the government resigned. But the proponents of intervention raised a violent protest against the parliamentary majority; part of the press led a heated campaign against the neutralists, for only participation in the war would enable Italy fully to achieve its national aspirations. This current of opinion displayed itself "in the street": at Rome, Gabriele D'Annunzio's appeal to the people; at Milan, Florence, Turin, processions of people forming to the cry of "We want war!" The demonstrations were effective: The King rejected the government's resignation, and the Parliament submitted to voting the war allocations, by a large majority, on May 20. Yet only a minority of the population actually wanted intervention, for the mass of the peasants remained passive. But it was enough for the partisans of intervention to demonstrate their resolution and their strength in numbers in the big cities for their will to be imposed. It was this current of opinion that furnished the decisive stimulus.

The role of public opinion was equally important in the decision of the United States, but it was defined in different terms. The question of what posture to adopt toward the European conflict had, of course, given rise to broad discussions in 1915 and 1916, particularly since the considerable increase in American exports had been somewhat checked by the blockade and submarine warfare; but the Presidential elections in November, 1916, clearly demonstrated that the great majority of citizens, while evincing moral disapproval of Germany, wanted neutrality maintained—to keep the United States "out of the war" had been the slogan adopted by both the Democrats and the Republicans.

In early February, 1917, when Germany had decided on submarine warfare "to the death," President Wilson was well aware that neutrality was no longer possible; he was convinced that the United States had to enter the war. However, he temporized for two months longer because he wanted to be able to count on the support of public opinion. In fact, opinion was very largely favorable to intervention in the Eastern states after Germany repudiated the promises it had made in May, 1916; but in the Central and Western states it was quite reserved. The economic congestion created in American ports by the submarine warfare shook loose the neutralism of the Midwestern farmers and Southern cotton planters; the publication of the Zimmermann telegram aroused indignation in the West, echoed in the sense of national honor expressed throughout the press.

Yet the President was still uneasy, because he feared that public opinion was not yet ripe. He was reassured only when he saw the vibrant welcome the vast majority of the public gave his message to Congress announcing America's entrance into the war on April 2. In this case, the opinion trends did not act as a *stimulus,* they did not provoke the government's decisions, but they provided the President's policy with an indispensable buttress. Without them, could Wilson have made his final decisions?

In 1915 and 1916 the public in France and Great Britain, as in Germany, persisted in the main in vigorously supporting the war effort; pacifist ideas, which had almost completely disappeared from view at the outset of the hostilities, nonetheless reappeared in the early months of 1915, though they found only timid expression.

The Zimmerwald movement, which aimed to end international conflict, but in order to substitute civil war for it, had few adherents as yet. Only in Russia was national unity badly shaken and a broad segment of public opinion agitated. Yet this agitation was not pacifist; it carried a reproach to the government for its inability to give a vigorous stimulus to national defense.

But in 1917, signs of lassitude were appearing. The duration of a war whose end no one could perceive, the mental suffering, the economic difficulties led a large part of the population in all the belligerent states to hope for a compromise peace. At the moment when the general conditions of the struggle were being transformed by the threat of Russian defection and the intervention of the United States, this idea of peace was being openly envisaged.

It is important to compare the forms, the characteristics, and the practical implications of this crisis in morale in the major belligerent nations.

This decline in morale was least serious in Great Britain. The big metalworkers' strike in April–May, 1917, which hampered the manufacture of armaments, had the unique purpose of protecting the interests of "qualified" workers against the invasion of "unqualified" manpower; it was decided on contrary to the views of the trade-union chiefs; it was condemned by the great majority of the newspapers and does not seem to have been a sign of a pacifist trend in the thinking of the mass of the population. On August 10, it is true, the Trades Union Congress declared its approval of sending a delegation to the Stockholm conference, but it abandoned the project three weeks later. In November the public letter of a political liberal of great authority, Lord Lansdowne, recommending the conclusion of a peace with "no annexations," was at first favorably received by a goodly segment of the public, but the Labour Party and the trade unions disavowed this vein of thought on December 28 and declared that the peace should allow France to recover Alsace-Lorraine and Italy to satisfy its irredentist claims. Thus, on every major occasion, the ranks of the union movement provided backing for the policy of Lloyd George's Cabinet.

In Germany, war weariness reached critical proportions in April and July, 1917. The immediate cause of the strike movements, which were as serious in mid-April as in Great Britain, was the shortage in the food supply, but they rapidly took on a political cast: The Socialist press stressed the desire for peace. In July, economic difficulties were again at the bottom of protests and disturbances in several country towns. This time the question of peace was at the forefront. The Social Democratic Party declared itself in favor of a peace of "conciliation" and rejected any notion of annexation; it got support from the Progressives and Catholic Centrists. The peace resolution voted for by the majority of the Reichstag on July 19 was intended to impose a political orientation on the government, and the vote gave rise to vehement protests from the rightist parties in the press. Public opinion thus seemed capable of providing a stimulus, but it quickly weakened; six weeks later, when the Social Democrats mounted an attack against nationalist propaganda at a Reichstag session, they were not supported by the Progressives and Catholics. This decline of the movement for a peace of conciliation was connected with the signs of distintegration of which Russia was the prime example and with the hope of concluding a separate peace with that country.

From January, 1917, onward, lassitude quickly overran "all parts of the country" in Austria-Hungary, as the president of the Austrian Council observed at a session of the Council of Ministers. The Minister of Foreign Affairs told the German Chancellor in March that the Dual Monarchy was at the end of its strength and that it wanted an early peace; he renounced any annexation and wished to induce the German government to abandon Alsace-Lorraine. The press, which gave considerable space to the question of "war aims" during the summer, rarely referred to eventual territorial annexations. It printed much discussion on the nationalities issue and the right of peoples to self-determination, and it envisaged the "renovation" of the Dual Monarchy—that is, its transformation into a federal state. The leaders of the national groups nonetheless affirmed their loyalty with regard to the dynasty and envisaged, they said, only a reform of the institutions. This was doubtless a necessary precaution to sidestep the exactions of the censors and the police. But these opinion trends had an undeniably broad base, at least among the bourgeois and trade unionists. Yet at no point did they take on a revolutionary character in 1917; the workers' protest was indeed much less active than in the other belligerent states in the same period.

In France and Italy, the opinion trends at certain moments during that critical year had features with more serious implications for national solidarity and the war effort.

In June and October–November, 1917, all the reports from the administrative officials, police, and postal inspectors in France signaled a crisis in morale. In June, the causes of this were the concern aroused by Russia's situation, economic difficulties, and, above all, the failure of the April 16 offensive. The loss of morale was serious in the Army, where 68 out of 112 infantry divisions were hit by mutinous uprisings, though actually most of these were short-lived flare-ups. It was also serious among the civilian populace; only ten department prefects stated that morale remained "satisfactory," all the others reporting a decline—"weakening," "edginess," "uneasiness," "sharp change in the public spirit." Several departments recorded "confusion" among a majority of the populace, and four of them spoke of an opinion trend which demanded peace "at any price."

In the course of the summer, this restlessness died down; the people again adopted an attitude of weary resignation. But in the autumn, the Italian defeat at Caporetto and especially the Bolshevik Revolution, which opened up the possibility of a separate peace with Russia, reawakened pessimism. Mid-November saw new and vehement expressions of pacifist feeling. The postal inspection services picked up allusions in letters to an imminent revolutionary movement. Only five or six weeks later, when the impetus furnished by Clemenceau began to be felt, did observers report a recovery of public spirit.

Public opinion was even more sensitive in Italy, where economic deprivation was severer than in France and neutralist propaganda more active, since only a minority of the population had wanted the country to enter into war. This climate of doubt was already noticeable in the spring of 1917. In August and September, the crisis showed itself simultaneously in renewed neutralist activity (the public's reception of Pope Benedict XV's peace note and of Giolitti's address at Cuneo), popular disorders (the serious disturbances at Turin, which led the government to declare a "state of siege" in three provinces), and demonstrations by Socialist municipalities, which did not want to participate in the war effort. The government did not submit to these opinion pressures, but its opposition to them was rather weak. In fact, it was the military defeat, the Battle of Caporetto, which ended the internal crisis; the Austro-German invasion of Venetia provoked a tide of patriotism in the labor associations as in Catholic groups. The great majority of the public agreed that it was no longer possible to hope for peace, for the conditions would now be disastrous.

In sum, no more in Italy than in France did the opinion trends and the increasing pacifist feeling succeed in influencing government policy in 1917.

But in Russia, public opinion played an important role in the development of the revolution. Does it alone explain the revolution's course? Surely not. Economic difficulties must be taken into account; the shortage in the bread and coal supplies was the immediate cause of the revolutionary disorders at Petrograd which were to end in the fall of the czarist regime, and the stagnation of industry, aggravated by the transportation crisis, markedly weakened the authority of the provisional government. Consideration must also and particularly be given to the undertakings of the militants, who exploited the trends of public thinking, and the activities of Lenin personally, who at an opportune moment proposed a program of immediate action to the "anonymous revolutionary masses."

Yet on at least two occasions, public opinion furnished a decisive stimulus.

The first instance was the rise of the February Revolution. Well before finding itself at grips with the workers' protests, the government had lost the confidence of a good number of the businessmen, who would no longer put up with the inefficiencies of the bureaucracy; it was this revolution of attitude among the bourgeoisie that opened the way to the political revolution. But this segment of opinion was not pacifist. The workers' protest, on the contrary, was, not so much from ideological choice as from the desire to escape the hardships the war imposed on the mass of the people in their daily life. During the first two days of the revolutionary uprising, this protest was spontaneous; it surprised even the revolutionary leaders, who thought it premature. Thus, the trend of public opinion here did play a determining role.

It still retained that role in the days following the fall of the Czar, when the provisional government and the Soviet received petitions, manifestos, proposals by the thousands from every quarter, expressing the aspirations of the peasants, workers, soldiers, but also the middle classes, artists, intellectuals, without prior suggestion from the revolutionary organizations. It was a great spontaneous flood, remarkable for the vigor of the convictions and the ardor of the feelings expressed. Public opinion "outran" the public powers.[1]

But it was not public opinion which laid the way for the October Revolution, whose plan had been drawn up and whose timing had been set by Lenin. The central committee of the Bolshevik Party decided on an armed coup, because it thought that the Constituent Assembly elections would not be favorable to it. It anticipated only that a large part of public opinion would remain passive and that the promise of immediate agrarian reform and peace would ensure

---

[1] On this point, see Marc Ferro, *La Révolution de 1917: La Chute du tsarisme et les origines d'Octobre* [The Revolution of 1917: The Fall of Czarism and the Origins of the October Uprising] (Paris, 1967), with a preface by Roger Portal.

it the sympathies or at least the neutrality of the rural population. The events proved this prediction correct.

In the final analysis, is it possible to weigh the role of public opinion trends in the outcome of the conflict? After the sharp turn in the military situation on July 18, 1918, the Allied and Associated armies marched toward victory. Doubtless that victory did not seem very close until the early days of October, but it was assured, thanks to the influx of American troops. The prospect of a fifth winter of war was, therefore, fairly easy for the combatants and the civilian population to accept. When the German petition for an armistice in early October made it possible to believe that the end would perhaps arrive before the end of the year, public opinion expressed deep satisfaction, of course, but exhibited no impatience.

In the United States, what was most often read in the papers and heard in Congressional debates was the intention to impose "unconditional" surrender on the Central Powers; only gradually was President Wilson able to rally a segment of opinion to his policy of a negotiated armistice. The press in Great Britain, except for the labor papers, was distrustful of the German initiative. In France, at the heart of the radical groups, as well as on the extreme right, a portion of the opinion wanted Germany's petition to be rejected and the Allied armies to enter Germany, so as to give the enemy a direct and painful taste of the horrors and devastations of the war; but the majority wanted an immediate armistice, provided that the conditions were severe, while only a small minority wanted peace at any price. These currents of opinion effectively allowed the governments rather broad freedom of action. When all was said and done, the Armistice of November 11, 1918, was cordially received, even by those who a month earlier had protested against undertaking negotiations with Germany.

But the opinion trends whose influence it is important to assess were those in Austria-Hungary and Germany.

Public opinion had a considerable share in the breakup of Austria-Hungary, where the Slavic nationalities found themselves under a political regime structured to benefit the Germans and Magyars. The right of peoples to self-determination had already been invoked, in 1917, to demand statutory autonomy within the framework of the Empire.[2] Since the defeat of the Central Powers had become a certainty, the national groups were no longer content with that demand: They sought independence. It was the threat of

---

2 See above, p. 445.

separatist movements in Czech lands and among the southern Slavs that led the Emperor Charles to make a peace offer on September 14, which was immediately rejected. As soon as Bulgaria's defection on September 28 was a *fait accompli,* the Austro-Hungarian government expected to see these opinion trends develop speedily; the signs of disintegration worsened during the first two weeks of October.

On October 21, 1918, when President Wilson declared that autonomy could no longer be considered an adequate solution, his note fell "like a bomb" that blew up the framework of the state. The Austro-Hungarian Empire was dead. The news from the interior, spread by the papers and the Italian propaganda services, ruined the discipline and sense of duty in the Army. Why should the contingents recruited from the national minorities agree to fight to defend a state which they had no patriotic attachment for? On October 23, in two sectors of the front, small units made up of Hungarians, Czechs, and southern Slavs refused to obey orders; these mutinous troops declared that they would no longer fight in the ranks of the Imperial Army, but were prepared to defend the territory of the new national state to which they would henceforth belong. The next day the Archduke Joseph informed the Emperor that it was necessary to conclude an armistice with little delay if he wanted to prevent the disintegration of the Army.

It was this very unsound Army which took the first shock of the Italian offensive that day. The Austro-Hungarian defeat at Vittorio Veneto on October 30 was a direct result of the national movements working for the dissolution of the Dual Monarchy. The Villa Giusti armistice was negotiated by a moribund government which no longer possessed even the semblance of power. Thus public opinion was the determining force in this dislocation of the state and the Army.

The same was not true in Germany. It was not prior to the great battle but in keeping with the pace of the fighting that the decline in morale developed. Of course, a major strike of the metalworkers in January, 1918, in which the demands were predominantly political, had shown that a portion of the workers wanted peace. But during the following months, when the Treaty of Brest-Litovsk had established the victory in the east and the German offensive on the French front had met with great success, these demonstrations of war weariness and inclinations toward pacifism had disappeared. Only in mid-August, a month after the shift in the military situation, did public opinion begin to show signs of uneasiness and edginess. At the beginning of September, the press was reporting on the progress of a "tide of skepticism" which was overtaking even the Army. The political parties began to revive their disputes, and the criticisms addressed to the government were bitter: Why had it maintained false hopes so long? The conviction thus began to take hold that Germany should seek an occasion to make peace. Yet even the pessimists did not believe that this move toward peace was urgent; they thought they had several weeks' time ahead of them.

Then, at the end of September, Ludendorff suddenly decided to present President Wilson with not just a peace offer but a petition for an armistice; he imposed his decision, not without trouble, on the new Chancellor, Prince Max of Baden. This was an admission of defeat; it staggered public opinion. Reports from provincial government officials were almost unanimous in signaling profound lassitude; those from industrial regions noted signs of agitation. It was at this point that the far-left Spartacus League sent out a call to revolution through secret channels. After President Wilson issued his notes inviting the German people to free itself from "its masters," the government soon realized that it was losing control over public opinion. The mutiny of the ships' crews at Kiel and the pacifist demonstrations at Munich in early November were followed by the revolutionary actions which took place on November 8 and 9, at the same time that Marshal Foch was presenting the German delegation at Rethondes with the conditions for armistice set by the Allied and Associated governments.

These currents of German public opinion thus had an incontestable breadth and influence. It is certain that when the government and the military leaders learned the conditions for an armistice, they were no longer in a position to discuss them; the revolutionary threat at that point eclipsed all other preoccupations. But this decline of morale, these violent reactions of the public mind were not the cause of the military collapse; they were the result. The public resolve showed itself to be weakening when it became evident that the Army was pursuing a hopeless struggle.

Do these very hasty notes allow us to sketch out a general interpretation? They do at least suggest two observations.

1. Aside from Italy, public opinion trends did not have a *determining* influence on government decisions at the time the belligerent states entered into conflict. The government of each state indubitably took the set of public thinking into account; if a broad current of opinion had showed itself hostile to the war, the government obviously would have weighed the risks of the undertaking and would in all likelihood have given it up. But wherever the

public expressed an opinion, it was positive. Yet it did not provide a stimulus. It was not tides of feeling, waves of passion that directed governmental actions; it was political interests.

2. These public opinion trends had far greater influence when war weariness and the burden of long suffering led the peoples to contemplate peace. In two instances—Russia in February–March, 1917, and Austria-Hungary in October, 1918—these trends opened the way to revolutionary disturbances, in which the desire to put an end to the war played an active role. Yet these two cases were quite different. In Russia, all segments of opinion wanted or were willing to see a transformation of the social condition; in Austria-Hungary, the appeal to the right of peoples to self-determination provided the impetus. Everywhere else, the crises of low morale were not sharp or enduring enough to seriously threaten public order or impel the government to reorient its policy. They were most often directly related to the disappointments caused by war operations, and they abated as soon as the news from the front lines of combat improved. Actually, the signs of weariness and discouragement did not hinder the war effort in cases where the administrative and societal structures remained steady. But here again, Italy was the exception; the crisis in morale, which was serious in the summer of 1917 at a time when the situation on the Italian front was satisfactory, lightened in November at the moment when the defeat at Caporetto confronted the nation with grave peril.

These provisory conclusions must indeed be re-examined and modified when the study of public opinion trends has given rise to further research. But they may at present suggest reflections which studies of social psychology will perhaps be called on to evaluate.

Bishop John W. C. Wand

BISHOP WAND *was born in Grantham, England, in 1885; he was educated at the King's School in that town and later at St. Edmund Hall, Oxford, and at Bishop Jacob Hostel, Newcastle-on-Tyne.*

He was ordained in 1908, and after serving two curacies, he became a minor canon of Salisbury Cathedral and tutor at the Salisbury Theological College. During World War I he served as chaplain in the Dardanelles, France, and Germany. On his return he became vicar of St. Mark's, Salisbury, but in 1925 was appointed fellow, dean, and tutor of Oriel College, Oxford, later being made lecturer on church history at the same university.

In 1934 he was consecrated as Archbishop of Brisbane, Australia, but after nine years he was recalled to England to become Bishop of Bath and Wells. Less than two years later, in 1945, he was translated to the see of London. There he had the heavy task of restoring the leading diocese of the Anglican Communion after the ravages of war. He retired from the bishopric of London at the age of seventy and was made canon and treasurer of St. Paul's in 1955, a double post which he still holds.

He has been a member of Her Majesty's Privy Council since 1945 and was made K.C.V.O. (Knight Commander of the Royal Victorian Order) ten years later. He is an honorary D.D. of Oxford, Toronto, and West Ontario, an S.T.P. (Professor of Divinity) of Columbia, and a D.Litt. of Ripon; Honorary Fellow of Oriel College and St. Edmund Hall, Oxford, and also of King's College, London. He is the author of forty volumes, including histories of the early church and the modern church, the Westminster Commentary on I and II Peter and Jude, Anglicanism in History and Today, *and* Changeful Page *(autobiography). For ten years he was an editor of the* Church Quarterly Review.

THE EFFECT OF WORLD WAR I
ON RELIGION

THE PERIOD just before the war saw the heyday of religious observance in the West. In Rome there was a pronounced move to greater paternalism on the part of Pius X, which led to a closer centralization through the codification of canon law in 1917 and the reorganization of the Curia. In England the beginning of the twentieth century had marked the peak of the Anglo-Catholic movement. There was also a great emphasis on churchgoing. It is true that England had never caught up in the provision of churches with the needs provoked by the Industrial Revolution and that members of the new proletariat had seldom acquired religious habits. But among the middle classes, to absent oneself from church was to become *déclassé*. At weekend house parties in the country, Sunday morning church formed a regular part of the hospitality.

In the United States the upward movement became really marked a little later. But when it came, it was prolonged and raised the figures of church affiliation to the highest point (more than 60,000,000) they had reached since the union.

In Greece, Christian activity had received especially vital expression in the Zoë movement (1907). This had done much to bring the Orthodox Church up-to-date. Its struggle to free Christian social influence from the dead hand of unthinking traditionalism had spread to Orthodox churches far beyond the limits of Greece. But the only Orthodox Church doing missionary work outside its own borders at the beginning of the twentieth century was that of Russia.

"From the date of Waterloo to the beginning of the First World War Christianity had enjoyed the greatest century of its expansion and the largest influence it had ever exerted." If we are to estimate the extent of the decline that came about as the result of the war and investigate its cause or causes, we may be well advised to begin with external features and try to penetrate later to the underlying causes. For this purpose we might start with habits, pass on to morals, and end with theology.

I

Perhaps the greatest blow to the Christian religion, regarded as a habit, was the abdication of the Czar of Russia in 1917 and the subsequent establishment of an atheistic regime. That the greatest Christian country in the world, which had been Christian for nearly 1,000 years, should repudiate its connection with religion was bound to loosen the hold of the Christian faith everywhere.

On the whole the Treaty of Versailles (1919) improved the position of Protestants as against Roman Catholics. Communism met Protestantism first in East Germany, where four-fifths of the population were Protestant. A by-product of these relations was seen in Czechoslovakia, where 1,000,000 people broke away from the Roman obedience and formed the Czech National Church (1920). In Russia the declension was from Orthodoxy; in Mexico, as in Czechoslovakia, it was from Roman Catholicism. The new constitution, accepted in 1917, nationalized church property and restricted the power of the clergy. The church's constitutional demotion in these instances weakened the influence of religion in millions of lives.

There was one comparatively small instance where the opposite has been noticed. The Anglican Church in the principality of Wales was disestablished in 1920. The result has been to increase, rather than diminish, the efficiency and zeal of its members. It is now estimated that the standing of the church in that country and its influence in the community are greater than at any time since the Reformation.

In England the war brought a definitive end to what is known as the Victorian period. The few intervening years of Edwardian license had affected only the more dubious strata of the aristocracy and their hangers-on, but the loosening of the bonds between church and society that had been then begun was carried a great deal further as a result of the war.

The war effort itself assisted the decline. The dislocation of families and the long hours spent in Sunday labor tended to break up the churchgoing habit among the elderly, and the discomfort of unheated churches did not encourage it among the young. On the Continent women were employed as members of the fighting services and, being divorced from their homes, were divorced also from the habits of family religion. The men, resting at some base town before going up to the front, saw for the first time in their lives queues forming outside the brothels as for a cinema. Violence, which the vast majority of all classes repudiated with horror during times of peace, had become a virtue under conditions of war. The theft on behalf of one's mess of anything that might add to the amenities of life under the appalling conditions of trench warfare was regarded as commendable and even necessary.

All this administered a decided shock to conventional religion. When the war was over, many failed to pick up again the old religious habits. Families were no longer so closely united. Family prayers were resumed by only a few old-fashioned people. The churches as a whole, with the notable exception of the Roman Catholics, never recovered their old swelling congregations. Nor were parents able to recover family discipline, which had perforce been intermitted during the separation caused by the war.

The intention to develop peaceful relations on international lines was seen in the creation of the League of Nations. This attempt at a new world order was not originally inspired by President Wilson of the United States, but it was his idealism which insisted, rightly or wrongly, on its incorporation into the peace treaty of 1919. He was, in the long run, unable to carry his countrymen with him, and the ultimate failure of the League was one of the severest blows that Christian utopianism has received in modern times.

In the ecclesiastical sphere a parallel effort to effect some kind of world organization was seen in the tentative approaches to the reunion of the churches. Of these the most notable example was the statement issued by the bishops of the Anglican Communion meeting at Lambeth Palace (the Archbishop of Canterbury's residence) in 1920. They announced that if other terms of union could be suitably arranged, they would be prepared to offer themselves for an interchange of rites of ordination with other Christian bodies. The effect of this would be to create a ministry mutually acceptable to all the denominations concerned. It would thus be the most valuable step toward complete unity. For the time being the appeal was not seriously regarded. But it sowed a seed which was to germinate later.

Certainly, as far as statistics and other external tests go, this was a period of very serious decline in religious habits. A significant clue to the narrowing limits of practicing churchmanship may be seen in the difficulty experienced in compiling the parochial rolls which had become the basis of the English electoral system leading to the new Church Assembly. Out of an estimated total of 30,000,000 nominal members of the Church of England not much more than a tenth could be induced to register themselves as qualified electors (3,601,782 in 1925).

In general, we may say that the most important religious effect of the war was to produce throughout mankind a new habit of mind. Whereas hitherto the majority had looked at least nominally beyond space and time for its incentives and rewards, now the outlook became frankly this-worldly. Man himself, rather than his gods, became the measure of all things. The example of Russia and later also of China seemed to show that this theory actually worked.

Inevitably such a mental attitude first expressed itself in an upsurge of nationalism. The individual was taught to merge his personality in that of the local community, and the community was determined to exercise its right to run itself. The self-determination that had been accepted as a governing principle in the Treaty of Versailles soon showed itself a dangerous expedient, but it was too late for the great powers to recall it. Soon it was working like leaven among the tribes and races of Africa and Asia. As the great powers began to lose their grip on their colonies, the peoples hastened to take advantage of the situation prematurely to free themselves from outside tutelage. Having no adequately trained civil service to run their affairs, they began to fall upon each other in an effort to gain by a ruthless display of power the wealth that they could not gain by good management.

In such a situation religion for the time being was the loser. In many countries where education and health were departments of especial missionary concern, schools and hospitals fell under government suspicion, which was not lightened by the fact that most of the trained personnel were Christian. In many instances the resultant tension between government and missions has not yet been resolved.

The effect of this kind of reasoning was seen most clearly in Japan, which even now has "a smaller proportion of Christians than any major country" and has deliberately rejected Christianity as a possible national religion. In other parts of what used to be known as the mission field, however, in spite of the rude shocks received, Christians have increased their numbers at a surprising rate. In Africa south of the Sahara between 1912 and 1956 the numbers rose from something over 1,000,000 to 21,000,000. In India, in spite of the rapid increase in population, the proportion has more than trebled, while, what is perhaps more significant, 3 out of every 4 trained nurses are Christians. In China the number of Christians had trebled before the revolution came and the missionaries were excluded.

Another feature in the postwar religious situation, of which due account must be taken, is the resurgence of other religions. No doubt this movement is partly to be accounted for by the rise of a perfervid nationalism. It was natural that emphasis should be placed on what were believed to be national characteristics in language, art, and religion. The movement grew as fresh efforts were made to reduce the large rate of illiteracy in the respective countries. In many instances there is a good deal of imitation of Christianity. Nevertheless, it does obviously mean that the lasting effect of the war was not universally detrimental to religion.

II

Habits are in large measure a reflection of moral attitudes. It is natural, therefore, in an effort to reach to the deeper consequences of the war to ask how far changing habits revealed a change in the moral standards of the nations engaged in it. Here we are helped by the fact that rapidly growing ease of communication began to make the whole world kin in a measure that had never been true before. Radio and telegraph, to say nothing of the gramophone and the cinema, made great cities aware of one another's life and thought the world over, and news penetrated with unprecedented rapidity even to the jungle and the desert. The latest women's fashions began to appear in the streets of Hong Kong and Achimota while they were still in the shop windows of Oxford Street and Fifth Avenue.

Sport, like fashion, began to give nations a common interest. The war had spread the knowledge of English team games to almost every part of the globe. Association football achieved a popularity never before reached by any national pastime. Compared with this extraordinary development, even the Olympic Games must probably take second place. Their modern history begins from 1896. They were canceled in 1916, when the four-year meeting should have been held in Berlin, but they were resumed when the war was over, the sixth Olympiad being convened at Antwerp in 1920.

If the optimists, who saw in common sport a panacea for the ills of the world, were disappointed, the pessimists, who thought that every kind of encounter between nations was bound to lead to internecine strife, were compelled to take shelter in a little mild cynicism. But inasmuch as the more important games everywhere are governed by a set of rules internationally enforced, sport may serve its part in the slow education of the nations in the acceptance of a commonly agreed supranational law. Its moral potentiality is, therefore, very great.

Something must be said about morals in the narrow and limited sense of the term. The traditional view of sexuality, at least in Anglo-Saxon countries, may have sufficed to keep the majority within the bounds of conventional respectability before the war. But when the soldier has lived several years in an atmosphere quite alien to the puritan spirit, during which every time he went on leave, he was offered prophylactics under the apparent assumption that that spirit no longer had any meaning for him, it is likely that after he has returned to civilian life, whatever may be his personal conduct, his mental attitude to moral questions will have suffered some considerable change.

It may be said that every change in moral attitude comes about through the questioning of hitherto accepted authority. The present instance was no exception to the rule. A common view is that the Victorian era was the last age in which tradition was accepted without question. There are, of course, some world-famous examples to the contrary, but by and large the judgment may be allowed to pass. In the intellectual sphere it had been only the favored few in the universities who were trained to accept nothing on authority and to think things out for themselves. The refusal to accept tradition at its own valuation now began to spread throughout the nations and all classes within the nations. This was to be the main element in the process which was a generation later to be described by Bonhoeffer as "the world's coming of age." It meant that man had begun to take a hand in his own evolution: He was at last an adult, grown up.

We have already remembered the violence with which the revolution broke down all existing authorities in Russia. In the United States change was not so marked, perhaps because it was not so necessary. The American way of life spelled the utmost possible freedom for the individual, and where poverty and want still existed, they were generally considered to be due to the individual's own fault. Further, on its religious side the American way of life was generally identified with the Protestant form of Christianity, and it has been pointed out that Protestantism, although there is no established religion in America, is generally regarded as the "national" religion. Before the outbreak of war the prevailing tendency in American religion had been clearly marked as activist. Great stress was laid on social service: Unkindly critics were wont to say that for the American the Kingdom of Heaven was deemed to have arrived as soon as the plumbing was right. The movement had already produced one important book in Rauschenbusch's *Christianity and the Social Crisis* (1907).

The social gospel was one of the chief casualties of the war so far as the United States was concerned. Its facile optimism seemed too superficial to stand up to the devastating calamities of the period. Presently the influence of Karl Barth and "Biblical theology" began to seep in from the Continent and ran parallel with the fundamentalism that took its place among the unlearned. The progress of both was helped by the combined psychological and economic depression of the middle of the century. As a result, religion reported a steady rate of progress during the first half century or so; as against 36 percent of the population in 1900 no less than 63 percent admitted affiliation to some religious body in 1959.

In other countries the revolution was more thorough, even where it came short of the horrors of violence. By a process of gradually increasing taxation the old aristocratic landlords of England were either forced out of their properties or compelled to turn themselves into limited liability companies. Mounting death duties broke up the great estates. Increasing government grants changed the character of the universities. Instead of being the finishing schools of a hereditary governing class, they became the training ground for the professional and managerial classes. With characteristic differences the same movement went on in various parts of the Commonwealth. But it was in the British Isles that the changeover was most complete. That so great a revolution could have taken place without bloodshed is perhaps the clearest evidence of Christian forbearance that civilization has achieved in the course of the century.

Nor is it to be thought that in other respects the effect of the war on the moral fiber of the people was wholly bad. So much heroism and self-sacrifice could not go wholly for nothing. The sense of comradeship engendered among troops on campaign was not completely lost. Not only did veterans' associations continue to encourage the spirit of mutual aid long after the war was over, but more definitely religious organizations such as Toc H (soldiers' club founded by P. B. Clayton and Neville Talbot, 1915) tried to preserve the memory of spiritual dedication that had been first aroused or quickened on active service.

In addition to all this, we must not fail to remember the effect of the war in making even the most careless face the issues of life and death. The fundamental questions of religion and philosophy had to be tackled afresh by each thinking individual according to his ability.

To this issue we must now turn and ask what was the effect of the war on theological thinking.

III

Of course, the first and most relevant question was one of theodicy: Why did God allow the war? The question grew more insistent as the horrors of trench warfare became more fully known and as the appalling lists of the dead piled up to millions. If God was good and omnipotent, as Christianity had always claimed, why did He allow such misery to affect His children?

For the professional theologian this situation was only a particular instance, though a specially poignant one, of the problem of evil, which is always his bugbear. Simple people who made much of the epithet "Almighty" were apt to think of God as a kind of policeman on point duty, who had only to hold up his hand to stop the traffic. Many did not get beyond this idea and allowed the dilemma to ruin their faith. Others by slow and painful steps learned to see God's governance of his universe exercised within the consciences of men, showing them the bitter consequences of man's inhumanity to man and teaching them to avoid war as a child learns to avoid the fire. It was in this atmosphere that some of the future theological leaders such as Barth, Brunner, and Tillich were nurtured.

In spite of such difficulties, many national leaders felt that so devastating an experience as worldwide war in its most horrible form ought to lead to a revival of religion. In England an effort to reassure the doubters and to strengthen the faithful was made in the National Mission of Repentance and Hope (1916). Either the people were too preoccupied or too many of the spiritual guides were away at the war. In any case, whatever the reason, the effort, made at the cost of considerable time and energy, was not voted a success.

Perhaps the most noteworthy result of the stresses of the period was a marked increase in spiritualism. Some inquirers were led to take an interest in it on what might be termed a scientific basis, hoping to establish beyond reasonable doubt the presence or absence of living beings on the other side of the grave. As usual, however, these inquiries proved indecisive. It was not by such mechanical means that the uncertainties stirred up by the war would be put to rest. A way must be found to the deeper springs of religion and reason. But it was just here that conditions were most difficult.

The latter part of the nineteenth century had been taken up largely with discussions of the theory of evolution. Although theologians had called in aid the Logos doctrine from the early apologists and had shown that evolution was more at home with that doctrine than was any theory of instantaneous creation, the faith of many never recovered from the shock of initial discovery.

When the evolutionary method was applied to the Bible itself and the Scriptures were read as a library of books with a complicated history of composition, the blow to the old unitary conception of inspiration and revelation was equally severe. Although the theologians themselves were responsible for this development and although they were able to adjust it to a more adequate and likely theory of revelation, the general effect was to make recovery from the intellectual malaise of the war still more difficult.

To this one must add the corrosive effect of the new theory of relativity (Einstein, c. 1919), which, beginning with physics, presently invaded philosophy and many other regions of thought. Even when it did not achieve precise formulation, the theory produced an attitude of mind in which there was no recognition of an absolute or an ultimate. However illogical the transition, there was produced in the minds of many a feeling that not only standards of taste but also rules of morals were merely relative and could, therefore, be adjusted to suit the ideas of each individual and occasion. For many, there remained no sound basis on which to rest, no solid rock on which to build.

A despairing effort to weld the new attitude of mind with Christian apologetics was made by the modernists. Of these there were two schools: the later in England and the earlier in France, the one Protestant and the other Catholic. The former was prepared to accept the "assured results" of current natural science and Biblical criticism as fundamental truth with which Christian dogma, whether to be found in the Bible or not, must be made to square. By the same token the doctrine of the Incarnation must be approached from the side of the humanity rather than the divinity of Christ. The certain fact was the high quality of His humanity: How and to what extent He was divine was a matter of debate.

French modernism seems to have begun in much the same way. Certainly Loisy struggled long and learnedly to find a reliable substratum in the Gospels upon which to erect an authentic image of Jesus which would square with traditional portraits, only in the end to abandon the unequal struggle. The philosophers of the movement, such as Blondin, took the more characteristic line of dissociating the practical importance of Christian dogmas from their allegedly doubtful historical origins. Relying on Ritschl's philosophy of values, they taught that one could dispense with the whole historical foundation of dogma so long as one could see that the doctrines themselves were useful for the salvation of souls.

As far as Roman Catholics were concerned, the modernist movement had been driven underground by the papal decree *Lamentabili* (1907), only to reappear in a modified form at the middle of the century in the *Aggiornamento* of Pope John XXIII. In England the storm burst after the notorious Girton Conference of Modern Churchmen in 1921. This meeting may be regarded as the peak of the movement. Characteristically no official action was taken to subdue it; it gradually died down, but not without imbuing nearly all other church movements with some, more or less liberal, elements of its spirit.

Among the members of most churches there remained a group of conservatives, for the most part of an evangelical persuasion, who clung to the literal interpretation of the Bible. Those who went so far as to retain the view of precise verbal inspiration were known as fundamentalists, from their emphasis on the "fundamental" truths of Christianity at the Niagara Bible Conference of 1895.

Others, who were not prepared to take quite so rigid a line, preferred to be described as conservative evangelicals. As such they have shown remarkable devotion and have produced a large and growing proportion of candidates for the ministry.

On the whole it can be said that "science" and theology reached an agreement to differ in their respective methods. It was admitted that whereas exact measurement was of the very essence of science, it was not applicable to religion any more than to morals or art. A generation was to elapse before it was widely realized that such a view necessarily involved that there could be no scientific proof of religious truth—or disproof either. No doubt there were those who had already reached this conclusion. "Nothing worth proving can be proven, nor yet disproven," was the way in which Tennyson had settled the question. But this was regarded as a piece of poetic hyperbole, and the majority still stuck to the view that somewhere and somehow there must be a logical and indisputable proof of the correctness of Christian teaching.

The attitude of mind that demands proof was further developed under the influence of the amazing advance in technology. The tendency of war is always to speed up research and inventiveness in those areas where advance is likely to be most favorable to its successful prosecution. The impetus will carry on into the peace; and in this case did carry on until a Second War came to rejuvenate it and multiply its energy. Radar and sound ranging led to the splitting of the atom and the lunar sputnik. As at the Renaissance five centuries before, man seemed again to become master of his environment. While everything else was in disarray, he could congratulate himself on the concrete successes achieved in his understanding and control of the material universe in which he lived. This temperament was not conducive to religion—"Glory to Man in the highest! for Man is the master of things."

What made matters worse was the spread of doubt into a fresh intellectual sphere. Christianity had always been regarded as a historical religion, and it had often boasted against its rivals that whereas they belonged to myth and legend, it had its roots firmly planted in historic fact. But now the philosophers of history—not the historians themselves (they have always rested confident in the value of their own technique), but the historical philosophers— began to question whether anyone can ever arrive at historical fact. Ranke's dictum that the historian's first duty is to establish the facts as they really happened gave way before the recognition that in every piece of reporting there must always be an element of interpretation.

Croce in Italy had put this big question mark beside history at the very beginning of the war, but England, because of its preoccupations, was slow in receiving the message. It was not until 1941 that *La Storia* was translated into *History as the Story of Liberty* and made a somewhat astonished public aware of the axiom that "all history is contemporary philosophy." This was soon followed by R. G. Collingwood's *Idea of History* (1946), which naturalized the point of view in Oxford lecture rooms.

As far as theology was concerned, the soil was already prepared for the new seed by the steady progress of Biblical criticism. Documentary analysis had given way to "form criticism" (Dibelius' *Fresh Approach to the New Testament*, 1936), and the endeavor to reach the *ipsissima verba* of oral tradition had made even the general reader realize how difficult it was to be sure that one had got back to the original word or act. History thus appeared to provide no safer "proof" for a Biblical religion than did science.

In this impasse the religious man is thrown back on his faith. This faith is not, as many suggest, an unreasoning credulity, but a reasoned acceptance of the tradition of his church combined with a consciousness of his personal contact with the unseen. Of such a faith the Bible remains a corroboration and an explanation. This is the point, succinctly expressed, to which he has been brought as the result of influences stemming from the First World War.

Sir Richard Rees

"A few years ago I published my autobiography. It contained so few facts about myself and such a lot of preaching that I subtitled it An Essay in Didactic Reminiscence. In order to preach, it is, of course, not necessary to have a doctrine, but it does help, and in 1924, when I joined the Labour Party in the fatuous belief that I was escaping from my upper-class background and education, I had thought I agreed with people like Bernard Shaw and H. G. Wells. After discovering my mistake, I met an author whose didacticism was much more congenial, J. Middleton Murry, and through him, D. H. Lawrence. (Not that I met Lawrence personally, though after his death I knew and greatly admired Frieda.) From 1930 to 1936 I edited Murry's magazine, The Adelphi. Murry's thought was anything but static, and he was prone to intellectual lapses, but he possessed critical genius (compare, for example, Bertrand Russell's puerile gibes against Rousseau in his History of Western Philosophy with Murry's luminous essay on him in Selected Criticism, 1916–1957). The Adelphi's course was erratic, but it fostered, and in many cases virtually discovered, a number of remarkable talents, among them George Orwell and Dylan Thomas. The contemporary intellectuals who chiefly influenced me, however, were T. S. Eliot and Lawrence, with Murry—in some ways the most intelligent of the three—as a sort of mediator between them.

"Between 1937 and 1945, in the Spanish Civil War and the Second World War, I was successively an ambulance driver, a gunnery rating, an obscure secretary in the same department of the Admiralty as Ian (James Bond) Fleming, and interpreter afloat, sometimes in more than one sense, in a French cruiser. After all this I was still prepared to be didactic, though still a little short on doctrine.

"Not long after the war I began to read Simone Weil's books, in which I found a synthesis of much of the best that I had learned from the others. And I continued to be as didactic as ever."

NEMESIS

THE FIRST WORLD WAR was the background of my schooldays. On leaving school, a boy went straight into the Army, and his chance of being alive and unwounded by the end of the war was not much better than 50-50. Of the boys who left during my time at school, which was exactly from 1914 to 1918, the number killed was 157.[1]

But the mind of youth is conformist, as we see today in the conformism of "protest," and to us this 50 percent tax on youth in the form of death and wounds seemed in the nature of things. I think indeed that when the tax was lifted in 1918, there were even some who felt vaguely cheated. A very junior boy in the school at that time called Blair, later to be known as George Orwell, was almost certainly one of these. And yet I doubt if there were many who felt any particular animus against the Germans. They were the baddies, of course, and we were the goodies, and we had been brought up to think of them as the opposing team. But there was hardly more to it than that.

> Cuff the Kaiser!
> The Kaiser cuff'd the cat.
> King George never never did a thing like that.

From our point of view, this version of "Rule Britannia" said just about all that needed saying.

Maybe I underestimate my schoolfellows' interest in public affairs, but what brought the situation home to me personally, perhaps more than anything else was the number of soldiers on leave to be seen in London restaurants and theaters and the fact that so many music hall songs and sketches were about the war. However, since it is the main theme of this essay that the war was, above all, symptomatic of a cultural decadence which had been in process for at least two centuries and which has accelerated since 1918, it would be dishonest to omit one other recollection which may appear to contradict this thesis. In the early days of the war I

---

[1] Total figures for the school (Eton), including those who had already left before 1914: out of 5,688 who served in the war, 1,159 killed and 1,469 wounded.

saw a regiment of soldiers in training pass along the road outside our house. They were workingmen from the north of England, and I suppose I had never before seen such a large number of workingmen all at once. I was astonished at how small most of them were.

I do not know the average height of contemporary Englishmen, but there is no class of the population today which strikes me as conspicuously shorter than any other class, and even if I should be wrong about this, there is still no doubt that standards of health and well-being have enormously improved during the last fifty years, while many inequalities have been greatly reduced. But whether the soldiers I saw in 1914, so stunted in growth and many of them from slum homes, were less happy than those of 1939, or than the Englishmen of today, is perhaps a question. They were certainly not less brave and humorous and friendly.

In any case, however, the theme of this essay is unaffected, because a civilization whose culture is in decay is not necessarily for that reason technologically incompetent. In spite of decadence, it may continue for a long time to improve its standards of health and physical comfort, and both the world wars of this century seem to have actually stimulated progress of this kind in all the participating nations. But they also intensified the process of cultural decay, and by the end of the First World War many of the civilized, as well as many of the barbarous, aspects of the world I knew as a child had been swept away forever.

In reality, of course, although as a child one could not know it, for at least fifty years the world had been changing more rapidly and more spectacularly than ever before. But that only takes us back to the 1860's, and the process had begun much earlier still. It was the French Revolution and then the first great expansion, in Britain, of modern industry that politically and economically disrupted the old world. (I shall argue in this essay that the psychological disruption began long before.) But it was not until after 1860 that the snowball began to turn into an avalanche.

In the 1860's, after the Civil War, it began to be possible for North America to develop its full industrial potential. At the same time the victories of Prussia began to upset the balance of power in Europe. The new plague of jingo nationalism, or idolatry of the nation-state, was growing more virulent throughout the West, and the population explosion was spreading from Britain to the other industrial countries. But Asia, except for those parts of it that were being modernized under European control, was static or decadent. It had become clear during the eighteenth century that the Turkish, Persian, and Mogul empires could no longer compete against the rising European power, which had already achieved world maritime supremacy two centuries earlier. And in Far Eastern Asia the West had begun to penetrate Japan in the 1850's, at about the same time as the shameful Opium War against China, which had still been a great power in the eighteenth century.

Between the 1860's and the outbreak of the Great War in 1914 there seems to have been little awareness in the West of the revolution in world economics and politics that was implicit in the gigantic strides being made by applied science and machine industry. There were very few who perceived that the world empires of the European powers and the mentality that went with them were doomed or that the privileged status in the world of both Europeans and Americans was soon to be challenged. I believe few people were any more aware of all this than I myself was aware, as a schoolboy, that the world of my childhood had gone forever.

Today, fifty years after 1918, the world is so different that the mind can hardly grasp the extent of the change. North America, Europe, Japan, and several other parts of the world are urbanized and industrialized to a degree that would have been unimaginable in the 1860's. Russia hopes to catch up with them, and China has thrown off its lethargy and become at least potentially a great world power again. Imperialism in the old sense of the word is dead, having been replaced by new forms of nationalistic, racial, economic, and ideological—or quasi-religious—power politics. And there is a population explosion almost everywhere.

Looking back, from our viewpoint in the 1960's, one can see that it was the First World War which was the great catalytic agent. And one of the most striking effects of the transformation is that the world has become much smaller. Journeys that still took months in 1914 take a few days in 1968. Long-distance verbal and visual communications are instantaneous, and the great powers are in continual nerve-racking and unneighborly proximity to one another.

In the days of the later Han dynasty and of the Antonine dynasty, the Chinese and the Roman empires were not absolutely isolated from each other. Both were affected by wars and migrations in the countries that separated them, and their tenuous trade relations fluctuated accordingly. A Chinese victory over the Mongols could lead to displacements of population which had repercussions on the Roman frontiers. A Hun or Turkic invasion of Bactria or Persia could cut the silk route. But for nearly all practical purposes the two empires could ignore each other's existence. And through all the succeeding centuries, until our own, war has been a more or less local and limited phenomenon, and every war has been waged for more or less definite and intelligible aims. Not even the wars of Napoleon were total war in the sense of the great wars of the twentieth century.

But in addition to being worldwide in its political repercussions, the war of 1914–18 was the first large-scale demonstration of what modern science and industry can contribute to man's powers of destruction.

For all these reasons, then, and many others, no one is likely to deny that the war of 1914–18 was a major event in world history. It was also one of the most frightful events in all history. Nevertheless, those who feel on the whole optimistic about the new world that has developed since 1918 can perhaps contrive to see that war as one of the sanguinary crises through which mankind progresses toward new and better ways of life. But those who feel otherwise will see it rather as a sinister warning that our civilization has gone astray. And that is how the most perceptive thinkers saw it at the time: Paul Valéry in France, for example, and D. H. Lawrence, Middleton Murry, and T. S. Eliot in England. When Eliot and Valéry agreed after the war that it was "the end of Europe," they meant, of course, the end of European culture. A glimpse into the future, revealing a Second World War followed by the booming, swinging Europe of the 1960's would only have confirmed their judgment. By comparison, those who scolded and tried to belittle the war as an irrelevant interruption and intrusion into a tidy Fabian evolutionary progress toward world Socialism—I am thinking of Bernard Shaw and H. G. Wells, for example—appear shrill and shallow today.

Thirty years after the First World War Eliot published a small book with the title *Notes Towards the Definition of Culture*. In one short passage of this book[2] he suggests a theory of religion and culture which is extremely relevant to the study of cultural declines. It is put forward with characteristically cautious reservations, and it looks very modest alongside the grandiose historicist theses of a Spengler or a Toynbee, and yet it touches on a profound and luminous truth. It could be developed into a theory of culture which sets the two great wars of the century in their true perspective.

Culture, says Eliot, never exists except in connection with a religion, although the culture may outlive the associated religion

---

[2] London, 1948, pp. 28–31.

and even achieve some of its most brilliant successes long after the religion has been more or less abandoned. But it cannot do this indefinitely, because the association is even closer than interdependence. Rather, it is as if they were two aspects of the same thing: the culture being, as it were, the incarnation of the religion. It is the religion as it is actually lived by the people who profess it or who formerly used to do so.

But what does Eliot mean by "religion"? Obviously he does not confine it to the rather prim Anglo-Catholicism which he himself professed, and one can probably assume that he intended to define the essential common factor in everything that can be called a religion when he wrote the following passage in his essay "Second Thoughts About Humanism": "Man is man because he can recognise supernatural realities, not because he can invent them. Either everything in man can be traced as a development from below, or something must come from above. There is no avoiding that dilemma: you must be either a naturalist or a supernaturalist."[3] When certain realities are recognized as supernatural, there is religion; when everything is assumed to be traceable as a development from below, there is not. But since the word "supernatural" has come to be associated with ghosts, miracles, and superstitions, it is perhaps better to use instead the word "transcendent," in its simple meaning of "existing apart from the material universe." In the terms of Eliot's theory we can then say that every culture ultimately derives from a belief in some reality apart from that of the material universe and that when a culture becomes completely saturated with antitranscendental thought, such as Marxism, positivism, and the contemporary form of humanism, it is a proof that the culture is in decline, even though it may still be achieving brilliant successes.

The belief that the good is a human invention or that the universal human hunger for goodness and justice is a product of the material universe implies the belief that the less good can produce something better than itself. An even more remarkable thinker and moralist than Eliot, the French Jewish philosopher Simone Weil, reduced this belief *ad absurdum* by describing it as the theory that "matter is a machine for manufacturing good."

It would no doubt be impossible to fix an exact date in European history when the belief that matter is a machine for manufacturing good, that evolution is a moral process, and that a corrupt tree can bring forth good fruit began to prevail over the Christian (and

---

[3] *Selected Essays* (London, 1932) , p. 447.

Judaic, Platonic, Islamic, Indian, Egyptian, and Persian) belief in a supernatural or transcendental source of morality. But if such a date could be fixed, it would mark the point where, in European culture, decline began to prevail over growth. But both tendencies were no doubt always present, or at least ever since the religious faith began to weaken, and the declining period has been so brilliant that the decline was for a long time unperceived.

Before attempting to show the relevance of these thoughts to the war of 1914–18, it may be desirable to emphasize more clearly the sense in which the word "religion" is being used, and this, unfortunately, involves a brief recapitulation of arguments which have been bandied to and fro ever since the human mind began to meddle with the problem of good and evil. First, then, religion as here understood is entirely distinct and independent from a number of ideas and phenomena which are often associated with it: emotional satisfactions, consolations for the ego, personal rewards in the sky, providential interferences with the course of nature, and so on. Second, religion is perfectly compatible with materialism, so long as the materialism is pure and not adulterated with a surreptitiously introduced morality, as both Marxism and naturalistic humanism are.

It is only the supernaturalist in Eliot's sense of the word who has no difficulty in admitting that the whole of the universe as known to or knowable by a human mind is purely material. And this, of course, includes the human mind itself, since all its thoughts and imaginings are to be regarded as psychic matter, which contains no mysterious material factor capable of generating *ex nihilo* an evolving and progressive morality. (In this résumé I am relying largely on terms borrowed from Simone Weil, but many others are available. Bergson, for example, whose *élan vital* is a concept almost antipodal to those of Eliot and Weil, nevertheless establishes clearly that what he calls an "open morality" is incompatible with any kind of naturalism or positivism. "We can never proceed," he says, "by a method of expansion from the closed society to the open, from the city to humanity. They are not of the same essence."[4])

The existence of a universal human aspiration toward an unknown good is totally anomalous in the material universe, but the existence of evil is less so, because what we call evil is simply matter, insofar as matter (including psychic matter) can obstruct, oppose, or confuse the aspiration toward the good. Apart from that, and in itself, matter is not evil, but amoral. But the good itself remains

---

4 *Les Deux Sources de la morale et de la réligion* (Paris, 1933) , p. 288.

always inconceivable. We can define it only by negatives, by the degree to which everything in which we think to find it always in the end falls short of our desire.

To be a supernaturalist or transcendentalist in the sense here used means recognizing this state of affairs, recognizing that the good is unattainable in the universe as we know it, except in degraded and ultimately unsatisfying forms. The essential act of religious faith is the recognition that goodness and justice and our aspiration toward them belong to a different order of reality from the only one we know; and that, nevertheless, every human being in the world is connected, in a totally mysterious way, with that reality; and, further, that it is only through this connection that any approximation to goodness and justice is ever effectively realized within the material universe.

The implications of this belief are all-embracing, and they can and should be indefinitely explored; but all that is necessary here is to establish that this belief is the essential religious belief and is, therefore, according to Eliot's theory, a prerequisite for the development of culture.

There is no need to labor the point that Christianity, the religion which inspired the development of Western culture out of the remains of Roman civilization as inherited by the Germanic invaders of Europe, was a transcendentalism according to our definition of the term, and the great cultural achievements of the twelfth, thirteenth, and fourteenth centuries—the cathedrals, Franciscanism, the *Divine Comedy*—are of quintessentially Christian inspiration. But just as every religion is indebted to earlier religion, so every culture includes elements from earlier culture, and medieval civilization, of course, included elements from Judaism, Islam, Hellenism, and, mainly through the latter, from Egyptian, pre-Islamic Persian and Babylonian culture as well. At the Renaissance it received a fresh infusion of Hellenism. But already in the fifteenth and sixteenth centuries the religious faith was beginning to weaken, and from the seventeenth century onward the cultural sphere of the profane, including science, and the sphere of religion became separated in two distinct compartments in the human mind.

This was an entirely new historical phenomenon. European science was derived from Greek science, and the Greeks would have been astonished at the post-Renaissance dichotomy between scientific and religious thought. The subsequent history of Europe, with the growth of the hitherto unknown idea of "progress," conceived not merely as technological development, but also as ethical improvement, would have struck them as a sinister example of what they called hubris. But there was worse to come. In the nineteenth century the belief in progress was thought to be confirmed by the biological theory of evolution, with the result that fantasies of Communist or anarchist millennia and other earthly paradises began to dizzy the minds of many educated people and even the heads of the uneducated as well, who are usually saner and more tough-minded, and, finally, in the twentieth century it has been believed by progressive thinkers in all classes that mankind, by the sole use of scientific know-how and by lifting itself up morally like an Indian juggler performing the rope trick, might create in the future a superstate inhabited by "men like gods," as H. G. Wells put it in 1923.

This essay is not concerned with prophecy but with history, so the future is outside its scope. But we may note parenthetically that if the obvious dangers of world famine and atomic war are averted, it does now seem to be conceivably within the bounds of technological possibility that a sort of Marxian or Wellsian utopia might in the end be established on a worldwide scale. And since, by our hypothesis, this irreligious earthly paradise could possess no culture of any kind, it would be something almost too horrible to contemplate, but of which one's everyday experience in technologically sophisticated countries and, still more, almost every issue of almost every newspaper already provide horrifying intimations: It would be a worldwide barbarism de luxe.

In case I seem to exaggerate, here is an example of the inroads already made by barbarism in the field of higher education. I have heard references in the highest academic circles to the "producers" and the "consumers" of culture—these words being used seriously and not as a joke. Culture is seen as a sort of prestige commodity, which ought to be available for every citizen of the democratic status state. Thus, if a citizen feels a lack of culture one morning, he can acquire some by visiting a culturama after lunch and consuming a few hundredweights of solid-culture producer Henry Moore or some decibels of the famous eighteenth-century producer of aural culture, W. A. Mozart, or if he is more serious-minded, he can visit a swami and join a group of pop singers and top models in a brief bout of deep meditation. But to speak seriously, it is the dismal truth that there are learned academics today who think of culture as a commodity or product, produced by producers for consumption by consumers, and who are incapable of grasping that culture is a way of life created collectively by a whole community, both in its work and in its play.

As a complement to their word "hubris" (approximately, insolence) the Greeks had another word: "nemesis" (approximately, vengeance). The nemesis for creating an earthly paradise without religion or culture is not difficult to foresee: It would be boredom, frustration, and finally desperation—with the consequences that can be imagined.

Of the wars known to historians, some appear to have been in the nature of things while others appear to have been unnecessary. That upland tribes like the Elamites, Medes, and Persians should have invaded the rich kingdoms of Mesopotamia seems natural. But the wars of the Greek city-states seem more like the result of political incompetence. We have described the war of 1914–18 as the precipitating agent of worldwide changes which appear to have been the inevitable result of the progress of Western technology. But the form taken by the precipitating agent seems to have been quite unnecessary. It was fratricidal strife between kindred peoples and attributable, like the wars of the Greek city-states, very largely to political and diplomatic incompetence.

"The war was a lie. . . . It never happened," says a character in D. H. Lawrence's *Aaron's Rod*[5] (1922), and when he is pressed to explain himself, he insists that none of the millions who took part in the war really experienced it. They lived through it or died in it somnambulistically, in a nightmare. And this was Lawrence's own view. He saw the war as a form of mass hypnosis by which millions of brave, kindhearted, and decent men were turned into flocks of sheep and driven to slaughter.

The theory of culture which I am trying to state can make this view intelligible. It gives a more precise and definite meaning to the old familiar commonplace that man's physical power has broken free from his spiritual, mental, and psychological control. In the course of the twentieth century religion and science have become completely divorced in the minds of civilized men. And alongside the spectacular triumphs of applied science and technology, religion has appeared increasingly irrelevant. It has, therefore, been on science, guided by the promptings of a supposedly natural and evolutionary morality, that man has come to rely for the fulfillment of his millennial hopes. But in minds that were not sophisticated, intellectual, or corrupt enough to accept the belief in evolutionary moral progress as an ersatz religion, the waning of real religious belief left a void. It is difficult to turn science into a satisfactory idol

---

5 London, Penguin Books, 1950, p. 144.

for focusing the human need of self-dedication and devotion, but there was another candidate for the role, an idol which had become popular in the nineteenth century and had grown very powerful long before the year 1900—namely, the nation-state.

The worshipers of the nation-state disguise their idolatry as patriotism, which is itself a humane and beautiful emotion, akin to the love of family and of one's home and traditions. But the modern nation-state has almost no connection with such things. It consists of a bureaucratic administrative machine and of the population and territory administered by it, which need not have any cultural, traditional, historical, or even geographical coherence, and the bureaucracy, like all bureaucracies, is self-centered, self-perpetuating, imperialistically expansive, and amoral. But for lack of anything better in an age of waning religious faith and materialistic culture, the nation-state became idealized and personified in millions of minds as the focus of patriotic and quasi-religious devotion.

Or is all this too cynical? It may be objected that the young volunteers who joined the British Army in 1914 were not fighting for the British state machine; they were fighting for the British way of life against Prussian militarism; they were defending democracy and the rights of small nations. And the objection is true. That is precisely what the British thought they were fighting for, and just as sincerely the young Germans opposing them believed they were fighting for Germany's "place in the sun." But one can see today, fifty years later, that insofar as the war can be regarded as an intra-European struggle the real issue was a shift in the European balance of power—which might, at least in theory, have been effected by diplomatic, instead of military, action—and from this point of view the illusion of the young German soldiers was less remote from twentieth-century reality than that of the young Englishmen. The causes for which the English fought—antimilitarism and the rights of small nations—have scarcely prospered in Eastern Europe since 1918, whereas Germany, in spite of her disasters in two world wars, seems almost certain to obtain sooner or later a more important place in the European sun. In a sense, therefore, it appears that Britain, whose efforts in the two wars were no less heroic than Germany's and whose suffering was hardly less, has been in the long run the chief loser in the two world wars. Certainly, by her complacent isolationist lethargy, to give it no worse a name, since the Second War, she has lost weight as a factor in the European balance of power, and she has done less than nothing to counteract the nation-state idolatry which is what De Gaulle means by a *Europe des patries*—though it must be admitted that in the world as it is today the only alternative to De Gaulle's stuffy obsession is the equally squalid totalitarian progressive myth.

In spite of the great "War to End War" of 1914–18, this century has seen the bellicose European nation-state idolatry imitated in every continent of the world—most recently and most dismally in black Africa. In its most powerful and highly developed form this ersatz religion becomes an ideological imperialism; in its elementary form it is little more than a rationalized xenophobia. But in all its forms it is a sterile substitute for religion, and if sufficiently highly developed, it would lead to humanity's self-annihilation. But in the twentieth-century world, what is the alternative? There is nothing but the progressivist dream of a materialistic utopian world-state inhabited by Socialized world citizens, each of them fitted with a built-in, self-perfecting mechanism, and this, according to our thesis, could be, at best, only a deluxe barbarism incapable of developing any culture. It would end by inducing frenzies of frustration and desperation which might culminate in a paroxysm even more frightful than a war of ideological imperialisms.

The 1914–18 war brought two facts to light: first, that technological development had reached a point where it could continue without disaster only in a unified world and, second, that the existing political and social organizations in the world made its unification impossible. It will certainly continue to be impossible for a very long time, but it will never be possible at all so long as we continue to believe that morality is independent of religion in the transcendental sense defined in this essay. To repeat Bergson's point: You cannot proceed by any method of expansion from the closed morality to the open, from the city to humanity. "They are not of the same essence." (If space allowed, how many examples one could give from the contemporary scene of the difficulty of promoting goodwill, harmony, or even tolerance, among dissimilar national, racial, or social groups, when the only dynamic is a well-intentioned humanistic rationalism, to say nothing of the so frequently toxic effects of similar good intentions in private life.)

But how can any two things be in the last resort "not of the same essence"? For some 200 years educated people have been finding it more and more difficult to conceive the possibility of any essence apart from the one we fancy we know something about, probing it with our minds and our scientific instruments. It is now the official doctrine of the world's two largest states, China and Russia, that there *is* no other essence, and this is also the opinion of, probably, the great majority of what we call educated people in the West. Not only have they been conditioned to disbelieve in superstition and in wishful fantasies about "the next world"—which would be all to the good—but they have been educated into a mixture of skepticism and hubristic complacency which makes them see what Eliot called "supernatural realities" either as unreal or else as natural. And this is precisely the sign of a culture whose religious roots have withered. To believe that goodness and justice are natural products is to believe that matter is a machine for manufacturing good and that a corrupt tree can bear good fruit. Whatever its technological virtuosity, a culture which harbors such a belief is sterile, and that is why Western culture has been a poison, where it might have been a stimulus, to the cultures of the surviving older civilizations.

If Eliot's theory of the relation between culture and religion is true, there can be no future either for Western culture or for any of the others, unless there is a revival of religious inspiration. It is far beyond the scope of this essay to speculate whether and in what way such a revival might occur. Eliot himself believed or hoped that, for the West, a revived inspiration might come sooner or later from the existing Christian churches. Or so I deduce from his sketch *The Idea of a Christian Society*. Simone Weil was much more critical of the churches, and of the two thinkers mentioned earlier, Middleton Murry and D. H. Lawrence, whose reaction to the war of 1914–18 was comparable to Eliot's, the attitude of Murry was very similar to Simone Weil's. His continual debate with Eliot concerning heresy and orthodoxy was the most serious intellectual controversy in England between the two wars, and it is regrettable, though not at all surprising, that it attracted much less interest than Marxism, psychoanalysis, surrealism, and the other talking points of the post–1918 decadence.

As for Lawrence, it is difficult to imagine, in spite of his passionately religious spirit, that he could ever have entertained the idea of a Christian revival. But nobody recognized more clearly or exposed with more perceptiveness, and vehemence, the sterility of modern Western culture. And nobody suffered more excruciatingly at the prospect of the barbarous utopia which is the worldwide political objective of our age. He would certainly have agreed that the war of 1914–18 was the first installment of the nemesis which awaits a civilization dedicated to such an ideal.

Literature of War

Maurice Genevoix

MAURICE GENEVOIX *was born on November 29, 1890, at Decize (Nièvre) of a father from Paris and a mother from Orléans. He spent his childhood in a borough of Loiret, Châteauneuf-sur-Loire, then studied at the lycées of Orléans and Lakanal and at the École Normale Supérieure (Lettres), which he left for the combat zone in August, 1914.*

Commissioned on August 2, 1914, as a second lieutenant in the 106th Infantry Regiment, he took part in the combat and the retreat at the end of August, at the battles of the Marne, of Hauts-de-Meuse, of Éparges, of the trenches of Calonne. Promoted to lieutenant and later to major of the 15th Company, he was wounded on April 25, 1915, and discharged after spending seven months in the hospital.

The next several years he spent in Paris. Then he returned to Châteauneuf-sur-Loire and, after 1930, to St.-Denis-de-l'Hôtel, where he still resides during the summer months. He has traveled extensively across Europe and also in Tunisia, Algeria, and Morocco. Before the last war he visited the United States and Canada. Since that war he has traveled in Senegal, Guinea, the Ivory Coast, Sudan, British Nigeria, Mexico, etc.

Maurice Genevoix has been publishing literary works for more than fifty years, beginning with Sous Verdun *(1916). He has written more than twenty novels and was awarded the Prix Goncourt in 1925 for his novel* Raboliot. *On October 24, 1946, he was elected to the Académie Française, and in 1958 he became its* secrétaire perpétuel *(permanent secretary).*

COMMENTARIES ON THE WAR:
SOME MEANINGS*

———————◆———————

TODAY more than ever, after celebrating the fifty-second anniversary of the Battle of Verdun, how could we, the veterans, not feel
drawn by the magnet of memory? For most of us, the return in time
is at once bitter and sweet, a paradoxically nostalgic pilgrimage
back to the years of our great suffering. But how, too, in the actual
time when we relive these battles, these trials, can we push away
the thought that soon there will be no more witnesses left of that
drama which was simultaneously individual and worldwide in scale
and whose dimensions, therefore, cannot be encompassed either by
personal recall or by collective remembrance?

Quite naturally, then, in the reawakened sense of truly brotherly
companionship—that of my comrades whom I joined in this recent
celebration—have I found myself led to question myself anew. As
the crowd of witnesses thins out from year to year, as the moment
approaches when they all will have disappeared, what can have
been the real meaning and the import, ephemeral or lasting, of the
testimony they will have left?

The final years of the war, I remember, were peppered with an
extraordinary superabundance of the writings called war literature—private diaries, field notes, narratives, essays, books written
"in the heat of battle," so to speak, in actual touch with the
happening and as if dictated by the events. Even so, this superabundance was only the residue of an enormous mass of written
accounts. Rare in fact were the men of arms who, gripped from the
outset by the feeling that they were participating in an unparalleled
experience, did not bow to the need to record its sights and vicissi-
tudes. However assorted it may have been, the war literature, it is
appropriate to stress, thus stands witness—and this is its reason for
being, as well as its justification—for all the fighting men.

Responding to this very keen need, to a kind of internal obligation, these testimonials would constitute a mine of firsthand infor-

---

* Translated from the French by Sally Abeles.

mation which would give the reader, knowledgeable or not, the chance of seeing the war not as a military staff problem or a historic account, but as a human event, through the life of a soldier or line officer, in its most concrete or I should say its most carnal aspects.

Some of these reports are still in our minds: Jean-Marie Carré's *L'Histoire d'une division de couverture,* Jacques Meyer's *La Biffe,* Galtier-Boissière's *En Rase Campagne;* similar books by René Naegelen, Georges Gaudy, Pierre Paraf; Jean Pottecher's *Les Lettres d'un fils;* or, more fictionalized, Henri Barbusse's *Le Feu,* Roland Dorgelès' *Les Croix de bois,* Georges Duhamel's *Vie des martyrs,* Henri Massis' *Les Impressions de guerre 1914–1915,* Henry Malherbe's *La Flamme au poing.*

The very variety of these records is such that even today it is hard to list a few without immediately wondering whether they or the hundreds of other titles that could have been cited fulfilled their purpose, whether they or the others are up to the level of the experience they were concerned with transmitting.

From this a basic dispute arose among the witnesses—some holding that literary creation allowed them to reach a deeper truth, a verisimilitude which was less slavish and which stepped back only in order to go further, beyond the specific; others considering, on the contrary, that in this case a truth was involved whose very nature and compelling dimensions constrained the witness to subjugate himself entirely to the subject. To put it another way, after 1919 wasn't there a risk of confusion, and weren't many of these records already highly unreliable from the viewpoint of the future historian?

This is quite likely; the best and the worst stood side by side. From which it follows that in order to test their genuineness, one would have to have known the realities of the war through personal experience. This was not always the case. Yet one man wanted to make the attempt, without waiting any longer for the requisite discrimination. His name was Jean Norton Cru. A serviceman and hence a witness himself, this French-born American professor, who returned to fight in the army of his native country, devoted fifteen years of his life to this task of discriminating. He read all the books by soldiers, testing their veracity in the light of his own recollections and little by little, from comparison to comparison, in the illumination of his readings themselves.

His large work *Témoins,* which appeared in 1929, had the primary purpose of addressing itself to future historians of the war. He intended above all to make their task easier, to clear the ground, to pave the way for them, to furnish them with an Ariadne's thread which would allow them at least to direct and assure their progress. He was inspired and sustained by that horror of falsification, of the fabricated tale, that thirst for truth blended with the need for fairness which were common to all the veterans.

It was high time. Already "histories of the war" were beginning to appear which themselves in turn mixed the best and the worst, too often taking up suspect reports and, for want of guidelines grounded in experience, combining them with others more trust-worthy. Norton Cru remarked on this bluntly in his introduction: "Military history up to the present has been written solely on the basis of documents issuing from people who could not have seen or heard or had the direct experience of combat, but who are familiar with orders that together, along with those of the enemy, only partly influenced the combat areas." In thus stressing the impor-tance and enormous value of eyewitness accounts, classifying them by degree of truthfulness, Norton Cru intended primarily to serve history.

Very quickly, we can say in fact beginning in 1920, war literature was lost and buried in the sand drift of indifference. The success of Erich Maria Remarque's book [*All Quiet on the Western Front*], a war novel, is thoroughly exceptional, for example. Public interest found new objectives and demands. Having exhausted feeling in a way, it now called to reason, to understanding. What awaited the reader in the future were cool-headed works, reflective and analyti-cal, works by moralists, sociologists, philosophers, historians.

It seems to be only just today—that is, after fifty years of docu-mentation and reflection—that the propitious time has finally come for the vast syntheses. We are in sum close enough to the event for its reality not yet to have escaped our memory, but far enough from it to be able to think about it tranquilly.

On the basis of these comments, I would like now to consider two works among others, both books of quality which seem to me to coincide well with the two viewpoints I have posited. They come to my hand by chance and not by predetermined choice. The parallels I find in them seem all the more significant, and more so still because they suggest points of agreement and even lines of con-vergence that we may henceforth no longer merely wish for but hope for.

One is a *Histoire de la guerre 1914–1918,* which will appear very shortly and whose editors are General Valluy and the historian Pierre Dufourcq. The other, *Vie et mort des Français, 1914–1918,* is the work of three infantrymen, Jacques Meyer, André Ducasse, and

Gabriel Perreux, all three former students at the École Normale Supérieure, certified through qualification in different specialties— philosophy, literature, and history—but all three molded according to the highest cultural traditions.

What particularly struck me on reading the first work is a kind of universality, not so unusual in itself as new in this sort of under-taking. In terms first of nationalism, or rather internationalism, the contributors observe war operations not by taking position in only one of the hostile camps, as it were, but from the viewpoint—actu-ally indivisible—of both. This leads rather naturally to parallel analyses of the psychology of peoples (and hence of the fighting men, since the subject is a war and national armies) and of the ethnic characteristics through which the dominant notes of their collective behavior are revealed. These create something like illu-minating cipher keys which help, almost always considerably, to decode paradoxical or at least baffling facts.

Here are some examples, intentionally taken at random: What were the determining causes of the evolution that led the United States to enter a war whose principal battlefields were in Europe? What were the reasons for the subsequent American delay which—I remember well—kept us on the boil a long time? Again, how was the Russian Revolution, a huge occurrence with enormous reper-cussions, prompted, made possible, triggered? Finally, how did the differences (and what sorts of differences) that intervened among the Central Powers themselves come into play, from interference to interference, from reaction to reaction, sometimes to frustrate an event and sometimes, contrary to apparently reasonable expecta-tions, to hasten its ripening and picking, as of a ripe fruit?

Who could really have answered all these questions in the year 1919?

It would be easy to cite many other examples of these cipher keys that would have remained hidden had not enough time elapsed. Who would have thought, under the still painful shock of the event and the grip of the early-born stories, even to recall the military regulations, French and German, in force in 1914? If both affirmed the primacy of the infantry, they parted ways on the role of the artillery. While the first, holding that the artillery "does not pre-pare the way for attacks" and carrying the logic of the system to its worst conclusions, described the movement of the infantry, the assault, and hand-to-hand combat as continuing "until the last enemy combatant is disabled, has laid down his arms, or has fled," the second, more realistic, wrote about the infantry's role that it should stand to battle "together with the artillery" and even with heavy field artillery, which was to be used both against the opposing batteries and to prepare the way for an infantry attack supported by light cannon. Another fundamental difference that likewise only today explains many things about yesterday: the concept of discipline. Contrary to prevailing notions, it was the regulations of the "sheeplike" Germans that gave credit to the individual, to the initiative of the individual as circumstances demanded. On the contrary, what did the French regulations say? "Discipline constituting the primary strength of armies, it is essential that each superior officer obtain from his subordinates total obedience and submission at all times." Fortunately, the French Army and its chiefs were on the whole more intelligent than were their regulations.

It has thus become possible, without appearing hereafter to resort to paradox or Procrustean solutions, to show how unforeseen factors, and which ones, eluded the planners and seized the most perfect and formidable war machine there was, though all the conditions were present which, according to the notions of modern warfare, should logically and almost inevitably have asserted victory to the Central Powers. Given this, moreover, the nature of the check is all the more dramatic, and psychologically the more charged with meaning and moral.

Thus, by a detour which has become possible and from now on almost inevitable, we have necessarily come back to the man, the fighter, the footsoldier, the poilu. And that is why, in counterpoint to the commentaries of today's historian—and this for the first time—something in me, an old warrior, is stirring, agreeing, and echoing. Even if, like everyone who harks back, I have all my life deplored the impossibility of transcribing our harsh experience, it is nonetheless true (and I have proof of it now) that there are meeting grounds where the most visceral experience and the most rigorous objectivity become one.

At this point, it would perhaps be appropriate to evoke some of the accounts that might be called intermediate, written not "in the heat of battle" like those I was speaking of a moment ago, but, while objectively, with fellow feeling. I am thinking of certain novels, Jules Romains' *Verdun* being the most striking example to me. It is perhaps thanks to books of this kind, where talent never overrides honesty and concern with reality, that the surviving witnesses of battles have not surrendered to the temptation to give up, that they have preserved any feeling that they have not been thoroughly and definitively disregarded and thus betrayed. How often, indeed, have they been disillusioned and even, in their innermost selves, disgusted! How often have they felt as though dispossessed, reading certain accounts, hearing certain words! Not that they saw traces of any ill will in them, but that the kind of objectivity these accounts laid claim to *sounded false* to their ears, that they sinned by levity, by coldness, and, therefore, by the omission of what the survivors knew to be essential.

This exigency in them has not weakened. On the contrary. As their vitality declines, as they see the shadow of evening advancing to meet them, their thoughts return increasingly to their martyred youth, take them back with all the strength of their being to what they know to be, beyond *their* truth, *the* truth. It is stronger than they. They would like not to leave this world with such sadness in their hearts.

This leads me directly back to the books by my professorial comrades. For their work responds to this need that haunts the surviving soldiers. In this connection, we have seen a sort of new war literature come to life during the last several years. It constitutes a new testimony, which is really testamentary. Raymond [Marcel Edmond] Naegelen, brother of the author of *Les Suppliciés,* has turned again toward the well-traveled path, and he, too, has found, *Avant que meure le dernier,* the truth that is an integral part of us. Pierre Jolly wanted to retrace his steps on the battlefields of the Somme once more, for *Les Survivants vont mourir.* There have been others, many others. How could we not be struck by this anxiety, this poignant, haunting memory, and this unanimity? All these essays, otherwise and likewise concerned with the generalities and generalizations of history, strain almost desperately to bring back that sort of visceral tremor they remembered in their bodies.

There is something here, obviously, that transcends conscious will. I have said it. It is an internal obligation that is involved. And all the more so because the preestablished ideas, the prejudices, the legends have shown themselves hard to kill. Almost always dangerous, baneful, and having demonstrated this too well, they can exercise their harmfulness tomorrow still. If they indeed offend intellectual rectitude and a certain honesty of feeling, less than ever do the men who fought the war consent to pardon them the extra sufferings they sustained because of these works, or the useless deaths which they are responsible for in their eyes, or the distorted images which are given out as truthful but in which they do not recognize themselves.

In this regard the book by Meyer, Ducasse, and Perreux is a summation. Its subtitle alone is significant: *Simple Histoire de la grande guerre*. A "simple" history in the sense that while it does not aspire to making systematic and authoritative syntheses, it nonetheless presents an objective and complete overview—that is, one which attempts to communicate what by nature was little or not at all communicable. Rather than a history of the war, what we who fought it have always hoped for and what these three writers have tried to give us is a history of men at war.

What does this mean? It is neither desirable nor good that the professional historian prevail over the veteran; it is also not good that the veteran prevail over the historian. This is why the history of the 1914–18 war remains so hard to write. When, in fact, one aspect is isolated—for instance, the study of military events—a given episode will seem to have been sacrificed or omitted for the sake of closely related events whose importance will thus tend to appear disproportionate. Where was the mud the stickiest, the heaviest? Where were there the most frozen feet? Which sector had the heaviest bombardments, the most savage counterattacks, the most monstrous mines? What sector did not have its "Death Gully" or "Plague Ravine"? This is a veteran's approach, not a historian's. But the historian who was blind to it would be a poor historian.

On the other hand, if the veteran came to write a history of the war, he would also be a poor historian if he did not forget his sector loyalty and determine his choices for reasons better detached from his personal memories. For some the Battle of Verdun is the capital battle, for instance; hasn't it become a symbol, and rightly so? For General Erich Ludendorff, it was the Somme. According to the fighters in the hottest sectors, it was the Yser, Artois, Argonne, Éparges, the hills of Champagne, the Vardar, or the Dardanelles. But it is well for the historian who relates the Battle of Verdun and describes the calvary of the infantryman there to know that this calvary did not last only a few months, but four years and more, and that its stations spread along a front extending hundreds of miles.

Everyone agrees in recognizing that in the whole history of mankind, few dates have had the importance of August 2, 1914. First Europe and soon after almost all humanity found themselves plunged into a dreadful event. Conventions, agreements, moral laws, all the foundations shook; from one day to the next, everything was called into question. The event was to exceed both instinctive forebodings and reasonable anticipations. Enormous, chaotic, monstrous, it still drags us in its wake.

Consequently we concur, so important is it not only to us, men of this time, but to the generations to come, that the historian must broach this event with a deep, unwavering sense of his responsibility. Mild or minor errors, distortions, levities, flights of imagination on lesser events would seem here to have no excuse. Jean de Pierrefeu, writing somewhere of an obviously inspired and tendentious staff document, added sadly: "Here is how history will be written in fifty years, when, with the witnesses dead, conscientious historians, wanting to go back to sound sources, will read the staff records."

Forty years have passed since he wrote these lines. We now have reason to believe that "conscientious historians" will no longer write the history of the Great War as Pierrefeu feared they would. To this end, and with the selectivity they now have the means to apply, they will need to take account of the experience of the witnesses thrown into the core of the event and matured in its pain.

"Those who say," wrote Maurice Donnay fifty years ago, "that there will always be wars, that war is a necessary evil, perhaps do not understand exactly what this war is. . . . We are not out of the moving sand of events, we do not have the necessary perspective. But when the frightful drama can be judged as a whole. . . ." So did Donnay understand in advance the demands on us today.

These demands are not contradictory. They must in actuality complement each other. I would like simply to compare Maurice Donnay's reflections with a few lines taken from a letter written by one of Captain Jean Vigier's* sergeants shortly after his chief's death: "We were glorying in combat. . . . Two months of war showed us the inanity of this way of looking at things. When we were in disarray, our captain told us: 'The duty of a true soldier is not where you've put it. The present war has nothing glorious about it; we are monks of nomadic monasteries, whose rule is honor, and our rule is to suffer. . . .' "

Perhaps this is what they called the spirit of the front. For myself, I would rather speak of a kind of collective soul, elementary but admirably lucid, courageous, fraternal under every circumstance. Suffering, yes, involved in painful flesh, but this is its stirring beauty and its greatness, measuring up to our human condition.

No, emphatically no: Because of this soul, it will no longer be possible to write the history of the Great War like the histories of bygone wars. Pierrefeu has to have been wrong.

---

* Jean Vigier, who had also been studying to teach, first in his class, a resident student at the Fondation Thiers, was already a master whose profound and enduring influence as a professor, as a writer, could be foreseen. A light infantry officer, he was killed in 1916.

G. Wilson Knight

Described by one critic as an "interpreter of genius . . . concerned with bringing to consciousness the experience of literature," George Wilson Knight has enhanced students' understanding of Shakespeare in such volumes as The Wheel of Fire (1930), The Imperial Theme (1931), The Shakespearian Tempest (1932), Principles of Shakespearian Production (1936; as Shakespearian Production, 1964), The Crown of Life (1947), The Mutual Flame (1955), The Sovereign Flower (1958), and Shakespeare and Religion (1967). Moreover, Knight has not restricted himself to Shakespeare. He has gone on to analyze Milton, Swift and Byron in The Burning Oracle (1939; as Poets of Action, 1968); Wordsworth, Coleridge, Shelley, and Keats in The Starlit Dome (1941); Byron in Lord Byron: Christian Virtues (1952), Lord Byron's Marriage (1957), and Byron and Shakespeare (1966); Pope in Laureate of Peace (1954); and John Cowper Powys in The Saturnian Quest (1964). He has also produced and acted in dramatic productions at Hart House Theater, Toronto, from 1932 to 1940, and at the University of Leeds from 1946 to 1960.

Born in Sutton, Surrey, England, on September 19, 1897, he was educated at Dulwich College, London, and at St. Edmund Hall, Oxford. From 1916 to 1920 he served with the British forces in Mesopotamia, Persia, and India as a motorcyclist dispatch rider. After the war he became English master at Dean Close School, Cheltenham (1925–31); Chancellors' Professor of English, Trinity College, University of Toronto (1931–40); master at Stowe School, Buckingham (1941–46); reader and later professor of English literature, University of Leeds (1946–62), and subsequently emeritus professor at Leeds. He is an honorary fellow of St. Edmund Hall.

Apart from his work as a literary critic, Knight has written Atlantic Crossing (1936), The Dynasty of Stowe (1945), the play The Last of the Incas (1954), and the poems Gold-Dust (1968). He is a C.B.E., an F.I.A.L., and an F.R.S.L., and has received honorary doctorates of letters from the universities of Sheffield (1966) and Exeter (1968).

RUPERT BROOKE

ON THE MENTION of Brooke's name we think first either of his five war sonnets or of the famous bare-shouldered photograph by S. Schell, used for the 1914 collection of his *Poems* and the original of the plaque in Rugby Chapel by Harvard Thomas, whose version is in the National Portrait Gallery, where copies are sold. I shall indicate a relation between Brooke's poetry and this portrait, called by Christopher Hassall in his biography *Rupert Brooke*[1] "A visual image that met the needs of a nation at a time of crisis" (390; my numerals refer to Hassall's volume).

Brooke was not obviously fitted for the role of patriot. He had, it is true, certain social advantages. He struck a figure at Rugby and Cambridge, his poetic powers rapidly won attention, and he mixed with leading personalities in literature and politics. He had brilliance and wit. But the general tone of his conversation and writing was iconoclastic and unorthodox; he was a Socialist in politics and a pagan if not atheist in religion. His poetry was often of a kind to shock. He links the estheticism of the nineties to the realisms of postwar writing; he has affinities with both Wilde and Eliot.

Like Byron and Wilde, he had a strong personal impact. His appearance was striking; men such as Henry James, Walter de la Mare, and Sir Ian Hamilton were conquered by it. The many records are extraordinary: "astounding apparition" with eyes "like the sky" (221); "so beautiful that he's scarcely human" (258); "a young man more beautiful than he I had never seen" (399); one who summed "the youth of all the world" (441). But the accounts vary. Though he had the "rosy" skin of a "girl" (240), of "girlish" smoothness (442), his appearance was all male, "there was nothing effeminate" (441), and we hear also of a deeply tanned face and sturdy form, large feet and hands, and clumsy movements (241–42). It seems that he could appear variously male and female, clumsy and ethereal, according to mood. His complexion was rich, as though the blood "was near the surface" (242). An inward power radiated out through the blood to the complexion, the eyes,

---

1 London, 1964.

and red-gold waves of hair, and it was some inner, spiritual, reality that gave him "a shining impression" as of one "from another planet" (524), so that he entered a room "like a prince" (527). According to Henry James, much of Brooke's importance as both poet and person could not be conveyed to posterity, since it depended on "the simple act of presence and communication" (523).

He was an *embodiment* of poetry: "There are only three good things," he once said, "in the world. One is to read poetry, another is to write poetry, and the best of all is to *live* poetry"; it "kept one young" (143). Siegfried Sassoon felt poetry in his presence, as of a "being singled out for some transplendent performance, some enshrined achievement" (451). He had the baffling bisexuality of such persons. Though he could oppose bisexual doctrines, he also admitted that "the soul of persons who write verse is said to be hermaphroditic" (442, 446; and see 440). He was well aware of his endowments—"I looked at myself, drying, in the glass, and I thought my body was very beautiful and strong, and that I was keeping it and making it splendid for you" (304)—but also, perhaps more, for himself, since there was in him an element of Whitman-esque narcissism. He was bodily conscious: "While the Samoans," he once wrote, "are not so foolish as to 'think,' their intelligence is incredibly lively and subtle"; even a European living among them "soon learns to *be* his body (and so his true mind) instead of using it as a stupid convenience for his personality, a moment's umbrella against the world" (460).

He preserved a child's bodily self-interest and a child's integrity; as "both man and boy" he was "the child he had grown from" (231); he was "a symbol of youth for all time," doing up his shoes with "the absorbed seriousness of a child" (277). Brooke remembered as a child often touching a "higher level" of existence and recognizing that we are normally "asleep," and the experience could be repeated in maturity, when he could say "I more than exist" (257). In the South Seas he came near to a full recapture of this childhood magic (421).

He was obsessed with nakedness, usually in relation to bathing, at Grantchester and the South Seas or by a Canadian lake, "lying quite naked on a beach of golden sand" (409). In the South Seas he wrote of himself "in a loin-cloth, brown and wild" by a "sun-saturated sea," among "naked people of incredible loveliness" (419). Here men were strong and beautiful in their unclothed bodies, and with finer sensibilities than Europeans (427–28), so that "one's European literary soul begins to be haunted by strange doubts" (421). When war came, Brooke expected to "find incredible beauty in the washing place, with rows of naked, superb men," either by sun or moon (463) . If the many revulsions in his poetry point on to Eliot, his body obsession points to Lawrence. It is less likely that this obsession (other relevant references occur in Hassall's biography at pp. 255, 265, 266, 280, 282, 304, 390, 410, 413, 418, 424, 427, 429, 443, 523, 526) came from knowledge of his own beauty than that that beauty flowered from the inward obsession. He was, in fact, an integrated, or near integrated, man.

His sex life was difficult. Living within the presexual or supersexual, Nietzschean, and lonely, integration at an age of physical maturity may be hard. His experience in the South Seas was not, he said, that of a love paradise; it was the opposite to alcohol according to the Porter's definition in *Macbeth*, "for it promotes performance but takes away desire" (422) . That is, sex functioned without a partner. Brooke knew intense love in England, but his artistic and political interests combined with "some obscure emotional distemper" (521) to make him unable to love. His biographer leaves the "root of his unsureness" undefined (445) . Here is Brooke's own account:

Oh, I've loved you a long time, child: but not in the complete way of love. I mean, there was something rooted out of my heart by things that went before. I thought I couldn't love wholly, again. I couldn't worship—I could see intellectually that some women were worshipful, perhaps. But I couldn't find the flame of worship in me. I was unhappy. Oh, God, I *knew* how glorious and noble your heart was. But I couldn't burn to it. I mean, I loved you with all there was of me. But I was a cripple, incomplete. [462]

In some moods he was an antifeminist (445) , rating friendship above love (425) . But he does not appear to have experienced male romantic friendships: imagination was turned inward, narcissistically, on himself.

We pass now to the poetry. It strongly attacks romantic love. The two sonnets "Menelaus and Helen" show knightly romance giving place to blear-eyed impotence and nagging. "The Beginning," "Sonnet Reversed," "Beauty and Beauty" tell the same story. In "Kindliness" youth's infinite hunger has to make terms with a "second-best." In "Mutability" our "melting flesh" aims at impossible absolutes. "Jealousy" contrasts young love with the slobbering age which follows, and in "A Channel Passage" there is little difference between "a sea-sick body or a you-sick soul." In "Dead Men's Love" love is reduced to "dust and a filthy smell." There appears to be some achievement in "Lust," but the only real gleams are, as we shall see, in some new dimension beyond earth.

Brooke's sense of physical perfection led to a corresponding reaction. Man's body could so easily be repellent: In "Wagner" and "Dawn" physical nausea is emphatic. Brooke questions the human form itself: In "Heaven" the fishes must see God as a great fish, and "On the Death of Smet-Smet" shows savages worshiping a hippopotamus goddess. Our human valuations are arbitrary. "Thoughts on the Shape of the Human Body" is a critique of sexual intercourse:

> . . . We love, and gape,
> Fantastic shape to mazed fantastic shapes,
> Straggling, irregular, perplexed, embossed,
> Grotesquely twined, extravagantly lost
> By crescive paths and strange protuberant ways
> From sanity and from wholeness and from grace.

What is wanted is a more harmonious love "disentangled from humanity," "whole," a "simplicity" like a "perfect sphere," loving "moon to moon"—the kind of love so often found in Platonic-homosexual engagements, though there are none recorded of Brooke. The moon's radiance is white, and whiteness is Brooke's color for beyond-earthly intimations.

Brooke was thrown back on himself. In "Success" his love's "white godhead," "holy and far," is entangled with "foul you," "shame" and a "black word," leaving the poet "alone." In "I said I splendidly loved you" he admits the lie, conscious that he has been following "phantoms" or "his own face." "Waikiki" shows him correspondingly "perplexed." In "The Voice" a love assignation horribly interrupts his lonely meditations in the night-darkened woods: "By God! I wish—I wish that you were dead!" Elsewhere, in the dark woods of "Flight," he has left daytime loves for the night's scents, weeping and stroking his own face. "Paralysis" shows him in his "white neat bed" laughing in his "great loneliness." In "Town and Country" two lovers may be "drunk with solitude" in the city, but in the woods by night love dissolves away into a vaster, cosmic, loneliness. "The Chilterns" tells us that:

> . . . a better friend than love have they,
> For none to mar or mend,
> That have themselves to friend.

He will have freedom enjoying the roads and winds and hedgerows. He is with Wordsworth and John Cowper Powys, for whom the natural partner of the human soul is, not a sexual partner, but the objective universe (*In Spite Of*, IV, 116; in my study of Powys, *The Saturnian Quest*,[2] 90). "The Great Lover" is a key poem, listing a fine assortment of loves ranging through all the senses from wet roofs, the smell of burning wood, "the rough male kiss of blankets" and "furs to touch," to the miracles of earth nature. This Powysian mystique is expanded in a remarkable letter to Ben Keeling, quoted in Hassall's biography (236–39).

Perfection is attainable in young beauty or in sense enjoyment of external objects. But what of the future? In "The Great Lover" he knows that life beyond death must be very different. He is ready to distinguish body from soul or spirit. In sleep the "soul" leaves the body like a "dress" laid by, and yet why then can the countenance appear troubled? Or smile? Surely, too, the sensuous is itself spirit-born, as in the mysterious sleep of "Doubts":

> And if the spirit be not there,
> Why is fragrance in her hair?

This was Powys' concern. On its bodiless excursions the soul still, even at a great distance, uses the senses of the body it has left behind. (*In Spite Of*, IV, 109; VII, 215; *The Saturnian Quest*, 88, and see 75).

This thought-teasing paradox of soul and body is brilliantly handled in a poem from Fiji, on the old cannibal practice of letting the victim see parts of himself eaten. Will this be his own fate? In brilliant if almost unreadable couplets, composed as for a past lover, he traces the horrors:

> Of the two eyes that were your ruin,
> One now observes the other stewing. [Hassall 426]

The verses are simultaneously a critique of physical glamor and an assertion of the mind, or soul's, independence. Perhaps nowhere else, apart from Byron, are crucial metaphysics so lightly handled.

Brooke was as strongly obsessed with the spiritual as with the physical. Though love fails on earth, there is hope for it beyond. "The Goddess in the Wood" sets, in mythological terms, a type. In "The Call" lovers may be "one" *above* the "Night," and in "Victory" "beyond all love or hate," "perfect from the ultimate

---

[2] London, 1964.

height of living," they challenge "supernal" hosts. Wounded on earth, love may win success at the "eventual limit of our light," in "The Wayfarers." "Choriambics II" balances solitude in dark woods and some "face of my dreams" gleaming down through the forest "in vision white." White is for Brooke, as for Powys (*The Saturnian Quest*, 24, 26, 48), a mystical color. In "Blue Evening," after "agony" and "hatred" the poet's love is felt within the moon's "white ways of glamour," blessing him with "white brows." "Finding" shows him after love's failure "lone and frightened" in the "white" moonlight's "silver way," with around him trees "mysteriously crying," "dead voices" and "dead soft fingers," and "little gods" whispering, and he sees his love radiant beyond "the tides of darkness," so that nothing was true

> But the white fire of moonlight
> And a white dream of you.

Such love is not sexually limited. "Sleeping Out: Full Moon" shows him alone under the lonely Moon-Queen, and he feels the whole world pressing toward "the white one flame" of a "heatless fire" and "flameless ecstasy"; "earth fades"; "radiant bands" and "friendly" presences help the stumbler to the "infinite height" and *maternal* eyes. We remember Brooke's desire for a perfect, unentangled, love, loving "moon to moon" in "Thoughts on the Shape of the Human Body." The visions are beyond sexuality in line with the contrast in "Success" of "white godhead" with "that foul you"—a contrast, in some vital way, of spirit with personality. We are all, already, part of some other, spiritual dimension. "In Examination" develops a vision of ordinary life transfigured, revealing "scribbling fools" as with flaming hair, God-like, "white-robed" in the "white undying Fire" among archangels and angels—beings in a dimension of which our normal seeing refracts only a miserable simulacrum. "Desertion," on the death of a loved friend, asks pathetically *why* he has gone? Had he known something that made him distrust earth's "splendid dream"? Is perhaps earth's seeming splendor—and often to Brooke it seemed sordid enough—a mere nothing in comparison?

Such intuitions touch spiritualism. Though "The True Beatitude" asserts "an earthly garden hidden from any cleric" Brooke's poetry can be intensely spiritualistic, as when in "Oh, Death will find me. . . ." he imagines his love's arrival in Hades tossing her hair "among the ancient Dead." "Dust" vividly exploits the freedoms of an afterlife. Though the "white flame" of love's earthly visions has gone and we "stiffen" in darkness, yet, in the manner of Byron's *Childe Harold* (III, 74) :

> Not dead, not undesirous yet,
>   Still sentient, still unsatisfied,
> We'll ride the air, and shine, and flit,
>   Around the places where we died . . .

Beyond "thinking" and "out of view" (*i.e.*, in an existence impossible to define) :

> One mote of all the dust that's I
> Shall meet one atom that was you.

The old love reflames in the "garden"; all senses are mixed—is it "fire," "dew," of "earth" or the "height," "singing, or flame, or sense, or hue"? All that can be said is that it is "light" passing on to "light."

Brooke had extrasensory experience. "Home" recounts how, returning by night to his room, he was aware of

> The form of one I did not know
> Sitting in my chair.

Then it goes. All night he "could not sleep."

He wonders variously about the afterlife. "The Life Beyond" imagines it as hideous. "Mutability" asks if indeed there is "a high windless world and strange" beyond time? "Our melting flesh" fixes Beauty there and "imperishable Love," but all we actually know is earth experience, where kisses do not last. "Clouds" ponders the belief that "the Dead" remain close to those on earth but suggests rather that they pass above like clouds, reflecting "the white moon's" beauty, and "break and wave and flow" like a silent sea. But shall we remember the past? "Hauntings" imagines a "poor ghost" "haunted" by vague recollections of earth life—as earth beings are "haunted" by spirit life—which are unintelligible:

> And light on waving grass, he knows not when,
> And feet that ran, but where, he cannot tell.

Official spiritualism is given the fine "Sonnet (Suggested by some of the Proceedings of the Society for Psychical Research.) " After death we shall

> Spend in pure converse our eternal day;
>   Think each in each, immediately wise;
> Learn all we lacked before; hear, know, and say
>   What this tumultuous body now denies;
> And feel, who have laid our groping hands away;
>   And see, no longer blinded by our eyes.

The lines report what spiritualism tells us: speech by telepathic immediacy, halls of learning and progress; the earth body as a limiting factor which narrows and constricts, so that we feel more keenly and see more clearly without it, as in Marvell's *Dialogue Between the Soul and Body*. The next plane, where sound and color are one, is richer, not poorer, in sense experience, depending not on a mentalized summation derived from separate sense inlets. We shall respond directly to the totality of which these allow parts only to trickle through and which we can on earth only approach by attempts at some total dramatic art blending intellectual awareness with sound and color.[3]

Brooke came near such a total experience in the South Sea Islands. "Tiare Tahiti," rejecting the "broken things" of earth, introduces us to a world of Platonic archetypes, to "the Face, whose ghosts we are" and to "Dance" without "the limbs that move," all lovely things meeting in "Loveliness." All colors, white especially, but also coral, pearl, green, gold, red, are there; all earth beauty recaptured and eternalized. And yet—must "feet" become "Ambulation," and what of kisses? Meanwhile, let us enjoy the "flowered way" and "whiteness of the sand," "well this side of Paradise." We may be nearer the spirit reality at choice, sense-summing moments of earthly life than with *mental* accounts, however accurate, of that reality, which is all, and more, of what we experience on earth. Such is the truth flowering from this cleverly balanced poem.

Brooke lived and wrote on the border between earth and paradise, life and death. The transition, as with Powys, involves what may be called the elemental. In nature Brooke loved night woods and the moon, and also his own, and others', nakedness, swimming, and water. These are as transition mediums between modes of existence.

Herein lies the importance of the poem "The Old Vicarage, Grantchester." It contrasts the regulated officialdom of Berlin, where the lines were composed, with the luxuriant freedoms and "unofficial rose" of Grantchester—more widely, civilized constrictions and elemental freedom. At Grantchester one runs on "bare feet" to the river "deep as death":

> In Grantchester their skins are white,
> They bathe by day, they bathe by night. . . .

Spirits are here: "His ghostly Lordship swims his pool," and among the trees flits "the sly shade of a Rural Dean." It is a place of "lithe

---

3 See my discussions in *The Starlit Dome* (London, 1959), 318–20 and *The Christian Renaissance* (London, 1962) 328–29.

children lovelier than a dream" and "youth," where suicide is preferable to "feeling old."

The phrase "deep as death" is important. In the Hades of Byron's *Cain* and in Ibsen's *Lady from the Sea* and *Little Eyolf* water naturally blends with the dimension of death. Brooke once, in imaginative vein, described his Grantchester night bathing:

I stood naked at the edge of the black water in a perfect silence. I plunged. The water stunned me as it came upwards with its cold, life-giving embrace. . . . [Hassall, 208]

Then a figure appeared, some "local deity" or "naiad of the stream," who urged him as Powys often urged us, not to search beyond present existence. But with the elements, especially by night, we are already on the border line, living life and death. Diving into blue waters at Fiji was perhaps more ultimate than poetry (Hassall, 421). Water is death and life. The dead of "Clouds" "break and wave and flow" like a silent sea. The visionary figure of "Blue Evening" comes "rippling" down the moon's "glamour." "Day That I Have Loved" imagines the day as a dead loved one, gone out to sea, and darkness. "Finding" tells of "the words of night" and "dead" spirit-voices and "the dark, beyond the ocean." Brooke's lines in "Seaside":

> In the deep heart of me
> The sullen waters swell towards the moon,
> And all my tides set sea-ward

correspond exactly to the conclusion to Powys' *Rodmoor*. In both Powys and Brooke we meet a mystique of water, darkness, and a great *white* peace (*The Saturnian Quest,* 26). In "The Jolly Company" the stars are "a white companionship" of "lonely light."

Sea life is as a new dimension. "The Fish" blends life and death:

> The strange soft-handed depth subdues
> Drowned colour there, but black to hues,
> As death to living, decomposes—
> Red darkness of the heart of roses,
> Blue brilliant from dead starless skies,
> And gold that lies behind the eyes,
> The unknown unnameable sightless white
> That is the essential flame of night. . . .

As elsewhere, *darkness* is one with the *white* vision. "Behind the eye" corresponds to Eliot's "More distant than stars and nearer than the eye" in "Marina." A fish's life contrasts with love's unrest; it is a lonely self-enjoyment of the blood rhythms. In Powysian vein, for these cool, atavistic depths are exactly Powysian, "His bliss is older than the sun."

Brooke's progress through love agony and love failure to a lonely delight in his solitary, narcissistic, childlike, integrated self, body and soul, to a superb culmination of swimming naked among the glorious nakednesses of the South Sea Islanders, was not all easy and innocent. It had its violent, nonmoral aspect: "I had to have a bath and dance many obscene dances, in lonely nakedness, up and down my room, to get sober" (Hassall, 443). In the early "Song of the Beasts" we leave the house by night when "shameful" desires awake, going

> Down the dim stairs, through the creaking door,
> Naked, crawling on hands and feet. . . .

We are "Beast and God," serving "blind desire," past "evil faces" and "mad whispers," out of the "city," "beyond lust," to level moon-lit waters, and the "calling sea." An embarrassment, half-shame, half-pride, is written into "Mary and Gabriel," wherein Mary feels both "her limbs' sweet treachery" and her "high estate," to be used for some high purpose. She feels "alone," her "womb"—or Brooke's own beauty—"not" exactly hers, and yet it *will* be; some half-glimpsed purpose will be fulfilled and known.

Death is, and yet is not, the end. In the early (1908) "Second Best" the poet is "alone with the enduring Earth, and Night." Death, he thinks, is the end. If so:

> Proud, then, clear-eyed and laughing, go to greet
> Death as a friend!

The poem advances to sense of death as containing all that was life:

> Exile of immortality, strongly wise,
> Strain through the dark with undesirous eyes
> To what may lie beyond it. Sets your star,
> O heart, for ever! Yet, behind the night,
> Waits for the great unborn, somewhere afar,
> Some white tremendous daybreak. And the light,
> Returning, shall give back the golden hours,
> Ocean a windless level, Earth a lawn
> Spacious and full of sunlit dancing-places,

And laughter, and music, and, among the flowers,
The gay child-hearts of men, and the child-faces,
O heart, in the great dawn!

Brooke's earthly poetry is mostly a nighttime poetry. The gold, the sun, the white dawn—like that in the penultimate chapter of Powys' *Weymouth Sands* (*The Saturnian Quest*, 48) —all lie, except for his experiences in the South Seas, beyond.

"The Little Dog's Day" is an early forecast of his death. After these supreme experiences in the South Seas, he had had his day: on his chosen line, there was little more. He had realized himself on the border where supreme self-enjoyment touches a new dimension, and he knew himself ripe for death. There was, he said, "point in my not getting shot," but "also there's point in my getting shot"; "death might be an admirable solution" (Hassall, 491). The famous war sonnets are less like patriotic trumpetings than paeans in praise of death. As in Sherriff's *Journey's End,* war is simply an elemental power, or death force: the sonnets could be applied, *mutatis mutandis,* to a young German.

The first, "Peace," contrasts the inadequacies of poetry and love with "swimmers into cleanness leaping" and a consequent "release." Only the body will be broken, and Death is both "enemy" and "friend."

In the second, "Safety," war, or death, "knows no power." One will be "safe" whatever happens: "And if these poor limbs die, safest of all." "Poor" registers both Brooke's emotional self-involvement and a recognition of the body's inadequacy.

"The Dead" celebrates "honour" but remains typical in "the rich Dead" who "poured out the red sweet wine of youth." Youth's sacrifice is more than patriotism: Called "holiness," it is a thing in itself, youth's perfect hour.

The fourth, also called "The Dead," remembers how they, as in "The Great Lover," had known the varied sense impressions of earth. "All this is ended." Instead, the glittering wavelets are now frosted to

> a white
> Unbroken glory, a gathered radiance,
> A width, a shining peace, under the night.

Moonlight is assumed, or stars.

In "The Soldier" Brooke concentrates on his body, made by England, after dying. The "heart," now "a pulse in the eternal mind," preserves the sounds and scents of its earthly experience; it is a "rich dust." The impressions are both physical and eternal.

These sonnets necessarily avoid explicit statements on spirit life. The problem of war sacrifice is one mainly of *body* sacrifice, as in Masefield's remarkable quatrain, printed in the *Times,* September 16, 1938, on the occasion of Neville Chamberlain's meeting with Hitler in 1938:

> As Priam to Achilles for his Son,
>> So you into the night, divinely led,
>> To ask that young men's bodies, not yet dead,
> Be given from the battle not begun.

Those lines and Brooke's five sonnets preserve necessary limits.

We now return to the Schell portrait. The mockery it at first received at Cambridge as "obscene" or as "your favourite actress" (Hassall, 390) signals the nature of its importance. It was used as a frontispiece to the 1914 collection of his poems and copied for the Rugby Chapel plaque. It became symbolic: "bare-shouldered, long-haired, Greek god-like, mystic, wonderful," it was "on the retina of the public eye, the soldier poet, the nation's sacrifice" (Richard Usborne, "The Lost Heroes," *Sunday Times Magazine,* pictorial supplement, January 29, 1967).

What is its secret? The head rising from bare shoulders suggests a totality unconstricted by the mufflings of civilization. The profile of lips and nose, the waves of hair, the upward tilt of the head and eager eyes, are riveting. Its deliberated pose may have seemed "a travesty" of one whose attractions were normally "unconscious," lacking the "candour" of glance his friends knew (Hassall, 390–91); but though critics thought the Rugby plaque "sentimentalized," his mother saw it as the living image of the youth she had loved, and liked its appearance of "pressing forward" (Hassall, 525).

The upward challenge of its meaning corresponds to Brooke's desire in the early "Second Best" to "meet Death as a friend," "clear-eyed and laughing," and to the use of "lift" in the 1913 poem "The Night Journey," wherein a rushing train symbolizes human destiny:

> Hands and lit faces eddy to a line;
>> The dazed last minutes click; the clamour dies.
> Beyond the great-swung arc o' the roof, divine,
>> Night, smoky-scarv'd, with a thousand coloured eyes

Glares the imperious mystery of the way.
　Thirsty for dark, you feel the long-limbed train
Throb, stretch, thrill motion, slide, pull out and sway,
　Strain for the far, pause, draw to strength again . . .

As a man, caught by some great hour, will rise,
　Slow-limbed, to meet the light or find his love;
And breathing long, with staring sightless eyes,
　Hands out, head back, agape and silent, move

Sure as a flood, smooth as a vast wind blowing;
　And, gathering power and purpose as he goes,
Unstumbling, unreluctant, strong, unknowing,
　Borne by a will not his, that lifts, that grows,

Sweep out to darkness, triumphing in his goal,
　Out of the fire, out of the little room . . .
—There is an end appointed, O my soul!
　Crimson and green the signals burn; the gloom

Is hung with steam's far-blowing livid streamers.
　Lost into God, lights in light, we fly,
Grown one with will, end-drunken huddled dreamers.
　The white lights roar. The sounds of the world die.

And lips and laughter are forgotten things.
　Speed sharpens; grows. Into the night, and on,
The strength and splendour of our purpose swings,
　The lamps fade; and the stars. We are alone.

Compulsion that "lifts"; the darkness; the white lights roaring,
sound and sight one in the new dimension; the intoxicating purpose and the conclusion on "alone"—here is Brooke's total meta-
physic, nobly stated.

The Schell portrait is, in its quiet way, a statement of this
empowered message. It shows, necessarily, nothing of the blood
radiance or red-gold hair which Brooke's friends knew. The definition is faint, a shadow kills the head's outline at the nape, and the
far shoulder is lost in light. The dominating effect is of whiteness, as
of a spirit body, its nakedness that of the "naked seraph" of Shelley's
additional lines to "Epipsychidion" or the "immortal nakedness" of
the young Caponsacchi's ecstatic sacrifice in Browning's *The Ring
and the Book* (VI, 971) . Some lines of Brooke's 1908 "Choriambics
II" were prophetic:

Somewhere lay, as a child sleeping, a child suddenly reft from
　mirth,

> White and wonderful yet, white in your youth, stretched upon
>   foreign earth,
> God, immortal and dead!

The child, or youth, may seem to sleep, but the seraph awakes, eager, as in the portrait. "Immortal" yet "dead": death in youth, and youth in death.

The bare-shouldered portrait was Brooke's own idea. Of it he wrote:

> Nothing's happened: except that my American photographer has sent me a photograph of me—very shadowy and ethereal and poetic, of me in profile, and naked—shouldered. Eddie says it's very good. I think it's rather silly. But anyhow, I don't look like an amateur popular preacher —as in those others.
> And no one will ever be able to put it into an interview, with the words "We want great serious drama" underneath. [Hassall, 390]

His self-exploitation might, he knew, incur mockery, but at least it distinguished him from conventional religion and the literary intelligentsia.

Brooke's death was in attunement with his life and thought. It came as an inevitable, half-willed, instinctive flowering. This does not detract from the sacrifice but rather raises it to artistic and universal status. It was not by chance but rather, to quote *Coriolanus*, by a certain "sovereignty of nature" that his dying became, like Byron's, symbolic, and his memorial at Skyros (Hassall, 528) was well devised by the sculptor Tombros as a nude statue not so much of Brooke himself as of "a young man symbolizing Youth."

Walter Allen

WALTER ALLEN, English novelist and critic, professor of English studies in the New University of Ulster, was born in Birmingham, England, in 1911. He is a graduate in English of the University of Birmingham. For most of his adult life he has been a free-lance writer. His novels include Innocence Is Drowned, Blind Man's Ditch, Rogue Elephant, Dead Man over All [Square Peg in the United States], and All in a Lifetime (Three Score and Ten in the United States). His critical books, The English Novel: A Short Critical History and Tradition and Dream (The Modern Novel in the United States) are familiar to students of English and American literature throughout the world. He has also written critical biographies of Arnold Bennett and George Eliot. As a literary journalist and a book reviewer, he has contributed to most of the leading British literary periodicals. For many years he was closely associated with the New Statesman and for a time was its literary editor. He now reviews books for the London Daily Telegraph and is a frequent contributor to the New York Times Book Review. He says that he has lost count of the number of times he has broadcast on literary subjects on the BBC's internal and external services.

He has visited the United States on several occasions and has been a visiting Professor of English at, among others, Vassar College, the University of Kansas, and the University of Washington. His main interest now is in American literature.

Married, with four children, he now divides his time between Northern Ireland and London, the only place in the world in which he would wish to live permanently, though, failing London, he would put up with New York.

A LITERARY AFTERMATH

IT CANNOT be merely the persistence of habit that prompts us, after fifty years and the experience of another war more widely ranging, more devastating, and more terrifying in its cruelty and barbarity, still to think of the war of 1914–18 as the Great War. Initially, perhaps, the phrase records the sense of awe with which the British, at any rate, contemplated what for them was the sudden and almost incredible end of a hundred years of peace. It had not, of course, been a century of total peace, but the wars the British had known at firsthand during the period, in the Crimea, in India, in South Africa, had been peripheral to the lives of most Englishmen, conflicts fought thousands of miles away from Britain by small professional armies. Yet the continued use of the phrase "Great War" must denote something beyond this—the recognition that the war destroyed a relatively stable world and substituted for probable evolutionary development violently revolutionary change, and as we know, the Second World War itself, though not a continuation of the First, was one of its consequences.

For us, it is difficult not to think of the war as one of the catastrophic turning points in history; like the fall of Constantinople, it seems to mark the end of one cycle of history and the beginning of another. Because of this, it appears at first sight strange that the literature it inspired, at least in English, should prove, when the wheat is sifted from the chaff, so small in bulk. Still, there are things to be remembered. It was not until more than fifty years after the French invasion of Russia that *War and Peace* appeared and almost a hundred years after the end of the Napoleonic threat to England that *The Dynasts* was published. It may be significant that Tolstoy and Hardy were born years after the events they describe.

Then, too, most of the best writers in English of our time did not fight in the war. "The lives of us all," Eliot remarks in his introduction to David Jones' *In Parenthesis*—the "all" meaning himself, Joyce, and Pound, but he might have added Yeats, Lawrence, and Forster as well—"were altered by that war, but David Jones is the only one to have fought in it." In a general sense this must be true, as it was true for everyone who lived through the period, whether as soldier or civilian. It is possible to doubt whether *Ulysses* and *Finnegans Wake* would have been much different from what they are had there been no war, but the effect on Pound is plain for all to see in the *Mauberley* poems, while *The Waste Land* is a typical product of the bitter disillusionment that was the immediate aftermath of the war, though it is also much more. To discover how the war impinged on Lawrence, for whom it was the final degrading triumph of industrialism, one has only to read *Kangaroo*.

So, it is tempting to say, the best writers of the time were not there. But that, as David Jones' title *In Parenthesis* reminds us, is too easy. One meaning of the title Jones explains in his preface: ". . . for us amateur soldiers (and especially for the author, who was not only amateur, but grotesquely incompetent, a knocker-over of piles, a parade's despair) the war itself was a parenthesis—how glad we thought we were to step outside its brackets at the end of '18. . . ." This must have been true for hundreds of thousands, no doubt the majority, of soldiers. J. B. Priestley confirms it. He joined the Army in September, 1914, aged nineteen, and spent the next four and a half years in it, mostly in the front line or not far from it. More than forty years later, we find him saying in his reminiscences, *Margin Released:*

There are those—and Hemingway may stand for many writers—who found in war, however much they hated it, the deeper reality we all look for. . . . And almost all these men . . . seemed to feel more confused and unhappy as the war receded, as if they felt they were drifting away from reality, as if a world with its guns silenced was an uneasy dream. To this class, neither inferior nor superior but different, I never belonged. The dream for me began when the guns roared. Except at certain rare moments, and these were far outnumbered by their peacetime counterparts, I did not discover any deeper reality in war. . . . Its obvious one-sidedness soon made it seem to me a vast piece of imbecility.

For Priestley the war was essentially an affair in parenthesis, a boring, though nightmarish, interruption of real life.

But there were also those for whom the war was not an affair in parenthesis but a dead stop. Writing on the literature of the Great War, inevitably today one thinks first of Wilfred Owen, killed on the eve of the Armistice at the age of twenty-five, of Isaac Rosenberg, killed at twenty-eight, of Charles Hamilton Sorley, killed at twenty. Speculation about what they might have done had they survived is futile; they were the best of the poets who wrote, as it were, straight from the front. For them no recollection of emotion in tranquillity was possible; they wrote, it still seems as one reads them, in the white heat of the experience itself; and Owen especially has conditioned the thinking on war of all who read him at an impressionable age. As for Sorley, he was given scarcely time enough before he died to do anything at all, but the handful of poems he did write, together with his letters, reveals an astonishingly tough and mature mind that must, one feels, have been capable of enduring work.

But these were not the only deaths. It has become a cliché to say that the best of a generation of Englishmen were wiped out in the years 1914–18. It is a little too easy and emotional. Excellent men in all walks of life survived. Nevertheless, the country lost thousands of talented young men, and among them there must have been many who would have become good writers and some who might have been great. The slaughter itself is one reason why the writing that came out of the war is less in quality and in quantity than, on the surface, might have been expected.

It was not until the last years of the twenties, ten years after the war's ending, that war books—novels, autobiographies, reminiscences—suddenly appeared in spate, more or less simultaneously from all the major combatant countries except Russia. It was as though a dam had burst, a dam of repression, imposed by common consent, on all memories of the war. The first breach in the dam was made by Arnold Zweig's *Case of Sergeant Grischa* in 1927. It was followed in the next year by Remarque's *All Quiet on the Western Front*, Edmund Blunden's *Undertones of War,* and Robert Graves' *Goodbye to All That*. Richard Aldington's *Death of a Hero* and Hemingway's *A Farewell to Arms* appeared in 1929, and Siegfried Sassoon's *Memoirs of an Infantry Officer* a year later. The spate became a trickle in the years that followed but even now has not yet quite died away. War books, products of personal experience of the Great War, still appear. There is Henry Williamson's *roman fleuve, A Chronicle of Ancient Sunlight,* of which five volumes, the last being published in 1960, are devoted to the hero's experience of war. Inadequate as novels as these books seem to me, they are still impressive as what appears to be an act of total recall of one man's life as a soldier. Even as recently as 1962 yet another important book, Gerald Brenan's autobiography, *A Life of One's Own,* appeared; the last two chapters can be compared only with the war chapters of *Goodbye to All That*.

From Zweig's onward, these books I have mentioned were works of prose: Time had to pass before the perspective necessary for prose, whether in fiction or autobiography, could be gained. The only work of value that has lasted from the war years themselves is lyric poetry. Here the great names are Owen, Rosenberg, and Sassoon. I have listed them in what seems to me the order of their poetic achievement, but Sassoon was the first of them to appear and, immediately, the most effective. He was also the only one of the three to survive the war, and its effect on him seems typical of that of many other writers who survived, for example, Graves, Blunden, Herbert Read, Wyndham Lewis, and perhaps Hemingway in the United States, all writers of distinction in their various fields whose achievements still seem conditioned by their war experience, which for them had the quality of a trauma to be lived through again and again before release was possible. And perhaps it has proved wholly possible for only one of them, Robert Graves, who has found something like salvation in his worship of the White Goddess.

In a sense, Sassoon remains the standard of reference by which one judges the other British writers of the war and their achievements. He was the first British soldier-poet to capture public attention as the opponent of the war. He was the first to expose its miseries, and the attitude he expressed toward it in his verse he translated into actuality, so that for a time, until he was persuaded otherwise by Graves and W. H. R. Rivers, the medical psychologist who was so great an influence on both poets, he even opted out of the war, committing an act of private rebellion that might have been construed as mutiny. The record, in fact, is anything but crystal clear. There can be no doubt that the Sherston trilogy, which consists of *Memoirs of a Fox-Hunting Man, Memoirs of an Infantry Officer,* and *Sherston's Progress,* is artistically much superior to the three volumes of straight autobiography that followed a decade later as more or less a gloss on the earlier books. *The Memoirs of George Sherston* is already an English classic, containing, as it does, some of the best accounts of fox hunting, steeplechasing, village cricket, and trench warfare that we have. But it does at crucial points fall, at times disastrously, between autobiography and fiction. Sherston is only one side of Sassoon; he is, so to say, Sassoon minus the poet, and it is that which makes his behavior in the later pages of *Memoirs of an Infantry Officer* incomprehensible.

Sassoon joined the Army as a private soldier in September, 1914, at the age of twenty-eight, several years older than Owen, Graves, Blunden, and Herbert Read, who joined as little more than schoolboys, and, indeed, a year older than Rupert Brooke. Though he had nothing like Brooke's reputation, he had published one book of verse by the time he joined up, and he was the friend of such figures of the Literary Establishment as Edmund Gosse and Eddie Marsh.

He was, in other words, much more than the amiable young fox-hunting cricketer that is George Sherston as we first meet him. As his early war poems, some of which were published in the London *Times,* show, he went to the war in much the same spirit of idealistic patriotism as Brooke. He was commissioned as an officer and proved himself an extraordinarily brave man; he won the highest honor but one for courage in action and, as Graves tells us in *Goodbye to All That,* was known as "Mad Jack." Then, already famous as the protesting war poet, he signed, under the influence of Bertrand Russell, a separate peace. He publicly denounced the war. Later—the British Establishment has never exhibited its qualities of tact and skill, its capacity for assimilating alien bodies, more strikingly than in its treatment of Sassoon—he returned to the war and the trenches. His gesture was at once noble and futile—and the logical consequence of his poems.

They are not, the poems of *The Old Huntsman* and *Counter Attack,* great poems. They are crude and immediate, and it is here that their power, which seems to me still great, resides:

> I'd like to see a Tank come down the stalls,
> Lurching to rag-time tunes, or "Home, sweet home,"
> And there'd be no more jokes in Music-halls
> To mock the riddled corpses round Bapaume.

What we have, immediately transcribed, almost without pause for reflection, is the impact of the war on lacerated nerves. Sassoon's response to trench warfare and its horrors, though not conceived in intellectual terms, is generous and disinterested. These are not egotistical poems; they are the poems of a man responsible for the lives of others, who has made himself the spokesman of the inarticulate. Chesterton has a line: "We are the people of England, who have not spoken yet." Through Sassoon, part of that silent England, the part that served in the trenches in the P.B.I.—the Poor Bloody Infantry—spoke.

In Sassoon's verse, the poetry, to adapt Owen's famous phrase, is the indignation, and it survives. Better, no doubt, that the poetry should be the pity, as it was with Owen. Owen's poetry, which is rooted in trench warfare as fully as Sassoon's, is the more universal because compassion is there as well as indignation. Lines such as:

> Move him into the sun—
> Gently its touch awoke him once,
> At home, whispering of fields unsown,
> Always it woke him, even in France,

Until this morning and this snow.
If anything might rouse him now
The kind old sun will know.

Think how it wakes the seeds,—
Woke, once, the clays of a cold star.
Are limbs, so dear-achieved, are sides,
Full-nerved—still warm—too hard to stir?
Was it for this the clay grew tall?
—O what made fatuous sunbeams toil
To break earth's sleep at all?

have a quality beyond Sassoon, a quality that comes from Owen's ability to stand back from his subject and see it *sub specie aeternitatis*. And this is associated with, perhaps is even in part the product of, a much greater command of poetic techniques than Sassoon ever had. Owen was the greater poet partly because he devised the medium—conspicuously, the use of assonance and half rhyme—fitting to his subject matter, though this should still not tempt us to minimize the achievement of Sassoon.

It seems clear now that one important factor that influenced writers' attitudes toward the war was the age at which they entered it, and age implies experience of life. Isaac Rosenberg is a case in point. Younger than Sassoon, older than Owen, his experience had been very different from theirs. He was from the working class, had left school at fourteen and become a painter. He was a Jew who had, one feels, not become assimilated into traditional English life as Sassoon had. As Bernard Bergonzi has noted in his valuable study of the English literature of the war, *Heroes' Twilight*, Rosenberg's working-class background, which was mainly Cockney, meant that he had "no English pastoral nostalgia to set against front-line experience." Moreover, when he returned from South Africa to join the Army in 1915, he was inspired by no such patriotic impulses as fired Brooke and Sassoon. He strikes a down-to-earth, working-class note in a letter in which he writes, "I thought if I'd join there would be the separation allowance for my mother." Killed in 1918, he remained throughout his service a private soldier, in contradistinction to Sassoon, Owen, Graves, Blunden, and Herbert Read. To that extent, he had it "cushy," to use the slang word of the P.B.I. that reechoes through the writings of the war, meaning something like not too bad or bearable and a notable example of what is called Anglo-Saxon understatement.

This is not to say that the private soldier's lot was a comfortable one; once behind the lines his material condition was much worse than the junior officer's. But at any rate he was spared the burden of responsibility for men under him that was the junior officer's. As we know it from its literature, from Sassoon, Owen, Graves, the Great War was largely a junior officer's war. But if only because he who is down need fear no fall, the private soldier could be his own man as the officer could not be, as Frederic Manning's *Her Privates We* seems to suggest. So that Rosenberg in his poems is detached from his material, as the officer-poets, who were mostly younger than he, were not. He was helped here, perhaps, by his training as a painter; his attitude toward the scenes of war is partly esthetic; they exist in a sharp and sure perspective that is impersonal. It would be both futile and small-minded to attempt to set off Rosenberg's achievement against Owen's; but it is very difficult to imagine the kind of poetry Owen would have gone on to write if he had lived, since so much of what we have is the lyrical response to immediate experience, whereas Rosenberg's verse, one feels, was the response to war of a man who was already mature, formed and set, as it were, before he went to the war.

In this he resembles a much older writer, Ford Madox Ford, who volunteered for the Army when he was forty-two. He was, of course, already very well known as a novelist, poet, and editor, the intimate, for longer or shorter periods, of men such as James, Conrad, Stephen Crane, and Wells. He recorded what one assumes to be his own war experience through the character of Tietjens in his *Parade's End* sequence of novels. He cannot be said to have had a "good war," to use the phrase of a later one. He was not long in the trenches, but long enough to be gassed and shell-shocked, and he did not hit it off with his superior officers. His military career, indeed, reflected remarkably the pattern of his civilian life; rightly or wrongly, he was a man toward whom the usual English reaction was suspicion and distrust, so much so that even now his reputation as a novelist is smaller in Britain than in the United States. There is irony here, for whatever else Ford may have been, he was certainly a patriotic Englishman. It is in *Parade's End* that both his patriotism and his notion of Englishness, which I must admit seems to me largely a sentimental dream, come together.

Parade's End is only incidentally a war novel. Primarily, it is Ford's dramatization of the breakup of the Edwardian era, of the degeneration of a ruling class. Seen from this point of view, the war, one cannot help feeling, came as a godsend to Ford: it proved his point. His hero, Tietjens, is done down by those who control the running of the war exactly as he is done down by their counterparts in civil life. There is a critical problem here. Tietjens was the final and most complete version of what may be called the Ford man. Whatever his name, whether Moffatt in *The Benefactor*, Ashburnham in *The Good Soldier*, Tietjens in *Parade's End*, he is the English gentleman, sometimes called the Tory, who does his duty regardless of consequences and who is done down precisely because of this. The problem is one that can be solved only by reference to Ford's own life; it seems plain that Ford saw himself as just such a man. The character, in other words, is a projection of his own paranoia. But this, though it may raise questions about *Parade's End* as a whole, does not invalidate the treatment of the war in the novel. In his impressionistically vivid style Ford renders the scene of Flanders brilliantly, and the picture is the more impressive because it is the work of a man who in a sense was an incurable civilian, already middle-aged, able to compare and contrast the war with the years of peace, the "summer afternoon" of Edwardian England, and to see the war as the consequence of those years of peace.

In Ford's sequence there is no nostalgia for the past, for the years of peace. The war is necessary almost to the conception of Tietjens; it is part of the "lasting tribulation"—Ford's words—that he must endure. In this absence of nostalgia Ford differs sharply from most of the poets, who were men in many instances more than twenty years younger. In Owen and Sassoon alike, nostalgia alternates with indignation; *Memoirs of a Fox-Hunting Man* in particular is a loving celebration of the "summer afternoon" of Edwardian England. In Edmund Blunden's poetry, as in his prose work *Undertones of War*, the horrors of the trenches are counterpointed against memories, almost visions, of a pastoral England. The title of one of Graves' wartime volumes, *Fairies and Fusiliers*, indicates the conflict in the poet's mind at the time. He was, as we know from *The Memoirs of George Sherston*, in which he appears as David Cromlech, a singularly tough, efficient, almost arrogantly self-confident and courageous officer; but the verse he was writing, based on nursery rhymes and ballads and with obvious affinities to the poetry of Walter de la Mare, seems now a wistful dream of childish innocence and arcadian simplicity. In the years immediately after the war, when he was much preoccupied with theories of depth psychology and was using the writing of verse as a kind of self-therapy, his poetry deepened and became darker. The simple wish-fulfillment dreams turn into nightmare. This period ended with the writing of his autobiography, *Goodbye to All That*, one of the great autobiographies, the most complete account we have of a young poet at war, a poet whose complexities include a pride in the soldierly virtues and in the traditions of his regiment. It is the self-portrait of a remarkable man characterized by what one is tempted to call a crotchety integrity and an independence that have allowed him to go his own way regardless of praise, neglect, and changes in literary fashion and to write probably more good poems than any other living poet writing in English, poems that, however traditional they may seem at first glance, are wholly original.

So far the writing we have looked at, with the partial exception of Rosenberg's, is the literature of personal response, almost of the private agony. Its value largely consists in this, but all the same one asks for something else as well, for the synoptic view as we find it in Tolstoy's and Hardy's renderings of the Napoleonic campaigns. Owen seems to have been working toward something like this in the months before he was killed, especially in his poem "Strange Meeting," in which, as Bergonzi has said, a "double vision" is imposed on the reader. Two works there are, possibly three, that attempt a synoptic vision, that attempt to speak not for one man, a single individual, but generically. They are Frederic Manning's novel *Her Privates We,* David Jones' *In Parenthesis,* a work that defies categories but may best be read as a long poem in a form related to *The Waste Land* and Pound's *Cantos,* and, more dubiously, Herbert Read's poem "The End of the War." I say "more dubiously" because I find it lacking in a certain quality of sensuousness, magic, unexpectedness, that for me is essential to poetry. Having said this, I must also say that it is greatly admired by better critics than I, critics who are themselves fine poets. Allen Tate has called it "a great poem on a great subject: the impact on the contemplative mind of universal violence, whether the violence be natural or man-made." I find the poem cold and abstract; even so, I recognize the nobility of Read's intention and the high seriousness of the work. His prose piece "In Retreat" is certainly one of the best descriptions of one aspect of the war that we have, the more moving because of its objectivity.

I think there can be no such reservations about *Her Privates We* and *In Parenthesis.* Manning's novel was published in 1930. Manning himself died five years later, a somewhat mysterious figure who had been writing since 1910, a more or less wealthy Australian who, as his early verse shows, had come under the influence of Pound. *Her Privates We* seems to me the best of the English war novels and to possess enduring merit. The central character is named Bourne; we are not told his Christian name or anything about his antecedents. He is wealthy: he is a connoisseur of wine and gets food parcels from Fortnum & Mason. He is not—and this is important—an officer, but a private soldier, though at the end of the novel he has submitted to the pressure brought upon him to take a commission. He is a very accomplished private soldier; he can scrounge—the Second War's word for it was "liberate"—with the best. His position as a rich man in the ranks is ambiguous, but he becomes the leader of a small group of very tough privates with whom in peacetime he could have had almost no conceivable contact. One of the themes of the novel is comradeship, which, Manning makes clear, is not the same as friendship, but something more impersonal and in some ways closer. *Her Privates We* is not an antiwar novel; rather, war is seen as life heightened, intensified; as Bourne reflects: "Life was a hazard enveloped in a mystery, and war quickened the sense of both in men: the soldier also, as well as the saint, might write his tractate *de contemptu mundi*, and differ from him only in the angle and spirit from which he surveyed the same bleak reality."

Her Privates We, then, is not a personal cry of anguish, indignation, or pity. It is a very impersonal novel, and the impersonality seems stressed by the fact that we never know the hero's Christian name; whether there is symbolic intention in his surname I do not pretend to know. The impersonality, which is bound up with a striving for universality, is reinforced by the references implicit in the structure of the book. The title is from *Hamlet*, and the mottoes affixed to the chapters are also from Shakespeare. As one reads, one feels more and more that the novel is rooted in Shakespeare, though I think one would search in vain for any correspondence between Manning's characters and those in the plays. The closest parallel is with *Henry V*. One chapter seems quite certainly based on Act IV, Scene 1, in which the King, incognito, talks to the private soldiers Bates, Court, and Williams on the eve of Agincourt, though there is one essential difference between Manning and Shakespeare: in Manning the King, or any equivalent of him, is missing.

Nevertheless, the Shakespearean echoes provide a frame of reference that compels us to look at the Great War in a long perspective of time, to see the war in the context of English history, and this Manning succeeds in doing, while at the same time rendering the very feel of trench life as experienced by the private soldier, the man without privileges on whom, ultimately, everything depends. And he does this in part through the extreme vividness of his realization of individual private soldiers, of, for example, the half-Caliban figure of "Weeper" Smart, one of the most memorable and challenging minor figures in modern fiction.

In Parenthesis, as I have suggested, is probably best approached as a work with a general affinity to both *The Waste Land* and *Cantos*. It is not presented formally as a poem, though punctuation and typography are used, as Jones says, "to indicate some change of tone, inflexion, or emphasis." Its initial difficulty, like that of Eliot's and Pound's poems, is that it demands of the reader knowledge, in the way of allusion and mythology, that he cannot be expected automatically to have. The matter of ancient Welsh poetry is one of Jones' constant references. Jones is liberal with his notes, and the poem is much less difficult than it might otherwise have been because of the author's view of the British, whom he sees as at once Celtic and Anglo-Saxon. In his preface he tells us that his companions in the war were mostly Londoners, together with some Welshmen. "Together they bore in their bodies the genuine tradition of the Island of Britain, from Bendigeid Vran to Jingle and Marie Lloyd. These were the children of Doll Tearsheet. Those are before Caractacus was. . . . It was curious to know them harnessed together, and together caught in the toils of 'good order and military discipline.' "

The Cockney elements in the poem, along with the recurring echoes of *Henry V*, seem to me an essential factor in the success of *In Parenthesis*. They peg down and give immediate actuality to the older, more esoteric matter on which the work is based, the world of Welsh legend and Malory's *Le Morte d'Arthur*. And in Jones these juxtapositions between past and present, between medieval myth and grimy reality, work toward a quite different end from the comparable juxtapositions in *The Waste Land*. Neither intent nor effect is satirical. Past and present are fused into one, as is suggested by the name, John Ball, that Jones gives to the private soldier who is at the center of the action.

The result is a poem that may be taken as an expression of a whole people throughout their history, but focused in one specific episode of that history, the Great War. Nothing is burked; there is no palliation of the horrors of war; yet the poem exists in a strange beauty, even in a serenity, which comes in part, it is difficult not to think, from Jones' Catholicism, his habit of seeing his immediate subject, the Great War, *sub specie aeternitatis*. There is a simple instance of this in the preface, in which Jones notes: " . . . the 'Bugger! Bugger!' of a man detailed, had often about it the 'Fiat! Fiat!' of the Saints." Perhaps the last lines of the poem, the final sentence of which is from the *Chanson de Roland*, may be quoted as an instance of its serenity and acceptance as well as of its method:

Lie still under the oak
next to the Jerry
and Sergeant Jerry Coke.
   The feet of the reserves going up tread level
with your forehead; and no word for you; they
                       whisper one with another;

pass on, inward;
these latest succours:
green Kimmerii to bear up the war.

Oeth and Annoeth's hosts they were
who in that night grew
younger men
younger striplings.

The geste says this and the man who was on the field . . .
and who wrote the book . . . the man who does not know
this has not understood anything.

There seems to be an obvious contrast between the English
literature of the Great War and the American. The war brought
the United States into the world, but its effect on American writers
was slight, and different in kind from that on the English. So far as
one can tell, Fitzgerald's few months of service in the United States
Army was the merest parenthesis in his life. He saw no action, and
it seems significant that the Americans we think of as war writers
were volunteers in other armies: Faulkner in the Royal Canadian
Air Force, Cummings and Dos Passos as ambulance drivers with the
French, Hemingway with the Italians. They were fighting some-
body else's war, which makes it possible for Hemingway's Frederic
Henry in *A Farewell to Arms* to desert and make his separate peace.
There is, in other words, an absence of the sense of commitment
and obligation. This is strikingly apparent in Dos Passos' *Three
Soldiers;* at times while reading it, it is difficult not to think that the
author conceives the major tragedy of the war to be the loss of John
Andrews' symphony. There is, of course, hatred of the war in Dos
Passos' novel, but the deeper hatred is for Army life itself and the
restrictions it imposes on individual rights. All of which is merely to
say that for Americans the Great War was not the traumatic experience it was for the British. For anything comparable America had
to wait for the economic depression of the thirties.

Frederick J. Hoffman

FREDERICK J. HOFFMAN, *who died suddenly on December 24, 1967, was born in Port Washington, Wisconsin, on September 21, 1909, and was educated at Stanford, Minnesota, and Ohio State universities. He taught at the universities of Ohio State, Oklahoma, Wisconsin (at Madison), California (at Riverside), Harvard, Stanford, Washington, and Duke before joining the University of Wisconsin (at Milwaukee) faculty in September, 1965, as distinguished professor of English.*

He was the author of more than 300 articles and reviews and more than 20 books, some of which were translated into other languages. His most well-known volume, The Mortal No *(1964), attempts, in the words of one critic, "a redefinition of modern literature in terms of a new set of metaphors, concerned with the intruding presence of the secular in the midst of the religious, of the spatial in the midst of the temporal, of the decorous in the midst of the violent." The theme of violence in modern literature, as well as the theme of death, is seen in* The Mortal No *as being significantly affected by the events of World War I and the postwar temper.*

In works like Freudianism and the Literary Mind *(1945),* The Modern Novel in America *(1951),* The Twenties *(1955), and* Samuel Beckett: The Language of Self *(1962), he was to elaborate on his belief that literature "helps us to see the reality of any idea in a full, clear, and meaningful form; the form is the matter, the matter is in the form, and the reality which is thus formally given is a moral and aesthetic anecdote of one or another aspect of the time."*

THE NOVEL OF WORLD WAR I:
A DOCUMENT IN THE
HISTORY OF SURPRISE

IF THERE is a major fact of the war novel of World War I, it has to do with the rude contrast between expectations and reality. Any number of adjustments had to be made to the immense acceleration of violence since the Franco-Prussian War of the 1870's and to the shock of discovering that this was no longer either a "gentleman's war" or a war in which the assailant and the victim had a clear view of each other.[1] The sense of outrage which followed upon a too naïve set of determinations and propaganda enterprises that were much more successful than their agents dreamed was interpreted in many ways. Of course, there were novels which preached the Great Crusade (Edith Wharton's, Dorothy Canfield Fisher's, Arthur Train's), but these are rather crude efforts to retain a tradition that had already been running down in the late nineteenth century.

It is possible to measure the energy of the postwar novel in terms of a calculus of violence and of its relation to rhetoric.[2] At its simplest, we can only say that the propaganda preceding the entrance of the United States into the war was very erratic and that the consequences for literature were quite explicit. It was not just a matter of disillusion; as a number of novelists asserted (Thomas Boyd, E. E. Cummings, and Ernest Hemingway among them), there was a violent disruption of the conventional and traditional ways of defining man and his moral responsibilities. In one of my attempts to describe this situation, I suggested following the lead of Kenneth Burke, in *Counter-Statement* (1931), in his definitions of violence and the mitigating effects of "eloquence":

. . . The purpose of eloquence is to direct the reader's attention away from fact, or to link fact with one or several of the systems of larger

---

[1] A recent book by Stanley Cooperman, *World War I and the American Novel* (Baltimore, 1967), is perhaps the best book on its subject. Especially relevant to the war's backgrounds are Parts I and II, pp. 3–125.

[2] This I have tried to do in several parts of *The Mortal No: Death and the Modern Imagination* (Princeton, 1964), and I depend much upon that book for this essay. The two are, however, quite separate from each other.

meaning which in any period circumscribe fact. Eloquence also acts to slow the rhythm of factual succession. . . . The more intensely violent fact becomes, the more solicitous is eloquence to mitigate its intensity.

A related problem is that of the pace of experience. Eloquence funcions to moderate the pace, by interjecting matters that are only relatively pertinent to fact. This function is most successful in circumstances that are not in themselves shocking, though they may be profoundly disturbing. . . . [*The Mortal No,* pp. 158–62.]

As Stanley Cooperman has so accurately pointed out, there was a vast difference between local heroics and the "filth of no man's land." (*World War I and the American Novel,* p. 33.) The rhetoric of prowar propagandists sounded a refrain that must have sickened the air; it had little or no recognizable relation to the war's reality. The shock of discovery led to a form of postwar nominalism, signalized by Lieutenant Frederic Henry's thoughts, after his return to the front from the hospital in Milan. These famous remarks deserve at least one more repetition because they are so representative of the postwar decade:

I was always embarrassed by the words sacred, glorious, and sacrifice and the expression in vain. We had heard them, sometimes standing in the rain almost out of earshot, so that only the shouted words came through, and had read them, on proclamations that were slapped up by billposters over other proclamations, now for a long time, and I had seen nothing sacred, and the things that were glorious had no glory and the sacrifices were like the stockyards at Chicago if nothing was done with the meat except to bury it. . . . Abstract words were obscene beside the concrete names of villages, the numbers of roads, the names of rivers, the numbers of regiments and the dates. [*A Farewell to Arms,* p. 196.]

These reflections fit so well into a pattern that it is as though they had been machine-tooled. Henry begins his participation in the war on the Italian front equipped with the usual illusions and expectations. He is not sure just why he is at the front at all. And he almost passively lets the war experience happen to him. He obeys orders, to the point when they no longer make any sense to him. Having submitted to a depersonalized machine, whose closest approximation to reality is its frequent accesses to confusion, he has gradually to disembarrass himself of the war world and to reassert himself, as individual man, lover, husband, father. All these last roles are apparently out of place in a condition of war, so Henry has to remove himself via a "separate peace," to a world in which the sound of the war is remote. We must note that Hemingway's novel was published in 1929, after a full decade of looking back at the events which are its setting. Hemingway deliberately set up his soldier as the man open to influences, not yet educated or firmly convinced regarding the justice of any acts or rhetorics. Henry is, nevertheless, of a group of American heroes (his immediate predecessor was probably Huckleberry Finn) who seem to have an instinctive sense of justice, a cautionary view of imbalances, and a proper view of what is wrong and right. So that he acts as a gauge of morality and has a basic moral sense.

There are two facts of the war that disturb him: The violence of it overwhelms all attempts to understand it rationally, and, of course, there is a point at which people behave irrationally in it. Henry's wound is perhaps symbolic of all the meretricious violence of the war. He is eating cheese and drinking wine when it happens, and it is least expected when it does: "There was a flash, as when a blast-furnace door is swung open, and a roar that started white and went red and on and on in a rushing wind. . . . I went out swiftly, all of myself, and I knew I was dead and that it had all been a mistake to think you just died. Then I floated, and instead of going on I felt myself slide back." (*Arms*, p. 58.) The unexpected, sudden violence and the fact that Henry was not "face to face" with his assailant are facts of the modern violent situation. As for the irrationality of the war scene, he encounters that later, during and at the end of the retreat from Caporetto, when the behavior of men toward one another could not be explained on any rational level. At the inquisition before the Tagliamento River the Italian military police "had the beautiful detachment and devotion to stern justice of men dealing in death without being in any danger of it." (Pp. 240–241.)

To these irrationalities, Henry opposes the love of Catherine Barkley, an English nurse who has already lost one lover in the war. The love begins in the sullen and tawdry world of the house of prostitution: Catherine, at least, is better than the girls in the brothel. Both of them accept it at first as "a rotten game we play." (P. 32.) But it becomes much more than that—in fact, a genuine assertion of his humanity and his manhood, in an inhuman situation. There are times when he even considers the affair close to being religious, in the presence of Count Greffi and of the priest. Mainly, the love for Catherine Barkley becomes a romantic affirmation in the midst of impersonal calamity. As such, it is doomed. It is true that the affair superficially turns out to be a biological "trap" and that success or failure in the maternity hospital represents the margin of loss. Yet the affair and the pregnancy are in themselves assertions of the humane in defiance of war. The margin is great between the girls in the house provided as an accommodation for the officers (they are, in the movements about the war scene, parts of the "baggage") and the figure of Catherine, dedicated wholly to her man ("There isn't any me any more." P. 113). In the end, however, the affair has turned out to be a gamble, and a losing one. Henry walks out of the Swiss hospital in the rain back to his hotel. His physical and sexual assertions have not prevailed. In the true economy of Hemingway's work, as Malcolm Cowley has said, the Lieutenant Henry of *Arms* walks away from the hospital to become the Jake Barnes of *The Sun Also Rises*. The affair has from the beginning been disturbed by its setting. Both Henry and Catherine have had trouble avoiding the atmosphere of casual prostitution, simply because *all* evidence of permanence is out of order in the war scene. On the evening of his departure from Milan, they rent a hotel room which has all the appearance and the trappings of a lavish and expensive whorehouse.

I went to the window and looked out, then pulled a cord that shut the thick plush curtains. Catherine was sitting on the bed, looking at the cut glass chandelier. She had taken her hat off and her hair shone under the light. She saw herself in one of the mirrors, and put her hands to her hair. I saw her in three other mirrors. She did not look happy. She let her cape fall on the bed.

"What's the matter, darling?"

"I never felt like a whore before," she said. I went over to the window and pulled the curtain aside and looked out. I had not thought it would be like this.

"You're not a whore."

"I know it, darling. But it isn't nice to feel like one." Her voice was dry and flat.

The real meaning of this and several other scenes is that the war scene, as Henry once put it, is not for virgins. It is not, in brief, the place for responsible behavior. The violence, the suddenness and unseemliness of death, the furtive nature of catch-as-catch-can pleasures—all militate against anything that may remotely be called normal. Hemingway's favorite image for this idea is that of the confusion of the retreat, when all semblance of normal human relationships are thrown into imbalance: "In the night many peasants had joined the columns from the roads of the country and in the column there were carts loaded with household goods; there were mirrors projecting up between mattresses, and chickens and ducks tied to carts. There was a sewing machine on the cart ahead of us in the rain." (P. 211.) The most familiar objects are piled in a helter-skelter, absurd arrangement, suggesting a hasty retreat before the threat of violence.

The violent upheaval had different meanings for the nationalities engaged in the hostilities. The Americans were likely to be the more shocked, because the less emotionally prepared. As Stanley Cooperman has said, "After the revolution-in-morals of the 1920's, it is not always easy to remember that the soldiers setting out in 1917 were leaving what was an essentially puritan, Victorian society, modified by frontier-developed emphasis on the virtues of righteous struggle, for a world in which every standard seemed torn apart." (P. 43.) There was variety, of course, in the war fiction, but the best of it usually represented a slide down into the experiencing of mud, filth, and surprise. As a result, the hero of our postwar fiction thought of the war as a devastating criticism of the society that preceded it. The two landscapes, those of war and of peace, continue to amaze, as the following lines from a recent poem by Philip Larkin suggest. The poem is cryptically called "MCMXIV":

> Never such innocence,
> Never before or since
> As changed itself to past
> Without a word—the men
> Leaving the gardens tidy,
> The thousands of marriages
> Lasting a little while longer:
> Never such innocence again. [*Poetry 1967*, p. 19.]

This is by way of retrospect of some fifty or so years. The immediate reaction was often more vivid, as in this portion of Ezra Pound's "Hugh Selwyn Mauberley" (1920) :

> There died a myriad,
> And of the best, among them,
> For an old bitch gone in the teeth,
> For a botched civilization,
>
> Charm, smiling at the good mouth,
> Quick eyes gone under earth's lid,
>
> For two gross of broken statues,
> For a few thousand battered books. [*Selected Poems*, p. 176.]

"It was the entire concept of the proving ground," says Cooperman, "that was broken in World War I; and it was broken violently enough to affect permanently the literature of a generation." (P. 48.)

War as a "proving ground" of heroism, of manliness, and of maturity had apparently disappeared forever. Perhaps the major reason is that force and energy were gradually being put to maximum utility. The American soldiers often found themselves in a war for which they had not prepared themselves, or they were commanded by officers who had learned to fight another kind of war. Friedrich Juenger speaks of the man-made transformation of entire landscapes; at Flanders, for example, "The artillery barrages which had hailed down for weeks had turned this theater of war into a sort of moonscape covered with craters." (*The Failure of Technology*, p. 117.)

In many cases there was an almost absolute loss of decorum, caused by indiscriminate saturation bombing. Pound speaks with bitterness and irony, in another part of his "Hugh Selwyn Mauberley":

> Died some, pro patria,
>   non "dulce" non "et decor" . . .
> walked eye-deep in hell
> believing in old men's lies, then unbelieving
> came home, home to a lie,
> home to many deceits,
> home to old lies and new infamy.

His shock here is obviously the direct result of a disappointment in expectations. But the effect is not only this; it comes from the fact of what Pound calls "wastage as never before." World War I was a war of attrition, on a scale never before seen; men were used (deliberately or aberrantly) as so much matériel against the enemy's force.

It was a violent experience, but there were cases in which it was not unwelcome. Willa Cather's *One of Ours* (1922) portrayed what Cooperman calls the "war drive seething beneath the peaceful surface of American life during these years." (P. 51.) Its hero, Claude Wheeler, is an example of what he calls "the midwesterner reaching for war as a means of achieving what his society simply ruled out as unthinkable (unless for missionary work) : adventure, daring, 'the bright face of danger.' " (P. 52.) In a number of cases the war came, or seemed to have come, as an opportunity to escape tedium; in others, it appeared to be a chance for a quick rise in society, through whatever dynamics it offered. Almost universally, it proved a shock and a disillusionment. Louis-Ferdinand Céline speaks of the war in *Journey to the End of Night* (1934) as follows:

It was an occasion when "everyone queued up to go and get killed."
(P. 26.) This phrase suggests a degree of impersonality almost
unheard of before. The tactics of attrition led to about 10,000,000
casualties. Men were killed without being able to face, even to
identify, their assailants. As Cooperman says, "The man was separated from the act; the potential hero could be—and often was—
splattered by a stray shell under circumstances that had nothing
whatever to do with soldiering." (P. 63.)

The psychology of war literature correspondingly changed, to
adjust to the alterations made in the machinery of war. One of the
most important protective reactions was the abandonment of personal attachment to causes, ideals, principles. The adjustment to
violence almost invariably meant the denial of the self; the pressure
of force was too great for the individual to perform matching
stratagems. The soldier, after having been saturated by abstractions
concerning a heroism that was passé, had almost no genuine re-
course when he became involved with reality. Cooperman says that
only 23 percent of the casualties "earned their red badges of
courage in any sort of direct encounter with the Hun." (Pp.
63–64.) The American soldiers did learn about the harsh realities of
mass war, but they were also introduced to the disillusioning truths
of a depersonalized and despiritualized war world. Nothing is more
appalling than the total collapse of cause and reason. The soldier
must readjust quickly and totally to radically new circumstances. In
the trench warfare of World War I especially, he had to imagine
himself in several dangerous positions and to improvise defenses for
them. The consequences are several forms of dislocation, both
physical and psychological. Sequences of events and the interpretations of them change radically. Since death is so frequent, it becomes less a climax of events as a small event itself, as in this case,
the death of Aymo in *Arms:* ". . . We went down the north side of
the embankment. I looked back. Aymo lay in the mud with the
angle of the embankment. He was quite small and his arms were by
his side, his puttee-wrapped legs and muddy boots together, his cap
over his face. He looked very dead. It was raining. I had liked him
as well as any one I ever knew. . . ." (P. 229.)

The full flush of naturalistic stench and filth was recorded in
many of these novels, whose authors for the most part had suddenly
come upon the facts of indiscriminate killing. "Things were getting
all mixed up in his mind," says Humphrey Cobb in *Paths of Glory*
(1935), one of the most popular of World War I novels. "It seemed
to be filled with flesh, cloyed with the sweetish smell of flesh that is
torn open and over which blood is pouring." (P. 31.) In another

place, Cobb describes the scene of death: ". . . a rat climbed noiselessly up the jamb of the gallery entrance and watched Paolacci for a while, then it stepped onto the lieutenant's chest and squatted there. It looked to the right and to the left, two or three times, then lowered its head and began to eat Paolacci's under lip." (P. 48.) In some such way as this, the phenomenon of what Erich Kahler has called the *neue Sachlichkeit* (new factuality) can be illustrated:

> . . . Factuality is handled so pointedly that it becomes symbolic; abruptness produces compression. Indeed, this peculiar factuality radiates an atmosphere which reflects the overstrained neutrality of the author—a neutrality that appears like an inversion of all the bitter experiences and disillusionments of the generation. The detachment and self-restraint of the author weighs upon the story like a tense aura, like a ghostly presence of fate. [*The Tower and the Abyss*, p. 99.]

It is obvious that the situation of modern violence required a full measure of *Sachlichkeit*. The central ambiguities of the postwar situation were rhetorical equivalents of the fragments of body and machine strewn about the landscape. Hemingway developed his famous style with close attention to the scene. The scene was itself disjunct, and its design was a ghastly and deadly, but calculated, disarray, directly related to the expenditure of mechanized force within an area. Cooperman speaks of the impact of twentieth-century fire power on the American troops first opposed to it: It "helped produce the combination of absurdity, protest, and numbness which were to become characteristics of the antihero in the post–World War I novel." (P. 73.) The circumstances were almost altogether antiheroic: soldiers being ordered mistakenly into a trap; the errantry of flying objects and parts of bodies; coffins exploding into midair, in effect celebrating the ritual of the funeral a second time; the trench itself taking on the appearances of an open grave. Cooperman quotes with some effectiveness a passage from Theodore Fredenburgh's novel *Soldiers March* (1930) :

> . . . On all sides lay great holes, half-filled with water. The chalky soil had been churned and rechurned until its vitals were spewed to the surface. Fragments of stained and rotten uniforms projected from the ground. The dirty bones of corpses reached despairingly from the soil that gave them no rest. . . .
> On the floor of the valley a sickly stream flowed. Its banks of yellow mud looked slimy and unclean in the sun. As far as the valley continued —a yellow, pestilent muck-heap. [P. 112.]

From this bewildering mass and mess of thoughtless, aimless, aberrant carnage, what conceivable types of hero, or antihero, could emerge? There were the "quiet types" of English gentlemen who seemed at least to die willingly to save their England. But in the best of these there is no denial of the confusion and the desperate world of fighting to no immediately clear purpose. Edmund Blunden's war world is "punctured" a bit, but he is alert to its dangers:

> . . . [We] enter Mailly, and turn at the church, still neatly jacketed with straw, but with a new hole or two in it, along a leafy side-road; another turn, and we are between excellent meadow-grounds, which lack only a few fat sheep, an old mole-catcher, and some crows. Groups of shell-holes, however, restrain the fancy from useless excursions, and, sitting under some tall slender elms on a convenient bank for a few minutes' rest, we keep our ears eastwardly attentive. [*Undertones of War*, 1928, pp. 124–25.]

But in American equivalents, the surprise of the soldier was neither contained within gentility nor discounted by illusion. As in *Paths of Glory*, the protest was often leveled against the leadership, which was frequently unprepared and stupid. In a real sense, the "separate peace" of Lieutenant Henry was based on the assumption, as Cooperman puts it, that "the war has deserted him"—that is, that its absurdity and its meaningless violence had in effect deserted any principle or basis according to which he can serve in it any longer. In the American image of him, the soldier "suffers, and is broken and coarsened by a military environment which he never expected and which, in many ways, never expected him." (P. 83.)

Cooperman has a number of ingenious classes of war heroes: the war lover (Willa Cather's *One of Ours;* the phrase is taken from John Hersey's novel about World War II) ; the surprised innocent (Zorn of Fredenburgh's *Soldiers March*) ; the depraved opportunist (Richard Savage of John Dos Passos' *1919*) ; the "Babbitt in Khaki" (James Stevens' *Mattock*) ; the lost souls (Elliot Paul's Irwin and Fuselli of John Dos Passos' *Three Soldiers*) ; the residents of hell (Donald Mahon of Faulkner's *Soldiers' Pay* and William Hicks of Thomas Boyd's *Through the Wheat*) . But for reasons that ought to be obvious, he saves his major analysis for what he calls the anti-heroes of World War I: the narrator of E. E. Cummings' *The Enormous Room*, John Andrews of *Three Soldiers*, and Lieutenant Henry. It is not hard to accept the preference. The last three represent the cry of agonized protest against the irrationalities of an

impossible circumstance. Each of them has, or temporarily enter-
tains, an alternative: Cummings, the quaint, erratic version of the
American underground, called by him the "Delectable Mountains"; Dos Passos' Andrews, art, in a strangely pseudoromantic
antiwar gesture; and Lieutenant Henry, the assertion of virility,
love, and the prospect of fatherhood—in short, a normal "life" as
opposed to the dark night and the shrapnel bursts of the northern
Italian front.

There are many gestures like this, many attempts to rescue the
ego from an incredible landscape destroyed by violence. The major
facts (at least for American authors) have to do with the elements
of surprise in the war scene. Perhaps there is some naïveté in these
demonstrations of shock, as well as in the resulting reactions. But
the shock was genuine, and however naïve the response, it, too, was
genuine. Cummings' love of the little man, the special and unique
"antimostarian" (as he called him in another place), has a special
role in the literature of the 1920's. In the last paragraph of his book,
he describes his sense of a newly found New York City, seen in the
perspective of the small unknown men and women of La Ferté
Macé prison camp:

> The tall, impossibly tall, incomparably tall, city shoulderingly up-
> ward into hard sunlight leaned a little through the octaves of its parallel
> edges, leaningly strode upward into firm hard snowy sunlight; the noises
> of America nearingly throbbed with smokes and hurrying dots which are
> men and which are women and which are things and curious and hard
> and strange and vibrant and immense, lifting with a great ondulous stride
> firmly into the immortal sunlight. [*The Enormous Room*, p. 271.]

The fact is that the best American writers prepared for the
twentieth century by rejecting the nineteenth and resenting their
nineteenth-century education into "realities" that were no longer
true or viable. There were fragments of romanticism left: John
Andrews of *Soldiers Three* just isn't quite real to any audience
observing his protest against the world he was thrown into. In
Lieutenant Henry's choice of values, there is a sense of the lavishly
romantic, a pseudometaphysical interpretation of the conjunction
of souls and bodies. But in these and in other interpretations of the
war, there are both realism and wisdom. We have the view of a man
shortly out of a prewar, post-Victorian, still largely puritan world
thrust into a world antithetically opposed to it. More important, he
has been assured that: (1) his cause is just; and (2) Germans cut
off the hands of Belgian infants. The explosion of mistrust, surprise,

and rebellion is comparably strong and violent. These men are antiheroes only in the sense that they cannot conceive of heroism in the altered circumstances. The political and military history of World War I is only on the periphery of the personal history of engagement and disengagement, which is the literary history of this segment of the 1920's. The difference from World War II is enormous. The mechanics of violence are sometimes similar. But in World War II men were sure (almost always) that there was an enemy; they believed, and justly so, their propaganda. In World War I the soldier suffered many surprises, mainly because he had not been sophisticated or aware of the historical circumstances of the war. The major element was surprise. Surprise is in itself the result of a lack of being briefed or it is a consequence of being briefed erroneously. The American soldier withdraws from the primary engagement, declares a separate peace, finds himself in the wrong company, and eventually describes the horrendous results of impersonal warfare in a realistic splurge of shocked acknowledgment. This act appears to be temporary, though it probably has a permanence not initially seen. The reaction to Vietnam in 1967 owes something to Lieutenant Henry's amazement over the sheer absurdity of Caporetto.

J. K. Johnstone

*J. K. JOHNSTONE was born on February 12, 1923, at Ferintosh, Alberta,
Canada, where he lived on a farm until 1945. He attended the University of
Alberta from 1945 to 1950, receiving his B.A. in 1948 and an M.A. in English
literature in 1950. He then studied at the University of Leeds, England, where
he received the degree of Ph.D. in English literature in 1952.*

His book The Bloomsbury Group: A Study of E. M. Forster, Lytton
Strachey, Virginia Woolf, and Their Circle *was published in London and
New York in 1954. He was elected a Fellow of the Royal Society of Litera-
ture, London, in 1955.*

*He has taught at Mirfield Grammar School, Yorkshire; the College of
General Education, Boston University; and the University of New Brunswick.
He is now a professor of English at the University of Saskatchewan, Saska-
toon.*

*He is married and has three children. He and his wife led a Boston Univer-
sity summer course in Europe in 1955 and a Nasson College semester abroad
in Vienna in 1965. In 1966 he was awarded Canada Council and Nuffield
Foundation grants for study in London of the contemporary English novel.*

WORLD WAR I AND THE NOVELS OF
VIRGINIA WOOLF

IT IS, of course, impossible to measure accurately the effect of World
War I on Virginia Woolf's fiction. Yet the effect was stronger than
might be expected in the work of a feminine novelist whose main

concern was the inner life. The ultimate effect of the war on the individuals who survived it was, however, on the inner life, and Virginia Woolf, to a much greater extent than has been generally recognized, is a chronicler, if not of contemporary events themselves, of what is at least as significant, the effect of contemporary events on individuals.

"Virginia was the least political animal that has lived since Aristotle invented the definition," says her husband, Leonard Woolf, "though," he goes on with cranky, but understandable, hyperbole, "she was not a bit like the Virginia Woolf who appears in many books written by literary critics or autobiographers who did not know her, a frail invalidish lady living in an ivory tower in Bloomsbury and worshipped by a little clique of aesthetes. She was intensely interested in things, people, and events, and, as her new books [after the war] show, highly sensitive to the atmosphere which surrounded her, whether it was personal, social, or historical. She was therefore the last person who could ignore the political menaces under which we all lived."[1]

Virginia Woolf apparently did not anticipate war. "Suddenly, like a chasm in a smooth road," she said, "the war came."[2] Most of her friends, successors to a liberal optimism of the Victorians, though rebels to some other aspects of Victorianism, had buoyant hopes for the future.[3] Maynard Keynes speaks of a belief among his friends of "the Society" at Cambridge, who became Virginia Woolf's friends in Bloomsbury, in "the beginning of a renaissance, the opening of a new heaven on a new earth."[4] Leonard Woolf says, "We found ourselves living in the springtime of a conscious revolt against the social, political, religious, moral, intellectual, and artistic institutions, beliefs, and standards of our fathers and grandfathers. . . . We were out to construct something new; we were in the van of the builders of a new society which should be free, rational, civilized, pursuing truth and beauty. It was tremendously exhilarating."[5] Clive Bell, Virginia Woolf's brother-in-law, planned a book to be entitled *The New Renaissance*. Roger Fry introduced Post-Impressionist paintings to Britain in 1910 and 1912 in two of the liveliest and most significant exhibitions in London's

---

1 *Downhill All the Way* (London, 1967) , p. 27.

2 "The Leaning Tower," *The Moment and Other Essays* (London, 1947) , p. 111.

3 E. M. Forster, as *Howards End* (London, 1910) makes clear, with its concern about certain aspects of life in contemporary Britain and Germany and its suggestion that force can be "kept in its box" for only brief periods of civilization, was an exception.

4 *Two Memoirs* (London, 1949) , p. 82.

5 *Sowing* (London, 1960) , pp. 160–61.

history and established in 1913 the Omega Workshops to provide employment for young artists and to improve British design. "At last, he felt," Virginia Woolf tells us in her biography of him, "after the hypocrisy of the Victorian age, of which he had many anecdotes drawn from his own past, a time was at hand when a real society was possible. It was to be a society of people of moderate means, a society based upon the old Cambridge ideal of truth and free speaking, but alive, as Cambridge had never been, to the importance of the arts. . . . 'We are at last,' he summed it up, 'becoming a little civilised.' And then of course the war came."[6]

Virginia Woolf and her friends of the Bloomsbury group regarded the war as an unmitigated disaster. It was unsoftened for them by a belief in the popular shibboleths that helped men into battle or by the hope that the catastrophe might accelerate desirable social change.[7] "It destroyed, I think, the bases of European civilization," says Leonard Woolf, looking back on the war in the recently published volume of his autobiography.[8] The mood and tense of the verb have changed; otherwise, the statement might have been made by Leonard Woolf in 1914, expressing, as it does, the disappointed hopes of a Fabian who had looked forward to peaceful, rational social evolution and of an artist, or rather, of a man in close association with artists, who valued art of the past. "I hoped never to see this mad destruction of all that really counts in life," said Roger Fry in that first year of the war. "We were just beginning to be a little civilised and now it's all to begin over again."[9] Though to superficial contemporary observers the social attitudes of the Bloomsbury group and the works of art of its members sometimes seemed revolutionary, its background was Victorian liberalism,[10] and unlike T. E. Hulme, who found the war less unpalatable, it saw no need for a break between twentieth-century and nineteenth-century European art.[11]

The few references that Virginia Woolf makes in her published writings to life in England during the war are consistent in their emphasis on dreariness. The person who goes out to buy a newspaper at the end of "The Mark on the Wall" curses the war and,

---

6 *Roger Fry* (London, 1940) , pp. 184, 199.

7 For two quite different expressions of this hope, see Edward Carpenter, *My Days and Dreams* (London, 1916) , pp. 311–15, and D. H. Lawrence's letter of May 29, 1915, to Bertrand Russell, *The Collected Letters of D. H. Lawrence*, Harry T. Moore, ed. (New York, 1962) , Vol. I, p. 346.

8 *Downhill All the Way, op. cit.*, p. 9.

9 Quoted by Virginia Woolf, *Roger Fry, op. cit.*, p. 200.

10 Noel Annan, *Leslie Stephen* (London, 1951) . "We were not part of a negative movement of destruction against the past," says Leonard Woolf, *Sowing, op. cit.*, p. 161.

11 T. E. Hulme, *Speculations*, Herbert Read, ed. (London, 1924) .

apparently, the stalemate on the western front.[12] Because of the personal tone of the story, or reverie, one is inclined to associate this speaker with Leonard Woolf, whose comments about civilian life as he experienced it during the war, about the sound of the guns in Flanders as they were heard near the Woolfs' country house, Asham, in Sussex, and the report of the death of his brother in France, are of interest not only in this context, but also in relation to imagery in *Jacob's Room* and *To the Lighthouse* that will be considered later:

The horror of the years 1914 to 1918 was that nothing seemed to happen, month after month and year after year, except the pitiless, useless slaughter in France. Often if one went for a walk on the downs above Asham one could hear the incessant pounding of the guns on the Flanders front. And even when one did not hear them it was as though the war itself was perpetually pounding dully on one's brain, while in Richmond and Sussex one was enmeshed in a cloud of boredom, and when one looked into the future, there was nothing there but an unending vista of the same boredom. When the telephone rang on December 2, 1917, and they told me that Cecil had been killed in France, in the dull, static greyness of one's days it was as if one had suddenly received a violent blow on the head.[13]

Cold and mist outside, squalor inside, characterize the wartime scenes in Virginia Woolf's novel *The Years.* In 1917 Eleanor Pargiter dines with her cousins in an untidy house. They begin their meal in the basement, since there are no servants to bring it up from the kitchen, and are forced, because of an air raid, to complete it in the cellar. On November 11, 1918, the old servant, Crosby, drags herself across Richmond Green to shop, complaining to herself, shortly before sirens and guns announce the Armistice, about "the Belgian who called himself a Count," whose spittle she has had to clean from a bathtub. In *To the Lighthouse* Mrs. McNab struggles, successfully at last, against the decay which nearly destroys the Ramsays' summer house during a vacancy of ten years, brought about in part by the war. In *Roger Fry* Virginia Woolf describes, in biography as she had in fiction, the cold drabness of the war years. Fry's charwoman, Mrs. Filmer, whose name is given to Septimus Warren Smith's landlady in *Mrs. Dalloway*, less heroic than Mrs. McNab, left untouched more than the arrangement for a still life that Fry was painting. "Rows of dusty medicine bottles stood on the mantelpiece; frying pans were mixed with palettes; some plates

---

[12] *A Haunted House and Other Stories* (London, 1944) , p. 48.
[13] *Beginning Again* (London, 1964) , p. 197.

held salad, others scrapings of congealed paint. The floor was strewn with papers." Amid the squalor of the studio, however, it was the still life that was important: "those symbols of detachment, those tokens of a spiritual reality immune from destruction, the immortal apples, the eternal eggs." Virginia Woolf conjectures that it was the application of esthetic theory both to art and to "the problems of private life" which gave Fry the detachment necessary to enable him to survive the war, "and not with his intellect merely."[14]

Statements such as that about the miseries of life at home during the war, trivial miseries when compared to the misery of the trenches and of battle, may seem histrionic. Yet Virginia Woolf, if not Roger Fry, did struggle for survival as a person and an artist during the war, and her struggle, though not caused by the war, was intensified by it. At the beginning of the war she was suffering from an attack, which had begun in 1913, of the mental illness that recurred four times in her life and led, finally, to her suicide. "Her mental breakdown lasted in an acute form from the summer of 1913 to the autumn of 1915, but it was not absolutely continuous," Leonard Woolf says. "There were two insane stages, one lasting from the summer of 1913 to the summer of 1914 and the other from January, 1915, to the winter of 1915; there was an interlude of sanity between the summer of 1914 and January, 1915."[15] After her recovery she began her second and perhaps her dullest novel, *Night and Day,* which she completed in March, 1919.

She had so far written nothing which would have caused her to be remembered for long, but she had begun, in 1917 in "The Mark on the Wall," to experiment and to find the discursive, but disciplined, method which was to be characteristic of her future work. Other significant experimental short stories followed from 1919 to 1921: "Kew Gardens," "Monday or Tuesday," "A Haunted House," "The String Quartet," and "An Unwritten Novel." An essay, "Modern Fiction," if it did not explain the method very clearly, expressed, in 1919, the excitement of its discovery.

Since all these stories deal with immediate experience, attempting to catch it, one might say, at the moment of its creation, as sensation, memory, intellect, and emotion interact in the psyche, it is inevitable that there should be references in them to the war and its aftermath: to spiritualism, the influenza epidemic, the peace treaty. In Virginia Woolf's next three novels, *Jacob's Room, Mrs. Dalloway,* and *To the Lighthouse,* published, respectively, in 1922, 1925, and 1927, the war is more central.

---

14 *Roger Fry, op. cit.,* pp. 214–15.
15 *Beginning Again, op. cit.,* p. 160.

In *Jacob's Room* Jacob Flanders, whose name suggests his fate, grows from childhood to maturity or near maturity and is then killed in the war. In *Mrs. Dalloway* Septimus Warren Smith is the victim of the war and of arbitrary authority. Suffering from hallucinations and a feeling of guilt as a result of his war experiences, he leaps to his death, in a moment of clarity, to escape the doctors who would confine him. In *To the Lighthouse,* as has already been mentioned, the war contributes to the vacant period, in the Ramsays' summer home and in the novel, when nonhuman forces are dominant and human things disintegrate. During this period, Andrew Ramsay, like Jacob Flanders, is killed in battle.

The aural imagery of the sound of guns is heard in *Jacob's Room,* as the sound itself was heard on the downs near Asham. In an early page of the novel Mrs. Cranch, Mrs. Flanders' neighbor, beats a mat against a garden wall, as she watches Mrs. Flanders feeding chickens. Mrs. Jarvis, another neighbor, is aware, a few pages later, of "distant concussions in the air" as she walks on the moor. On the night, apparently, of Jacob's death, Mrs. Flanders is awakened by what she at first, though she lives in Scarborough, takes to be the guns:

> "The guns?" said Betty Flanders, half asleep, getting out of bed and going to the window, which was decorated with a fringe of dark leaves.
> "Not at this distance," she thought. "It is the sea."
> Again, far away, she heard the dull sound, as if nocturnal women were beating great carpets. There was Morty lost, and Seabrook dead; her sons fighting for their country. But were the chickens safe? Was that some one moving downstairs? Rebecca with the toothache? No. The nocturnal women were beating great carpets. Her hens shifted slightly on their perches.[16]

Clearer, more vivid sounds are heard by Jacob. In his childhood a tree fell near him at night as he sought specimens in a forest for his collection of butterflies and moths. He recalls the incident twice (we see it only in his memory), and each time, in the description of it, it is associated with pistol shots and with death, as indeed it was already associated with death through the moth that he had collected that night:

> The tree had fallen the night he caught it. There had been a volley of pistol-shots suddenly in the depths of the wood. And his mother had taken him for a burglar when he came home late. . . .
> The tree had fallen, though it was a windless night, and the lantern,

---

16 *Jacob's Room,* pp. 14, 25, 175. All references to Virginia Woolf's novels are to the Hogarth Press uniform edition.

stood upon the ground, had lit up the still green leaves and the dead beech leaves.[17]

A terrifying volley of pistol-shots rings out—cracks sharply; ripples spread—silence laps smooth over sound. A tree—a tree has fallen, a sort of death in the forest.[18]

The first recollection occurs as Jacob examines the moth in his collection; the second, in the present tense, as he attends a service at King's College Chapel and is reminded of a lantern by the light coming through the stained-glass windows. Memory, it may be observed, extends the metaphorical pistol shots and their association with death into a kind of continuous present. Meanwhile, other, more common sounds contribute more quietly to the aural pattern of the novel and to the ominous suggestion, linked with it, of death. Doors slam as Jacob goes out of his lodgings in London; swing doors open and shut "with a soft thud" as the diners go in and out from the hall at Cambridge; after dinner, objects fall in the college rooms with a thud.[19]

In *Mrs. Dalloway*, which is set in London on a June day in 1923, the pattern of sound is based on the striking of clocks and other sounds of the postwar city, in place of the sharp report of a pistol, the pounding of guns, and, one is tempted to conjecture, the thud of a falling body, which echo in *Jacob's Room*. It is worth noting, however, that Clarissa Dalloway saw, in her youth, her sister killed by a falling tree; that she is startled in the morning in a Bond Street flower shop by an explosion from a car in the street, which she at first takes to be a pistol shot; and that the explosion provides a means of transition to the street, where Septimus Warren Smith is encountered for the first time. The incident brings traffic to a standstill, and "the throb of the motor engines sounded like a pulse irregularly drumming through an entire body."[20] That night, when Clarissa hears at her party of Septimus' suicide, she vividly imagines his fall onto Mrs. Filmer's area railings: "Up had flashed the ground; through him, blundering, bruising, went the rusty spikes. There he lay with a thud, thud, thud in his brain, and then a suffocation of blackness."[21] In the "thud, thud, thud," with its suggestion of both a pulse and Septimus' fall, life and death are inextricably mixed, as they are mixed also in the thudding of the

17 *Ibid.*, p. 21.
18 *Ibid.*, p. 30.
19 *Ibid.*, pp. 37, 41, 88.
20 *Mrs. Dalloway*, p. 17.
21 *Ibid.*, p. 202.

waves on the beach, measuring time and suggesting eternity, in *To the Lighthouse* and in the novel that followed it, *The Waves* (1931).

From one point of view, the war is in the distant background in *To the Lighthouse*; from another, it is at the heart of the novel as the most violent of those blind forces described in the middle part of the book, "Time Passes," which destroy the order, the significant form, which humans impose on life. Time and decay are Mrs. Ramsay's chief antagonists as she guards her home and her family and attempts to give significance to their lives. The war, which coincides with her death, hastens and intensifies the destructiveness of time.[22]

War is foreshadowed and depicted in *To the Lighthouse*, as in *Jacob's Room*, chiefly through the aural imagery. Early in the book Mrs. Ramsay hears the waves on the beach and finds in their sound suggestions of life and death. Within the passage the sounds of drums and guns are heard:

. . . the monotonous fall of the waves on the beach, which for the most part beat a measured and soothing tattoo to her thoughts and seemed consolingly to repeat over and over again as she sat with the children the words of some old cradle song, murmured by nature, "I am guarding you—I am your support," but at other times suddenly and unexpectedly, especially when her mind raised itself slightly from the task actually in hand, had no such kindly meaning, but like a ghostly roll of drums remorselessly beat the measure of life, made one think of the destruction of the island and its engulfment in the sea, and warned her whose day had slipped past in one quick doing after another that it was all ephemeral as a rainbow—this sound which had been obscured and concealed under the other sounds suddenly thundered hollow in her ears and made her look up with an impulse of terror.[23]

In "Time Passes" there are further premonitions of war. The shawl that Mrs. Ramsay had wrapped around the boar's skull that her son, James, had collected and that frightened his sister, Cam, loosens and begins to unwind.[24] "As summer neared . . . there came to the wakeful . . . imaginations of the strangest kind—of flesh turned to atoms which drove before the wind."[25] Then the distant sounds of the war itself are heard:

---

22 Leonard Woolf's and Roger Fry's comments about the destructiveness of the war and Virginia Woolf's conjectures about the way in which Fry survived the war, cited above, are relevant here.

23 *To the Lighthouse*, pp. 29–30.

24 *Ibid.*, pp. 202, 206.

25 *Ibid.*, p. 204.

. . . there came later in the summer ominous sounds like the measured blows of hammers dulled on felt, which, with their repeated shocks still further loosened the shawl and cracked the tea-cups. Now and again some glass tinkled in the cupboard as if a giant voice had shrieked so loud in its agony that tumblers stood inside a cupboard vibrated too. Then again silence fell; and then, night after night, and sometimes in plain mid-day when the roses were bright and light turned on the wall its shape clearly there seemed to drop into this silence this indifference, this integrity, the thud of something falling.

[A shell exploded. Twenty or thirty young men were blown up in France, among them Andrew Ramsay, whose death, mercifully, was instantaneous.][26]

Death is emblemized in *To the Lighthouse* by James's boar's skull, which is nailed to the nursery wall.[27] In *Jacob's Room*, Jacob is associated with death from the first scene, in which, as a toddler, he picks up a jawbone from a sheep's skull and insists on taking it with him, in spite of his mother's protests. On the last page of the book, as Jacob's mother and his friend gather up his belongings after his death, carvings over the doorways of his lodgings of "a rose or a ram's skull" are mentioned. The two images, the one intensifying the other, remind us of what is now fully evident: the beauty and brevity of Jacob's life. This double truth has been stated throughout the novel by other images. By the account of the fad for "little paper flowers which opened on touching water" and then sank in finger bowls.[28] By the comments on real flowers: "But real flowers can never be dispensed with. If they could, human life would be a different affair altogether. For flowers fade. . . ."[29] By the sadness perceived by Jacob and his friend in the "sunny peace" of the Cornish countryside: "But imperceptibly the cottage smoke droops, has the look of a mourning emblem, a flag floating its caress over a grave."[30] By the moonlight, chalk, and bones that Mrs. Jarvis and Betty Flanders see on the moor.[31] Above all, by the frequently recurring images of butterflies, consistently associated, as in Jacob's collection, with death: "The pale clouded yellows had pelted over the moor; they had zigzagged across the purple clover. The fritillaries flaunted along the hedgerows. The blues settled on little bones lying on the turf with the sun beating on them, and the painted ladies and the peacocks feasted upon bloody entrails

---

26 *Ibid.*, pp. 206–7.
27 See the images of stoats nailed to a stable door and jays nailed to a wall in *The Waves*, p. 12.
28 *Jacob's Room*, pp. 81–82.
29 *Ibid.*, p. 82.
30 *Ibid.*, p. 47.
31 *Ibid.*, p. 131.

dropped by a hawk."[32] "The chestnuts have flirted their fans. And the butterflies are flaunting across the rides in the Forest. Perhaps the Purple Emperor is feasting, as Morris [an authority on butterflies] says, upon a mass of putrid carrion at the base of an oak tree."[33] Like the lives of the butterflies, Jacob's life is ephemeral, beautiful, doomed.

His life is, of course, the more significant for the reader because of its brevity, as it would be for Jacob himself, could he catch the hints of his early death that the reader is given in the novel. Similarly, the experiences of the Ramsays in the first part of *To the Lighthouse* are made more significant by the realization, given to the reader of this novel, as we have seen, by Mrs. Ramsay herself, that "it was all ephemeral as a rainbow." "There was no treachery too base for the world to commit; she knew that. No happiness lasted; she knew that."[34] She may wrap a shawl around the boar's skull to make it less frightening for Cam, she may say, as Lily Briscoe, a painter, thinks of her as saying, "Life stand still here,"[35] but older and more aware than Jacob, she knows that her creative powers can resist destruction and death only briefly.

It is this mood of a happy present made more vivid and valuable by the knowledge that it cannot endure that dominates *Mrs. Dalloway*. In the near past is the war and in the present some of its aftereffects: Miss Kilman's bitterness at having been dismissed from her job for suspected German sympathies; Septimus Warren Smith's insanity and suicide. A keen awareness of death is present in Septimus' and in Clarissa Dalloway's minds, and for Clarissa, at least, it intensifies the awareness of life. Septimus has seen his officer and friend killed in battle; Clarissa is pale and fifty-one, she has recovered from influenza, but her heart has been affected; "year by year her share was sliced," she thinks; "narrower and narrower would her bed be."[36] Septimus' suicide is a dark fact in the novel, and Clarissa learns of it at her party. Yet it is the beauty of the June day and Clarissa's enjoyment of it and of other ephemeral things, flowers, her party, which are most apparent. "In people's eyes, in the swing, tramp, and trudge; in the bellow and the uproar . . . was what she loved; life; London; this moment of June."[37] "What she liked was simply life."[38]

Clarissa's outlook is like the state of mind that Siegfried Sassoon

32 *Ibid.*, p. 22.
33 *Ibid.*, p. 123.
34 *To the Lighthouse*, p. 102.
35 *Ibid.*, pp. 249–50.
36 *Mrs. Dalloway*, pp. 34–35.
37 *Ibid.*, p. 6.
38 *Ibid.*, p. 134.

describes as his during a convalescent leave in 1916: "The war had taught me one useful lesson—that on the whole it was very nice to be alive at all; and I had also acquired the habit of observing things with more receptiveness and accuracy than I had ever attempted to do in my undisciplined past."[39] Richard Dalloway has similar thoughts as he goes home with roses for Clarissa: "Really it was a miracle thinking of the war, and thousands of poor chaps, with all their lives before them, shovelled together, already half forgotten; it was a miracle. Here he was walking across London to say to Clarissa in so many words that he loved her."[40]

Clarissa's happy alertness as she sets out at the beginning of the novel to buy flowers for her party is composed partly of the fine June morning, partly of anticipation of her party, but chiefly of the realization that the war and the influenza epidemic are over and that she is still alive:

For it was the middle of June. The War was over, except for some one like Mrs. Foxcroft at the Embassy last night eating her heart out because that nice boy was killed and now the old Manor House must go to a cousin; or Lady Bexborough who opened a bazaar, they said, with the telegram in her hand, John, her favourite, killed; but it was over; thank Heaven—over. It was June.[41]

One may conjecture that the happiness and vivid beauty that Clarissa experiences, set against the dark experience of Septimus, is ultimately derived from the relief, transformed by art, that Virginia Woolf herself felt that the war was over and that she had survived it, sane, and with increased powers as a writer. Certainly her ability to portray Septimus so well was derived from her own experience of insanity and attempted suicide.[42]

Moreover, Virginia Woolf was more optimistic than her husband about postwar society, if his attitude in this respect is reflected accurately in his autobiography, written after World War II. Peter

39 *Siegfried's Journey, 1916–1920* (London, 1945) , p. 16.

40 *Mrs. Dalloway*, p. 127.

41 *Ibid.*, pp. 6–7. Why, with this emphasis, Virginia Woolf set *Mrs. Dalloway* in 1923, instead of 1919 or 1920, is unexplained. Perhaps the dates of the writing (1922–1924) and the publication (1925) of the novel affected the year of its setting, and Peter Walsh, who has returned to England after five years in India, can observe more changes in postwar London in 1923 than he might have done in 1919 or 1920.

42 Like Septimus, but less successfully than he, she attempted to commit suicide after seeing a consultant who recommended that she have a few weeks' rest in a nursing home. Her own hallucination of sparrows singing Greek words is given to Septimus rather inappropriately, since he is scarcely well enough educated to have studied Greek. See Leonard Woolf, *Beginning Again, op. cit.*, pp. 148–65.

Walsh, back from India, observes with approval, in *Mrs. Dalloway*, changes that have taken place in London since the war, "more than suspecting from the words of a girl, from a housemaid's laughter— intangible things you couldn't lay your hands on—that shift in the whole pyramidal accumulation which in his youth had seemed immovable. On top of them all it had pressed; weighed them down, the women especially. . . ."[43] In *The Years*, published in 1937, Eleanor Pargiter, at the wartime dinner already referred to, reflects that the war removes barriers and discusses with Nicholas, a Polish homosexual, how a better society and freer individuals might be created.

In a paper read to the Workers' Educational Association at Brighton in 1940, Virginia Woolf differentiates the writers of the generation of Auden and Isherwood from those who were educated and began to write before August, 1914. The latter writers, she says, "when the crash came in 1914 . . ., had their past, their educa- tion, safe behind them, safe within them. They had known security; they had the memory of a peaceful boyhood, the knowledge of a settled civilization."[44] Virginia Woolf herself belonged to that fortunate generation, and undoubtedly she owes much to the calm development which Victorian and Edwardian civilization made possible for her. She had learned in that quieter time the value of art and of personal relations and, as she believed, of the application of esthetic theory and of detached observation and reflection to the problems both of art and of the private life, lessons which, in her opinion, had enabled Roger Fry to survive the war as an individual and an artist.

Yet her sensibility, if one may generalize for a moment about something so individual, is not Edwardian, much less Victorian. She is intensely aware of flux and of the impermanence of individual human experience, an awareness which the war sharpened and which caused her, like Mrs. Ramsay and Mrs. Dalloway, to value the significant moment the more and to attempt to make it, as Lily Briscoe did, permanent in art. Death, violent or natural, is usually sudden in her novels, not the conclusion of a long decline. When she attempts a novel in what may broadly be called the Edwardian manner, as she did in *Night and Day* and in *The Years*, which has affinities with both *The Forsyte Saga* and *The Old Wives' Tale*, she fails.

Her own style as a novelist, which she set aside briefly as she

---

43 *Mrs. Dalloway*, p. 178.
44 "The Leaning Tower," *op. cit.*, pp. 110–16.

wrote *The Years*, was not developed until after the war. It is associated always with a concentration on the inner life, which, fluid and impermanent as it is, she finds not only more valuable, but also more reliable, in a changing world, than the outer life. This style and subject are found in *Jacob's Room*, *Mrs. Dalloway*, and *To the Lighthouse*, in which, as we have seen, the war has a significant place; in *The Waves*, in which her concentration on the inner life and on personal relations is most singleminded and profound and the war plays no part (though the central, silent figure, Percival, dies violently in India, as Jacob Flanders and Andrew Ramsay died in the war) ; and finally, in *Between the Acts* (1941) , in which Isa Oliver anticipates personal annihilation and her husband foresees bombs shattering the English countryside as another war threatens.

The evidence in *Jacob's Room*, *Mrs. Dalloway*, and *To the Lighthouse*, Virginia Woolf's first novels of major significance, suggest that her sensibility as a novelist, though not formed by the war, was strongly affected by it and by her experience, coincidental with war, of insanity and that war and mental illness gave her materials which she used to express her vision of life. The war heightened her awareness of flux, impermanence, and death, causing her to value personal experience the more and to examine the more closely the experience of the present moment, seeking what permanence she could find in it and in its representation in fiction. It increased her astonishment at the miracle, which it made plainer, of being alive, and it intensified her presentation of the beauty of that miracle, as the bloody entrails, the putrid carrion, and the bones on the turf intensify the beauty of the butterflies in *Jacob's Room*.

Melvin J. Friedman

MELVIN J. FRIEDMAN *was born in Brooklyn, New York, in 1928, and was educated at Bard College, Columbia University, and Yale University. He served in the Army from 1954 to 1956. He has taught at the University of Maryland and the University of Wisconsin and is presently a professor of comparative literature at the University of Wisconsin at Milwaukee. He has held fellowships from Yale University and the American Council of Learned Societies and was a Fulbright predoctoral fellow in Lyon, France, in 1950–51.*

His published writings—in English, French, German, and Italian—are mainly concerned with twentieth-century fiction and drama. He has contributed essays and reviews to The New Republic, Modern Age, Comparative Literature, Modern Drama, La Revue des lettres modernes, Symposium, The French Review, Yale French Studies, Commonweal, Books Abroad, Journal of Popular Culture, *and* Umanesimo, *among others. He has written and edited books on the twentieth-century experimental novel, Samuel Beckett, Flannery O'Connor, and William Styron.*

He has served as editor or associate editor of three learned journals and now is assistant managing editor for comparative literature of The Modern Language Journal. *He has served as secretary and chairman of the Franco-American group of the Modern Language Association of America and is presently chairman of the nominating committee of the group.*

He is preparing a book on Samuel Beckett and editing a book on the Roman Catholic novel of the twentieth century, as well as a collection of Beckett criticism.

THREE EXPERIENCES OF THE WAR:
A TRIPTYCH

———•———

This book is Art—War—Art, in three panels. War is the centre panel.—
Blasting and Bombardiering, Part II

WHEN WE THINK of the First World War, we are reminded dramati-
cally of the way so many younger writers, in midcareer, lost their
lives: Rupert Brooke, Wilfred Owen, and Isaac Rosenberg among
the English; Alain-Fournier, Charles Péguy, and Guillaume Apollinaire among the French; Ernst Stadler, Reinhard Sorge, and Walter
Flex among the Germans. Péguy's death in the first year of the war
at the Battle of the Marne is perhaps the most heroic; Apollinaire's
death probably from influenza, some six months after being
wounded at the front, is perhaps the most ironical. Literary historians have concentrated valuable attention on the mythos of the
Kriegstod but have tended, unfortunately, to romanticize its conditions and circumstances. The following inscription which appears
on a memorial to Spain's war dead is not untypical of these
sentiments: "*Corona de la vida es morir por la patria pero esa
corona brilla más si la acompaña el Heroísmo.*" The Romans,
through Horace, expressed this somewhat differently, but with
much the same feeling: "*Dulce et decorum est pro patria mori.*"
The compassionate response is probably even stronger when a
writer was killed in the war, especially in the Great War—as World
War I historians still fondly refer to it.

The case of Alain-Fournier is fairly typical. His life has been
turned into legend, and his single novel, *Le Grand Meaulnes*
(translated as *The Wanderer*), has been treated as a delicate case
apart—almost as if it deserved a special place by itself, not part of
any tradition, in the history of the French novel. Havelock Ellis'
description of Fournier's death (in his introduction to the standard
American translation of *Le Grand Meaulnes*) has this quality of the
legendary:

When the Great War broke out in the summer of 1914 Fournier
happened to be in the south of France. Like others he was hurried

among many hardships to the front, and found himself eventually in the Meuse, near Vaux-les-Palameix. Fournier, "timid but fearless," for whom life was a "great game," never drew back. The inevitable end swiftly ensued. On the 22d of September at Saint-Rémy a vague figure was seen in the enemy's lines. The captain rushed forward, revolver in hand, followed by Fournier, but only by a small number of men. They were being led into an ambush on the edge of the wood. Most of them were shot down. Fournier fell struck in the forehead, according to the only report that could be obtained, but his body was not recovered.

Fournier the romantic, the figure of myth, and Fournier the author of perhaps the finest "adventure" novel written by a Frenchman in the twentieth century are often hopelessly confused. Our image of him is further distorted because of our tendency to connect him with that other writer-hero, Charles Péguy, whose literary spell and warm friendship Fournier succumbed to in the years preceding the war in which they both lost their lives.

I

There is certainly a quite different literary reaction to the war which Leonard Woolf soberly described as ending "19th-century civilization." The title he gave the third installment of his autobiography, *Beginning Again* (New York, 1964), gives us fair warning that for him and for others connected with the Bloomsbury group the world of Victorian values was officially over and a new one had to be negotiated. This is a far less romantic view than the one usually associated with the English war poets—a *Weltanschauung* which spoke in terms of *ends* rather than of *beginnings*.

It is the more sober, less spectacular concern with the war which we shall concentrate on here. The three writers whose experiences we shall examine are Wyndham Lewis, Virginia Woolf, and James Joyce. It is interesting to note that in his "Chronology of Publications," found at the end of his fine book on the literature of the First World War, *Heroes' Twilight* (New York, 1966), Bernard Bergonzi lists only one book by any of the three , Lewis' *Blasting and Bombardiering*. And this autobiography of the years 1914–26 is given only two pages in Bergonzi's study. *Blasting and Bombardiering* is clearly not a book about twilight; it is a book about beginnings rather than ends.

The grouping of the three now seems particularly timely. Within the past year we have seen the appearance of the second and third volumes of Joyce's letters, which completes the image of the Irish writer which Richard Ellmann has been painstakingly giving us since the publication of his monumental biography in 1959; the appearance of the collected essays of Virginia Woolf in four volumes, as well as the fourth installment of her husband Leonard's autobiography, *Downhill All the Way;* the appearance of the second, revised edition (Berkeley, 1967), of Lewis' *Blasting and Bombardiering* (long out of print). It is interesting that these writers who reached early primes during or just after the First World War have now reached enviable maturities posthumously as we approach the fiftieth anniversary of the end of the Great War. None, I am afraid, would have much cared about celebrating the golden anniversary if he were still alive.

One of England's most talented novelists, Anthony Burgess, has recently brought the three together in his *The Novel Now* (New York, 1967). In a chapter entitled "Giants in Those Days" he says:

The humour of Lewis's books is usually too clotted with detail to hit home, but, because of the highly individual manifesto they exemplify—"I am for the Great Without, for the method of *external* approach," said Lewis—the books have to be read. They are the best possible foil to Virginia Woolf and Joyce. [P. 28.]

Burgess has already written a loving study of Joyce, called *Re Joyce* in its American edition, and is perhaps himself the happiest blending we have today of Lewis' "Great Without" and Joyce's and Virginia Woolf's *"tellers-from-the-inside"* (Lewis' own special vocabulary found in his chapter on himself in *Men Without Art*). Burgess can calmly assess this literary problem, writing as he does about an earlier generation at a comfortable remove from it.

The Woolf-Joyce-Lewis confrontations were in their own time stormy and often unsettling. Yet they bring to the fore certain essential issues concerned with the development of twentieth-century literature. Lewis is at his most polemical when he attacks the effeteness of Bloomsbury. He speaks of E. M. Forster, in *Blasting and Bombardiering,* as "a quiet little chap, of whom no one could be jealous, so he hit it off with the 'Bloomsburies,' and was appointed male opposite number to Virgina Woolfe [*sic*]."[1] (Pp. 235–36.) He gets at Virginia Woolf more directly in his chapter on her in *Men Without Art*; here her work is dismissed as the "feminine" expression of the " 'Bloomsbury' technique" (which is in

---

[1] It is likely that Lewis intentionally misspelled Virginia Woolf's last name. We have this other striking example of it: "We were all in the post-war, but that period produced nothing but a lot of sub-Sitwells and sheep in Woolfe's clothing. . . ." (P. 249.)

itself, according to Lewis, singularly lacking in masculinity). We know how much this attack disturbed the always sensitive Virginia Woolf when we open her *A Writer's Diary* dated "Thursday, October 11th," "Sunday, October 14th," "Tuesday, October 16th," and "Friday, November 2nd" (all 1934). It takes her from Thursday, when she first discovers *Men Without Art* advertised in the *"Lit. Sup."* until the following Tuesday to recover: Thus we have the entry for Tuesday, October 16, beginning: "Quite cured today. So the W.L. illness lasted. . . ."

Virginia Woolf mildly disapproved of Joyce's *Ulysses* but had fond words for his experiments with consciousness in her most influential essay, "Modern Fiction" (see Volume II, *Collected Essays*, New York, 1967). In this essay, which features the suggestive metaphor of "a semi-transparent envelope surrounding us from the beginning of consciousness to the end," she speaks of *Ulysses:*

. . . there can be no question but that it is of the utmost sincerity and that the result, difficult or unpleasant as we may judge it, is undeniably important. In contrast with those whom we have called materialists, Mr. Joyce is spiritual; he is concerned at all costs to reveal the flickerings of that innermost flame which flashes its messages through the brain, and in order to preserve it he disregards with complete courage whatever seems to him adventitious, whether it be probability, or coherence, or any other of these signposts which for generations have served to support the imagination of a reader when called upon to imagine what he can neither touch nor see. [P. 107.]

Her response is more qualified in the entry of Wednesday, September 6, 1922, of *A Writer's Diary:*

I finished *Ulysses* and think it a mis-fire. Genius it has, I think; but of the inferior water. The book is diffuse. It is brackish. It is pretentious. It is underbred, not only in the obvious sense, but in the literary sense. A first rate writer, I mean, respects writing too much to be tricky; startling; doing stunts.

Leonard Woolf, in *Beginning Again*, reports on the ambiguous circumstances leading to the Hogarth Press' final inability to publish "this remarkable piece of dynamite," *Ulysses*.

Joyce did not answer Virginia Woolf; his silence was rather like Virginia Woolf's confiding her "hurt," received at the hands of Wyndham Lewis, to the muted pages of her *Writer's Diary*. There is no mention of her anywhere in *The Critical Writings of James*

Joyce (edited by Ellsworth Mason and Richard Ellmann) and only a single passing reference—Joyce mentions that he had received a copy of *The Voyage Out* from Mrs. Woolf—in the three volumes of Joyce letters.

The Joyce-Lewis relationship is quite different from the others we have spoken of. It is a case study in literary polemic. Lewis attacked Joyce in a variety of places: in the chapter entitled "An Analysis of the Mind of James Joyce" in *Time and Western Man;* in an essay entitled "The Diabolical Principle," which first appeared in *The Enemy*[2]; more obliquely in *The Apes of God* and *The Childermass.* Lewis is not consistently harsh with Joyce as we observe from the fond, if at times foolish, portrait he gives of him in *Blasting and Bombardiering* ("First Meeting with James Joyce"). Joyce retaliated with the fable of the Ondt and the Gracehoper in *Finnegans Wake*—putting the Joyce-Lewis conflict in superb poetic relief.[3]

We have given only a few details of these various literary confrontations involving Virginia Woolf, James Joyce, and Wyndham Lewis. The essential point to be made is that Lewis distrusted the post-Bergsonian "time-books" which Joyce and Mrs. Woolf were writing; he was especially hard on Virginia Woolf, probably because of her Bloomsbury affiliations. Virginia Woolf could not quite stomach a book of the physical dimensions and erotic leanings of *Ulysses;* she would have preferred something more classically lean and morally reticent. Joyce used the elaborate pastiches of *Finnegans Wake* to have his say against Lewis.

II

I have spent so much time on matters which seem to have little to do with the First World War because of a basic irony involving these three writers. Each was more involved in the proverbial war of words than in the war contested on the battlefields of Europe. None could agree with Wilfred Owen: "My subject is War, and the

---

2 Sylvia Beach tells us in her *Shakespeare and Company* (New York, 1959) how Wyndham Lewis had asked Joyce for a section of *Finnegans Wake* (then known as "Work in Progress") for the literary review he was then launching. The first issue of *The Enemy* appeared, we are told: "Joyce's text was not in it. All the space was taken up by a violent attack on Joyce's new work by Wyndham Lewis." (Pp. 168–69.)

3 See Geoffrey Wagner's chapter "Master Joys and Windy Nous" in his brilliant book *Wyndham Lewis: A Portrait of the Artist as the Enemy* (New Haven, 1957) for the most complete and convincing discussion of the Joyce-Lewis relationship. My discussion here is indebted to it. Wagner concludes, "In his lampoon of Lewis Joyce was as fair as Lewis was unfair to him." (P. 174.) See also Richard Ellmann's *James Joyce* (New York, 1959) for revealing details on the same subject.

pity of War./ The poetry is in the pity." Wyndham Lewis, the only one of the three who actively participated in the war, puts the case for all three when he says at the beginning of Part II of *Blasting and Bombardiering:*

I show, too, going from the particular to the general, how War and Art in those days mingled, the features of the latter as stern as—if not sterner than—the former. This book is Art—War—Art, in three panels. War is the centre panel. But for me it was only a part of Art: my sort of life— the life of the "intellect"—come to life. A disappointing imitation. I preferred the real thing: namely Art. [P. 63.]

Neither Joyce nor Virginia Woolf was capable of this glibness or this Wilde-inspired paradox, yet the sentiment is one they doubtless would have approved. *Blasting and Bombardiering* is filled with the notion that all experience, even fighting in the war, must be turned into art; for Lewis that meant painting and literature. Lewis left for the war in 1916 after neatly and meticulously bringing his "early period" to a close; by this time he had finished the first version of *Tarr* (not published as a book till 1918) , brought out two numbers of his Vorticist review *Blast,* and had successfully exhibited some of his drawings.[4] Lewis made the transition from peacetime blaster to wartime artilleryman with exemplary ease. He could say in *Blasting and Bombardiering,* with a trace of a smile, "All Europe was at war and a bigger *Blast* than mine had rather taken the wind out of my sails." (P. 85.) He went to the front, appropriately enough, with a copy of *La Chartreuse de Parme* in his baggage; he delighted in the ineptitude of Fabrice del Dongo at Waterloo. Mixing Stendhal with the battlefields of World War I was Lewis' way of showing "how War and Art in those days mingled."

Lewis' brief period as editor of *Blast* was considerably more unsettling than his experience in the war. His *engagement* was always a matter of art, never of causes. He was more interested in blasting "ROUSSEAUISMS" (he capitalized all its letters in *Blast*) than Germans. He was, as Geoffrey Wagner has told us, an outspoken enemy of Romanticism; he joined, intellectually, those who gathered around the *Action française* in their hatred of the flabbiness of the nineteenth century (summarily dismissed by Léon Daudet as *"le stupide dix-neuvième siècle"*) . War was a kind of interlude for him, a time for catching up with himself and regroup-

---

[4] See Geoffrey Wagner's introductory section of his book on Lewis for more details. See also *The Art of Wyndham Lewis,* Charles Handley-Read, ed. (London, 1951) , and Hugh Kenner's excellent little book *Wyndham Lewis* (New York, 1954) .

ing his moral and intellectual forces. Yet some of his descriptions of battle scenes in *Blasting and Bombardiering* are as vivid and compelling as any we have:

Going through the lines of "the Field" the shelling was heavy—though on the whole there was every evidence that the enemy were not replying with their customary aggressiveness. Their artillery was being moved back.

A Field Battery beside which we were making our way was having a rough time, however. There were several casualties while we were passing its guns, but my little O.C. [officer commanding] might have been taking a walk with his dog for all the notice he took. [P. 13.]

A kind of romanticism creeps into descriptions of this sort, but it is always a romanticism tempered by irony. Despite his uneasiness with this kind of sentiment, he is forced reluctantly to admit:

Need I say that there is nothing so romantic as war? If you are "a romantic," you have not lived if you have not been present at a battle, of that I can assure you. I am very sorry to have to say this. Only a care for truth compels me to avow it. I am not a romantic—though I perfectly understand romance. And I do not like war. It is under compulsion that I stress the exceedingly romantic character of all the scenes I am about to describe. [P. 114.]

(Later on, in quite a different context, Lewis admits: "Perhaps I am *half* a romantic." [P .195.])

The most eloquent and compelling chapters in *Blasting and Bombardiering* are probably the two which deal with T. E. Hulme and Gaudier-Brzeska—both admired by Lewis and killed in the war. Hulme, who was in a neighboring battery, was killed, "within a quarter of a mile of where [Lewis] was standing." (P. 99.) The death of Gaudier-Brzeska seemed at the time more remote because Lewis learned of it indirectly from Ezra Pound. Yet later in *Blasting and Bombardiering* there is a courageously forthright statement, quite worthy of Voltaire's famous suggestion that the Lisbon earthquake should have occurred in a less populated area if indeed there were a Providence: "When I had first attested, I was talking to Ford Madox Hueffer about Gaudier's death. I'd said it was too bad. Why should Gaudier die, and a 'Bloomsbury' live? I meant that *fate* ought to have seen to it that that didn't happen. It was absurd." This gives Lewis his occasion to describe the "military" activities of his favorite literary group:

The "Bloomsburies" were all doing war-work of "National importance," down in some downy English county, under the wings of powerful pacifist friends; pruning trees, planting gooseberry bushes, and haymaking, doubtless in large sunbonnets. One at least of them, I will not name him, was disgustingly robust. All were of military age. All would have looked well in uniform. [P. 184.]

Lewis then mockingly singles out Lytton Strachey and supplies us with the terms of his "exemption" from military service. Strachey, one of the Bloomsbury "faithful," had written Virginia Woolf on March 19, 1918 (see *Virginia Woolf and Lytton Strachey Letters*, New York, 1956, p. 95) about his eagerness for things military: "My 'medical board' yesterday pronounced me 'permanently & totally unfit for any form of Military Service'—which is a great relief. The whole thing was infinitely more civilised than I've ever known it before. The doctors, and even the clerks, were positively polite."

Lewis wants very much to be identified with the "Men of 1914," as he calls them. Among this group, which curiously enough includes Joyce and Eliot (the "pseudoist," as Lewis once called him), he shows the most profound attachment for Ezra Pound. We might even say that the "mask" he chose as a point-of-view character for certain sections of *Blasting and Bombardiering*, Cantleman, bears a likeness in certain ways to Pound's Hugh Selwyn Mauberley. When Lewis insists, "Need I repeat that this hero of mine is not to be identified with me?" (p. 84), we are reminded of the complex relationship which exists between Pound and his persona. The war sections of Pound's poem "Hugh Selwyn Mauberley" are more to the point here than the esthetic forays (like the famous lines, "His true Penelope was Flaubert,/ He fished by obstinate isles;"). Lewis, through Cantleman, would be capable of the sentiment, if not the poetic splicing, of Pound's well-known reworking of Horace: "Died some, pro patria,/ non 'dulce' non 'et decor'. . . ." When Lewis bemoans the death of Hulme, "in one of England's stupidest wars," one is surprised he didn't quote the first stanza of Part V of "Mauberley":

> There died a myriad,
> And of the best, among them,
> For an old bitch gone in the teeth,
> For a botched civilization.[5]

---

[5] For the best discussion of "Mauberley" and its relationship to the ambience of World War I, see Frederick J. Hoffman, "The Temper of the 1920s," in *The Twenties* (New York, 1962), pp. 21–66.

The language should be sufficiently un-Bloomsbury to attract Lewis.

The war, for Lewis, was more a matter of persons than of causes. He can be unconcerned and even disdainful when faced with the rhetoric of war; the idea of losing his life in combat did not seem especially frightening to him. He could make very light of the possibility, as in a letter to Pound: "If I get my head blown off when I am pottering about Flanders. . . ." (*The Letters of Wyndham Lewis*, W. K. Rose, ed., New York, 1963, p. 67.) He is much more serious about the whole thing when confronted with the deaths of Hulme and Gaudier-Brzeska or with the "war-work" of the "Bloomsburies." He seems to ask for an imaginary court of military justice to intercede in favor of Hulme and Gaudier-Brzeska against the "effete" Lytton Strachey, E. M. Forster, Virginia and Leonard Woolf, and the others associated with Bloomsbury. While Lewis again and again reveals unconcern for his own safety, both in *Blasting and Bombardiering* and in his letters of the war years, he still can express a metaphysical hurt in the name of the "Men of 1914." He could write to Herbert Read just after the war ended: "What a nightmare this wicked war has been! . . ."

Lewis saw very active combat for a sustained six-month period in 1917. He was hospitalized following a siege of "trench-fever." He ended the war by serving as what he called "a painter-soldier, attached to the Corps-headquarter Staff of the Canadian Army." (P. 191). W. K. Rose mentions, in his excellent edition of Lewis' letters, how Pound had tried for more than a year to get him to leave the trenches for a cushier position and quotes Pound's splendid remark from one of his letters to Lewis: ". . . you should not be allowed to spill your gore in heathen and furrin places."

The year 1917 found Lewis vigorously publishing again, especially in *The Little Review*. Pound led off the May issue with his famous editorial about what he planned to do with Margaret Anderson's magazine: "I wished a place where the current prose writings of James Joyce, Wyndham Lewis, T. S. Eliot, and myself might appear regularly, promptly, and together, rather than irregularly, sporadically, and after useless delays." Lewis published "Imaginary Letters" in five issues between May, 1917, and April, 1918. He also placed in the pages of *The Little Review*, during this period, "Cantleman's Spring-Mate" (included in the 1967 edition of *Blasting and Bombardiering*) , "A Soldier of Humour," the essay "Inferior Religions," an abstract drawing called "The Starry Sky," and the three-scene playlet "The Ideal Giant." He missed appearing in only two issues during the year from May, 1917, to May, 1918—a remarkable record for anyone, especially for an artilleryman recently turned "painter-soldier." (His "Imaginary Letters, VIII," by the way, appeared in the same issue as the first install-ment of Joyce's *Ulysses*—March, 1918.) [6]

Lewis emerged from the war, then, as active creatively as when he entered it. (We are fortunate to have this new edition of Lewis' brilliant book of 1937, *Blasting and Bombardiering*, for what it tells of this transitional period; it is, along with Leonard Wolf's, clearly one of the finest literary autobiographies of the century.) The lines were perhaps more firmly drawn between the "Men of 1914" and the "Bloomsburies"—which was entirely to Lewis' liking. *The Little Review* took the place of the defunct *Blast*, at least until Lewis could start another review of his own.

III

Virginia Woolf's experience during the war was quite different from the one which Lewis ascribed to her "group": ". . . the 'Bloomsburies' all exempted themselves, in one way or another." (P. 185.) We know from Part III of *Beginning Again* some of the details of Virginia Woolf's nervous breakdown, "neurasthenia" as her doctors called it, which corresponded roughly with the first two years of the war. Leonard Woolf remarked about them: "In many ways 1914 and 1915 were years which we simply lost out of our lives, for we lived them in the atmosphere of catastrophe or im-pending catastrophe." (*Beginning Again*, p. 166.) Leonard himself was "exempted" (he uses the very word which Lewis was fond of directing against the "Bloomsburies") from military service be-cause of Virginia's illness and because of a "nervous disease" he himself had. He spent the middle years of the war admirably investigating the causes of it and working on solutions for its curtailment in the future; he did this under the auspices of the Fabian Society. Although he was very far away from the trenches, Leonard Woolf could experience the same sense of irony about the war as Wyndham Lewis. When he speaks about his brothers at the front, he could be borrowing a page from *Blasting and Bombardier-ing*: "Cecil was killed and Philip severely wounded and it was appropriate that the death of the one and the wounds of the other were caused by the same shell. The episode was characteristic of the 1914 war." (P. 181.)

---

[6] Geoffrey Wagner's "Checklist of the Writings of Wyndham Lewis," placed at the end of his *Wyndham Lewis*, has proved very helpful here. I have also had occasion to examine *The Little Review* papers in the special collection at the library of the University of Wisconsin at Milwaukee.

It is unfortunate that Leonard Woolf's edition of his wife's *A Writer's Diary* offers as its first entry August 4, 1918. Virginia makes no mention of the war, which was to end in three months. However, if we turn to her entries for 1939 and 1940, we find a person profoundly distressed with the horror and meaninglessness of war. There is nothing feminine or Bloomsbury (in Wyndham Lewis' sense) about her responses. Leonard, in *Beginning Again,* made the crucial distinction between the First and Second World Wars; the 1914 war, he felt, was characterized by a dullness and boredom ("Nothing seemed to happen") , while in the 1939 war "things moved and happened and one was kept keenly alive by the danger of death continually hanging just above one's head." (P. 197.) It was this sense of danger—perhaps psychologically anticipating Virginia Woolf's suicide in 1941—which seems to get into the texture of her prose in the later entries of her *A Writer's Diary;* thus, we have reactions like: "The war is like a desperate illness. For a day it entirely obsesses: then the feeling faculty gives out; next day one is disembodied, in the air. Then the battery is re-charged and again—what? Well, the bomb terror. Going to London to be bombed." (May 20, 1940.) Unlike the years of World War I, when Virginia Woolf was relatively unproductive, she was able during this later period to advance her brilliant novel *Between the Acts* (always referred to in *A Writer's Diary* as *P.H.*) . She seems to echo Lewis' sentiments about the convergence of war and art. There are many passages in which only a delicate thread divides the two. Virginia Woolf's imagination moves along wearily, often without the benefit of transition: "The Press [Hogarth Press]—what remains—is to be moved to Letchworth. A grim morning. How can one settle into Michelet and Coleridge? As I say, we have need of courage. A very bad raid last night on London—waiting for the wireless. But I did forge ahead with *P.H.* all the same." (September 18, 1940.)

There is an essay to be written, certainly, on Virginia Woolf's great courage and her reaction to World War II, but that is not our intention here. Still *A Writer's Diary* is a valuable document for the study of a "neurasthenic" in civilian war conditions. One should look also at several of her later essays, especially "Thoughts on Peace in an Air Raid" (contained in Volume IV of her *Collected Essays*) , which was written in 1940 and contains much of the ambience of war. We can begin to see the desperation building up and perhaps understand James Southall Wilson's remark that her suicide was, in the end, a choice between death and insanity.

Perhaps Viriginia Woolf's most revealing statement about the effects of war on the writer is found in her late essay "The Leaning Tower" (included in Volume II of her *Collected Essays*). She wrote this essay during World War II, but something of what she had to say pertained to the war of 1914. She makes an important distinction between the nineteenth and twentieth centuries: "War then we can say, speaking roughly, did not affect either the writer or his vision of human life in the nineteenth century." (P. 164.) She points out, for example, how little the Napoleonic Wars affected the novels of Jane Austen and Scott. The change seems to come with the 1914 war, which for her, as for Leonard, ended "19th-century civilization." She clearly takes the Bloomsbury position and insists on the enviable priority of the "educated class" over the "working class" in shaping modern British literature. She notices a change in the generation which began to write in 1925 and uses the metaphor of the leaning tower to express their displacement. This generation wrote "under the influence of change, under the threat of war." (P. 170.) Almost all the writers Virginia Woolf uses to illustrate her theories in "The Leaning Tower," by the way, have Oxford or Cambridge backgrounds. The embarrassing exception is D. H. Lawrence, whom she manages to dismiss with her accustomed delicacy.

While Wyndham Lewis is for persons and "things," the Woolfs are for causes. Virginia Woolf is haunted by the very notion of war while Lewis can calmly dodge every variety of enemy fire at the front. There is no possible meeting except in the matter of art, which for both is the "real thing." It does not matter that Virginia Woolf's *A Writer's Diary* has nothing to say about World War I; the fact that it comments so poignantly about World War II is quite enough. Lewis, on the other hand, if he had written in such depth about his experiences in World War II, would probably have written a very different book from *Blasting and Bombardiering*.

IV

In "The Leaning Tower," Virginia Woolf speaks of Jane Austen's and Walter Scott's literary careers during the Napoleonic Wars: "each wrote through them." We can say this also about James Joyce, that he "wrote through" the First World War. He divided the war years between Trieste and Zurich, quite out of touch with events at the front. Joyce had considerably less involvement with the Great War than even Virginia Woolf had. We know how much, for example, Virginia Woolf's novels of the twenties were crucially involved with the 1914 war and its aftermath; we need only recall Jacob Flanders' death (*Jacob's Room*) ; the shell-shocked condition leading to the suicide of Septimus Warren Smith (*Mrs. Dalloway*) ; the report, in brackets, of the death of Andrew Ramsay (the "Time Passes" section of *To the Lighthouse*) . There is nothing quite like this in Joyce's work.

These were the years when he was writing *Ulysses* and suffering publishing and financial indignities. The war rarely finds a place in his creative work, and it is singularly absent from his letters. It does enter through the back door of *Finnegans Wake*, but as an almost indistinguishable part of war from the beginning of time. There is the brief lyric in *Chamber Music* (1907) , number XXXVI, which starts in this way:

> I hear an army charging upon the land,
>   And the thunder of horses plunging, foam about
>   their knees:
> Arrogant, in black armour, behind them stand,
>   Disdaining the reins, with fluttering whips,
>   the charioteers.

This was written many years before the war, and W. B. Yeats, for one, who placed it highest among Joyce's lyric poems, spoke of it in a letter to Joyce as "a poem of yours about the sea." We remember the presence of Private Carr and Private Compton in the Nighttown section of *Ulysses*, but there is little about them and their behavior to remind us of the Great War. Nor is Major Tweedy, who also turns up briefly in Nighttown, of much help.

The letters are scarcely more revealing. Joyce's private epistolary war with his publishers dominates the years when others were at the front. He even blithely disregards his brother Stanislaus' internment during a significant part of the war. In Richard Ellmann's edition of the Joyce correspondence we find a letter from Stanislaus, dated May 25, 1919, expressing contempt for Joyce's methods: "I have just emerged from four years of hunger and squalor, and am trying to get on my feet again. Do you think you can give me a rest?" A later letter, dated February 26, 1922, reinforces Stanislaus' sense of outrage: "In fact this seems to me only part and parcel of the careless indifference with which you have always acted in affairs that concerned me."

The only compelling statement about the war, in the three volumes of Joyce letters we have, is in a letter to Joyce from his sister May:

Have you heard from Stannie [Stanislaus] lately? I was expecting a letter from him. I sent him shoes about six weeks ago. I dont know whether he got them or not. He is wonderful to keep up so well during all this time, it must be dreadful for him being a prisoner and idle all this time, but he says he has nothing to complain of in his treatment, which is some consolation. Will all this never end? When the war started it was said it could not last more than six months, but now there seems as much prospect of a finish as then. [Ellmann edition, September 1, 1916.]

Joyce's remoteness from the war perhaps explains a sentence from a letter he wrote to Harriet Shaw Weaver on December 1, 1918 (Stuart Gilbert's edition) : "I hope you are well in these dangerous days." Could Joyce not have realized that the Great War ended on November 11?[7]

V

It might perhaps seem arbitrary to bring these three writers together under the same umbrella. Yet they will always be connected through literary history, whether one refers to them obliquely as social reactionaries as C. P. Snow has done[8] or whether one confronts the "Great Without" position of Lewis with Joyce's and Virginia Woolf's *"tellers-from-the-inside"* position. But most interesting, for our purposes, are the extremes in respect to the war: Lewis the ironical combatant, Virginia Woolf the psychologically disrupted observer, Joyce the detached nonobserver. All three are very far from the literature of *Kriegstod* celebrated in books like Bernard Bergonzi's *Heroes' Twilight.*

---

[7] Joyce does mention in a letter to Ezra Pound of about July 15, 1915 (Ellmann edition), that he read about an Italian raid of the Trieste shipyard, which was located a few minutes from his house there. In an "open letter" of April 28, 1919, Joyce offers this interesting autobiographical information: "I am a prisoner of war liberated on parole to Switzerland in July 1915 by the Austrian Government in consideration of my health. Three months after the occurrences narrated, Mr. Consul Bennett summoned me for combatant military service in the United Kingdom and threatened that if I did not comply with his proposal within 48 hours he would blacklist me. I declined to accept service of this monstrous document and sent it back to him by return of post with two lines of courteous refusal."

[8] See Rubin Rabinovitz, "C. P. Snow vs. The Experimental Novel," *Columbia University Forum,* X (Fall, 1967), pp. 37–41.

The Guilt

Correlli Barnett

CORRELLI BARNETT was born in Norbury, Surrey, on June 28, 1927. He was educated at Whitgift Middle School, Croydon (now the Trinity School of John Whitgift), and at Exeter College, Oxford, where he read modern history with, as a special subject, military history and the theory of war. He graduated in 1951 with second-class honors. He also won a college naval history prize with an essay on the development of aircraft carriers.

From 1945 to 1948 he served with the British Army, mostly in Palestine, and held the rank of sergeant.

His first work of military history, The Desert Generals, published in 1960, excited both praise and heavy attack. It has been translated into four languages. His second work of military history, The Swordbearers: Studies in Supreme Command in the First World War (critical portraits of the younger Moltke, Jellicoe, Pétain, and Ludendorff), was also widely praised.

In 1963 Correlli Barnett was one of the historical consultants for the BBC television series The Great War, and wrote a third of the programs. In 1964–65 he was a historical consultant for the television sequel, The Lost Peace. 1918–1933, and wrote nearly all the programs.

Currently he is finishing a short history of the British Army, considered as a national institution. He also teaches part time at the University of East Anglia and lectures elsewhere by invitation of such institutions as the Staff College, Camberley. He is a Fellow of the Royal Society of Literature, a member of the Royal United States Institution, and a member of the Institute for Strategic Studies. He is married, has two daughters, and lives in Norfolk.

THE ILLOGICAL PROMISE

THERE IS, successive generations have discovered, a persuasive force about a victory that is lacking in even the most cogently argued diplomatic note. War is, therefore, a continuation of policy by other means. History bears Clausewitz out: Where negotiation and nonviolent pressure have failed to secure an object, the armies have marched. Such is the diversity of human interests that armies have marched to decide the candidature of vacant thrones, to determine how much of Europe should believe in transubstantiation and accept papal authority, to define the English constitution, and conclude whether or not the United States of America should be dissolved. The armies have marched in pursuit of provinces and of markets. War, or threat of war, has been one of the essential tools of statecraft.

The immediate and fundamental difficulty with the Great War is that it, biggest of all wars, does not fit Clausewitz's definition. It was not consciously embarked on by any power (except Austria) in pursuit of positive objectives of policy. The greatest war in history was a meaningless accident: It went on to a finish of exhaustion because no one could see how to stop it.

Austria alone went into war deliberately to achieve a limited and perfectly rational objective: the crushing of Serbia and the ending of the unrest Serbia had encouraged among Austria's south Slav peoples. Every other nation in 1914 entered the war for negative reasons—not in pursuit of aims, but because of obligations and fear of others. Russia did not go to war to win Constantinople or destroy Austrian influence in the Balkans, but defensively, in support of her Serbian clients. France did not go to war to reverse the verdict of 1870 and make France the dominant great power of Europe again in place of Germany; she did not even go to war, as Déroulède would have wished, to regain Alsace-Lorraine; she went to war in fulfillment of her treaty obligations to Russia. Germany did not go to war to conquer Russian territory in the East or industrial areas and Channel ports in France and Belgium, or even to speed up her commercial defeat of British industry by naval and military victory over Britain: She went to war because her ally Austria was going to war. All the nations went to war defensively, believing themselves threatened, believing they must support their allies and fight now if they were not to be left fatally exposed to attack alone later. The Schlieffen plan, often wrongly thought to be a miscarried master-piece of long-matured and arrogant aggression, was, in fact, stra-tegically defensive. It was a gamble, a desperate gamble, to save Germany from overwhelming onslaught from east and west. Ger-many's weakness, not her strength, was the leitmotiv in the thinking of her prewar chiefs of the General Staff, from the elder Moltke, through Waldersee and Schlieffen, to the younger Moltke in 1914. And Britain did not declare war in order to crush the German Navy or destroy the growing German threat to British world markets and industrial supremacy; she declared war reluctantly, and in troubled mind, because of informal obligations to come to the aid of France.

Whatever the underlying rivalries between the nations and the social tensions within each state, war itself had thus come about by accident, by nobody's design, out of a chain of defensive obligations. No statesman of any nation (except the Austrians) had any idea of what sort of settlement might follow the swift military victories so confidently expected. The great battles of 1914 therefore took place in a vacuum so far as grand strategy, or national policy, was concerned. They were what Clausewitz had believed impossible: meaningless acts of violence, irrelevant contests of strength, the instrument of nothing.

The chains of treaty obligations that had pulled the nations into this meaningless war had been the work of the narrow prewar ruling classes. Their peoples had been spectators, crowds at the back of the stage, although their own racial and nationalist hatreds had been felt by the governments, and had helped create the prewar atmosphere of mutual fear in Europe. But once war was declared, the peoples began to take it over. The exquisite courtesies between ambassador and foreign minister when a declaration of war was delivered—the common memories even in such a moment of the single international world of the upper classes—were one thing. The hatreds being bayed and screeched in the streets of European capitals were another. The masses had been let out of their cage— the cage of a colorless and shabby, highly disciplined life in the dreary rats' nests of modern industrial cities. The existence of the masses was boring, monotonous, and insecure, their leisure short and lacking in outlet, their emotional and sexual life deprived and repressed. Even before the war, contemplation of their own coun-try's strength and glory had served to give vicarious color and ful-fillment to the narrow lives of the lower-middle and working classes. These urban masses were people without the peasant's understanding of life and of his own familiar world, without his hard, if limited, realism and sagacity. These people—like Hitler and H. G. Wells' early heroes—had no roots, no secure emotional foundations, no personal independence, no education but the ability haltingly to read and write. They had not the ability to analyze and reason or the information by which such an ability could form sound judgments. Instead, they were ruled by emotion and romance. Men like Pearson and Harmsworth had grown rich by providing them with reading matter: nothing boringly factual or closely argued, of course, but highly colored and exciting stuff to flatter prejudice and bring artificial excitement and action to the lives of people like pet mice on a wheel in a cage.

On this aimless conflict in fulfillment of prewar defensive treaties there thus impinged the quenchless hate of the common man for any person who was different. The ever-responsive popular press gave its readers what it wanted: atrocity stories by the columnful. The dreariness of urban life was reflected in the torrent of volunteers to British recruiting offices seeking escape, a bit of foreign travel and adventure, the opportunity legitimately to clobber other human beings, the splendor of uniform instead of the baggy shabbiness of shiny hand-me-downs.

The consequence of letting the little man and his wife out of their cage of obscurity might yet not have been disastrous if only one of the combatants had won a clear victory in the field in August and September, 1914, and ended the war before it really got started. There was no such decision. Instead, there was stalemate in the worst possible circumstances. Had the stalemate come about with both sides having enjoyed roughly equal success in the 1914 battles, a peace on the basis of the *status quo ante* might just have been possible. Instead, when the armies came to rest, Germany occupied eleven departments of northern France and most of Belgium. In the east, although the Serbs had chucked the Austrians back over the Danube, the Germans had also won great successes against the Russians. Stalemate it might be, but the visible balance of the war was wholly and greatly in Germany's favor. Peace by negotiation was thus impossible, for Germany could legitimately make claims that would be utterly unacceptable to the Allies. The Allies would have been bound at least to demand the evacuation of the German armies from their conquests as a preliminary to negotiation, an evident impossibility. There were therefore not the faintest beginnings of hope that the stalemate would lead to early peace negotiations; the Allies were bound to fight on in the faith that victories would give them a better platform for negotiation. Just as the nature of the stalemate on a line of German success meant the war must go on, so in terms of strategy it meant that the Allies must attack and keep on attacking. The course of the war from November, 1914, till March, 1918, was thus determined by the initial German partial success.

It gradually dawned on the nations that this was going to be a long war, that all conceptions of a large-scale, but quick and purely military, effort had been misguided. A long war, either side of a trench system well wired and fortified and densely held by troops, meant the total mobilization of the human and material resources of the combatants. In British and French industry the years 1915 and 1916 saw the replacement of Victorian small-scale organization and handicraft attitudes with modern (German and American) conceptions of huge-scale and mass production. In Germany the transition to the needs of total war implied no such revolution: Her mercantilist tradition, the large-scale organization of her industries, and the cooperative attitude of her trade unions all favored massive coordinated effort, in a way that the British tradition of small-scale enterprise and the British trade-union system, with its endless proliferation of specialist craft unions and elaborate and rigid demarcation of jobs, did not.

However, in all the combatant countries industrial mobilization meant that the ardent participation of the masses in the war had to be enlisted. It could not be a "Cabinet" war, a relatively precise instrument of realistic policy firmly under the control of the cool judgment of statesmen. Governments therefore had to meet the uncaged little man halfway: the little man had to be flattered, encouraged, filled with a sense of his importance, of the glory and righteousness of the cause, and of the criminal depravity of the enemy. Primitive government propaganda machines were created. They disseminated lies and hatred with the willing cooperation of privately owned newspapers and journals. It cannot be said that they created or "fanned" the hatred of the little man, which existed spontaneously and which seized eagerly on the gratifications offered by the press. From the end of 1914 till the end of 1916 the nations sought "victory." "Victory"—whatever that really meant in hard terms of a settlement or a prior military achievement—was the only outcome of the conflict that now would satisfy the little man's hatred of the enemy or compensate for his heroic exertions.

The state of mind of Europe at this juncture hardly boded well for any kind of ultimate, constructive peacemaking. The phlegmatic British broke out into anti-German riots, with plenty of looting of shops with German names, on account of the Germans having sunk the liner *Lusitania,* which carried a consignment of arms and which sailed from New York in defiance of a public German warning that it would be in danger. In every country, men like Horatio Bottomley thrived by publishing what the little man wanted to read. Bottomley referred constantly to "Germ-huns" in his journal *John Bull,* whose contents so appealed that its circulation became the largest in the country.

There was little to choose between the ignorance and the violence of the opinions expressed by the peoples of the different belligerents. A German, for example, made this penetrating diagnosis of the causes of the war:

"What is the war itself but the outcome only of British cunning, British lying, British hypocrisy and cant and treachery? No means can be too unholy to combat this hideous octopus, whose tentacles have too long encircled the peoples of the world."

A Briton outlined a long-term policy for the war:

"The huns—vicious in victory, cowardly in defeat—deserve no more consideration than a mad dog or a venomous snake and it is our duty to humanity to carry death and devastation into the heart of their country. We're out for War—let it be War to the death!"

Then there was another important question, with evident bearing on the peace settlement: Was the enemy human? On the one hand a Briton pointed out that "There are only two divisions in the world today—human beings and Germans," while on the other a German no less closely reasoned that "The Englishman, indeed, is not to be classed among human beings."

Above all, there was the question of why everybody was going on fighting, other than that it was a meaningless predicament from which nobody knew how to escape. The common man would not fight for anything so prosaic as coal and iron fields or to weaken a trade competitor. His mind was above such things. His purpose was as Christian as his sentiments. A war begun without aims had now been allotted an aim—total victory over evil. As a British bishop put it from the fire step of his cathedral pulpit: "Such a war is a heavy price to pay for our progress towards the realization of the Christianity of Christ, but duty calls."

However, there was a German claim as well to godliness: "One thing is clear. God must stand on Germany's side. We fight for truth, culture and civilization and human progress and true Christianity." A picture was thus conveyed by the religious ecstasies of the combatants that the soldiers were beating each other's heads in with crucifixes.

In fact, of course, at the front, where the reality was instead of the fantasy, the emotional transports that filled the silly heads of the masses had no place. The soldiers of all the combatant nations were unfortunately placed between the enemy barbed wire and machine guns in front, and their relatives behind demanding total victory at all costs.

What is especially depressing is the degree to which men who ought to have known better—politicians, diplomats, soldiers, writers —were unable to preserve their good sense and detachment, but themselves caught the popular mood. The only people bucking the tide—pacifists of one kind or another—were just as emotionally in the fidgets as the war winners. Virtually nowhere was to be found the political realism, the practical good sense, the sagacity of judgment of a Talleyrand, a Metternich, a Castlereagh, a Bismarck. In its combination of boy scout idealism and romanticized aggression, Europe seemed to have regressed to a mental age of thirteen.

However, not only were there journals like *John Bull* to read; but there were casualty lists. Although evey patriotic German, Frenchman, or Briton knew that one of his soldiers was worth three of the enemy and that every offensive had been a brilliant demonstration of military superiority over a cowardly and despicable enemy, the fact remained that the front stayed much where it was. By the end of 1916, when both sides had made a supreme effort to win and failed, even the British people, last to commit a great army to battle, began to notice that a lot of their sons, husbands, fathers, nephews, cousins, uncles, and friends had been killed or wounded.

The autumn of 1916 and the winter of 1916–17 (cold and long) mark the point at which some dawning sense of reality about the war came to the bemused mind of the common man of Europe, rather like sobriety returning to drunks who have just unloaded a vast cargo of inhibited lusts and aggressions by wrecking a pub and fighting everybody in reach. Or perhaps like a man falling out of love. The war was no longer so glorious and colorful and exciting. How long would it go on for? Could anybody win? Would it be worth winning?

In the absence of public opinion polls it is impossible to judge to what extent a shift of opinion (so to dignify the varying moods of the common man) had taken place among the warring peoples. It was certainly enough to create a climate where it seemed worthwhile to various diverse individuals—Lord Lansdowne, Bethmann-Hollweg, Henry Ford, the Pope, and the new Austrian Emperor Karl—to try for a compromise peace, not all at the same time. However, opinion in favor of carrying on the war until total victory apparently remained the stronger, among both governments and peoples. The mood of the war winners was now grim and dour, more of obstinacy than of wild passion. New leaders like Lloyd George and Ludendorff brought a promise of new ideas and talent, a sense of a second wind. The war went on to the final, sterile conclusion of the total victory demanded by the masses.

The common man did not so much enjoy the latter half of the war; it ceased to be like an exciting serial story in his paper. People he was related to or knew socially kept getting killed or wounded. The war came right home when the Germans bombed Paris and London, and the Allies bombed the Rhineland. The indignation, uproar, and damage to war production owing to absenteeism caused by these trivial attacks indicated that the common man's appetite for battle was strictly vicarious. Then there was rationing and substitute foods: Who could enjoy a Christian, patriotic war against subhuman monsters on cod steak and unsweetened tea?

The "aim" of victory over evil was no longer quite enough in itself. Something more was now needed to keep up flagging spirits and interest—to provide some kind of justification for the unending waste and killing. The idea of war aims gradually emerged. Nobody noted that the time to decide on war aims is before you get into a war. The course and character of the war now molded the evolution of these war aims; the peoples demanded compensation for their enormous efforts, sacrifices, and losses since the beginning of the war. The French looked beyond the recovery of Alsace-Lorraine to a French puppet state in the Rhineland and the breakup of united Germany. The Germans looked to a protectorate of some kind over Belgium and the Channel ports and a colonial empire in Poland and the Baltic. Both the French and the German aims were concrete enough, despite their ambition, given that total victory could first be achieved. It was the Anglo-Americans who produced a new fantasy, a new focus for the simple emotional reactions of the common man, that partly replaced the earlier fantasy of a crusade against evil. This fantasy was a Better World, to be created by a Postwar Reconstruction. It was just the stuff for people who were thinking more about peace, now they had got bored with war. Within national society, a Better World was to take the form of social reform, industrial reorganization, greater equality and political democracy, an attack on poverty and misery. In terms of a European and world peace settlement it was to take the form of a League of Nations. The genuine and spontaneous idealism of the Better-Worlders was never better expressed than in the disastrous figure of Woodrow Wilson.

With the advent of Wilson and those who passionately believed with him in Better Worlds and Leagues of Nations, there evolved the ultimate in war aims. It was proclaimed that this was a War to End War. Thus, after four years of hapless slaughter, a war that had begun unintentionally, because of treaty obligations intended to *preserve* the existing European political system, ended with such vaulting and visionary aims as had no previous war in history.

However, the mood of Wilson and the victorious Allies in November, 1918, was not all passionate idealism; there was a good deal still of earlier sentiment that the enemy was a wild beast to be castrated, hobbled, and caged forever. Some people managed to blend relentless hatred of the Germans with Christian hopes for future international amity; others specialized in one or the other. The climate of the peacemaking was thus determined by the evolving psychology of the common man and his prophets in the course of war. Unlike their happier predecessors at the Congress of Vienna, the statesmen gathered in Paris in 1919 were acutely conscious of, and had to be responsive to, public opinions that had not really existed in so powerful and vociferous a form even in 1914. Promises both to squeeze Germany till the pips squeaked and to usher in a millennium of peace and love had in some way to be simultaneously redeemed by the ingenuity of statesmen. At the same time, some hard and practical questions of the old, sordid kind familiar to the realistic past had also to be arranged.

There was thus at the base of the peacemaking the same irrationality that had determined the people's attitudes to the war. It made sense only in terms of psychological explanation to say that *because* this had been the most hideous and pointless war in history, the peace by compensation must be the most beautiful, just, idealistic, and long-lasting. It can be understood how people who think with their guts instead of their heads came to believe that such unspeakable hatred, cruelty, and horror must naturally lead to a world of love, kindness, and international understanding, came to believe that people who had wrestled with each other to the last gasp would now abjure force. It is also understandable that ignorant people of weak understanding should see social justice and unprecedented prosperity as the consequence of all the destruction and waste of the war. The logic of the urban common man, like that of all primitives, was emotional and symbolical, not reasonable or analytical. What is less comprehensible is that intelligent and educated men with a knowledge of history, as well as of affairs, from Wilson himself down to young idealists like Harold Nicolson of the British delegation to the Peace Conference, could believe that the

Great War provided a wonderful springboard to a better world. The gulf between the real state of the world and the blueprint of the idealists was absolutely unbridgeable. The gulf within the personalities of the idealists themselves—between Wilson the toughened politician and Wilson the prophet, for example—was no less wide.

Thus a war of irrationality paved the way for a peace of irrationality: The emotional fantasies of the emancipated masses were the key to the making of both.

The core of the postwar European problem, as it had been of the war and of the prewar problem, was a united Germany. Germany occupied the center of Europe, the largest single nation-state (excepting Russia) and the most powerful and enterprising industrial nation in Europe, bar none. Despite her defeat in the Great War, the conflict only proved Germany's dominating strength: She had beaten Russia, had held off France and Britain, and had succumbed only to the fresh and overwhelming weight of America. The verdict of victory could be only temporary; German relative weakness would last only as long as the Allied wartime coalition stayed in being. There were two answers to this problem of German power. First, the peacemakers could accept that, willy-nilly, Germany would always dominate Europe and therefore make a very lenient peace so that Germany would harbor the least resentment. Unfortunately the war had come to be fought just to deny this German domination, and the common man had been taught to expect that Germany would be heavily "punished." In any case, Wilson had already broken up the German monarchy and reduced the country to political chaos. So the kind of peace that had been granted France in 1814 was impossible.

There was the second alternative: Weaken Germany so that she no longer dominated Europe; in other words, so that she was no stronger than another single great power, *i.e.,* France. This meant either breaking up the united Germany made by Bismarck into small states (which the French in fact wanted to do) or reducing the German population and industrial resources to the level of France by cession of territory to the victors. However, such a solution would be too brutal for Wilsonian idealism, for the new world of justice being created in Paris. Instead, a compromise was finally evolved that tried to take in punishment, reconciliation, self-determination (even for Germans), *and* the weakening of German power. It was a compromise that reflected the conflicting pressures of political reality and idealistic fantasy. It did not solve the central problem of power. Postwar Germany matched 60,000,000 of population against 40,000,000 in France. The Ruhr and Silesian industrial areas made her still the most powerful industrial country in Europe. Cessions of territory to Poland and Belgium, reparations, French occupation of the Rhineland, and German disarmament eroded only the edges of German strength: The core remained intact. At the same time the Allies had ensured that this potentially still-powerful Germany would have a weak and unpopular republican regime and would harbor strong resentments. Owing also to the collapse of the Austrians in the last days of the war enforced by Wilson, there was no great power to balance Germany in the center of Europe, as Austria had balanced Prussia until the 1880's. The new Germany, though itself weakened, was bordered by second-class states like Poland, Czechoslovakia, and Austria (the German-speaking rump). The prewar balance of power in Europe (how good a balance it was is proved by the stalemate of the war) had in fact been replaced by arrangements that left Germany relatively stronger in potential, not weaker.

More irrationality is found in the painstaking drawing of borders for the new states so as to get people speaking one language all on one side of a frontier. Harold Nicolson in his diary of the Peace Conference portrays the conscientious agonizing of the peacemakers as they tried to apply the principles of self-determination to areas where the populations were hopelessly jumbled up. The state lines drawn according to this doctrinaire ideal divided up the balanced economic system of the Austrian Empire into peasant agricultural states without access to their old urban markets or industrial supplies, and cities and industrial areas with no agriculture to feed them and no markets for their products. To, therefore, the ruin of industry, trade, and agriculture throughout central and eastern Europe caused by the war was gratuitously added further dislocation instead of a settlement realistically based on economics. A further irrationality was found in the colossal reparation demands on Germany made by the Allies, which were based on the proposition that Germany *ought* to pay for all damage incurred by the Allies in the course of the war. How much Germany *could* pay was a question dealt with only in the Dawes and Young plans later in the 1920's.

It is not merely hindsight to perceive how unrealistic and incoherent a peace had emerged; there were those who were aghast even before the draft was rammed down the German throat without negotiation.

To recapitulate: The war began without purposes; it became a meaningless dilemma; it entailed the participation of the common man to a novel extent; the common man's demand for total victory over "evil" helped lead to the war's immense destruction and Europe's final exhaustion; and increasingly statesmen were trapped (or at least hindered) by their own tributes to the common man's sentimentality, whether sugary-idealistic or romantically aggressive and indignant. By 1918, therefore, a powerful element of sentimentality had been injected into the conduct of international affairs, where, instead, sober and materialistic calculation is required for businesslike and workable settlements. The anatomy of the urban little man's unreason and sentimentality has never been better laid out than in *Mein Kampf* by Adolf Hitler, himself a prime example of what he was dissecting.

Henceforward, the machinery of mass communications grew more sophisticated and placed leaders and led in closer intimacy: radio, cinema, mass-circulation press. The spread of parliamentary government and universal suffrage demolished autocracy and oligarchy everywhere, sometimes replacing them with plebiscitary dictatorships. It was impossible to place complicated political issues factually before the masses, impossible to appeal to their reason, which did not exist. The trend of the war and the peacemaking continued: Advertising and statesmanship went forward together in appealing to the irrational in the mind of the masses, to their primitive emotional drives. The new statesmanship of the mass age was a matter of slogans evoking or exploiting sentimental moods. A double standard evolved: what a politician wrote and said in private and what he said to his gormless electors. No longer could statesmen come to arrangements in private according to the merits of the case and the reality of the balance of bargaining power, for there were always the sentimental expectations of their own masses to cumber their freedom of maneuver.

Since these sentimental expectations were subject to all the violent swings of emotion and mood, and not to the consistent guidance of reason and information, they were often untimely and disastrous. At the end of the 1920's a deep and irrational refusal to think about the true nature of the Great War and its causation led to a blind faith in the League of Nations and in unilateral disarmament as preservatives of peace. Those who had been filled with bloody desires for vengeance and victory in 1914–18 now espoused the cause of peace at all costs, and funk replaced vicarious enjoyment of violence. The masses ducked their own responsibility for the xenophobic tension of the prewar period, and they ducked their responsibility for the length and violence of the war. They refused to see that the demand for total victory plus a trench system (without flanks) inevitably equaled stalemated slaughter. Instead, the masses eagerly swallowed fables that blamed the origins of the war on armament manufacturers, that blamed the long duration and unspeakable horror of the fighting on the generals. As a result of this escapist mood of the masses, Baldwin was unable to swing British public opinion behind timely rearmament and opposition to Hitler. By their escapism in the 1930's the masses ensured that they would catch the full consequences of the muddled peace that their irrational hopes and inconsistent attitudes had done so much to make: another war.

"The Promise of Greatness," therefore, so fruitily expounded by such men as Wilson (and Lloyd George in public utterances to the masses), was surely in the short term a baseless self-delusion. The physical destruction and dislocation of the war, the human loss, pointed toward exhaustion and poverty, not toward a bounding prosperity more fairly shared. Four years of unleashed hatred and violence and the destruction of social ties and habits pointed logically to a future of neurotic restlessness, suspicion, and more violence, not to a new social order of self-discipline, calm mutual understanding, and brotherly love. However, the Promise of Greatness itself made worse the universal and insidious disintegrating effects of war by raising hopes incapable of fulfillment and demanding of statesmen what they could not possibly deliver, by making a peace which was fundamentally ill-adapted to the practical requirements of Europe in 1919.

Thus, to recapitulate, the nature of the Great War after 1914 and the nature of the peace from 1919 to 1939 are the immediate consequences of the uncaging of the little man, the eruption of mass opinion as a force of which statesmen must take continuous account. This eruption marks the advent of the irrational, of fantasy and ignorance, into the higher conduct of human affairs to a degree never before seen in modern times. The short-term consequences were disastrous in 1914–19. The long-term consequences are still manifesting themselves. The pattern established during the Great War is still with us: Great international questions are seen in simple moralistic and idealistic terms, as emotional crusades; statesmen still find their freedom to strike realistic bargains hampered by the ingenuous expectations of electorates at home. In an attempt to manipulate the fantasies of the masses in support of their real, but rarely publicly expounded policies, statesmen have developed the double personality: the actor-statesman, all ideals and generalized goodness for the television, and the real statesman behind the TV makeup. The influence of the masses has introduced falsity, as well as rigidity, into international affairs.

In so many ways the Great War began or quickened the transi-

tion of Western society from one of privilege to one of mass participation. Optimists can therefore point to all the contemporary
phenomena of mass enjoyment and prosperity ("Greatness"?) that
have their origins in aspirations awakened during the Great War.
However, the influence of ignorance and unreason in the higher
conduct of affairs, national and international, is a less agreeable and
more dangerous product of the Great War. It never has carried—
and it does not carry now—any Promise of Greatness. It carries
rather the promise that in questions vitally affecting national well-
being or international relations, the measures demanded by the
reality of a problem are precisely those which are most difficult to
carry out because of public opinion.